GOVERNING
AT THE GRASSROOTS

3rd edition

GOVERNING AT THE GRASSROOTS

state and local politics

NICHOLAS HENRY
Arizona State University

PRENTICE-HALL, INC., ENGLEWOOD CLIFFS, NEW JERSEY 07632

Library of Congress Cataloging-in-Publication Data

Henry, Nicholas, (date)
Governing at the grassroots.

Bibliography.
Includes index.
1. State governments. 2. Local government—
United States. I. Title.
JK2408.H46 1987 320.8′0973 86-30364
ISBN 0-13-360678-3

Editorial/production supervision
and interior design: Edie Riker and Virginia L. McCarthy
Cover design: Ben Santora
Manufacturing buyer: Barbara Kelly Kittle

Printed in the United States of America

10 9 8 7 6 5 4 3 2 1

ISBN 0-13-360678-3 01

Prentice-Hall International (UK) Limited, *London*
Prentice-Hall of Australia Pty. Limited, *Sydney*
Prentice-Hall Canada Inc., *Toronto*
Prentice-Hall Hispanoamericana, S.A., *Mexico*
Prentice-Hall of India Private Limited, *New Delhi*
Prentice-Hall of Japan, Inc., *Tokyo*
Prentice-Hall of Southeast Asia Pte. Ltd., *Singapore*
Editora Prentice-Hall do Brasil, Ltda., *Rio de Janeiro*

To Muriel

CONTENTS

PREFACE

"Shame! Shame!" The cry is occasionally heard from the back benches of Parliament when a speaker has said something that strikes the opposition party as dreadful. It is a cry that might be echoed after perusing the literature on state and local politics.

The third edition of this book, like the first, attempts to rectify at least some of the dullness associated with the study of state and local politics. The better examples of significant research on various facets of state and local politics are put forth, but are put forth somewhat differently from standard texts. An emphasis is placed on suburban politics, the politics of bureaucracies, regional politics, politicians as social-psychological actors, and the policy conflicts between social classes. While some of these themes are present in other books, *Governing at the Grassroots,* 3rd ed., stresses these facets of state and local government. It covers topics that are either omitted or present only peripherally in other texts—notably, the "second civil war" between the Sunbelt and the Snowbelt, the politics of a suburbanized America, the women's movement (including the issue of "comparable worth"), the grassroots bureaucrats, state and urban planning, public administration, government corporations, the emerging American underclass, political corruption, and organized crime among others.

The organization of *Governing at the Grassroots,* 3rd ed., reflects these emphases. Part One examines some of the dramatic issues confronting state and local politicians and bureaucrats, focusing on the high comedy of politics at the grassroots as well as the high drama of the political process. It traces the sweep of people and power across the breadth of this vast nation and shows the political implications of the large-scale demographic shifts this country has experienced during the twentieth century. The third edition features in Part One an expanded chapter on political participation, which suggests that Americans participate in the grassroots political process more than is commonly believed; the chapter provides new information on those forms of political participation that are found only at the grassroots: the referendum, the initiative, the recall—and the riot. A newly developed chapter on interest groups is featured, including a discussion of that relatively recent phenomenon, political action committees, and their impact on states and communities.

Part Two approaches the politics of the states, focusing on political parties, legislatures, the governors, and the courts. New material includes expanded treatments of legislative leadership, party caucuses, and gubernatorial campaigning.

Part Three moves to those eighty thousand creatures of the states—counties, towns, townships, suburbs, cities, special districts, and school districts—and examines the structures of government in the United States, which are many and are constantly evolving. We also consider the increasingly strained relationships between those governments and Washington, D.C., the complex dimensions of community power (including the role of the federal government in the conscious development of that power), and the urban chief executives. New discussions are featured on county government, town meetings, urban lobbying, interlocal cooperation, federal involvement in state and local affairs, citizen participation in local policymaking, and the remarkable black-versus-white mayoral election of 1983 in Chicago.

Part Four is an unusual one in state and local government books; it discusses public administration at the grassroots. Some of the major political issues of our time are centered within the bureaucracy, and these include affirmative action policies, fiscal federalism, the issue of comparable worth, strikes by public employees, tax revolts, and the growing independence of the "fourth branch of government"—bureaucracy itself. Part Four features a unique chapter on government corporations and government contracting that highlights the career of that spectacular public administrator in New York, the late Robert Moses. A new discussion on the biggest default in municipal history also is included—that of the Washington Public Power Supply System (WPPSS), known to critics as "Whoops!"

Part Five considers public policies formed and implemented by state and local governments; it approaches these policies from the viewpoint of conflict between social classes. Thus, policies for the poor include welfare policies and policies for crime in the streets. Policies for the middle class include education, state and urban planning efforts, land use, and transportation. The third edition includes new material on school finance, the states' new aggressiveness in reformulating educational standards, poverty among children, the governance of higher education, and urban zoning.

The book concludes with a chapter on corruption and organized crime. Although everyone knows that corruption is a fact of life in all levels of government—not merely state and local ones—few textbooks talk about it. One reason is that there are little empirical data available on what is usually a highly secretive area of politics, but another reason seems to be the grim determination of political scientists to uphold civic text virtues at any expense. This book does not take that approach.

Much of the third edition of *Governing at the Grassroots* is new, and many people deserve credit for its successful completion and production. No book can be produced without a corps of dedicated typists, and I have been extraordinarily fortunate in having a group of devoted and talented secretaries work on this manuscript. Fran Mularski (especially Fran Mularski), Karen Neese, and Gwen Weaver all turned out reams of manuscript. They did this not only with a high degree of professionalism, but with unflagging good will, and for that I am most grateful. Catherine Osborn and Valerie Kime, my graduate assistants, proved to be most insightful critics of the manuscript.

I also am in debt to my editor, Stan Wakefield, for his encouragement in pursuing this project. Stan is now a film producer—a fitting career change for one who has such an unerring eye. Stan was succeeded in midrevision by Karen Horton who has been both helpful and patient. Prentice-Hall also provided the professional talents of Edie Riker and her able staff.

Most of all I am grateful to my family; my wife, Muriel, my son, Miles, and my daughter, Adrienne, were most understanding. Their support, as always, is deeply appreciated.

N.H.
Tempe

1

THE JOY OF POLITICS:

the sweep of people and power

State and local politics is high theater—either comic or tragic, depending on the point of view. Keep in mind, however, that the line between tragedy and comedy can be a fine one.

POLITICAL FOLLIES

Whether the subject is funny or sad, we should approach the study of state and local politics as we would approach going to a movie; and grassroots politics is considerably more entertaining than most movies. Consider some examples. During the late 1960s Georgia had a governor who kept the nation in stitches: Lester Maddox. Governor Maddox was a man of the people, or at least, some of the people. In 1967, Maddox answered a query from *Esquire* magazine about whether he had an eye on Washington when his term expired. He answered, according to *Esquire,* "Naw suh. I jus' wanted to see how fer a li'l feller could go. I wanted to see if this wuz still America. . . . Son, you jus' come on back down here fo' years from now and you gon' fin' me givin' up this here guv'nor stuff and right back to my furniture store, jus' a pickin' and a rickin'."[1] In 1968 Maddox ran for president.

The former governor of Georgia delighted in making spectacular entrances. One of his favorite stunts was to ride a bicycle backwards; another was to enter political rallies through a large paper hoop while riding on the hood of a car. On one occasion, however, the driver picked up a little too much speed; the governor went through the hoop all right, but he was spread-eagled over the hood. Some objected that such a posture was less than dignified for a governor.

State politicians often seem to revel in the kind of behavior exemplified by Governor Maddox. Sometimes such behavior is intentional and other times not. Consider another example, that of State Senator Fred Berry of Tennessee, who in 1976 came very close to being named the official state fossil. Berry proposed that the state designate an official rock, an official gem, and an official fossil, and he introduced a bill toward this end in the Tennessee legislature. The legislators, engaging in their usual high jinks at the end of the session, amended the portion concerning the fossil and elected to name Berry the official fossil; the senator hastily withdrew his proposal. On the other hand, Nevada legislators in 1977 actually did consider seriously the adoption of an official fossil for the state. The legislature of Nevada, a state now located in desert, gave solemn thought to adopting the ichthyosaur, a prehistoric reptile that dwelt exclusively in the earth's early oceans, as the state's official fossil.

Nor are fun and games limited to the legislature in grassroots politics. One of the more entertaining campaigns in recent years was that of Senator S. I. Hayakawa's upset of Senator John V. Tunney in California. Hayakawa, campaigning in a state that some contend practically invented the Oriental Exclusion Act, is of Japanese descent, sports a tam-o'shanter as a campaign symbol, and is a respected academic in semantics. He amazed his audiences with the absolute candor of his positions. Asked at a fund-raising reception in Orange County, "What is your assessment of the United Nations situation involving the Libyan delegation?" Hayakawa responded, "I'm not terribly informed on this one. What is the Libyan delegation?" When queried about the Panama Canal question, a hot issue at one point in the 1976 campaign for president, Hayakawa replied, "We should hang on to it; we stole it fair and square." When informed by a McDonald's hamburger franchise owner that McDonald's had 100 outlets in Japan, Hayakawa retorted, "That was too high a price to pay for Pearl Harbor." Hayakawa won handily against an opponent who had achieved a responsible record in Congress.[2]

Of course, part of the reason why Hayakawa won may have been California itself. Politically, California is unpredictable, and culturally it is often where things happen first in America. One sociologist has called California the world's largest outdoor asylum. California has Disneyland; it has both the highest and the lowest geographical points in the contiguous 48 states; it has the Hollywood Pet Cemetery, the Golden Yoga Dream Hermitage, and the Golden Gate Bridge; it had the Symbionese Liberation Army, a governor (later president) who said, "If you've seen one redwood tree, you've seen them all," and a U.S. senator who rationalized that Mexicans made the best farm workers because they were short and, therefore, closer to the crops. No attempt is made here to single out California; it simply happens to be one of the nation's more spectacular political systems and one endowed with an almost unconscious sense of humor.

A sense of humor pervades most statewide politics. In our bicentennial year, the state of Washington put up as a gubernatorial candidate a Mr. Red Kelly, who represented the OWL party. OWL stood for "Out With Logic, On With Lunacy," and, indeed, the party fronted a full slate (which lost) in the Washington election. Kelly promised to abdicate immediately if elected, printed bumper stickers reading "A vote for Red Kelly is two giant steps backward," and maintained that on most issues he was "for everything and against everything else," noting for good measure that "the buck starts here." For lieutenant governor, the OWL party nominated Jack "The Ripoff" Lemon, who campaigned with the slogan: "If you care enough to send the very least, vote for a Lemon and throw the rascals out." "Fast Lucy" Griswold was the nominee for secretary of state, who trumpeted, "I have developed two new recipes, one for welfare rolls and the other for unemployment rolls, using a new special yeast. You can't raise the dough no matter how much you need it."[3]

Then there is Oklahoma, which was the home state of the presidential campaign of one Larimore Hustle, who qualified for the official ballot in several states during the 1976 presidential election. Candidate Hustle was a 1,000-pound pig who ran on the platform that, according to his agents, was anything but hogwash. Hustle, said his staff, was four-square against swine flu, felt that foreign policy was an area in which we should "bring home the bacon," and subscribed to the view that in energy use "one shouldn't be a hog."

State legislators long have been a source of political humor at the grassroots. The Texas legislature, known in that state as "the Ledge," provides a particularly rich source.[4] In 1964, for example, half of the 150 members of the Texas House of Representatives were simultaneously involved in an all-out fistfight over an issue long forgotten. During the riot, four members mounted the Speaker's dais and began singing, "I Had a Dream, Dear," as a barbershop quartet. The incident led to a tradition of providing a legislative sing-along in moments of catastrophe. For example, ten years later, after the Texas legislators had spent six months and $6 million in a futile attempt to rewrite the state constitution (futile because the legislators ultimately voted down their own efforts), members of the House started singing "Nearer My God to Thee."

Nor do Texas legislators always give their colleagues the respect that they might be due. For example, when Senator Walter Mengden—known as "Mad Dog" Mengden because of his extreme right-wing views—would make speeches on the floor, his legislative brethren would begin to bark and howl like (what else?) mad dogs. This is not to say, however, that the Texas legislators do not have their own brand of common sense. For example, "the Ledge" once passed a law rounding off the mathematical function of pi (3.1416) to an even 3, on the grounds that it would be simpler to work with.

Legislators of liberal persuasion are not common in Texas and, in fact, liberal groups in the legislature have been labeled with such monikers as the Gas House Gang (a group that wished to put a tax on natural gas, not a particularly popular concept in Texas), the Dirty Thirty, and the Killer Bees, a group of 12 Texas senators who hid out for five days to delay consideration of a bill that they opposed, despite the fact that the Texas Rangers had been sent to find them.

Legislators also have their own way of clarifying issues. Consider the following examples drawn from remarks that have been made by members of the Michigan legislature:[5]

> "Before I give you the benefit of my remarks, I would like to know what we are talking about."
>
> "There comes a time to put principle aside and do what's right."
>
> "I don't see anything wrong with saving human life. That would be good politics, even for us."
>
> "This bill goes to the very heart of moral fibre of human anatomy."
>
> "It's a step in the right direction, it's the answer, and it's constitutional, which is even better."

"Some of our friends wanted it in the bill, some of our friends wanted it out, and Jerry and I are going to stick with our friends."

"I'm not only for capital punishment, I'm also for the preservation of life."

"From now on, I'm watching everything you do with a fine tooth comb."

"Now we've got them right where they want us."

"I don't think people appreciate how difficult it is to be a pawn of labor."

"Let's violate the law one more year."

"Mr. Speaker, what bill did we just pass?"

Local governments also have their share of color. One of the less known but certainly more entertaining examples of local political color occurred in the nation's capital in 1976, when the Washington Police Department and Federal Bureau of Investigation set up a major fencing operation.[6] The operation, dubbed "The Sting," was designed to net a number of burglars in the District of Columbia and was eminently successful. "The Sting" involved undercover officers posing as out-of-town Syndicate members; over a period of months they bought more than 3,500 pieces of stolen property estimated at $2.4 million. The fake fence operation paid the alleged thieves $67,000 for television sets, stereos, appliances, cars, guns, and $1.2 million in federal government checks, which apparently had been stolen from a vault during office hours in the Department of Housing and Urban Development. They had business cards printed that identified their fencing operation as "PFF, Inc.," which actually stood for Police-FBI Fencing, Inc., although the suspects were told that the initials stood for Pasquale's Finest Fencing. The operation eventually grew so big that it had to be terminated because the investigation was becoming overwhelmed with administrative tasks, since about 200 people had made sales to the fencing company, with most becoming regular customers.

All those involved thought that the supposed fencing operation was so successful—evidently, it had become the largest one in the city—that its operators (who, of course, were police officers) invited the suspects to a warehouse for a "victory night party" to celebrate the profits of their fencing ring. The police wanted to save thousands of dollars by having the suspects come to them rather than going to the suspects to arrest them.

The guests arrived at the warehouse driving expensive cars and wearing tuxedos and heavy jewelry, possibly their own. The suspects were asked to check their guns at the door and were told they were going to get to see "the big boss, the don, who is so proud of what you did for us." A Washington policeman, one Carl Mattis, was selected to play the role of "the don." Mattis, 43 years old, the father of six, and a member of the Elks, the American Legion, and Veterans of Foreign Wars, had no idea what a don was supposed to do, so he sat in a highbacked chair (mainly because he had a back problem) as the host of the supposed party and greeted each incoming arrival with "Bless you, my son." Mattis was introduced as "the boss himself, the man from New York," and gave such a winning performance as the don that more than one guest knelt in front of him and kissed his wedding ring. Hors d'oeuvres were, of course, served. The suspects then were escorted into a back room, where they were met by police officers who advised them of their rights, arrested and handcuffed them, hustled them into rented "U-Haul" trucks parked at the rear of the warehouse, and hauled them off to the police station. One hundred eight suspects were arrested.

The police and FBI had gone into the fencing business with style. Sally Quinn stated in her social column in the *Washington Post,* "It may well be remembered in these unexciting times as THE party of the year."

Pasquale's Finest Fencing operation is just one example of the theatrics of grassroots government. There are others. The town of Brawley, California, passed a resolution forbidding snow within the city limits; Coral Gables, Florida, enacted a law against snoring at night; Atlanta, Georgia, made it unlawful to tie a giraffe to a telephone pole or street lamp within the city limits; Greenville, South Carolina, came out foursquare against selling and buying whiskey unless the sun was shining[7]; and the city of Florence, Oregon, took the matter of population growth and morality firmly in hand by passing an ordinance making it illegal to practice sexual intercourse "while in or in view of a public or private place."[8] Officials of Florence later decided not to enforce the new ordinance until they could amend it.

Any town, of course, can make mistakes. But some local governments in America seem to have a pervasive, if unconscious, whackiness in everything they do. Consider the case of Loving County, Texas. Loving County is a stretch of virtually uninhabitable desert that locals call "Kuwait West." Its nickname derives from the fact that there are oceans of natural gas within its boundaries. Loving County has a per capita income of $25,000, more than double, in fact, the per capita income in the oil-rich sheikdom of Kuwait. On the other hand, Loving County is the least populated county in the country, with only 91 citizens in its 647 square miles. (Somehow, however, there are 95 voters registered in Loving County. When asked why, the county clerk replied, "Don't ask me.")[9] According to one Texas historian, "The place is already so small, they don't even have a village idiot."[10]

Despite its natural wealth, it is not surprising that Loving County is underpopulated. It freezes in the winter, and in the summer temperatures climb to 115 degrees Fahrenheit. There are no trees, no crops, and no drinking water. In fact, what little water Loving County has is infused with gypsum, a principal ingredient of plaster of Paris. Gypsum "leaves a thick coat of milky gunk on all it touches. It can eat through the hood of a car, smother plants, harden into rock and stop up a commode. Cows drink it, but people, dogs, and horses do not."[11] Loving County was founded in 1893 by an irrigation company that wanted to dig canals, turn the desert into a garden, and sell the land to settlers. However, the water was not only too loaded with gypsum, but was also too salty. Soon, as a consequence of their financial failure, the founders of the irrigation company elected themselves to all the county offices and then departed with the entire county treasury. According to the Loving County clerk, the only thing left behind was "a pile of clothes on the banks of the Pecos River." The Texas legislature was sufficiently incensed that it dissolved the county, which was founded again later when oil was discovered; Loving County, of Texas's 254 counties, is the only one to have been officially reborn.

Loving County is conservative politically, and revenues are not spent on frills such as water, gas, and roads; water and propane gas are shipped in from other counties. The county judge has stated, "People say you got all this money, why don't you have water? Well, you could get it . . . but . . . we can't pipe it to everybody."[12] Similarly, despite the fact that Loving County sits on one of the largest natural gas reservoirs in the world, there is no pipeline to residences because county officials disapprove of such luxuries. There is only one paved road in the county—a two-lane state highway. All other roads are dirt ones. As the county judge has put it, "Sure, we could pave the streets with gold, but I don't believe in spending it just because you can get it. We just use what we need to operate. We could afford more, but why do it if you can get by without it?"[13]

Loving County puts its money where its mouth is (or, more accurately, it does *not* put its money where its mouth is). Although the county has been collecting revenue sharing funds from the federal government ever since the program was implemented in 1972, it has never spent a penny of it. As the county judge states, "We just put it in the bank and let it draw interest. They can have it back if they ever ask us to do anything. This way, we are not obligated." In fact, the assessed value of property in Loving County burgeoned from $16 million in 1976 to $450 million in 1983, but taxes on property have been reduced during those seven years from $1.15 per $100 of property value to 10 cents per $100. In spite of its great natural wealth, folks in Loving County remain downhome people. As the county clerk observed about Jim Wheat, a millionaire rancher who owns many of the oil wells in the county, who dresses in diamond-studded clothes, and who drives a Rolls Royce on the county's rutted dirt roads, "About all we do here is sit by the window and watch Jim Wheat's Rolls Royce break down."[14]

If Loving County is one of America's more peculiar counties, one of the country's more peculiar towns may be Pembroke Park, Florida, which has long provided material for bored journalists in the region. Pembroke Park's difficulties began with the brief but spectacular administration of Mayor Tom Courtney, who, in 1977, decided that despite the fact that Pembroke Park has fewer than 5,000 residents, he would develop the most formidable municipal police force in the country. Toward that end, he hired 30 police officers, a SWAT team, a K-9 Corps, and two helicopters. As it turned out, there was not a great deal to do with this arsenal. For example, one grand jury of Broward County, in which Pembroke Park is located, found that at least one helicopter was used to buzz a nearby nudist camp.

A third helicopter was on order when some of the members of the city council (which, under Pembroke Park's charter, elected a mayor from their own ranks) began to have second thoughts. As one commissioner put it, "I told Tom there were problems with the sewer lines and we couldn't just go on buying helicopter parts." Or, as one of Pembroke Park's public administrators tried to explain, the mayor appeared to hire people "under the misunderstanding that wages were a one time expense."[15]

Mayor Courtney ultimately resigned and moved to the Midwest, where he eventually was imprisoned for 15 years on the grounds that he had taken up robbing banks. One resident stated that it was his opinion that the chunky Courtney had been driven "over the bend" through his constant consumption of diet pills.[16]

Courtney was succeeded by Gerald Yourman, who was noted in the local press for driving a Honda 1000 motorcycle and living in a trailer that was parked under a television broadcasting tower. Yourman turned out to be somewhat controversial, too. For example, he typically referred to the county commissioners as "a bunch of idiots," took steps to rent out part of the town hall to a local karate academy, and fired many of the city workers (most of whom were police officers) who had organized and campaigned for his election. In 1982, Mayor Yourman announced his resignation from the office of mayor, stating that "I find that marital bliss and sexual sensation and a sensuous life are important to me. . . . the King of England gave up his throne for the woman he loved," and Yourman could do no less.[17]

It is perhaps because of such incidents that the press has referred to Pembroke Park as the "Rodney Dangerfield of municipalities," "that wacka-wacka town," and "Bozoville, U.S.A."[18]

The politics of the grassroots, as "Bozoville, U.S.A.," exemplifies, is frequently the politics of fun. But if some state and local governments, like Rodney Dangerfield, "don't get no respect," the fact remains that the people have more faith in state and local governments than they have in the national government. A 1976 Harris survey found that the public rated state government more worthy of trust than the federal government by a 3-to-1 margin. State governments legitimately can claim more grassroots support: 65 percent of those polled believed that the state government was closer to the people. By more than 3-to-1, they believed that the federal government was more corrupt than state government.[19] Surveys taken every year since 1972 by the Advisory Commission on Intergovernmental Relations have found that state and local governments combined have consistently been rated higher than the federal government when respondents are asked from which level of government they feel they got the most for their money—federal, state, or local. In the 1979 and 1981 polls, respondents indicated that local governments gave them more for their money than did either the federal or state governments, and in 1984, for the first time, the federal government ranked last on this question, after both local and state governments.[20]

STATE CONSTITUTIONS: THE RULES OF THE GAME

Why people seem to have greater faith in their state and local governments than they do in the federal government is attributable to a variety of factors. State and local governments are more convenient to the people, often operate more openly, and are far more restricted in the potential damage that they can cause. Yet, these governments form policy on and administer the most basic elements of the public's common interests: justice, safety, health, order, education, and welfare. These are the grassroots governments, and they show the American people and the political systems that they have devised in their most vivid colors. Through these governments, each of us has the most likely chance of making and changing public policy.

The fundamental vehicle that state and local governments use to implement changes in public policy are the state constitutions, which express the basic political parameters of each state and its local governments. Like the national Constitution, all state constitutions contain a bill of civil rights (although, technically, such bills are unnecessary, since state citizens are guaranteed these rights by the Fourteenth Amendment) and set up an organization of the government. Invariably, three branches of government (legislative, executive, and adjudicative) are specified, and their powers and limitations are enumerated in a manner similar to the federal checks and balances system. A bicameral (two-house) legislature is specified in all but one state, Nebraska, which has a unicameral (one-house) legislature.

The 50 state constitutions frequently are as inelegant as the state governments themselves. They lack the intellectual brilliance, stylistic grace, and verbal parsimony of the federal Constitution of 1789. Most are ponderous tomes (the estimated length of state constitutions is more than 26,000 words)[21] that revel in the pretentious. According to their constitutional preambles, Alaskans are "grateful to God," Puerto Ricans are "fully democratic," and Hawaiians are not only "mindful of our Hawaiian heritage," but possess "an understanding heart toward all the people of the earth."

Almost two-thirds of the state constitutions were written in the last century or even earlier (three states, Massachusetts, New Hampshire, and Vermont, still use constitutions that were drafted in the eighteenth century), and the average age of state constitutions in 1985 was about 85 years. Over the years, the American states have discarded and adopted no fewer than 145 constitutions. Between 1776, when the first state constitution was adopted, and 1981, a total of 7,953 proposed constitutional changes were submitted to voters in 49 states, and of these, 4,988 were adopted. The exception is Delaware, where legislative action alone is sufficient to change the constitution. Figure 1-1 illustrates periods of activity and lethargy among the states in revising their constitutions since the Revolution.

Figure 1-1 Number of state constitutional revisions by decade, 1776–1979. (*Source:* Advisory Commission on Intergovernmental Relations, *The Question of State Government Capability,* Washington, D.C.: U.S. Government Printing Office, 1985, p. 34.)

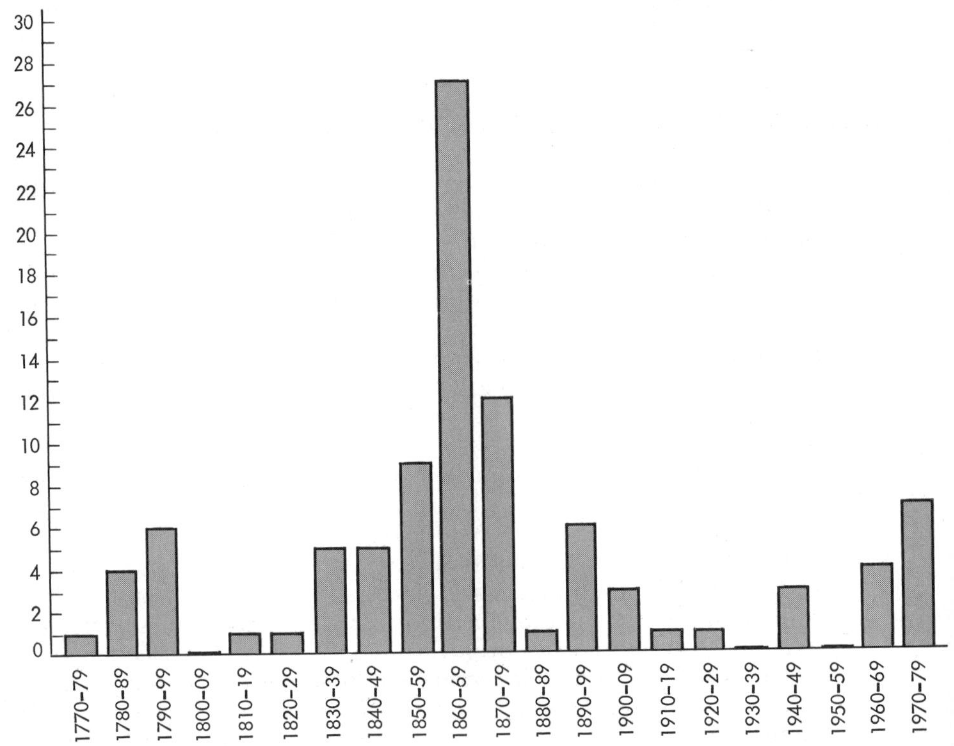

Does not include adopting of original constitution.
Hawaii was added to the decade of the 1970s because of extensive revisions to its 1950 constitution.

Table 1-1 indicates the kinds of changes that have been incorporated into state constitutions between 1970-1971 and 1980-1981. As it shows, the types of substantive alterations made in state constitutions range across the spectrum, from adjustments in the bill of rights to far-reaching amendments in finances and debt policies. By far the most popular category of constitutional change is that of state and local finance.

States may change their constitutions in one or more of the following four ways:

1. Proposals made by the state legislatures.
2. The constitutional initiative.
3. The constitutional convention.
4. The constitutional commission.

Only Florida provides specifically for the use of all four methods of constitutional revision, and every state except Delaware requires that the voters approve of any proposed change in the state's constitution; in Delaware, only the state legislature needs to vote on proposed constitutional amendments.

The most common approach that the states use to change their constitutions is through proposals by the legislature, which account for approximately 90 percent of the constitutional revisions that have been enacted by the states. State legislatures clearly play the major role in enacting constitutional change in all states.

The constitutional initiative is a device through which the citizens may directly propose constitutional change by acquiring a certain number of signatures on petitions to place the proposed constitutional change on the ballot. Oregon was the first state to use this method of changing its constitution when it adopted the device in 1902, and 17 states now use it. Dramatic political changes have been proposed through the constitutional initiative, such as California's tax-slashing Proposition 13, which was enacted by the voters in 1978. Critics contend that the constitutional initiative encourages proposals for constitutional amendments by special interests and that many of these initiatives are poorly drafted. By 1982, 539 constitutional initiatives had been submitted to voters in 17 states, although only 34 percent were adopted. It is clear that voters think less of proposals for constitutional change that are put forth through the constitutional initiative method than of those that are proposed by the legislature.

A third method of constitutional change is the constitutional convention, which may be used in all states, although only 41 states expressly permit it in their statutes. At least 230 such conventions have been held in the American states since 1776, and more than a quarter of these have been held in this century. Of the 35 referenda placed before the voters since 1930 to hold constitutional conventions, 27 have been rejected at the ballot box.

A final way in which states revise their constitutions is through the constitutional commission. Constitutional commissions have two major purposes: to study the state constitution and recommend changes (known as "study commissions") and to make preparations for a constitutional convention (or "preparatory commissions"). By far the most popular version is the study commission, which usually serves the legislature. Constitutional commissions may be set up by action of the legislature, through executive order by the governor, or, in the case of Florida, by the state constitution itself. Eighty-eight

Table 1-1 Substantive Changes in State Constitutions: Proposed and Adopted, 1970–71 to 1980–81

	TOTAL PROPOSED						*TOTAL ADOPTED*						*PERCENTAGE ADOPTED*					
Subject matter	*1980 –81*	*1978 –79*	*1976 –77*	*1974 –75*	*1972 –73*	*1970 –71*	*1980 –81*	*1978 –79*	*1976 –77*	*1974 –75*	*1972 –73*	*1970 –71*	*1980 –81*	*1978 –79*	*1976 –77*	*1974 –75*	*1972 –73*	*1970 –71*
Proposals of statewide applicability	254	295	283	253	389	300	160	200	189	171	275	176	63.0	67.8	66.8	67.6	70.7	58.2
Bill of rights	13	17	10	9	26	13	10	15	6	6	22	11	76.9	88.2	60.0	66.7	84.6	84.6
Suffrage and elections	5	12	17	23	34	39	5	9	14	20	24	23	100.0	75.0	82.4	86.9	70.6	59.0
Legislative branch	43	37	40	40	46	42	21	25	18	27	25	19	48.8	67.6	45.0	67.5	54.3	45.2
Executive branch	21	16	32	34	36	27	10	12	23	20	25	22	47.6	75.0	71.9	58.8	69.4	81.5
Judicial branch	23	25	34	20	35	17	17	19	32	18	26	11	73.9	76.0	94.1	90.0	74.3	64.7
Local government	11	27	7	13	30	21	4	13	3	12	23	15	36.4	48.1	42.9	92.3	76.7	71.4
Taxation & finance	77	68	56	49	85	50	52	39	41	33	56	29	67.5	57.4	73.2	67.3	65.9	58.0
State & local debt	20	19	36	18	24	25	13	9	20	6	15	10	65.0	47.4	55.6	33.3	62.5	40.0
State functions	23	31	42	23	40	46	16	24	25	16	36	26	69.6	77.4	59.5	69.6	90.0	56.5
Amendment & revision	9	11	2	8	19	13	7	10	1	7	12	7	77.8	90.9	50.0	87.5	63.1	53.8
General revision proposals	1	1	1	12	2	7	0	1	1	3	1	3	0	100.0	100.0	25.0	50.0	42.9
Misc. proposals	8	31	6	4	12	*	5	25	5	3	10	*	62.5	80.6	83.3	75.0	83.3	*
Local amendments	134	100	116	99	141	103	112	77	91	85	93	48	83.6	77.0	78.4	85.9	65.9	46.6

[1] Not compiled for 1970–71.

Source: Albert L. Sturm and Janice C. May, "State Constitutions and Constitutional Revisions: 1980–81 and the Past Fifty Years," *Book of the States,* 1982–83 (Lexington, Ky.: Council of State Governments, 1982), p. 126.

commissions have been established since 1930 (only a dozen of which were preparatory commissions) in 43 states. This method reached its apex of popularity during the late 1960s, and the increased use of constitutional commissions has been one of the more important developments in the process of state constitutional revision for the past three decades. Constitutional commissions save time and energy in the legislatures, and often come up with useful ideas for revising the state's constitution.

The 1960s and 1970s saw an unprecedented wave of comprehensive revisions of state constitutions, and the principal methods used were the constitutional convention and the constitutional commission. One analysis[22] of why states enthusiastically undertook major revisions of their constitutions emerged with three theories of constitutional change: the *renovation-relearning model,* which contends that states reinforce a tendency to revise their constitutions by interacting with each other; the *federal model,* which holds that the federal government is a central source in stimulating state constitutional revisions; and the *state system model,* which argues that social, economic, and political variables within the state are the main reasons behind the initiating of a constitutional revision.

The renovation-relearning model, in which neighboring states stimulate each other to revise their constitutions, probably served as the most accurate description of why the states have been changing their constitutions so prolifically in recent years. The states that are the most actively pursuing constitutional revision tend to have significantly larger populations, to be more industrialized, and to have higher levels of professionalism in their legislatures and in the bureaucracy.

State constitutions are indeed "living documents" in the sense that they can be changed and frequently are. Nevertheless, most contain a proliferation of obsolete clauses, and one must speculate on whether these supposedly living documents might simply be the "undead." This juxtaposition of vitality and obsolescence epitomizes politics at the grassroots. In the statehouses, county courthouses, and city halls, democracy is displayed in the raw, exhibiting not only the warts on the body politic, but also the genius of the American political mind. State constitutions, with their odd amalgam of modernity and antiquity, express this continuing duality at the grassroots. They are documents of both political principle and political expedience.

TWO EXAMPLES OF GRASSROOTS POLITICS: SEX AND LIFE

Within the frameworks established by state constitutions, the grassroots political process is almost unbelievably rich and varied. This richness is often unappreciated by students of American politics. Despite the fact that state and local governments are the governments closest to each of us, some have contended that the study of state and local politics is dull and boring. Although it is unfortunately true that some of the analyses of state and local government constitute less than racy reading, it does not necessarily follow that the subject matter itself is dry. Quite the contrary, state and local governments form and execute not only some of the most fundamental public policies in the nation, but some of the most intellectually intriguing and emotionally laden as well. Consider just two examples: the women's movement and policies for some of the most dangerous scientific research currently being conducted in the world.

States and Sexism

Most people have heard of the women's liberation movement, or "women's lib," a major social reality of our time. Although the roots of the women's movement can be traced back for hundreds of years in this country, it is fair to say that much of the turmoil surrounding feminism today is a relatively recent development.

In terms of their attempts to reform fundamental social mores concerning the status of women, the states historically have been the major political target of the women's movement, chiefly because of laws enacted by state legislatures concerning the place of women in American society. For example, an Arizona statute provides that a person who "in the presence of or hearing of any woman or child, or in a public place, uses vulgar, abusive, or obscene language is guilty of a misdemeanor," and at least 12 states make it a criminal offense to impugn the chastity of a woman.[23]

There also is evidence of a double standard when the sentences for criminal offenses dealt to women by courts are examined. For example, the New York State Family Court Act provides that youths who are "habitually truant, incorrigible, ungovernable, or habitually disobedient and beyond lawful control of parent or guardian" may be imprisoned. The law applies to boys only up to the age of 16, and a boy may be kept in confinement only until age 18; but a girl can be imprisoned until the age of 20. A study of juvenile delinquents in jails and retention centers across the country found that more than half of the female delinquents were incarcerated for noncriminal conduct, whereas only 20 percent of the boys were incarcerated for noncriminal matters; the study concluded that girls served significantly longer terms than did boys.[24]

Married women also are often discriminated against in state law, purely on the basis of their marital status. In five states the wife must acquire court approval to engage in an independent business, and in Florida a wife must present a petition giving her name, age, and "her character, habits, education, and mental capacity for business" and she must "briefly set out the reasons why such disabilities [to engage in her own business] should be removed."[25] Indeed, it was not until 1921 that women gained the right to practice law in all states, and many states still bar women from such vocations as mining, wrestling, and tending bar.

State-legislated prohibitions as to the kinds of work in which women may engage lead us to the area of protective labor laws that apply to women only (for example, laws stating that women may not lift more than 30 pounds of weight on a job). Protective labor laws generally set out such regulations as maximum hours, minimum wages, and related standards. States vary greatly in the kinds of protective labor laws they have enacted, and a number of these laws use sex as a basis for protection. The effects of these laws, in the view of many, have been to exclude women from job opportunities for which they, in reality, are quite qualified, and it has been argued that protective labor laws are really designed to protect men's job opportunities at the expense of women's.

In 1963 and 1964, federal legislation designed to eliminate sex discrimination was enacted and quickly came into conflict with a number of state protective laws. This national legislation was the Equal Pay Act of 1963 and Title VII of the Civil Rights Act of 1964. The Equal Pay Act was an amendment to the Fair Labor Standards Act of 1938 and was later extended in 1968. The act has been helpful in eliminating artificial qualifications that prevent women from even being considered for certain jobs.

Title VII of the Civil Rights Act is more significant, stating that it "shall be unlawful employment practice" to discriminate on the basis of sex. The act also established the Equal Employment Opportunity Commission (EEOC) to investigate discrimination complaints against companies with 25 or more employees. In 1972 the Commission was given power to sue an employer in court for violation of the Civil Rights Act, a power that applies to educational institutions and government employers as well as to the private sector.

Title VII allows an employer to discriminate on the basis of sex only where such discrimination constitutes "*bona fide* occupational qualification reasonably necessary to the formal operation of that particular business or enterprise." This provision has resulted in a number of court actions seeking to define what constitutes a "*bona fide* occupational qualification" under Title VII of the Civil Rights Act.

Two major cases occurred in 1968 and 1969. In 1968 the Supreme Court upheld, in *Rosenfeld* v. *Southern Pacific Company,* that certain weight-lifting limitations for women established by California were invalid. In the famous case of *Weeks* v. *Southern Bell Telephone and Telegraph Company* in 1969, the Court of Appeals held that "an employer has the burden of proving that he had reasonable cause to believe . . . that all or substantially all women would be unable to perform safely and efficiently the duties of the job involved." This was the argument used to permit Ms. Weeks to become a "switchman," voiding a 30-pound weight-lifting limit for women established by the state. In effect, the two cases held that certain state protective labor laws cannot be used to deny women a job or promotion and that the burden of proof regarding the fairness of a *bona fide* occupational disqualification is on the employer rather than on the employee.[26] In summary, state protective labor laws are increasingly coming under fire by both the courts and the Equal Employment Opportunity Commission as laws that discriminate against women in terms of employment opportunities.

How effective the pressures brought by feminist groups have been in opening more job opportunities to women must be conjectural. On the one hand, there has been a huge influx of women into the nation's labor pool. Fifty-two percent of all women over the age of 16 were working or looking for work in 1980, and women made up 43 percent of the labor force. In 1950, only 34 percent of women worked or were in the job market, and they constituted only 29 percent of the labor pool. Projections indicate that perhaps as many as 65 percent of all women will be in the labor force by 1995.[27] On the other hand, women earn about six dollars for every ten that a man earns, and their share of the occupational dollar has actually declined since 1955.[28] Overall, the median weekly income of full-time women workers in the professions is less than three quarters that of men in comparable jobs, less than two-thirds of men's pay in clerical positions, and 45 percent of men's salaries in sales jobs. Male college graduates earn about 70 percent more than their female counterparts do.[29] Nevertheless, as state laws continue to come under fire as discriminating against women, the vocational opportunities available to women can only increase over time.

While state protective labor laws and what constitutes a *bona fide* occupational qualification are under attack in the courts, another route women are taking to eradicate discriminatory practices is purely political. The most notable example, perhaps, is the Equal Rights Amendment (ERA) passed by Congress in 1972, which required the ratification of 38 states. The Equal Rights Amendment was resisted by such powerful groups as the AFL-CIO, which viewed it as a threat to job opportunities for men. By 1974, however, organized labor had reversed its position and was supporting the ERA.

Labor's slow support of the Equal Rights Amendment may have been a case of too little, too late. Despite an unprecedented extension by Congress of the time limit in which states could approve the proposed Amendment, from 1979 to 1982, only 35 states had endorsed the ERA when it went down in defeat.[30] Those states that did not approve the ERA were largely the same states that did not approve the amendment granting women the vote back in 1920.

More effective than the fight to pass the Equal Rights Amendment has been the gradual entrance of increasing numbers of women into grassroots politics. Women, who make up 53 percent of the voting-age population, occupy 9 percent of all the nation's state and local elected offices. Although still low, the gains being made by women in elected politics are nonetheless impressive; in 1975, women occupied only 5 percent of the country's state and local elected positions.[31]

In brief and to the point, states are "where the action is" in one of the major social movements of our time. The women's movement is an example of how most major political movements really happen—in the states, not in some entity called "the nation." It is state laws that often are the most discriminatory against women, and it is state legislatures that have felt the brunt of feminist activity.

Science and the City

A second example of policies debated and made by state and local governments occurred in 1976 in Cambridge, Massachusetts, when the Cambridge city council took on Harvard University and the Massachusetts Institute of Technology, both located within its city limits, and voted to terminate temporarily the research underway in their respective biology departments on recombinant DNA.

Before we can appreciate the significance of this vote, we need to understand what is involved in biological research in recombinant DNA. DNA, the basic genetic molecule, is the molecular basis of heredity in most organisms, including human beings. Biologists have been attempting—with increasing success—to recombine the basic genetic molecule in new formats. Research involves (in grossly oversimplified terms) cutting the DNA molecule into various segments and sticking them back together in a new way. Most biologists who are doing recombinant DNA research are inserting animal genes into human intestinal bacteria.

The implications for this kind of research are profound but unknown. In 1974, Paul Berg of the National Academy of Sciences called for a worldwide moratorium on certain experiments involving recombinant DNA. This moratorium was observed for two years by all nations when, after much debate, the National Institutes of Health (NIH) of the federal government developed security guidelines for recombinant DNA research. These guidelines were deemed necessary by many biologists because, when one is creating new forms of life at the bacterial level, one might also be creating new forms of diseases for which there would be no control. As one biologist observed, "What we are doing is almost certainly irreversible. Knowing human frailty, these structures will escape, and there is no way to recapture them. The hazard, if there is a hazard, will not be like DDT or PCBs or aerosols, which you can just stop manufacturing."[32] *Science* magazine commented: "After the first atomic devices were successfully developed, Robert Oppenheimer remarked that physicists had now known sin. That biologists may be at least moving out of an 'age of innocence' may be heralded by research on recombinant DNA."[33]

Much potential social good, of course, could come from this research, notably new vaccines against viruses. But still, research in recombinant DNA can create new organisms that may spread uncontrollably about the planet, for better or worse. *Science* magazine quoted the head of the Division of Biology at the California Institute of Technology, who warned "of the potential broader social or ethical implications of initiating this line of research—of its role, as a possible prelude to longer-range, broader-scale genetic engineering of the fauna and flora of the planet, including ultimately, man. . . . Do we want to assume the basic responsibility for life on this planet—to develop new living forms for our own purposes? Shall we take into our own hands our future evolution?"[34]

Such are the issues that the National Institutes of Health grappled with, eventually developing guidelines that established four classes of recombinant DNA research, which were designated from P1 (research safe to conduct in virtually any kind of laboratory) to P4 (to be conducted only under conditions of very strict physical surveillance); P4 research, for example, should be conducted only in such places as military fortresses.

In short, recombinant DNA is exciting, but dangerous, involving not only life, but new forms of life. So why would the city council of Cambridge interfere with recombinant DNA research?

On July 7, 1976, the Cambridge city council, seven men and two women who normally handled such matters as road repairs and taxes, took on one of the most perplexing problems in biology today and debated whether or not recombinant DNA research was safe for Cambridge.

Harvard and M.I.T. wanted to put a P3 class laboratory on the Harvard campus. The faculties of both Harvard and M.I.T. were divided on the wisdom of establishing such a laboratory at Harvard, and the issue centered around security reasons. The meeting of July 7, which lasted until 1:00 in the morning, was described by observers as a "circus." Meanwhile scientists at Harvard and M.I.T., who had been waiting nearly two years for establishment of NIH guidelines and an end to the worldwide moratorium, suddenly found themselves confronting the Cambridge city council. The council was saying, and with authority, that it was an open question as to whether these biologists could conduct such research.

Cambridge is largely a working class town of 100,000 people. That its city council became embroiled in an issue involving a highly sophisticated level of biological research was, to say the least, an interesting policy process. The mayor of Cambridge characterized the DNA researchers as "those people in white coats" who could "build a Frankenstein" or visit upon the populace some deadly organism along the lines of the fictional *Andromeda Strain*. *Science* magazine quoted one city councilman as saying, "The Harvard and MIT people thought that, because Washington had said it was okay to go ahead, that was that. They were flabbergasted to discover that Al Vellucci [the mayor of Cambridge] could have a noose around their neck in just a few days' time. Here's a guy ranting and raving about monsters and germs in the sewers and they have to stop what they want to do because of him. They just didn't understand."[35]

Mayor Vellucci had been approached by a member of the Harvard faculty, who expressed his concern about the proposed lab for recombinant DNA research. Some argued that Vellucci then used this concern as a political gambit, since Vellucci already had gained a good deal of political mileage out of the Harvard campus, arguing loudly that Harvard Yard should be converted into a parking lot.

Scientist after scientist appeared before the Cambridge city council, arguing both for and against the proposed P3 facility and the continuation of recombinant DNA research. Then the biologists made a grievous political error. One of the scientists stated that the health commissioner of Cambridge had been invited to attend meetings of the Harvard Committee on the Regulation of Hazardous Biological Agents. While the city council members may not have known much, if anything, about recombinant DNA, they did know that they did not have a health commissioner. The city had not had a health commissioner for 19 months, and, in one observer's view, it was "something of a sore point with them." Thus, what had started off as a good political gambit for the mayor was not ending well. Ultimately, the city of Cambridge voted that a Cambridge Laboratory Experimentation Review Board comprised of scientists and citizens be established to investigate recombinant DNA and, in the future, other types of dangerous research. They also voted that once a health commissioner was appointed, he or she would have the authority to recommend a course of action for the city council. The city declared a three-month "good faith" moratorium on recombinant DNA research, which Harvard and M.I.T. observed; eventually, the city permitted the two universities to proceed with its P3 facility at Harvard.

How the Cambridge city council wrestled with one of the most complex, controversial, and explosive scientific issues of the twentieth century is a fine example of what local governments do. Although admittedly a more exotic example than most, it highlights the fundamental kinds of issues that governments at the grassroots must grapple with. Consider the opinion of one Cambridge council member: "I tried to understand the science, but I decided I couldn't make a legitimate assessment of the risk. When I realized I couldn't decide to vote for or against a moratorium on scientific grounds, I shifted to the political."[36] That is probably the way most of the council members felt, but "political" is not used here in a pejorative sense. The council members of Cambridge seemed to want to involve the public in realms where the public had never been involved before, although these decisions could determine the very form of their lives—and not just *their* lives, but all of *ours*. Moreover, the Cambridge city council did this in defiance of federally established guidelines that the global scientific community assumed would end the two-year-old worldwide moratorium. Local government in America is not only fun and vital, it is also powerful.

But even the most autonomous of subnational governments are subject to forces beyond their control. After all, America is a big country. Its people are as different as its regions, its politics as varied as its climates. But where are the people in this nation, and why are they there?

The people are scattered throughout a plethora of political jurisdictions administered by 82,341 governments. Although the numbers of all types of American governments have remained roughly constant (with the exception of school districts, which have declined) since 1960, the number of people and the movements of people have not.

Two major trends emerged in the 1970s that will determine the political realities of our time. One is the *sub*urbanization of the nation; for the first time, the historic migrations of Americans to cities is reversing. The other is the rise of the Sunbelt states in the South and Southwest as economic and political competitors to the Eastern Establishment and the Snowbelt.

THE SUBURBANIZATION OF AMERICA

To appreciate what *suburbanization* means, a bit of background is necessary. In 1790, when the first census was taken, 95 percent of our people were farmers and 5 percent city dwellers; by 1970, these figures essentially had been reversed. Related to this migration to the central cities was the black exodus from the South to the North. From 1900 until the 1970s, approximately 10 percent of the South's black populace moved from Dixie every decade. Even though black migration rates to the North peaked in the 1950s and began to decline in the 1960s, between 1950 and 1970, some *four million* blacks moved to the North. Most went to the metropolises of Yankeeland, in what amounted to the biggest population shift in world history. There, blacks carved neighborhood enclaves for themselves out of what was usually the cities' cheapest housing and, over time, became entrapped in those same central cities in what we now call "black ghettoes."

Beginning at midcentury, certain countertrends and variational shifts began to emerge. The census of 1970 detected a hefty minority of blacks who were "going home" to the Old South, an area that has changed considerably since 1900. By 1974, for the first time since Emancipation, more blacks were moving south than north. More significant, however, was the departure, starting around 1945, of white middle-class families, pressured by competition for housing from blacks, rising property taxes, and other forces, from the core cities to the suburban fringe. By the early 1960s the overall rate of population growth in the inner cities had begun to decline.

During the 1970s, these trends accelerated. Between 1970 and 1983, the central cities endured a net loss of nearly 18.7 million people, who departed for the suburbs and nonmetropolitan areas. Figure 1-2 indicates the patterns of these migrations. This fleeing to suburbia and the countryside by inner-city residents reversed demographic patterns that can be traced as far back as 1820, when the urbanization of America began.

Of course, a few middle-class people have recently entered the central cities from the suburbs, but these movements—what some have called the "regentrification" of the inner cities—have never amounted to much more than "mini trends" in a demographic sense.[37] Americans love suburbs, and between 1970 and 1983, a net total of more than 15.5 million people left the cities to live in them. Overall, the suburban share of all metropolitan residents has risen from 50 percent in 1960 to more than 60 percent.[38]

Note that in this discussion of suburbanization since 1970 we have not used the term "white flight," the well-worn phrase used to indicate that whites were fleeing the inner cities and leaving them to blacks and browns. This was once true, and, to a degree, still is. But, increasingly, blacks are fleeing to the

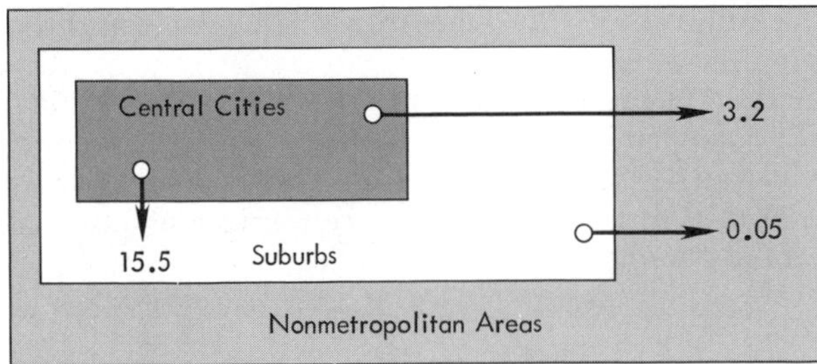

Figure 1-2
Net residential flows 1970–1983, central cities, suburbs, and nonmetropolitan areas (in millions). (*Source:* Bureau of the Census, *Current Population Reports,* Series P-20, No. 353, Washington, D.C.: U.S. Government Printing Office, March, 1975–March, 1979, p. 2; Bureau of the Census, *Current Population Reports,* Series P-20, No. 377, Washington, D.C.: U.S. Government Printing Office, March, 1980–March, 1981, p. 3; Bureau of the Census, *Current Population Reports,* Series P-20, No. 384, Washington, D.C.: U.S. Government Printing Office, March, 1981–March, 1982, p. 2; and Bureau of the Census, *Current Population Reports,* Series P-20, No. 393, Washington, D.C.: U.S. Government Printing Office, March, 1982–March, 1983, p. 1.

suburbs along with whites—in fact, faster than whites. In 1970, slightly more than 11 percent of the residents of the "urban fringe" (a Census Bureau term that more or less covers suburbs) were blacks; by 1980, nearly 19 percent of these residents were blacks. Yet, the percentage of central cities' residents who are black (57 percent) remained virtually the same over the decade, declining by only 1 percent. In part, this stability was attributable to influxes of blacks to central cities from rural areas; between 1970 and 1980, the proportion of rural dwellers who were black fell by half (from nearly 19 percent to more than 9 percent), but also because many blacks still remain trapped in inner cities.[39] Still, as the trends verify, blacks are leaving central cities for the suburbs in larger numbers and more rapidly than ever before. The phenomenon of "white flight" becomes more a misnomer with each passing year.

Nevertheless, people are deserting the central cities. But who are they? Increasingly, the people leaving the cities are those who can afford to get out. Until 1960, most poor people lived in small towns or rural areas. By 1978, however, 60 percent of the nation's poor lived in metropolitan regions, and 60 percent of the metropolitan poor, in turn, lived in the inner cities. Only 7 percent of the suburban population was below the poverty line, compared to 16 percent of the central city population. Between 1960 and 1978, the percentage of all poor people living in suburbs had risen by only five points, while the inner cities' proportion of poor people rose by ten points.[40] The flight from the cities is quintessentially middle-class, regardless of race. "Poverty," to quote the president's *National Urban Policy Report,* "has increasingly become a central city phenomenon."[41] Increasingly, big American cities are "hardship" cases.

"THE WORSE THINGS GET, THE WORSE THINGS GET"

In a sophisticated analysis of "urban hardship" in 55 major cities, the Brookings Institution ranked the disparities that existed between inner cities and their suburbs on the logic that, "Such disparities often lead to the population movement and economic decline typical of distressed central cities."[42] As the authors observe,

The picture is familiar. As more residents and businesses move to the suburbs, the city's tax base is driven down. Property or other tax rates must be raised to compensate, in turn causing more people and industries to leave. A natural law seems to govern these high-disparity cases: "The worse things get, the worse things get." It is a continuous process, feeding on itself.[43]

The upshot of the black-white, poor-rich imbalance between cities and suburbs is that those local governments with the greatest demand for public services are least able to afford them because of inordinately weak tax bases. Funds for education, fire protection, police protection, public health, and other basic functions of government are lacking for significant portions of the population.

Table 1-2, which updates the Brookings studies along comparable criteria, lists the nation's "worst off" and "best off" big cities in 1970 and 1980. The term "resident need," in the table's title refers to a composite of a city's percentage of population below the poverty line, the net change and the percentage of growth in real per capita income over the decade, and the unemployment rate in 1980. The table indicates massive shifts among regions of the country. In 1970, 7 of the 10 cities with the highest need were in the Sunbelt and West, but a decade later only one was; in 1970, the 10 big cities with the lowest resident need were split evenly between Snowbelt and Sunbelt, but 10 years later only 2 of these cities were found outside the South and West.

THE METROPOLITAN MORASS

Compounding the disparities in public service that are inflamed by demographic shifts are the minions of governments proliferating in Metropolitan Statistical Areas (MSAs), or regions containing at least one city with 50,000 people or moreor an urbanized area (as defined by the Census Bureau) of 50,000 or more inhabitants and a total MSA population of at least 100,000 (but 75,000 in New England).[44] Of the 82,341 governments in the United States, more than a third—29,861 of them—are found in the MSAs, and they are growing; governments

Table 1-2 Big Cities with the Highest and Lowest Levels of Resident Need: 1970 and 1980

	10 HIGHEST NEED		*10 LOWEST NEED*	
Rank	*1970*	*1980*	*1970*	*1980*
1	Newark	Newark	Honolulu	Tulsa
2	New Orleans	Detroit	Nashville	San Jose
3	El Paso	Atlanta	Indianapolis	Wichita
4	St. Louis	Cleveland	Virginia Beach	Houston
5	Birmingham	Baltimore	St. Paul	Virginia Beach
6	Sacramento	Buffalo	Omaha	Seattle
7	Miami	Philadelphia	Dallas	Honolulu
8	San Antonio	New York	Minneapolis	Austin
9	Oakland	Chicago	Toledo	Charlotte
10	Cleveland	St. Louis	Austin	Denver

Source: National Urban Policy Advisory Committee to the Subcommittee on Investment, Jobs, and Prices of the Joint Economic Committee of the Congress, *Urban America, 1984: A Report Card* (Denver, Co.: Center for Public/Private Cooperation, Graduate School of Public Affairs, University of Colorado, 1985), p. 5.

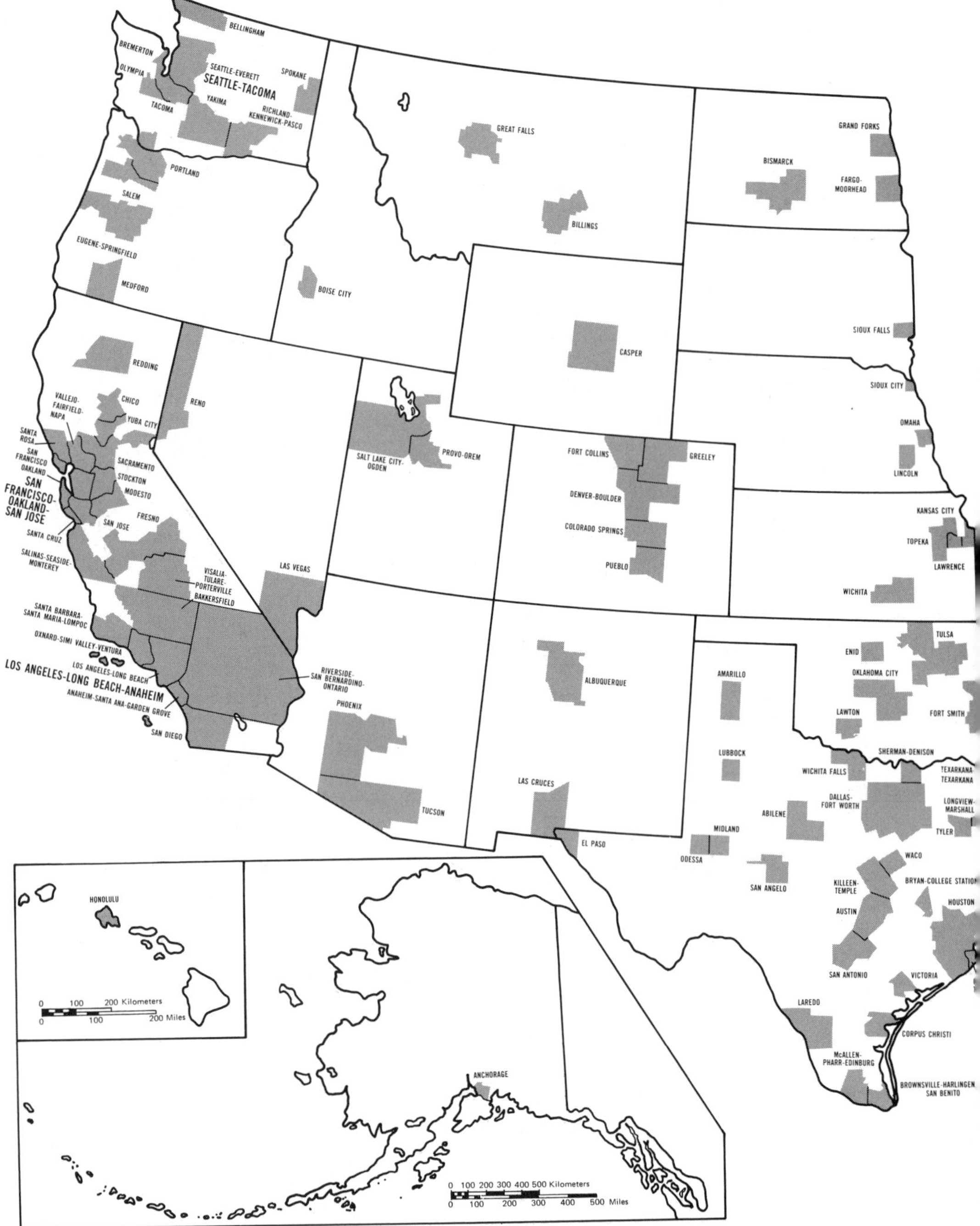

Figure 1-3 Metropolitan statistical areas of the United States, 1981. (*Source:* Bureau of the Census, *State and Metropolitan Data Book, 1982,* Washington, D.C.: U. S. Government Printing Office, 1982, pp. xii–xiii.)

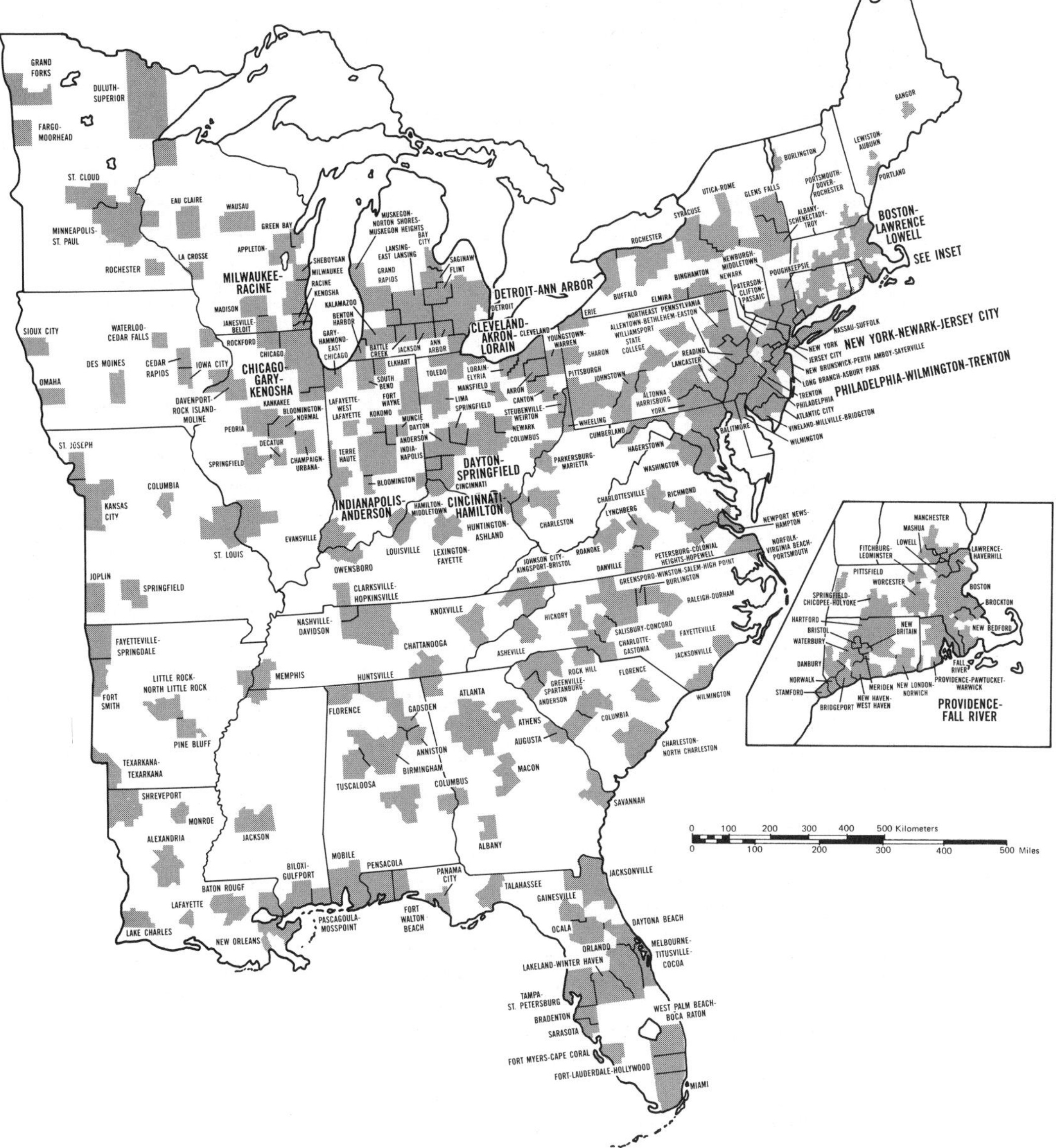

Figure 1-3 (continued)

inside MSAs have burgeoned by more than a fourth since 1972. These are independent governments, not agencies or departments. The nation's 277 MSAs (shown in Figure 1-3) contain more than three quarters of the total population, cover only 16 percent of the nation's land, and average almost 98 local governments per metropolis.[45] Despite this median figure, there is considerable variation in the number of governments found in different metropolitan areas. Chicago has the most (more than 1,200 governments); metropolitan areas in the South are usually leaner. An MSA's population size seems primarily related to the number of governments that the area has. For example, metropolitan areas with a million people or more have, on the average, nearly 300 governments within them, while metropolises between 50,000 and 100,000 people average fewer than 30.

The upshot of this kind of ultralocal arrangement of America's metropolitan governments is that the structure, or lack of it, may add to the public's problems. Consider the evaluation made by the National Research Council:

> Fragmentation rather than correspondence to the scale of metropolitan activity is the rule, not the exception. Administrative disabilities are widespread. Overlapping responsibility is prevalent. Fiscal externalities persist. Control of environmental pollution is impeded. Residents with higher incomes continue their migration to the suburbs. The central city finds it more and more difficult to raise necessary revenues. Differences between city and suburban tax burdens reflect inequitable distribution of metropolitan costs. Efforts to increase metropolitan unity are hampered. The state of metropolitan transportation, water supplies, and waste disposal, for example, remains precarious in many areas. Meanwhile, jurisdictions, like the small enterprises they often resemble, calculate and compete for additional sources of tax revenue. The social problems of the metropolis—crime, inadequate education programs, unemployment, and inadequate housing—slowly spread. Fragmentation of government is only in small part a cause of these social problems, but it makes them much more difficult to solve.[46]

Perhaps a more pithy assessment of the human dimension of the problem, as opposed to the governmental dimensions, was made by a mother of two teenage boys: "We live in East Meadow. I work in Garden City. My husband works in Syosset. We shop for clothes in Hempstead. My husband's Pythias Lodge meets in Great Neck. Our temple is in Merrick. The children's doctor is in Westbury. And we pay for our parking tickets in Mineola."[47]

POLITICAL CULTURES: THE POLITICS OF REGIONALISM

Our discussion of the nation's political demography thus far has centered on urban and suburban areas. But the relationships between people and power on a state and regional level are also important and in many ways more interesting.

In his classic study of federalism, Daniel J. Elazar drew a "map" of political cultures for the mainland 48 states. He defined three major cultural types: moralism, individualism, and traditionalism.[48] A *moralistic* political culture, in Elazar's view, blankets the West Coast, Midwest, and Northeast. It fosters a high concern for public issues, is directed toward the common man and his search for the good society, views government's place in society positively, disparages partisan politics, is change oriented, has a high intolerance of political corruption, and is relatively accepting of a professionalized public bureaucracy.

An *individualistic* political culture peppers most of the country, with comparatively high concentrations in the Southwest, Midwest, and Northeast. It stresses the concept that democracy is a marketplace and places a premium on the value of the private sector as opposed to the public sector; it sees the role of the government as one permitting the growth of prosperity in the private sector. Party affiliation counts for much, issue orientation is eschewed. It is felt that government should play a passive role in society, and it is deemed relatively legitimate for an officeholder to distribute political rewards, both to himself or herself and to others.

A *traditionalistic* political culture dominates in the South, Southwest, and portions of the Midwest. It is in part a hybrid between the moralistic and individualistic cultures. Although the traditionalistic culture believes in a positive role for government (as does the moralistic culture), its members also assume that a person's first obligation is to himself or herself, and, therefore, it is legitimate to benefit personally from one's political office (as in the individualistic culture). Partisan politics is played down, as with the moralists, and the development of a professional corps of public officials is resisted in very elemental terms. The overriding reality of a traditionalistic culture is the role of a paternalistic political elite, usually comprised of people with "old family" ties. Its mission is the preservation of the *status quo*. To this end, a widespread citizen disinterest in political issues is the norm.

Aspects of all these political cultures are found in all parts of the nation, but there are particular concentrations in various regions. The population changes that many regions have undergone may have far-reaching consequences for state and local politics, especially in light of differing political belief-sets among the regions of the country.

THE POWER SHIFT: ENTER THE SUNBELT

Americans are doing more than moving out of the inner cities. They also are moving out of the Northeast and Midwest—the "Snowbelt"—and to the milder climes of the South and West—the "Sunbelt."[49] More than 90 percent of the country's population growth between 1970 and 1980 occurred outside the Snowbelt.[50] Figure 1-4 shows these trends. Between 1970 and 1983, the Northeast increased its share of the nation's population growth by less than 6 percent and the Midwest by 11 percent. But the South's share of the country's population growth burgeoned by 110 percent during the same period and the West's by nearly three-fourths. The nation's bicentennial year was a benchmark in regional terms: for the first time in the country's history, a majority of Americans lived in the South and West.

The migrations to the South and West during the 1970s and early 1980s were dramatic. The population of the Northeast grew by 1 percent between 1970 and 1983 and the Midwest by 5 percent. But the South's population exploded by more than 25 percent and the West's by more than 30 percent.[51] Moreover, it is continuing. The U.S. Bureau of the Census has projected that the population of the South and West may grow by four times the rate of the Northeast and Midwest between 1980 and 2000.[52]

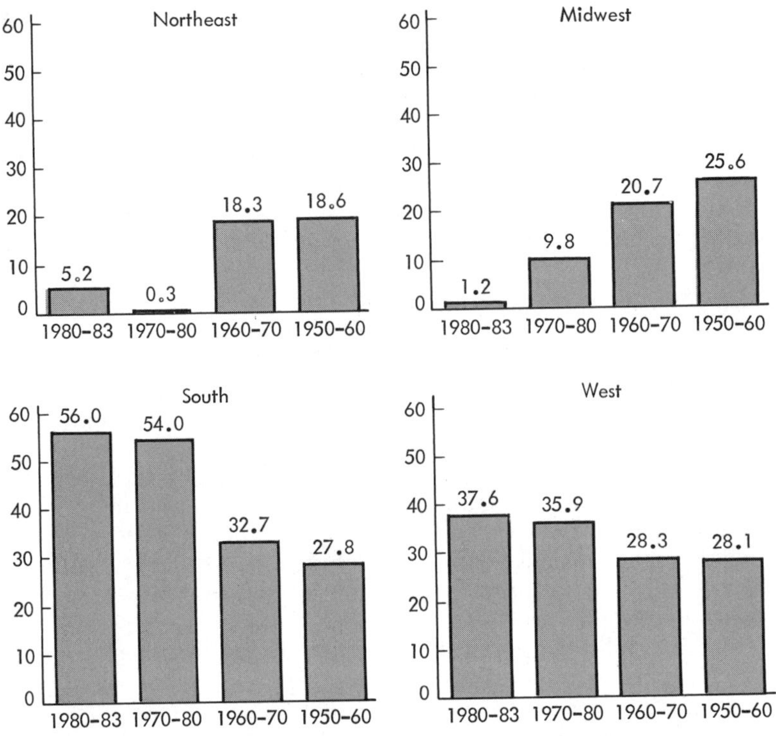

Figure 1-4 Percent share of U.S. population growth, by region, for selected periods: 1950 to 1983. (*Source:* Bureau of the Census, *Current Population Reports,* Series P-25, No. 957, "Estimates of the Population of States: 1970 to 1983," Washington, D.C.: U.S. Government Printing Office, 1984, p. 1.)

Table 1-3 displays the meaning of these regional migrations in terms of the 30 largest American cities. Note that 16 of the 22 biggest cities that gained population from 1970 to 1983 were Sunbelt and Western cities, while none of the 11 largest cities that lost people was in the Sunbelt or West.

These massive shifts have had an economic and political impact. Between 1970 and 1980, almost 60 percent of the expansion of the service sector of the nation's economy occurred in the South and West, and the Snowbelt lost more than 750,000 jobs in manufacturing.[53] A study of the nation's 131 largest cities underscored the grim meaning of these figures for the Snowbelt. The analysis ranked cities according to the decline or increase in their real total incomes from 1970 to 1980. Of the 54 cities that actually suffered a drop in real income during the decade, 49 were in the Northeast or Midwest. Of the 30 cities that experienced the greatest gains in real income, 29 were in the South or West![54]

Despite a fast-track economy in the Sunbelt, much of it remains a less developed portion of the nation. Median family income for residents of the South is significantly lower than is that for Snowbelt denizens, although the West now surpasses the Midwest (but not the Northeast) on this measure.[55] What we

Table 1-3 Population Changes in Major Metropolitan Areas, 1970–1983 (Population 1,000)

Growing	*1983 Ranking in size*	*1970*	*1983*	*Percentage Gain 1970–1983*
Boston	7	3,939	3,997	+1
Baltimore	16	2,089	2,232	6
Chicago	3	7,779	8,016	3
Kansas City, Mo.	25	1,373	1,464	6
Indianapolis	32	1,111	1,182	6
Columbus	28	1,149	1,263	9
Memphis	42	834	930	10
Washington, D.C.	9	3,040	3,370	10
San Francisco	5	4,754	5,624	15
New Orleans	27	1,100	1,318	16
Seattle	18	1,837	2,187	16
Los Angeles	2	9,981	12,191	18
Nashville	45	699	878	20
Jacksonville	50	613	773	21
San Antonio	33	888	1,169	24
Atlanta	15	1,684	2,305	27
Dallas	10	2,352	3,266	28
Denver	21	1,238	1,768	30
El Paso	70	359	510	30
San Diego	19	1,358	2,015	33
Houston	8	2,169	3,561	39
Phoenix	23	971	1,664	42
Shrinking				*Percentage Loss 1970–1983*
Milwaukee	24	1,575	1,571	−0.2
Philadelphia	4	5,749	5,738	0.2
St. Louis	14	2,429	2,396	1
Springfield	69	528	515	2
New York	1	18,193	17,687	3
Youngstown	67	537	522	3
Detroit	6	4,788	4,605	4
Dayton	41	975	936	4
Cleveland	11	3,000	2,803	7
Buffalo	30	1,349	1,226	10
Pittsburgh	13	2,556	2,400	10

Source: Bureau of the Census, *Statistical Abstract of the United States, 1985* (Washington, D.C.: U.S. Government Printing Office, 1984), pp. 19–21.

are witnessing, as Figure 1-5 dramatically illustrates, is economic catch-up among the regions.

We also may be witnessing a political equalization as well. The South and West gained 17 seats in the U.S. House of Representatives as a result of the 1980 Census. With the decline of the seniority principle in Congress during the past two decades and the corresponding rise of the "juniority," Sunbelt freshmen may have a more immediate impact in the national legislature than congressional

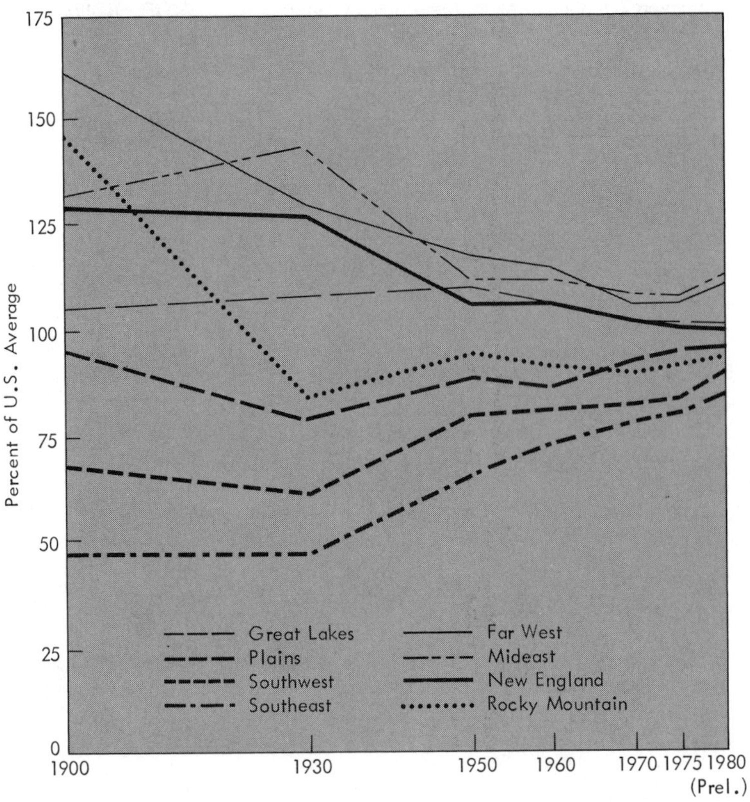

Figure 1-5 Regional per capita income as a percentage of U.S. average, selected years, 1900–1980. (*Source:* Advisory Commission on Intergovernmental Relations, Washington, D.C.: U.S. Government Printing Office.)

newcomers have had in the past. It is equally worth noting that three of the past four presidents have been sons of the Sunbelt.

More fundamentally, perhaps, we may be witnessing a rather precipitous conflict between peoples reared in fundamentally different political environments and holding incompatible political values. The Moralists from the North are invading the western and southern preserves of the Traditionalists. People who believe in widespread political participation, aggressive government programs for social change, and political self-direction suddenly are rubbing shoulders with people who value political apathy, view government as a necessary evil for maintaining the *status quo*, and accept as only meet and proper the political dominance of paternalistic elites.

The transfer (or diffusion) of people and power from cities to suburbs and countryside, and from the Northeast and Midwest to the South and West, constitutes the primary political reality during the last quarter of this century. These shifts imply that not only will the supposed Eastern Establishment gradually fade as an object of national (or at least regional) resentment, but that Americans may lose some of their preoccupation with politics in Washington and perhaps refocus their attention on their state and local governments.

WHY STUDY STATE AND LOCAL POLITICS?

We have seen that state and local governments are important and powerful, and that alone makes the study of subnational politics worthwhile. There is a more practical reason, however, for acquiring a smattering of knowledge about state and local politics: towns, cities, counties, and states have jobs for college graduates; indeed, they have more jobs than any sector of the national economy. More than three quarters of all nonmilitary public employees work for state or local governments, and state and local employers have been hiring college graduates at a rate seven times that of the federal government. Of the nation's labor force, roughly one employee in six works for one level of government or another, and almost one in five is hired by a government other than the national government. Since the mid-1950s, employment by state and local governments has increased at a rate four times that of the economy as a whole. State and local governments are not only where the power is, they are where the jobs are.

But while a practical turn of mind is an asset in learning about state and local politics, the field offers intellectual fascination quite aside from the practical. *Governing at the Grassroots* displays the gleaming threads that weave the nation's political brocade, whose richness is the result of citizens, groups, governments, and regions contributing their colors, strengths, weaknesses, and tensions to the tangle of yarns that have been woven into a varied political cloth on the loom of the earth's most complex democracy. The warp and weft of American politics—that tensile, underlying strength of the nation's political fabric—are what *Governing at the Grassroots* is about.

NOTES

[1]Rex Reed, "Lester Maddox as a Leader of Men," *Esquire* (October, 1976), p. 172.
[2]Harold Lavine, *The Arizona Republic* (October 7, 1976).
[3]United Press International, *The Arizona Republic* (October 11, 1976), syndicated nationally.
[4]"Killer Bees Prove Shenanigans Are Just a Way of Life in Texas Legislature," *The New York Times*, as reprinted in the *The Arizona Republic* (May 27, 1979).
[5]Eugene Carlson, " 'Now,' the Senator Said, 'We've Got Them Right Where They Want Us'," *The Wall Street Journal* (March 19, 1982).
[6]Information in the following paragraphs is drawn from Alfred E. Lewis and Ron Shaffer, *Washington Post* (March 1, 1976); Shaffer, *Washington Post* (March 5, 1976); Timothy S. Robinson, *Washington Post* (March 5, 1976); and Sally Quinn, *Washington Post* (March 5, 1976).
[7]Dick Hyman, *The Trenton Pickle Ordinance and Other Bonehead Legislation* (Brattleboro, Vt.: Stephen Greene, 1975).
[8]"City's Sex Ban Needs Surgery," *Washington Post* (December 2, 1979).
[9]County Clerk Edna Dewees, as quoted in Bill Rose, " 'Kuwait West' Encourages Little Else than Humor to Grow," *The Arizona Republic* (January 30, 1983).
[10]Frank Tolbert, as quoted in *ibid.*
[11]*Ibid.*
[12]County Judge Don Creager, as quoted in *ibid.*
[13]*Ibid.*
[14]County Clerk Edna Dewees, as quoted in *ibid.*
[15]Charles Feighan and Hewitt Wagner, as quoted in Calvin Trillin, "U.S. Journal: Pembroke Park, Florida," *The New Yorker* (April 12, 1982), p. 136.
[16]Phil Bryan, as quoted in *ibid.*, p. 139.
[17]*Ibid.*, p. 136.
[18]*Ibid.*, pp. 134-136.
[19]*State Government News* (July, 1976), p. 3.

[20]Thirty-five percent of those interviewed in 1984 said local governments gave them the most for their money, compared to 27 percent for the state governments and 24 percent for the federal government. See Advisory Commission on Intergovernmental Relations, *Significant Features of Fiscal Federalism, 1985 Edition* (Washington, D.C.: Advisory Commission on Intergovernmental Relations, 1985), p. 139.
[21]As of 1982, and the estimate excludes the extensive local amendments to the Georgia constitution. See Albert L. Sturm and Janice C. May, "State Constitutions and Constitutional Revisions: 1980-81 and the Past Fifty Years," *Book of the States, 1982-83* (Lexington, Ky.: Council of State Governments, 1982), p. 116. Unless noted otherwise, the following discussion is drawn from *ibid.,* pp. 116-120.
[22]Edward D. Grant III, "State Constitutional Revision and the Forces That Shape It," *State and Local Government Review,* 9 (May, 1977), pp. 50-64.
[23]Barbara Deckard, *The Women's Movement* (New York: Harper & Row, 1975), p. 143.
[24]Sally Gold, in New York City Commission on Human Rights, *Women's Role in Contemporary Society* (New York: Avon, 1972), pp. 512-513 and 515, as cited in Deckard, *The Women's Movement,* p. 149.
[25]*Ibid.,* p. 154.
[26]*Ibid.,* p. 165.
[27]Linda J. Waite, "U.S. Women at Work," *Population Bulletin,* 36 (May, 1981), p. 37.
[28]*Ibid.,* pp. 29-33.
[29]Associated Press, "Survey Reports Sex, Race Biases Still Pervasive," *The Arizona Republic* (January 21, 1979).
[30]Unprecedented, that is, since 1917, when Congress first set deadlines for the amendment process.
[31]Figures are for 1982. See Bureau of the Census, *Statistical Abstract of the United States, 1985* (Washington, D.C.: U.S. Government Printing Office, 1984), p. 251.
[32]Nicholas Wade, "Recombinant DNA: Guidelines Debated at Public Hearing," *Science,* 191 (February 27, 1976), p. 835.
[33]*Ibid.,* p. 834.
[34]Nicholas Wade, "Recombinant DNA: The Last Look Before the Leap," *Science,* 192 (April 16, 1976), p. 237.
[35]Barbara J. Culliton, "Recombinant DNA," *Science,* 193 (July 23, 1976), p. 300.
[36]*Ibid.,* p. 301. See also Arlen J. Large, "Science and the Politics of Gene Splicing," *The Wall Street Journal* (January 25, 1982).
[37]Only one-half of 1 percent of the inner cities' nearly 20 million housing units were revitalized or restored between 1968 and 1979, and more than 70 percent of the "gentry" who moved into these refurbished brownstones (or whatever) already lived in the inner city, as opposed to moving in from the surrounding suburbs! See President's Commission for a National Agenda for the Eighties, *Urban America in the Eighties: Perspectives and Prospects* (Washington, D.C.: U.S. Government Printing Office, 1980), p. 30.
[38]Department of Housing and Urban Development, *The President's National Urban Policy Report, 1980,* (Washington, D.C.: U.S. Government Printing Office, 1980), pp. 1-10. Figure is for 1980.
[39]U.S. Bureau of the Census, *Statistical Abstract of the United States, 1985,* Table 24, p. 22.
[40]Department of Housing and Urban Development, *The President's National Urban Policy Report, 1980,* pp. 1-13 and 1-16.
[41]*Ibid.,* pp. 1-13.
[42]Richard P. Nathan and Paul R. Dommel, "Understanding the Urban Predicament," *The Brookings Bulletin,* 14 (Spring-Summer, 1977), p. 9.
[43]*Ibid.*
[44]In 1983, the U.S. Office of Management and Budget dropped the term "Standard Metropolitan Statistical Area" (SMSA) and replaced it with "Metropolitan Statistical Area" (MSA). The Office also altered the definition of an MSA, as noted in the text. For details (and there are many details), see Bureau of the Census, *Statistical Abstract of the United States, 1985 Edition,* Appendix II, pp. 872-874.
[45]The 98 local governments per metropolitan area figure is based on 305 Standard Metropolitan Statistical Areas, as opposed to the newer, 277 Metropolitan Statistical Areas, because SMSAs still were used in 1982, when the last Census of Governments was taken. (See footnote 44.)

[46]National Research Council, *Toward an Understanding of Metropolitan America* (San Francisco: Canfield, 1975), pp. 104-105.
[47]Samuel Kaplan, *The Dream Deferred* (New York: Seabury Press, 1976), p. 9.
[48]Daniel J. Elazar, *Federalism: A View from the States* (New York: Thomas Y. Crowell, 1966), pp. 86-94.
[49]The national debate over the "Sunbelt" versus the "Snowbelt" is notable in its lack of intellectual rigor. Definitions of which states comprise the Sunbelt and which constitute the Snowbelt vary from analysis to analysis. Moreover, most data from the U.S. Bureau of the Census refer to the West and South, as opposed to the Northeast and Midwest. For our purposes, the Sunbelt consists of the following 18 states: Alabama, Arizona, Arkansas, California, Colorado, Florida, Georgia, Hawaii, Louisiana, Mississippi, Nevada, New Mexico, North Carolina, South Carolina, Tennessee, Texas, Utah, and Virginia. The Census Bureau uses the following breakdowns of the nation's four major regions: *Northeast*: Connecticut, Maine, Massachusetts, New Hampshire, New Jersey, New York, Pennsylvania, Rhode Island, and Vermont. *Midwest*: Illinois, Indiana, Iowa, Kansas, Michigan, Minnesota, Nebraska, North Dakota, Ohio, South Dakota, and Wisconsin. *South*: Alabama, Arkansas, Delaware, District of Columbia, Florida, Georgia, Kentucky, Louisiana, Maryland, Mississippi, North Carolina, Oklahoma, South Carolina, Tennessee, Texas, Virginia, and West Virginia. *West*: Alaska, Arizona, California, Colorado, Hawaii, Idaho, Missouri, Montana, Nevada, New Mexico, Oregon, Utah, Washington, and Wyoming. Of the 18 Sunbelt states, 7 are in the West (which is comprised of 14 states) and 11 are in the South (which holds 16 states and the District of Columbia). Among the more interesting analyses of regional shifts are (1) a series of seven articles in *The New York Times,* beginning with Robert Reinhold, "Sunbelt Region Leads Nation in Growth of Population Section's Cities Top Urban Expansion" (February 8, 1976), pp. 1 and 42; James P. Sterba, "Houston, as Energy Capital, Sets Pace in Sunbelt Boom" (February 9, 1976), pp. 1 and 24; Wayne King, "Federal Funds Pour into Sunbelt States" (February 9, 1976), p. 24; Roy Reed, "Sunbelt Still Stronghold of Conservatism in U.S." (February 10, 1976), pp. 1 and 22; Reed, "Migration Mixes a New Southern Blend" (February 11, 1976), pp. 1 and 30; and B. Drummond Ayres, Jr., "Developing Sunbelt Hopes to Avoid North's Mistakes" (February 12, 1976), pp. 1 and 24. (2) "The Second War Between the States," *Business Week* (May 17, 1976), pp. 92-114. (3) Joel Havemann, Rochelle L. Stanfield, and Neal R. Pierce, "Federal Spending: The North's Loss Is the Sunbelt's Gain," *National Journal* (June 26, 1976), pp. 878-891. (4) John Ross and John Shannon, "Measuring the Fiscal 'Blood Pressure' of the States: Some Warning Signs of Our Federal System and Alternative Prescriptions," paper presented at the Conference on State and Local Finance, University of Oklahoma, Norman, Oklahoma, June, 1976. (5) Carol L. Jusenius and Larry C. Ledebur, *A Myth in the Making: The Southern Economic Challenge and Northern Economic Decline,* Economic Development Administration, U.S. Department of Commerce, 1976. (6) Robert W. Rafuse, Jr., *The New Regional Debate: A National Overview,* (Washington, D.C.: National Governors Conference, 1977). And, (7) Kirkpatrick Sale, *The Power Shift: The Rise of the Southern Rim and Its Challenge to the Eastern Establishment* (New York: Random House, 1975). There are others.
[50]Jacqueline Mazza and Bill Hogan, *The State of the Region, 1981: Economic Trends in the Northeast and Midwest* (Washington, D.C.: Northeast-Midwest Institute, 1981), p. 2.
[51]U.S. Bureau of the Census, *Current Population Reports*, Series P-25, No. 957, *Estimates of the Population of the States: 1970 to 1983* (Washington, D.C.: U.S. Government Printing Office, 1984), p. 1.
[52]Mazza and Hogan, *The State of the Region,* p. 2.
[53]*Ibid.,* pp. 1-2.
[54]Advisory Commission on Intergovernmental Relations, *Fiscal Disparities: Central Cities and Suburbs, 1981* (Washington, D.C.: U.S. Government Printing Office, 1984), Table 13, pp. 34-37.
[55]U.S. Bureau of the Census, *Statistical Abstract of the United States, 1985,* Table 752, p. 451. Data are for 1982.

2

THE PARTICIPATION PUZZLE

Why people participate in politics has long been a puzzling subject. The mystery stems in part from the fact that political participation can take so many and varied forms: from complaining to a public bureaucrat about a deficiency in services or carping to a politician about an excess of taxes to rioting in the streets. A surprising number of Americans, in fact, have some kind of contact with public officials; some 76 percent of the citizenry has had some sort of contact with their congressional representatives, and 14 percent have actually met their congressman or congresswoman at one time or another.[1] Another survey found that 58 percent of Americans had had some sort of formal contact with a government administrative office, and almost three quarters of these said that their encounters with the bureaucracy had been helpful.[2]

POLITICAL PARTICIPATION: FROM VOTING TO VIOLENCE

There are, of course, a variety of other, and more concentrated, forms of political participation. Table 2-1 indicates that Americans participate in political life in a variety of ways. As it shows, despite declining voting rates, almost two-thirds of Americans try to vote regularly. Table 2-1 concentrates on the more orthodox modes of political participation, such as voting, becoming involved in community organizations, talking to local government officials, or even founding organizations that attempt to solve community problems. There are also less orthodox ways of participating in the political process.

One of these, which has gained increasing popularity during the last two

Table 2-1 How Much Americans Participate in Politics

Mode of Participation	*Percentage*
Vote regularly in national and local elections	63%
Are active in at least one organization involved in community problems	32
Have worked with others trying to solve some community problems	30
Have attempted to persuade others how to vote	28
Have ever actively worked for a party or candidate during an election	26
Have ever contacted a local government official about some issue or problem	20
Have attended at least one political meeting or rally in last three years	19
Have ever formed a group or organization to attempt to solve some local community problem	14
Have ever given money to a party or candidate during an election campaign	13
Presently a member of a political club or organization	8

Sources: Sidney Verba and Norman H. Nie, *Participation in America* (New York: Harper & Row, 1972), p. 31; and Lester W. Milbrath and M. L. Goel, *Political Participation,* 2nd ed. (Chicago: Rand McNally, 1977), p. 22.

decades, is joining a protest demonstration. Although only 2 to 3 percent of Americans have ever engaged in a protest march of some kind, as many as 20 percent would be willing to do so, given the right circumstances.[3] In addition, the American public has shown a steadily increasing tolerance of protest activities such as sit-ins and marches, and a majority now approve of these kinds of participation. This represents a significant opinion shift among Americans. In 1968, three quarters of the populace disapproved of civil disobedience activities that were undertaken to protest "unjust" laws.[4] Moreover, Americans' tolerance of political protests seems to have increased among every significant demographic and ideological group in society.[5]

The least acceptable form of protest is the riot. The 1960s were a decade of riots, and these were almost exclusively race riots. Most of the race riots occurred in the big cities of the North. In the 5 years between 1963 and 1968, there were 283 racial disturbances of varying degrees of intensity in cities of more than 25,000 people, while during the 50 years between 1913 and 1963, there were only 76 major racial disorders. Among the major ones were the Watts riot of 1965 in Los Angeles, which scorched an area of more than 45 square miles, killing 34 people, 31 of them black, and damaged or destroyed more than 600 buildings; the rioting in Newark, New Jersey, that erupted in 1967, killing 23 people, of whom 21 were black, and requiring more than 4,000 legal officers to restore order; and in Detroit that same year, where the worst disorders occurred—5 days of concentrated rioting that left 43 people dead, 39 of whom were black, leveled more than 1,300 buildings, looted more than 2,700 businesses, and required deploying 15,000 peace officers and soldiers to quell. In 1967 alone, the most explosive year of the riots of the 1960s, 139 riots or serious racial incidents in 114 cities and towns erupted in virtually every section of the country, killing 95 people, maiming more than 1,700, and resulting in more than 12,000 arrests. The National Guard and Army paratroopers were brought in to restore order in 15 cities in 1967, and property damage in 8 communities alone that year totaled more than $250 million.[6]

Virtually all the disturbances in the 1960s occurred in black neighborhoods. They were usually directed against symbols of white authority. In most cases, no single incident precipitated the riots; rather they were preceded by a series of tension-heightening occurrences culminated by a final incident (usually police related) that led to violence. Riots occurred, however, only in those cities with large black populations, and particularly in cities with high population density that had experienced recent upsurges in the size of their black population. The "typical" rioter was a young black male, a lifelong resident of the city in which he rioted, underemployed or working in a menial job, hostile to whites and middle-class blacks alike, racially proud, politically informed, alienated, and better educated than blacks in his neighborhood who did not riot.[7]

Why did they riot? A survey taken by the National Advisory Commission on Civil Disorders of 20 riot-torn cities of the 1960s indicates that at least a dozen reasons could be listed, but the three major "causes" of the riots were, first and foremost, police practices, followed by unemployment or underemployment, and inadequate housing.[8]

During the 1960s, Benjamin L. Hooks, now national director of the National Association for the Advancement of Colored People, told a white audience that, "Pragmatically, riots work."[9] Did the riots of the 1960s accomplish anything for blacks?

While it is clear that blacks have made political gains since the riots (in 1967, the peak year of the rioting, there were only 400 elected public officials in the nation who were black, but by 1984 their number was more than 5,650), it requires something in the nature of a leap of faith to associate those gains with the urban riots of the 1960s. More to the point, in the riot areas themselves, the ruins of destruction persisted ten years later. Although the riots brought federal, state, and local aid to the Twelfth Street neighborhood in Detroit, to the Fourteenth and Seventh Street corridors in Washington, D.C., and to Watts in Los Angeles, these and other riot centers of the 1960s clearly are worse off than they were in 1967. Of the 200,000 people who left Detroit between 1967 and 1977, 12,000 were from the Twelfth Street area alone, and vacant lots that once supported small businesses abound. Only ten stores that were in operation before 1967 were still doing business along Washington's Fourteenth Street, and the percentage of poor people in the neighborhood has increased since the rioting. Blacks have fled Watts since the devastation, leaving behind the poorest families, and unemployment is estimated at more than 25 percent—considerably higher than it was in the mid-1960s.[10]

While blacks have made some major political gains, and some less dramatic social and economic advances, the problem of the black poor is little changed and may have become worse since the 1960s. In sum, Hooks may have been wrong; rioting did not work, at least not for the very poorest members of society. To quote one Willie Alexander of Rochester, New York, "I threw a few stones, but I don't think it did no good, though. I didn't have a job then and I'm still not workin'." Or, as another participant noted, "In some ways it might have been better then. At least then we had decent places to shop. What's there now? A big hole in the ground."[11]

This frustration has continued to explode intermittently since the 1960s. In 1977, New York City experienced a major power failure, and during the blackout hundreds of stores were sacked by residents of their own neighborhoods, an action in stark contrast to the city's power failure of 1965. In 1977, roughly 3,500 people were arrested for looting during the power failure; in

1965 only 100 or so were arrested on similar charges. A conclusion one might draw from this contrast is that, as frustration in the ghetto mounts, the poor have turned on themselves.

But not always. In 1980, a virtual war erupted between blacks and whites in the all-black Liberty City area of Miami, Florida. Its cause was the verdict of a jury in Tampa. The all-white jury had been hearing the state's case against four white Dade County police officers who had beaten to death a black insurance executive after arresting him for reckless driving and found the officers innocent. For two days in May, Liberty City blew up. Three whites returning from a fishing trip were dragged from their car and killed. An elderly Hispanic butcher was burned alive. Three blacks were shot by whites cruising in trucks or cars on Liberty City's streets. Police killed a black man who, they said, was threatening them with a knife. Total damage to Miami, including its tourist trade, may have been as high as $250 million and 3,000 jobs lost, at least temporarily. Some 400 people were injured, more than 1,250 people were arrested (almost all of whom were black men), and 67 buildings were damaged, two dozen of which were gutted totally. It took the Miami police and 3,600 National Guardsmen to restore order. A psychologist at a local university commented, "I've never seen anything like it. In the 1960s people got hurt because they got in the way. But in this riot, [black] people have set out to kill white people."[12]

There can be no question that large scale violence in the 1980s is a political act.

A CONTINUUM OF POLITICAL PARTICIPATION

Given the aftermath of the rioting during the 1960s, 1970s, and 1980s, it appears that the more orthodox forms of political protest and participation are likely to be more politically and economically rewarding to their participants, and within this less violent context, Americans participate in varying degrees. Table 2-2 represents some of the most careful research on the degrees of participation among Americans.

About 20 to 25 percent of all Americans simply do not participate.[13] These people have a low sense of political self-worth and are disproportionately poor, elderly or young, and black.

Another 20 percent of the electorate votes conscientiously but does very little else politically. They are highly partisan, working class or poor, and tend to be found in the inner cities of large metropolitan areas. Older people are overrepresented in this group.

A small number of Americans, about 4 percent, are single-issue participants, or what researchers have called "parochial participants." They tend to concentrate their activities at the local level and to zero in on special-issue concerns. They are quick to contact public officials, come from lower-class backgrounds, and tend to be found in big cities. Catholics are overrepresented, but blacks are underrepresented in this group.

"Community activists," on the other hand, comprise a fifth of the population and, unlike the single-issue participants, concern themselves about a broad spectrum of social issues. They vote reasonably regularly (unlike, for the most part, their parochial counterparts), although they tend not to participate in election campaigns. Again, in contrast to the single-issue types, they come from

Table 2-2 The Participation Input: A Summary

TYPE OF PARTICIPANT	*PATTERN OF ACTIVITY*	*LEADING ORIENTATIONS*	*MAIN SOCIAL CHARACTERISTICS*
Inactives (22%)	They exhibit no activity.	Totally uninvolved. No interest, skill, sense of incompetence, or concern with conflict.	Lower socioeconomic levels and blacks are overrepresented, as are older and younger citizens (but not middle-aged ones) and women.
Voting specialists (21%)	They vote regularly, but do nothing else.	Strong partisan identity but otherwise relatively uninvolved; low skills and competence.	Lower socioeconomic levels are overrepresented. Older citizens are overrepresented as are those in big cities. Underrepresented in rural areas.
Parochial participants (4%)	They contact officials on particularized problems, but are otherwise inactive.	Some political skill (information), but otherwise exhibit no political involvement.	Lower socioeconomic groups are overrepresented, but blacks are otherwise underrepresented. Catholic rather than Protestant. Big cities rather than small towns.
Communalists (20%)	They contact officials on broad social issues and engage in cooperative activity. Vote fairly regularly, but avoid election campaigns.	High sense of community contribution, involvement in politics, skill and competence. Nonpartisan and avoid conflict.	Upper socioeconomic levels are very overrepresented; blacks are underrepresented. Protestant rather than Catholic. Overrepresented in big cities.
Campaigners (15%)	They are heavily active in campaigns and vote regularly.	Politically involved, relatively skilled and competent, partisan, and involved in conflict, but little sense of community contribution.	Upper-status groups are overrepresented. Blacks and particularly Catholics are overrepresented. Big-city and suburbs rather than small towns and rural areas.
Complete activists (11%)	They are active in all ways.	Involved in politics in all ways, are highly skilled and competent.	Heavy overrepresentation of upper-status groups. Old and young are underrepresented.
Unclassified (7% of sample)			

Source: Sidney Verba and Norman H. Nie, adapted from *Participation in America: Political Democracy and Social Equality* (New York: Harper & Row, 1972), pp. 118, 119.

the upper social and economic levels and tend to be Protestants. However, they parallel their more parochial colleagues in that blacks are underrepresented.

The "campaigners" are far more partisan than any other type of participant and constitute about 15 percent of the population. They vote regularly and have a broader view of political issues (like the community activists), and there is an overrepresentation of the upper-level social and economic groups. Blacks, Catholics, suburbanites, and big-city residents are heavily represented among the campaign activists. Small-town types and dwellers in rural America are underrepresented.

Finally, the "complete activists" may comprise as much as a tenth of the population, and they are active in politics across the board. They are skilled political actors, and the upper economic groups are heavily overrepresented, although both the elderly and the young are quite underrepresented.

WHO PARTICIPATES?

Degrees of political participation are one thing, but what kinds of Americans participate in politics? Who are the politically active? Who are the politically inert?

Among the clearest conclusions that political scientists have drawn about political participation is that the higher the social and economic status of an American, the more likely he or she is to participate in politics. (Social and economic status is comprised of three characteristics: income, occupation, and education.)

Figure 2-1 indicates this relationship. About 60 percent of the nonparticipants in politics are Americans of low social and economic status, while approximately 57 percent of the most active political participants in the country earn substantial salaries, hold professional jobs, and have spent a great deal of time in school.

Age is another factor that correlates with political participation, and people in their forties tend to be the most politically active. Participation rates tend to build to that point, and afterward they decline. Figure 2-2 indicates this relationship. Among the most apathetic participants, particularly when it comes to voting, are the young. Eighteen-year-olds received the franchise in 1971 and, as a result, 18- to 21-year-olds added another 8 percent to the eligible voting population. Nevertheless, not much more than a third of the people in this age group have registered to vote and only a fifth to a fourth have actually voted.[14]

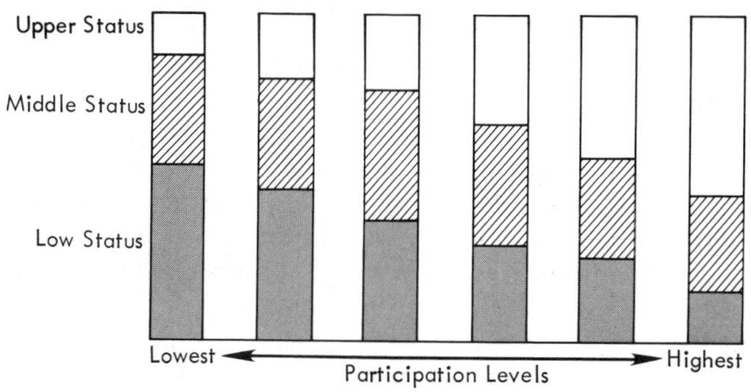

Figure 2-1
Socioeconomic status and political participation. (*Source:* Figure 8-3 on page 131 from *Participation in America: Political Democracy and Social Equality* by Sidney Verba and Norman H. Nie. Copyright © 1972 by Sidney Verba and Norman H. Nie. Reprinted by permission of Harper & Row, Publishers, Inc.)

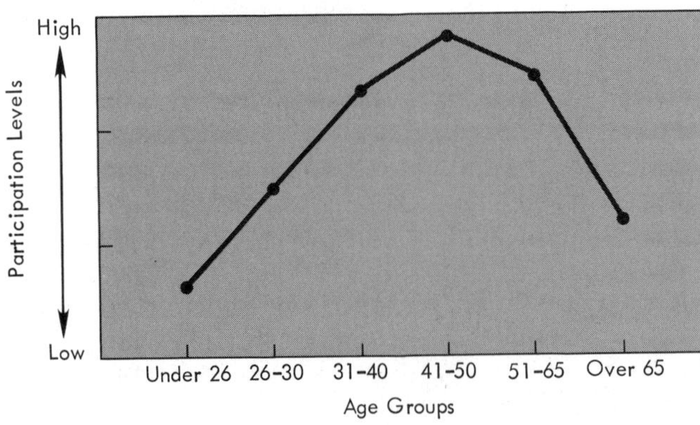

Figure 2-2
Age and political participation. (*Source:* Figure 9-1 on page 139 from *Participation in America: Political Democracy and Social Equality* by Sidney Verba and Norman H. Nie. Copyright © 1972 by Sidney Verba and Norman H. Nie. Reprinted by permission of Harper & Row, Publishers, Inc.)

Sex, as someone noticed, also makes a difference, and women (who constitute more than 52 percent of the nation's eligible voters), at least in the 1980s, now appear to participate in politics at roughly equivalent rates as men, and in some areas actually exceed the rates of male participation. This is a recent development.[15]

Among blacks, the story is much the same. As blacks gained the suffrage during the 1960s and 1970s, especially in the South, black political activity soared. Figure 2-3 traces the dramatic increase in campaign activity by blacks. What is of interest here is that race seems to have very little, if anything, to do with determining the likelihood of whether or not a person will vote. A much more influential factor is the level of education, and well-educated blacks vote in the same proportions as do comparably educated whites.[16]

On the other hand, the kinds of political participation that blacks perceive as legitimate differ markedly from that of whites. Blacks are far more likely to join a delegation to make a protest to a public official, to attend protest meetings, to join in protest marches and demonstrations, and to believe that an occasional riot is necessary to get the attention of public officials and to correct political wrongs. Given the fact that blacks have been denied their basic political rights for most of this nation's history, such attitudes are not surprising.[17]

Finally, one's involvement in organizations has a real impact on whether one is likely to be politically active or not. Figure 2-4 indicates this relationship, and the intensity of the organization-membership/political-participation connection is uniquely American. Americans are a society of joiners. About two-thirds of them belong to some kind of professional, economic, religious, or social group; about 40 percent of the population is active in some kind of group. As Figure 2-4 indicates, the more groups to which one belongs, the more likely one is to be politically active as well. Interestingly, it appears that membership in organizations is more likely to lead to potential activity by blacks than by whites.[18] Although people who belong to a multiplicity of organizations also tend to be well-educated people of a higher social and economic status (characteristics that associate strongly with high levels of political participation), even when these attributes are factored out of the equation, membership in a number of groups still correlates strongly with high levels of political participation.

We have reviewed some of the research on political participation of all types, but among the most important single kind of political participation in a

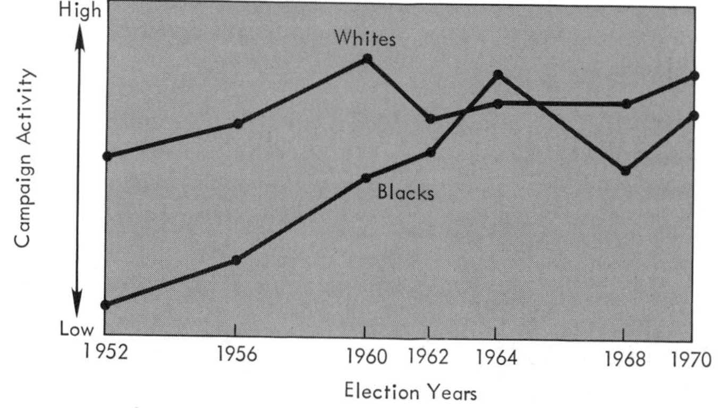

Figure 2-3
The political participation of blacks and whites. (*Source:* Figure 14-4 on page 255 from *Participation in America: Political Democracy and Social Equality* by Sidney Verba and Norman H. Nie. Copyright © 1972 by Sidney Verba and Norman H. Nie. Reprinted by permission of Harper & Row, Publishers, Inc.)

democracy is the simple act of voting, and it is time to devote some special attention to this piece of the participation puzzle.

VOTING: THE ULTIMATE DEMOCRATIC ACT

Until quite recently, voting has been in decline. Figure 2-5 indicates the percentage of voter turnout in presidential and off-year congressional elections from 1954 to 1984. Presidential elections draw the most voters, but, as the graph indicates, turnout for both types of elections had been falling off for a number of years until 1982 and 1984, when turnouts went up fractionally. The proportion of eligible voters who have been turning out to vote in presidential elections has been declining steadily since 1960, when 63 percent of the eligible population voted; but by 1980, barely 53.2 percent exercised their right to vote. The Committee for the American Electorate, after surveying the decline in turnout, concluded that some 15 million voters have "dropped out." In other words, some 15 million people who are registered to vote, and who have voted in the past, no longer do so. In the view of some pundits, American voters are not voting with their feet but with their bottoms. This situation brightened marginally in 1984, when voting turnout in presidential elections went up, for the first time in two dozen years, to 53.3 percent.

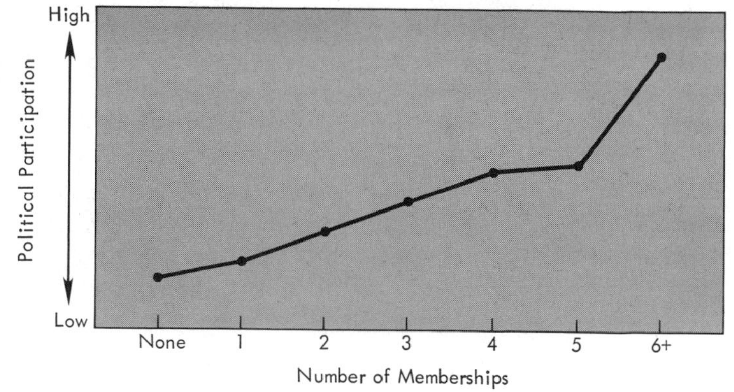

Figure 2-4
Organizational involvement and political participation. (*Source:* Figure 11-1 on page 184 from *Participation in America: Political Democracy and Social Equality* by Sidney Verba and Norman H. Nie. Copyright © 1972 by Sidney Verba and Norman H. Nie. Reprinted by permission of Harper & Row, Publishers, Inc.)

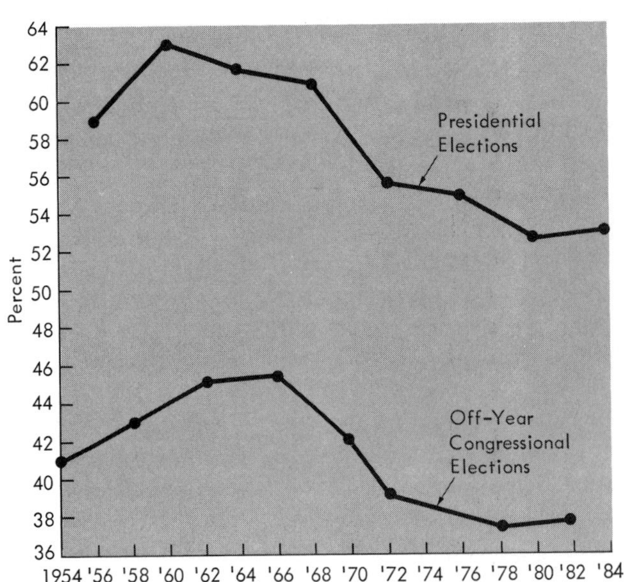

Figure 2-5
Voter turnout as a percentage of voting-age population, 1954–1984.

The pattern is repeated in off-year congressional elections. Participation has been declining in these elections since 1966, with turnout reaching an all time low in 1978 when only 37 percent of the eligible voters voted; in three southern states, in fact, fewer than a fifth of the voting-age population voted. In 1982, the trend of a dozen years executed an exceedingly modest reversal, when 38 percent of the electorate turned out, or about 1 percent more than in 1978.

MACNELLY. Courtesy of *Chicago Tribune*—New York News Syndicate, Inc.

The Convenience of Elections

Although these trends are ominous, it should be recognized that the United States conducts an unusually large number of elections and there are considerably more elections than simply those in which congressional representatives and presidents are chosen. As Table 2-3 shows, 60 percent of all cities and towns hold their municipal elections independently of congressional and presidential elections, which means that voters must make a separate trip to the polls to vote in these elections. Another 23 percent of municipalities hold their elections only with other local elections; only 17 percent of cities and towns hold their municipal elections concurrently with state or national elections.[19]

Convenience of election scheduling does make a difference in turnout. As Table 2-4 indicates, in 1975 those municipal elections that were held independently of all other elections had a median voter turnout of 27 percent; in those city elections that were held concurrently with other local races, the turnout was 30 percent; and in those city elections held in conjunction with state and national elections (the "most convenient" scheduling), the voting turnout was 38 percent.[20]

Elections, Regions, and States

Although not much more than half of the eligible voters vote in presidential elections, some regions traditionally have evidenced much higher turnout, particularly in the Midwest, New England, and the Rocky Mountain states. For example, in 1980 more than 65 percent of the voting-age population voted in Idaho, Maine, Minnesota, Montana, South Dakota, and Wisconsin. The South typically has the lowest voter turnout in the country. However, in contrast to other regions of the country, Southern voting is increasing. The primary reason why appears to be attributable to dramatically increased participation rates by

Table 2-3 Independent and Concurrent Municipal Elections, 1962 and 1975

			METHOD OF HOLDING LAST ELECTION					
	Number of Cities Reporting		*Independent (Percent)*		*With Other Local Elections[1] (Percent)*		*With State or National Election[2] (Percent)*	
Classification	*1962*	*1975*	*1962*	*1975*	*1962*	*1975*	*1962*	*1975*
Total, all cities	529	782	66	60	20	23	14	17
Form of election								
Partisan	137	216	51	50	22	23	27	27
Nonpartisan	391	566	71	64	19	22	10	14
Unknown	1		—		—		—	

Dashes (—) indicate data are unknown.

[1] Excludes cities that also held elections concurrent with stater or national elections.

[2] Includes cities that held elections concurrent with state or national and with other local races.

Source: Adapted from Albert K. Karnig and B. Oliver Walter, "Municipal Elections: Registration, Incumbent Success, and Voter Participation," *1977 Municipal Yearbook* (Washington, D.C.: International City Management Association, 1977), p. 69. Reproduced by permission of the publisher.

Table 2-4 Percent of Adults Voting, by Type of Municipal Elections: 1962 and 1975

	ALL CITY ELECTIONS				*ELECTIONS HELD WITH STATE OR NATIONAL RACES*				*ELECTIONS HELD WITH OTHER LOCAL RACES*[1]				*INDEPENDENT ELECTIONS*			
	No. of Cities Reporting		*Median Voter Turnout (%)*		*No. of Cities Reporting*		*Median Voter Turnout (%)*		*No. of Cities Reporting*		*Median Voter Turnout (%)*		*No. of Cities Reporting*		*Median Voter Turnout (%)*	
Classification	*1962*	*1975*	*1962*	*1975*	*1962*	*1975*	*1962*	*1975*	*1962*	*1975*	*1962*	*1975*	*1962*	*1975*	*1962*	*1975*
Total, all cities	461	739	33	29	63	125	50	38	87	173	44	30	303	441	29	27
Form of government																
Mayor-council	137	271	50	38	31	54	51	38	28	59	50	35	78	158	44	39
Council-manager	281	419	27	24	29	64	43	38	54	105	35	26	193	250	23	22
Commission	41	49	38	34	3	7	33	38	5	9	57	43	32	33	38	31
Form of election																
Partisan	109	201	50	36	31	52	51	40	22	48	53	37	56	101	41	34
Nonpartisan	350	538	30	27	32	73	43	38	65	125	35	27	246	340	27	25
Unknown	2		—										1		—	

[1] Excludes cities also holding elections concurrent with state or national elections.

Source: Adapted from Albert K. Karnig and B. Oliver Walters, "Municipal Elections: Registration, Incumbent Success, and Voter Participation," in *The Municipal Year Book 1977* (Washington, D.C.: International City Management Association, 1977), p. 70. Reproduced by permission of the publisher.

Southern blacks and Southern white women. In the case of blacks, this increase in voting participation associates with the passage of the Voting Rights Act of 1965 (to be discussed later); the voting rates of blacks more than doubled between 1960 and 1968. Why Southern white women are showing up in greater numbers at the polls is more difficult to ascribe to any one specific reason, but the women's movement cannot be dismissed as a factor.[21] It appears that as more women enter higher education and the work force (as they are), their likelihood of voting increases substantially.[22]

Figure 2-6 indicates the voting turnout in each state and region by presidential and off-year congressional elections. The variations obviously are wide. Generally speaking, however, we know that states with higher family incomes and relatively well-educated populations tend to have greater voting participation. Higher turnouts are also seen in states where political parties are relatively competitive with each other and in states in which the "hassle" of voting has been minimized. In these states there are fewer registration laws, the minimum residence requirement is considerably shorter, and the registration procedure for absentee voting is simpler.

There are, of course, exceptions for every rule, and certain states defy the norms of voting turnout. For example, Utah has a higher turnout in statewide elections than does any other state of the Union, and some observers have attributed this to the influence of the locally powerful Church of Jesus Christ of Latter Day Saints, which encourages a high civic consciousness among its members. Similarly, voting behavior in West Virginia is unique. One of the poorest states in the nation, West Virginia is a Southern border state with a very low level of formal educational attainments and only moderate competition between its two political parties. Nevertheless, West Virginians go to the polls in large numbers. Apparently, this turnout has to do in part, at least, with the presence of the United Mine Workers Union, a major power in West Virginia politics, which has long encouraged its members to vote along organized labor lines and has established a tradition of voting participation.[23]

Personal Factors

Beyond local and regional factors, a variety of more personal characteristics enter into a person's propensity to vote: sex, race, age, residence, education, and employment, all are relevant. Table 2-5 indicates some of these elements. As it shows, men, whites, older people, rural dwellers, college graduates, people with jobs (particularly those with government and professional jobs), and people who own their own homes are the most likely to exercise their rights of suffrage.

THE STATES AND THE SUFFRAGE

The variations in voting turnout reflect in part how parsimonious or generous state governments have been in the past in letting their residents vote. Considering where the nation started in its views of who was "qualified" to vote, enormous progress has been made. Prior to the adoption of the Constitution in 1789, most of the original 13 states stipulated that only males who owned specified amounts of property and supported the state's dominant religion could vote.[24] The property-owning barriers fell first (although a few states required that vot-

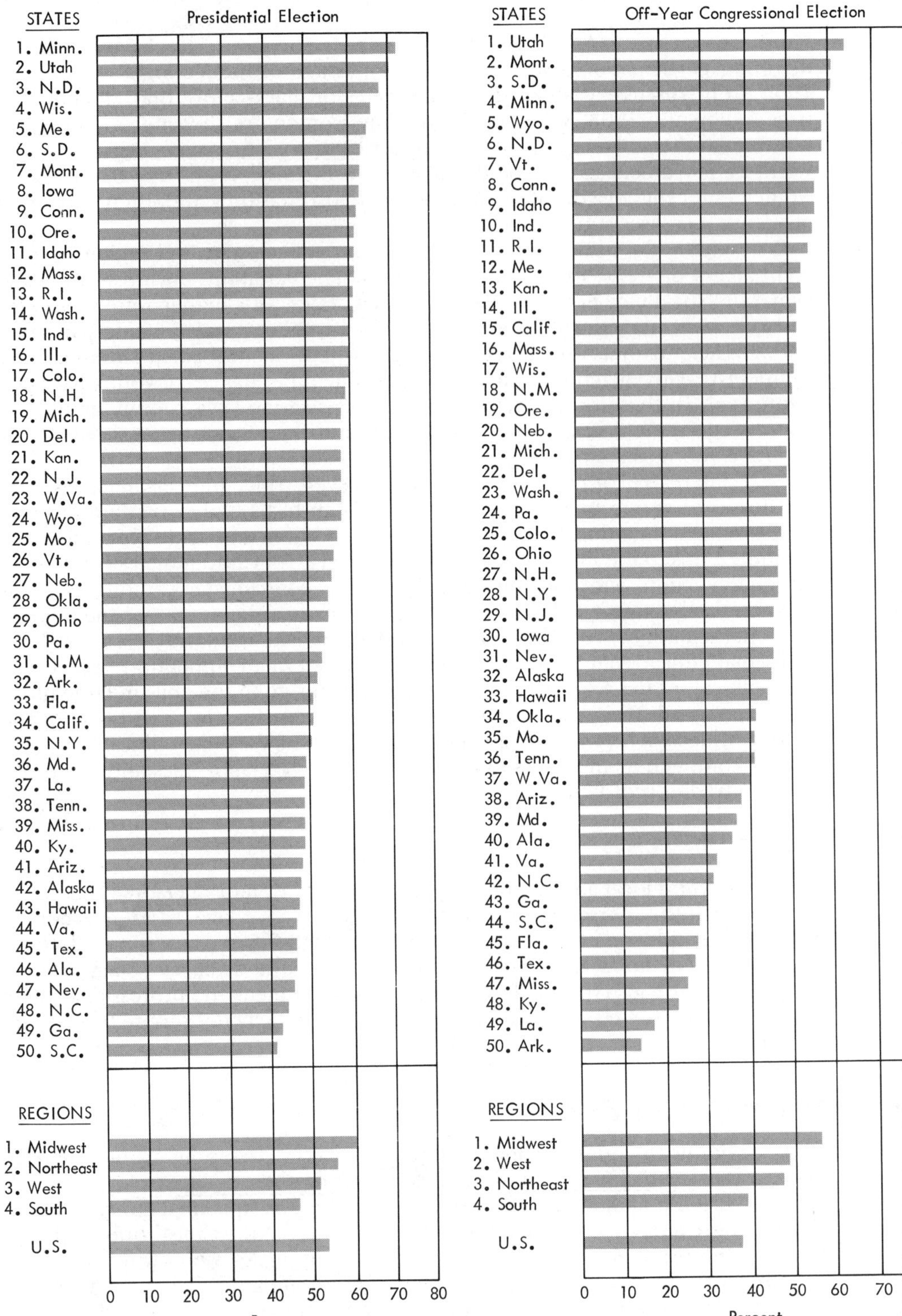

Figure 2-6 Percentage of voting-age population casting votes by state and region. (*Source:* U.S. Bureau of the Census, *Statistical Abstract of the United States, 1985,* Washington, D.C.: U.S. Government Printing Office, Table 425, p. 254.)

ers be taxpayers well into the late 1800s), followed by religious tests; by the midnineteenth century, universal white male suffrage was the norm.

In 1889, the year of the Constitution's one-hundredth anniversary, Florida introduced the nation to the poll tax, a charge levied on anyone who wanted to vote, and by 1910 most of the Southern states had adopted the device. The poll tax was designed to reduce the numbers of blacks being registered in the South, which it did effectively. It also reduced the number of poor whites being registered to vote, which was probably not an entirely unforeseen development.

More than half of the states that originally passed poll taxes had abolished them by 1950. By 1962 only five states still had a poll tax, and in 1966 the Supreme Court, in *Harper* v. *Virginia State Board of Elections,* in effect obliterated the last remaining poll taxes in the country.

Another major obstacle to voting was the age requirement. Traditionally, most states had stipulated that 21 be the required age for exercising the right to vote; Georgia (the first to lower the age to 18 during World War II), Kentucky, Hawaii, and Alaska were the exceptions. With the passage of the Twenty-sixth Amendment to the United States Constitution in 1970, however, all states were required to allow citizens 18 years of age and over to vote in local, state, and national elections.

Yet another barricade to voting thrown up by the states was the literacy test. By 1965 more than a third of the states had some kind of literacy examination. Some of the states allowed an alternative in the form of a thinly veiled property requisite or required the potential voter to show an understanding of the "principles of republican government"—whatever that meant. Literacy tests eventually came under fire from the national government, and in 1965 the Supreme Court, in *Louisiana* v. *United States*, ruled that the use of "understanding tests," which gave voting registrars discretion to determine who passed or failed the literacy test, was unconstitutional. The Supreme Court's decision did not cover all literacy tests and in the same year, Congress enacted the Voting Rights Act which made possible the suspension of literacy tests, and in 1970 Congress actually did suspend them; Congress has kept literacy tests "suspended" (i.e., effectively abolished) ever since.

ENFRANCHISING THE PEOPLE: WASHINGTON MOVES IN

The welter of obstacles erected by the states to prevent citizens from voting was attributable to the political conservatism often found at the state level. But, as we have noted, these state hindrances to voting have been increasingly circumscribed by national statute and by amendment to the Constitution. Indeed, the federal government has been most forceful in removing suffrage restrictions and enabling citizens to vote. Consider some of the major enactments in this regard.

The Fifteenth Amendment

The Fifteenth Amendment to the Constitution, enacted in 1870, states that a person may not be denied the right to vote because of race. The amendment, enacted by a Reconstruction Congress and a victorious North, also gave Congress the power to enforce black voting rights "by appropriate legislation." In effect, this clause permitted the states to retain the right to determine voter qualifications, provided that they did not use race as a criterion. This proviso,

Table 2-5 Participation in National Elections, by Population Characteristics, 1982

CHARACTERISTICS	*PERSONS OF VOTING AGE (MIL.)*	*PERSONS REPORTING THEY REGISTERED*	*PERSONS REPORTING THEY VOTED*	*PERCENTAGE OF VOTING AGE POPULATION NOT A CITIZEN*
Total	165.5	64%	49%	4%
Male	78.0	64	49	4
Female	87.4	64	48	4
White	143.6	66	50	3
Black	17.6	59	43	3
Spanish origin	8.8	35	25	32
By age				
18–20 yr old	12.1	35	20	5
21–24 yr old	16.7	48	28	5
25–34 yr old	38.8	57	40	6
35–44 yr old	28.1	68	52	5
45–64 yr old	44.2	76	62	3
65 yr and over	25.6	75	60	2
Median age (yr)	40.4			
Metropolitan locale	113.1	63	48	6
In central cities	46.8	60	47	7
Outside central cities	66.2	64	49	5
Nonmetropolitan locale	52.4	67	49	2
School years completed				
8 yr or less	22.4	52	36	11
High school				
1–3 yr	22.3	53	38	4
4 yr	65.2	63	47	3
College				
1–3 yr	28.8	70	53	3
4 yr or more	26.9	79	67	4

Civilian labor force composition	108.0	64	48	4
Employed	97.2	66	50	4
Agriculture	3.3	64	48	8
Nonagriculture industries	94.0	66	50	4
Private wage and salary workers	70.9	62	46	4
Goverment workers	15.5	80	67	2
Self-employed	7.6	72	57	3
Unemployed	10.8	50	34	6
White-collar workers	53.4	73	58	3
Professional and technical	17.3	77	64	3
Managers and administrators	11.7	75	60	2
Clerical and kindred workers	18.0	68	52	3
Blue-collar workers	28.2	56	39	5
Craft and kindred workers	12.0	60	44	3
Operatives, except transport	8.9	52	36	9
Service workers	13.0	57	41	6
Farm workers	2.6	67	51	8
Not in labor force	57.5	64	49	5
Owner occupied	44.5	77	62	2
Renter occupied	16.0	47	32	8

Source: U.S. Bureau of the Census, *Statistical Abstract of the United States, 1985* (Washington, D.C.: U.S. Government Printing Office, 1984), Table 427, p. 255.

nonetheless, permitted the states, and particularly the Southern states, to practice *de facto,* if not *de jure,* racial discrimination through poll taxes, literacy tests, and so forth.

The Nineteenth Amendment

The next major action by the federal government to enfranchise large numbers of voters came in 1920 with the passage of the Nineteenth Amendment, which enfranchised women by stating that no voters could be disenfranchised because of sex. The federal government thus doubled the number of potential voters with a single amendment.

The Twenty-fourth Amendment

The Twenty-fourth Amendment, while not making quite so dramatic an expansion of voting rights as the Nineteenth, is perhaps the most significant expression of regional politics that appears in the Constitution. It was (and is) directed primarily at the South; in effect, it prohibited the collection of poll taxes by voter registrars. The Twenty-fourth Amendment was ratified in 1964, the same year in which the Civil Rights Act was passed by Congress. Together, these two statements of public policy represented a dramatic expansion of the franchise for black voters.

The Civil Rights Act

The Twenty-fourth Amendment affected only the five states that still retained their poll taxes: Alabama, Arkansas, Mississippi, Texas, and Virginia. The Civil Rights Act of 1964 made it illegal for registrars to discriminate on the basis of race in registering voters, or to reject an application for registering to vote on the basis of inconsequential mistakes made by the applicant. The act thus went farther than the Twenty-fourth Amendment, which prohibited the poll tax only in national elections.

The Twenty-sixth Amendment

Because the Supreme Court by its 1970 decision in *Oregon* v. *Mitchell* had, in effect, invalidated congressional ability to extend the vote to 18-year-olds in state and local elections, a drive was initiated to pass the Twenty-sixth Amendment to the Constitution. Ratified in 1971, the amendment prohibits the denial of the right to vote on the basis of age to citizens 18 years old and above in *all* elections—national, state, and local.

The Voting Rights Acts

Neither the Twenty-fourth Amendment, which made poll taxes unconstitutional, nor the Civil Rights Act, which prohibited discrimination by voting registrars, was as successful in enabling blacks to register and to vote as they might have been. In 1965, therefore, Congress passed the first Voting Rights Act. It was designed to make the Fifteenth Amendment more effective in practice. The act applied to any state or county where the literacy test, or some similar test, was enforced and where more than 50 percent of voting-age residents either were not registered or could not cast ballots in the 1964 national election. Where there was evidence of voter discrimination, the U.S. attorney general could replace local registrars with federal voting registrars. Federal registrars could abolish literacy tests, and they could register voters under federal procedures, which were considerably simpler than those found in some states and localities. In 1966, the Supreme Court upheld the Voting Rights Act as an appropriate piece of national legislation with which to combat bigotry at the ballot box. Table 2-6 indicates the number of jurisdictions covered by the Voting Rights Acts and where they are located. In all, 7,296 cities, towns, counties, and states are covered by the Voting Rights Act, and between 1965 and 1980, the Civil Rights Division of the U.S. Department of Justice prereviewed almost 35,000 changes that were submitted to it by these subnational governments. Of these proposals, only 811 resulted in objections by the Justice Department, and the proposed changes in the laws were subsequently negotiated between the governments in question and the Department.[25]

A second Voting Rights Act was passed in 1970. In this legislation, Congress extended the vote to all persons 18 years old and above, abolished residency requirements of more than 30 days for voting in national elections, and suspended all literacy tests. This law was immediately challenged in court, and, as noted earlier, in the 1970 case of *Oregon* v. *Mitchell*, the Supreme Court ruled that Congress had the power to extend the vote to 18-year-olds in national elections, but not in state or local elections. In 1975, the Voting Rights Act was further amended to require bilingual ballots in those jurisdictions that had a substantial number of residents who could not speak English.

Table 2-6 State and Local Governments Covered by the Voting Rights Acts of 1965 and 1982

STATES	*NUMBER OF COUNTIES*[1]	*NUMBER OF COUNTIES*[1] *COVERED BY VOTING RIGHTS ACTS*
Alabama	—	All
Alaska	—	All
Arizona	—	All
Georgia	—	All
Louisiana	—	All
Mississippi	—	All
Texas	—	All
Virginia	—	All
California	58	4
Colorado	63	1
Connecticut	169 (towns)	3
Florida	67	5
Hawaii	4	1
Idaho	183	1
Massachusetts	312 (towns)	9
Michigan	1,254 (townships)	2
New Hampshire	233 (towns)	10
New York	62	3
North Carolina	100	40
South Carolina	67	2
Wyoming	23	1

[1] Unless another type of jurisdiction is specified.

The impact of the 1965 legislation and its later extensions was profound. As Table 2-7 indicates, between 1960 and 1984, the Voting Rights Acts essentially doubled the number of Southern blacks who had registered to vote. Moreover, this legislation also seems to have had a favorable impact on white registration rates in the South, which showed a modest increase over the 24-year period.

In 1982, Congress passed a new Voting Rights Act that extended all of the provisions of its predecessors to the year 2007. There was an added fillip, however. The Voting Rights Act of 1965 and its extensions had rested on the idea that any challenges to state or local voting procedures must be demonstrated in court by proof of intentional discriminatory acts. Such a proviso (which has been reinforced over the years by the bench) opened a juridical can of worms. Plaintiffs, challenging the behavior of local voting procedures, had to prove in court that they were being *intentionally* discriminated against. In extending the act in 1982, Congress came very close to, but ultimately drew away from, inserting a new passage in the law that stated that any practice that resulted in the denial or abridgment of the right to vote on account of race would be illegal. One observer called this attempt "not a stiff dose of medicine designed to restore a sick law to health, but more like a sex change operation intended to alter fundamentally the nature of the law itself."[26] What this attempt represented was the elimination of a "fair shake" in getting minorities elected to public office in exchange for a "fair share" for minorities of all elected offices.

Congress watered down this concept considerably in its final version. The Senate Judiciary Committee, in reporting the bill out, explicitly stated that no substantive right to proportional, racial representation exists. But it did urge any court reviews of the law to consider "the totality of circumstances" in determining whether the political process was "equally open" to people of all races. In other words, the emphasis of the 1982 Voting Rights Act is on participation in the election process. A jurisdiction's failure to elect minority candidates to office is a fact that can now be considered by the courts, but only as one component of a larger body of evidence that points toward the exclusion of minorities from the political process.

It appears that the Voting Rights Act of 1982 may well make it easier for litigants to challenge both the tradition of at-large electoral districts (which are the norm in local elections) and cumbersome voting registration practices in those jurisdictions that are covered by the act.

Table 2-7 Voter Registration in 11 Southern States, by Race, 1960 and 1984

	1960		*1984*	
Registered Voters	*Number (000)*	*Percentage of Voting Age Population*	*Number (000)*	*Percentage of Voting Age Population*
White	12,276	61%	24,744	67%
Black	1,463	29	4,948	59

Source: Bureau of the Census, *Statistical Abstract of the United States, 1985* (Washington, D.C.: U.S. Government Printing Office, 1984), p. 253.

THE WRANGLES OF REGISTRATION AND RESIDENCY REQUIREMENTS

Property ownership, religious requirements, gender justifications, poll taxes, literacy tests, racial discrimination, and age minimums have all been eliminated or (in the case of age) modified to make the ballot box more accessible to more Americans. But there remains a worrisome wrangle that discourages voting: registration and residency requirements in state and local governments.

To vote, one must first register as a voter in one's state of residence. The sole exception is North Dakota, which allows its residents to vote without first registering. Most states require that a prospective voter appear in person before a registration board or a voting supervisor to establish his or her qualifications. In some states these qualifications can be manifold, although some are attempting to simplify registration.

There are two basic kinds of registration for voters. Virtually all states have some sort of *permanent registration;* a few require *periodic registration.* Vermont requires a voter to register every year. South Carolina, at the other extreme, requires its voters to register every ten years.

These voting registration requirements presuppose a stable population, which, of course, is hardly the case in the United States. The Census Bureau tells us that, on the average, Americans make 12 moves throughout their lifetimes. Although the number of Americans who move every year has declined slightly in the 1980s (from 20 percent of all households before 1976 to 16 to 17 percent thereafter), the country nonetheless is one that is "on the move." Peak mobility occurs between the ages of 20 and 35, or during those years that citizens are entering the pool of qualified voters.[27] This means that, in a typical year, one in every six Americans who is eligible to vote has to reestablish his or her legal residency in order to do so. It has been estimated that more than 6 percent of the nearly 170 million Americans who would otherwise have been eligible to vote in national elections are disenfranchised by these state residence requirements.[28] Another study concluded that the state registration laws probably reduced voter turnout in presidential elections by 10 percent.[29]

In short, residency requirements have a clear, negative effect on the propensity of American citizens to vote. Table 2-8 demonstrates this relation-

Table 2-8 Residence, Registration, and Voter Turnout, 1980

Years in Current Residence	*Percentage of Voting Age Population Who Voted*	*Percentage Registered*	*Percentage of Registered Who Voted*
Zero to Two Years	48%	56%	87%
Three to Five Years	58	66	88
Six to Ten Years	60	73	82
Eleven or More Years	72	82	88
Total	60	69	87

Source: Peverill Squire, Raymond E. Wolfinger, and David P. Glass, "Residential Mobility and Voter Turnout," Paper presented at the 1985 Annual Meeting of the American Political Science Association, August 28–September 1, 1985, New Orleans, Table 8.

ship. As it shows, the percentage of adults registered to vote is quite low among those Americans who have been living in their present residences for less than two years. By and large, the longer the period of residence, the higher the level of voter registration.

The U.S. Supreme Court, in a series of cases that it decided from 1969 to 1972, became involved in the states' manipulation of residence requirements. These decisions justified the states' right to stipulate that its voters be *bona fide* residents, but denied the validity of lengthy residence requirements as a test of voting qualifications. In 1972, the Court invalidated Tennessee's one-year residency requirement. The Voting Rights Act of 1970 had firmed up the issue by stipulating that residency requirements may not exceed 30 days' residence for voting in presidential elections, or 50 days for state and local ones.

Regardless of the complexity of state registration procedures and residency requirements, such requisites clearly have a negative impact on voting turnout. A Gallup poll found that 38 percent of the eligible voters did not vote in the last presidential election and gave as the reason that they were not registered.[30]

Innovations for Easing Registration

Simplifying registration is one of the easiest and most direct ways that states can raise voting levels, and, in recent years, some states have moved to make voting and registration more convenient. California and Oregon have begun permitting their local governments to conduct elections by mailed ballots. Among the more notable efforts in this regard are registering voters by mail and permitting voters to register when they vote.

Postcard registration. Registering voters by mail is a new idea. Indeed, prior to 1974, only 6 states permitted voter registration by mail, but by 1982, 18 states, plus the District of Columbia, permitted voter registration by mail. This device covered more than 40 percent of the nation's eligible voters.

It is too early to determine how well voter registration by mail works in practice. A study conducted for the Council of State Governments concluded that, while mail registration likely adds to the overall convenience of voter registration (depending on how well the system is administered), "It seems unlikely that mail registration has an immediate and dramatic impact on registrations and turnout rates."[31] In 1976, only two "postcard" states, Missouri and Minnesota, did not report reduced voting levels. Moreover, there is always the possibility of increased fraud in voter registration schemes when conducted through the mails. For example, one researcher had 500 nonforwardable voter registration forms sent by first-class mail to 500 totally nonexistent people in Maryland. Had Maryland's fraud protection plan worked, all 500 forms should have been returned, but about 10 percent of the forms were not returned. Conclusion? "A small conspiracy . . . might be highly successful."[32]

Election-day registration. The latest suggestion to ease registration requirements proposes that voters be allowed to register on election day. Four states—Maine, Minnesota, Oregon, and Wisconsin—already have adopted election-day registration, and it is likely that the device encourages voting.

THE STATES, THE NATION, AND THE VOTE: A CONTINUING BALANCE

Thanks largely to the federal government, and most clearly so during the last two decades, more Americans than ever before have the right to vote. In the 1780s, when the nation had just been founded, only 120,000-odd of the residents in a country of more than 2 million people were allowed to vote—or about 6 percent of the population. Now, however, nearly 170 million people in a country of 226 million—or better than 70 percent—have the right to vote if they wish to exercise it. The federal government, at least in this century, has taken an aggressive and wholly admirable lead in expanding the suffrage for all Americans, and often it has done so against recalcitrant and balky statewide political establishments.

We should not overlook, however, the active role that states have played in expanding the right to vote, although the federal government has taken the lead in most instances. For example, the Fifteenth, Nineteenth, Twenty-fourth, and Twenty-sixth Amendments to the Constitution could not have been passed unless two-thirds of the states had ratified them. In addition, the states have proven themselves to be innovative leaders in reducing a number of registration and residency requirements, and they have done much of this without encouragement from the federal government.

In fact, it appears that the states may take a wholly new tack in encouraging people to vote. In 1982, an enterprising promoter in California (where else?), in an attempt to expand voter participation, created an "election sweepstakes" for the California primaries. California's voters simply sent in their election stub, on which they had written their name and address, and winners were drawn on a lottery basis. The prizes included a trip to Hawaii, a lifetime supply of french fries, a pair of rollerskates, and a date with Linda Evans, star of the television series "Dynasty," among other prizes totaling $5 million. Whether or not the promotion was successful we shall never know. But according to the California secretary of state, between 50 and 55 percent of the state's nearly 12 million voters had cast ballots in the primary election—a considerably higher percentage than the national average.[33]

Thanks in large part to federal intervention, but thanks, too, to a determination by some state governments to make the ballot more accessible to more citizens, the suffrage has been significantly expanded. Prior to 1955, state residency requirements ranged from six months to two years, but counties and even precincts had their own residency requirements that could be as long as half a year. Felons, lunatics, and idiots were barred from voting in most states. Thirty years later, however, state residency requirements never surpassed 30 days, and some states (Iowa, Kansas, and Nebraska) had no residency requirements. Permanent registration covering all elections, absentee registration, absentee voting, absentee ballot application by mail, and voting booths open from early morning to early evening—all major conveniences for the voting public—were commonplace.[34]

THE CITIES AND THE SUFFRAGE

Voting turnout is highest in presidential elections, it is next highest in off-year congressional elections, and it is lowest in local elections. We can expect more than 50 percent of the nation's eligible voters to vote in a presidential election, but only from 25 to 50 percent vote in local ones, and sometimes even fewer. Studies of voters in St. Louis and Dayton concluded that more than a quarter of those eligible to vote in local elections have never voted at all. These investigations also indicate that, although those who do vote in local elections are also likely to vote in state and national ones, the reverse is seldom true. In other words, those who vote for national and state officeholders do not necessarily vote for local ones.[35]

As we discussed earlier, a major reason why Americans tend to vote less in local elections than in state and national ones is that many of these elections are held at inconvenient times. An additional cause, however, seems related to partisan versus nonpartisan elections. In cities that identify the partisan affiliations of candidates on their ballots, about 50 percent of the eligible voters usually turn out, whereas in cities that do not, about 30 percent generally turn out (see Table 2-4). The fact that voter turnout in partisan elections is almost two-thirds more than that in nonpartisan ones is doubtlessly a product of higher popular interest in partisan political campaigns and the greater likelihood of a dedicated core of party workers being available to get out the vote.

The pattern of partisan versus nonpartisan city elections is paralleled by big city versus small city. Big cities in America are more apt to use partisan elections than are small cities, and voter turnout for municipal elections is higher in the larger cities than in smaller ones.

Overall, we may expect a lower voter turnout in cities that are located in the Midwest, West, and South; that have middle-class and homogeneous populations; that are small or medium size; that hold their elections separately from state or national elections; and that have a council-manager form of government and nonpartisan electoral systems. Higher voter turnout can be expected in the East in cities that include many different kinds of ethnic and economic groups; in the big cities; in elections that are held simultaneously with state and national elections; in cities with a strong mayor form of government; and in cities with partisan elections and competitive party systems.[36] In contrast to national and state elections, the number of citizens registered to vote in local elections does not relate to the percentage of voter turnout; there can be many potential voters registered in a city but few real voters in a municipal election.[37]

The Suburbs and the Suffrage: The Smugness Factor

The number of suburbanites who vote in their own suburban elections probably represents the bleakest tribute to democracy in the nation. The smaller, more homogeneous, richer, and more smugly self-satisfied a suburb is, the less likelihood that its residents will vote. While the findings supporting this contention are mixed, a major investigation concluded that suburbs have the lowest overall participation rates of any six types of urban areas studied. Sidney Verba and Norman Nie held social status constant and categorized urban areas according to (1) villages or rural areas, (2) isolated towns, (3) isolated larger towns and nonmetropolitan cities with more than 10,000 people, (4) small suburbs, (5) large suburbs, and, of course, (6) central cities. Participation was lowest in the small suburbs, a fact that Verba and Nie attributed to the absence of strong local ties. The authors argue that their data confirmed that "community" is declining as the nation urbanizes.[38]

Additionally, as cities "reform"—as they adopt nonpartisan, at-large elections, eliminating the ward system—voting turnout declines. One investigation concluded that such reform movements discouraged political participation in American cities with more than 50,000 people.[39] Since suburbs often favor nonpartisan, at-large elections, this "reform" factor may contribute to low voter turnout there as well.

But it also may be that, quite aside from the reform factor, suburbanites simply are satisfied, and this very satisfaction may be attributed to the fact that they feel less of a need to get out into the political arena and brawl over policy issues. As a consequence, "suburbs are not beehives of political activity."[40]

DIRECT DEMOCRACY: REFERENDA, INITIATIVES, AND RECALLS

Most states and cities allow their citizens to vote on policy matters and to eject elected officials who have overstayed their welcome in ways that the federal government has never considered.

The Referendum

Forty-two states use the *referendum,* a device through which legislatures may allow voters an opportunity to accept or reject proposed legislation through popular balloting.[41] In 35 of those states that have the referendum, local ordinances as well as state laws are included.[42]

The use of referenda in this country can be traced back to the seventeenth century, well before the United States ever considered becoming the United States, but perhaps the first state referendum was conducted by Massachusetts, when it submitted its constitution to a popular vote immediately following independence.[43] Since then, referenda have evolved into several types. One is the *compulsory referendum,* which is referendum required by a state's constitution; all proposed amendments to constitutions, for example, must be submitted to the voters in every state except Delaware. An *optional referendum* is a straw vote; legislatures may submit a proposal to the voters to determine their preference, but the vote is not binding on the legislature. A *popular referendum* provides voters with an opportunity to vote to approve or disapprove legislation enacted by the legislature. Usually this vote must be taken shortly after the legislature adjourns (typically 90 days), and for the measure to be placed on the ballot requires that a petition be circulated and a fixed number of voters' signatures be secured. The number of signatures ranges from 2 percent of the votes cast in the last general election (in Massachusetts) to 15 percent (in Wyoming).[44]

The use of state referenda is burgeoning. Their popularity peaked in 1982, when 185 referenda were submitted to voters in all 42 states that use the device,[45] but its use is still going strong, and typically more than 150 referenda are submitted to the electorate every two years in 40 states.[46] These were the highest figures since 1932.

Local governments, like the states, also are heavy users of referenda. Seventy-seven percent of all municipalities have the power of the referendum written into their codes.[47] The issues voted upon in referendum elections run the gamut, but fiscal ones predominate. Thirty-five percent of all cities, for example, are legally required by their own charters or ordinances to hold referenda if their officials are considering changes in the municipal tax limits—and about a third of these cities held such referenda over the course of one three-year period.[48] Between 1975 and 1977, from 28 to 31 percent of American municipalities and from 18 to 19 percent of the counties held a referendum of some type; Southern and Western local governments, central cities, metropolitan counties, and council-manager cities and counties with county administrators use the device most frequently.[49]

The propensity among local governments to shift decision-making authority from elected representatives directly to the people is a move that receives high marks among local policymakers themselves. One survey of more than 1,800 cities and counties found that "there were no criticisms" by local officials "of public ratification of the multitudinous issues" that had been decided in their jurisdictions through popular referenda—issues that ranged from selling bonds to selling beer in the Orange Bowl.[50]

Perhaps public officials like to submit issues directly to the electorate because a certain kind of voter tends to dominate in referendum voting. Suburbanites and residents of small cities, well-informed citizens, Republicans, whites, high-income earners, the upper-middle class, and well-educated people possessing a strong belief in their own political effectiveness turn out measurably more heavily to vote on referenda than do residents of large cities and rural areas, poorly informed citizens, Democrats, blacks and other minorities, low and moderate income earners, working and middle-class people, and people who have not attended college and who do not hold a high level of confidence in their political efficacy.[51] Moreover, these voters vote more frequently on referenda than they vote on candidates for public office! Referenda voters "are likely to be the political elite."[52]

The Initiative

An even more direct form of democratic participation that the states have encouraged is the initiative. An *initiative* (a notion originated by South Dakota in 1898) is direct citizen balloting on issues that are initiated by citizen petition; typically, the petitioners must submit the signatures of a jurisdiction's registered voters in the amount of 5 to 15 percent of the ballots cast in the last election. Unlike the referendum, the initiative does not depend on the legislature to put an issue before the voters.

Twenty-three states[53] and more than half of all municipalities (51 percent)[54] use some form of the initiative. Writing initiatives into state constitutions was popular in the first two decades of the century, when the Progressive Movement—a political reform, "good government" movement—was in full flower; in fact, only 4 of the 23 states that have the initiative adopted it after 1918,[55] although 21 of the 27 states without the initiative have considered adopting it since 1980,[56] so it may be making a comeback.

As with referenda, initiatives come in more than one type. The *direct initiative* procedure, used in 15 states, permits petitioners to collect the needed signatures, has the state government verify them, and puts the measure on the ballot; it bypasses the legislature completely. The *indirect initiative* inserts a new step after the petition's signatures are verified. Rather than placing the measure directly on the ballot, it is sent to the legislature, which may accept it and vote it into law (in which case, it is not submitted to the electorate), fail to act on it, reject it, or propose a substitute measure. In these instances, the measure is placed on the ballot, as well as any substitution the legislature may have proposed; in most states, the measure receiving the most votes wins. In addition, about half the states using the initiative place certain subject matter restrictions on what the people may propose, such as appropriations, creation of courts, and civil rights.

Like referenda, the presence of initiatives on the ballot peaked in 1982, when 52 initiatives (the greatest number in 50 years) appeared in 19 states, representing the wishes of 16 million registered voters who had signed their petitions.[57] Since then, the number of initiatives making it to the voters per election has declined to around 40.[58] The issues ranged from the recall of elected officials, to "bottle bills" (requiring deposits on soft drink and beer bottles), to handgun controls, to tax and revenue limitations, to calls for a freeze on American nuclear weapons development. Often, these votes are of major consequence to a state, as in the case of California's "Proposition 13" or Massachusetts' "Proposition 2 1/2," both of which severely limited the government's abilities to tax and resulted in serious fiscal straits for both states. Still, voter approval of state initiatives is surprisingly marginal: only about a quarter get approved at the ballot box in contrast to approximately two-thirds of referenda that are proposed by legislatures.[59] Moreover, initiatives typically have a tough time even making it to the ballot: only 13 percent of the more than 300 petitions circulated in 1984, for example, were presented to the voters.[60]

Opinions on the value of the initiative vary. Those who support it cite its provisions for direct democracy, its assurances as a check on unbridled legislatures, and its educational value for the citizenry. Those who are against it point out that measures often are poorly drafted or duplicate existing laws, render compromise impossible, give the legislature "an out" on controversial issues, and open the door to out-of-state special interests who can influence electoral outcomes through heavy media campaigns.

When moral issues are featured in an initiative election, the voter turnout is highest, while questions of government structure and reform elicit the lowest interest.[61] Minorities, poor people, and uneducated citizens tend not to vote on initiatives, while organized interest groups tend to use the initiative as yet another weapon in their political arsenals;[62] when a special interest is stymied in the legislature, it can, with a lot of money and media "hype," go directly to "the people." Studies indicate, however, that the political results are mixed when either referenda or initiatives are judged by the people. The " 'scoreboard' for the continuing political Superbowl of conservatives versus liberals shows the same close game. . . . Most voters are less concerned with whether a particular measure represents a 'liberal' or a 'conservative' position than with whether it is right or wrong."[63]

Between them, the referendum and the initiative are the grassroots governments' twin pillars of direct democracy. Table 2-9 indicates those states that permit the use of the referendum and the initiative. Fifteen of these states provide maximum democratic participation; that is, they use all five procedural

Table 2-9 States with Direct Democracy Provisions

State	Constitutional Initiatives	Statutory State	Initiatives Localities	Statutory State	Referendum Localities
Alabama					
Alaska		X	X	X	X
Arizona	X	X	X	X	X
Arkansas	X	X	X	X	X
California	X	X	X	X	X
Colorado	X	X	X	X	X
Connecticut					
Delaware					
Florida	X			X	X
Georgia			X	X	X
Hawaii					
Idaho		X	X	X	X
Illinois	X			X	X
Indiana					
Iowa				X	X
Kansas				X	X
Kentucky			X	X	X
Louisiana			X		
Maine		X	X	X	X
Maryland				X	X
Massachusetts	X	X	X	X	X
Michigan	X	X	X	X	X
Minnesota			X		X
Mississippi					
Missouri	X	X	X	X	X
Montana	X	X	X	X	X
Nebraska	X	X	X	X	X
Nevada	X	X	X	X	X
New Hampshire				X	
New Jersey			X	X	X
New Mexico				X	
New York				X	
North Carolina				X	
North Dakota	X	X	X	X	X
Ohio	X	X	X	X	X
Oklahoma	X	X	X	X	X
Oregon	X	X	X	X	X
Pennsylvania			X	X	X
Rhode Island				X	x
South Carolina			X	X	X
South Dakota	X	X	X	X	X
Tennessee					
Texas			X		X

Table 2-9 (Continued)

State	*Constitutional Initiatives*	*Statutory State*	*Initiatives Localities*	*Statutory State*	*Referendum Localities*
Utah		X	X	X	X
Vermont			X	X	X
Virginia			X	X	X
Washington		X	X	X	X
West Virginia			X		X
Wisconsin				X	X
Wyoming		X	X	X	X
Total	17	21	32	39	38

Source: Council of State Governments, *The Book of the States, 1976–77* (Lexington, Ky.: Council of State Governments, 1976), pp. 176, 216–218.

forms of direct democracy—constitutional initiatives, statutory initiatives at the state and local levels, and statutory referenda at the state and local levels.

The Recall

The *recall* is a type of initiative used to throw public officials out of office by calling a special election before the official's term of office has expired; if a majority votes to expel an officeholder from office, he or she is expelled.

Los Angeles was the nation's first government to implement the recall mechanism, when the city inserted it in its charter in 1903. Oregon, in 1908, was the first state to adopt the device for state officials, and by 1914 10 additional states permitted the recall; only 2 states have adopted the recall since that year.[64] However, 37 states permit their local governments (or at least certain types of their local jurisdictions) to recall local officials.[65] Twenty-one states permit most or all local officials to be recalled, and only 14 flatly deny the recall of local officeholders.[66] To put up an official for reelection by recall requires that a petition attain the signatures of registered voters ranging from 4 to 55 percent of the votes cast in the last general election; 25 percent is the typical requirement.[67]

The recall has been used successfully only once against statewide elected officers—in 1921, when North Dakotans recalled the governor, attorney general, and secretary of agriculture.[68] However, district voters in Michigan recalled two state legislators in 1983, a recall unique in the annals of American politics.[69] Generally, judges and officers in the executive branch are the objects of state recall drives.

The recall is more popular at the local level. Although precise data are not available, one study found a surprising propensity among local voters to use it. On a per capita basis, Oregon emerges as the clear leader, with more than 1 recall per 10,000 people, but, overall, Californians use the recall most, with nearly 400 recalls during the 1970s. Oregon, Nebraska, Alaska, Idaho, Michigan, Nevada, California, Washington, and Arizona are the states most likely to employ the recall (at least when calculated on a recall-per-population basis), and their relative likelihood of using it follows the order just presented. The study estimated that about 60 to 70 percent of recall petitions qualify for the ballot and that approximately half of local officials subjected to a recall election are voted out of office.[70] The recall, then, is not merely a symbol of direct democracy; it is very direct democracy indeed.

The referendum, initiative, and recall all stand as strong testaments to the grassroots governments' commitment to full citizen participation in democracy. This commitment exceeds that of the federal government, where questions of public policy are never placed directly before the people.

AMERICANS: A PEOPLE WHO PARTICIPATE AT THE GRASSROOTS

But if America's grassroots governments are uniquely determined in providing more opportunities for political participation to their citizens, do citizens care? Can we extend our earlier suburban metaphor to all Americans? Is the nation something less than a beehive of political activity?

Several analyses indicate that Americans, as a nation of joiners, are far more involved in their communities and, by implication, in their politics, than more superficial data might suggest. It is true that Americans vote relatively less frequently in national elections than do their Western European counterparts. But in some ways, these comparisons are unfair. Richard M. Scammon, for example, argues that European democracies count their voting turnout rates differently from the U.S. practice. In Europe, voting turnout is computed on the percentage of registered voters who vote, while the American Census Bureau bases its calculations on the percentage all those eligible to vote (i.e., all those citizens 18 years of age and older) who vote. Scammon suggests that if the United States determined its turnout rate in the same way that Europe does, the American turnout rate would rise by 8 to 10 percentage points, thus making it comparable to the turnout rates in Switzerland, Canada, Ireland, Japan, and Britain.[71]

It is also worth keeping in mind that, because the United States is a federal system, there are many more elections in which to vote than there are in most democracies. When we account for the local, state, as well as national elections in which Americans are asked to vote, we find a population very prone to vote. One study of electoral participation in 27 major democracies around the globe concluded that "although the turnout rate in the United States is below that of most other democracies, American citizens do not necessarily do less voting than other citizens; most probably, they do more."[72]

Limiting the analysis of voting turnout only to elections for national offices tends to result in an understatement of voting participation in the United States. One analysis of voting turnout between 1972 and 1976 indicated that the average adult had voted 3.4 times during this four-year period, while the average registered voter had voted 4.5 times. By this analysis, only about 25 percent of all American adults and 5 percent of all registered voters had failed to vote in any election during the four years, while a third of all adults and 45 percent of registered voters had voted in at least five elections.[73]

In another view, there are many forms of political participation besides voting. One study of Americans and the citizens of four Western European democracies tried to analyze these other forms of political participation sepa-

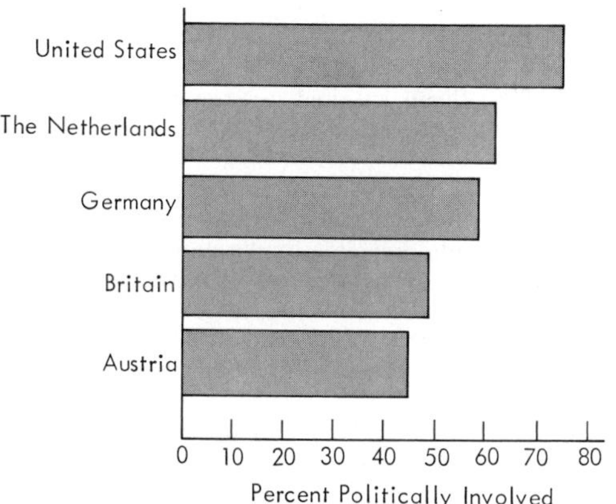

Figure 2-7
Political involvement other than voting in five countries. (*Source:* Samuel H. Barnes et al., *Political Action Mass Participation in Five Western Democracies.* Beverly Hills, Calif.: Sage Publications, 1979, p. 169.)

rately from the single political act of voting, on the logic that European elections differed radically from the elections in the United States. The study concluded that Americans participated in a far richer variety of political acts than did their European counterparts.[74]

Figure 2-7 indicates this relative involvement by Americans in the political life of their country in comparison to citizens of the four Western European countries studied. As it shows, almost 75 percent of Americans can be categorized as politically involved. By contrast, the next highest country (The Netherlands) shows roughly a 65 percent involvement. Other evidence of the high rate of political participation by Americans includes such mundane activities as letter writing: the number of Americans who write letters to public officials has nearly doubled since 1964.[75] A reasonable conclusion is that, despite relatively low voting turnout patterns, "political apathy, by a wide margin, is lowest in the United States" when compared to other countries of comparable democratic development.[76]

A major reason why this high level of political participation by Americans has been obscured is the fact that Americans generally (with the exception of voting turnout in national elections) are much more involved at the grassroots than at the national political level. Protests, community groups, citizen contacts with state and local policymakers—these are among the primary modes of American political participation.[77] "If . . . we concentrate our attention on national elections we will find that the United States is the least participatory" of five democracies examined in the study cited. "On the other hand, data from empirical studies show that the United States has a very participation-oriented culture on the local level of government."[78]

These realities make the study of governance at the grassroots all the more vital. It is in the states and communities of our country where the most intense politics are played, where political participation is the broadest, and where public policies are formed.

NOTES

[1]Center for Political Studies, University of Michigan, as cited in Samuel C. Patterson, Roger H. Davidson, and Randall B. Ripley, *A More Perfect Union,* rev. ed. (Homewood, Ill.: Dorsey, 1982), p. 119.

[2]Daniel Katz et al., *Bureaucratic Encounters* (Ann Arbor, Mich.: Institute for Social Research, 1975). For a review of this literature as it pertains to local governments, see Philip B. Coulter, "Citizen-Initiated Contacting: A Methodological Exploration of Rates and Reasons," paper presented at the Annual Meeting of the American Political Science Association, August 31 - September 2, 1985, New Orleans.

[3]Max Kaase and Alan Marsh, "Political Action Repertory: Changes Over Time," in Samuel H. Barnes and Max Kaase, eds. *Political Action: Mass Participation in Five Western Democracies* (Beverly Hills, Calif.: Sage, 1979), p. 155.

[4]Jack Citrin, "Changing American Electorate," in Arnold Meltsner, ed., *Politics and the Oval Office: Towards Presidential Governance* (San Francisco: Institute for Contemporary Studies, 1981), pp. 37-39.

[5]*Ibid.;* also Jack Citrin, "Political Alienation as a Social Indicator: Attitudes and Action," *Social Indicators Research* (1977), p. 4.

[6]David L. Langford, "Black Plight Changed Little Since Turbulent '67 Summer," United Press International, *The Arizona Republic* (July 10, 1977).

[7]Seymour Spilerman, "The Causes of Racial Disturbances," *American Sociological Review,* 35 (August, 1970), pp. 617-649.

[8]National Advisory Commission on Civil Disorders, *Report* (Washington, D.C.: U.S. Government Printing Office, 1968).

[9]Quoted in Langford, "Black Plight Changed Little."

[10]"Those Riot Torn Cities: A Look at Progress Ten Years Later," *U.S. News and World Report* (August 29, 1977), pp. 50-51.

[11]Quoted in Langford, "Black Plight Changed Little."

[12]Marvin Dunn, quoted in Manning Marable, "The Fire This Time: The Miami Rebellion, May, 1980," *The Black Scholar* (July-August, 1980), p. 4.

[13]The source for the following discussion is Sidney Verba and Norman H. Nie, *Participation in America: Political Democracy and Social Equality* (New York: Harper & Row, 1972), pp. 79-91.

[14]Census Bureau's survey as cited in Robert Rheinhold, "American Voters Fall into Elite Category," *The New York Times* Syndication, as reprinted in *The Arizona Republic* (November 3, 1976).

[15]John W. Soule and Wilma E. McGrath, "A Comparative Study of Male-Female Political Attitudes at Citizen and Elite Levels," in Marianne Githens and Jewell Prestage, eds., *A Portrait of Marginality: The Political Behavior of the American Woman* (New York: Longman, 1977), p. 187.

[16]Census Bureau Survey, 1976, as cited in Rheinhold, "American Voters Fall into Elite Category."

[17]Lester W. Milbrath and M. L. Goel, *Political Participation,* 2nd ed. (Chicago: Rand McNally, 1977), as derived from Table 1-1, p. 16. These conclusions are based on a survey of residents of Buffalo, New York.

[18]Verba and Nie, *Participation in America,* p. 175.

[19]Albert K. Karnig and B. Oliver Walter, "Municipal Elections: Registration, Incumbent Success, and Voter Participation," *Municipal Year Book, 1977* (Washington, D.C.: International City Management Association, 1977), p. 69.

[20]*Ibid.,* p. 70.

[21]Carol A. Cassel, "Change in Electoral Participation in the South," *Journal of Politics,* 41 (August, 1979), pp. 907-917.

[22]Susan Welch, "Women as Political Animals? A Test of Some Explanations for Male-Female Political Participation Differences," *American Journal of Political Science,* 21 (November 1977), pp. 711-730; and Kristi Andersen, "Working Women and Political Participation, 1952-1972," *American Journal of Political Science,* 19 (August 1975), pp. 439-454.

[23]Jae-On Kim, John R. Petrocik, and Stephen N. Enokson, "Voter Turnout in the American States: Systematic and Individual Components," *American Political Science Review,* 69 (March, 1975), pp. 359-377.

[24]Advisory Commission on Intergovernmental Relations, *The Question of State Government Capability* (Washington, D.C.: U.S. Government Printing Office, 1985), p. 265.

[25]Richard E. Cohen, "Will the Voting Rights Act Become a Victim of Its Own Success?" *National Journal,* 13 (August 1, 1981), p. 1365.

[26]James F. Blumstein, "Minority Civil Rights in Voting Rights," *The Wall Street Journal* (May 27, 1982).

[27]U.S. Bureau of the Census, "Geographic Mobility: March 1975 to March 1976," *Current Population Reports,* Series P-20, No. 305 (Washington, D.C.: U.S. Government Printing Office, 1977).

[28]Robert Thornton, "Election Legislation," *The Book of the States, 1972-73* (Lexington, Ky.: Council of State Governments, 1972), pp. 26-27.

[29]Steven J. Rosenstone and Raymond E. Wolfinger, "The Effect of Registration Laws on Voter Turnout," paper presented at the 1976 Annual Meeting of the American Political Science Association (September, 1976), Chicago. The study was of the 1972 presidential election only.

[30]Cited in Virginia Graham, *Voter Registration (National),* Issue Brief IV 74003 (Washington, D.C.: Congressional Research Service, Library of Congress, 1977), p. 2. Data are for the 1976 election only.

[31]Jack E. Rossotti and Charles L. Miller, Jr., *State Voter Registration by Mail* (Lexington, Ky.: Council of State Governments, 1976), p. 9.

[32]Richard G. Smolka, *Registering by Mail: The Maryland and New Jersey Experience* (Washington, D.C.: The American Enterprise Institute, 1975), pp. 78-80.

[33]Ed Shaw, quoted in "$5 Million in Prizes for Voting," *Washington Times* (June 4, 1982); and Associated Press, "Hook'em Danno: Register to Vote, Win a Date with Television Star," *The Arizona Republic* (June 11, 1982).

[34]Advisory Commission on Intergovernmental Relations, *The Question of State Government Capability,* pp. 268-271.

[35]John C. Bollens, ed., *Exploring the Metropolitan Community* (Berkeley: University of California Press, 1961), p. 82; and John C. Bollens, *Metropolitan Challenge* (Dayton, Ohio: Metropolitan Community Studies, 1959), p. 231.

[36]Thomas R. Dye, *Politics in States and Communities,* 4th ed. (Englewood Cliffs, N.J.: Prentice-Hall, 1981), p. 285.

[37]Albert K. Karnig, "Registration and Municipal Voting: Putting First Things Second," *Social Science Quarterly,* 55 (April, 1974), pp. 159-166.

[38]Verba and Nie, *Participation in America,* pp. 229-247.

[39]Robert Lineberry and Edmund Fowler, "Reformism and Public Policies in American Cities," *American Political Science Review,* 61 (September, 1967), pp. 165-166.

[40]John Rehfuss, "Suburban Development and Governance," *Public Administration Review,* 37 (January/February, 1977), p. 116.

[41]Advisory Commission on Intergovernmental Relations, *Citizen Participation in the American Federal System,* A-73 (Washington, D.C.: U.S. Government Printing Office, 1979), p. 9.

[42]*Ibid.*

[43]Advisory Commission on Intergovernmental Relations, *The Question of State Government Capability,* p. 280.

[44]*Ibid.*

[45]"Freeze Success Highlights Ballot Measures," *Congressional Quarterly Weekly Reports* (November 6, 1982), p. 2809.

[46]Austin Ranney, "Referendums and Initiatives 1984," *Public Opinion* (December/January 1985), p. 15. In 1984, about 160 referenda were submitted.

[47]Sanders, "The Government of American Cities," p. 180.

[48]John Rehfuss, "Citizen Participation in Urban Fiscal Decisions," *Municipal Year Book, 1979* (Washington, D.C.: International City Management Association, 1979), p. 92.

[49]*Ibid.,* pp. 92-94.

[50]*Ibid.,* p. 95.

[51]Jerome M. Clubb and Michael W. Traugott, "National Patterns of Referenda Voting: The 1968 Election," in Harlan Hahn, ed., *People and Politics in Urban Society* (Beverly Hills, Calif., Sage, 1972), pp. 144-146.

[52]Advisory Commission on Intergovernmental Relations, *The Question of State Government Capability,* p. 282.
[53]*Ibid.*, p. 279.
[54]Sanders, "The Government of American Cities," p. 180.
[55]Advisory Commission on Intergovernmental Relations, *The Question of State Government Capability,* p. 278.
[56]Lucinda Simon, "Representative Democracy Challenged," *State Legislatures* (August, 1984), p. 13.
[57]David D. Schmidt, "Initiative Pendulum Begins Leftward Swing," *Public Administration Times* (September 15, 1982), p. 1.
[58]Donald W. Lief, "Initiatives Gain Support," *Intergovernmental Perspective,* 11 (Winter, 1985), p. 27.
[59]Advisory Commission on Intergovernmental Relations, *Citizen Participation,* pp. 247-250. In 1984, however, an unusually large percentage of initiatives were granted voter approval: about 50 percent. See Lief, "Initiatives Gain Support," p. 27.
[60]Lief, "Initiatives Gain Support," p. 27.
[61]Hugh A. Bone and Robert C. Benedict, "Perspectives on Direct Legislation: Washington State's Experience, 1914-1973," *Western Political Quarterly,* 28 (June, 1975), pp. 330-351.
[62]Eugene C. Lee, "The Initiative and Referendum: How California Has Fared," *National Civic Review,* 68 (February, 1979), pp. 69-76, 84.
[63]Ranney, "Referendums and Initiatives 1984," p. 16. See also Lief, "Initiatives Gain Support," p. 27.
[64]Advisory Commission on Intergovernmental Relations, *The Question of State Government Capability,* p. 275. The 13 states using the recall are Alaska (which adopted it after 1914), Arizona, California, Colorado, Idaho, Kansas, Louisiana, Michigan, Nevada, North Dakota, Oregon, Washington, and Wisconsin (also after 1914).
[65]Charles M. Price, "Recalls at the Local Level: Dimensions and Implications," *National Civic Review* (April 1983), p. 200.
[66]*Ibid.*
[67]*Ibid.;* and Advisory Commission on Intergovernmental Relations, *The Question of State Government Capability,* p. 274.
[68]*Ibid.*, p. 278.
[69]*Ibid.*, p. 283.
[70]Price, "Recalls at the Local Level," p. 203. Price based his estimate on California data.
[71]Richard M. Scammon, as cited in, "The Technical Difficulties," *Public Opinion* (October/November, 1983), p. 19.
[72]Ivor Crewe, "Electoral Participation," in David Butler, Howard R. Penniman, and Austin Ranney, eds., *Democracy at the Polls: A Comparative Study of Competitive National Elections* (Washington, D.C.: American Enterprise Institute, 1981), p. 261.
[73]Richard W. Boyd, "Decline in U.S. Voter Turnout: Structural Explanations," *American Politics Quarterly,* 9 (April 1981), p. 148.
[74]Max Kaase and Alan Marsh, "Distribution of Political Action," in Barnes and Koose, eds., *Political Action,* p. 168.
[75]Richard A. Brody, "The Puzzle of Political Participation in America," in Anthony King, ed., *The New American Political System* (Washington, D.C.: American Enterprise Institute, 1978), p. 317.
[76]Kaase and Marsh, "Distribution of Political Action," p. 168.
[77]Gabriel A. Almond and Sidney Verba, *The Civic Culture* (Princeton, N.J.: Princeton University Press, 1963), p. 13.
[78]Kaase and Marsh, "Distribution of Political Action," p. 168.

3

POLITICAL PRESSURE

Special interests, pressure groups, and lobbies (all of which mean essentially the same thing) are integral to the very idea of democratic government. Indeed, James Madison, writing close to 200 years ago in *The Federalist, No. 10,* discussed the powers of a "landed interest, a manufacturing interest, a mercantile interest, a monied interest, and many lesser interests" that fought each other for policies favorable to themselves within the confines of the political process.

Madison and his contemporaries saw this situation as being quite normal in a democratic polity and, indeed, felt that the workings of such a system could enhance the general public's interests. Harmon Zeigler and G. Wayne Peak call Madison's view "the hydraulic theory of politics."[1] That description permits us to visualize a system of forces pushing against each other and emerging with the public policy that satisfies all interested parties and in proportion to their relative degrees of power in the system.

A real question has arisen as to whether the "hydraulic theory" still serves as a moral justification of a political process that results in policies that are supposedly in the "best" interests of the public. We shall return to this question at the close of this chapter.

Philosophic questions aside, whether the "hydraulic theory" is accurate as a description of how public policy is made is an open question. Researchers who have tried to test the theory in the real world have found that sometimes it applies, and sometimes it does not. For example, one study of the legislatures in three states (California, Iowa, and Texas) found that there was no particular correlation between the number of interest groups involved with a bill and the eventual success or failure of the bill, but that the "balance" of groups on a bill (i.e., groups were either heavily for or against a bill) did make a significant difference. For instance, if some powerful groups were arduously pushing a bill that had little or no opposition, then it was likelier to be passed. Beyond these generalizations, however, the researchers found that the "group struggle . . . clearly associated with legislative outcomes in California . . . marginally so in Texas . . . and hardly so in Iowa. . . . This suggests that the pluralists' theory of countervailing power [i.e., the hydraulic theory] works in some systems but not in others."[2]

PRESSURE GROUPS, POWER, AND PECKING ORDERS

An interest group is any collection of people with a common political goal that makes a concerted effort to attain that goal through the normal political channels. One of the favorite methods, and certainly the most notorious, that a group may use to attain political objectives is lobbying. Lobbying often is performed by professionals who are hired staff members of a particular special interest. Lobbyists normally ply their trade by developing personal contacts among policymakers—both legislators and bureaucrats. Lobbying, of course, is only one technique that interest groups use to affect the policymaking process in their favor; public relations and influencing elections are others.

There is a clear pecking order among interest groups in the states, and this pecking order has remained remarkably stable over the years. In 1962, John C. Wahlke and others interviewed state legislators in California, New Jersey, Ohio, and Tennessee, and, in all four states, legislators cited business interest as the "most powerful" group more often than any other. Educational interests ranked second in three of the four states, and labor interest came in third.[3] Five years later, Wayne L. Francis also found that business lobbyists were by far the most likely to be regarded by legislators as powerful.[4] In 1971, Francis and Robert Presthus found that lobbyists for business interest were clearly the most likely to be perceived politically powerful by state legislators.[5] In 1976, L. Harmon Zeigler and Hendrick Van Dalen also concluded that business interests were similarly dominant, at least in terms of being the majority of registered lobbyists (58 percent, on the average) in the states.[6] And in 1981, Sarah McCally Morehouse, in a 50-state study, also determined that business interest groups were the most powerful in the states.[7]

Table 3-1 describes the major interest groups by state and also categorizes the states according to whether or not they are dominated by powerful special interests, or whether special interests are relatively weak.

Table 3-2, which is derived from Table 3-1, categorizes the types of groups regarded as powerful. As it notes, whether or not a state is dominated by powerful interest groups or is relatively free of them, business still emerges as the most powerful single lobby. A variety of factors are important in determining whether or not a special interest has power within a state political system. These include:

1. The size of the groups.
2. The cohesion of factions within the groups.
3. The geographic distribution of the lobby (for example, statewide versus localized).

Table 3-1 Pressure Groups Reputed to be Influential, by State

States in which pressure groups are strong (22)	
Alabama	Farm Bureau Federation, utilities, highway interests, Associated Industries of Alabama
Alaska	Oil, salmon, mining, contracting, labor unions, Chamber of Commerce
Arkansas	Transport, agriculture, utilities, natural resources (oil, timber, bauxite), insurance, local government (County Judges Association, Arkansas Municipal League), labor, Chamber of Commerce, Arkansas Free Enterprise Association
Florida	Associated Industries, utilities (Florida Power Corp., Florida Power and Light), Farm Bureau, bankers, liquor interests, chain stores, race tracks, Phosphate Council
Georgia	Atlanta business group, Citizens and Southern Bank, Coca-Cola, Fuqua Industries, Delta Airlines, Trust Company of Georgia, Woodruff Foundation, education lobby, Georgia Municipal Association
Hawaii	Big Five Companies: C. Brewer and Co. Ltd. (sugar, molasses, insurance, ranching); Thro. H. Davies & Co. (sugar, merchandising, foreign investment); Amfac, Inc. (sugar and merchandising); Castle and Cooke, Inc. (sugar, pineapple, bananas, seafoods, coffee, macadamia nuts, discount stores, steamship agent in Hawaii, land development, and property management); Alexander and Baldwin, Inc. (docks and warehouses, sugar, pineapples, merchandising); Dillingham Corporation (construction)
Iowa	Farm Bureau Federation, truckers
Kentucky	Coal companies, Jockey Club, liquor interests, tobacco interests, Kentucky Education Association, rural electric cooperatives
Louisiana	Oil companies (Exxon, Chevron, Texaco, Gulf, Shell, Mobil, Mid-Continental Oil and Gas Association); gas pipeline interests, Louisiana Chemical Association, forest industry, rice industry, Louisiana Manufacturers Association, Farm Bureau, AFL–CIO
Mississippi	Mississippi Economic Council, Farm Bureau, manufacturers; association, medical association, public school teachers, association of local officials (county supervisors, mayors, sheriffs, etc.), segregationist groups (Citizens' Council, John Birch Society, Association for Preservation of the White Race, Women for Constitutional Government)
Montana	Anaconda Copper Company, Montana Power Company, State Chamber of Commerce, Northern Pacific Railroad, Great Northern Railroad
Nebraska	Farm Bureau, Omaha National Bank, Northern Natural Gas Company, Union Pacific Railroad, Northwest Bell Telephone, education lobby
New Hampshire	Public utilities, paper manufacturing, lumber, racetrack lobby
New Mexico	Oil and gas, school teachers, liquor dealers, banks, truckers, cattle breeders, business groups
North Carolina	Textile, tobacco, furniture, utilities, banks, teachers
Oklahoma	Phillips Petroleum, Kerr-McGee, other oil companies (Texaco, Mobile, Humble, Atlantic-Sinclair, Sun-Sunray, DX Division, Hess Oil), transportation companies, power companies, local public officials
Oregon	Utilities (Pacific Power & Light, Portland General Electric), lumber companies, public school teachers (Oregon Education Association), railroads and truckers, organized labor (AFL–CIO, Teamsters, Longshoremen), Farm Bureau, Agricultural Association, insurance lobby

Table 3-1 (Continued)

South Carolina	Planters, textiles (DuPont, Stevens, Deering-Milliken, Fiberglass, Textron, Chemstrand, Lowenstein, Burlington, Bowaters), Electric and Gas Company, banks
Tennessee	Manufacturers association, County Service Association, Farm Bureau, Municipal League, Education Association, liquor lobby
Texas	Chemical Council, Mid-Continent Oil and Gas Association, Independent Producers and Royalty Owners, State Teachers' Association, Manufacturers' Association, medical association, Motor Transport Association, insurance organizations
Washington	Boeing Aircraft, Teamsters, government employees, school teachers, AFL–CIO, highway interests (oil, asphalt, contractors, car builders), timber, banking, commercial fishing, pinballs, public and private power, gravel, wine and beer, Grange
West Virginia	Union Carbide, Bethlehem Steel, Occidental Petroleum, Georgia Pacific, Baltimore and Ohio Railroad, Norfolk and Western Railway Company, Chesapeake and Ohio Railway Company, United Mine Workers
States in which pressure groups are moderately strong (18)	
Arizona	Copper companies (Phelps Dodge), oil companies, farm groups, Arizona Power Company, "school lobby," liquor lobby
California	Pacific Gas & Electric, Standard Oil of California, Bank of America, California Teachers Association, Lockheed Aircraft, Transamerica, Kern County Land Company, Bankers Association of America, California Real Estate Association, California Growers Association, University of California, AFL–CIO
Delaware	DuPont Chemical Company, insurance lobby
Idaho	Idaho Power Company, Idaho Farm Bureau, stockmen, mining and forest industries, railroads, county courthouses, Mormon church, Idaho Education Association, AFL–CIO
Illinois	Illinois Manufacturers Association, Illinois Chamber of Commerce, coal operators, insurance companies (State Farm and Allstate), Illinois Education Association, Illinois Medical Society, AFL–CIO unions (steelworkers), retail merchants, race tracks, Farm Bureau, *Chicago Tribune*
Indiana	AFL–CIO, Farm Bureau, Indiana State Teachers' Association, Chamber of Commerce
Kansas	Banks, power companies, pipeline companies, railroads, Farm Bureau
Maine	Big three: electric power, timber, textile and shoe manufacturing; Farm Bureau; grange; liquor and beer lobby; horse-racing lobby; conservation groups
Maryland	Bankers, industrialists, AFL–CIO, liquor lobby
Missouri	Missouri Farmers Association, AFL–CIO, Missouri Bus and Truck Association, Teamsters, Missouri State Teachers Association, brewers
Nevada	Gambling, utilities, banks, mining, livestock, insurance, railroads
Ohio	Insurance, banking, utilities, savings and loan association, Chamber of Commerce
Pennsylvania	Steel companies (U.S. Steel, Republic, Jones and Laughlin, Bethlehem); oil firms (Standard, Gulf, Sun, Atlantic); public utilities; service industries; Pennsylvania State Teachers Association; Welfare Rights Organization; AFL–CIO

Table 3-1 (Continued)

South Dakota	Farmers Union, rural co-ops and rural electrification interests, Farm Bureau, Chamber of Commerce, banks, South Dakota Wheat Growers Association, South Dakota Stockgrowers Association, Northern States Power, Homestake Mine, liquor lobby
Utah	Utah Mining Association, Utah Manufacturers Association, Utah Industrial Council, Utah Bureau Federation, Salt Lake City Chamber of Commerce, Utah Education Association, AFL–CIO, Farmers Union
Vermont	Farm Bureau, Associated Industries of Vermont
Virginia	Virginia Electric Power, Virginia Manufacturers Association, Chamber of Commerce, railroads
Wyoming	Wyoming Stock Growers Association, Rocky Mountain Oil and Gas Association, Farm Bureau Federation, Wyoming Education Association, Wyoming Association of Municipalities, Union Pacific Railroad, Truckers
States in which pressure groups are weak (10)	
Colorado	Colorado Cattlemen's Association, Denver financial interests, oilmen, Chamber of Commerce, billboard interests, Colorado Education Association, Colorado Municipal League, AFL–CIO, Colorado Farmers Union, League of Women Voters
Connecticut	Connecticut Manufacturers Association, Insurance Lobby, Farm Bureau Federation, grange, AFL–CIO
Massachusetts	Labor, Catholic Church, public utility interests, real estate lobby, Associated Industries of Massachusetts, Chamber of Commerce, insurance companies, Massachusetts Federation of Taxpayer's Association, racetrack interests, state employees, liquor interests
Michigan	General Motors, Ford, Chrysler, American Motors, United Automobile Workers, AFL–CIO
Minnesota	Railroads Association, 3M, Dayton Hudson Corporation, Northern States Power Company, Honeywell, Northwestern Bell Telephone, banking, beer, iron mining, liquor, Minnesota Education Association, Teamsters, Minnesota Association of Commerce and Industry, AFL–CIO, Farm Bureau, Farmers Union, League of Women Voters
New Jersey	Johnson & Johnson, Warner-Lambert Pharmaceuticals, Prudential Insurance, Campbell's Soup, Becton Dickinson, First National State Bank in Newark, New Jersey Manufacturers Association, Hess Oil, Garden State Race Track, New Jersey Farm Bureau, New Jersey Education Association, Chamber of Commerce, AFL–CIO
New York	Education Lobby: Board of Regents, N.Y. State Teachers' Association, N.Y. Federation of Teachers, Associated Industries of New York, Empire State Chamber of Commerce, Bankers Association, AFL–CIO, Teamsters, state medical association, Roman Catholic Church, New York City lobby
North Dakota	Education lobby: North Dakota Education Association, PTA, School Boards, Department of Public Instruction, Farmers' Union; Farm Bureau; North Dakota Stockmen's Association; Association of Rural Cooperatives
Rhode Island	AFL–CIO, Associated Industries of Rhode Island, insurance companies, public utilities, banks, racetrack associations
Wisconsin	AFL–CIO, United Auto Workers, business interests, Farmers' Union, liquor lobby, local public officials

Source: From *State Politics, Parties and Policy*, by Sarah McCally Morehouse. Copyright © 1981 by Holt, Rinehart and Winston, Inc. Reprinted by permission of Holt, Rinehart and Winston, CBS College Publishing.

4. The social status of the group (the California Education Association probably has more political clout than does the Western Nudist Association, for example).
5. The organization and leadership of the lobby.
6. The program that the lobby espouses (for example, the National Association for the Advancement of Colored People probably has a more attractive program to most people than does the Ku Klux Klan).
7. The general political environment in which the interest group must function.

Of these seven sources of interest group strength, perhaps that elusive variable of status is the most important. The term *status* refers to the social standing and economic well-being of the members of the interest group. One study concluded that 44 percent of all members of all kinds of groups are described as "upper middle class" by the professional staff directors of their respective associations. Less than 20 percent are seen as working class. "Those who join groups possess disproportionate amounts of such political resources that typically accompany such properties, including conceptual and forensic skills, an appreciation of one's stake in society, and the political knowledge and interest inspired by this definition of one's situation."[8]

The South, long dominated by a single party, has particularly strong interest groups. According to one analysis, fully half of the strong interest group states are in the South; in fact, 83 percent of the Sunbelt states are considered to be strong lobby states. The states with the weakest interest groups are found most frequently in New England and the Midwest.[9]

Although a high level of economic development tends to associate with weak interest groups, there appears to be very little relationship between party competitiveness and the strength of interest groups. States can have both competitive (and presumably vibrant) parties and strong interest groups. States in which parties are competitive and interest groups are strong include Alaska, Iowa, Montana, Nebraska, New Hampshire, and Washington.[10]

Parties do not seem to act as a countervailing force against interest group strength. This is not to say that interest groups dominate all states, but only that parties do not necessarily provide a buffer. One observer has noted that even in states where parties are strong, interest groups are "less junior partners than traditional analysis would suggest. In weak party states, groups work directly with

Table 3-2 Types of Groups Regarded as Powerful

Type of Group	*TYPE OF INTEREST GROUP SYSTEM*		
	Strong	*Moderate*	*Weak*
Business	125 (75%)	76 (71%)	46 (58%)
Labor	9 (5%)	7 (7%)	12 (15%)
Farm	12 (7%)	14 (13%)	11 (14%)
Education	11 (7%)	8 (2%)	10 (14%)
Government	9 (5%)	2 (29%)	—
Total	166	107	79

Source: Derived from Table 3–1. As in Table 3–1, states are categorized according to strength of interest groups. Morehouse reached her conclusions from reading available state literature. From L. Harmon Zeigler, "Interest Groups in the States," in Virginia Gray, Herbert Jacob, and Kenneth N. Vines, eds., *Politics in the American States: A Comparative Analysis,* 4th ed. (Boston: Little, Brown and Company, 1983), p. 103.

candidates, and successful candidates understand well to whom they are beholden. In strong party states, single-issue groups and political action committees work more closely with party organizations. The sources of the money are the same: the actual distribution changes, however, in different group systems."[11]

As we elaborate in Chapter 5, what does seem to be the most effective public defense against the influence of a special interest is a combination of legislative professionalism, the size of the state executive branch, the strength of the governor and the legislative leadership, and the extent to which the parties are cohesive in the legislature. "Legislative professionalism" refers to such variables as the size of the legislature's professional staff, the amount of compensation paid to legislators, and the legislature's use of relatively advanced managerial techniques. Most of the states with more professional legislators tend to associate with weaker interest groups.[12] This correlation appeals to common sense. When legislators have staff to whom they can go for information about policy issues, they become less reliant upon lobbyists as sources of information on which to base policy.

It seems probable that the same kind of effect pertains when the state bureaucracy is strongly staffed; legislators can go to state bureaucrats for information as easily as they can go to their own staffs and avoid relying on lobbyists for information in the process. It follows that there is "a clear relationship between the size of the state bureaucracy and the strength of interest groups; strong lobby states have smaller bureaucracies than weak lobby states."[13] Morehouse found, in a related vein, that states with strong governors also were likely to have less powerful interest groups: those states in which the governors have longer terms of tenure, and strong powers of appointment, budget formulation, and the veto associate with weak interest groups.[14]

Finally, how well the party can exercise discipline over its members in the legislature also equates with weak interest groups. If the party can command loyalty, legislators have less ability to respond to interest groups demands. Legislative party discipline is measured on the basis of "party cohesion," or the percentage of votes in which a majority of one party opposes a majority of the other. Those states with more cohesive legislatures also tend to be weak interest group states.[15] We can detect at least four distinct types of interest group conflict in the states.

POWER PATTERNS AND PRESSURE POLITICS

Zeigler and Van Dalen have done some provocative work on why some interest groups are more powerful in some states than in others. Basically, their argument is that interest groups have the weakest political impact in the more industrialized and urbanized states with more heterogeneous populations. The logic continues that the more open and competitive the conflict between pressure groups in the states is, then the correspondingly less chance there is of any single group becoming dominant in the making of public policy.

Obviously, those states that have combative and tough pressure groups should be the most interesting. Zeigler and Van Dalen have forwarded four distinct patterns of interest group conflict in the 24 states that they categorize as having strong pressure group politics. These patterns are (1) an alliance of dominant groups, (2) a single dominant interest group, (3) a conflict between two dominant groups, and (4) what Zeigler and Van Dalen call "the triumph of many interests." We shall consider each of these patterns in turn.

An Alliance of Dominant Groups

A good example of powerful interests working together politically is provided by the state of Maine. "In few American states are the reigns of government more openly or completely in the hands of a few economic interest groups than in Maine."[16] Maine's "Big Three" are the electric power, timber, and manufacturing industries, which long have been in clear and cohesive alliance with each other. In his study of New England state politics, Lockard points out that when Edmund Muskie was governor, he suffered most of his defeats on those legislative matters that were opposed by the Big Three. For example, Muskie was unable to establish a statewide minimum wage, a state labor relations commission, a state income tax, or a corporate tax. In 1955, the state legislature defeated handily a proposed water pollution law. By the 1969-1970 session, however, there were strong indications that the overwhelming impact of the Big Three was diminishing in Maine.

First, new groups of legislators who were consumer minded, ecology conscious, and politically active entered the Maine assembly. These legislators were also aware that tourism is Maine's second largest and fastest growing business, bringing more than $500 million a year to the state. Moreover, old interest group patterns were changing. While the Big Three remained a solid block, real estate agents, fishermen, and summer residents in Maine were beginning to form an ecology-conscious conservation coalition. Summer residents would not normally be a particularly powerful force in any state's political system. "However, when the summer residents are named Rockefeller, Cabot, and Du Pont, the picture changes."[17] These and other prominent families maintained vacation homes in Maine and had no desire to see their pleasant summer retreats marred by industrialization.

The more a state urbanizes and industrializes, the more these changes seem to work against formerly dominant economic groups. An example is Alabama, which was dominated by "the big mules," a big farmer and big-money amalgam. As Alabama industrialized and urbanized, however, organized labor and civil rights interests carved out an increasingly potent role for themselves in Alabama politics.

The Single Dominant Interest

The primary example is Montana. Since becoming a state, Montana has been dominated politically by the Anaconda Company, the single largest employer in the state. The Anaconda Company is based on copper mining, but it also owns forests and runs mills, railroads, and similar operations. Politicians in Montana win elections either because of their opposition to or their alliance with "the company," as it is known in Montana.

Anaconda's dominant role in Montana was evident when the state was admitted to the Union. It had in its constitution a clause that mining claims could be taxed only "at the price paid the United States therefor" and that the taxes could be levied only on "net proceeds." This constitutional clause meant, in effect, that oil production, for example, which grossed only 18 percent as much as mines, paid twice as much as the mines in state taxes. Mines contributed less than 9 percent to Montana's revenues, whereas agriculture contributed 32 percent. In 1918, a faculty member of the University of Montana reviewed these inequities in the state's tax system and, as a result, was dismissed by the chancellor. Anaconda's role in the suppression of a book that the professor published on the state's tax system quickly became well known. The professor eventually was reinstated, but only after a considerable controversy. In 1924, the legislature finally revised the tax structure so that each ton of ore produced was taxed, and this revision resulted in a substantially more equitable tax structure for the state.

Such setbacks persuaded the company to change its political strategies. Anaconda owned approximately half of the state's newspapers, and the company's editorial treatment of political opponents from the 1920s to the 1950s can be traced as becoming steadily less vitriolic. In the late 1950s, the company sold its newspapers, and since then Anaconda has become a quiet but still highly influential political force. Anaconda has changed its strategy rather than its position, and now it works directly through the legislative process.

More recently, Anaconda has been challenged by a growing coalition of environmentalists and smaller business interests in Montana. They have been spurred to more intense political action by the knowledge that, since 1961, Anaconda actually has had the right of eminent domain. Eminent domain is an authority usually reserved to governmental bodies; it allows them to condemn private properties if such condemnation is in the public interest—for example, buying land for a road. To give such governmental authority to a private interest is an entirely different matter; it gives the company the legal authority to level an entire city and dig an open pit mine on the location. The rise of environmental interests, however, reflects a pattern of political resistance similar to that seen in Maine, where these and other interests coalesced against the Big Three.

Like Anaconda's growing mellowness in the political frays of Montana, other dominant economic interests in other states have found it expeditious to keep the cap on vitriol in policy disputes. Oil interests in Texas have become increasingly less overt in their tactics; business interests in Delaware have tried to establish a "good guy" image in that state's politics. Big economic interests in state politics, in spite of their money and influence, can lose and lose consistently when public opinion is mobilized.

Conflict Between Two Dominant Groups

Maine, Alabama, and Montana are similar in that they all have rather underdeveloped economies that have contributed to a bipolarization of political infighting. We have yet to consider a state with competitive political parties, with strong grassroots organizations, which is industrial, urban, and has relatively high educational and income levels. Michigan provides an example of this kind of economy and social structure. Although its economy may be even less diversified than Montana's, it is dominated by the automobile industry, which constitutes the largest single employer in Michigan. Hence, two dominant groups have emerged in Michigan, the automobile industry and organized labor. But they differ from dominant groups in the previous examples in that they work through two strong and cohesive political parties. The United Automobile Workers uses the Democratic Party to attain its political ends; the automobile manufacturers are deeply involved in the Republican Party. Neither of these two interest groups controls its respective parties, but both are extremely powerful and influential within those parties' inner workings.

One national ranking placed Michigan sixth among the states in the degree of partisan conflict, as perceived by a sample of legislators, and fourth in the amount of pressure group conflict, as perceived by Michigan's representatives to the state assembly. Unlike interest groups in the preceding two categories, interest groups in states like Michigan, which have two dominant groups competing for influence, work through the political parties rather than rely on their own political organizations.[18] They are the "junior partner" in their alliance with political parties.[19]

The Triumph of Many Interests

The example here is an obvious one—California. Early in its history, California developed as the railroads developed, and the Southern Pacific Railroad clearly dominated California politics. Around the turn of the century, however, a wave of political reform rolled over California, weakening the parties and clearing the way (quite unintentionally) for the rise of extraordinarily powerful pressure groups. These pressure groups emerged in large part because California actively discouraged the development of political parties; from 1917 until 1954, California laws stated that a person could enter both the Democratic and Republican primaries (known as cross-filing), and then enter the general election without his or her party affiliation appearing on either ballot. After 1954, party labels were required on the ballot, but until 1959 cross-filing was retained. These requirements seriously weakened the development of any political party within the state; candidates for the state legislature and other elective offices were virtually on their own and were forced to develop their own personal organizations if they wished to run for office effectively. Organized interest groups were more than willing to help a candidate gain office if he or she was sympathetic to their needs.

This situation is reflected by Wahlke's finding that 9 percent of all legislators in California referred to interest groups as the chief sponsors of their political careers, in contrast to only 1 percent in New Jersey and 2 percent in Ohio. In Tennessee 16 percent of the legislators referred to interest groups as the primary sponsors of their legislative careers, a higher portion than in California, but it is noteworthy that parties in Tennessee are even less competitive than are those in California.[20] Thus, the notion seems to be validated that weak political parties in a state tend to pave the way for the emergence of powerful interest groups that function very similarly to parties. As we observe in Chapter 5, however, interest groups usually do not appear to substitute for political parties in the legislative process, no matter how weak a state's party structure might be.

From 1942 to 1953 public policy formulation in California was a product of interest groups. It was during this period that the notorious lobbyist Artie Samish arose as king pin in the California pressure group system. Samish began his career in the 1930s working for the bus companies in California, but soon he represented other interests as well, including brewers, railroads, horse racing and gambling interests, the motion picture industry, and a number of others. Samish's influence was not so much a product of "filthy lucre" being poured into California's legislature by the interest groups that he represented, but rather of his organizational talents in welding the many interests he represented into an organization that worked as a political party would have worked. Samish's primary drive was to prevent the industries he represented from being taxed.[21] It was ironic that in 1959, the same year in which cross-filing was abolished in California, the legislature passed the first significant hike in beer taxes. In the 1960s and 1970s, other interest groups became politically active in California, and, as in Maine and Montana, the environmental issue provided the main rallying point for a number of diverse groups. In the early 1970s a coalition of California oil companies, utilities, and organized labor was influential in preventing the formulation of a statewide antipollution agency, but in 1974, when the environmentalists were joined by the 65,000-member California chapter of Common Cause, the Political Reform Act was enacted, much against the wishes of the oil, labor, and utilities combine. Among other reforms, the act prevented lobbyists from spending more than ten dollars per month (including campaign contributions) in a manner designed to influence state officials. The Political Reform Act (also known as Proposition 9) in California may spell the end of the traditional pressure group system in that state—as, indeed, it was designed to do.

POLITICS WITHOUT PRESSURE GROUPS

The four categories considered in the preceding section all apply to states with high levels of pressure group activity. In those states where there is not a symbiotic relationship between political parties and pressure groups, the interest groups take the place of political parties and actually function as political parties.

Missouri, however, presents an example of a state without a dominant pressure system. Missouri has a pressure system of temporary alliances rather than permanent and ongoing ones. This shifting pattern is attributable to a high issue orientation among competing economic interests in Missouri that is unable to offset the very stable and competitive party system. Interest groups do not work closely with parties, nor do they function as parties, and the existence of this typically weak interest group situation is due principally to the fact that there are no major economic interests that dominate the state.[22]

THE NITTY-GRITTY OF LEGISLATIVE LOBBYING

Zeigler and Van Dalen have shown by their study of pressure group patterns in the states that, even in those states where there is a concentrated economic and political influence structure, the situation is hardly monolithic. Challenges can arise to even the most established economic and political powers in these states through the mobilization of contrary interests. Recognizing this fact, how do lobbyists, who represent special interests in a state, work? How do lobbyists have their way with legislators?

Lobbying, in its essence, is a communications process. Lobbying is conducted quite differently in the state capitals than in Washington. Both the lobbyists and legislators in our nation's capital consider state-level lobbying to be substantially more corrupt, blatant, and crass. According to one analyst, "Lobbying is very different before state legislators; it is much more individualistic. Maybe this is the reason they have more bribery in state legislatures than in

Congress. . . . In the state legislatures, lobbying is definitely on a lower plane. The lobbyists are loose and hand out money and favors quite freely. . . . Lobbying at the state level is cruder, more basic and more obvious. . . . Lobbying at the state level is faster and more free wheeling and less visible; that is why it is more open to corruption."[23]

Whether or not this assessment is correct, lobbying is a subtle process even at the state level, involving sophisticated interplay between raw political clout and strategic finesse. An adroit lobbyist quickly learns that it can be counterproductive to threaten a legislator. For example, if the Anaconda Company in Montana threatened to "punish" legislators who voted the "wrong" way, certain representatives would feel it necessary to vote against Anaconda simply for the sake of showing the public that they were independent.

Figure 3-1 indicates this tendency among legislators. For example, in Massachusetts, one of four states studied by Zeigler and Michael A. Baer, only 66 percent of the legislators who felt that they were being pressured by organized education lobbyists favored an increase in the state education budget, whereas 90 percent of those who felt no pressure from education were predisposed to favor an increase.

Lobbyists in the states often seem to be wiser and more experienced in the workings of their legislatures than the legislators themselves. Zeigler and Baer found that in three of the four states they studied intensively, the lobbyists had longer experience in their positions than the legislators did in theirs, and there were fewer "freshmen" among lobbyists than among legislators.

On the other hand, lobbyists do not appear to visit legislative chambers very frequently. In a study of lobbying in Oklahoma, it was found that more than 60 percent of lobbyists in that state spent half their time or less engaged in actual lobbying.[24] In Zeigler and Baer's study, only in Oregon (which is a weak-party/strong-lobby state) did the time spent in actually lobbying by lobbyists approach anything close to an eight-hour day on a regular basis.

Nevertheless, lobbying at the state level appears to be professionalizing. In a study of more than 550 registered lobbyists in ten states, it was found that 82 percent have at least a bachelor's degree (nearly half have taken some graduate classes), and a fourth are full-time professional lobbyists. As Table 3-3 shows, relatively few state lobbyists are lawyers (only 15 percent), in contrast to lobbyists in Washington, D.C., where it appears that most are; a plurality of state

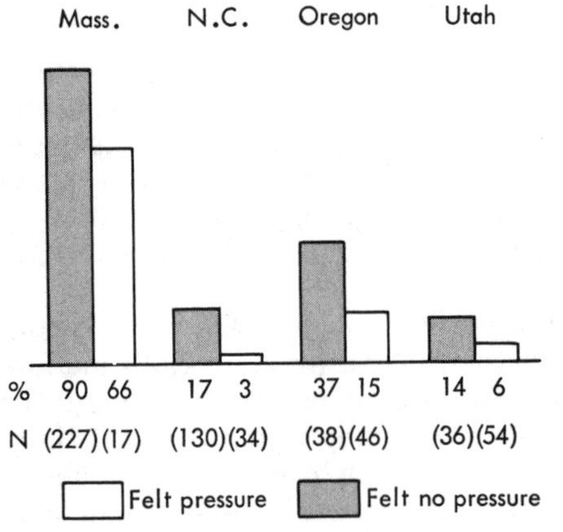

Figure 3-1
Relation between legislators' belief that they were "pressured" by education lobbyists and their attitude toward education goals: Percentage favoring increased education budget. (*Source:* L. Harmon Zeigler and Michael A. Baer, *Lobbying: Interaction and Influence in American State Legislatures.* Belmont, Calif.: Duxbury Press, Div. of Wadsworth, 1969, p. 118.)

Table 3-3 Social and Political Backgrounds of State Lobbyists, 1984

	Percentage of All Lobbyists (N = 530)	*Percentage of "Amateur" Lobbyists (N = 194)*	*Percentage of "Professional" Lobbyists (N = 185)*
Age			
Under 35	24%	17%	35%
36–44	27	26	27
45–55	24	29	19
56 and over	25	28	20
Sex			
Male	81	73	85
Female	19	27	15
Education			
Two years of college or fewer	18	20	13
B.A./B.S.	33	33	36
Some Graduate Work/M.A.	25	28	22
Advanced Professional Degree	24	19	30
Occupation			
Full-time Lobbyist	25	19	33
Lawyer	15	9	21
Business/Professional	30	35	25
Government Employee	8	9	3
Other	22	29	17
Party			
Democrat	47	49	48
Republican	33	30	34
Independent	19	20	16
Other	1	1	2
Years as a Lobbyist			
3 or Fewer	28	31	31
4–6	26	20	31
7–10	22	21	19
More than 10	24	28	19
Held Elective Office			
Yes	22	25	16
No	78	75	84

Percentages have been rounded.

Source: Derived from Mark S. Hyde and Richard Alsfeld, "Role Orientations of Lobbyists in a State Setting: A Comparative Analysis," Paper Presented at the 1985 Annual Meeting of the American Political Science Association, August 29–September 1, 1985, New Orleans, Tables 1 and 2.

lobbyists are business and professional people who, presumably, lobby only part-time. Fewer than a quarter of state lobbyists have ever held an elective office.

The researchers who collected this information on state lobbyists concluded that 37 percent could be categorized as "amateurs," or those lobbyists who were committed to particular issues and who would work only for special interests with which they agreed on the issues, and 35 percent were rated as "professionals," or lobbyists who were committed to winning in the political arena and would work for any client, regardless of whether or not they shared the same political values. (The remaining lobbyists were in between, and were categorized as "semiprofessionals.") Amateurs were more likely than professionals to be women, older, less educated, part-time lobbyists, government employees, and to have held an elective office. Professionals were more likely than amateurs to be quite young, highly educated, full-time lobbyists, Republican, and recent entrants in the lobbying field. Table 3-3 provides details.

If it is true that lobbying at the state level may be cruder in style and form than lobbying at the national level, one reason why may be that state legislatures convene less often and for shorter periods of time than Congress does, thereby preventing the evolution of a set of rules of conduct (both formal and informal) such as those adopted by the U.S. House and Senate. Such rules, at least in theory, should discourage legislators from the kind of unethical behavior that has contributed to an image of political corruption.

The turnover rate is also much higher among state legislators than among members of Congress. About half of the legislators in the Zeigler and Baer study were first-term members of their respective chambers (today the proportion of first term members is closer to a third of the membership);[25] and, as a consequence, legislators not only were unfamiliar with the mores and norms of the state legislature but frequently had to rely on lobbyists for information about how their state assemblies worked. State legislators are, despite trends to the contrary, still less likely to be professional lawmakers than are members of Congress and more likely to regard a stint in the legislature an interesting, but secondary, avocation.

Finally, state legislators often are not well paid and, as a result, incur more expenses stemming from their legislative duties relative to their income than do members of Congress. This situation, of course, can increase the temptations when dealing with lobbyists. Fortunately, the lobbying process is not as corrupt as one might infer; both lobbyists and legislators in the Zeigler and Baer study ranked bribery as the least effective lobbying method.

Legislators, like most people, tend to communicate with and listen to people who support their views. This certainly happens in the lobbying process. Zeigler and Baer found that lobbyists are most effective with those legislators who are predisposed to agree with them on ideological grounds.[26]

Legislators, for their part, use lobbyists as sources of influence with other legislators. They ask lobbyists to influence other legislators by mobilizing public opinion in favor of the legislator's position, by including lobbyists in strategy sessions on how to move legislation through the assembly, and in negotiating their bills through the legislature.

In summary, the techniques of lobbying, while perhaps more crass at the state level than at the national, have gravitated toward a subtle interchange between lobbyists and legislator and away from the more brutal power-play mode that often dominated state legislative politics in the past. Contacts, access, and who knows whom (as well as who knows what) are more important variables in swinging legislation in one's favor than is pure political clout.

AN "EXPLOSION" OF SPECIAL INTERESTS?

It is well documented that interest groups at the national level have been proliferating in recent years,[27] but far less is known about interest groups at the state level. Nevertheless, although "no analysis of interest group growth at the state and local level has been done . . . it is [generally] assumed [by political scientists] that a concomitant increase has occurred subnationally."[28]

Figure 3-2 indicates the number of lobbying organizations that have registered with their state governments. As it shows, Florida is the leader, with more than 800 registered lobbies, followed by California, Pennsylvania, and Texas, each of which has more than 700 state interest groups; most states tend to have 200 to 400 registered lobbies, and many have fewer than 100.

These are not overwhelming numbers, at least not when compared to the number of Washington lobbyists; there are more than 15,000 lobbies registered with the federal government, up from only 2,000 in 1947.[29] Moreover, at least one study indicates that, except perhaps in the very largest states, interest groups in the states have not aped the national phenomenon of multiplying

DUNAGIN'S PEOPLE by Ralph Dunagin. Courtesy of Field Newspaper Syndicates.

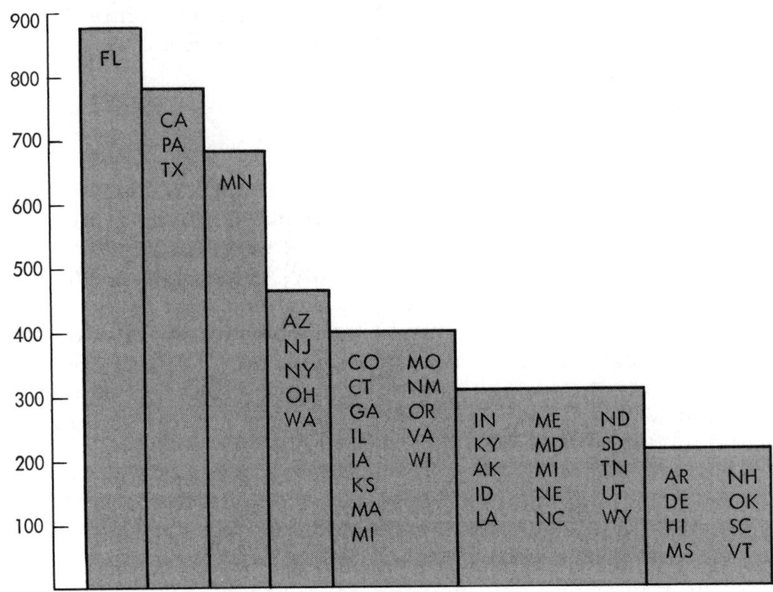

Figure 3-2 Number of registered lobby groups, by state, 1980. (*Source:* Virginia Gray, "Fundamental Changes in Group Life at the State Level." Paper presented at the 1984 Annual Conference of the American Political Science Association, Washington, D.C., August 30–September 2, 1984, p. 31.)

special interests: "The level of interest representation [in the state capitols]. . . is modest and proportionate to the size of the state's population. . . . the picture that emerges is one of political stability."[30] Nevertheless, numbers do not necessarily equate with power, and the possibility remains that state interest groups, while not proliferating as they have in Washington, have gained political clout.

PACS AMERICANA

One reason why this possibility deserves attention is the emergence of political action committees, or PACs. A PAC is not the same creature as a registered interest group. A *political action committee* is the electoral funding arm of an interest group (it can collect dues or accept donations for purposes of influencing an election), and the states register their lobbyists and their PACs on separate rosters. All states require that lobbyists register,[31] and 38 states register political action committees and make these lists public.[32]

Like interest groups, PACs have bred like proverbial rabbits at the national level; in 1970 there were no political action committees, but by 1985 there were some 3,200 in Washington alone.[33] The proliferation of national PACs was accelerated by the Federal Election Campaign Act of 1971 and subsequent amendments to it, particularly those enacted in 1974 and 1976, which permitted businesses, organized labor, ideological groups, and other associations to establish political action committees empowered to contribute campaign funds to candidates, parties, and candidate support organizations of their choosing. This national legislation has had an impact on the states.

As with the literature on interest groups, scholars largely assume that the explosion of national political action committees has been paralleled at the subnational levels as well. And, although data are fragmentary, this seems to be a more valid assumption than that about interest groups;[34] state political action committees are multiplying in number and are spending more on elections.

Although national statistics are unavailable, consider some examples. In Oregon in 1970, there were 36 PACs contributing less than $200,000 to state political races; ten years later, Oregon registered 151 PACs contributing almost $1 million. In Washington in 1978, there were 114 PACs with receipts of $2 million; by 1980, there were 200 political action committees with receipts of more than $4.3 million. In Idaho, PAC spending went up by 20 percent between 1978 and 1980. In California, the number of PACs contributing to state campaigns more than tripled between 1976 and 1980. In Arizona, the number of PAC contributions of more than $100 to state legislative races exploded by 1,218 percent between 1974 and 1980; the average donation by Arizona PACs to a winning candidate for the legislature was less than $3,000 in 1974, but by 1980 the median PAC campaign contribution was more than $11,500 per winner in a state that pays its legislators $15,000 a year.

Figure 3-3 indicates the numbers of political action committees by state for the 38 states that publish PAC registration lists. As with registered lobbies, the more PACs that a state has, the more people and the more complex economies it is likely to have as well; 14 states, in fact, have 100 or fewer PACs.

State political action committees representing business and the professional interests are growing faster than are those of any other special interest. Records in California, Kansas, and Missouri indicate this, and a parallel trend is evident at the national level. These business and professional PACs seem to favor Republican candidates.

It is considerably more apparent that all PACs favor incumbents, winners, and legislative leaders. In Washington state, campaign donations in 1980 constituted 37 percent of the campaign expenditures of all legislative races, but comprised 47 percent of all campaign war chests raised by incumbents and only 24 percent of the campaign budgets of challengers. In Iowa in 1980, incumbent representatives received 40 percent of the campaign funding from PACs, but challengers garnered only 25 percent of their campaign chests from political action committees. In Kansas, fully 50 percent of the campaign budgets of incumbents were donated by PACs in 1980, while their challengers could claim that only 25 percent of their campaign contributions were from PACs.

By favoring incumbents, PACs increase their chances of backing winners. As we note in Chapter 5, fewer than a fifth of incumbent legislators are defeated at the polls, so investing in incumbents is reasonably effective as a strategy designed to maximize an interest group's access to state senators and representatives.

Similarly, PACs contribute heavily to the campaigns of legislative leaders as a means of enhancing their clout. In 1980, the legislative leadership of Kansas gathered 57 percent of its bulging campaign treasuries from PACs, and the major leaders of the Iowa legislature gained more than half of their campaign funds from special interests. PACs are, above all, pragmatic.

Whether these pragmatic practices count when it comes to winning legislative votes is open to speculation, since research on the topic is mixed.[35] Nevertheless, state-level PACs, like their national counterparts, seem destined to

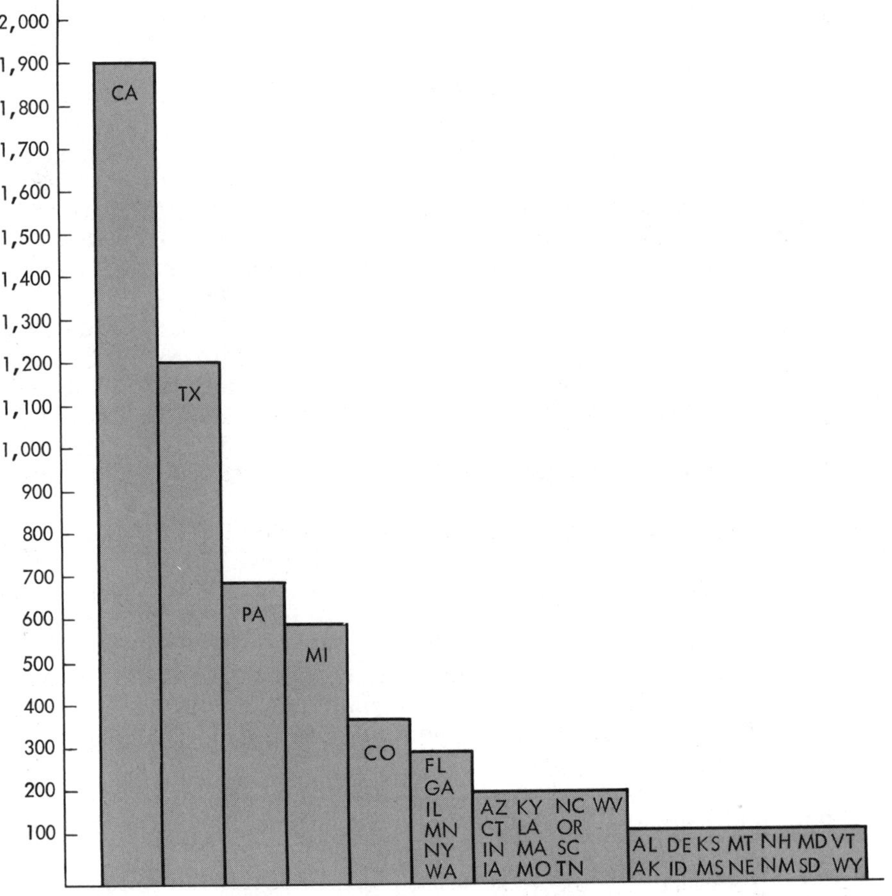

Figure 3-3 Number of registered PACs by state, 1983. (*Source:* Virginia Gray, "Fundamental Changes in Group Life at the State Level." Paper presented at the 1984 Annual Conference of the American Political Science Association, Washington, D.C., August 30–September 2, 1984, p. 30.)

become an integral part of political pressure at the grassroots. Of more concern, perhaps, is their role in enhancing the power of special interests in state government.

PRESSURE AND THE PUBLIC INTEREST

Irrespective of the emergence of political action committees in the states, the question first asked at the beginning of this chapter on interest groups still must be addressed: Does the conflict between pressure groups in the political system result in a public policy that is in the "best" public interest? In other words, does Zeigler's "hydraulic theory of politics" work most effectively toward the public interest?

The standard answer forthcoming from political scientists is, yes, it does.

Those with more power in the political system have that power because they represent more people; therefore, if a policy tends to favor the more powerful groups, then it is necessarily closer to being in the public interest. Competitive interest groups, in effect, offset any policy that would tend to run over minority rights. It is a classic world view of political science.

Perhaps Zeigler's hydraulic theory still "works," and interest group compromises really are in the public interest in those areas of public policy that are made largely by legislatures or by the courts. But to work, the hydraulic theory must rest on at least three basic assumptions concerning the American policymaking process:

1. That all people affected by any one particular policy question (for example, public transit) are aware that the resolution of the question actually will affect them and the way they live.
2. That all people affected will have a reasonable understanding of the issues in question and how their resolution will impact on the way they live.
3. That if the people affected are not aware of the policy question, then it is only a matter of time before they find out about it and join in the policymaking battles simply to protect their own self-interests.

These assumptions of the hydraulic theory of policymaking have provided a well-accepted and not entirely unreasonable explanation of the policymaking process in our democracy—at least until recently. But in the late twentieth century, there are new forces at work that have not been dealt with satisfactorily by political thinkers. Primarily, these forces are (1) the emergence of a bureaucracy employing many millions of government workers and (2) the simultaneous development of an advanced technology. Indeed, America is the archetype of technological society in the world today. Both technology and bureaucracy deny the basic assumptions underlying the hydraulic theory of politics.

Bureaucracy denies the first and third assumptions. Bureaucrats, as has been amply documented, have a penchant for secrecy, and there is mounting evidence that neither bureaucrats nor the citizenry always act in their most rational self-interest; these facts undercut the basic premises that people are informed of what matters to them—and that they will act on what matters to them.

Technology denies the second assumption. Technology is very complicated; because of its complexity, it is difficult for most people to understand the political problems that are brought about by technology. How many people, for example, really understand the technical and political issues behind nuclear energy? Therefore, it would seem that the classic view of interest groups, in which they are viewed as battling out the most beneficial public policy to all the people, must come under increasing scrutiny by citizens who are interested in a just society. Interest groups only rarely, if at all, represent anything close to all the people. More often they represent elites. These elites have control of knowledge about the issues in question. Consequently, they are extremely influential in making policies that affect all the people in our increasingly interrelated society. Hence, when we discuss interest groups from the traditional perspective of political science, we should be aware that pressure politics may be how the policymaking process works. But is special interest pressure in the best interest of all the people in a complex, technological, and increasingly bureaucratized society?

NOTES

[1]L. Harmon Zeigler and G. Wayne Peak, *Interest Groups in American Society,* 2nd ed. (Englewood Cliffs, N.J.: Prentice-Hall, 1972), p. 12.
[2]Charles G. Bell, Keith E. Hamm, and Charles W. Wiggins, "The Pluralist Model Reconsidered: A Comparative Analysis of Interest Group Policy Involvement in Three States," paper presented at the 1985 Annual Meeting of the American Political Science Association, August 29 - September 1, 1985, New Orleans, abstract page.
[3]John C. Wahlke, Heinz Eulau, William Buchanan, and LeRoy C. Ferguson, *The Legislative System* (New York: John Wiley, 1962).
[4]Wayne L. Francis, *Legislative Issues in the Fifty States: A Comparative Analysis* (Chicago: Rand McNally, 1967), pp. 44-45.
[5]Wayne L. Francis and Robert Presthus, "Legislators' Perception of Interest Group Behavior," *Western Political Quarterly,* 14 (December, 1971), p. 705.
[6]L. Harmon Zeigler and Hendrick Van Dalen, "Interest Groups and State Politics," in Herbert Jacob and Kenneth N. Vines, eds., *Politics in the American States: A Comparative Analysis,* 3rd ed. (Boston: Little, Brown, 1976), pp. 110-111.
[7]Sarah McCally Morehouse, *State Politics, Parties, and Policy* (New York: Holt, Rinehart and Winston, 1981).
[8]Robert Presthus, *Elites in the Policy Process* (Cambridge: Cambridge University Press, 1974), p. 110.
[9]L. Harmon Zeigler, "Interest Groups in the States," in Virginia Gray, Herbert Jacob, and Kenneth N. Vines, eds., *Politics in the American States: A Comparative Analysis,* 4th ed. (Boston: Little, Brown, 1983), pp. 113-114.
[10]*Ibid.,* p. 116.
[11]*Ibid.,* p. 118.
[12]John G. Grumm, "The Effects of Legislative Structure on Legislative Performance," in Richard I. Hofferbert and Ira Sharkansky, eds., *State and Urban Politics* (Boston: Little, Brown, 1971), pp. 307-322.
[13]Zeigler, "Interest Groups in the States," p. 122.
[14]Morehouse, *State Politics, Parties, and Policy,* pp. 493-494.
[15]Thomas R. Dye, *Politics in States and Communities,* 3rd ed. (Englewood Cliffs, N.J.: Prentice-Hall, 1981), p. 147.
[16]Duane Lockard, *New England State Politics* (Princeton, N.J.: Princeton University Press, 1959), p. 79.
[17]Zeigler and Van Dalen, "Interest Groups and State Politics," p. 97.
[18]Wayne L. Francis, *Legislative Issues in the Fifty States: A Comparative Analysis* (Chicago: Rand McNally, 1967), pp. 44-45.
[19]V. O. Key, Jr., *Public Opinion and American Democracy* (New York: Alfred A. Knopf, 1961), p. 524.
[20]Wahlke et al., *The Legislative System,* p. 100.
[21]William Buchanan, "Legislative Partisanship: The Deviant Case of California," *University of California Publications in Political Science,* 13 (Berkeley: University of California Press, 1963).
[22]Nicholas A. Masters, Robert H. Salisbury, and Thomas H. Eliot, *State Politics and the Public Schools* (New York: Alfred A. Knopf, 1964), pp. 37-38.
[23]Lester Milbrath, *The Washington Lobbyists* (Chicago: Rand McNally, 1963), pp. 241-243.
[24]Samuel C. Patterson, "The Role of the Lobbyist: The Case of Oklahoma," *Journal of Politics,* 25 (1963), p. 79.
[25]Kwang S. Shin and John S. Jackson III, "Membership Turnover in U.S. State Legislatures: 1931-1976," *Legislative Studies Quarterly,* 4 (February, 1979), pp. 97-99.
[26]L. Harmon Zeigler and Michael A. Baer, *Lobbying: Interaction and Influence in American State Legislatures* (Belmont, Calif.: Wadsworth, 1969), p. 82.
[27]See, for example, Dennis S. Ippolito and Thomas G. Walker, *Political Parties, Interest Groups, and Public Policy* (Englewood Cliffs, N.J.: Prentice-Hall, 1980), p. 281; Ronald J. Hrebenar and Ruth K. Scott, *Interest Group Politics in America* (Englewood Cliffs, N.J.:

Prentice-Hall, 1982), p. 257; and Jeffrey M. Berry, *The Interest Group Society* (Boston: Little, Brown, 1984), p. 18.

[28]Virginia Gray, "Fundamental Changes in Group Life at the State Level," paper presented at the 1984 Meeting of the American Political Science Association, Washington, D.C., August 30 - September 2, 1984, p. 4. See also, however, Mancur Olson, *The Rise and Decline of Nations* (New Haven, Conn.: Yale University Press, 1982).

[29]Nicholas Henry and John Stuart Hall, *Reconsidering American Politics* (Boston: Allyn & Bacon, 1985), p. 111.

[30]Gray, "Fundamental Changes in Group Life at the State Level," pp. 21-22.

[31]Advisory Commission on Intergovernmental Relations, *The Question of State Government Capability* (Washington, D.C.: U.S. Government Printing Office, 1985), p. 109.

[32]Gray, "Fundamental Changes in Group Life at the State Level," p. 20. Thirty-eight states register PACs *and* make their registration lists public. The remaining dozen states either do not permit PACs or do not make the registration lists public.

[33]Henry and Hall, *Reconsidering American Politics,* p. 129.

[34]Much of the following discussion is drawn from Ruth S. Jones, "Financing State Elections," in Michael Malbin, ed., *Politics and Money* (Washington, D.C.: American Enterprise Institute, 1984), pp. 180-193. But see also Frank J. Sorauf, *What Price PACs?* (New York: The Twentieth Century Fund, 1984), p. 39; and Samuel C. Patterson, "Legislators and Legislatures in the American States," in Gray, Jacob, and Vines, *Politics in the American States,* p. 146. The works refer to PACs in Wisconsin and California, respectively.

[35]James Eisenstein and Roger Karapin, "The Relationship Between Political Action Committee Contributions and Roll Call Votes in the Pennsylvania House of Representatives: A Preliminary Analysis," paper presented at the Annual Meeting of the Pennsylvania Political Science Association, University Park, Pa., March 28, 1981; and Michael B. Binford, "PAC Campaign Contributions and the State Legislature: Impact on Legislators and the Legislative Agenda," paper presented at the Annual Meeting of the Southern Political Science Association, Memphis, Tenn., November 5-7, 1981, p. 15. Eisenstein and Karapin found no significant relationship between legislators' votes and PACs' contributions in Pennsylvania, while Binford's study of the Georgia legislature found a "substantial connection" between the two.

4

PARTIES

whirlpools of politics

The party is one of America's several unique contributions to the world's political workings. "The first modern political parties arose in the United States decades before they appeared in Great Britain and other nations; and this has meant that the first experiments in party politics were made in the American arena."[1] William Nisbet Chambers traces the evolution of the nation's party systems through three stages: (1) the period when parties were instrumental in "establishing the nation as a going entity" (roughly 1789 to 1815), or the nation-building stage; (2) the establishment of significant form (1828 to 1860), when parties set up their grassroots organizations, conventions, procedures, and so forth; and (3) the derivative stage (1865 to the present), the time when parties became adjustive and reactive to their political environments, rather than innovative and creative in making policy.[2] During the more recent years of this phase, American political parties "have lost the virtual monopoly over nominations, campaigning, and elections which they once enjoyed . . . and the party system has come to play a less significant role than it once did. If party once was king in a democratic polity, it no longer reigns."[3]

Still, political parties perform irreplaceable functions of government. Chambers lists these functions as (1) assisting in the maintenance of the political system's legitimacy, (2) promoting the efficiency of the political system, and (3) rendering the political system more adjustive to social change. Parties have been crucial to the workings of these three interrelated functions largely because, generally speaking, "the American party systems have been moderate in character and less ideologically oriented than party systems in other nations."[4] Although there have been signs that the parties have grown more ideological in tone during the last decade, the "saving illogicality" of the American parties, as one observer described it, has remained a feature unique to the American political system.[5]

TYPES OF PARTIES

But if American political parties are relatively nonideological, they are all the more difficult to categorize. In a useful attempt at such a categorization, however, Malcolm E. Jewell and David M. Olson have described three types of American parties that exist at the state level by degree of internal factionalism: cohesive parties, bifactional parties, and multifactional parties.[6] Table 4-1 summarizes the attributes of state political parties in terms of the categories described by Jewell and Olson.

A cohesive party, while hardly one that has an absence of factions or a dearth of squabbles, nonetheless has the capacity to compromise differences among factions internally and to present a unified front in both primary and general elections. Currently, 12 state Republican parties and 4 state Democratic parties seem to be relatively cohesive. As Table 4-1 indicates, cohesive parties are quite active in all stages of the electoral cycle (i.e., the recruitment and nomination of candidates, and campaigning for them through general elections); they tend to wage campaigns for all offices listed on the ballot; state, county, and city leaders of the party coordinate candidacies and nominations on an ongoing basis; party staff positions are generally filled to capacity and the people in them are active; the state party chair is likely to be autonomous and powerful; and candidates for office typically wage a joint campaign among all levels within the state.

In the bifactional parties, each of the party's two factions tends to recruit its own candidates and work for their nomination and election, as opposed to working together as a party for those candidates; the factions tend to wage campaigns for the entire ticket; each faction tends to control a separate set of

Table 4-1 Attributes of Types of State Political Parties

	PARTY TYPES		
Attributes	*Cohesive*	*Bifactional*	*Multifactional*
Electoral cycle stage	All	All	Segmented: varied
Scope of office	Wide	Wide	Office or candidate specific
Geographic coordination	High	High	Low
Staffing and activity	High	High	Low
Formal structure	Independent chairman	Conflict between governor, chairman	Agent chairman
Electoral reliance	Party	Faction	Candidate

Source: Malcolm E. Jewell and David M. Olson, *American State Political Parties and Elections,* rev. ed., Dorsey Series in Political Science (Homewood, Ill.: Dorsey, 1982), p. 67.

Table 4-2 State Laws Governing Party Roles in the Electoral Process

State	*Nominating Convention*[1]	*Party Endorsement*[2]	*Closed or Partly Open Primaries*[3]	*Sore Loser Provision*[4]	*Straight Party Ballot*[5]	*Cumulative Party Support Index Scores*[6]
			Generally Unsupportive			
Alaska						0
Hawaii						0
Louisiana						0
Montana						0
Vermont						0
Mississippi			X			1
Florida			X			2
Idaho				X		2
Nevada			X			2
New Jersey			X			2
Washington				X		2
Arkansas		X		X		3
Minnesota		X		X		3
North Dakota		X		X		3
Tennessee			X		X	3
Texas			X		X	3
			Moderately Supportive			
Arizona			X	X		4
California			X	X		4
Illinois		X	X		X	4
Kansas	X		X			4
Maine			X	X		4
Maryland			X	X		4
Nebraska			X	X		4
New Hampshire			X		X	4
Oklahoma			X		X	4
Oregon			X	X		4

Virginia	X	X	X			4
West Virginia			X	X		4
Wyoming			X		X	4
Alabama	X		X		X	5
Delaware		X	X	X		5
Georgia	X		X		X	5
Massachusetts		X	X	X		5
Missouri			X	X	X	5
Ohio		X	X	X		5
Rhode Island		X	X		X	5
Kentucky			X	X	X	6
New York	X	X	X			6
North Carolina			X	X	X	6
Generally Supportive						
Iowa	X	X	X		X	7
Michigan	X	X		X	X	7
Pennsylvania		X	X	X	X	7
South Carolina	X		X	X	X	7
South Dakota	X	X	X		X	7
Colorado	X	X	X	X		8
Connecticut	X	X	X		X	8
Indiana	X	X	X	X	X	8
New Mexico		X	X	X	X	8
Utah	X	X		X	X	8

[1] Does the state allow or require nominating conventions?
[2] Do any of the state's parties make candidate endorsements before the general election?
[3] Does the state have a closed primary or require voters to acknowledge a party preference?
[4] Does the state have a "sore loser" provision?
[5] Does the state provide a straight party voting mechanism on its ballot?
[6] Scores are determined by the state's positions on the five issues examined. Minimum score is 0; maximum score is 10.
Source: Timothy Conlan, Ann Martino, and Robert Digler, "State Parties in the 1980s: Adaptation, Resurgence, and Continuing Constraints," *Intergovernmental Perspective*, 10 (Fall, 1984), p. 13.

counties and cities throughout the state; party staff positions are typically filled to capacity, but party staffers are split by the two major factions in the state; the state party chair may well belong to a different party faction than the governor; and the factions might eliminate one another's candidates from their own campaigning throughout the general election, in contrast to waging a coordinated campaign. Currently, 21 state Republican parties and 7 state Democratic parties seem to bisect along factional lines.

Finally, in multifactional party types, candidates create their own personal campaign organizations and often bypass the party structure completely; campaigners tend to concentrate on a single office or set of offices in a particular geographic area or level of government; factions tend to concentrate on specific regions of the state, as opposed to waging a coordinated statewide campaign; party staff positions are often empty and activity is low; the party state chair is highly dependent upon the governor, and, in fact, the party is little more than an instrument of the governor; and the party organization (such as it is) is largely bypassed altogether by party nominees in the electoral process. Presently, 17 state Republican parties are considered to be multifactional, and 39 state Democratic parties are equally splintered.

According to this analysis, it seems that the statewide GOP parties are relatively more "together" organizationally. Two-thirds of them are cohesive or bifactional. In fact, the Republicans' cohesive state parties alone outnumber the Democratics' by 4 to 1, and the GOP's bifactional state parties outnumber the Democrats' counterparts by 3 to 1. By contrast, only 22 percent of the state Democratic parties are cohesive or bifactional.

REGULATING THE CENTER: PARTIES IN THE STATES

Unlike most democracies, the American states give legal recognition to their political parties. This came about because, following the Civil War, state parties were seedbeds of corruption, and legislatures gradually passed laws designed to stem their influence. In some states, in fact, regulations of parties were written into the state constitutions themselves. One study of state regulations and party bylaws found that together they had listed nearly 250 different powers for the state parties and party chairs.[7] In general, these laws limit state parties in a number of ways.[8]

One such way is party finance. We review this area of considerable importance later in the chapter.

A second area regulated by the states is the parties' role in the electoral process. Parties in most of the states have very little say on how they will select their candidates for office. Most states *require* direct primaries (i.e., popular votes on who will be the party's nominee) as opposed to private caucuses, conventions, or any other form of smoke-filled room. Only five states (Alaska, Hawaii, Louisiana, Montana, and Vermont) have not regulated the parties' role in the electoral process in a significant way. Table 4-2 lists this legislation by state and ranks the states according to the supportiveness of their legislation. An "X" in the table means that the legislation is supportive of the parties' role in elections; a blank indicates the opposite. Four-fifths of the states do not provide a positive role for state and local parties in the electoral process.

A third area of legislation concerns the organization of the parties themselves. Ninety percent of the states stipulate to a significant degree the legal organizational structure of its state parties.

Finally, there is the area of access to the ballot. All states specify how an organization may qualify as a political party and, as such, have its candidates' names and party affiliations listed on the ballot. The state legislatures view their political parties primarily as organizations for nominating candidates and arguing over issues in elections. As a result, most states prescribe the structure and duties of committees, conventions, and caucuses of their parties in detail. Only five states have not enacted major legislation regulating the internal composition of state parties: Alaska, Delaware, Hawaii, Kentucky, and North Carolina. Table 4-3 describes this kind of legislation by state. Only 28 percent of the states can be considered light regulators of their political parties.

THE CASUAL ORGANIZATION OF POLITICAL PARTIES

In all states, the political party serves as a highly unstructured arena where coalitions form and reform over political issues and personalities. The consummate scholar of political parties, V. O. Key, Jr., observed that state parties may be described "as a system of layers. . . . Yet each higher level of organization, to accomplish its ends, must obtain the collaboration of the lower layer."[9]

Perhaps the essential remark by Key is the final one, which dwells on the concept that American political parties do not have a military command hierarchy. What we have instead is a loose negotiation structure, in which the state parties must wheel and deal with the urban and county parties. How successful this process of negotiation is depends on a number of factors, but particularly on whether the party structure in a state is cohesive, bifactional, or multifactional. Figure 4-1 sketches the formal structure of state political parties. Like the federal structure itself, the structure of state political parties is more in the nature of a marble cake than a layer cake.

Nevertheless, the most important single feature of state party structures is the presence of the county organization, which is an important factor in every state party organization. Within county parties, there are two main organizational patterns. The most favored pattern relies on the precinct as the smallest unit of the party. There are an estimated 178,000 precincts for the Republican and Democratic parties,[10] which nominally report to some 6,202 county organizations (or their functional equivalents). In this version, the precinct chair is elected either at a precinct convention or by the party primary. The precinct chair becomes a member of the county committee, which then elects a county chair. The solid lines of the county-level portion of Figure 4-1 indicate this pattern.

The other form of organization bypasses the precinct, and makes the city or ward the lowest level of party organization. Chicago uses this model, in which precinct captains are appointed from the ward or citywide level. The dashed line in the county-level portion of Figure 4-1 indicates this general pattern.

In a few states, notably, California and Wisconsin, the legal party organizations as stipulated by the legislature are controlled by what are known as "political clubs." In both states, the clubs have been spawned as a result of

Table 4-3 Index of State Laws Regulating Political Parties

State	*State Comm. Selection*[1]	*State Comm. Composition*[2]	*State Comm. Meeting Date*[3]	*State Comm. Internal Rules*[4]	*Local Comm. Selection*[5]	*Local Comm. Composition*[6]	*Local Comm. Internal Rules or Activities*[7]	*Cumulative Regulatory Index Score*[8]
Light Regulators[9]								
Alaska								0
Delaware								0
Hawaii								0
Kentucky								0
North Carolina								0
Alabama							X	1
Georgia							X	1
Minnesota							X	1
New Mexico							X	1
Oklahoma							X	1
Virginia							X	1
Connecticut						X	X	3
Maine	X		X		X		X	4
New Hampshire	X				X		X	4
Moderate Regulators								
Arkansas	X				X		X	5
Florida		X	X	X		X	X	5
Nebraska	X				X		X	5
Rhode Island				X	X	X	X	6
Pennsylvania	X	X	X	X			X	7
Colorado	X	X	X	X	X	X	X	8
Idaho	X	X			X	X	X	8
Iowa	X	X			X	X	X	8
South Carolina	X	X		X		X	X	8
South Dakota	X	X			X	X	X	8
Utah	X	X		X	X	X	X	8
Mississippi	X	X		X	X	X	X	9

State	1	2	3	4	5	6	7	Score
Nevada	X	X		X	X	X	X	9
Vermont	X	X	X	X	X	X	X	9
Washington	X	X			X	X	X	9
Wisconsin	X	X			X	X	X	9
Heavy Regulators								
Indiana	X	X	X	X	X	X	X	10
Michigan	X	X		X	X	X	X	10
New York	X		X	X	X	X	X	10
North Dakota	X	X	X	X	X	X	X	10
Oregon	X	X	X	X	X	X	X	10
Arizona	X	X	X	X	X	X	X	11
California	X	X		X	X	X	X	11
Maryland	X	X	X	X	X	X	X	11
Massachusetts	X	X	X	X	X	X	X	11
Missouri	X	X	X	X	X	X	X	11
Tennessee	X	X	X	X	X	X	X	11
West Virginia	X	X	X	X	X	X	X	11
Kansas	X	X	X	X	X	X	X	12
New Jersey	X	X	X	X	X	X	X	12
Texas	X	X	X	X	X	X	X	12
Wyoming	X	X	X	X	X	X	X	12
Illinois	X	X	X	X	X	X	X	13
Ohio	X	X	X	X	X	X	X	13
Louisiana	X	X	X	X	X	X	X	14

[1] Does state law regulate the manner of selecting the parties' state central committees?
[2] Does state law regulate the composition of the parties' state central committees?
[3] Does state law regulate when the parties' state central committees will meet?
[4] Does state law regulate any of the internal procedures of the parties' state central committees?
[5] Does state law regulate the manner of selecting the parties' local organizations?
[6] Does state law regulate the composition of the parties' local organizations?
[7] Does state law regulate any of the internal rules or activities of the parties' local organizations?
[8] Scores are determined by state regulatory actions in the seven areas examined. Minimum score is 0; maximum score is 14.
[9] "Light" regulators are defined as having an index score of 0–4; "moderate" regulators are those states having index scores of 5–9; and "heavy" regulators are those states having index scores above 10.

Source: Timothy Conlan, Ann Martino, and Robert Digler, "State Parties in the 1980s: Adaptation, Resurgence, and Continuing Constraints," *Intergovernmental Perspective,* 10 (Fall, 1984), p. 12.

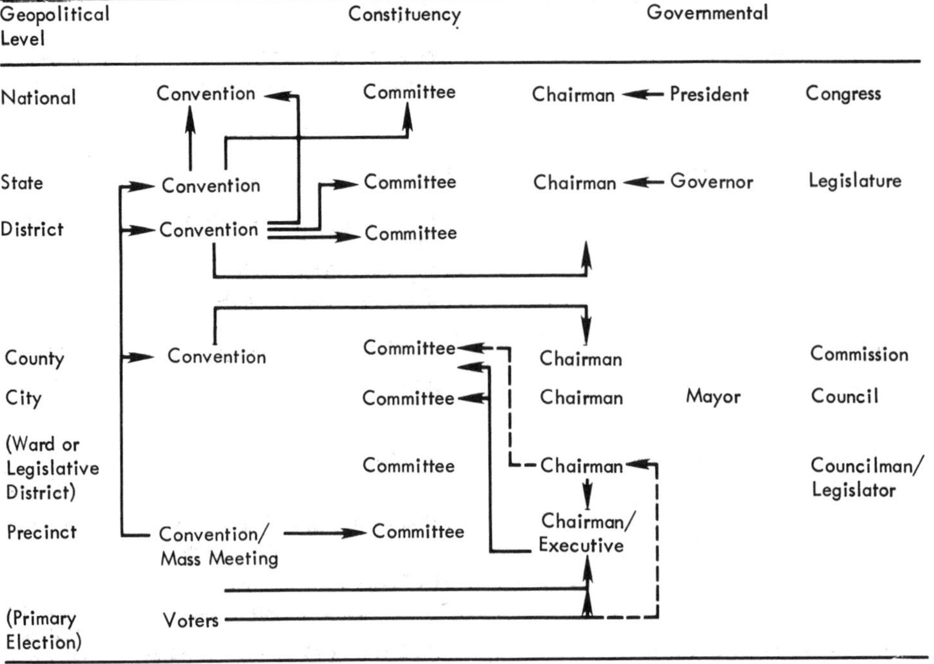

Figure 4-1 Formal structure of state political parties. (*Source:* Malcolm E. Jewell and David M. Olson, *American State Political Parties and Elections,* rev. ed., Dorsey Series in Political Science. Homewood, Ill.: Dorsey Press, 1962, p. 74. © 1982 by Dorsey Press.)

rebellious factions attempting to wrest political power from entrenched interests that control the traditional machinery of the party.[11]

State parties normally are comprised of the state committee, a state chair, and some other offices, and typically hold a state convention every two years. Some state party committees are quite large, with more than 500 members, but about 25 percent of them have fewer than 50 members. Approximately a third have between 100 and 500 members.[12]

All state parties have a central committee, also called an executive committee, that is influenced in varying degrees by state law. In many instances, these central committees are large to the point of organizational unwieldiness, although they can serve useful purposes as a central coordinating agency for election campaigns. The real grassroots organization in the state political parties, however, is represented by the local committees, and these organizations are made up of the groups that get out the vote by serving as poll watchers, campaigners, and doorbell ringers.

Perhaps the most significant development in the state parties is their dramatically accelerating professionalism. Ninety-six percent of state parties have at least one full-time staffer, up from around a third in the 1960s. Republicans tend to be more professionally staffed than Democrats; 44 percent of state Democratic parties have only one or two full-time staff people, compared to only 8 percent of state GOPs. State party budgets are up, too, and Republicans again have the edge; most state Democratic parties have budgets of $250,000 or more, but most state Grand Old Parties have annual budgets of at least $500,000.[13]

WHO'S IN CHARGE HERE?

Who controls these party organizations? Are they run by the methods of the traditional political machine of the past, or are they more responsive to the brand of citizen politics that we have seen emerging in recent years? A partial answer is furnished in a study of six states by John Fenton. He classified three state party systems as "issue oriented" or "programmatic" (Michigan, Minnesota, Wisconsin) and another three as "job oriented" or "traditional" (Illinois, Indiana, and Ohio).[14] The issue-oriented parties corresponded to Daniel Elazar's concept of moralistic political culture (see Chapter 1); this is a party system that is interested primarily in public issues in an ideological sense. In contrast, the job-oriented political party system will evolve from a job-oriented to an issue-oriented system if the following conditions apply:

1. Strict civil service systems, which reduce a party's control over the distribution of state offices.
2. Continued and sustained defeat of one party at the polls, reducing it to a shell.
3. Powerful interest groups that seize control over the party's machinery.
4. The existence of an electorate that is issue oriented along national lines.[15]

Whether or not Fenton's analysis is correct, the state political parties are made up of people who are the political grassroots of this country. In this light, it is of note that a study of how grassroots party officials see themselves found that more than three quarters of them saw their proper role as related primarily to campaigns or party organization. Less than 10 percent saw their most important role as being "ideological," that is, increasing political information and forming policy.[16]

Similarly, state party chairs take a more traditional view of their role and see themselves primarily as fund raisers and campaigners, and as recruiters of candidates. In fact, the differences between Republican Party chairs and Democratic Party chairs at the state levels are negligible in terms of their perceptions of their own roles.[17] State chairs concentrate their energies on county and legislative offices.[18] Increasingly, the role of the state party chairs is institutionalizing, and most state parties now have a permanent headquarters—virtually all of which have opened only since the early 1960s—and typically vary in size from about five staffers in nonelection years to ten during election years.[19]

Beyond agreeing on a basically traditionalistic model of what their role involves, state party chairs can be categorized as being one of three differing types.[20] One is the "agent chair," who generally is appointed by the governor on the understanding that he or she will be the governor's personal political agent. Another type is the "independent chair," who is not necessarily the governor's choice. Such chairs may or may not be at odds with their party's governor, but clearly are powers in their own right. A final category is the "chair of the out party," or the party that has lost the governorship. Often these chairs are important political figures with considerable authority of their own, but occasionally they are the agents of high-level elected officeholders, such as a U.S. senator, who is a member of the party. Of the three types of state party chairs, the independent in-party chair probably has the most difficult job in that he or she must balance the wishes of the governor *and* the state party committee. The agent chair, on the other hand, simply is an instrument of the governor, while the independent out-party chair does not have a governor to contend with and simply must keep his or her political fences mended with the state committee.

Although the employment of full-time professionals as party chairs or executive directors is now the norm, elected politicians are quite active in the inner workings of their state parties. This is particularly the case with governors; in a survey of state party chairs, 63 percent of the Democratic respondents and 45 percent of the Republican chairs said that their governors were "very active" in the affairs of their state parties. About a third of the chairs ranked congressmen and congresswomen as very active, followed by state legislators and (at least among the Republicans) local officeholders. Republican state party chairs said that all elected officials, but especially state legislators and congress members, had become considerably more active in their party's business over the last 25 years. Among Democrats, only governors and congress members were perceived as having increased their interest in the party, and then only modestly. But the engagement of local officials in the workings of the Democratic Party had fallen sharply over time (by a fifth), a finding "consistent with the widely perceived decline in political influence by big city mayors and political 'machines' in state politics."[21]

GETTING CANDIDATES: CAUCUSES, CONVENTIONS, AND PRIMARIES

Nominating candidates for a public office is a vital party function. But the way in which parties nominate candidates has changed and, in the view of most observers, has been made more democratic over the years. American political parties have moved from the relatively tightly controlled *party caucus,* to the more expansive *party convention* and, finally, to the relatively democratic *party primary.*

The Caucus

A *caucus* is a series of multitiered meetings of state party leaders. The first tier usually involves a meeting of all registered party voters who participate at the precinct level. Typically, the number of people who attend these precinct meetings is quite small, with perhaps only 1 percent of registered party voters doing so. Recent party reforms, however, particularly among the Democrats, have radically increased the number of participants in precinct meetings in some states, with participation as high as 10 to 16 percent of the voting turnout for presidential elections.[22] At these precinct meetings, delegates (who usually are registered party voters who have openly declared their favorite candidates) are elected to the next stage, which is normally a districtwide or countywide caucus. From that level, delegates are elected to the statewide caucus or convention.

The caucus is the most traditional nominating procedure. It is what John Adams had in mind when he first coined the term "smoke-filled room." Adams was describing a meeting of the Boston Caucus Club in 1763, which had been held in a smoke-filled attic. He disapproved of this meeting, not only because the caucus was entirely extralegal and unpublic, but also because, as he observed, "there they drink, flip, I suppose," and determine who will be "selectmen, assessors, collectors, wardens, fire wards, and representatives" before they ever "are chosen in the town."[23]

The Convention

In John Adams's day, the caucus controlled the entire nominating process. Today, however, the precinct caucus is used primarily as a means of electing delegates to the statewide party conventions, or as members of county party committees, and the statewide party nominating conventions have, since the middle of the eighteenth century, displaced the caucus as the method principally used to nominate candidates. Delaware, the first state to adopt such a device, inaugurated it during the administration of Thomas Jefferson, and by 1930, most of the Northern states had gone over to it.[24] A *convention* is simply a meeting of delegates who have been elected by registered party voters during a series of meetings held at the substate level, for example, precinct caucuses and county conventions or caucuses.

State conventions usually meet once every two years to elect officers of the state party and adopt a party platform. They also endorse candidates who have been selected in the party primaries. Statewide party conventions are not small. Most state party conventions have fewer than a thousand delegates attending, but 30 of the state parties have more than a thousand delegates.[25]

The Primary

Today, yet a more participatory form of nominating procedure has displaced the convention. This is the primary election. The *primary* is a means of making party nominations for office by direct popular election. The first direct primary took place in Crawford County, Pennsylvania, where both Democrats and Republicans adopted the idea prior to the Civil War. The idea caught on rapidly, and was seen as a means of leveraging control of the party machinery from the grasp of the party bosses. Wisconsin adopted the first statewide compulsory primary law in 1903, and by 1917 virtually all states had adopted it. Connecticut was the last state to adopt a form of direct primary in 1955.

The adoption of primary election laws in all 50 states, in effect, displaced the convention system as the principal means of nominating party candidates. The convention has not been completely displaced, and in Colorado, Connecticut, New Mexico, New York, North Dakota, Utah, and Virginia, the endorsement of a candidate by the party convention remains extremely important in winning the primaries. Nevertheless, primaries are virtually the only means by which a prospective candidate for a party's nomination can hope to acquire that nomination.[26]

As with most political processes at the state and local levels, primary elections are not simple. Twenty-six states use the "closed primary," in which only members registered in a particular party may vote in that party's primary. The remaining 24 states use various kinds of "open primaries." A dozen of these states use an open primary that requires an element of party selection; typically, a voter must state his or her party preference at the polls, and request that party's ballot. Even so, voters in these states need not register with a party in advance, and no permanent record is kept of party preference. As a consequence, there is no hindrance in the event that the voter wishes to change party preference between elections.

Another dozen states have completely open primaries, and in these states voters do not have to state their party preference publicly. They can vote in either primary, and voters can move from year to year from one primary to the other. Two of these states, Alaska and Washington, use a "blanket primary," in which voters may participate in both party primaries during a single primary election. Louisiana has gone so far as to adopt (during the 1970s) a "nonpartisan primary" for its congressional and statewide campaigns. In a nonpartisan primary, voters and candidates of all parties participate in a single primary, one that usually involves a runoff election between the top two candidates. Nonpartisan primaries also are used in some local elections, and in most elections for judges.

Table 4-4 indicates the regional distribution of statewide primaries by type. As can be seen, states that have (or have had) a strong two-party system, particularly those in the Northeast and the Midwest, favor the closed primary, while open primaries largely are favored in states that have had weak party systems or are in the South and West.

Table 4-4 Regional Distribution of State Primaries with Varying Voter Qualifications

Type of primary	*Northeast*	*Midwest*	*Border*	*South*	*West*
Closed	Conn. Del. Maine Md. Mass. N.H. N.J. N.Y. Pa.	Iowa Kans. Nebr. Ohio S. Dak.	Ky. Okla. W. Va.	Fla. N.C.	Ariz. Calif. Colo. Nev. N. Mex. Oreg. Wyo.
Open; party selection required	R.I.	Ill. Ind.	Mo.	Ala. Ark. Ga. Miss. S.C. Tenn. Tex. Va.	
Open	Vt.	Mich. Minn. N. Dak. Wis.			Hawaii Idaho Mont. Utah
Open; blanket					Alaska Wash.
Nonpartisan				La.	

Source: Malcolm E. Jewell and David M. Olson, *American State Political Parties and Elections,* rev. ed., Dorsey Series in Political Science (Homewood, Ill.: Dorsey, 1982), p. 10.

ELECTING CANDIDATES: IS THE PARTY OVER?

Regardless of how a party nominates its candidates, the influence of that party on the governments of states and localities obviously is determined, in large part, by the number of potential officials that may be put up for election. State and local governments elect 490,265 officials, that is, 23 elected officeholders for every 10,000 inhabitants in the nation, or 6 officials per government. Table 4-5 indicates that state governments have the most elected officials of any type of government (almost 306 per state), followed by county governments, which elect almost 21 officials per county. The number of elected officials per state varies widely, from 172 in Hawaii to more than 40,000 in Illinois. Ten states elect more than 18,000 officials and account for 47 percent of all elected officials in the country. Almost half (7,562) of all elected state officials are members of the legislature, 1,229 are elected members of state boards, and 6,503 are executive and judicial officials.[27]

The Recruitment Game

With an average of 306 publicly elected positions to fill per state, the challenge of finding qualified candidates for these positions is an obvious one. Available research indicates that statewide parties take this job fairly seriously, although the clear focus of candidate recruitment by parties is on state legislative races. As many as 60 percent (or more) of the legislators or candidates for the legislature in some states have been recruited by their states' political parties.[28]

The propensity of party staffers to recruit candidates for public office relates, unsurprisingly, to the vitality of party organization. But there seem to be no particular correlations between such factors as recruitment activity and urbanism, or even with the competitive status of the parties.[29]

Organizing for Elections

Once candidates are recruited, the problem becomes one of getting them elected. Increasingly, the available evidence indicates that candidates for

Table 4-5 Popularly Elected Officials, 1977

Type of Government	*Number of elected officials*	*Average per government*
United States	490,265[a]	6.1
State governments	15,294	305.9
Local governments	474,971[a]	6.0
Counties	62,922	20.7
Municipalities	134,017	7.1
Townships	118,966	7.1
School districts	87,062	5.7
Special districts	72,377	2.8

[a] Adjusted to avoid duplicate counting of elected officials serving both a county and another local government.

Source: U.S. Bureau of the Census, *1977 Census of Governments,* Vol. 1, *Governmental Organization,* No. 2, *Popularly Elected Officials* (Washington, D.C.: Government Printing Office, October 1979), p. 1.

state and local offices rely less and less upon the party organization to help them in their campaigns. One study found that only 17 percent of the elected executives of statewide agencies attributed even some of their success to the support of their party. By contrast, 27 percent felt that their personal campaign organization was among the more significant reasons for their success.[30]

Such findings may not be too surprising when we recall that only about a quarter of the 100 state parties can be classified as cohesive organizations and the remainder as bifactional or multifactional parties. We can infer from this that fractionalized parties are of not much utility to individuals wishing to be elected to office. Other studies, however, do indicate a marginal effectiveness of parties in getting candidates elected. One estimate, in fact, is that intensive work at the precinct level by party organizations can increase the parties' vote by perhaps 5 percent.[31] Although two authorities on state political parties have concluded, after reviewing the literature, that "party activity does seem to make a small difference" in winning campaigns,[32] such a conclusion does not stand as an especially glowing testimonial to the political effectiveness of the parties.

Interestingly, these opinions by the parties' nominees for public office contrast with the increasingly sophisticated techniques being used by state party organizations to support candidates.[33] In the early 1960s, only 39 percent of the state parties sponsored voter mobilization programs (e.g., voter identification, registration, and get-out-the-vote drives), but by the early 1970s, the proportion had increased to 70 percent. Half of the parties research and develop campaign issues, and four-fifths of the state party organizations publish newsletters (up from two-thirds in the early 1960s). Public opinion polling, campaign seminars, and media consultation are additional professional services provided by parties to candidates, and Republicans generally are better at providing them than are Democrats; Table 4-6 indicates these services and how many state parties provide them.

Yet, while these party activities help, they are largely incidental to getting elected, in the opinions of most candidates for state and local offices. What, then, does get candidates for office elected? A major factor is the personal campaign organization, and central to the creation of such an organization is the candidate's relationships with the more powerful interest groups. One technique that candidates for state and local offices use is simply to join every available group in sight: churches, lodges, professional associations, civic groups, luncheon clubs, and so on. Occasionally, membership in such groups will result in letters of endorsement for their candidacies.

Those interest groups that are more dedicated to the political process (because they have more to gain from it), such as unions of public employees, for

Table 4-6 Services Provided by State Parties to Candidates for State Office

Services Provided	*Republicans*	*Democrats*
Polling	78%	50%
Media consulting	75	46
Campaign seminars	100	76
Coordinating PAC contributions	52	31
State party chairs responding	(38)	(30)

Source: Timothy Conlan, Ann Martino, and Robert Digler, "State Parties in the 1980s: Adaptation, Resurgence, and Continuing Constraints," *Intergovernmental Perspective,* 10 (Fall, 1984), p. 10.

example, often will provide direct staff services to candidates, and it is not unknown for such groups to turn their own offices over to the candidate for his or her personal use. One study, in fact, cites the case of the Los Angeles County AFL-CIO that contributed more than 100 precinct workers paid by the union to each district of the California Assembly on the day of the election.[34]

Money, Money, Money!

Needless to say, interest groups also supply money. Although information for states and localities concerning campaign contributions to candidates is sporadic, it has been estimated that special interests contribute as much as $10 million to $20 million in state legislative races alone.[35] We know that campaigning for these offices grows increasingly expensive. For example, at least three winning candidates for governor's races during the 1970s spent between $4.8 million and $6.8 million in their gubernatorial campaigns, and, in a fourth case, an estimated $10 million was expended to win the governorship. Generally, estimates earmark around $1 million in a typical gubernatorial campaign.[36]

One study of about a dozen state legislatures found that the campaign expenditures for both primary and general elections combined during the 1978 election cycle indicated that spending for a contested seat in the state senate ranged from $10,000 to almost $65,000 and in the house from about $3,000 to $44,000. (The high sides of the scales were for California.) The figures were considerably lower in a number of states, mostly in the South and in the underpopulated states, but it is clear that, as legislators professionalize, so do their electioneering techniques and expenditure levels of their campaigns rise to accommodate their new sophistication.[37] Although there are no comprehensive measures for the costs of running for state and local offices, the tab for running for Congress typically exceeds the Consumer Price Index by about one-third, while the costs of running for president exceeds the rising rate of the Consumer Price Index by more than 50 percent.[38] If this rate is at all comparable for the state and local races, then we may infer that candidates must get their money somewhere.

Political parties rarely provide their own candidates with very much money, but state parties appear to do a better job of it than do their national counterparts. In 1982, for a typical example, national party committees contributed less than 3 percent of the campaign budgets of candidates for the U.S. House of Representatives and less than 1 percent of the war chests of U.S. Senate candidates.[39] By contrast, one examination of the campaign contributions made by 53 state parties in 27 states during the 1978 election found that 40 of the 53 organizations did donate campaign funds to candidates, and that, on the average, these contributions comprised a third of the candidates' campaign budgets. The remaining 13 parties, however, contributed nothing to their own candidates' campaigns. The candidates derived their remaining funding from their own pockets, individual contributors, and special interests. State parties make their biggest contributions, first, to the campaigns for the governorship, followed by races for state legislative seats, U.S. House and Senate seats, and statewide offices, such as attorney general.[40] State Republicans tend to be more financially supportive of their candidates than are state Democrats, as Table 4-7 indicates.

Data from California amplify our understanding of the relatively minor financial role that parties play in state campaigns. During the 1978 election, the

Table 4-7 Contributions by State Parties to Candidates

Forms of Assistance	*Republicans*	*Democrats*
Percentage providing campaign contributions		
For state candidates	90%	70%
For congressional candidates	70	56
Percentage providing fund-raising assistance		
To state candidates	95	63
To congressional candidates	63	63
State party chairs responding	(40)	(30)

Source: Timothy Conlan, Ann Martino, and Robert Digler, "State Parties in the 1980s: Adaptation, Resurgence, and Continuing Constraints," *Intergovernmental Perspective,* 10 (Fall, 1984), p. 10.

Republican Party of California donated almost $600,000 to legislative candidates and concentrated $500,000 of that sum on just 21 campaigns. This meant that these candidates received from $10,000 to $25,000 apiece. Nevertheless, it cost the typical California campaigner some $65,000 to run for the senate and $44,000 to run for the house in 1978, so while the party's contribution was substantial in these 21 cases, it was nonetheless not even half of what they needed to run. Moreover, the remaining GOP campaigners in California in that year apparently received virtually nothing from the party.[41]

When parties provide state and local candidates with campaign funds and other services, they generally earn a return on their investment. Not only do they increase the likelihood of their candidates winning the election, but the parties apparently garner the loyalty and personal involvement of the candidates whom they back as well. At least this correlation seems to be valid among the Democrats, for whom "the more campaign assistance state parties provide to gubernatorial and state legislative candidates, the more likely it is that those candidates will be active in party affairs."[42]

Whatever the sources, campaigners for state and local political offices spend their campaign contributions on a number of devices that they can use to get themselves elected, but which are seldom provided by the party. For example, media have become a major object of expenditure for political contenders at the state and local levels. The typical governor's race will devote from 15 to 30 percent of its total campaign budget to television alone.[43]

Another object of expenditure is the professional campaign management firm, which has become an industry unto itself since the 1950s. Although the parties increasingly are trying to professionalize their campaign management skills (and are making significant progress), it appears that the private sector has overtaken them in this regard and often provides more effective services. Increasingly, these firms use skilled statisticians, computer-based information technology, telephone banks, and mass media techniques to get their candidates recognized by the voters. Increasingly also, these technologies are extremely expensive, but they appear to be worth the investment. For example, if only 2 percent of the addresses solicited for contributions returned their self-addressed envelopes to campaign headquarters, the cost of the mailing would be covered.[44]

Do big spenders win? Although it cannot be determined precisely, it appears that money definitely helps. One analysis of all gubernatorial elections found that 10 of the 15 incumbents who outspent their challengers won, while only 2 of the 7 challengers who outspent incumbents won. In campaigns in which an incumbent was not running, the candidate who spent the most money won three quarters of the time. When party strength and incumbency were controlled in the study, higher spending did associate positively with the votes won by the candidates.[45] Among state legislative races, studies have indicated that there is a solid correlation between the amount spent by the challenger and the outcome of the election.[46]

MONEY, PARTIES, AND CAMPAIGN REFORM

Because of the mounting rates of expenditures that are increasingly needed to run for state and local office (and the occasionally questionable sources of the funds acquired to do so), state governments during the 1970s began to interest themselves in the public financing of state and local elections. In part, state legislatures began to do this as a result of cues from Washington in the form of the Federal Election Campaign Act of 1971, and its subsequent amendments of 1974 and 1976. But it is a tribute to the creativity of state legislatures that they did this in a way that differed significantly from the model provided by Washington. Unlike Congress, state legislatures were particularly sensitive to the legitimate place in parties in the electoral process. Seventeen states use tax monies to finance statewide campaigns. Of these, 11 states contribute funds directly to the political parties, and, in 5 additional states, state funds are channeled to parties with various restrictions. Seven of the 17 states that publicly finance elections send checks directly to the candidates. This jibes with the federal model, which also bypasses the party structure.

State public funding of campaigns began only in 1973, so it is difficult to draw many conclusions of significance. It does appear, however, that Republicans seem to benefit less than Democrats. In the 9 states that permit taxpayers to check off a portion of their tax bill to the party of their choice, Democrats generally garner anywhere from two-thirds to three-fourths of the total state contribution; only in Utah, among the states that permit taxpayers to specify party, has the GOP received more dollars than the Democrats.[47] Table 4-8 indicates the states that engage in the public financing of state elections. The choice made by 11 states to channel funding directly to the parties likely has strengthened those party organizations. For example, we know that those states that have traditionally had lackluster party organizations have seen those parties revitalize, in some cases significantly, with infusions of public funds. Those states that already have competitive parties[48] have tended to bypass those organizations and have contributed directly to candidates.

The states also have attempted to blunt the influence of the special interests on the electoral process and to strengthen the role of the parties in ways other than that of direct public financing of campaigns. The 1970s were a decade of aggressive and wholly admirable efforts by legislatures to limit the amounts that individual citizens and groups could contribute to campaigns, and to assure that the public could find out who contributed how much to whom. By 1980, every state required some form of disclosure by candidates on the nature of their campaign contributions, and about half the states had enacted limits on individual donations to campaign organizations and parties. Eighteen states limit the amounts that may be spent on campaigns by candidates.[49]

Table 4-8 Public Finance of State Elections

Year First Bill on Public Financing Was Passed	States	Years in Which Public Monies Have Been Allocated to Parties/Candidates
1973	Iowa	1974–78
1973	Maine[1]	1974–78
1973	Rhode Island	1974–78
1974	Minnesota	1976–78
1975	Montana[1]	1976
1974	Maryland[1]	—
1974	New Jersey	1977
1973	Utah	1975–78
1975	Idaho	1976–78
1975	Massachusetts[1]	1978
1975	North Carolina	1977–78
1976	Kentucky	1977–78
1976	Michigan	1978
1977	Oregon	1978
1977	Wisconsin	1978
1978	Hawaii	—
1978	Oklahoma	—

[1] States with tax surcharges; all others have tax checkoffs.

Source: Ruth S. Jones, "State Public Financing and the State Parties," in Michael J. Malbin, ed., *Parties, Interest Groups and Campaign Finance Laws* (Washington, D.C.: American Enterprise Institute, 1980), p. 303.

In enacting limitations on campaign contributions and expenditures, the states had been forced to reckon with the case of *Buckley* v. *Valeo,* which was decided by the Supreme Court in 1976, and which struck down laws in 31 states that had dealt with campaign finance. The Court had held that it was unconstitutional to limit the funds that could be spent by an individual to publish his or her own views of public issues or elections, although contributions by individuals to candidates and to the parties could still be limited. While it could be argued that the Court's ruling amounted to a somewhat precious legal distinction, *Buckley* v. *Valeo* nonetheless provided an impetus for legislatures to readdress state campaign reform legislation throughout the remainder of the decade.

THE COMPETITION QUESTION

If legislators wrestled with the formidable problem of campaign finance during the 1970s, political scientists have been grappling with a knotty intellectual dilemma for a considerably longer period of time, and one that lies at the heart of the political place of parties in America. This is the question of interparty competition. To phrase it succinctly, Which states have parties that more closely reflect state issues, those with highly competitive electoral contests or those dominated by a single party? Political scientists differ in their answers to this question, and their conclusions range from a belief that interparty competition yields public policies that are substantially different in states that have it when compared to states that do not, to views that partisan competitiveness does not make much, if any, difference in the process and results of policy formation.

Ideology Equals Competition

One school of thought, represented by V. O. Key, Jr., is that states possessing highly competitive party systems are likely to have more ideologically oriented state legislatures and executive branches.[50] Therefore, different public opinions on policy issues will result in sharp competition between political parties.

The Illusion of Competition

Another school of thought, represented by Thomas R. Dye, argues just the opposite, that interparty competition has at best a minor influence on the form taken by public policies in states.[51] Dye related social welfare expenditures—notably, old age assistance, unemployment compensation, and education—to a measurement of interparty competition and found that, statistically, a state's level of welfare expenditures was only weakly related to its degree of interparty competition. On the other hand, the amount spent on such social welfare programs is very strongly related to the level of wealth and resources in the state—a less than surprising conclusion.

The Reality of Competition

A final variant is represented by Ira Sharkansky and Richard Hofferbert. They argue that high levels of interparty competition do indeed relate to high levels of social welfare expenditures and that the correlation between the two is higher than Dye recognizes.[52] Sharkansky and Hofferbert's analysis uses a somewhat more sophisticated set of correlational methods than does Dye's, and their statistics bear out this contention.

An even more sophisticated attempt to place the role of party competition in political perspective has been attempted by Gerald C. Wright, Jr. Wright concludes that competitiveness between a state's parties can result in very real policy differences, at least in terms of welfare policies, when compared to noncompetitive state systems. But Wright has discovered an interesting caveat to this generalization. Differences in levels of party competition among the states result in "relatively little policy impact where there is little threat to the governing party," a condition that can arise even in those states that have long traditions of interparty competitiveness. But, Wright found, where "the minority party does have some reasonable chance of winning at the polls, the same small differences in party competition are related to rather significant changes in social welfare policies."[53] In other words, competition equates with highly responsive welfare policies in the states when it is perceived by the party in power that the opposition might win.

The Rise of Competition

Regardless of whether competition is ideological, illusory, or real, on the whole, political scientists seem to accept the idea that competitive political parties equate more or less with a healthy political system, and they generally agree that five major patterns of interparty competition have appeared in the United States during this century.[54]

One form is comprised of *one-party Democratic systems,* or states in which the politics are dominated completely by the Democratic party. These states are entirely in the South. A second form is the *modified one-party Democratic system,* or states where the Democratic party has a general predominance, but can be effectively challenged on occasion. These, with some exceptions, largely are the border states, or those on the rim of the old Confederacy. A third form is clear *two-party systems,* including virtually all of the Western and Midwestern states and many of the Northeastern states. A few states have a *modified one-party Republican system.* They are Iowa, Kansas, Maine, New Hampshire, North Dakota, Vermont, and Wyoming. Until recently, both New Hampshire and Vermont could be considered to constitute a fifth form of interparty competition, as they were *one-party Republican systems.*

Recent studies indicate that interparty competition in the states is clearly on the rise. A few states, all in the South, still can be properly categorized as one-party Democratic states. But the number of one-party states (e.g., the 12 Democratic states of the Old South and the 2 Republican states of New Hampshire and Vermont) has fallen precipitously since 1950. Between 1930 and 1950, the dominant party in the 14 single-party states lost not one election. But between 1950 and 1975, the "post office Republicans" in the South (so named because their only purpose was to acquire jobs in the federal government when a Republican president was in office) won elections in half of the solid Southern states. Similarly, the underdog Democrats began winning a higher percentage of the vote in both New Hampshire and Vermont. Table 4-9 shows the diminishing margins of partisan dominance, as measured by gubernatorial elections, in these one-party states since 1950.

Another 20 states normally vote a traditionally favored party into power. Nine of these states tend to favor the Democrats and 11 usually favor the Republicans. As Table 4-10 shows, however, competition between the parties is on the rise in these states, too. As it indicates, not only is the underdog party in these states winning the governorship at an increasing rate, but the registrants of the major party in these states are defecting at increasing rates in gubernatorial elections. Table 4-11 indicates that even among the remaining 14 states that have maintained a tradition of fierce party rivalry since 1930 (excluding Alaska and Hawaii, both of which are two-party states but which were granted statehood after 1950), it appears that competition is intensifying as well.

In sum, party competition at the state levels is growing considerably sharper. In 1950, only 14 states could be clearly considered two-party competitive states, but today the number of states that are clearly competitive is 31. If we look at the important indicator of gubernatorial elections, the number of one-party states had shrunk by half (from 14 to 7 during this same 25-year period), and between 1961 and 1982 there was no state outside the Deep South in which any one party could claim a consistent "lock" on the governorship. Importantly, even in the South the Republicans elected at least one governor or U.S. senator during the 1961-1982 period.[55]

Figures 4-2 and 4-3 indicate the shift in patterns of party competition between the states and contrast the 1932 to 1958 elections with the 1960 to 1980 elections. As one might infer, the rise of interparty competition in the states, on the whole, has accrued largely to the advantage of the Republicans. This has happened despite the infamous "Watergate election" of 1976, an election that, to quote the chair of the Republican National Committee, represented for the GOP

Table 4-9 Metamorphosis in Party Control in the One-Party States, 1930—1980

	YEARS 1930–1950		*YEARS 1951–1980*	
	DEMOCRATIC STATES			
	% of Gubernatorial Elections Won by Democrats	*Average % Democratic of Major Party Vote for Governor*	*% of Gubernatorial Elections Won by Democrats*	*Average % Democratic of Major Party Vote for Governor*
Georgia	100.0	100.0	100.0	79.8
Mississippi	100.0	100.0	100.0	80.9
South Carolina	100.0	99.9	85.7	74.5
Louisiana	100.0	99.2	87.5	80.8
Alabama	100.0	90.6	100.0	84.0
Texas	100.0	89.0	92.3	70.4
Arkansas	100.0	88.6	80.0	67.1
Florida	100.0	78.5	88.9	62.8
Virginia	100.0	74.0	57.1	54.0[a]
Tennessee	100.0	73.8	75.0	73.7
North Carolina	100.0	68.5	85.7	59.4
Oklahoma	100.0	57.7	71.4	56.1
	REPUBLICAN STATES			
	% of Gubernatorial Elections Won by Republican	*Average % Republican of Major Party Vote for Governor*	*% of Gubernatorial Elections Won by Republican*	*Average % Republican of Major Party Vote for Governor*
Vermont	100.0	68.5	66.7	52.0
New Hampshire	100.0	58.6	66.7	50.2

[a] Figure includes the percentage won by Henry Howell, though officially an independent, received the "commendation" of the Democratic party.

Source: Larry Sabato, *Goodbye to Good-time Charlie: The American Governorship Transformed,* 2nd ed. (Washington, D.C.: Congressional Quarterly Press, 1983), pp. 122-123. Reprinted by permission of Congressional Quarterly Inc.

Table 4-10 Metamorphosis in Party Control in the Normally Democratic or Republican States, 1930–1980

	YEARS 1930–1950		*YEARS 1951–1980*	
	DEMOCRATIC STATES			
	% of Gubernatorial Elections Won by Democrats	*Average % Democratic of Major Party Vote for Governor*	*% of Gubernatorial Elections Won by Democrats*	*Average % Democratic of Major Party Vote for Governor*
Arizona	90.9	64.1	41.7	48.3
New Mexico	90.9	53.3	58.3	51.3
West Virginia	83.30	54.6	62.5	52.7
Kentucky	83.3	54.5	87.5	56.1
Utah	83.3	53.6	62.5	55.4
Rhode Island	81.8	55.4	73.3	54.7
Nevada	66.6	55.5	57.1	56.4
Missouri	66.6	54.0	75.0	53.5
Maryland	66.6	52.0	71.4	58.8
	REPUBLICAN STATES			
	% of Gubernatorial Elections Won by Republican	*Average % Republican of Major Party Vote for Governor*	*% of Gubernatorial Elections Won by Republican*	*Average % Republican of Major Party Vote for Governor*
California	83.3	66.7	42.9	49.1
Pennsylvania	83.3	53.1	42.9	49.4
Maine	81.8	59.0	30.0	47.6
South Dakota	81.8	55.9	69.2	53.2
Kansas	81.8	54.5	46.2	48.7
Iowa	72.7	55.2	61.5	50.5
Wisconsin	72.7	47.2[a]	58.3	51.0
Oregon	66.6	59.4	75.0	53.3
North Dakota	63.6	56.3	45.5	53.7
Minnesota	63.6	49.8[a]	40.0	49.9
Nebraska	54.5	50.1	45.5	51.3

[a] The Republican percentages are low due to the presence of active third parties in both Wisconsin (the Progressives) and Minnesota (the Farmer-Laborites) during much of the period surveyed.

[illegible] 2nd ed. (Washington, D.C.: Congressional Quarterly Press, 1983), pp. 122-123.

Table 4-11 Metamorphosis in Party Control in the Two-Party States, 1930–1980

	YEARS 1930–1950		*YEARS 1951–1980*	
	DEMOCRATIC LEANING			
	% of Gubernatorial Elections Won by Democrats	*Average % Democratic of Major Party Vote for Governor*	*% of Gubernatorial Elections Won by Democrats*	*Average % Democratic of Major Party Vote for Governor*
Indiana	66.6	52.2	25.0	46.3
Montana	66.6	51.6	50.0	52.5
Massachusetts	63.60	51.4	45.5	49.3
Ohio	54.5	50.1	44.4	49.4
Colorado	54.5	52.8	55.6	50.4
New York	54.5	52.8	42.9	48.7
Idaho	54.5	51.8	42.9	53.2
Connecticut	54.5	49.8	85.7	55.2
	REPUBLICAN LEANING			
	% of Gubernatorial Elections Won by Republican	*Average % Republican of Major Party Vote for Governor*	*% of Gubernatorial Elections Won by Republican*	*Average % Republican of Major Party Vote for Governor*
Delaware	66.6	51.8	62.5	53.5
New Jersey	62.5	51.4	14.3	45.4
Michigan	54.5	54.6	54.5	51.1
	EVENLY DIVIDED			
	% of Gubernatorial Elections Won by Republican	*Average % Republican of Major Party Vote for Governor*	*% of Gubernatorial Elections Won by Republican*	*Average % Republican of Major Party Vote for Governor*
Washington	50.0	54.5	37.5	48.1
Illinois	50.0	54.8	37.5	47.4
Wyoming	50.0	49.7	42.9	48.0

Source: Larry Sabato, *Goodbye to Good-time Charlie: The American Governorship Transformed,* 2nd ed. (Washington, D.C.: Congressional Quarterly Press, 1983), pp. 122-123
Reprinted by permission of Congressional Quarterly Inc.

"the lowest point in forty years in terms of elective offices, membership and public perception."[56] In the nation's bicentennial year, only 26 percent of the governors were members of the Republican Party and only a third of the state legislators belonged to the GOP. But the Republicans already were making gains in the South, and were able to keep this momentum going. By 1980, the Republicans had captured almost 600 additional offices in state and local governments, controlled the legislature and governor's mansion in 6 states, the governorship in 23 states, and both houses in 15 states. In 1982, however, the Republicans slipped significantly, and endured their first losses since 1976. The party lost 7 statehouses, and its control of both legislative chambers in 15 states fell to 11. Nineteen eighty-four saw modest Republican gains, and in 1985 the GOP held 16 governorships and 32 of the nation's 98 state legislative chambers. Figure 4-4 illustrates the fluctuating fortunes of the Republicans in those 42 states that have some degree of interparty competition. As it indicates, the GOP's star is in the ascendancy, but there is still a considerable way to go.

The base of the Republicans' strength long has been the growing suburban population. "There is little question that suburbia has remained a major problem for the Democrats . . . just as it has remained a bastion for the Republicans except when they occasionally slip."[57] For an example of this occasional slip, consider Robert Dill, who ran as a Republican for the county executive of Nassau County in New York. Among other slips, Dill characterized the Democrats as "greasy, slimy pigs," and despite a two-to-one Republican registration ratio in Nassau County, Dill's Democratic opponent won the election. But such

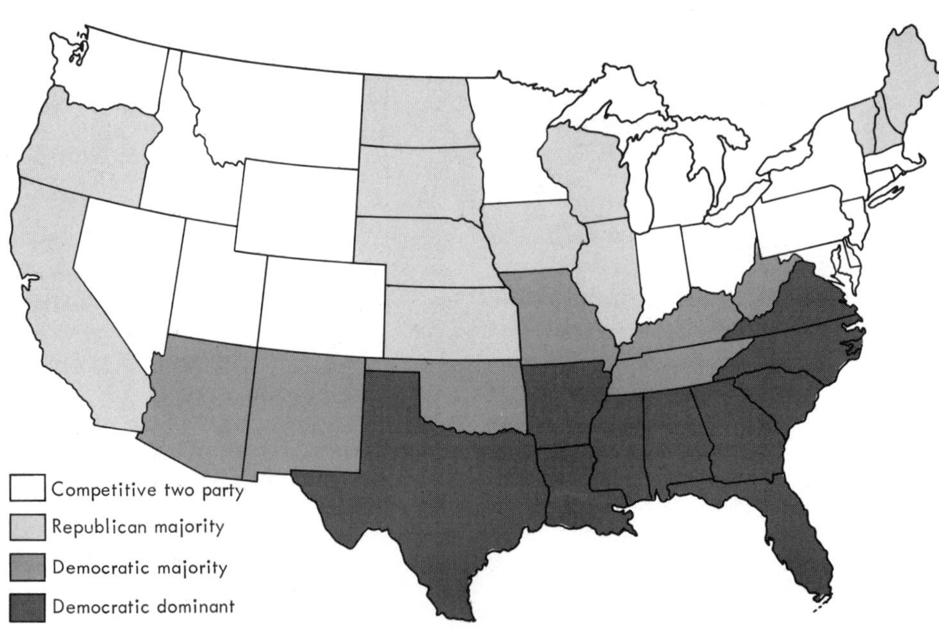

Figure 4-2 Patterns of party competition in states, 1932–1958 elections. (*Source:* Malcolm E. Jewell and David M. Olson, *American State Political Parties and Elections,* rev. ed., Dorsey Series in Political Science. Homewood, Ill.: Dorsey Press, 1982, p. 25. © 1982 by Dorsey Press.)

a win for the Democrats certainly was an exception in suburban, middle-class, largely white Nassau County.[58]

While it is by no means clear that the suburbs tend consistently to vote Republican in municipal elections, it nonetheless seems to be the case that suburbanites tend to vote for the Grand Old Party. Political scientists have evolved two theories as to why this may be true: the conversion theory and the transplantation theory. The *conversion theory,* as espoused by Robert C. Wood, argues that when inner-city residents move "up" to suburbia, their desires to be accepted by the community overwhelm their traditional voting preferences. "Green grass, fresh air and new social status work their magic; class and ethnic appeals lose their potency . . .. The ownership of land, the symbol of community, these provide the sources for suburban loyalty and interest."[59] This becomes particularly true when the new suburbanite receives his or her property tax bill, or when the new suburbanite learns that the community may somehow be rezoned.

The other theory, that of *transplantation,* holds that those voters who move to the suburbs have always in fact been conservative, which is one reason why they moved to suburbia in the first place. When these "transplants" get to suburbia, they simply come out of the closet and vote Republican. In support of the transplantation theory, it does seem that, as migration from the central cities to the suburbs has increased, so the proportion of Republican votes has increased in the suburbs while declining in the central cities. In any case, the literature on the subject seems to indicate that, although the notion of "pure Republican suburbs" in contrast to "pure Democratic cities" has been overstated,

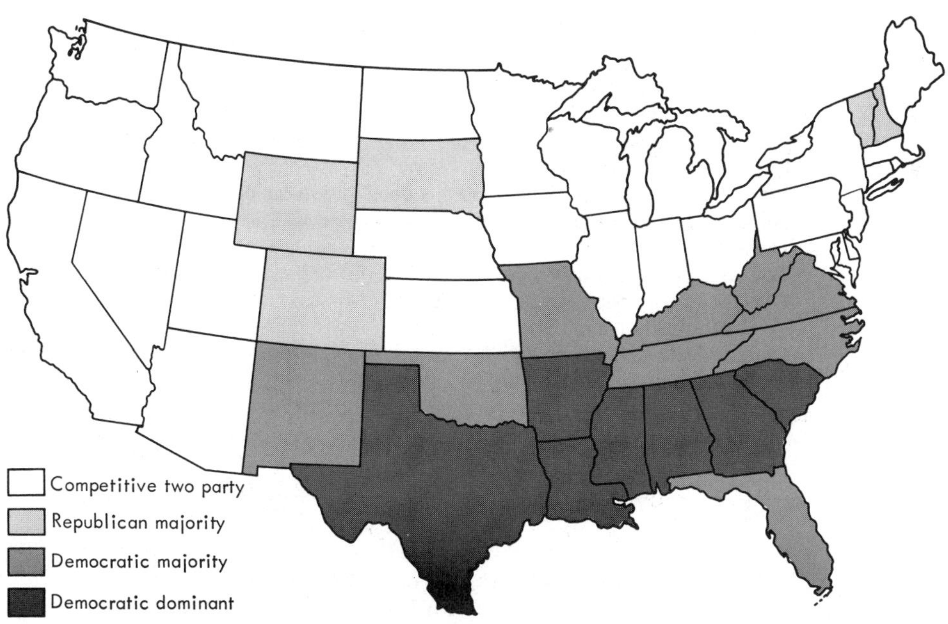

Figure 4-3 Patterns of party competition in states, 1960–1980 elections. (*Source:* Malcolm E. Jewell and David M. Olson, *American State Political Parties and Elections,* rev. ed., Dorsey Series in Political Science. Homewood, Ill.: Dorsey Press, 1982, p. 26. © 1982 by Dorsey Press.)

the "typical suburb" (whatever that is) tends to vote Republican while the "typical central city" (ditto) tends to vote Democratic. Whether or not this inclination can be attributed to a conversion or transplantation theory is a moot point, but the tendency nonetheless is there.

If the suburbs are the Republicans' traditional base, youth may be their future. Thirty-four percent of young voters (18-to-21 year-olds) just entering the electorate in 1985 favored the GOP, in contrast to 27 percent of this group who favored the Democrats. Moreover, young voters who had entered the electorate in 1981 had significantly shifted their allegiances toward the Republicans four years later. In 1981, 24 percent of 18-to-21 year-olds favored the GOP and 33 percent preferred the Democrats; by 1985, however, 31 percent of this same group (who were by then four years older) favored the Republicans (a 7 percent gain for the GOP) and 28 percent preferred the Democrats (a 5 percent loss). Older voters also exhibited a tilt toward the Republicans during the first half of the 1980s, but not nearly as emphatically as did younger voters; only 2 percent of prospective voters born before 1958 shifted away from the Democrats and toward the GOP during this period.[60] The Grand Old Party, it seems, legitimately could consider changing its moniker to the Grand Young Party—but then its acronym (GYP) might not be as appealing.

HOW TO TELL REPUBLICANS FROM DEMOCRATS

Democrats buy most of the books that have been banned somewhere. Republicans form censorship committees and read them as a group.

Republicans consume three-fourths of all the rutabaga produced in this country. The remainder is thrown out.

Democrats give their worn-out clothes to those less fortunate. Republicans wear theirs.

Republicans enjoy exterminators. Democrats step on the bugs.

Republicans tend to keep their shades drawn, although there is seldom any reason why they should. Democrats ought to, but don't.

Republicans study the financial pages of the newspaper. Democrats put them in the bottom of the bird cage.

Most of the stuff alongside the road has been thrown out of car windows by Democrats.

Republicans raise dahlias, Dalmatians, and eyebrows. Democrats raise Airedales, kids, and taxes.

Democrats eat the fish they catch. Republicans hang them on the wall.

Republican boys date Democratic girls. They plan to marry Republican girls, but feel they're entitled to a little fun first.

Democrats make up plans and then do something else. Republicans follow the plans their grandfathers made.

Republicans sleep in twin beds—some even in separate rooms. That is why there are more Democrats.

Congressional Record (October 1, 1974).

In part, these impressive gains made by the GOP during the early 1980s are largely attributable to a grassroots emphasis by the national Republican Party. In 1980, the typical contribution received by the Republican National Committee was less than $30, and more than a million people donated these contributions. Among the Democrats, however, approximately four-fifths of the contributions in 1980 were contributed in amounts of $500 or more.[61] As a consequence of these patterns (i.e., one of the "little people" contributing on a

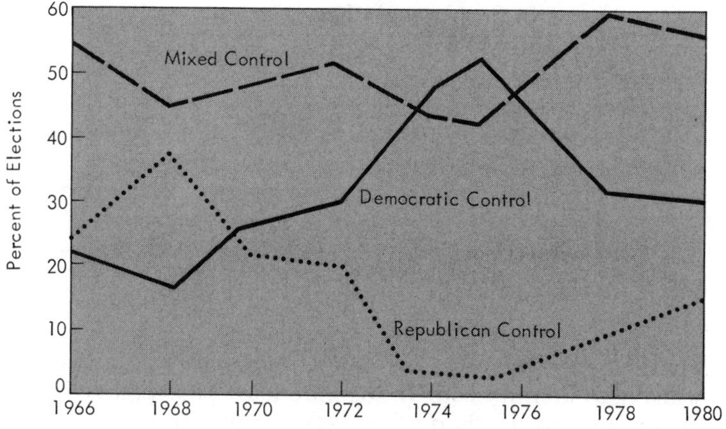

Figure 4-4 Party control of state legislatures and governorships in two-party competitive states, 1966–1980.* (*Source: The Book of the States.* Lexington, Ky.: The Council of State Governments, appropriate years.)

* Percent of the elections in 42 states, resulting in the governorship and both houses of the legislature in partisan control or mixed control between the governorship and one or both houses. Seven solid Democratic states (Alabama, Georgia, Louisiana, Mississippi, South Carolina, Texas) were not included nor was Nebraska which has a nonpartisan legislature. Minnesota was not included prior to 1972 because its legislature was nonpartisan.

massive scale to the Grand Old Party, as opposed to selected "fat cats" contributing large amounts to the Democrats), the Republican National Committee outspent the Democrats by almost 5 to 1 during the 1980 election.[62] When we combine what appear to be superior organizational abilities by the Republicans with the demographic shifts noted in Chapter 1—that is, the movement from the Snowbelt and the East to the Sunbelt and the West, a migration that resulted in 17 additional seats in the House of Representatives for the South and the West, together with the accelerating flow to the suburbs and the Party's increasing appeal to youth—it appears that the "permanent minority" Republicans may become a little less permanent as minorities generally go.

PARTIES IN DECLINE?

Despite the emergence of a newly combative Grand Old Party, the traditional vibrancy of the parties over time in this country seems to be waning. More than one pollster has observed the "disgust" and "disillusionment" of the people with both parties.[63] And the numbers seem to support the validity of these assessments. Table 4-12 indicates the decline in partisan identification by decades, from the 1950s through the 1980s. As it shows, Americans who identify with either major party have declined in numbers from about three-fourths to less than two-thirds of the voting-age population.

Currently, the number of people who think of themselves as Independents almost equals the number of people who identify with the nation's dominant party. Thirty-seven percent of Americans call themselves Democrats, 27 percent say they are Republicans, and 34 percent state they are Independents.[64] Not only are Independents gaining strength at the expense of both parties (in

Table 4-12 Party Identification by Decade, 1952–1984

	1950s	*1960s*	*1970s*	*1980s*
Partisans	74%	73%	63%	64%
Independents	23	24	36	34
Apoliticals	3	2	1	2

Percentages have been rounded.

Source: As derived from Martin P. Wattenberg, "The Hollow Realignment: Partisan Change in a Candidate-Centered Era," Paper presented at the 1985 Annual Meeting of the American Political Science Association, August 29–September 1, 1985, New Orleans, Table 1.

the 1950s and 1960s, less than a fourth were Independents), but younger voters are the most likely to identify with Independents.[65] Hence, it is likely that partisanship will continue its steady decline well into the future.

These national trends, indicating a declining partisan identification, seem, however, to be less intensive at the state levels. In gubernatorial races, for example, survey data indicate that voters who are partisans are still influenced by their party loyalty in voting for governors. On the other hand, the smaller share of those who vote in gubernatorial elections is now made up of partisan voters. In those states, notably in the South where one party has dominated but is being increasingly challenged by the opposition, it appears that party loyalties are weakening the most rapidly.[66]

Related to the variable of voters' identification with parties are trends concerning how many voters bolt their declared party of choice in the voting booth and vote for the competition. Party "defection rates" among voters have increased, at least in the national elections, since 1950. Defection rates among Democrats who strongly identified with their party soared from about 4 percent in the 1950s to almost 18 percent in the 1970s. Among the Republicans, we find considerably higher levels of loyalty, and among Republicans who identify strongly with the GOP, defection rates have never exceeded 4 percent, on the average, during the last three decades.[67]

Split-ticket voting, or elections in which a voter votes for selected candidates in both parties, is yet another measure of the ability of parties to attract and retain loyalists, and ticket splitting is clearly on the rise. Figure 4-5 indicates this increase. Note particularly the increase in split-ticket voting for local offices, a practice that increased from about 35 percent of the voters in 1952 to almost 60 percent of them in 1980. Indeed, split-ticket voting at the local level exceeds that of any other type of election. Figure 4-5 indicates reasonably conclusively that a shift in party loyalty is occurring over time in subnational elections.

These trends, that is, the decline of party identification by the electorate and the rise of the Independent voter over the past 30 years, seem to have been encouraged by a variety of developments that have been both internal to the parties and external to them. Among the internal developments are those reforms that have been initiated by the parties themselves and that have had the effect of reducing party discipline and undermining the parties' own rewards systems for faithful service.

One of these reforms is the adoption of the direct primary by the parties in all states. As the late V. O. Key noted several years ago, "the adoption of the direct primary opened the road for disruptive forces that gradually fractionalized the party organization."[68]

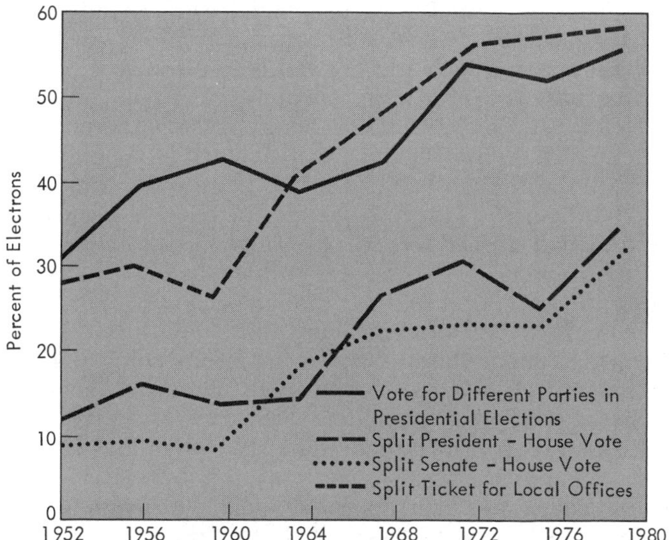

Figure 4-5
Trends in split-ticket voting, 1952–1980. (*Source:* Arthur H. Miller and Martin P. Wattenberg, "Policy and Performance Voting in the 1980 Election." Paper presented at the 1981 Annual Meeting of the American Political Science Association, New York, September 3-6, 1981.)

Key insightfully observed that the direct primary had eroded the control of the party pros over the party machinery. But even Key could not anticipate the rise of the "open primary," in which voters whose political sympathies actually are with the opposing party can take a hand in determining the party's candidates. It is difficult to conceive of a system more skillfully designed to undermine the expressed values of a political party than one in which members of the opposition choose its candidates for office.

A second set of internal reforms initiated by both parties involved the composition of the delegates to the quadrennial national conventions. The process began in 1968 for both parties. Among the Democrats, quotas were established by 1972 for the young, the minorities, and women. This meant that the delegates attending the national Democratic Convention had to equal, in percentage terms, the numbers of young people, minorities, and women in the national population.

Among the Republicans, the changes were less demographic in nature but far more regional in concept. The Republicans arranged that a much larger contingency of delegates from Western and Southern states would be represented at their national conventions, a change that assured that the "Eastern Establishment" (and relatively liberal) Republicans would be squeezed out of the party structure.

The effects of these reforms, particularly among the Democrats, were to toss out party loyalists who had given years of dedication to their parties and to replace them with delegates whose primary claim to distinction was their loyalty to particular candidates. For example, only 47 percent of the Democratic governors were delegates or alternates to their national party convention in 1976 compared to almost double that proportion in 1968.

Simultaneously, the number of delegates committed to a particular candidate and who viewed their primary loyalties as being to a candidate rather than to a party increased dramatically. In 1968, more than half of the delegates to both parties' conventions were unpledged to any candidate, but by 1980 only 3 percent of the Democratic delegates and fewer than half of the Republican delegates were uncommitted.[69]

These kinds of dynamics are reflected in the shifting attitudes of party members about their own parties. In 1972, approximately 70 percent of the Republican delegates to the National Convention saw themselves as representing the party as opposed to the candidate. By 1980, this had changed to roughly 30 percent. Among the Democrats, more than half of the delegates to the National Convention in 1972 perceived themselves as representing the party as opposed to the candidate. By 1980, this had slipped to approximately 45 percent.[70]

These reforms by the national parties appear to have had some detrimental effects on their state and local counterparts, although we do not know the precise extent of those effects. However, it seems likely that when loyalty to a particular candidate is rewarded more than loyalty to an overarching party; when party loyalists and party pros with years of experience are actively booted out of the party structure in favor of political amateurs who have no particular loyalty to party principles beyond their favorite candidate; and when there is no particular hierarchy for advancing up the party to positions of power—then one must ask, What can devotion to a party gain the individual? Who is going to pound the pavement in those 178,000 precincts come election time?

Another major influence that has undermined the parties stems less from internal reforms and more from changes in the parties' outside environments. One of these changes is the rise of the welfare state. More than one in every three American households receives some sort of welfare from the federal government.[71] The rise of welfare throughout the nation has rendered the parties increasingly anachronistic as providers of subsidies to party loyalists. No longer is a family dependent upon the party for a Thanksgiving turkey, complements of the local ward heeler, or the many other services once provided by the party.

Among those services, of course, was the ability to provide jobs (if often menial ones) for its voters. The federal government assumed the lead in displacing the parties in this area by its passage of the Civil Service Act of 1883, which ultimately expanded from its original scope of only 10 percent of all federal employees to more than 90 percent. The rise of merit-based public personnel systems in the federal government substantially undercut the traditional role of the parties in providing government jobs to their workers and voters. In 1939, Congress also enacted the Political Activities Act, which effectively prohibited federal employees from taking an active role in campaigns.

More important for the state and local parties, however, was that Washington aggressively pushed the parties out of their traditional role as the government's chief personnel agencies in states and communities. When Congress passed the Social Security Act of 1940, it inserted a proviso that effectively ordered states to adopt merit-based public personnel systems if they wished to receive federal funding for welfare, health, and a variety of other grant programs that were tied to the adoption of merit systems in the states. As a result, Washington, D.C., and 33 states now have statewide merit, and another 17 states have partial merit systems. All cities of more than 250,000 people have some sort of provision for a professional civil service.[72] Additionally, state and local governments have imitated the federal government by enacting their own versions of the Political Activities Act of 1939, to prohibit political activity by state and local employees.

Finally, state and local governments have depoliticized not only themselves, but their elections as well. The rise of the nonpartisan election, among local governments especially, has undercut the very idea of partisan politics. A nonpartisan election simply means that a candidate's party is not identified on the ballot (assuming, of course, that the candidate even belongs to a party, which he or she may not). The use of the nonpartisan election in the nation's cities has been increasing since 1930 and currently accounts for three quarters of all the municipal elections in the country.[73] Moreover, a variety of other local governments increasingly are moving toward it. About 85 percent of all school board members are elected in school districts that use nonpartisan ballots, and the available evidence indicates that a majority of elections in the nation's 28,588 other kinds of special districts also use it. A significant minority of counties are nonpartisan, including all the California and Wisconsin counties.[74] Even state governments are moving slowly to the adoption of the nonpartisan ballot. Seventeen of the 33 states that elect statewide judges use nonpartisan elections;[75] one state (Louisiana) has adopted nonpartisan primary elections, Nebraska has a nonpartisan ballot for all legislative races, and Minnesota had a nonpartisan legislature until 1972.

Political scientists argue that the nonpartisan ballot increases the clout of the Republican Party, and they point to the suburbs as their example in supporting this contention. Suburban voters not only favor the nonpartisan ballot, but they have tended to vote Republican more heavily than Democratic. But the blade cuts two ways. In partisan elections, the Democrats have the edge: "Nonpartisan elections more often than not facilitate the elections of Republicans in cities which usually vote Democratic in partisan races."[76] Why this is so is unclear, although some have argued that Republicans are more adept in working behind the scenes through various "good government" committees that have no overt party affiliation.

Unless a candidate is identified by party, it is very difficult to know what the candidate stands for as a political figure. This has been the principal utility of parties in the past—that is, identifying the values and principles of the candidate—and one that is denied them in the nonpartisan election, a form of ballot that is now the norm in American local governments. Because of these factors, "State and local party organizations in the near future are not likely to wither away, but they are likely to be less disciplined, more fluid in membership, and less capable of influencing the decisions of voters than used to be the case a few years ago. They will often become empty shells, filled from time to time by the supporters of particular state or national candidates."[77]

NOTES

[1]William N. Chambers, "Party Development and the American Mainstream," in William N. Chambers and Walter Dean Burnham, eds., *The American Party Systems,* 2nd ed. (New York: Oxford University Press, 1975), p. 4.
[2]*Ibid.,* p. 23.
[3]*Ibid.,* p. 15.
[4]*Ibid.,* p. 4.
[5]Herbert Agar, *The Price of Union* (Boston: Houghton Mifflin, 1950), pp. 689-690. The new penchant for ideology in both major political parties has been noted, for example, in Warren J. Mitofsky and Martin Plissner, "The Making of the Delegates, 1968-1980," *Public Opinion* (October/November, 1980), pp. 42-43; and Barbara G. Farah, "Convention Delegates: Party Reform and the Representativeness of Party Elites, 1972-1980," paper presented at the Annual Meeting of the American Political Science Association, New York,

September 3-6, 1981, p. 17. Despite such trends, American political parties are notably practical when compared to their Western European and Japanese counterparts.

[6]The following discussion is drawn from Malcom E. Jewell and David M. Olson, *American State Political Parties and Elections,* rev. ed. (Homewood, Ill.: Dorsey, 1982), pp. 57-73.

[7]David Davis, as cited in Robert J. Huckshorn, *Party Leadership in the States* (Amherst: University of Massachusetts Press, 1976), pp. 14-15.

[8]National Municipal League, *State Party Structures and Procedures: A State-by-State Compendium* (New York: National Municipal League, 1967).

[9]V. O. Key, Jr., *Southern Politics in State and Nation* (New York: Alfred A. Knopf, 1949), pp. 395-396.

[10]Ruth K. Scott and Ronald J. Hrebenar, *Parties in Crisis: Party Politics in America* (New York: John Wiley, 1979), p. 94.

[11]See, for example, Frank J. Sorauf, "Extra-Legal Parties in Wisconsin," *American Political Science Review,* 48 (September, 1954), pp. 692-704; Hugh A. Bone, "New Party Associations in the West," *American Political Science Review,* 45 (December, 1951), pp. 1115-1120; and James Q. Wilson, *The American Democrats* (Chicago: University of Chicago Press, 1962).

[12]Andrew D. McNitt, "Gubernatorial and Senatorial Nominations: An Empirical Analysis of the Influence of Party Organizations," paper presented at the Annual Meeting of the Southern Political Science Association, 1976, Table 17A, as cited in Jewell and Olson, *American State Political Parties,* p. 77.

[13]Timothy Conlan, Ann Martino, and Robert Dilger, "State Parties in the 1980s: Adaptation, Resurgence, and Continuing Constraints," *Intergovernmental Perspective,* 10 (Fall, 1984), p. 7; and John F. Bibby et al., "Parties in State Politics," in Virginia Gray, Herbert Jacob, and Kenneth N. Vines, eds., *Politics in the American States: A Comparative Analysis,* 4th ed. (Boston: Little, Brown, 1983), p. 76. The study by Conlan, Martino, and Dilger is a survey of all state party chairs conducted in 1984.

[14]John Fenton, *Midwest Politics* (New York: Holt, Rinehart and Winston, 1966), p. 116.

[15]*Ibid.*

[16]Lewis Bowman and Robert Boynton, "Activities and Role Definitions of Grass Roots Party Officials," *Journal of Politics,* 28 (February, 1966), pp. 121-143.

[17]Huckshorn, *Party Leadership,* p. 100. An earlier study of party chairs came up with similar results, although administration of the state party apparatus and promotion of the party's image ranked first in this survey of party chairs; however, campaign management and fund raising were considered important as well. See Charles W. Wiggins and William L. Turk, "State Party Chairmen: A Profile," *Western Political Quarterly,* 23 (June, 1970), pp. 321-333.

[18]Huckshorn, *Party Leadership,* pp. 103-105.

[19]*Ibid.,* pp. 254-257.

[20]*Ibid.,* Chapter 4.

[21]Conlan, Martino, and Dilger, "State Parties in the 1980s," p. 8.

[22]Jewell and Olson, *American State Political Parties,* p. 78.

[23]Charles Francis Adams, ed., *The Works of John Adams,* Vol. 2 (Boston: Little, Brown, 1850), p. 144. Citation from diary entry of February, 1763.

[24]Daniel R. Grant and H. C. Nixon, *State and Local Government in America* (Boston: Allyn & Bacon, 1975), p. 172.

[25]McNitt, "Gubernatorial and Senatorial Nominations," as cited in Jewell and Olson, *American State Political Parties,* p. 77.

[26]Jewell and Olson, *American State Political Parties,* pp. 105-120.

[27]Bureau of the Census, *1977 Census of Governments,* Vol. 1, *Popularly Elected Officials,* No. 2, *Governmental Organization* (Washington, D.C.: U.S. Government Printing Office, 1978), p. 1.

[28]This figure applies to both parties in Connecticut, Pennsylvania, New Jersey, and Minnesota and to the Republicans in Washington State. See Heinz Eulau et al., "Career Perspectives of American State Legislators," in Dwaine Marvick, ed., *Political Decision-Makers* (Glencoe, Ill.: Free Press, 1961), p. 226; and Richard J. Tobin and Edward Keynes, "Institutional Differences in the Recruitment Process: A Four-State Study," *American Journal of Political Science,* 19 (November, 1974), p. 674.

[29]David M. Olson, "U.S. Congressmen and Their Diverse Congressional District Parties," *Legislative Studies Quarterly,* 3 (May, 1978), p. 250.

[30]Nelson C. Dometrius, "State Government Administration and the Electoral Process," *State Government,* 53 (Summer, 1980), pp. 132-133.

[31]John C. Blydenburgh, "A Controlled Experiment to Measure the Effects of Personal Contact Campaigning," *Midwest Journal of Political Science,* 15 (1971), pp. 365-381.
[32]Jewell and Olson, *American State Political Parties,* p. 170.
[33]The following data are for the late 1970s and are drawn from Bibby et al., "Parties in State Politics," pp. 79-81.
[34]Totton J. Anderson, "The 1958 Election in California," *Western Political Quarterly,* 12 (March, 1959), pp. 276-300.
[35]Kevin P. Phillips, "Campaign Funding Arms Are Gaining Muscle," *The Arizona Republic* (July 20, 1979). The figures are for the 1978 election.
[36]Herbert E. Alexander, *Financing Politics: Money, Elections, and Political Reform,* 2nd ed. (Washington, D.C.: Congressional Quarterly Press, 1980), pp. 120-123.
[37]Jewell and Olson, *American State Political Parties,* p. 184.
[38]Congressional Quarterly, *Elections '80* (Washington, D.C.: Congressional Quarterly Press, 1980), pp. 129-132.
[39]U.S. Bureau of the Census, *Statistical Abstract of the United States, 1985* (Washington, D.C.: U.S. Government Printing Office, 1984), p. 257, Table 431.
[40]James Gibson et al., "Assessing Institutional Party Strength," paper presented during the Annual Meeting of the Midwest Political Science Association, Cincinnati, Ohio, April, 1981.
[41]Jewell and Olson, *American State Political Parties,* p. 187.
[42]Conlan, Martino, and Dilger, "State Parties in the 1980s," p. 8. The gamma correlation for Democratic gubernatorial candidates was 0.46 and for state legislative candidates it was 0.75.
[43]Larry Sabato, "Gubernatorial Politics and the New Campaign Technology," *State Government,* 53 (Summer, 1980), p. 150.
[44]Jewell and Olson, *American State Political Parties,* p. 182.
[45]Samuel C. Patterson, "Campaign Spending and Contests for Governor," unpublished paper cited in *ibid.,* p. 192.
[46]*Ibid.,* pp. 192-193.
[47]Alexander, *Financing Politics,* pp. 137-140.
[48]Ruth S. Jones, "State Public Financing in the State Parties, in Michael J. Malbin, ed., *Parties, Interest Groups, and Campaign Finance Laws* (Washington, D.C.: American Enterprise Institute, 1980), p. 303.
[49]Richard G. Smolka, "Election Legislation," *Book of the States, 1980-81* (Iron Works Pike, Ky.: Council of State Governments, 1980), pp. 52-75.
[50]V. O. Key, Jr., *American State Politics: An Introduction* (New York: Alfred A. Knopf, 1956), p. 201.
[51]Thomas R. Dye, *Politics, Economics and the Public: Policy Outcomes in the American States* (Chicago: Rand McNally, 1966).
[52]Ira Sharkansky and Richard I. Hofferbert, "Dimensions of State Politics, Economics, and Public Policy," *American Political Science Review,* 63 (September, 1969), pp. 867-879.
[53]Gerald C. Wright, Jr., "Interparty Competition and State Welfare Policy: When a Difference Makes a Difference," *Journal of Politics,* 37 (February/May, 1975), p. 803.
[54]See, for example, Seymour Martin Lipset, *Political Man* (Garden City, N.Y.: Doubleday, 1960), Chap. 2, for a lucid expression of the argument that partisan competitiveness leads to broader democratization. Unfortunately, however, the data do not consistently support this contention. See, for example, Charles M. Bonjean and Robert L. Lineberry, "The Urbanization-Party Competition Hypothesis: A Comparison of All United States Counties," *Journal of Politics,* 32 (May, 1970), pp. 305-321.
[55]Jewell and Olson, *American State Political Parties,* p. 43.
[56]William Brock as quoted in Timothy B. Clark, "The RNC Prospers, The DNC Struggles as They Face the 1980 Elections," *National Journal* (September 27, 1980), p. 1617.
[57]Samuel Kaplan, *The Dream Deferred* (New York: Seabury, 1976), p. 140.
[58]*Ibid.,* pp. 144-145.
[59]Robert C. Wood, *Suburbia: Its People and Their Politics* (Boston: Houghton Mifflin, 1959).
[60]Helmut Norpoth, "Changes in Party Identification: Evidence of a Republican Majority?" paper presented at the 1985 Annual Meeting of the World Association for Public Opinion Research, September 1-5, 1985, Wiesbaden, West Germany, Table 3.
[61]Clark, "The RNC Prospers," pp. 1618-1619; Congressional Quarterly, *Dollar Politics* (Washington, D.C.: Congressional Quarterly Press, 1982), p. 71; and Nick Thimmesch, "Brock Claims GOP Is Strong," *The Arizona Republic* (September 10, 1980).

[62]*The New York Times,* citing the Federal Election Commission figures as reprinted in "The GOP Outspent Democrats 5 to 1 in 79-80," *The Arizona Republic* (February 21, 1982); and Congressional Quarterly, *Dollar Politics,* p. 71.

[63]Lou Harris, quoted in Associated Press, "Presidential Choices Disgust Voters, Pollster Harris Says," *The Arizona Republic* (October 21, 1980); and Patrick Caddell, as quoted in Kevin Phillips, "Polls: Few Americans Think Democrats Can Do Better," *The Arizona Republic* (April 18, 1982).

[64]Martin P. Wattenberg, "The Hollow Realignment: Partisan Change in a Candidate Centered Era," paper presented at the 1985 Annual Meeting of the American Political Science Association, August 21 - September 1, 1985, New Orleans, Table 1. Figures are for 1984.

[65]Everett Carll Ladd, "As the Realignment Turns: A Drama in Many Acts," *Public Opinion* (December/January 1985), p. 6.

[66]Andrew Cowart, "Electoral Choice in the American States," *American Political Science Review,* 67 (September 1973) pp. 835-853; Paul T. David, *Party Strength in the United States, 1872-1970* (Charlottesville: University Press of Virginia, 1972); and Jewell and Olson, *American State Political Parties,* pp. 205-209.

[67]Center for Political Studies as reported in Arthur H. Miller and Warren E. Miller, "Partisanship and Performance: 'Rational' Choice in the 1976 Presidential Election," Washington, D.C., Annual Meeting of the American Political Science Association, September 1-4, 1977, p. 12.

[68]V. O. Key, Jr., *Politics, Parties, and Pressure Groups* (New York: Thomas Y. Crowell, 1964), p. 352.

[69]Mitofsky and Plissner, "The Making of the Delegates," pp. 42-43.

[70]Farah, "Convention Delegates," p. 17. Farah distinguishes between delegates selected by the primary route and delegates selected by caucuses, so overall percentages are approximations. Among the Democrats, according to Farah, 19 percent of those delegates selected to the 1972 National Convention by the primary route saw themselves as representing the party, and 36 percent selected by caucus perceive themselves as representing the party. By 1980, those selected by primary had risen slightly to 22 percent, while those selected by caucus had fallen to 26 percent. Among the Republicans, the figures are more dramatic. Sixty-five percent of those delegates selected by the primary and 77 percent of those selected by caucus saw themselves as representing the party as opposed to the candidate. But by 1980, 26 percent of those delegates selected by the primary and 31 percent of those selected by caucus saw themselves as representing the party as opposed to the candidate.

Among the ironies for the Democrats is that even though proportions of those delegates who thought that they represented the candidate as opposed to the party has actually declined somewhat, Democratic candidates were far more bound during these years to the candidates whom they represented than were the Republicans. From 1974 through 1981, the Democrats enforced a rule that gave the presidential candidates a *personal* veto over which delegates could represent them to the convention. This rule resulted in delegates who were astoundingly loyal to their candidates.

[71]U.S. Bureau of the Census as cited in United Press International, "Federal Aid Went to One in Three Families," *The Arizona Republic* (March 14, 1981). The Census Bureau study was the first of its type and covered only food stamps, subsidized school lunches, subsidized housing, Medicare, and Medicaid. It did not cover such additional welfare programs as Aid to Families with Dependent Children, Social Security, unemployment insurance, and Supplemental Security Income, although virtually every household that received the benefits studied would be very likely to also receive one or more of the programs that were not studied. Out of the 79.1 million households in 1980, 27.2 million received some sort of federal assistance.

[72]O. Glenn Stahl, *Public Personnel Administration,* 8th ed. (New York: Harper & Row, 1983), pp. 42-43.

[73]Heywood T. Sanders, "Governmental Structure of American Cities," *Municipal Year Book, 1979* (Washington, D.C.: International Cities Management Association, 1979), p. 97.

[74]Willis D. Hawley, *Nonpartisan Elections and the Case for Party Politics* (New York: John Wiley, 1973), p. 17.

[75]Derived from *Book of the States, 1980-81* (Lexington, Ky.: Council of State Governments, 1980), table on pp. 156-157.

[76]Hawley, *Nonpartisan Elections,* pp. 165-166.

[77]Jewell and Olson, *American State Political Parties,* p. 281.

5

THE LEGISLATIVE LABYRINTH

Perhaps more than any other political institution, state legislatures are the object of Americans' love and hate. On the love side, we can visualize an image of concerned citizens working for the good of their people, grappling with problems that perhaps they are ill-equipped to understand, given the complexity of twentieth-century America, but nonetheless trying to do the right thing under difficult circumstances.

On the hate side, quotable observations are more plentiful. For example, John Gardner has stated of legislatures, "Most of them are riddled with conflict of interest, riddled with corruption and are wholly inadequate instruments of self-government. The conflict of interest in the state legislatures is the worst evil they have. There are men making laws who most of the time are in the employ of the interest they are making the laws about."[1]

THE LEGISLATIVE CONSTRUCTION

A less vitriolic (and likely more accurate) assessment of state legislatures has been offered by Herbert Jacob: "State legislatures may be our most extreme example of institutional lag."[2] And, indeed, when one recalls an evaluation of our state legislatures written nearly a century ago, Jacob's remark rings with discomfiting truth:

> There is in State Legislators . . . a restlessness which, coupled with their limited range of knowledge and undue appreciation of material interests makes them rather dangerous. Meeting for only a few weeks in the year . . . they are alarm-

ingly active . . . and run measures whose results are not apprehended until months afterwards . . . the meeting of the legislature is looked forward to with anxiety . . . and its departure is hailed as a deliverance.[3]

Outwardly, at least, state legislatures are relatively simple structures, although they grow more complex. All state legislatures have a bicameral, or a two-house, structure made up of the house and the senate. The exception, of course, is Nebraska, which became a one-house, or unicameral, legislature in 1934.

The arguments for and against unicameralism, as opposed to bicameralism, can be quickly stated. Those in favor of bicameral legislatures argue that they serve as checks on each other, bringing together the relative intellectual sophistication of the senate with the popular preferences represented by the house. The melding of the two value systems produces legislation that is in the best possible public interest. Those who argue for the unicameral system claim that it is relatively inexpensive and that it furnishes more responsible government because it discourages buck-passing between the two houses and delay in the policymaking process.

Size is an important consideration. Nebraska's unicameral legislature has varied, roughly, from 30 to 50 members. Normally, however, the upper house, or senate, in most states oscillates between 20 members, as in Alaska and Nevada, and 67 members, as in Minnesota. The lower house can range from 40 members, as in Alaska and Nevada, to the enormous New Hampshire House of Representatives with its 400 members. The average size of the lower house in the states is about 100 members; the average size of the senate, 38 members. State senators serve four-year terms in all but a dozen states while members of the houses of representatives serve two-year terms in all states except Alabama, Louisiana, Maryland, and Mississippi; in those states the terms of representatives are four years.

Each house of a state legislature is comprised of numerous functional committees, most notably, finance, taxation, education, judiciary, and rules committees. The lower house elects a speaker to preside over its session; the lieutenant governor presides over the senate in 29 of the 36 states that have the office. The 14 states that do not have a lieutenant governor elect a president *pro tempore* to preside over the senate. In states with a lieutenant governor, the president *pro tempore* presides in the absence of the lieutenant governor.

Traditionally, state legislatures met only every two years, or biennially. The national trend, however, has been toward yearly sessions. Forty-four states have annual sessions (although only 36 states have formally endorsed the idea), up from 10 in 1951. More than half the states limit sessions to 75 days or less.

What Do Legislatures Do?

What do legislatures do? While they act as a constitutional check to the judiciary and executive branches, conduct impeachments, and investigate public issues, their chief duty is to make laws. Each state legislature processes on the average more than 4,000 bills and resolutions; the average state enacts more than 1,000. The larger states were shouldered with huge work loads. In New

York, for example, almost 35,000 bills and resolutions were introduced during the 1975-1976 biennial session, and more than 2,500 were enacted. In the early 1950s all the nation's legislatures combined considered only about 25,000 bills a year; by the mid-1970s the figure had grown in excess of 150,000. During that same 20-year period, the total number of bills and resolutions enacted burgeoned from roughly 15,000 per year in the 1950s to more than 50,000 in the 1970s. Table 5-1 summarizes the typical state legislative procedure and what is involved in getting each bill passed. Of course, a bill may be defeated at any point along the way.

Table 5-1 Getting a Bill Through the State Legislature

1. Introduction of bill	One or more members file bill with clerk or presiding officer who gives it a number and refers it to a committee. This is the first reading.
2. Committee hearings	Important bills may be given public hearings at which all interested persons or groups may testify.
3. Committee report	Committee meets in executive (closed) session. Bills may be amended or pigeonholed or reported favorably or unfavorably.
4. Bill placed on calendar	Bills reported by committee are placed on calendar for floor consideration. Urgent or favorite bills may get priority by unanimous consent or informal maneuvering; other bills may be delayed, sometimes indefinitely.
5. Floor debate, amendment, vote	The second reading of the bill before the entire chamber is usually accompanied by debate and perhaps amendments from the floor. Often the crucial vote is on an amendment or on second reading.
6. Third reading and passage	Usually a bill is delayed one day before it is brought to the floor for third reading. On third reading debate is not customary, and amendments usually require unanimous consent. After final vote, bill is certified by presiding officer and sent to second house.
7. Referral to second chamber	Bill is sent to second chamber where steps 1 through 6 must be repeated. Bills must pass both chambers in identical form before going to governor.
8. Conference committee	If there are differences in wording in the bills passed by each house, one or the other house must accept the wording of the other house or request a conference committee. This committee is made up of members of both houses, and it arrives at a single wording for the bill.
9. Vote on conference committee report	Both houses must vote to approve conference committee wording of bill. Bills may be shuttled back and forth and eventually die for lack of agreement between both houses.
10. Governor's signature or veto	An identical bill passed by both houses becomes law with the governor's signature. It may also became law without his signature after a certain lapse of time (e.g., ten days) if the legislature is still in session. If the legislature has adjourned during his time, the governor's failure to sign is the same as a veto. A governor may formally veto a bill and return it to the house of origin for reconsideration. An unusual majority is generally required to override a veto.

Government by Committee

The concept of the committee is significant not only to the organization of the legislature, but to the enactment of legislation in the states as well. "The committee hearing is generally the most important source of information, for legislators and lobbyists tend to flock to the committee rooms as the focal point of their contact with legislators."[4]

The committee system is simply a division of labor into certain functional areas that the legislature must consider. The more important areas—appropriations, welfare, education, and labor—generally are consigned to *standing committees,* which are permanent committees of the legislature. *Special* or *select committees* are appointed to investigate passing problems that may or may not surface again—civil disorders, political scandals, and so on. There are also *interim committees,* which conduct studies between sessions of the legislature, and, of course, there are *joint conference committees,* composed of members from both houses and designated to reconcile differences between each house over particular pieces of legislation. Connecticut, Maine, and Massachusetts are among the states that make the most use of the joint committee device as a means of minimizing deadlocks between the two chambers.

The typical legislature has between 20 and 30 standing committees, and the trend has been to reduce the number of such committees in the legislature; the number of committees in state legislatures has been reduced by fewer than half the number that existed in 1931. Today, the average state house of representatives has fewer than 20 committees; the average senate has more than 15.[5]

An important but difficult-to-answer question is, How influential are committees in the legislative process? Some argue that state legislative committees actually have relatively little influence on legislation, particularly in comparison with committees in the United States Congress, because

1. Most legislatures meet relatively infrequently, thereby giving committees relatively scant time for meaningful review of bills.
2. State legislative committees seldom have adequate staff assistance.
3. Legislatures lack a prevalent seniority system comparable to that of Congress.
4. There are high levels of legislative turnover.[6]

Perhaps this final point is the most telling. A study conducted of committee service by legislators in 12 state legislatures, for example, showed that, in not a single one of these legislatures did more than half of the legislators who served on a particular committee in one session serve on the same committee in any subsequent session.[7] Another study of the lower chambers in all the states found that more than three quarters of the memberships of standing legislative committees turned over during a four-year cycle. While the major committees evidenced slightly more stability than the minor ones, the difference was marginal. Even more significantly, nearly 77 percent of the committee chairs changed hands, on the average, during the four-year period, even in legislatures that did not experience a change in party control! The researcher concluded that "the massive instability of state legislative committees seems to preclude them from becoming as effective as their national counterparts."[8]

If the studies on state legislatures agree on anything, it is that committees have less influence, as committees, over legislation in two-party states where there is a high degree of party discipline, and in two-party states where the governor and the legislative majority are of the same party. Committees, by contrast, are more likely to be influential in one-party states where the governor is not a particularly strong leader, where he or she has little legal authority, or where the government is divided along some other line, such as ideology or class.[9] One examination of state legislative committees in three states found that, of several hypotheses tested, the only conclusion that one could reasonably draw was that those committees that were "better performing and more central to decision making" also were those committees that were in agreement with the speaker on the issues, and when the speaker was relatively powerful.[10] Thus, the study implied that the leadership of the legislature, rather than the standing committees or their chairs, is the more powerful figure in enacting legislation in the states.

Although it has been a tradition in state legislatures that committees have less influence than do their counterparts in Congress, their power may be strengthening over time, and most of the reasons commonly cited for the relative weakness of state legislative committees pertain less and less as we enter the 1990s. For example, legislatures now convene increasingly frequently, thereby giving committees more time to consider legislation.

Professional staffing of standing committees and related legislative service units, which was virtually nil in 1960, is now the norm in virtually every state. Not a single state hired professional staff for its standing committees in both houses in 1960, but by 1980, 36 states had professional staffing for their standing committees.[11] Professional staffers always are able to strengthen a committee and improve its power position in any legislative system. As one study of Congress, for example, noted, "Whether a subcommittee has its own staff is literally an index of how independent a subcommittee is."[12] Presumably the same generalization applies to state legislative committees as well.

Finally, legislative turnover in the states is nothing what it once was, and this may add to the stability and continuity of the legislative committees. As we discuss later in this chapter, by the 1980s legislative turnover had decreased by about one-third from its levels in the 1950s.[13]

Committees, in sum, are important to the workings of any legislative body. Although their development has been hindered in the states—just as, to some degree, the development of the legislatures themselves has been hampered—by irregular sessions, a lack of staff support, and high rates of membership turnover, some of these conditions seem on the wane, and the legislative committee systems may grow healthier for it.

ELECTORAL SYSTEMS, REAPPORTIONMENT, AND GERRYMANDERING

It is a truism that the kinds of people who become legislators are put there more often than not by the kinds of people whom they nominally represent. How legislators get to represent particular kinds of people depends on the electoral system used in any particular state.

Electoral Formulas: Those Who Have, Get

Most American states use an electoral formula known as the plurality vote, which is associated with the single member district system. Under this formula, each electoral district in a state may elect one representative to the legislature by plurality (in contrast to majority) vote. The arrangement is called the *single-member district, plurality vote system.* As Table 5-2 shows, this system is by far the most popular one among state legislatures. More than four-fifths of the electoral districts and two-thirds of the representatives in the lower chambers and almost 95 percent of the senate districts and 86 percent of the state senators are elected in single-member districts.

Twenty lower chambers (down from 32 in 1969) and a dozen upper chambers (down from two dozen in 1969) use a *multimember district system.*[14] The multimember district, also known as the "at-large" system because candidates are competing with each other at large in a single electoral district, works against the success of candidates from minority parties. The party that accumulates the largest slice of a multimember district's votes will garner an even larger proportion of a district's legislative seats, while parties with relatively smaller percentages of the vote tend to acquire even fewer seats. This condition is known as the "Matthew effect," named after the passage in Matthew 13:12 that says, "To him who has will more be given, and he will have abundance; but from him who has not, even what he has will be taken away." When partisan gerrymandering is combined with the plurality vote formula, the Matthew effect is even more emphatic. Hence a party that may win between 55 to 60 percent of the popular votes in a state will in reality win between 65 to 70 percent of the legislative seats. On the other hand, the party that may win only 40 to 45 percent of that statewide vote will be allocated only 35 percent or less of the seats available in the legislature.[15]

Just as the multimember district works against the electoral success of minority parties, it also works against the representation of minority people. A spokesperson for the National Association for the Advancement of Colored People has stated that "multimember districts are the greatest retardant in black representation in state legislatures."[16]

Because of these antiminority biases brought about by the use of at-large districts, the judiciary has cautiously (and somewhat ambivalently) begun to question their continuance. In 1965, the U.S. Supreme Court addressed the

Table 5-2 Single-member and Multimember State Legislative Districts, 1979

	HOUSES		SENATES	
Type of Districts	*Number*	*Percent*[1]	*Number*	*Percent*[1]
Single-member districts				
Districts	3,567	83%	1.718	95%
Representatives	3,567	65	1,718	87
Multimember districts				
Districts	714	17	100	6
Representatives	1,934	35	263	13

[1] Percentages have been rounded.

Source: Derived from *The Book of the States, 1980–1981* (Lexington, Ky.: Council of State Governments), pp. 86–87.

issue of multimember districts by declining to state flatly that their use was unconstitutional, but nonetheless placed the nation on notice that at-large districts would be challenged if they operated "to minimize or cancel out the voting strength of racial and political elements of the voting population."[17] In 1970 the Court ruled that the creation of a multimember district in Indianapolis did not discriminate against blacks,[18] but in 1973 it upheld the lower court by stating that certain multimember districts used by the Texas house of representatives had, in fact, discriminated against particular racial and ethnic groups.[19]

In tilting against at-large districts, the courts have accepted the notion that they bias legislative representation against minorities (whether partisan or ethnic) and have rejected the contention that multimember districts are beneficial because they discourage "ward politics," "machines," and "political parochialism." It is clear that the courts have been helpful in promoting the gradual, grassroots movement away from the at-large election and its attendant, inequitable Matthew effect.

Reapportionment: Redistricting for "People, Not Trees"

The Matthew effect was considerably worse before the courts became involved in reapportioning legislative districts in the states. Because a number of state legislatures simply refused to reapportion on the basis of national censuses, rural interests dominated urban interests in many states. In Maryland, for example, a state senator from a rural county in 1961 represented 15,481 citizens, whereas a senator from urban Baltimore County represented 492,428 people. Although almost 80 percent of Maryland's population in 1960 lived in four counties, they elected only a third of the members of the Maryland senate. But Maryland was only one example among many. In fact, as of 1960 only five states were *not* heavily malapportioned.[20] Those legislators who were in power before court-ordered reapportionment began were determined to keep things as they were.[21] And such determination could last a very long time. Vermont had not reapportioned its legislature since 1793. Connecticut had not done so since 1818. Mississippi had refused to reapportion since 1890. Delaware's last reapportionment went back to 1897, and Alabama and Tennessee had not bothered to reapportion their legislatures since 1901. In the face of such stubbornness, only another branch of the government, such as the courts, could effectively change legislative malapportionment in the states.

This is precisely what happened in 1962 in the case of *Baker* v. *Carr*. This famous decision concerned the contention of urban residents in Tennessee that the largest district in the state's house of representatives was 23 times larger than the smallest district. They argued that such malapportionment denied them "equal protection of the law" as guaranteed by the Fourteenth Amendment of the Constitution. In response to this argument, the Supreme Court decided

1. That despite the fact that apportionment is a legislative concern, the federal courts can and should accept jurisdiction where a constitutional question is at issue.
2. That voters in underrepresented areas are entitled to judicial relief if apportionment laws have violated their constitutional rights.
3. That arbitrary state apportionment laws violate the Fourteenth Amendment's prohibition against laws that deny citizens equal protection.

Sanders in The Kansas City Star

"Great Scott! We've lost our vote!"

As a result of *Baker* v. *Carr,* citizens throughout the country started taking their legislatures to court, suing for reapportionment. The courts were responsive. In 1964, the case of *Westberry* v. *Sanders* was resolved: the presiding justice stated, "As nearly as practicable, one man's vote should be equal to another's." This was the one-person, one-vote principle.

Two years after *Baker* v. *Carr,* the Supreme Court decided a second major case known as *Reynolds* v. *Sims.* This case involved an attempt by Alabama to base representation in its upper house on counties. The Supreme Court decided that both houses of the state legislature had to be apportioned fairly and according to population. This was a second revolutionary decision, in that it went against the deep-running concept in mainstream American legislative thinking of bicameralism, which traditionally has one house based on political units (such as states or counties) rather than on population. It was in this decision that Chief Justice Earl Warren wrote,

> Legislators represent people, not trees or acres. . . . The complexions of societies and civilizations change, often with amazing rapidity. A nation once primarily rural in character becomes predominately urban. Representation schemes once fair and equitable became archaic and dated.

The impact of the Supreme Court's decisions was immediate and profound; by 1967, all states had been reapportioned, and only minor inequalities remained.

Redistricting continued throughout the 1970s, but the impact of the Court was made. In fact, by 1973 in the case of *Mahan* v. *Howell,* the Court evidently felt that a strict mathematical reapportionment mandated by the courts no longer was necessary, and it permitted the Virginia House of Delegates to reapportion on the basis of what it called a "rational approach" rather than requiring rigid mathematical formulas to be implemented. In any case, it is clear that state legislatures, purely because of the judiciary, now reflect a one-person, one-vote philosophy.

The States Adapt: Gerrymandering Under New Constraints

Within the bounds of the "one-person, one-vote" formula, the courts have established a series of other guidelines that governments must consider each time they reapportion their electoral districts. These guidelines can be reduced to the following and are presented in rough order of their importance:[22]

1. Redistricting must create districts that are as equal in population as is reasonably possible to achieve.
2. The integrity of county and city boundaries (and smaller divisions within those boundaries) must be retained as much as possible.
3. Districts must be as compact as possible.
4. Significant natural geographic barriers should not be crossed by district lines whenever possible.
5. Some unity of character or interest within districts should be retained; that is, "group interest," such as race or ethnicity, should not be artificially divided along politically expedient lines within a district.
6. The *status quo* of existing electoral districts should be retained when possible.

What these court-established guidelines represent is an effort to accommodate two political realities: parties and race.

Gerrymandering for Party

The judiciary has never addressed (beyond establishing the one-person, one-vote principle and promoting the idea that electoral districts should be compact) the problems of rigging political boundaries so that they accrue to the advantage of the party in power. This practice, called *gerrymandering,* is the creation of new electoral districts in such a way that a particular party gains an electoral edge that it likely would not otherwise have.

As a result of the courts' disinterest in addressing the partisan aspects of redistricting, states have addressed the issue in their own way. For example, three states do not even use the U.S. Census (as is their right to do) as a basis for redistricting. Kansas and Massachussetts use their own statewide censuses, while Hawaii redistricts according to registered voter lists.[23] Six states (Alaska, Delaware, North Dakota, South Dakota, Vermont, and Wyoming) do not have to bother redistricting for Congress since they elect only one congress member-at-large per state, although, of course, they must redistrict for their own legislatures.

Traditionally, state legislatures redraw their electoral districts after each decennial census, and the redistricting plan that the legislatures conceive are subject only to veto by the governor. Perhaps no other subject that state legislatures consider is more frankly partisan than redistricting, and legislative careers have been made or broken on the political boundaries that result from the political infighting that is forced by each census. One state legislator has noted, "I was a novice in the legislature and a novice at reapportionment—and it was probably one of the most traumatic things I ever went through."[24]

Perhaps as a consequence of this trauma, 15 states now have some sort of agency or advisory council concerned with redistricting. Another 11 states can create an agency to redistrict if the legislature fails to do so within a designated time.[25] Three of these states—Colorado, Hawaii, and Montana—have set up reapportionment commissions that are the most stringently antipartisan.

These commissions, which vary in clout and composition from state to state, represent an effort by some states to reduce some of the partisan intensity that usually accompanies any redistricting plan. These 26 states have moved in the direction of "plugging in" nonlegislative and nonpartisan elements into the redistricting process in part because the judiciary has been notably reluctant to enter the "political thicket" of partisan gerrymandering. Nevertheless, no state legislature has released its ultimate control of legislative redistricting.

Gerrymandering for Race

But if the courts have evaded the issue of partisan gerrymandering, they have dealt with the issue of racial gerrymandering somewhat more courageously. As early as 1960, the U.S. Supreme Court ruled in the case of *Gomillion* v. *Lightfoot* that the Alabama legislature could not redraw the city limits of Tuskegee so as to exclude virtually all black residents, and perhaps no other single decision by the Supreme Court opened the way for black representation in state legislatures more than this one. In 1973, the Court strengthened the idea that minorities' interests must be considered by deciding the important case of *Gaffney* v. *Cummings,* in which it addressed a Connecticut redistricting plan on the grounds of "political fairness," stating that districts may be equal in population, but were nonetheless vulnerable to complaints about denial of equal protection to individuals. In 1977, the Supreme Court heard the case of *United Jewish Organizations of Williamsburgh* v. *Carey*, which upheld a deliberate "racial gerrymander" in New York and effectively encouraged blacks and Puerto Ricans to move to districts where the majority of the voters belonged to the same race. This ruling went farther than the Court had gone in *Gomillion* because it was positive in tone: gerrymandering could be used to strengthen the electoral clout of minorities, but never to weaken it. With this decision, state and local policymakers entered an era of "affirmative gerrymandering."[26]

A more direct approach to the problem of racial gerrymandering has been initiated by Congress. In 1965, Congress passed the Voting Rights Act (discussed in Chapter 2), which requires that the nine states of Alabama, Alaska, Arizona, Georgia, Texas, Louisiana, Mississippi, South Carolina, and Virginia clear any reapportionment plans that they might develop either with the U.S. Department of Justice or the federal district court in the District of Columbia. The objective was to assure that the voting rights of minorities were fully considered in such reapportionment plans. In addition, 82 local governments in another 13 states also must submit their redistricting plans for review and clearance before implementation.

In sum, the national political system has confronted racial gerrymandering in part, and partisan gerrymandering barely at all. The federal government, largely through the Voting Rights Act of 1965, and less directly through a variety of Supreme Court decisions beginning in 1960, has tried to reduce gerrymandering by state and local governments on the basis of race. On the other hand, the national government has stayed largely away from interfering with the states' fondness for gerrymandering on the basis of political party. Instead, a number of state governments have shown themselves more concerned with this issue and have attempted to deal with it. It should be recognized, however, that redistricting is innately a political process and, while the worst abuses of partisan politics may be regulated in part, the nature of the redistricting process will never be metamorphosed into a nonpolitical, bloodless minuet.

The Results of Reapportionment

What has the wrench of reapportionment amounted to in real terms?[27] First and most obviously, the number of state legislators from urban and suburban areas has increased, while the number of legislators from rural areas has decreased. The states where this has happened dramatically include California, Florida, Georgia, and New York. Second, reapportionments probably have worked to the advantage of the Democratic Party in the North, and to the advantage of the Republican Party in the South. In this light, they seem to have stimulated party competition for seats in the legislature and more highly partisan voting behavior by legislators once they are in office. Partisanship seems to have increased most dramatically where malapportionment was the most serious. Finally, reapportionments may have contributed to the greater responsiveness of state legislatures. One reason for this is that in some states (notably, California, Florida, and New York), the turnover of membership in the legislature that has been induced by reapportionment seems to have produced a higher proportion of younger, better educated representatives and, in the South, a marked increase in the representation of minorities, particularly blacks.

What effects, if any, has reapportionment had on the public policies emanating from the state legislatures? There are a number of views on this issue. The most common opinion is that the urban interests have pushed aside the rural interests in the state assemblies and, as a result, the nation is getting more education- and welfare-oriented policies. This conventional wisdom, however, has been challenged by such scholars as Thomas Dye, Richard I. Hofferbert, and Malcolm Jewell.

Dye contends that the malapportionment-reapportionment variable has very little to do with the kinds of policies emanating from state legislatures, and that the causal variable is in fact the state's economic status. Dye addressed the major issues of education, health and welfare, highways, taxation, and what he called the "regulation of public morality." Of these, only education policy seemed to bear any kind of a relationship with reapportionment; after reapportionment, expenditures for educational programs in the states often went up.[28]

On the other hand Hofferbert's study, conducted at about the same time, concluded that a state's predisposition toward welfare programs is less a result of reapportionment and more of a reflection of the level of financial support for various educational and welfare programs and the level of direct state aid to the two largest cities in the state. Hofferbert, in fact, found no relationship whatever between policy and reapportionment.[29]

By contrast, Jewell and others argue that reapportionment does indeed make a difference in the kinds of policies adopted by a state legislature. To quote Jewell, "The effects of malapportionment on policy outputs can be best evaluated not by measuring differences among states with different degrees of malapportionment, but by studying the response of state legislatures as a whole to the challenges of the metropolis."[30]

More recent studies confirm this view. A careful examination of the legislative distribution of state welfare benefits to counties in New Jersey, New York, Oregon, and Wisconsin found that "significant malapportionment relates directly to aid distributions and that reapportionment relates directly to change in aid distribution."[31] After reapportionment, the more urbanized counties received considerably more state benefits than they had before.

But besides spending patterns among regions in the states, issues alter, too, with reapportionment. Table 5-3 lists and ranks the major policy issues identified as important by state legislators in 1963 and 1973. As it indicates, times change. In 1963, just before massive, court-ordered reapportionments were about to occur and legislatures were still dominated by rural interests, public policies on taxation, apportionment (not surprisingly), labor, highways, local government, gambling, liquor, and agriculture were considered to be more important issues by legislators than they were a decade later.[32] By contrast, in 1973, well after legislatures had been rescued from the grasp of rural interests, legislators regarded such issues as finance, administration, business, elections, land, and crime as more significant than did their colleagues of a decade earlier.[33]

Obviously, these shifts in legislative priorities over ten years are at least partly attributable to factors other than reapportionment. The decline in legislative interest in civil rights and apportionment and the rise in interest over the issues of environment and energy, for example, are likely more reflective of the nature of the times than they are of rural versus urban interests. But such policy questions as highways, gambling, liquor, and agriculture have long been associated with rural legislators, and the decline in legislative concern over these policy areas may reflect the decline in rural domination of state legislatures. Conversely, the rising legislative interest in such issues as finance, business, and crime may signify a resurgence of urban legislators.

But this is not the whole story, for there are many kinds of urban legislators. Although the inner cities have made some legislative gains, they are not as dramatic as the gains made by the suburbs. Therefore, we may predict that metropolitan areas will be reflected in the state legislatures as suburbs (that is, white, middle-class interests) versus the core city (that is, predominately black and other minority groups of lower income level). The suburbs will battle for such middle-class issues as education; the central cities may find the salient issues to be welfare measures and urban rejuvenation projects. If this inner-city/outer-suburb dimension waxes into a major division among state legislators, the suburbs will probably win. It is the suburbs that are gaining legislative representation, and it is the middle class (which is found most frequently in the suburbs) that has always been the most politically active in this country. As one observer has noted, "The United States is an urban nation, but not a big city nation. The suburbs own the future."[34]

Table 5-3 State Legislators' Opinions on the Importance of Policy Issues, 1963 and 1973

1963			*1973*		
	Issue Mentions[1]			*Issue mentions*[1]	
Policy Areas	*% of Total*[1]	*N (3,449)*	*Policy Areas*	*% of Total*[1]	*N (4,981)*
Taxation	19%	662	Finance	16%	808
Apportionment	14	472	Taxation	13	657
Education	14	466	Education	10	520
Finance	13	456	Administration	9	453
Labor	6	208	Business	8	372
Business	5	160	Election; primaries, conventions	6	297
Health	5	158	Land	6	292
Social welfare	4	120	Labor	6	275
Administration	4	120	Courts; penal, crime	5	247
Civil rights	3	113	Health	5	244
Highways; transportation	3	112	Environment	3	149
Local government	2	67	Apportionment	3	128
Courts; penal, crime	2	62	Highways; transportation	2	118
Land	2	58	Civil rights	2	104
Gambling	2	51	Social welfare	2	100
Liquor	2	51	Local government	1	56
Constitutional revision	1	33	Energy	1	45
Election; primaries, conventions	1	33	Gambling	1	34
Water resources	1	27	Water resources	1	31
Agriculture	1	20	Constitutional revision	1	29
			Agriculture	Less than 0.5	21
			Liquor	Less than 0.5	3

[1] Percentages have been rounded. Totals include primary and secondary descriptions.

Source: As derived from Wayne L. Francis and Ronald E. Weber, "Legislative Issues in the Fifty States: Managing Complexity Through Classification," *Legislative Studies Quarterly*, 5 (August, 1980), p. 410.

Recognizing that there are a number of sources of political conflict in society, what are the means of resolving conflict in state legislatures? Conflict in the political process is resolved through the use of power. To be tagged as a "nice guy" in politics is not necessarily a compliment. Duane Lockard has provided us with a cogent overview of the source of legislative power.[35]

One major power base is the use of legislative rules and structure. Those who understand the rules of the game and the terrain of the playing field have a natural power base. (We shall return to this point in our discussion of "Rules of the Game" in the legislatures.)

A secondary source of power is campaign contributions, patronage, and political support. Money, access, and votes always help a legislator get his or her way; we consider these power sources later in this chapter, in our reviews of political parties, interest groups, and constituents.

Finally, there is the state bureaucracy as a base of power. The symbiotic relationship between legislators and bureaucrats is complex, and this book has devoted several upcoming chapters to it.

Rules of the Game: Written Ones

As mentioned, a major method of reconciling conflicts between legislators is simply the use of rules. Rules are both formal and informal, and political scientists tend to stress the use of informal sanctions in legislative strategies and in the legislative process generally. Nevertheless, the formal rules should not be overlooked, and often provide a major and effective power base for blocking or enacting public policy. As Lockard observes, the written rules of the legislature are "utterly incomprehensible to many a fledgling legislator, and indeed some of those who stay on and gain legislative experience never learn the rules in detail."[36] Indeed, most legislators are not meant to. The "needless" complexity is there for reasons of power, and those who understand the parliamentary procedures gain some additional power as a result. It is the old saw revisited, "knowledge is power." Because of the enormous work load of some state legislatures, and because state legislatures are made up more of amateurs than professionals, such knowledge can give a legislator a power source of considerable significance.

Consider some major formal rules of the game in state legislatures: One such rule concerns the quorum—that is, the specific proportion of the total membership that must be present for any official action to be taken. This proportion varies from legislature to legislature, but normally it requires at least a majority of the membership.

Quorum calls furnish another vehicle of political strategy in a legislature. For example, members of the legislature in Tennessee have been known to break a quorum and delay legislation by crossing over the state border into Kentucky, a device that also renders them immune from arrest for noncriminal conduct, since it is against Tennessee law to deliberately stall legislation while remaining in the state.

Another major rule concerns the powers given to the officers of the legislature, notably, the speaker of the house and the president *pro tempore* of the senate. The speaker of the house usually has more power than his or her senate counterpart, primarily because the house in most states has far more rules to work with than the senate; a larger membership results in longer lists of regulations and rules.

Rules of the Game: Unwritten Ones

Patterson has observed that informal rules may be viewed either as "inside" influences on the legislature or "outside" influences on the legislature. Notable among the inside influences are basic rules of human behavior, including the roles played by friendship and expertise in swaying legislation one way or another.[37] Studies of the Michigan legislature, for example, found that when sources of expertise were relied upon in making policy, 59 percent of the responding legislators indicated that their "experts" on a subject were other legislators rather than outside sources.[38]

John C. Wahlke and his colleagues, in a study of four state legislatures, conducted a more systematic review of the internal, unofficial rules of the game.[39] These rules, they found, serve six functions:

1. *Rules that are intended to promote group cohesion and solidarity.* Such sanctions protect other members' "legislative rights" (for example, "support another member's local bill if it doesn't affect you or your district"; "don't steal another member's bill"). Some rules promote impersonality ("oppose the bill, not the man"; "don't criticize the moral behavior of members"); some govern personal behavior ("don't be a prima donna"; "don't talk for the press or the galleries"); some emphasize respecting other members' political rights ("don't embarrass him in his district"). Finally, there is the all-important rule, the rule of institutional patriotism—a legislator defends the institution and its members against outsiders.
2. *Rules that promote the predictability of legislative behavior.* This is perhaps the most important of the informal rules and involves the concept of keeping one's word. Quotations from legislators that illustrate this concept include "abide by your agreements," "be frank in explaining bills," and "don't conceal your opposition."
3. *Rules that channel and restrain conflict.* Rules in this area encourage a willingness to compromise and respect for the seniority system (for example, "accept half a loaf"; "don't try to accomplish too much too soon").
4. *Rules that expedite legislative business.* These rules center primarily around the value of self-restraint in debate ("don't talk too much").
5. *Rules that give tactical advantages to individual members.* In other words, it is expeditious for an individual legislator to recognize the tenets of courtesy, gracefulness in defeat, negotiation, and caution in making commitments simply because such politeness will accrue to his or her personal advantage in the long run.
6. Finally, *rules that revolve around the development of desirable personal qualities.* Legislators responding to these kinds of rules mention such characteristics as integrity, virtue, objectivity, and intelligence.

Breaking the Rules

Do legislators break these rules? What can legislators do to get their colleagues really "ticked off"? One study found at least nine areas of highly undesirable legislative behavior. Of these, the most important is never concealing the real purpose of a bill or misrepresenting it to assure its passage. No one likes to be "snookered," least of all legislators. Others include dealing in personalities in debates on the floor, refusing unanimous consent when the legislative leadership desires it, leaking confidential knowledge to the press, and being overly committed to a special interest group.[40]

When in the opinion of most legislators, enough of these rules are broken, a number of sanctions can be invoked against individual lawmakers. These include ostracism, loss of political perquisites, denial of certain privileges, and, most frequently, the obstruction of the personal bills of the legislator being disciplined.[41]

THE PROCESS: PUSHING AND PULLING IN THE LEGISLATURES

The foregoing discussion on how legislators "get" each other illuminates the darker side of the intensely human legislative process. But there is a brighter, more constructive aspect, and it concerns how legislators work with each other and with other people in making laws.

There are many forces that influence a legislator's thinking about making policy. One study of more than 1,200 responding state legislators across the country identified the sources of "cues," that is, influential people, in the legislative process. For example, and in keeping with other studies, legislators most frequently state that their personal friends in the legislature are the most influential people in shaping their own opinions about policy questions, followed closely by other legislators who specialize in the policy area.[42]

A variation of whose advice a legislator values is whose ideas are considered by the legislature in making policy. An examination of the legislature in California, the nation's most populous and one of its most economically and politically complex states, found that interest groups clearly led the way in suggesting legislation (including local governments, which must function as an interest group in the context of the state legislative process), followed by other branches of state government, individual legislators themselves (who, too, can originate ideas), other legislative and partisan sources, and individual constituents.[43] Although categories and definitions may vary, most research identifies three primary sources of influence on a legislator's vote: parties, pressure groups, and constituents. Let us consider these forces in turn.

The Party as an Influence

The political party's role in influencing the legislative process is difficult, if not impossible, to determine precisely. Wahlke and his coauthors concluded in their study of legislative behavior that "ambivalence and uncertainty about the meaning of 'party' is a fact of political life, felt by the legislators themselves; it is not just a reflection of the state of political research."[44] It was with this viewpoint in mind that Wahlke constructed Table 5-4, which is the ranking of evaluations of party influence on legislative behavior by state legislators. Researchers have found that the state in which a legislature operates determines to a large degree the influence of party on the legislative process. Although party influence in the legislatures is hardly a uniform phenomenon, certain patterns nonetheless emerge. It is obvious, for example, that parties in one-party states are not able to

Table 5-4 Evaluations of Party Influence on Legislative Behavior in Four States

Evaluation[1]	*New Jersey*	*Ohio*	*California*	*Tennessee*
Much/considerable influence				
Republicans have	37%	34%	1%	16%
Democrats have	22	1	5	3
Both parties have	33	16	—	1
Some/increasing influence				
Republicans have	—	7	5	16
Democrats have	1	6	15	4
Both parties have	—	5	34	3
Little/no influence				
Republicans have	1	2	8	2
Democrats have	—	17	—	4
Both parties have	6	12	32	51

[1] The percentages refer to the proportion of all interviewees making a specified evaluation of a particular party's influence on legislative behavior. The percentages do not refer to the proportion of legislators belonging to one party or the other or to the normal voting strength of each party in the legislature.

Source: John C. Wahlke et al., *The Legislative System: Explorations in Legislative Behavior,* p. 355. Copyright © 1962 by John Wiley & Sons. Reprinted by permission of John Wiley & Sons, Inc.

enforce any high degree of party discipline and lack a strong ability to bring their legislators "into line" on political issues.

The think-alike/vote-alike factor. Legislatures in which parties have high degrees of influence seem to develop most easily and completely in the urbanized and industrialized states. The memberships of political parties are relatively homogeneous in these states: Democratic legislators are from urban areas, are labor oriented and are relatively more representative of various minorities and low-income groups; Republican legislators come from the higher-income suburbs and smaller communities. Such homogeneity of membership makes party discipline easier to enforce; people who tend to think alike, vote alike.[45]

Although the economic and social makeups of legislators' districts do have a significant influence on determining the way a legislator votes, other studies have found that a legislator's loyalty to party often can supersede the type of constituency that he or she represents. For example, it does not appear that legislators representing urban interests will forsake their party and band together as an urban coalition—at least not on any kind of a regular basis.[46]

What appears to happen in many state legislatures is that the legislator's party acts as a modifying variable between the legislator and his or her constituency. On the one hand, the typical legislator tends to vote what he or she perceives as being in the economic interest of his or her constituency. On the other hand, this vote is not necessarily direct, but can be influenced by the demands of the legislator's party.[47]

The urban-rural factor. The degree of importance that the party serves as an intervening variable seems to relate, at least to some degree, to the urban-rural dimension. For example, studies of relatively urban Ohio and relatively agrarian Iowa indicate that legislative parties are more effective in influencing a legislator's vote in the more urbanized areas. It was found that only one-third of Ohio legislators who were interviewed disagreed with the precept of supporting their party's position on a policy issue in the legislature if the party's position conflicted with the views held by the legislator's constituency. In Iowa, however, more than half of the legislators interviewed felt this way—that is, they would not follow the party line if it were at odds with the overall opinion of their constituencies.[48]

The landslide factor. Another factor that relates to a legislator's constituency and party is just how close the legislator's race was in his or her district. It has been contended, for example, that legislators who won their seats by substantial margins—by electoral "landslides"—are more loyal to their parties because they run less risk of displeasing their constituencies to the point of being voted out of office. By contrast, legislators who won by a tight margin are likely to be much more sensitive to the perceived wishes of their constituencies.[49]

While this theory holds up in some cases, it does not hold up in others. For example, research done on the Pennsylvania and Michigan legislatures found no particular connection between the competitiveness of legislative races and whether or not legislators voted liberal or conservative. Similarly, the level of competitiveness in district primary elections had no particular effect on this dimension. More pointedly, the likelihood of a legislator being loyal to his or her party did not correspond with the closeness of the race for the legislature.[50]

In summary, it appears that given the right conditions—notably, as we discuss shortly, a strong governor of the legislator's party and strong party support in the legislature—the party organization can exert more influence on a legislator's vote than can either the social and economic composition of the legislator's district or whether or not the legislator ran a close race for his or her legislative seat. Interestingly, one study found that this combination was a more powerful influence among Democrats in influencing a legislator's vote than among Republicans. Although party support was less important to legislators from the Republican Party than to the Democrats, a strong governor of the same party could have a significant influence among Republicans as much as among Democrats.[51]

The issue factor. The type of political issue involved also affects the relative influence of a legislator's party affiliation on how he or she will vote on a bill. The issues where a party is most apt to influence a legislator's thinking concerning a particular bill are those that pertain to elections, proposed legislative reorganizations that might directly affect the party, local government, state administration, and so forth. Issues that concretely affect the party's status or its organization are likely to cause the party to behave like a normal interest group.[52]

Beyond issues that are directly related to a party's status, however, the party's impact on legislative behavior is considerably less clear. On those issues that entail a redistribution of resources from haves to have-nots, such as welfare policies, parties can have a heavy hand in determining the votes of their legislators—but only in those states where the parties cleave along economic and class lines (e.g., Democrats clearly are the party of the poor, and Republicans clearly represent the rich). In those states where the parties have more heterogeneous constituencies, the parties are not particularly effective influencers of legislative votes on welfare and other redistributive issues.[53]

Another issue where parties display influence is in the area of health care and hospitals, but again there is a caveat. In this case, health expenditures tend to be cut in favor of other policy areas in those states where there are high levels of interparty competition (perhaps on the logic that most voters do not "notice" cuts in health care, but they might notice cuts in more visible policies); party cleavage along economic and class lines, however, apparently is not related to health care issues, as it is with welfare issues.[54]

Finally, there are a number of issues where parties seem to exercise little or no influence. These include education expenditures, highway expenditures, total state budgets, and tax policies.[55]

The leadership factor. Finally, one more major variable should never be underestimated in assessing the party's influence on a legislator's behavior. That is the respective roles of the leadership of the legislature and of the party. The more "professional" legislatures—in other words, those that pay their members relatively high salaries and maintain large professional research staffs—tend to have less turnover of party leadership, longer periods of waiting for leadership positions by other legislators, established patterns of succession, and fewer brawls over who will succeed to leadership positions. In these legislatures, which normally are found in urban and industrial states, legislative leaders tend to be relatively powerful and to think in terms of party ideologies.[56]

As an indication of the active role that the party leadership assumes in many legislatures, one study of 20 representative states found that legislative party leaders possessed an acute understanding of just how many votes were needed for their parties to win. The leaders understand (as political scientists have discovered) that if their party has between 40 and 60 percent of the seats in the legislature, they can typically command on the average more than 80 percent of their party's members on any given vote in the legislature. On the other hand, when their party has more than 60 percent of the legislative seats, the party leaders do not need as many party loyalists to assure a given vote, and, in these instances, they are able to maintain a winning sequence of votes with 70 percent of the legislators from their own party in the average vote.[57] In other words, party leaders enforce party loyalty only as they need it; once party leaders believe they do need the loyalty of the membership, they can usually acquire it.

A relatively high influence of the party on state legislators is somewhat surprising in light of the fact that most legislators do not give high marks to the party either as an instrument that was effective in getting them initially elected to the legislatures or as a major factor in getting legislators reelected. Recall, in this regard, our discussion in Chapter 4, in which we noted that party activity does not seem to make a great difference in winning campaigns. Incumbency, however, counts for a great deal in winning legislative races. Information obtained from 29 states for elections running from 1966 through 1976 suggests that about 15 to 18 percent of the incumbents running in both the primary and general election for the senate are defeated, and only 10 to 15 percent of incumbents running in house elections are defeated in the primaries or general elections. Of these defeats, about one quarter occur in the primary elections as opposed to the general elections. In no state for which we have data do the number of incumbents defeated in a primary or general election exceed 25 percent for the senate or 20 percent for the house.[58]

Given the fact, then, that it is highly probable that a legislator will win reelection simply by dint of his or her incumbency, the influence of the party on a legislator's vote is all the more impressive. One might surmise that legislators listen carefully to the legislative party leadership on the commonsensical grounds that they are fully aware that getting one's way in the legislature requires a modicum of party teamwork.

The rise of the legislative party? It also appears that the power of parties in the legislative process may be waxing over time. An indication of this is the growth of party caucuses in the legislature.

The *legislative,* or *party, caucus* is those legislators who belong to the same party and who confer on how to vote on upcoming bills. The majority caucus elects legislative officers, and all caucuses elect party leaders. The existence and use of the party caucus in legislatures is a sign that parties are important influences on how a legislator votes.

In the early 1950s, majority party caucuses were found in 33 lower chambers and 33 upper chambers. Caucuses were "unknown" in 13 of the 18 states then classified as one-party states, and most caucuses concentrated in competitive, two-party states.[59]

Today, both houses in 45 state legislatures have party caucuses (only Alabama, Arkansas, Louisiana, Mississippi, and the nonpartisan legislature of Nebraska do not), and their expansion seems to associate with the growth in competitiveness between the parties in the states.[60] About a third of these party caucuses have their own professional staffs, whose primary duties are the provision of services to legislators, but which are also heavily involved in analyzing policy issues.[61] Legislators themselves clearly view the chief responsibility of the caucuses to be one of policy formation,[62] and a plurality of legislators believe that the role of the caucus (and hence the party) in the legislature had increased over the past five years.[63] If, in short, the use of party caucuses is an indicator of the impact of the parties on legislators, then their clout seems to be growing.

The Pressure Group as an Influence

Pressure groups, or lobbyists, constitute the second major influence on legislators when they are making policy. Of the three sources of influence under consideration—parties, pressure groups, and constituents—pressure groups are probably the most stereotyped; they supposedly have irresistible influence that they are able to exercise on state legislators. No doubt this image of relative omnipotency stems from the last century when certain interest groups, notably railroads, were able literally to buy whole legislatures—lock, stock, and senator.

The phenomenon of interest groups is discussed in Chapter 3, but let us consider here some of the specific ways in which lobbyists interact with legislators.

Perhaps the most succinct statement of the real influence lobbyists have on state legislators was made by a legislator: "Lobbyists do affect the vote. Maybe they don't change your vote—lobbyists are only effective with those that are undecided—but they can sure make you bleed."[64] Lobbyists probably cannot "buy" legislators, but they can make life uncomfortable for them.

The aggressiveness factor. Interest group lobbyists are more involved and more aggressive in the legislative process than anyone other than legislators themselves. Studies going back to 1948 have found that interest groups are among the principal sources of bills submitted to state legislatures,[65] and the evidence indicates that they are actively involved in promoting or resisting far more bills than are governors and parties.[66]

In their study of Massachusetts, North Carolina, Oregon, and Utah, Harmon Zeigler and Michael Baer found that legislators were more free to respond to the pleas of interest groups on relatively specific topics than on those bills dealing with major issues affecting the general public interest.[67] Beyond that relationship, however, there was a considerable difference of cause and effect between lobbyists and legislators. In Massachusetts and North Carolina, only about 20 percent of the respondents confessed that lobbying on an issue changed their position frequently, or at least occasionally. But in Oregon and Utah, almost 50 percent of the legislators agreed that this was the case. Of course, the more that legislators and lobbyists interact, the greater the degree of influence held by lobbyists over legislators. This is particularly so when both groups tend to share the same social and economic status and have similar professional backgrounds. Table 5-5 indicates the findings from the Zeigler and Baer study.

The party factor. Other researchers have found different patterns of relationships between kinds of legislatures and the influence of lobbyists. Wahlke and his coauthors found that even in the absence of strong party competition, such as in Tennessee, lobbyists had relatively little legislative influence, despite the fact that interest groups bulked large in Tennessee as the sponsors of candidates for the legislature.[68] Yet in Massachusetts, where the legislature is highly partisan, there were also relatively low levels of influence exercised by lobbyists.[69] In theory, one would surmise that when there is a power vacuum created by a lack of party competition, lobbyists would enter that vacuum and exercise increasing degrees of influence. But this does not seem to be so; as we discussed in Chapter 3, partisan strength in a state, or lack of it, does not appear to associate with interest group strength, or lack of it, and this absence of correlation appears to hold in the legislative process as well.

The professionalism factor. The degree of legislative professionalism also affects the power of pressure groups in a legislature. Information from California indicates that the more staff assistants provided to legislators, the less likely legislators are to rely solely on information provided by interest groups. Lobbyists are more likely to have power in those legislatures that have relatively limited professional staffs. Of course, it also holds that the larger the membership of the interest groups (notably teachers' associations), the more likely that it is going to have higher degrees of influence on the legislative process.[70]

And a few more factors. Party membership, leadership status, and length of service in the legislature also seem to relate to a legislator's closeness to interest groups. An analysis of the California legislature found that Democrats, legislators who were not part of the legislative leadership, and legislators who had been members of the legislature for some time were the most likely legislators to sponsor bills desired by private interest groups.[71]

Legislators and lobbyists. Individual legislators assume certain roles when interacting with lobbyists. Some act as *facilitators;* they tend to have a friendly attitude toward lobbyists and are relatively well informed about the groups the

Table 5-5 Perceived Effect of Lobbying by Legislators in Four States

	Massachusetts	*North Carolina*	*Oregon*	*Utah*
Persuasion: Percentage of legislators believing that they have been influenced to the extent of:				
Changing from one position to another	20%	18%	51%	42%
Leaning more to the views of lobbyist	31	20	42	38
Questioning a previously held opinion	34	22	45	32
Information: Percentage of legislators indicating that they				
Depend upon information from lobbyists	50	41	83	80
Have confidence in information from lobbyists	55	56	88	70
Find information from lobbyists helpful	41	28	61	43

Source: Derived from data in Harmon Zeigler and Michael Baer, *Lobbying: Interaction and Influence in American State Legislatures* (Belmont, Calif.: Wadsworth, 1969).

lobbyists represent. Others take the role of *resister;* they are relatively hostile toward lobbyists although, like facilitators, they also possess a fair amount of knowledge about the groups that lobbyists represent. Still others are *neutrals;* they have no particular attitude concerning an interest group, regardless of their level of knowledge about it, or they simply have very little knowledge about the group. Wahlke found an almost equal number of facilitators and neutrals (nearly 37 percent of each) in his four-state study; close to 27 percent were classified as resisters.[72] The group Wahlke categorizes as resisters is probably the group that has been primarily responsible for various laws enacted against lobbying activity, especially since resisters as a category most frequently express the opinion that pressure group activity "is a wholly disruptive force which ought to be eliminated."[73]

Still, recognizing that lobbying is less than a wholly pure activity, it is worth observing what happens when a legislature tries to enact bills without any organized group support (or resistance). Consider the following example.

During the 1955 session a Republican member of the Connecticut House of Representatives had singlehandedly and relentlessly attempted to get a bill enacted that advocated a more sensible psychiatric treatment of sexual deviates in prisons and mental hospitals. So unmitigated and so personal was her campaign that her colleagues had begun "to duck behind a pillar when she approached." She eventually made her views known to Governor Abraham Ribicoff during the last days of the session; the governor sent a messenger to the Democratic senate caucus room with the message that he had decided to support the bill, and he requested the support of the caucus. Given Connecticut's considerable partisanship in legislative voting, there would normally have been no dissent, but on this occasion the senators "blew the roof off and ranted and raved at the messenger. . . and almost bodily threw him out of the caucus room." The reason? There was no or very little organized support for the bill, and the governor had done for the bill's sponsor what he had not done for other individual members of the assembly—that is, he had given his support for a personal bill. Without organized support, the frustrations of a group of tired and aggravated legislators got the better of the suggested legislation, and the bill never made it to the floor for a vote.[74]

The moral of the story is that pressure groups do serve a purpose. They push legislation, for better or for worse, that might otherwise not even be considered.

Salvaging the public interest? But can pressure groups be resisted by legislators when their ends are contrary to the public interest? Available evidence suggests that they can, largely because statewide elected officials (notably, the governors) and party-oriented legislative leaders act as effective countervailing forces against organized interests.

Table 5-6 is a compilation of studies conducted of interest group success rates in the California, Iowa, and Texas legislatures. As it indicates, interest groups won on 67 percent of the bills that they wanted passed or defeated by the California legislature during the 1981-1982 session (see column 1 for California). But when the governor's office in California took on organized interests, their success rate sank dramatically, and interest groups won only 24 percent of the time (column 2). Interest groups' success rates dropped by 41 percent in California when they came into conflict with the governor's office (column 3).

Table 5-6 Success Rates of Interest Groups Versus Other Influence Agents in Three State Legislatures[1]

	CALIFORNIA (1981–82)			*IOWA (1977–78)*			*TEXAS (1983)*		
	1	*2*	*3*	*1*	*2*	*3*	*1*	*2*	*3*
Influence Agent	*Overall Success Rate*	*Success Rate of Interest Group When in Conflict with other Agents*	*% Decrease in Interest Group Success Rate*	*Overall Success Rate*	*Success Rate of Interest Group When in Conflict with other Agents*	*% Decrease in Interest Group Success Rate*	*Overall Success Rate*	*Success Rate of Interest Group When in Conflict with other Agents*	*% Decrease in Interest Group Success Rate*
Interest groups	67%	—	—	51%	—	—	55%	—	—
Governor's office	84	24%	−41%	69	27%	−19%	95	24%	−12%
Majority leadership	78	44	−30	80	33	−20	73	25	−41
Minority leadership	71	60	−14	74	82	+26	NA	NA	NA

Percentages have been rounded.

NA: No minority party leadership in Texas.

Source: As derived from Charles W. Wiggins, Keith E. Hamm, and Charles G. Bell, "Interest Groups and Other Influence Agents in the State Legislative Process: A Comparative Analysis," paper presented at the 1984 Annual Meeting of the American Political Science Association, Washington, D.C., August 39–September 2, 1984, pp. 24, 26.

Similar (though less striking) patterns emerge when interest groups are challenged by the legislative leadership of both the majority parties and the minority parties. In only one case, when interest groups did battle with the minority leaders in the Iowa legislature, did interest groups win more often than they lost.

Governors, majority party leaders, and even minority party leaders (with the marginal exception of California) also consistently enjoyed higher overall success rates on legislation than did organized interests. Thus, it appears that "popularly elected officials representing broad constituencies . . . dampen the power of special interests. . . . [and] that only strong, party-oriented leadership groups within government can thwart the power of interest groups."[75] Among government leaders, governors who are strong, party-oriented chief elected executives seem to be the most effective in controlling the excesses of organized special interests.[76]

The People as an Influence

Still a third source of influence on state legislators is the people who vote for them—that is, their constituencies. Of the three major sources of influence, the constituency is likely the most important, although its influence is seldom applied directly.[77] Indeed, it can be argued that even in strong two-party states, the constituency is the primary influence on the political party, which as we observed earlier, acts primarily as an intermediary in applying pressure to a legislator. When the party represents an effective coalition of social and economic groups, it usually is the result of constituencies that already happen to fall along these economic and social lines; the nature and make up of a constituency is more responsible than any other factor for party cohesion.

The elusive comfort of voting on principle. Legislators tend to vote for or against bills on the basis of how they think their constituents may vote for them as a consequence of their stand, and thus the constituency has more influence on legislators than does either the party or pressure group. Interestingly, research indicates that legislators are loathe to admit to this fact. Nearly two-thirds of the legislators Wahlke studied identified themselves with the "Burkean position" as opposed to the populist position. By this, Wahlke meant that most legislators seemed to agree with the statement by the "founder of conservatism," Edmund Burke, that the elected representative should be guided not by "local purposes and prejudices" but by "his unbiased opinion, his mature judgment, his enlightened conscience."

Legislators' cries that they are independent of their constituencies (or, for that matter, of political parties and pressure groups) should be taken with a grain of salt. Everyone, legislators included, likes to proclaim his or her independence of social institutions and to tell the world that they make their own decisions. But, common sense indicates that we can agree with the legislator who noted, "Basically you represent the thinking of the people who have gone through what you have gone through and who are what you are. You vote according to that. In other words, if you come from a suburb, you reflect the thinking of the people in the suburbs; if you are of a depressed people, you reflect that. You represent the sum total of your background."[78]

The bliss of political ignorance. Yet, it is a moot question as to whether legislators really know their constituents, whether they do vote as their constituents would have voted on particular issues. In studies of the Iowa and Florida legislatures, it was found that legislators could predict only in a very mixed way how their own districts would vote on certain proposed constitutional amendments and referenda. On highly salient and politically charged issues, such as home rule, reapportionment, and busing, the legislators accurately forecast their constituents' votes by as much as 90 percent and no less than 70 percent. The less salient issues had a considerably lower percentage of legislators accurately predicting their constituents' subsequent voting.[79]

The irony of legislative anonymity. The other side of the coin, of course, is not how well legislators know their constituents, but how well their constituents know them. In a national survey conducted by the Gallup organization, only 28 percent of those polled could name their state senator and only 24 percent knew who their representative was. Interestingly, people in small towns and in rural areas were much more likely to know their state representative than were those living in big cities.[80]

The next question that arises is whether the constituents of a state care what their legislature is doing. In a poll conducted in Minnesota during the middle of the legislative session, about one-third of the citizens of Minnesota indicated no interest whatever in what their own legislature was doing,[81] and a similar study completed in Iowa found that nearly 50 percent of those polled said they paid very little or no attention to the legislature.[82] Yet, both Iowa and Minnesota have reputations for politically active and interested citizenries. It may be that if such polls were conducted in other states, they would find even lower percentages of citizens expressing an interest in what their legislatures did or were doing.

If, indeed, most constituents neither know who their legislators are nor care what their legislatures are doing, then legislators can afford to be "Burkean." They can tell their constituents that they "vote their own mind" with impunity because the evidence indicates that few people are paying much attention to them anyway.

GETTING THERE

Even though relatively few citizens seem to be paying attention to them, the fact remains that being a member of the legislature is an attractive goal for a number of people. As we noted in Chapter 4, the parties play a surprisingly large role in the recruitment of legislative candidates, and party officials consider candidate recruitment to be one of their primary duties. Typically, the states that have the strongest parties are those states in which the parties have the greatest influence on candidate recruitment.[83] In states where the parties are relatively weak, however, candidates tend to be "self-starters" or are recruited by special interests, particularly business interests.[84]

Irrespective of the party's role in securing candidates for the legislature, prospective candidates almost always must have the endorsement of one of the major parties to win, and such endorsements increasingly are determined by victory in the party primary. The competitiveness of party primaries varies substantially among the states. Primary contests are more frequent among the Democrats than among the Republicans, and the races within the Democratic primaries often are closer. Over time, however, it appears that contested primaries for legislative seats are in decline, and this trend seems to relate to the growing tendency of incumbents to run again.[85]

In contrast to the primary races, contests in the general election are considerably more competitive. But competition must be viewed in relative terms, and, by most standards, legislative races generally do not involve particularly close calls. Figure 5-1 illustrates the lack of competition in legislative elections during the 1970s for 42 states. In 32 of these states, the winners won by more than 60 percent of the vote in more than half of the legislative districts, and in 13 states the victors walked away with more than 60 percent of the vote in more than three quarters of the legislative districts. "Although, on the average, state legislative elections are about as competitive as congressional elections, the fact is that most states have a majority of electorally safe legislative seats."[86]

As in Congress, the greatest single advantage in running for a legislative seat is if one already occupies it. Typically, incumbents seek reelection in about 80 percent of state legislative districts, and, as we have noted, incumbents are more likely since the mid-1960s to run for reelection. Approximately 90 percent of incumbent legislators are successful in their campaigns.[87]

Because of the advantages of incumbency, anyone challenging a sitting legislator generally must be willing to spend a considerable sum of money if he or she wishes to win. Research on campaign spending and legislative election races in California and Iowa in 1978 found that campaign spending made a real difference in determining the outcome of the election, even when party strength,

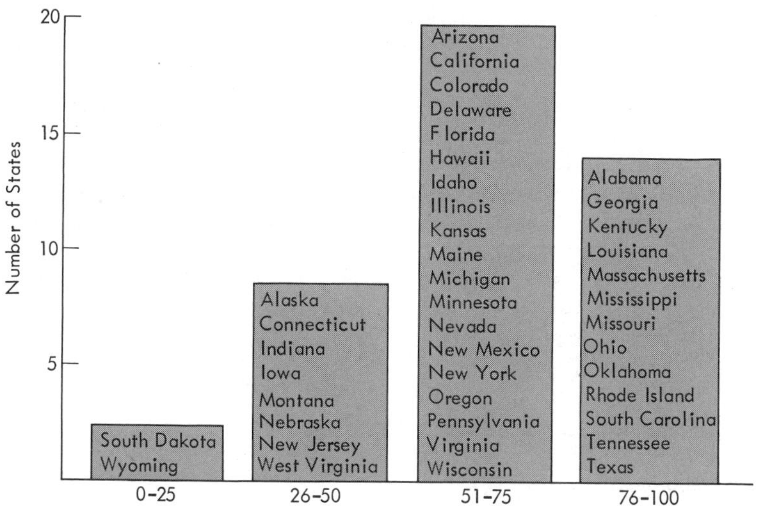

Figure 5-1 Competitiveness of House elections in forty-two states, 1974–1979.* (*Source:* Samuel C. Patterson, "Legislators and Legislatures in the American States," in Virginia Gray, Herbert Jacobs, and Kenneth Vines, eds., *Politics in the American States: A Comparative Analysis,* 4th ed. Copyright © 1983 by Samuel C. Patterson. Reprinted by permission of Little, Brown & Company.)

*Data not available for Arkansas, Maryland, New Hampshire, North Carolina, North Dakota, Vermont, Utah, and Washington.

incumbency, and the closeness of the races were factored out of the calculations.[88]

WHO ARE LEGISLATORS?

The 7,461 state legislators are an upwardly mobile group. In general, they enjoy higher social, economic, and professional status than their parents did, and they tend not to be from old-line, established families in their states. Politicians emanating from statewide "aristocracies" tend to enter gubernatorial and congressional elections and rarely, if ever, run for the state legislature.

Legislators as a Semielite

One's profession or occupation, of course, is closely related to one's upward mobility or lack of it. Lawyers are well represented, although the proportion who are lawyers has been declining—from a fourth in 1967 to a fifth in 1979. Business people comprise a plurality—36 percent—while professionals constitute 21 percent. Farmers, long an interest group with a particular concern over state politics, also are heavily represented in legislatures. Working people occupy a mere 5 percent of legislative seats, an apparent increase from only 2 percent more than 25 years earlier.[89] Table 5-7 lists the occupations of state legislators in greater detail.

Few legislators are women—fewer than 12 percent—but women have been steadily expanding their numbers in the statehouses.[90] Legislatures with larger numbers of women seem to be located in the Northeast and West and are less "professional" in their orientation.[91]

Minorities are more fully represented than are women as a proportion of their percentage of the population, although the underrepresented minorities, too, fall grossly short of their ratio in the American population.

Five percent of the state legislators are blacks.[92] Blacks are relatively well represented in the legislatures of northern urban industrial states and generally tend to come from the inner cities in those states. They are seriously underrepresented in the South and in the border states, largely because of the residency patterns and the nature of legislative districting in those states. In the South and rural border states, blacks are more or less spread around the countryside. In the North, blacks tend to be concentrated in the inner cities, where they make up larger portions of these districts' populations and are therefore more likely to be voted into office.[93]

Table 5-7 Occupations of State Legislators, 1979

Business	36%
Professionals	21
Lawyers	20
Agriculture	11
Clerical, service, blue collar, union officials	5
Other	7

Percentages have been rounded.

Source: Insurance Information Institute, *Occupational Profile of State Legislators* (New York: Insurance Information Institute, 1979).

A little more than 1 percent of state legislators are of Hispanic origin. Nearly two-thirds of these legislators are in the western states, and virtually all of the remainder are from the South.[94]

In keeping with their upward mobility, legislators have substantially more formal education than does the population at large. Indeed, approximately 75 percent of state legislators in the country have had some college education. Legislators also tend to be "home country boys," who enter the legislature in their early forties; most of them lived all or most of their lives in the district that they represent in the legislature.[95] They are not at all geographically mobile compared to the population generally. Along with having deep roots in his or her district, legislators also seem to reflect their district in social, economic, and religious characteristics as well. For example, a study of the Pennsylvania legislature found that Protestant candidates came from Protestant districts and Catholics from Catholic districts. These religious differences paralleled ethnic and economic differences as well.[96]

Roles Our Representatives Play

What kind of psychological factors do legislators bring to the business of representing the people? To aid in answering this question, a political scientist was somehow able to persuade a number of South Carolina legislators a number of years ago to undergo some rather thorough psychological testing. He found that the legislators from South Carolina were relatively self-sufficient, self-confident, and extroverted; somewhat more domineering; less neurotic; and less authoritarian than the average American.[97] A considerably more recent study of Iowa state legislators determined that this group also was generally more tolerant of others and more sympathetic toward minority groups than was a corresponding sample of Iowa voters.[98] These findings are not surprising. It would be an odd person in politics, for example, who was less than gregarious, self-confident, and flexible, which seems to be the typical mental makeup of state legislators.

Once a budding legislator runs for office and wins, what happens then? What roles do legislators assume in working with their colleagues? Although the number of roles a legislator can play is almost infinite, some political scientists have taken pains to describe a few of them.

James David Barber has categorized state legislators as *spectators, advertisers, reluctants,* and *lawmakers.*[99] *Spectators* are largely passive people who enjoy watching the circus of the legislative process, would like to stay on, and seem to have been attracted to the legislature by the social prestige of the office. Spectators are "compensating for feelings of social inferiority."

Advertisers, on the other hand, are quite active but are not especially keen on returning to the legislature because their primary purpose is to attain some personal publicity, usually for business reasons. Advertisers "show occupational insecurity and marked inner conflicts."

The *reluctants* are just that. They did not want to get into the legislature in the first place, but feel that they must do their civic duty for their friends and neighbors. They have difficulty in "adapting to a strange, fast-moving situation."

Finally, the *lawmakers* are about as close as legislators come to being inner-motivated professionals. They probably plan to stay in the legislature for some length of time, and they concentrate on the major issues of public policy because they are "freed for this by personal strength and powerful adjustive techniques."

Wahlke came up with quite a different set of roles, which he described as encompassing "the legislator as decision maker"; these were the *ritualist, tribune, inventor,* and *broker.*[100] The *ritualist* prefers the mechanics of the job. He or she is fascinated by procedures and rules and purposefully sets out to master this admittedly complex topic. Often, ritualists can become rather powerful individuals in the legislature simply because they understand the rules of the game.

The *tribune,* to put the matter bluntly, is a blowhard. Tribunes are close to being modern-day populists and are primarily concerned with knowing the needs and feelings of the people and becoming their spokespersons.

The *inventor* is frustrated. But inventors are also perceptive because they recognize that in the twentieth century, the center for public policy formulation and execution resides in the executive branch of government. They see themselves as thoughtful and farsighted, possessed of imagination, and eager to devise new ways of solving current problems. They maintain that legislators should "be in the front of things" but recognize that they are not.

Last, the *broker* is a legislator who provides the grease between the wheels. Brokers see their function as balancing competing interests, achieving compromise, and coordinating and integrating groups that are at loggerheads. The "sophisticated broker" perceives conflicting groups in terms of power potentiality and the "moral worth" of the groups in contention, whereas the "naive broker" tends to believe that a compromise can be achieved if he or she merely listens to the competing group (a naive broker might say for example, "Isn't this just a communications problem?").

A third unified theory of the roles that legislators play has been offered by Frank Sorauf.[101] Sorauf categorizes legislators as *trustees, delegates,* and *partisans.* A *trustee* is one who votes his or her conscience; a *delegate* tends to follow the instructions (at least as he or she perceives them) of his or her constituents; and the *partisan,* or *politico,* follows the orders of the party leadership. Of course, as with all the other theories concerning legislative role playing, these categories overlap considerably when applied to an individual legislator.

The Turnover Trauma

Regardless of the kinds of roles that legislators play, political scientists who have studied these peculiar creatures have concluded that it takes at least three terms before a legislator can become genuinely effective and have an impact on the formulation of public policy.[102] Yet, generally about a third of all legislators in any given session are new to the job.

The proportion of "freshmen" legislators (i.e., those legislators serving their first term), however, has been declining steadily, indicating a renewed stability in the statehouses. The average percentage of freshmen state representatives has fallen from 45 percent in the 1950s to 37 percent in the 1971-1976 period; for state senators, the figures are 40 percent and 32 percent, respectively.[103] Figure 5-2 illustrates the steady decline in legislative turnover.

Legislative turnover has been high, in part, because of the impact of reapportionment. During the years of unprecedented legislative reapportionment (1963-1971), for example, the overall turnover rate for the 50 state senates

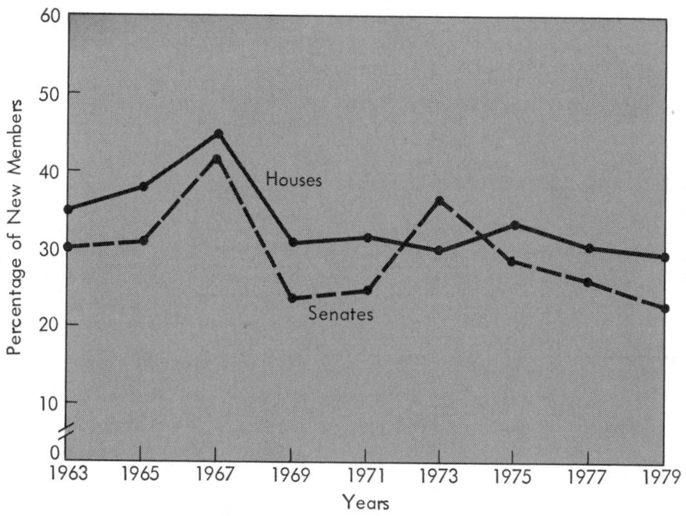

Figure 5-2
Membership turnover in the state legislatures. (*Source:* Samuel C. Patterson, "Legislators and Legislatures in the American States," in Virginia Gray, Herbert Jacobs, and Kenneth Vines, eds., *Politics in the American States: A Comparative Analysis,* 4th ed. Copyright © 1983 by Samuel C. Patterson. Reprinted by permission of Little, Brown & Company.)

was more than 30 percent, for the 49 lower chambers more than 36 percent.[104] Turnover rates have been declining since the mid-1970s.[105]

Neither reapportionment nor losing at the polls can completely account for the high legislative turnover in the states. Rather, many legislators voluntarily leave the legislature; they are defeated for reelection far less frequently than they "opt out." As we noted earlier, substantially fewer than a fifth of incumbent legislators running for reelection are defeated at the polls,[106] and from a quarter to a fifth of all legislators resign voluntarily after the session is over.[107]

Why do state legislators resign? Studies indicate that career ambitions, particularly in the form of running for a higher public office, and occupational, and family-related personal reasons are by far the most common motivations to retire; very few legislators (less than 10 percent) resign because they expect to lose the next election.[108]

Large states that have longer legislative sessions and more professionalized legislatures show a pattern of lower turnover rates. The declining turnover rate in state legislatures seems related to the fact that legislatures are professionalizing; bigger staffs, higher pay, increasing prestige, and the normal perquisites of political office seem to be slowly reducing legislative turnover.

THE PROFESSIONALIZATION OF THE LEGISLATURES

Professionalism implies working at one's job on a relatively full-time basis and trying to do the job well, as defined by standards that relate directly to the job. Just as a lawyer is supposedly a "professional," so is a legislator, at least in some of the states.

Making Laws and Making Money

One clear indication of the degree of professionalism possessed by a legislature is how much the legislators are paid. The average biennial wage of legislators has grown dramatically in the states—from about $4,000 in the early

1960s to more than $20,000 by 1980. Alaskan legislators are the highest paid, receiving a biennial compensation of more than $90,000. The low end of the continuum is represented by New Hampshire, whose constitution prohibits the state from paying its legislators more than $200 for the two-year session.

The Bureaucratization of the Legislatures

Another criterion indicating the professionalization of state legislatures is the growth of the professional staffs attached to the legislature. These staffs provide at least three major functions to a legislature: the legislative reference service, the bill drafting service, and the legislative council.

The legislative reference service is found in virtually all states. It was inaugurated in 1901 in Wisconsin and has since been adopted elsewhere. Usually located in the state archives, legislative reference services provide research on upcoming legislation.

Often the legislative reference service is integrated with the bill drafting service. Together, they draft bills that articulate (in lawyer-like fashion) the public policy that legislators really wish to accomplish. Normally both the legislative reference and bill drafting services are directly responsible to the legislature rather than to the executive branch of government.

A third type of professional staff is the legislative council, which got its start in 1932 in Kansas. Virtually all state legislatures now have a council whose purpose is to provide a continuous and ongoing research staff for the legislature, whether or not that body is in session. The average council has 15 members, but individual councils range in size from 5 in South Carolina to more than 250 in Pennsylvania. Frequently, the legislative council functions as a liaison between the chief executive and the legislature in the development of public policy.[109]

There has been a recent trend to abolish legislative councils and replace them with legislative management committees, as Connecticut, Florida, and Utah have done. The intent is to consolidate the administration of legislatures within a single organization. A related development is the recent establishment of permanent research staffs specializing in technical and scientific areas, such as energy. About a dozen legislatures have such staffs. Finally, all legislatures have budget review staffs, whose sole function is to analyze budgetary and fiscal matters. Almost all also have some sort of auditing staffs. Computer-based management information systems also have made their impact, and today all state legislatures have them, compared to only 28 in 1969.[110] Each legislator also has a personal staff of some kind, with the legislative leadership normally having a larger personal staff.

The rise in professional staffing in the state legislatures is one of the surest signs that the legislatures are professionalizing, and the legislative drive toward this kind of professionalization has occurred largely since 1960. As we noted earlier, no state staffed its standing committees in both chambers in 1960, but 36 now do.[111] In addition, however, all legislatures maintain both personal and committee staffs in at least one house, almost two-fifths of the legislatures fund personal staffs year-round, and the remainder do so when the legislature is in session.[112] Twenty years earlier, only 9 legislatures accorded their own legislative leadership with even partial staff assistance.[113] All the states now boast their own "legislative bureaucracies." The nation's 7,461 legislators pay more than 16,000 full-time legislative employees year round, a number that balloons to 25,000 employees when the legislatures are in session.[114]

Despite the growth of both salaries and staffs in the state legislatures, legislatures are not organized hierarchically, as is the executive branch and even the judiciary. Thus, legislatures have difficulty grappling with the problems of administration and expertise. It can be argued that the only reason legislatures have even bothered to professionalize at all is simply because professionalization provides the surest method for countering information "fed" to them by the executive branch of government. Legislators have felt a need to develop their own sources of expert information, and staffs provide this means.

But the drive to professionalize legislatures also brings with it implications for power relationships, and one of the consequences of legislative professionalization may be a more powerful staff. As a former staffer in the highly professionalized legislature in California put it, "The most remarkable discovery that I made during my tenure as a staff member was the amount of power I had over the bills on which I worked. The members relied almost entirely on staff to summarize accurately the legislation and also to develop compromises among the many interests which were brought into conflict by these bills."[115]

A study of state legislatures contrasted those states with high levels of legislative professionalization as measured by relatively large staff resources, office facilities, computer systems, and operating budgets with those legislatures that were less professionalized, and found that the more professionalized legislatures tended to make more centralized decisions. In the more professionalized legislatures, decisions frequently are made in the governor's office and legislative policy committees; decentralized legislative decision making occurs in party caucuses, regular legislative committees, and on the floor.[116]

Should Legislatures Professionalize? The Case for the Citizen Legislator

The original concept of legislatures was that of the citizens' assembly. According to this view, legislators ought to be full-time citizens and part-time policymakers. They should have jobs to earn their daily bread and should contribute to the formulation of public policy only as a civic duty. New Hampshire has adopted this view perhaps more completely than has any other state, and it is not a bad view.

The counterargument runs that the more the legislator is paid and the more professional staff support he or she receives, the more responsive the legislature will be and the better public policy will be for the state. The argument continues that social, economic, and political realities in the states have become far too complex; that America is in the throes of a technological revolution that has resulted in new relationships among traditional elements of society. A part-time legislature may result in legislation that is only partially responsive and responsible. California and New York, two states that are among the most complex socially of any states in the Union, have adopted this view most completely. In short, among the more interesting aspects of state politics are the structural alternatives that the states use to make public policy, and nowhere is this contrast more evident than in the "citizens' legislature" versus the "professional legislature."

But the question, if interesting, may also be academic. Whether or not "citizen legislatures" are "good" or "bad" for a democracy, legislatures are taking the road to professionalism, and this choice can be seen in the legislatures' growing enthusiasm for pulling the levers of the policy process on a regular basis. Not only are legislatures meeting more frequently and staffing themselves more professionally than ever before, but they are entering the world of fiscal oversight as never before.

Eighty percent of the state legislatures directly control their governments' audit functions (double the number in 1960), and many legislatures are expanding this function to include a systematic policy assessment capacity. Legislatures are also reviewing administrative regulations established by the executive branch (38 legislatures have such procedures); enacting sunset legislation, or laws requiring that programs terminate at a predetermined date unless the legislature specifically prevents it (two-thirds of the states have done so); and reviewing how state agencies use funds that they receive from the federal government (three quarters of the legislatures regularly review these uses).[117] Legislative concern in each of these areas had been essentially nil only two decades earlier. Yet, such "powers are close to the heart of legislative independence."[118] Legislative professionalism seems to bring with it additional increments of legislative power.

HOW GOOD ARE LEGISLATURES? A PROBLEM OF ASSESSMENT

Someone very wisely once observed that the making of laws, like sausage, should not be watched. Nevertheless, we still must ask, How well do legislatures perform in making public policy for their states? Virtually every citizen of every state has asked the question at one time or another, but the answer is elusive.

Do Legislatures Matter?

How much impact do legislatures actually have on the formulation of policies in their own states? Dye argues that legislatures are merely incidental in the policy processes of the states. The central realities, he claims, are such factors as wealth, education levels, degree of urbanization and industrialization, and related social and economic variables. Dye goes on to contend that most state legislatures are arbiters of public policy rather than initiators. Dye states that "policy initiation is the function of the governor, the bureaucrat, and the interest group," but not the legislature. He adds that legislatures "inject into public decision making a parochial influence" in that they represent local interests rather than the statewide interest.[119]

William L. Shade and Frank J. Munger take issue with Dye, arguing that the variables of legislative professionalism, levels of information available to legislators, and interparty competition are the strongest determinants of responsive state policies.[120]

Assessing Legislatures

It is admittedly difficult to determine how important legislatures are in making public policies in the states. Still the question remains: How well do they make public policy? We can measure and evaluate the quality of their performance in a number of ways.

The yardstick of professionalism. One way is to employ the criterion of professionalism. Legis 50 (formerly the Citizens' Conference on State Legislatures) evaluated the 50 state legislatures using five criteria: functionality (administrative quality), accountability, information-handling capability, independence, and representativeness.[121] California ranked highest; Alabama ranked fiftieth. Table 5-8 gives the ranking of the states.

An analysis of the state legislatures conducted by the U.S. Advisory Commission on Intergovernmental Relations in 1985, using the Legis 50 criteria, found that all the legislatures had made significant progress on all these dimensions.[122] However, as a former director of Legis 50 noted, despite considerable improvement, society has "changed more rapidly than legislatures. . . . We've improved the legislature's ability to tear apart a problem, to get information on it, and open it up to public debate. But we have not improved its ability to resolve a problem."[123] Indeed, the increasing tendency among state legislators to resort to the referendum, noted in Chapter 2, and send the tough problems to the people and let them resolve them, seems to support this assessment.

The yardstick of public opinion. A second major method of evaluating state legislatures is simply finding out what the citizens of the states think of their legislatures. We already noted that most citizens (at least in selected states) do not know who their legislators are or what their legislature is doing. Even so, Americans have definite opinions about the performance of their legislatures.

Table 5-9 shows how citizens in a national survey evaluated their legislatures' performance. It is apparent that many Americans are critical of the performance of their state legislatures. Even so, Americans rank their legislatures' performance, according to the survey, higher than they rank the performance of Congress; although 19 percent of the respondents gave their legislatures a rating of "poor," 30 percent accorded Congress an evaluation of "poor."[124]

The yardstick of responsiveness. A third way to evaluate legislative performance is to measure the legislatures' responsiveness to public demands. A comprehensive analysis of all 50 states found a reasonably high degree of close agreement between popular preferences in the states and the actual policies enacted by their legislatures—at least on such issues as civil rights, welfare policies, liquor and gambling laws, and unionization of public employees. There was considerably less congruence between the people's opinions and the policies legislated by their representatives on such issues as right-to-work laws, election legislation, firearms regulation, motor vehicle registration, and aid to parochial schools.[125]

The yardstick of illusion. All these efforts in evaluating the performance of legislatures and their worth in society are perhaps best summed up by philosopher T. V. Smith, who not only was a university professor of philosophy but

Table 5-8 State Legislative Performance as Measured by Selected Professional Standards

Overall Rank	*State*	*Functional*	*Accountable*	*Informed*	*Independent*	*Representative*
1	California	1	3	2	3	2
2	New York	4	13	1	8	1
3	Illinois	17	4	6	2	13
4	Florida	5	8	4	1	30
5	Wisconsin	7	21	3	4	10
6	Iowa	6	6	5	11	25
7	Hawaii	2	11	20	7	16
8	Michigan	15	22	9	12	3
9	Nebraska	35	1	16	30	18
10	Minnesota	27	7	13	23	12
11	New Mexico	3	16	28	39	4
12	Alaska	8	29	12	6	40
13	Nevada	13	10	19	14	32
14	Oklahoma	9	27	24	22	8
15	Utah	38	5	8	29	24
16	Ohio	18	24	7	40	9
17	South Dakota	23	12	15	16	37
18	Idaho	20	9	29	27	21
19	Washington	12	17	25	19	39
20	Maryland	16	31	10	15	45
21	Pennsylvania	37	23	23	5	36
22	North Dakota	22	18	17	37	31
23	Kansas	31	15	14	32	34
24	Connecticut	39	26	26	25	6

25	West Virginia	10	32	37	24	15
26	Tennessee	30	44	11	9	26
27	Oregon	28	14	35	35	19
28	Colorado	21	25	21	28	27
29	Massachusetts	32	35	22	21	23
30	Maine	29	34	32	18	22
31	Kentucky	49	2	48	44	7
32	New Jersey	14	42	18	31	35
33	Louisiana	47	39	33	13	14
34	Virginia	25	19	27	26	48
35	Missouri	36	30	40	49	5
36	Rhode Island	33	46	30	41	11
37	Vermont	19	20	34	42	47
38	Texas	45	36	43	45	17
39	New Hampshire	34	33	42	36	43
40	Indiana	44	38	41	43	20
41	Montana	26	28	31	46	49
42	Mississippi	46	43	45	20	28
43	Arizona	11	47	38	17	50
44	South Carolina	50	45	39	10	46
45	Georgia	40	49	36	33	38
46	Arkansas	41	40	46	34	33
47	North Carolina	24	37	44	47	44
48	Delaware	43	48	47	38	29
49	Wyoming	42	41	50	48	42
50	Alabama	48	50	49	50	41

Sources: Report on Evaluation of the 50 State Legislatures (Denver: Legis 50/The Center for Legislative Improvement, formerly the Citizens' Conference on State Legislatures, 1971), p. 29.

Table 5-9 Public Opinion of State Legislatures, 1979

Rating	*% of Total*
Excellent	2%
Pretty good	29
Only fair	42
Poor	19
Not sure	9
	100%

Source: Glenn Newkirk, "State Legislatures Through the People's Eyes," *State Legislatures,* 5 (August–September, 1979), p. 9.

served in the Illinois senate and the U.S. House of Representatives. He noted that legislators have

> a magnificent protection against external hostility in the friendly bosom of a "we group," nonetheless dependable because achieved ad hoc and perennially shifting in membership. By making it possible for representatives amiably to stand the gaf, this "we group" bulwark gives opportunity for a great many good citizens to do a great deal of criticizing harmlessly. Legislators become scapegoats. . . . what, for instance, would most editors have to work themselves into decent form upon were it not for the "extravagance," the "waste," the "inefficiency," the "stupidity," the "venality" and, in general "the never ending audacity of elected persons"? Nor are editors alone in this need . . . it is safe to say that no other institution today has half the effectiveness of the legislature in soaking up and sterilizing the wastage produced in society when the will to perfection meets the willpower in the lives of good men and women. To have a "show" that every citizen can "show up" without fear of retaliation (since he supports it) maximizes the fun and minimizes the fury of the social process.[126]

NOTES

[1]John Gardner, as quoted by United Press International, January 3, 1972, reprinted in Daniel R. Grant and H. C. Nixon, *State and Local Government in America,* 3rd ed. (Boston: Allyn & Bacon, 1975), p. 206.

[2]Herbert Jacob, "Dimensions of State Politics," in Alexander Heard, ed., *State Legislatures in American Politics* (Englewood Cliffs, N.J.: Prentice-Hall, 1966), p. 3.

[3]James Bryce, *The American Commonwealth* (New York: Macmillan, 1891), p. 521.

[4]Harmon Zeigler and Michael Baer, *Lobbying: Interaction and Influence in American State Legislatures* (Belmont, Calif.: Wadsworth, 1969), p. 126.

[5]William T. Pound, "The State Legislatures," *Book of the States, 1984-85* (Lexington, Ky.: Council of State Governments, 1984), p. 118. In 1983, the average state senate (including Nebraska's legislature) had 15.4 standing committees; the average house had 19.5 standing committees. For further discussion of these trends, see Advisory Commission on Intergovernmental Relations, *The Question of State Government Capability* (Washington, D.C.: U.S. Government Printing Office, 1985), p. 82.

[6]Malcolm Jewell, *The State Legislature* (New York: Random House, 1962), p. 93; and H. H. Basehart, "The Effect of Membership Stability on Continuity and Experience in U.S. State Legislative Committees," *Legislative Studies Quarterly,* 5 (February, 1980), pp. 55-68.

[7]H. Owen Porter and David A. Leuthold, "Acquiring Legislative Expertise: Appointment to Standing Committees in the States," paper presented at the 1974 annual meeting of the American Political Science Association and cited in Samuel C. Patterson, "American State Legislatures and Public Policy," in Herbert Jacob and Kenneth N. Vines, eds., *Politics in the American States,* 3rd ed., (Boston: Little, Brown, 1976), p. 184.

[8]James R. Oxendale, Jr., "Membership on Standing Committees in Legislative Lower Chambers," *State Government,* 54, No. 4 (1981), p. 127. The study covered the 1973-77 period.
[9]Alan Rosenthal, "Legislative Committee Systems," *Western Political Quarterly,* 26 (June, 1973), pp. 252-262.
[10]Keith E. Hamm, "Committee Unity and Influence on the Legislative Floor: A Comparative State Assessment," paper presented at the 1984 Annual Meeting of the American Political Science Association, Washington, D.C., August 29-September 2, 1984, p. 24.
[11]Advisory Commission on Intergovernmental Relations, *In Brief: State and Local Roles in the Federal System* (Washington, D.C.: U.S. Government Printing Office, 1981), pp. 8-9.
[12]Congressional Quarterly, *Inside Congress,* 2nd ed. (Washington, D.C.: Congressional Quarterly Press, 1979), p. 64.
[13]Kwang S. Shin and John S. Jackson III, "Membership Turnover in U.S. State Legislatures: 1931-1976," *Legislative Studies Quarterly,* 4 (February, 1979), pp. 97-99.
[14]Advisory Commission on Intergovernmental Relations, *The Question of State Government Capability,* p. 82. Figures are for 1982.
[15]For a fuller explanation of the "Matthew Effect," see Patterson, "American State Legislatures and Public Policy," pp. 153-155.
[16]Michael Sussman, as quoted in Andrea J. Wollock, "Reapportionment Now," *State Legislatures* (January, 1982), p. 11.
[17]*Forston* v. *Dorsey* (1965).
[18]*Whitcomb* v. *Chavis* (1970).
[19]*White* v. *Regester* (1973). In 1980, however, the U.S. Supreme Court, in *City of Mobile* v. *Bolden,* seemed to shy away from the tilt against at-large systems that it and lower federal courts had been expressing during the 1970s, and held that at-large systems were unacceptable only if it could be proven that they were used with the intent to discriminate against minorities.
[20]Advisory Commission on Intergovernmental Relations, *In Brief,* p. 7.
[21]For an excellent case study of this resistance, see Gilbert Y. Steiner and Samuel K. Gove, *The Legislature Redistricts Illinois* (Urbana: University of Illinois, Institute of Government and Public Affairs, 1956). The remaining information in this paragraph is drawn from this source.
[22]Harry Basehart, "The Nature of Representation: What the Court Guidelines Say," *National Civic Review,* 69 (November, 1980), p. 547.
[23]Wollock, "Reapportionment Now," p. 8.
[24]Senator Hal Runyan of Arizona quoted in Dan Pilcher, "Reapportionment: The New Ingredients," *State Legislatures* (April, 1980), p. 9.
[25]Carolyn Kenton, "Reapportionment—Dividing the Power," *State Government News* (October, 1981), p. 4.
[26]Kenneth Eshleman, "Affirmative Gerrymandering Is a Matter of Justice," *National Civic Review,* 69 (December, 1980), pp. 608-613, 620.
[27]This discussion is drawn from Samuel C. Patterson, "Legislators and Legislatures in the American States," in Virginia Gray, Herbert Jacob, and Kenneth N. Vines, eds., *Politics in the American States: A Comparative Analysis,* 4th ed. (Boston: Little, Brown, 1983), p. 139; and T. O'Rourke, *The Impact of Reapportionment* (New Brunswick, N.J.: Transaction, 1980).
[28]Thomas R. Dye, *Politics, Economics and the Public: Policy Outcomes in the American States* (Chicago: Rand McNally, 1966), p. 294.
[29]Richard I. Hofferbert, "The Relation Between Public Policy and Some Structural and Environmental Variables in the American States," *American Political Science Review,* 60 (March, 1966), pp. 73-82.
[30]Malcolm Jewell, "Will *Baker* v. *Carr* Save the States?" paper delivered at the National Conference of the Southern Political Science Association, 1966. Cited in Grant and Nixon, *State and Local Government,* 3rd ed., p. 261. See also Young Hyo Cho and H. George Frederickson, "The Effects of Reapportionment: Subtle, Selective, Limited," *National Civic Review,* 63 (July, 1974), pp. 357-362; and Douglas G. Feig, "Expenditures in the American States: The Impact of Reapportionment," *American Politics Quarterly,* 6 (July, 1978), pp. 309-324.
[31]James E. Lennertz, "The Policy Consequences of State Legislative Apportionment," paper presented at the 1984 Annual Meeting of the American Political Science Association, Washington, D.C., August 30-September 2, 1984.

[32]The 1963 survey results are in Wayne L. Francis, *Legislative Issues in the Fifty States* (Chicago: Rand McNally, 1967).
[33]The 1973 survey results are in Eric M. Uslaner and Ronald E. Weber, *Patterns of Decision-Making in State Legislatures* (New York: Praeger, 1977).
[34]William J. D. Boyd, "Suburbia Takes Over," *National Civic Review,* 54 (June, 1966), pp. 294-298.
[35]Duane Lockard, *The Politics of State and Local Governments,* 2nd ed. (New York: Macmillan, 1969), pp. 274-277.
[36]*Ibid.,* p. 275.
[37]Patterson, "American State Legislatures," p. 183.
[38]H. Owen Porter, "Legislative Experts and Outsiders: The Two Step Flow of Communication," *Journal of Politics,* 36 (August, 1974), pp. 703-730.
[39]John C. Wahlke, Heinz Eulau, William Buchanan, and LeRoy C. Ferguson, *The Legislative System* (New York: John Wiley, 1962), pp. 146-161.
[40]Ted Hebert and Lelan E. McLenmore, "Character and Structure of Legislative Norms," *American Journal of Political Science,* 17 (August, 1973), pp. 506-27.
[41]Wahlke et al., *The Legislative System,* p. 154.
[42]Eric M. Uslaner and Ronald E. Weber, "Changes in Legislator Attitudes Toward Gubernatorial Power," *State and Local Government Review,* 9 (May, 1977), p. 41. See also Porter, "Legislative Experts and Outsiders"; and Robert Zwier, "The Search for Information: Specialists and Nonspecialists in the U.S. House of Representatives," *Legislative Studies Quarterly,* 4 (February, 1979), pp. 31-42.
[43]Julie Davis Bell, "Legislative Genesis, Agenda Setting and Gatekeeping: A Study of the California State Legislature," paper presented at the 1984 Annual Meeting of the American Political Science Association, Washington, D.C., August 30-September 2, 1984, p. 10.
[44]Wahlke et al., *The Legislative System,* p. 376.
[45]Malcolm E. Jewell, "Party Voting in American State Legislatures," *American Political Science Review,* 49 (September, 1955), pp. 773-791; Thomas R. Dye, "A Comparison of Constituency Influences in the Upper and Lower Chambers of a State Legislature," *Western Political Quarterly,* 14 (June, 1961), pp. 473-481; and Bruce W. Robeck, "Legislative Partisanship, Constituency and Malapportionment: The Case of California," *American Political Science Review,* 66 (December, 1972), pp. 1246-1255.
[46]See, for example, Thomas A. Flinn, "Party Responsibility in the States: Some Causal Factors," *American Political Science Review,* 58 (March, 1964), pp. 60-71; and David R. Derge, "Metropolitan and Outstate Alignments in Illinois and Missouri Legislative Delegations," *American Political Science Review,* 52 (December, 1958), pp. 1051-1065.
[47]Frank J. Sorauf, *Party and Representation* (New York: Atherton, 1963), pp. 141-144.
[48]Patterson, "American State Legislatures," p. 178.
[49]See Duncan MacRae, "The Relationship Between Roll Call Votes and Constituencies in Massachusetts," *American Political Science Review,* 46 (December, 1952), pp. 1046-1055; and Samuel C. Patterson, "The Role of the Deviant in the State of Legislative System: The Wisconsin Assembly," *Western Political Quarterly,* 14 (June, 1961), pp. 460-472.
[50]Robert W. Becker, Frieda L. Foote, Mathias Lubegea, and Stephen V. Mosma, "Correlates of Legislative Voting: Michigan House of Representatives, 1954-1961," *Michigan Journal of Political Science,* 6 (November, 1962), pp. 384-396.
[51]Sarah McCally Morehouse, "Party Loyalty in a House Divided," paper presented to the 1981 Annual Meeting of the American Political Science Association, September 3-6, 1981, New York.
[52]See, for example, Hugh L. LeBlanc, "Voting in State Senates: Party and Constituency Influences," *Midwest Journal of Political Science,* 13 (February, 1969), pp. 43, 56; and Charles W. Wiggins, "Party Politics in the Iowa Legislature," *Midwest Journal of Political Science,* 11 (February, 1967), p. 94.
[53]See, for example, Wayne Peak, "The Effects of Politics on the Policy Choices of States: A Comparison Across Policy Areas and Across States," paper presented at the 1985 Annual Meeting of the American Political Science Association, August 29-September 1, 1985, New Orleans, p. 19; Thomas R. Dye, "Party and Policy in the States," *Journal of Politics,* 46 (August, 1984), pp. 1097-1116; and Edward T. Jennings, Jr., "Competition, Constituencies, and Welfare Policies in American States," *American Political Science Review,* 73 (March, 1979), pp. 414-429.
[54]Peak, "The Effects of Politics on the Policy Choices of States," p. 20.
[55]*Ibid.*

[56]Douglas Camp Chaffey and Malcolm Jewell, "Party Opposition in the Legislature: The Ecology of Legislative Institutionalization," *Polity,* 4 (Fall, 1972), pp. 744-766.
[57]Morehouse, "Party Loyalty in a House Divided," p. 19.
[58]Jerry Calvert, "Revolving Doors: Volunteerism in State Legislatures," *State Government,* 52 (Autumn 1979), pp. 174-181.
[59]Belle Zeller, *American State Legislatures* (New York: Thomas Y. Crowell, 1954), pp. 203-211.
[60]Robert Harmel, "On the Importance of State Party Caucuses: An Empirical Study," paper presented at the 1984 Annual Meeting of the American Political Science Association, Washington, D.C., August 30-September 2, 1984, p. 16. Data are for 1984.
[61]Alan Rosenthal, *Legislative Life: People, Process, and Performance in the States* (New York: Harper & Row, 1981), pp. 209-210; and Harmel, "On the Importance of State Party Caucuses," p. 4.
[62]National Conference of State Legislatures, "Legislative Caucus Procedures: Policy and Practice," State Legislative Report No. 6 (Washington, D.C.: Conference of State Legislatures, 1981), mimeo; and Harmel, "On the Importance of State Party Caucuses," p. 5.
[63]Harmel, "On the Importance of State Party Caucuses," p. 17.
[64]Quoted in Wahlke et al., *The Legislative System,* p. 340.
[65]See Harvey Walker, *The Legislative Process* (New York: Ronald, 1984); Boyd L. Wright, *Sources of Legislation in the Legislative Assembly of North Dakota* (Grand Forks: Bureau of Governmental Affairs, University of North Dakota, 1971); and Bell, "Legislative Genesis, Agenda Setting and Gatekeeping."
[66]Charles W. Wiggins, Keith E. Hamm, and Charles G. Bell, "Interest Groups and Other Influence Agents in the State Legislative Process: A Comparative Analysis," paper presented at the 1984 Annual Meeting of the American Political Science Association, Washington, D.C., August 30-September 2, 1984, p. 23.
[67]Zeigler and Baer, *Lobbying.*
[68]Wahlke et al., *The Legislative System,* pp. 323, 100.
[69]Zeigler and Baer, *Lobbying,* pp. 155-160.
[70]William Buchanan, *Legislative Partisanship: The Deviant Case of California* (Berkeley: University of California Press, 1963), pp. 101-107; see also Joel M. Fisher, Charles M. Price, and Charles G. Bell, *The Legislative Process in California* (Washington, D.C.: American Political Science Association, 1973), pp. 65-70.
[71]Bell, "Legislative Genesis, Agenda Setting, and Gatekeeping," p. 24.
[72]Wahlke et al., *The Legislative System,* p. 325.
[73]*Ibid.*
[74]Lockard, *Politics,* pp. 271-272.
[75]Wiggins, Hamm, and Bell, "Interest Groups and Other Influence Agents," p. 22.
[76]*Ibid.*
[77]See, for example, LeBlanc, "Voting in State Senates," pp. 33-57; Malcolm Jewell, "Party Voting in American State Legislatures," *American Political Science Review,* 49 (September, 1955), pp. 773-791; and Flinn, "Party Responsibility in the States," pp. 60-71.
[78]Quoted in Wahlke et al., *The Legislative System,* pp. 267-286.
[79]Ronald Hedlund and H. Paul Friesma, "Representatives Perceptions on Constituency Opinion," *Journal of Politics,* 34 (August, 1972), pp. 730-752; and Robert S. Erikson, Norman R. Luttbeg, and William V. Holloway, "Knowing One's District: How Legislators Predict Referendum Voting," *American Journal of Political Science,* 19 (May, 1975), pp. 231-234.
[80]Gallup Opinion Index, *Report No.* 20 (February, 1967), p. 17.
[81]Press release of the Minnesota poll, *Tribune,* July 11, 1965, as cited in Patterson, "American State Legislatures," p. 163.
[82]Independent Research Associates, Inc., "A Study of Voters' Opinions of State Legislatures: Iowa," prepared by Legis 50/The Center for Legislative Improvement, formerly the Citizens' Conference on State Legislatures (June, 1968), pp. 6-7.
[83]Richard J. Tobin and Edward Keynes, "Institutional Differences in the Recruitment Process: A Four State Study," *American Journal of Political Science,* 19 (November, 1975), p. 674.
[84]Lester G. Seligman et al., *Patterns of Recruitment: A State Chooses Its Lawmakers* (Chicago: Rand McNally, 1974); and B. D. Kolasa, "Party Recruitment in Nonpartisan Nebraska," in John C. Comer and James B. Johnson, eds., *Nonpartisanship in the Legislative Process* (Washington, D.C.: University Press of America, 1978).
[85]Jerome M. Mileur and George Sulzner, *Campaigning for the Massachusetts Senate* (Amherst: University of Massachusetts Press, 1974).

[86]Patterson, "Legislators and Legislatures in the American States," p. 150.
[87]Malcolm E. Jewell, *Legislative Representation in the American States* (Lexington, Ky.: University of Kentucky Press, 1982).
[88]Gregory A. Calderia and Samuel C. Patterson, "Bringing Home the Votes: Electoral Outcomes in State Legislative Races," paper presented at the 1981 Annual Meeting of the American Political Science Association, New York, September 3-6, 1981, p. 17.
[89]Zeller, *American State Legislatures,* p. 71.
[90]Bureau of the Census, *Statistical Abstract of the United States, 1985* (Washington, D.C.: U.S. Government Printing Office, 1984), Table 420, p. 251. Figure is for 1982, when there were 911 women state legislators.
[91]Emmy F. Werner, "Women in State Legislatures," *Western Political Quarterly,* 21 (March, 1968), pp. 40-50.
[92]Bureau of the Census, *Statistical Abstract of the United States, 1985,* Table 418, p. 250. The table reflects the inclusion of 21 black congressmen, and these have been subtracted in making the percentage calculation. There were 375 black state legislators in 1984.
[93]Frank J. Sorauf, *Party and Representation,* pp. 89-94.
[94]Bureau of the Census, *Statistical Abstract of the United States, 1985,* Table 419, p. 250. Figure is for 1983, when there were 108 Hispanic state legislators.
[95]Wahlke et al., *The Legislative System,* p. 488.
[96]Sorauf, *Party and Representation,* pp. 89-94.
[97]John C. McConaughy, "Some Personality Factors of State Legislators," in John C. Wahlke and Heinz Eulau, eds., *Legislative Behavior: Reader in Theory and Research* (Glencoe, Ill.: Free Press, 1959).
[98]Ronald W. Hedlund, "Psychological Predispositions: Political Representatives and the Public," *American Journal of Political Science,* 19 (August, 1973), pp. 489-505.
[99]James David Barber, *The Lawmakers: Recruitment and Adaptation to Legislative Life* (New Haven, Conn.: Yale University Press, 1965), p. 163.
[100]Wahlke et al., *The Legislative System,* pp. 249-257.
[101]Sorauf, *Party and Representation,* pp. 121-146.
[102]Charles S. Hyneman, "Tenure and Turnover of Legislative Personnel," *Annals of the American Academy of Political and Social Science,* 195 (January, 1938), pp. 30-31.
[103]Shin and Jackson, "Membership Turnover," pp. 97-99.
[104]Alan Rosenthal, "Turnover in State Legislatures," *American Journal of Political Science,* 18 (August, 1974), pp. 609-616.
[105]William Pound and Carl Tubbesing, "The State Legislatures," *Book of the States, 1978-79* (Lexington, Ky.: Council of State Governments, 1978), p. 7.
[106]Calvert, "Revolving Doors," pp. 174-181.
[107]*Ibid.* Approximately one-fourth of state senators and slightly less than a fourth of state representatives left the legislatures voluntarily after each session during the 1970s.
[108]Wayne L. Francis and John R. Baker, "Why State Legislators Vacate Their Seat," paper presented at the 1985 Annual Meeting of the American Political Science Association, September 29 - August 1, 1985, New Orleans, Table 1; and Diane Kincaid Blair and Ann D. Henry, "The Family Factor in State Legislative Turnover," *Legislative Studies Quarterly,* 6 (February, 1981), pp. 55-68.
[109]William J. Siffin, *The Legislative Council in American States* (Bloomington: Indiana University Press, 1959).
[110]Advisory Commission on Intergovernmental Relations, *The Question of State Government Capability,* p. 112.
[111]Advisory Commission on Intergovernmental Relations, *In Brief,* pp. 8-9.
[112]As derived from Table 21, Council of State Governments, *Book of the States, 1984-85,* p. 124. Figures are for 1983.
[113]Council of State Gòvernments, *1961 Survey,* as cited in Herbert L. Wiltsee, "Legislative Service Agencies," *Book of the States, 1961-62* (Lexington, Ky.: Council of State Governments, 1962), p. 67.
[114]Figures are for 1980. See William Pound, "The State Legislatures," *Book of the States, 1982-83* (Lexington, Ky.: Council of State Governments, 1982), p. 181.
[115]Michael J. BeVier, *Politics Backstage: Inside the California Legislature* (Philadelphia: Temple University Press, 1979), p. 229.
[116]Lynn B. Lehle, "Organizational Impact of Computer and Information Technology Resources on the Distribution of Decision Making Power in State Legislatures," paper presented at the 1985 Annual Meeting of the American Political Science Association, August 29 - September 1, 1985, New Orleans, p. 17.

[117]William Pound, "The State Legislatures," *Book of the States, 1980-81* (Lexington, Ky.: Council of State Governments, 1980), pp. 77-83. Figures are for 1980.
[118]Herbert L. Wiltsee, "Legislative Service Agencies," p. 66.
[119]Dye, *Politics in States and Communities,* pp. 160-161.
[120]William L. Shade and Frank J. Munger, "Consensus, Conflict, and Congruence: Policy-Making in the American States," paper delivered at the American Political Science Association, New Orleans, September 4-8, 1973.
[121]Legis 50/The Center for Legislative Improvement, formerly the Citizens' Conference on State Legislatures, *Report on an Evaluation of the 50 State Legislatures* (Denver, 1971), p. 29.
[122]Advisory Council on Intergovernmental Relations, *The Question of State Government Capability,* pp. 65-126.
[123]Larry Margolis, as quoted in David S. Broder, "Legislatures in Trouble," *Washington Post* (December 11, 1983).
[124]Glenn Newkirk, "State Legislatures Through the People's Eyes," *State Legislatures,* 5 (1979), pp. 8-9.
[125]Ronald E. Webber and William R. Shaffer, "Public Opinion and American State Policymaking," *Midwest Journal of Political Science,* 16 (November, 1972), pp. 683-691.
[126]T. V. Smith, "Two Functions of the American State Legislature," *Annals of the American Academy of Political and Social Science,* 195 (January, 1938), p. 187. See also T. V. Smith, *The Legislative Way of Life* (Chicago: University of Chicago Press, 1940).

6

THE GREENING OF THE GOVERNORS

Governors are moving up in the pecking order of American politics. It was not all that long ago that governors were referred to as "flowery old courthouse politicians" or "political pipsqueaks";[1] a famous columnist observed in 1962 that "the state capitols are over their heads in problems and up to their knees in midgets."[2]

But by the mid-1970s, an equally reputable observer could state, "There may have been, a decade ago, stronger individual governors in the Big Five States, but never, in this reporter's experience, a group of fifty governors—from New England to Dixie—as capable as the current crop."[3] Another student of the American governorship has stated that we now have as governors a "new breed of vigorous, incisive, and thoroughly trained leaders."[4]

Americans seem to agree. A Harris survey, for example, concluded that "Governors are easily the best known political figures in the country" with the sole exception of the president.[5] Another poll by Harris found that governors ranked higher than either members of Congress or state legislators; 9 percent of Americans rated their governors' performance as "excellent," compared to 2 percent for legislatures and 1 percent for Congress.[6] Table 6-1 indicates the results of this survey.

But among the most important indications of the burgeoning political prestige of the governorship is the reduction, over the last few decades, of the so-called "coattail effect" that presidents traditionally have had on gubernatorial elections. During the last few years of the nineteenth century, the party of the president could almost always pull the gubernatorial candidates who were running on his party's ticket into office with him. Between 1880 and 1892, more

Table 6-1 Public Opinions of Governors' Performance, 1979

Rating	*Percent*
Excellent	9%
Pretty good	35
Only fair	33
Poor	18
Not sure	5
	100%

Source: Glenn Newkirk, "State Legislatures Through the People's Eyes," *State Legislatures,* 5 (August–September, 1979), pp. 8–9.

than 93 percent of the governors elected belonged to the same party as the president, and even by midcentury more than three quarters of the governorships were still going to the party of the successful presidential candidate. But by 1960, things began to change, and between 1960 and 1980, less than 59 percent of the governors belonged to the party of the successful presidential candidate. Table 6-2 indicates the deteriorating "coattail effect" of presidents on gubernatorial candidates. The significance of this decline is that governors appear to be emerging more than ever before as political figures in their own right.

WHO ARE THE GOVERNORS?

Increasingly, governors are a well-educated lot. During the 1970s, virtually each one of the 146 men and women who were governors during that decade attended one or more colleges or universities. The 1970s were the first decade in which this was true, and the educational levels of the governors have increased every decade in this century. During the 1900-1910 period, fewer than half of the governors were college graduates. Educations in law predominate, although law degrees are in decline.[7]

Governors are typically elected to their first term of office in their mid-forties, and the age level of governors has been gradually declining since 1940. More than half of the governors have been attorneys, and another 20 percent

Table 6-2 The "Coattail Effect" of Presidents on Gubernatorial Elections, 1880–1980

Period[1]	*Percentage with Coinciding Party Results for Governor and President*	*Percentage with Different Party Results for Governor and President*
1880–1892	93.1%	6.9%
1896–1908	89.5	11.5
1912–1924	81.2	18.8
1928–1940	77.8	22.2
1944–1956	75.5	24.5
1960–1980	58.5	41.5

[1] Each time period includes four presidential elections, except the 1960–1980 period, which includes six.

Source: Larry Sabato, *Goodbye to Good-time Charlie: The American Governorship Transformed,* 2nd ed. (Washington, D.C.: Congressional Quarterly Press, 1983), p. 139.

come from the business sector. The state legislatures provide the largest single political pool of future governors, followed by holders of statewide elective offices, such as lieutenant governors, who move on to the governorship. Roughly a quarter of the governors who served their terms between 1970 and 1981 ran for the office as the occupant of a statewide elective office, while another 22 percent were state legislators.[8] About the only trends that have been observed in terms of "springboard offices" to the governorship are the decrease in law enforcement positions and the increase in congressional ones. Compared to the early part of the century, in other words, increasingly fewer governors have held, as their last political office immediately prior to becoming governor, a position in law enforcement, while more congress members and state legislators are running for the governorship than ever before.[9]

Few women have ever been governors. Prior to 1970, only three were elected to the governor's mansion, and in each case they had been immediately preceded in the governorship by their husbands. But beginning in the 1970s, women began making some real, if modest, gubernatorial gains. In 1974, the late Ella T. Grasso of Connecticut became the first woman governor to be elected governor in her own right, and Dixy Lee Ray of Washington became the second in 1976. In 1984 Martha Layne Collins made it a triumvirate when she became governor of Kentucky.

No black has ever been elected governor since Reconstruction, but two Hispanics won the office during the 1970s: Jerry Apodaca of New Mexico and Raul Castro of Arizona. Democrats habitually have outnumbered Republican governors during the past 50 years.[10]

GETTING THERE AND GETTING OUT

As with all other forms of state and local campaigning, the cost of getting to the governor's chair is increasingly expensive. One analysis of the reported campaign expenditures for 50 gubernatorial races during the 1978-80 election cycle totaled more than $175 million, or an average of $3.5 million per gubernatorial chair. In a half-dozen of these campaigns an average of more than $9 million was spent per state. In Louisiana, in fact, nearly $21 million were spent on campaigns, or more than $15 per voter, a record for recorded gubernatorial campaign expenditures. Without the six most expensive campaigns, the average cost during the 1978-80 cycle was $2.2 million per gubernatorial campaign.[11] As one observer has noted, "The good news is that you can still buy West Virginia. The bad news is, boy, is it expensive."[12]

Figure 6-1 indicates that the cost of running for governor clearly is on the rise (although the data on this topic are somewhat fragmentary). The figure traces the rise in gubernatorial campaign expenditures, controlling for inflation, in seven states. Although there are peaks and valleys, the general trend is upward.

Does money count? Is there a relationship between campaign expenditures and winning? Yes, there is. An analysis of 48 contested primary races for the governorship found that "the winning candidate was the one who spent the most money" in 36 of the campaigns.[13]

An increasing number of governors are eligible to run for a second term as incumbents, and a growing number of them are now doing so. From 1900 to

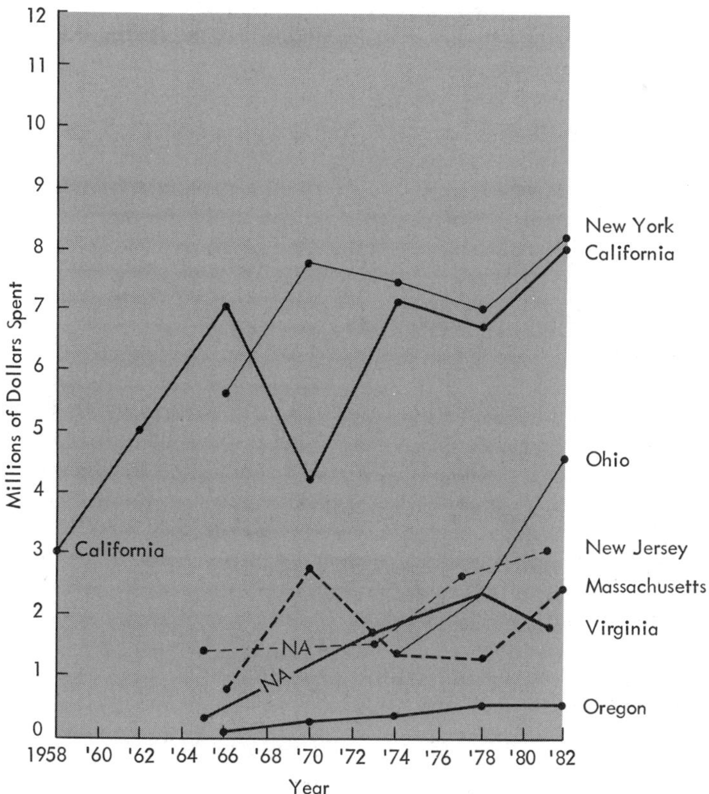

Figure 6-1 Trends in gubernatorial expenditures: Selected states, adjusted to 1967 dollars. (*Source:* Thad L. Beyle, "The Cost of Becoming Governor," *State Government* 56, No. 2, 1983, p. 76.

1909, there were 76 elections in which the governor could seek reelection, but in only 46 percent of them did an incumbent run. By the 1970-1979 decade, however, there were 113 elections in which the governor could seek reelection, and in 69 percent of those elections, an incumbent governor ran.[14]

Clearly, the attractions of the office are gaining on governors. But staying in office is, perhaps, a less certain proposition for governors than it is for incumbent legislators or members of Congress, since the proportion of governors who are defeated for reelection is higher than it is for either of these groups. From 1940 through 1969, approximately two-thirds of the incumbent governors who ran for reelection won, and during the 1970-1979 decade not quite three quarters of the incumbent governors won. The key issues in the defeats of incumbent governors were intraparty politics (31 percent of the incumbent and former governors running for reelection were defeated in their party's primary), tax issues (more than 20 percent of the governors were defeated for reelection because they had raised taxes), party competitiveness (16 percent of the governors were defeated by the superior campaign tactics of the opposition party), and scandal (13 percent lost because of scandals in their administrations).[15]

Increasingly, governors return to private life, usually in the form of a lucrative law practice, upon completing their stint in the gubernatorial chair; during the 1970s, more than three out of every five did so. The one-third of governors who went on to other offices typically took a federal job. Nearly 8 percent entered the United States Senate following their term as governor; almost 15 percent entered some federal administrative office such as a cabinet, subcabinet, or ambassadorial position; and not quite 8 percent became a governor again or received the presidential or vice-presidential nomination of one of the two major parties. Nearly 3 percent of the governors during the 1970-1980 decade followed their gubernatorial career with a term in prison.[16]

DO GOVERNORS MATTER? THE DEBATE BETWEEN DETERMINISTS AND HUMANISTS

A recurring theme in the literature of American political science is (for want of better terms) the dialogue between the "determinists" and the "humanists." Perhaps no reality of American politics has brought this debate into sharper focus than has the office of governor, and what the governorship means to America's civic life.

The determinist approach represents, in the view of one observer, "a much broader attempt to depoliticize the political process."[17] When this perspective is narrowed to the governorship, it can best be expressed as the "helpless state executive" thesis.[18]

The basic thrust of the determinists' argument is an economic one. It holds that a state's level of wealth, industrialization, urbanization, and education, among other variables that associate with a high social and economic status, correlate far more conclusively with the kinds of public policies that are enacted by states than anything that a mere governor—a transitory political executive—is able to do. Consider the following assessment made by a leader of this school of thought:

> There is little evidence that a governor's formal powers significantly affect policy outcomes in the fifty states. While "strong" and "weak" governor states pursue somewhat different policies in education, health, welfare, highways, and taxation, these differences are attributable largely to the impact of economic development rather than to the governor's power.[19]

There are variations on this deterministic hypothesis of politics. For example, Joseph A. Schlesinger has related the power of governors, as determined by the amount of certain legal powers they possess, to the states' levels of urbanism and population size. Schlesinger's index of formal gubernatorial power is comprised of four components: tenure longevity, appointive powers, responsibilities for preparing the budget, and veto powers. He found that the more urban and richer states tended to accord their governors more formal powers; the more rural and poorer states gave their governors fewer formal powers. All the larger states that are also highly industrialized, such as California, Illinois, New Jersey, New York, and Pennsylvania, were rated high on Schlesinger's formal power index, although Schlesinger was careful to note that the degree of formal legal powers granted to governors did not necessarily equate with powerful governors as such; gubernatorial power, he implied, still could be affected by a governor's personal skills.[20]

Relatedly, James E. Jarrett, in an effort to determine the capacity of governors to affect the size of their state government bureaucracies, found that governors were relatively helpless to alter the number of employees in their own executive branches.

> State government growth . . . is engendered primarily by population growth, economic growth, and intergovernmental aid increases . . . it follows that state elections for governors . . . do not provide a true opportunity for altering state government growth, even when clear-cut choices between candidates are provided. A broader implication . . . is that state government growth and changes in state government employment in this country, seem to stand largely outside the realm of intentional, political preferences of high elected state officials.[21]

These and other studies in the determinists' tradition implicitly take the point of view that the human being is not a terribly important factor in politics. Thomas R. Dye, for example, argues that certain welfare policies bear no relation to gubernatorial power or ability; Schlesinger takes the point of view that the formal power base of the governor is a factor of urbanism, wealth, and industrialization; Jarrett contends that such a basic phenomenon as the public employment level within a state cannot be affected by even the highest elected official of that state, and that there is a far more positive correlation between state governmental size and the growth of a state's population, economy, and success in securing federal grants. Governors, in short, do not count for much.

A counterview is taken by the humanists. Here, the central variable is not economics but politics.

Among the more articulate advocates of the humanists' tradition as it pertains to the governorship is Sarah McCally Morehouse. Morehouse contends, pointedly, that "the role of political leadership has been minimized in recent years as a result of studies that stressed the influence of socioeconomic variables over policy outcomes. In much of the literature in state policy output, the deterministic view of what leadership in the state can accomplish is a counsel of despair."[22] She goes on to note that the governor has at least six major political bases: patronage, publicity, the promise (or threat) of campaign support (or opposition) to other politicians, control over information, influence over the scheduling of local legislation, and the promise of advancement in the governor's party or his or her faction within the legislature.[23]

A similar position is taken by Ira Sharkansky. In a study of the governor's and bureaucracy's role in the budget process in 19 states, Sharkansky found that

> administrative agencies and the governor play more consistent roles than the legislature in the state budget process . . . the major agencies . . . requested an average of 24 percent increase in their current budgets, and that the governor's recommendations trimmed an average of 14 percent from their request. The legislature's final appropriation for these agencies typically remained close to the governor's recommendation. . . . The governor's support appears to be a critical ingredient in the success enjoyed by individual agencies in the legislature.[24]

The determinist's and the humanist's perspectives on the role of the governor (and, for that matter, on the role of politics) in the states present both a conflict and a paradox. The conflict centers on the fact that the determinists attribute social change and the creation of public policy to large-scale economic and social forces that are well beyond the ken and influence of mere mortal politicians. By contrast, the humanists take the view that the human being is at the center of the political process; therefore, it stands to reason that the higher the political official, the more critical that official is to the political process. Hence, the governor assumes considerable importance in the humanist's viewpoint.

The paradox centers on the fact that the foci of analysis used by the determinists and the humanists are quite different. The determinists are dealing with interstate aggregate data. For example, it may be interesting to learn that those states with wealth, industry, cities, and relatively literate populations spend more on welfare than do those states that are less blessed by such advantages, and that the formal (or even reputed) power of the governors shows little, if any, correlation with these expenditures. But this datum is irrelevant to the problem of how the policymaking process works *within* states, regardless of their social and economic status. If, instead of asking the question, "What kinds of states spend the most on welfare policies?" and we ask, "What impact does the governor have on policymaking within his or her state?" we may end up with entirely different answers. It also might be persuasively argued that the latter question has more importance than the former, at least if we are interested in determining how the process of policy formation actually works. As Coleman B. Ransone, Jr. (himself a member of the humanist camp), has put it, what the determinists do "is emphasize the fact that the economic conditions in a given state at a particular time, may set the parameters within which the policy process operates. However, these studies do not explain the process itself. The basic question of policy formation still remains: Who gets what, when, and where within a state?"[25]

In this chapter, we assume a humanist's perspective. We do it for two reasons. First, we believe that people do make a difference in politics, and second, the humanists' concerns go to the heart of the political process in that they ask *how* policies are made within political systems rather than what kinds of policies associate with what kinds of economic conditions. The question of how policy is made remains the central query of politics itself.

THE GOVERNOR AND THE PARTY

It appears from the available evidence that governors have increasingly little use for their own political parties. One major empirical study of governors found that the party was involved only marginally with the governors' appointments to state jobs, was "ideologically irrelevant" to the governor's legislative agenda, and had "no influence upon the course of policy development."[26] The investigation had found that partisan ideology was usually overruled by gubernatorial common sense and a "loose pragmatism," that governors "largely dismissed the party platform as meaningless," and that "patronage is in part the victim of the managerial image and the emerging conviction among governors that the business of state government is beyond politics."[27]

Within this context of disparagement of the party's role, however, the governors believe that the party still has a few functions left. For one, the party continues to provide a major linkage with legislators in getting a governor's program enacted, although the governor's interest in the party focuses on only one segment of it: the legislative party. We consider this later in the chapter.

A second reason why the party has some importance to governors deals with the complex of intergovernmental relations that has emerged since 1960. With the federal bureaucracy ever more involved in state and local finance, greasing the cogs of the intergovernmental machine becomes a far easier task when the governor is a member of the predominant party in Washington. As one governor has observed, "I learned quickly the difference when you are of the same party as the President—that's critically important . . . that is why governors who sit on the sidelines and say that selection of the president doesn't make any difference are misleading themselves. I found that it makes a lot of difference."[28]

Finally, each governor faces the necessity of obtaining a nomination for election or reelection from one of the two major parties of the state. Ironically, however, once that nomination is obtained, the gubernatorial nominee tends to leave the party behind rather abruptly. One governor has noted that "the party is a mechanism—there's really no other way to get the nomination. But very few people get elected because of the activities of the party . . . for the most part—with today's electronic media—it's the individual who gets elected; it's not the party."[29]

The declining role of the state party in nominating gubernatorial candidates is an important trend even in the states where only one party has dominated. Table 6-3 indicates the growing insignificance of the gubernatorial primary in one-party Democratic states. The vote in these primaries, as a percentage of the general election, has shrunk drastically. For example, between 1930 and 1950, the vote in the Democratic primary in 11 Southern one-party Democratic states was literally ten times the voting turnout in the general election. This was because the Democratic primary, not the general election, was the "real" election, or the one in which the governor was effectively elected. But during the 1950-1980 period, the turnout in the South's Democratic primaries fell precipitously. In only four of these states has the average gubernatorial

Table 6-3 The Fading Gubernatorial Primary in One-Party Democratic States, 1930–1980

	1930–1950 Primary Interest[1]	*1951–1980 Primary Interest*[1]
South Carolina	1009.1	98.2
Mississippi	550.1	149.2
Louisiana	511.1	152.0
Georgia	315.8	114.2
Alabama	211.1	128.7
Texas	194.8	78.8
Arkansas	139.4	76.8
Florida	111.4	61.0
Tennessee	108.2	87.2
Virginia	101.5	47.1
North Carolina	54.4	40.8

[1] Figures show the total vote in the gubernatorial primary as a percentage of the total vote for governor in the subsequent general election, on the average. If no primary was held in a given year, the general election vote in the same year was not used.

Source: Larry Sabato, *Goodbye to Good-time Charlie: The American Governorship Transformed,* 2nd ed. (Washington, D.C.: Congressional Quarterly Press, 1983), p. 124.

primary turnout been higher than the turnout for the general election, and, since 1971, only two states, Alabama and Mississippi, have persisted in this pattern. The decline of voter turnout in the primaries of these one-party states reflects the diminishing importance of the dominant party in determining the state's next governor.

THE GOVERNOR AND THE LEGISLATURE

The typical governor spends a sixth of his or her time (the largest single block of time, second only to managing state government itself) dealing with the legislature. Virtually every governor has at least one staffer whose full-time job is one of legislative liaison. Despite staff assistance, however, one survey of 56 governors and former governors found that of all the problems of running state government, working with the legislature rated as the most onerous.[30]

The Governors' New Powers

If legislative relations are the governor's biggest frustration, the office nonetheless has received new constitutional and statutory powers during the past two decades that have increased the governor's authority in dealing with the legislature and likely have eased the task considerably from years past.

The veto. Not the least of these new authorities is the strengthened use of the veto power. Only one state, North Carolina, does not permit its governor to veto legislation, but a number of other states have given their governors more comprehensive and sophisticated veto powers than the president has. For example, in 43 states, the governor may "item veto" appropriations bills. This means that the governor can veto a single item in the budget proposed by the legislature without rejecting the bill in its entirety. Such a power permits the governor to evade accepting objectional parts of appropriations measures simply because the bill is too important as a whole to veto.

Eleven states have strengthened even this considerable power and have granted the governor an "item reduction power," which permits a governor to reduce the appropriated amounts on specific items rather than simply to veto them.[31] Fifteen states (up from only four in 1950) grant the governor the power of "executive amendment," whereby the governor can return a bill that he or she has vetoed to the legislature, along with suggested amendments that, if enacted, would not be vetoed.[32] These powers and their various permutations grant the governors in most states a greater authority with legislatures than the president of the United States has with Congress. Table 6-4 rates the governors' veto powers by state.

Of course, legislatures retain the power of overriding the governor's veto, usually by a two-thirds vote, although in six states legislatures may override by a simple majority, and in five states three-fifths (60 percent) of the legislators can override. Nevertheless, legislatures are seldom able to do so. It appears that only 5 to 6 percent of bills vetoed by governors are ever passed into law by virtue of a legislative override (although this percentage represents an increase from 1 to 2 percent of the vetoed bills overridden by legislatures in the late 1940s) and, even then, such overrides occur in only about a third of the states in any given

Table 6-4 The Governors' Veto Powers

Very Strong		Strong	Medium	Weak
Alaska	Minnesota	Alabama	Massachusetts	Indiana
Arizona	Mississippi	Arkansas	Montana	Maine
California	Missouri	Kentucky	New Mexico	Nevada
Colorado	Nebraska	Tennessee	Oregon	New Hampshire
Connecticut	New Jersey	West Virginia	South Carolina	North Carolina[1]
Delaware	New York		Texas	Rhode Island
Florida	North Dakota		Virginia	Vermont
Georgia	Ohio		Washington	
Hawaii	Oklahoma		Wisconsin	
Idaho	Pennsylvania			
Illinois	South Dakota			
Iowa	Utah			
Kansas	Wyoming			
Louisiana				
Maryland				
Michigan				

[1] No veto power.

Source: The Book of the States, 1984–85 (Lexington, Ky.: Council of State Governments, 1985).

year. Still, governors tend to use the veto power gingerly and veto only about 5 percent of all the bills sent to them by their legislatures.[33]

In considering whether or not to veto a bill, governors often perform a complicated political pirouette. Governors and their legislative assistants tend to be very reluctant to threaten the use, or to confirm the lack of use, of a veto prior to legislation arriving on their desks. Similarly, governors touch a number of political bases when considering the use of the veto: legislators, agency heads, appeals procedures, and public hearings are all part of the process. But when all is said and done, if a governor really does not like the bill, he or she harbors few compunctions about vetoing it. A large portion of a sampling of governors are entirely willing to use the veto in a "hard-case" situation, that is, when a clearly popular bill is passed, but the governor believes that the legislation would be detrimental to the best interests of the state.[34]

When it comes to the item veto power held by the governors in 43 states, however, state legislative budget officers hold a more jaundiced perspective and generally believe that governors are more likely to use the item veto for reasons of partisan advantage rather than fiscal restraint. When governors do attain greater fiscal responsibility through the use of the item veto, it often is an incidental side effect of their partisan motivations.[35]

Another power that the governor has is the ability to call the legislature into special session. All 50 governors have this power, but in 23 states, they also have the power to set the agenda for the special session that they call; hence, legislators in these states may not go off on their own legislative tangents but must stick instead to the agenda set by the governor.[36]

The tenure. Another formal power that has been granted to governors during the past quarter century has been the dramatic extension of the governors' terms of office. Although the states have been moving steadily toward increasing the length of gubernatorial tenure since the founding of the country itself (at the close of the Revolutionary War, 10 of the 13 original states had gubernatorial terms of only a single year), this trend has picked up in the last two or three decades; in fact, seven states during the 1970s alone changed their gubernatorial tenures from two years to four. Table 6-5 indicates the extension of the governors' tenure from 1960 through 1984. Only 4 states still retain the two-year term (as opposed to 16 in 1960), and only 4 prohibit their governors from succeeding themselves (compared to 15 in 1960).

The increase in the governors' tenure potential has the obvious advantage of reducing the number of opportunities for a presiding governor to become a "lame duck." The lengthening of terms and the growing number of opportunities to succeed oneself as governor yield greater stability and continuity to the office. Partial evidence of this increased stability is reflected in a national survey of major state administrators. Only 30 percent of those public administrators who served under governors with two-year terms thought that their governors had high levels of authority. But more than 43 percent of those administrators serving under governors with tenures of four years felt that their governors had high authority levels.[37]

In addition to strengthening the governor's hand with his or her bureaucracy, longer terms of office have diminished the requirement that an incumbent governor campaign constantly to retain the governorship at reelection time. As an Ohio commission stated in recommending that Ohio's gubernatorial term be stretched from two to four years, "a two year term in office of governor, leaves him in the situation where, in the first term, he must spend the first year getting acquainted with his position, and the second year in campaigning for reelection. These necessities pose a severe limiting factor to his administrative contribution."[38] We might add, of course, that such necessities have posed an equally severe limiting factor to a governor's ability to work with a legislature.

Legislative reapportionment. A final structural reform that has enhanced the power of the governor has less to do with the executive branch and more to do with the legislative branch. With the implementation of the one-person, one-vote principle during the 1960s, rural, conservative interests lost political ground in

Table 6-5 Changes in Governors' Terms of Office, 1960–1984

	1960	*1984*
Four-year terms		
No consecutive reelections allowed	15	4[a]
Two terms allowed	7	24
No limitation on number of reelections	12	18
Total	34	46
Two-year terms		
Two consecutive reelections allowed	2	—
No limitation on reelections allowed	14	4
Total	16	4[b]

[a] Kentucky, Mississippi, New Mexico, and Virginia.

[b] States with two-year terms: Arkansas, New Hampshire, Rhode Island, and Vermont.

Source: Data from *The Book of the States, 1960* and *1984–85* (Lexington, Ky.: Council of State Governments, 1960 and 1985).

at least 45 states. Until reapportionment, rural interests had often dominated legislatures far beyond their numbers in the electorate, while the governors, more often than not, were elected by urban and suburban voters. Hence, the scene was set for policy conflicts between the governor's mansion and the statehouse. And the statehouse usually won. By 1970, however, this situation had been fully rectified. "For the first time, governors and the legislature were elected by and represented the same weighted constituency—a development that could only help them find a community of programmatic interests."[39]

In fact, the harmony that exists between the legislatures and the governors is, in contrast to the bickering relationships between the Congress and the president, quite remarkable. A survey of state senators in 11 diverse states

> revealed a surprisingly high degree of consensus among lawmakers that there *is* a proper balance in power relations between the legislature and the chief executive. Thus . . . it does not appear that most legislators actually believe that they are anything approaching vassals of the governor. If lawmakers acquiesce or even relinquish some of their power to the governor, it may be because they choose to do so.[40]

Gubernatorial Authority and Legislative Power

These increases in the formal powers of the governors (plus some others such as the governors' expanding control of the state budget process and the authority to make critical appointments, which we discuss later) correlate strongly and positively with the ability of governors to get legislation that they wish enacted. In a sophisticated regression analysis of 20 representative states, Morehouse isolated three factors that could be associated with the ability of a governor to secure legislative support for his or her program. These factors were the state's economy (i.e., industrialization, urbanization, and related variables), the governor's leadership of the party (i.e., strong to weak), and the governor's formal powers (i.e., the legal authority of budget making, veto capability, appointment control, and tenure potential).[41]

The condition of the state's economy, in Morehouse's analysis, was only "weakly to negatively" associated with the legislature's support of the governor's program. The next most useful factor in getting the governor's program enacted was the ability of the governor to lead his or her party. But by far the most important factor in strengthening the governor's hand with the legislature was the extent of the governor's formal powers.

Morehouse's conclusion—that formal powers carry more clout than partisan leadership—has found support in another analysis that employed a quite different methodology. A survey of governors discovered that those governors who possessed the fewest formal powers were also the most reluctant to enter the partisan "electoral thicket" in an attempt to build legislative support for their program. Paradoxically, however, governors invested with the most formidable legal and constitutional authority also were disinclined to involve themselves in such skirmishes. Although the results are the same—that is, most governors tend to avoid entering intraparty battles over leadership selection in the legislature and related partisan brawls that are "internal" to the legislature or involve the selection of legislative candidates—the motivations among governors to stay out of their legislative party's affairs are radically different. "Weak" governors avoid intense intraparty disputes because they fear that such fights might only weaken them further, but "strong" governors sidestep the same kinds of battles because fighting them usually is unnecessary in getting their programs through their legislatures—they have other weapons—and engaging in them is potentially counterproductive.[42]

Gubernatorial Skill: Luck, Lobbying, and Legislative Effectiveness

There are other problems confronting governors who must deal (as all of them must, to some degree) with their legislative parties. For example, it is entirely possible for a governor actually to have too much of a majority of his or her party. While a majority is positively related to the success of governors in getting legislation passed, once the majority becomes too large their success in acquiring enough votes to pass their legislative programs begins to diminish. "The governor can handle the modest majority, but when his party has an overwhelming majority, coalitions form against him, which he cannot undermine with his traditional stock of rewards and punishments. The optimum legislative contingent, then, would appear to be a comfortable majority—say about 55 percent in both houses of the legislature."[43]

On Being Gubernatorial

In the following excerpt, former Governor Milton Shapp of Pennsylvania makes a sound case for moving fast and moving hard when first walking into the governor's mansion.

Then I announced my cabinet positions. I was sworn in on January 17, 1971, at noon. There was a parade for an hour, and then my schedule called for lunch—and at one o'clock, the Senate was to go into session to confirm my appointments to the cabinet. At two o'clock, there was going to be a general reception in the House of Representatives for all the friends of the cabinet nominees—who at that point would all be cabinet officers. At 1:30, I was still on the reviewing stand, and had sandwiches and coffee brought out there—bands going by. I got a message from one my aides that the Senate Committee on Appointments—the Nominations Committee—had adjourned without bringing out any of the names of my appointees to the various cabinet positions.

So, I had my first crisis. About 2,000 to 2,500 people were there—friends, relatives and 17 to 20 people from the cabinet. Fortunately, the Attorney General, a man by the name of Fred Speaker, an attorney from Harrisburg whom I knew very well, a Republican, had not resigned his post. So I called a meeting of all my top advisors, and we decided that what I would do was take my Secretary-designee for Welfare, Helene Wohlgemuth, appoint her Special Assistant for Welfare, and give her instructions to go on over to the secretary's office and sit at the secretary's desk and run things in my name. And my Secretary-designee for Agriculture, Jim McHale, would be designated Special Assistant for Agriculture to do the same thing, and so on across the board. I couldn't do that with my Attorney General because of legal restrictions. So I had a meeting of all my cabinet-designees, and I appointed them all and just gave them a letter and signed it. They went over and started running things in my name. Fred Speaker, at my request, stayed on as Attorney General so I had an Attorney General, and so that when anything was challenged he could issue a ruling. After about a week, the Senate leadership came to me. I wouldn't say they capitulated, but the end of that meeting was that the appointments were all made. So, my first head-on clash with them showed that I was resolved to do things in a way that I thought fit.

Source: "Governors' Views on Management," *State Government,* 54, No. 3 (1981), pp. 66-67

In other words, governors have only a finite number of resources to expend among their fellow party members, and thus, while the number of party members in the legislature may increase, a governor's political resources with which to feed these additional mouths do not multiply proportionately with them.[44]

This dilemma becomes even more pronounced in states that are dominated by a single party, such as the 11 Southern states. In fact, governors appear to be more successful in those legislatures where there is a high degree of party competition than in those one-party states where the governor is a member of the same party.[45] In the one-party states, "the governor has no dependable, cohesive faction to support his program, nor does he face a cohesive opposition."[46]

Governors have the best chance of working effectively through their legislative parties when they can also exercise a substantial degree of control over the party apparatus that exists outside the state legislature, or those parties in the counties and cities, as well as the state organization itself. Morehouse found that there was a high and positive correlation between outside party cohesion and the legislative party's loyalty to the governor, and that the "governor's outside party organization generates discipline within the legislative party."[47] Such a combination works most efficaciously in pushing the governor's programs through the legislature.

Although formal executive powers, party cohesiveness, and gubernatorial party control all associate with high levels of gubernatorial success in enacting legislative programs, the governor's role in the legislative process remains a delicate and subtle one, about which few generalizations can be drawn because lobbying with individual members of the legislature by the governor's legislative liaison is a constant and frequent business. Two-thirds of the governors' legislative liaisons, in fact, have floor privileges when the legislature is in session, and three quarters of the governors maintain the policy of an open door for any and all legislators.[48]

State agency heads provide a formidable back up to the governors' immediate staffs in getting the governors' programs enacted. As "Big Daddy" Jesse Unruh of California once observed, "The governor is the biggest lobbyist in the state, and these [referring to the state bureaucracy] are his troops."[49]

Besides lobbying members of the legislature, governors also work with their party to bring along new members of the legislature who will be sympathetic to their programs. However, this is done with enormous tact and selectivity. Governors, for example, only rarely become actively involved in the candidate selection process of their own party; one survey found that only 15 percent were willing to do so in any systematic way. On the other hand, almost two-thirds of the governors would do so on a selective basis, although another fifth under no circumstances would become involved in selecting their party's candidates. Half of the governors think that a conscientious effort to campaign for their party's candidate is appropriate, but almost a tenth believe that they should not participate in even this aspect of their role as party leader. In fact, almost four-fifths of the governors feel that they should play absolutely no role in the process of the selection of the legislative leadership, since this is strictly an internal matter of the legislatures.[50]

Regardless of the sources of their power in dealing with the legislature, governors are surprisingly successful in getting their programs through. At least one investigation has indicated that legislatures enact into law approximately 70 percent of the recommendations that governors make to the legislature.[51] By contrast, the "success rate" of presidents in getting their proposed domestic legislation through Congress has been measured at around 40 percent.[52] When we combine this 70 percent success rate of governors with their considerable ability to fend off legislative overrides of their vetoes, the governor emerges as a figure of considerable legislative power in most states.

THE GOVERNOR AND THE BUREAUCRACY

A similar power curve can be traced in the governors' relations with their own bureaucracies, and in many ways the gains made by the governors in controlling their bureaucrats are actually more impressive than the progress they have made in working effectively with the legislature.

The public bureaucracy represents a considerable political challenge in its own right. In fact, governors accord the management of state government their largest single block of time (more than a fourth of their time is spent on this activity), even more time than they spend working with the legislatures.[53]

The Public Bureaucracy: A Wiley Beast

One reason why governors must spend more time managing their bureaucracies than in any other activity is attributable to the natural antagonism that exists between a governor and the state agencies. As an elected chief executive, the governor has considerable influence among the various agencies and organizations of the executive branch. But influence is not the same as power, and a governor is not a manager of the state's executive branch in the same sense that a chief executive officer manages a large corporation. On the one hand, governors are elected to represent the people of their entire state, and to do so they must convince the public that they are fulfilling their duty as a political executive. On the other hand, state government, like any bureaucracy, is large, diverse, and, to some degree, autonomous. Within the framework of these two realities, governors must provide a basic stewardship of the bureaucracy itself; respond to ongoing political crises; provide for basic administrative functions, such as accurate accounting; and manage and resolve "turf wars" and other problems among the state agencies.[54] In short, state chief executives must deal with a very different kind of bureaucratic animal than their counterparts in the private sector.

Perhaps, as a partial consequence of this difference, governors habitually seem to distrust their own state agencies. To a degree, this distrust is healthy, but it also can be an impairment to the evolution of a close working relationship with competent state officials. Consider the following evaluation expressed by one governor:

> For the first year or so of my administration, I used to carry a piece of paper with me in my pocket to meetings with bureaucrats, particularly middle-level bureaucrats. I don't use that as a perjorative term, although I know it sounds that way. Well, halfway through a meeting I would take that piece of paper out of my pocket and look at it. On it was written, "The bastards are lying." Well—they are.

Not consciously, not consciously at all, but the system produces an intense desire to tell the boss, the elective guy, particularly, what you think he wants to hear instead of what he really wants to hear.[55]

Consolidating the Governors' Management Powers

The governors' problems with their own bureaucracies had reached a critical point by the 1960s. Despite considerable pressures, especially from the nation's capitol, for state governments to begin dealing with problems of public administration and reorganization that had been building for years, not a single comprehensive statewide reorganization of the executive branch had taken place during the 1940s or throughout most of the 1950s.[56]

By the mid-1960s, the stultification of state bureaucracies had grown intolerable to most governors. According to a survey taken in 1965, more than 46 percent of the governors listed the lack of the power to reorganize their agencies as among their major problems, and two-thirds stressed the absence of the appointive power in certain areas as the most damaging single weakness in their role as chief executive.[57] The frustration of the governors in terms of bringing their own houses under control no doubt was compounded by the drive by the heads of state agencies to gain even more autonomy than they already had. A survey that was also taken in the mid-1960s of agency administrators in all 50 states found that only 42 percent wanted to be under the primary control of the governor.[58] The resistance by state agency heads to "interference" and management by their governors perhaps is summed up in the remark made by the head of a public agency in Mississippi, who was responding to a question about how he felt about consolidating various management functions in his state's government:

> I think this is one of the very best things that has ever been done in the state of Mississippi and I long have been of the opinion that this work should have been accomplished in the past. However, my department is of a type, character and kind that cannot be consolidated with any other agency, as its duties and functions are unique, and a reduction of personnel or a transfer of any duties of this department would work a hardship and prevent certain citizens from receiving benefits to which they are entitled.[59]

Eventually, state policymakers had had enough. The late 1960s and 1970s witnessed a spate of administrative reforms that accorded the governors far more management powers than they had ever had in the past. Besides increased veto powers and lengthened tenures, states consolidated executive functions, reduced the number of statewide elected offices, expanded the governor's reorganization powers, and increased the governor's control over the budgetary process.

The general consolidation of executive functions that occurred during this period was dramatic, and frequently was written into the states' constitutions. Between 1902 and 1963, only 5 states redrafted their constitutions, but from 1964 through 1980 10 states completely overhauled their constitutions, and these redraftings resulted in substantial gains for the governors' offices. Between 1972 and 1979, states considered 118 constitutional changes dealing specifically with the executive branch and enacted 80 of them.[60] Between 1965 and 1980, 22 states totally redesigned their executive branch, and in every case, the result was a concentration of power in the office of the governor. Virtually all the other states reorganized one or more departments during this period.[61]

Minimizing the "mini-governors." One of the thrusts of these consolidations centered on the gradual reduction in statewide elective offices. There were in 1965 (aside from the governors and lieutenant governors) 244 separately elected executive branch officials in the states, but by 1984 this number had been reduced to 219.[62] These officials are effectively "mini-governors" in their areas of authority—state finance, mines, agriculture, and so forth—and, as such, the more of them that a state has, the more competitors for statewide executive authority that a governor must face. Table 6-6 indicates the titles of these executives and how their numbers changed from 1965 through 1984. Only three states used the short executive ballot in 1960 (a ballot that permitted the election of only four statewide officers or fewer), but by 1980, the number had tripled to nine.[63]

Strengthening the appointment power. The governors' appointment powers have been strengthened in ways besides that of simply reducing the number of statewide officials who are elected by the people. Of the 1,992 major administrative positions existing in the states, almost 47 percent are appointed by the governors, more than 38 percent are appointed by independent boards and commissions or by the legislature, and only 15 percent are separately elected. More than a third of the governors' appointments do not need to be confirmed by anyone or anything else.

The authority to appoint is a major tool of control over the state bureaucracy. A survey of more than 3,500 state administrators found that only 9 percent of those administrators who were elected to their offices perceived that

Table 6-6 Separately Elected Executive Branch Executives, 1965–1984

Official	*1965*	*1984*	*Change*
Governor	50	50	—
Lieutenant Governor[1]	38	42	+4
Attorney General	42	43	+1
Treasurer	40	38	−2
Secretary of State	39	36	−3
Auditor	29	25	−4
Superintendent of Education, Public Instruction	22	17	−5
Board of Education	9	12	+3
Secretary of Agriculture	13	12	−1
Controller	9	10	+1
Insurance Commissioner	10	8	−2
Land Commissioner	7	5	−2
Secretary of Labor	6	4	−2
Commissioner of Mines/Minerals	4	1	−3
Public Utility Commissioner	14	11	−3

[1] Lieutenant governors and governors ran as a team in 7 states in 1965 and 22 states in 1984, representing a +15 change.

Source: The Book of the States, 1984–85 (Lexington, Ky.: Council of State Governments, 1985), p. 45.

their governors had a high level of authority over them. On the other hand, more than 20 percent of state administrators who served on independent boards and commissions (who could not be dismissed by the governor directly, but potentially could be eased out of office by the governor's political influence) felt that the governors' authority was high. And among department heads appointed by the governor (and who obviously could be fired by the governor), almost 40 percent felt that the governor had a high level of authority.[64]

Strengthening the reorganization power. Governors also gained increased powers to reorganize their own branch of government. Table 6-7 is an index of this authority. A high ranking is determined by whether the governor and lieutenant governor are elected as a team (22 states—up from none in 1953—elect their governors and lieutenant governors as a team, and the practice reduces the chances for administrative infighting brought on by partisan factionalism); whether the governor may appoint and fire his or her own officials, as opposed to their being separately elected; whether all or a significant majority of state agencies report directly to the governor; whether there are relatively few government corporations and regulatory boards that function independently of the governor; and whether the governor has the power to reorganize his or her own executive branch, subject to legislative concurrence. By these measures, most of the states where governors have strong powers of organization are in the Northeast, tend to have competitive parties, and have undergone a major and recent governmental reorganization. Five of the seven states, in fact, in which governors have the strongest authority to organize have been reorganized since 1965. The states that are the most parsimonious in granting their chief executives the power to reorganize are Southern, have low levels of partisanship, and have not reorganized their governmental structures in some time.[65]

Strengthening the budgetary power. Finally, governors have been granted more authority to formulate and control their state budgets; today 47 governors are the focal point of an executive budget process, compared to only 40 in 1960.[66] The increasing centralization of the budgetary power in the office of the governor has affected the executive branch's relations with the legislature. Morehouse, for example, found that the degree of budgetary authority of the governor was a critical component of the governor's formal powers, which, taken together, correlated far more positively with the governors' legislative success rates than did either the level of the states' industrialization or the governors' relations with their own political parties.[67] Similarly, a study of the budgetary process in all 50 states found that, "As the budget has increased in size and developed into a tool of executive leadership, the legislature has suffered a decline in its budget power . . . it no longer can play an effective role as 'watchdog of the treasury' and its oversight of administrative actions is confined to a few areas on a hit or miss basis."[68]

Still, it should not be forgotten that the state legislatures are professionalizing and increasing their research staffs as never before. One long-time observer of state governments contends that if we were to trace the governors' legislative success rates on budgetary issues today, we would likely "find that the legislatures have more clout in the budget process than they had in 1968. In many states, the greater institutionalization of the legislature has made it more difficult for the governor to secure the passage of his legislative package and,

Table 6-7 The Governors' Power of Organization, 1980: A 50-State Comparison

Very Strong	*Strong*	*Moderate*	*Weak*	*Very Weak*
New Jersey	Hawaii	Minnesota	California	Indiana
Alaska	Missouri	Rhode Island	Illinois	Louisiana
Michigan	Montana	Tennessee	North Carolina	Nebraska
Maine	Virginia	Vermont	Ohio	Nevada
Massachusetts	New York	Wisconsin	Kentucky	Mississippi
Maryland	Pennsylvania	Wyoming	Georgia	Alabama
South Dakota	Utah	Arizona	New Mexico	South Carolina
	Connecticut	Colorado	Arkansas	Texas
	New Hampshire	Delaware	North Dakota	Oklahoma
		Florida	West Virginia	
		Idaho	Iowa	
		Kansas	Washington	
		Oregon		

Source: Thad L. Beyle, "The Governors' Power of Organization," *State Government*, Vol. 55, No. 3 (1982), p. 84.

therefore, to act as a leader in the establishment of public policy judged in terms of legislation passed."[69]

Entering a new era in gubernatorial management. Overall, it is clear that the executive and political authority of the governors has increased since the 1960s. Fifteen years after the 1965 survey that found that governors were most frustrated over their lack of ability to appoint their own executive officers and their inability to reorganize their own branch of government, another survey found that virtually all the governors interviewed agreed that their powers, both formal and informal, had increased over the past decade, and in some cases quite significantly. The governors were, by and large, satisfied with their formal powers and the increased responsibilities that had been granted them, and very few mentioned any specific authorities that they did not possess, but which they still believed to be important for a strong and successful governorship.[70]

Table 6-8 summarizes much of what we have been discussing, and ranks the governors' overall formal powers by state. The table is an index comprised of the governors' tenure potential, powers of appointment, budget authority, power of organization, and veto authority.

GUBERNATORIAL STYLE: THE GURU OF CALIFORNIA AND THE KINGFISH OF LOUISIANA

Thus far, we have traced the renaissance of the governors during the last two decades, emphasizing the renewed political authority that most states have been granting them. We have demonstrated that there is more to being governor than how much formal power is invested in the office. To enliven this aspect of the governorship, consider the following two case studies of what talented governors can do with native intelligence, an instinct for exploiting political opportunities, and that most evanescent of qualities, style.

The Governor as Moonbeam: Edmund G. Brown, Jr., of California

"Jerry" Brown entered politics in 1969 when he ran for the Board of Trustees of the Los Angeles Community College District.[71] Son of Edmund G. (Pat) Brown, Sr., governor of California from 1959 through 1966, Jerry Brown already possessed high name identification in California politics. In 1970, Brown ran for secretary of state. Despite his unlikely prospects for victory, he won that election and subsequently brought some recognition to himself by attempting to bring about substantial campaign law reform.

In 1974, at the age of 36, he ran for governor on the Democratic ticket. His Republican opposition was Houston Flournoy, who at that time was the state's comptroller. The Republicans launched an aggressive campaign, charging that Brown was too young and inexperienced; moreover, Brown, as a bachelor, did not have the image of a sedate family man. Beyond that, however, there were allegations that Brown was simply far too "mystical" for the average electorate. Brown had spent four years in a Jesuit seminary studying to be a priest and maintained a peculiar life-style (at least by some standards): he lived a very spartan existence, eschewing the new, $1.3 million governor's mansion in favor

Table 6-8 Formal Powers of Governors: A Comparison

Very Strong	*Strong*	*Moderate*	*Weak (10–15 points)*	*Very weak (less than 10 points)*
New Jersey (25)	Alaska (22)	Indiana (19)	Mississippi	No current samples
Pennsylvania (25)	Maine (22)	Oregon (19)	Texas	
Utah (25)	Montana (22)	Rhode Island (19)	South Carolina	
Hawaii (24)	Tennessee (22)	Vermont (19)	New Hampshire	
Maryland (24)	Arizona (21)	Alabama (18)	North Carolina	
Massachusetts (24)	Colorado (21)	Arkansas (18)	Nevada	
Minnesota (24)	Delaware (21)	New Mexico (18)		
New York (23)	Idaho (21)	Oklahoma (18)		
	Iowa (21)	Washington (18)		
	California (20)	Florida (17)		
	Connecticut (20)	Georgia (17)		
	Illinois (20)	Kansas (17)		
	Michigan (20)	Kentucky (17)		
	South Dakota (20)	Louisiana (17)		
	Wyoming (20)	North Dakota (17)		
		West Virginia (17)		
		Missouri (16)		
		Nebraska (16)		
		Ohio (16)		
		Virginia		
		Wisconsin (16)		

Source: Thad L. Beyle, "Governors," in Virginia Gray, Herbert Jacob, and Kenneth Vines, eds., *Politics in the American States,* 4th ed. (Boston: Little, Brown and Company, 1983), p. 202.

of a $275-a-month apartment; drove a Plymouth; practiced transcendental meditation; and breakfasted on Granola. Nevertheless, Flournoy was fighting the Watergate scandals and, as a Republican, was tainted by them; he seems to have compounded this problem by asking President Gerald Ford to campaign for him, which Ford did. Brown won by the narrow margin of 2.9 percent.

As governor, Brown had to deal with the California Assembly. The assembly had a two-thirds Democratic majority, and the leadership of both houses supported his budget bills. Brown presented unusual policy packages to the legislature. In one sense he emulated his predecessor's policy of "cut, squeeze, and trim" as a budgetary approach, justifying this position on the grounds of reducing an inflationary economy and dwindling state revenues. But he also promulgated some major social reforms within the state. Not all of his programs met with success in the legislature, but Governor Brown's style helped to enact most of them. Brown would deliver extremely brief oral presentations to the legislature outlining his programs. He would follow these up with more ample written messages. Then he would personally participate in marathon conferences with key legislators and key interest group representatives.

Californians loved Jerry Brown. After his first two years in office, public opinion surveys showed that he received the highest approval rating ever recorded from citizens identifying with both parties in the history of California polling.[72] Perhaps his popularity inspired him to enter (quite late in the season) the Democratic presidential primaries in 1976. Brown's showing was impressive: at 37 years of age, he won five of the six primaries he entered. Jimmy Carter had

proceeded too far down the track to be derailed for the nomination, but Brown had made a very credible national showing, and it hardly hurt him at home: in 1978, Brown was reelected to the governor's mansion (or, more accurately, apartment) by one of the largest electoral margins in the state's history, 56 percent of the vote.

Besides his surprisingly formidable bid for the 1976 Democratic presidential nomination, Brown had shown himself to be an adroit political dancer in California politics. "Proposition 13," a successful 1978 initiative that mandated a sweeping restructuring and slashing of California's property tax, had been strongly opposed by Brown, organized labor, local governments, teachers, school districts, and virtually all the elected Democratic officeholders in the state. But with its enactment—by 65 percent of the voters—Brown reiterated his prior opposition and said that, as governor, it nonetheless was his solemn duty to execute Proposition 13. By election time, 40 percent of Californians assumed that Brown had always been for the proposition![73] One pundit said Brown's "slick reversal on Proposition 13 is among the finest examples of political opportunism since Italy switched alliances during World War I."[74]

Although Brown's political pirouette on Proposition 13 strengthened his hand in California's 1978 gubernatorial election, it also appears to have undercut his longer-range political plans. "The downturn in his image became dramatic after [Proposition 13's] advent, and it dogs him still."[75]

In 1979 these problems became evident when Brown entered the Democratic presidential primaries a second time. Unlike 1976, his showing in these primaries was dismal, and he won not one of them. Brown appears to have compounded his growing "image problems" during this period by taking rock star Linda Ronstadt with him on an African safari. (Ms. Ronstadt declared the trip to be "boring.") People were beginning to perceive him, paradoxically, as both an "opportunist" and a "flake." The "Governor Moonbeam" moniker began to stick. The "CBS Evening News" described his announcement of his decision to enter the primaries again as a blend of "Boy Scout Oath" and "Star Wars."[76]

These problems persisted, and no doubt were nourished by his handling of the Mediterranean fruit fly, or "Medfly," crisis in 1981. This pest was threatening California's immense ($14 billion a year) agribusiness, and the normal defense used against its predations on fruits and vegetables is the spraying by airplane of malathion. Brown appealed to environmentalists by characterizing this technique as an "aerial attack" that would endanger the health of Californians; instead, Brown ordered spraying of malathion by hand-held devices. This did not work, and the Medfly began to scatter around the state. Other states, such as Florida, Georgia, and Texas, and even Japan, began threatening to ban all California produce. Farmers initiated a drive to impeach the governor. The U.S. Secretary of Agriculture warned Brown that he would declare a national quarantine on California's harvest unless aerial spraying commenced immediately. Brown capitulated. But critics felt that he had come dangerously close to initiating an agricultural catastrophe for political ends and had cynically whipped up a public hysteria over the highly improbable health risks associated with malathion. The barbs became sharper: "There are only two things I don't like about Jerry Brown: his face."[77] Or (and this from a sitting president), "Governor Brown is California's way of celebrating the International Year of the Child."[78]

After the Medfly flap, Brown decided to get out of the governor business and enter the U.S. Senate. After a hard-fought campaign in 1982, he lost decisively. But he had done much for the good of California during his eight years as governor. For example, blacks, Hispanics, Asian-Americans, and women received fully half of his more than 6,000 executive appointments; under his predecessor, Ronald Reagan, less than 1 percent of the governor's top administrative appointments were women. Forty percent of Brown's judgeships went to women. He inserted substantially greater numbers of citizens instead of the representatives of special interests into the state's consumer commissions and regulatory boards; Brown drafted the nation's most comprehensive, renewable energy plan; adopted an ambitious state urban policy (the Sunbelt's first); pushed through a tough "right-to-know" law designed to alert factory workers when they are being exposed to hazardous substances; created an Office of Appropriate Technology and the acclaimed California Conservation Corps; developed a new medical malpractice insurance system for the state; and extended collective bargaining to public employees, among other policies that were both progressive and innovative.[79]

The Governor as Megalomaniac: Huey Long of Louisiana

A man who represents the antithesis of Brown in virtually every respect (or at least one would hope so) is Huey P. Long, Jr., the "Kingfish." He was born in 1893, the eighth of nine children, in an agricultural area of Louisiana "characterized by a large number of hogs and children."[80] Huey completed a three-year program at the Tulane Law School in less than one year and quickly passed the bar examination. At 26 he ran for his first public office, that of the representative from the Third District for the state's Railway Commission; this was the only office open under the state constitution for one of his age, since it had no age limitation whatever. He won. When the new state constitution of 1921 converted the Railway Commission to the Public Service Commission, Huey had his opportunity to build a political base. After a tilt with the Cumberland Telephone and Telegraph Company, Long managed to push through a retroactive refund to all telephone users, thus becoming a state hero overnight. For good measure, he also lowered rates for gas and electricity for Shreveport's street cars and all of the state's intrastate railroads. In 1924, when he was 30, the minimum legal age for a gubernatorial candidate, Long made his first bid for the governorship. He lost his campaign for the Democratic nomination (which was the only election that really counted in Louisiana), but used the next four years to mend his political fences. In 1928, he entered the campaign for governor with substantially more press and popular support than he had enjoyed during his first attempt.

Long's 1928 campaign can be summed up as "the redneck as reformer." He came out strongly and self-righteously against the notorious Choctaw Club of New Orleans, which was the controlling political machine of that city, mainly because it would not support him. On the positive side, he argued for free textbooks, free bridges, better roads, improved schools, repeal of the tobacco tax, and more taxes on Standard Oil, Inc., the state's major industry. He won, and he won largely with a class-based campaign; the poor and dispossessed consistently voted Long into office. The big planter parishes (counties) of Louisiana and the small dirt farmers traditionally voted against each other and, after Long's victory in 1928, the plantation interests joined with the major urban political machines in an effort to defeat Long. In 1929 these interests combined in an unsuccessful attempt to impeach Long. The impeachment process was conducted with incredible sloppiness, and Long was able to defeat it. But he remembered the attempt, saying, "I used to try to get things done by saying 'please.' That didn't work and I'm a dynamiter. I'll dynamite 'em outta my path."[81]

After only two years in office, Long announced that he was going to run for the U.S. Senate on the curious understanding with the people of the state that he would not leave the governorship for two years after his election to the Senate, and on a platform advocating a state "good roads" program. Long rationalized this situation by stating that Louisiana's representation in the U.S. Senate would not decline by Long's staying in Baton Rouge to complete his gubernatorial term for two more years because, with the incumbent Senator Ransdell in office, "the seat was vacant anyway."[82] Long won the Democratic primary of 1930, thus assuring himself a seat in the Senate. Under the state's constitution, the lieutenant governor should have moved into office after Long's election, and the lieutenant governor immediately had himself duly sworn into office by a Shreveport notary. The lieutenant governor was a political rival of Long's, so Long responded to this act by having the president *pro tempore* of the senate, one of his own men, take the oath as governor. He then informed the lieutenant governor that his oath was illegal and that he had forfeited his position as lieutenant governor by virtue of his illegal assumption of the governorship. This position was upheld by the Louisiana Supreme Court, which was under Long's dominance by that time, on the grounds that it "lacked jurisdiction." Thus, the Kingfish not only put his own man into the governor's office, but eliminated an irritating political rival.

In 1932, Long worked tirelessly for the nomination of Franklin Delano Roosevelt as president at the National Democratic Convention, but, during the same year, he introduced his "Share Our Wealth" program, which promised to make "every man a king, but let no man wear the crown." This program, which was in direct competition with FDR, by 1935 had more than 27,000 clubs located in every state and claimed more than 7,500,000 members. "Huey, along with the rude, plain-spoken agitators of the new South, was founding a personal dictatorship."[83] President Roosevelt, concerned about the rise of the Kingfish on the national scene, started working to undermine his Louisiana political base. Roosevelt had more than $10 million of federal public works projects curtailed in Louisiana and had Long and his aides investigated by the Internal Revenue Service for tax evasion charges.

These actions, plus other internal statewide factors in Louisiana, had an effect and, by 1934, Long was in some trouble. Still, he controlled the legislature absolutely, and in 1934 he had the Louisiana assembly pass measures very favorable to lower-class interests, he declared war on the "corrupt" Choctaw Club of New Orleans, and he "erected, through laws, the most thorough state dictatorship known to twentieth-century America."[84] By way of example, Long had his newly installed governor—with no proper warrant, or by invitation of the civil authorities, or by proclamation of martial law—order the National Guard to enter New Orleans and seize the voter registration offices. With the National Guard present, Long supervised the nomination of his candidates for Congress, the Public Service Commission, and the State Supreme Court from the city of New Orleans. Only then did he retire the National Guard from the city.

Later, Long had the state legislature enact a series of laws that allowed him to take supervisory control of New Orleans's finances and had the city officials in Baton Rouge and Alexandria replaced by gubernatorial appointments. He also established authority over nonelective municipal fire and police chiefs, and later this authority was extended to virtually every appointive municipal and parish employee in the state, including teachers, school bus drivers, and janitors. Long also pushed through legislation that enabled the governor to call out the militia at any time, without challenge from the courts, and empowered the governor to increase without limit the personnel of the State Bureau of Identification, which soon became known throughout Louisiana as "Huey's Cossacks." "Long had taken advantage of every inadequacy of the state constitution and every exigency of the Depression to centralize power and to suppress opposition. In terms of the controls he possessed, the Kingfish had swallowed the Pelican State. They tuk Sah Huey."[85] In 1935 there was a popular riot of anti-Longs, protesting his ruthless control over the state.

In September of that year, the Kingfish was in Baton Rouge to supervise the successor to his appointed governor. As he left the capitol, surrounded by bodyguards, he was assassinated by a medical specialist whose family members had been prominent anti-Longs; the assassin was killed immediately by Long's guards.

Long made an impact on Louisiana and may have made a larger impact on the nation had he lived long enough. There is no question that he was a tyrant, and a very shrewd one, capitalizing on the class biases of southern politics. Indeed, he was idolized in Louisiana after his death. The state presented a statue of the Kingfish, as one of its two great sons, to be recognized in statuary hall in Washington; it purchased his New Orleans home as a museum; and it made Long's birthday a legal holiday. For many years after Long's death, the personal columns in the New Orleans *Times-Picayune* frequently included such items as "Thanks to St. Peter, St. Joseph, St. Huey."

While it is difficult to conceive of two governors more dissimilar than Jerry Brown and Huey Long, they share two things in common: both built power bases without regard for the formal authorities granted them, and both had style.

Quite a different power base and political style are evidenced in the institution we consider in the next chapter: the courts.

NOTES

[1]Larry Sabato, *Goodbye to Good-time Charlie: The American Governor Transformed,* 2nd ed. (Washington, D.C.: Congressional Quarterly Press, 1983), p. 1.

[2]James Reston, *The New York Times,* 1962, as quoted in Andrew M. Scott and Earl Wallace, *Politics USA: Cases on the American Democratic Process,* 4th ed. (New York: Macmillan, 1974), p. 90.

[3]David Broder, *Washington Post* (June 12, 1976).

[4]Sabato, *Goodbye to Good-time Charlie,* p. 2.

[5]Louis Harris survey, as cited in National Governors' Conference, *The State of the States* (Washington, D.C.: National Governors' Conference, 1974), p. 5.

[6]Louis Harris survey, as cited in Glenn Newkirk, "State Legislatures Through the People's Eyes," *State Legislatures,* 5 (August-September, 1979), pp. 8-9.

[7]Samuel R. Solomon, "Governors: 1970-1980," *National Civic Review,* 70 (March, 1981), pp. 123-124.

[8]Thad L. Beyle, "Governors," in Virginia Gray, Herbert Jacob, and Kenneth L. Vines, eds.,

Politics in the American States: A Comparative Analysis, 4th ed. (Boston: Little, Brown, 1983), p. 184.
[9]Sabato, *Goodbye to Good-time Charlie,* p. 40.
[10]Solomon, "Governors: 1970-1980," pp. 131-132.
[11]Beyle, "Governors," pp. 187-190.
[12]D. P. Baker, "West Virginia's Deep Pockets: Rockefeller Lays Out $30 for Vote," *Washington Post* (November 29, 1980).
[13]Malcolm E. Jewell, "Political Money and Gubernatorial Primaries," *State Government,* 56, No. 2 (1983), p. 70. Figures are for 1982.
[14]Beyle, "Governors," p. 214.
[15]*Ibid.,* p. 215. The period covered in these figures is 1951-1971.
[16]*Ibid.,* pp. 216-217.
[17]Coleman B. Ransone, Jr., "The Governor, the Legislature, and Public Policy," *State Government,* 52 (Summer, 1979), p. 118.
[18]James E. Jarrett, "Gubernatorial Control of State Government Work Forces," *State Government,* 54 (Summer, 1981), p. 87.
[19]Thomas R. Dye, "Executive Power and Public Policy in the States," *Western Political Quarterly,* 27 (December, 1969), pp. 926-939.
[20]Joseph A. Schlesinger, "The Politics of the Executive," in Herbert Jacob and Kenneth N. Vines, eds., *Politics in the American States,* 2nd ed. (Boston: Little, Brown, 1965), pp. 210-237.
[21]Jarrett, "Gubernatorial Control," p. 91.
[22]Sarah McCally Morehouse, "The Governor as Political Leader," in Herbert Jacob and Kenneth N. Vines, eds., *Politics in the American States,* 3rd ed. (Boston: Little, Brown, 1976), p. 239.
[23]*Ibid.,* pp. 221-222.
[24]Ira Sharkansky, "Agency Requests, Gubernatorial Support and Budget Success in State Legislatures," *American Political Science Review,* 62 (December, 1968), p. 1224.
[25]Ransone, "The Governor, the Legislature, and Public Policy," p. 119.
[26]Lynn Muchmore and Thad L. Beyle, "The Governor as Party Leader," *State Government,* 53 (Summer, 1980), p. 123. The study was based on interviews with 15 former governors during 1978 and 1979, who had left office since 1976.
[27]*Ibid.*
[28]Governor Reuben Askew of Florida, as quoted in *ibid.,* p. 124.
[29]Governor James B. Edwards of South Carolina, as quoted in *ibid.,* p. 124.
[30]Thad L. Beyle, "The Governor as Chief Legislator," *State Government,* 51 (Winter, 1978), p. 2.
[31]Advisory Commission on Intergovernmental Relations, *The Question of State Government Capability* (Washington, D.C.: U.S. Government Printing Office, 1985), p. 129.
[32]Sabato, *Goodbye to Good-time Charlie,* p. 77.
[33]Beyle, "The Governor as Chief Legislator," p. 7; and Charles W. Wiggins, "Executive Vetoes and Legislative Overrides in the American States," *Journal of Politics,* 42 (November, 1980), pp. 1112 and 1115. Data in both articles are for the 1973-74 legislative sessions only.
[34]Beyle, "The Governor as Chief Legislator," p. 8.
[35]Glenn Abney and Thomas P. Lauth, "The Line-Item Veto in the States: An Instrument for Fiscal Restraint or an Instrument for Partisanship?" *Public Administration Review,* 45 (May/June, 1985), p. 377.
[36]Sabato, *Goodbye to Good-time Charlie,* p. 77.
[37]Nelson C. Dometrius, "The Efficacy of the Governor's Formal Powers," *State Government,* 52 (Summer, 1979), p. 123.
[38]Cited in Sabato, *Goodbye to Good-time Charlie,* p. 98.
[39]*Ibid.,* p. 79.
[40]E. Lee Bernick and Charles W. Wiggins, "Executive-Legislative Power Relationships: Perspectives of State Lawmakers," *American Politics Quarterly,* 9 (October, 1981), p. 475.
[41]Sarah McCalley Morehouse, "Party Loyalty in a House Divided," paper presented at the Annual Meeting of the American Political Science Association, New York, September 3-6, 1981, p. 22.
[42]Beyle, "The Governor as Chief Legislator," p. 2.
[43]Morehouse, "The Governor as Political Leader," p. 231.
[44]Morehouse, "Party Loyalty in a House Divided," p. 2.
[45]*Ibid.,* p. 23.
[46]*Ibid.,* p. 15.

[47]*Ibid.*, p. 23.
[48]Beyle, "The Governor as Chief Legislator," p. 6.
[49]Bruce Kappel, "The State's Biggest Lobbyist: Executive Agencies," *California Journal* (December, 1972), reprinted in Eugene C. Lee and Larry L. Berg, *The Challenge of California: Text and Readings*, 2nd ed. (Boston: Little, Brown, 1976), p. 175.
[50]Beyle, "The Governor as Chief Legislator," pp. 9-10.
[51]Alan J. Wyner, "Gubernatorial Relations with Legislators and Administrators," *State Government*, 41 (Summer, 1968), p. 202.
[52]Aaron Wildavsky, "The Two Presidencies," in Aaron Wildavsky, ed., *Perspectives on the Presidency* (Boston: Little, Brown, 1975), p. 449.
[53]Beyle, "The Governor as Chief Legislator," p. 2.
[54]Lynn Muchmore, "The Governor as Manager," *State Government*, 54, No. 3 (1981), pp. 71-72.
[55]Governor Dan Walker of Illinois (1973-1977) as quoted in "Governors' Views on Management," *State Government*, 54, No. 3 (1981), p. 66.
[56]Neal R. Peirce, "Structural Reform of Bureaucracy Grows Rapidly," *National Journal Reports*, 7 (April 5, 1975), pp. 502-508. The First and Second Hoover Commissions, which issued reports in 1949 and 1955, dealt with a number of problems of federal government reorganization and executive administration, and, as a result, a plethora of "little Hoover Commissions" was appointed throughout most of the states. Despite the existence of these bodies, however, essentially nothing was done in statewide administrative reforms.
[57]Thad L. Beyle, "The Governors' Formal Powers: A View from the Governor's Chair," *Public Administration Review*, 28 (November/December 1968), pp. 540-545.
[58]Diel S. Wright, "Executive Leadership in State Administration," *Midwestern Political Science Review*, 11 (February, 1967), pp. 1-26.
[59]Quoted by Carl Bosworth, "The Politics of Management Improvement in the States," *American Political Science Review*, 47 (March 1953), p. 90.
[60]Albert L. Sturm, "State Constitutions and Constitutional Revisions: 1978-1979 and the 1970s," *Book of the States, 1980-81* (Lexington, Ky.: Council of State Governments 1980), Table C, p. 5.
[61]James L. Garnett, *Reorganizing State Governments: The Executive Branch* (Boulder, Colo.: Westview Press, 1980), pp. 1, 5; and David B. Walker, "The States and the System: Changes and Choices," *Intergovernmental Perspective*, 6 (Fall, 1980), p. 7.
[62]Thad L. Beyle and Robert Dalton, "Appointment Power: Does It Belong to the Governor?" *State Government*, 54, No. 1 (1981), as derived from Table 1, p. 4. Only executives are included in these figures, and not other kinds of statewide elected officials, such as members of education commissions. If all statewide elected officers are counted, there were 557 in 1984 (down from 709 in 1955). See Thad R. Beyle, "The Executive Branch: Elective Officials and Organization," *Book of the States, 1984-85* (Lexington, Ky.: Council of State Governments, 1984), p. 44.
[63]Advisory Commission on Intergovernmental Relations, *In Brief: State and Local Roles in the Federal System* (Washington, D.C.: U.S. Government Printing Office, 1981), p. 6.
[64]Dometrius, "The Efficacy of the Governor's Formal Powers," p. 123.
[65]Thad L. Beyle, "The Governors' Power of Organization," *State Government*, 55, No. 3 (1982), pp. 79-81, 84-86.
[66]Advisory Commission on Intergovernmental Relations, *In Brief*, p. 6. Figure is for 1980.
[67]Morehouse, "Party Loyalty in a House Divided," p. 22.
[68]Allen Schick, *Budget Innovation in the States* (Washington, D.C.: Brookings Institution, 1971), p. 167.
[69]Ransone, "The Governor, the Legislature, and Public Policy," p. 119.
[70]Sabato, *Goodbye to Good-time Charlie*, p. 58.
[71]Unless noted otherwise, the following paragraphs on Jerry Brown are drawn from Winston W. Crouch, John C. Bollens, and Stanley Scott, *California Government and Politics*, 6th ed. (Englewood Cliffs, N.J.: Prentice-Hall, 1977), pp. 156-160.
[72]David Harris, "Whatever Happened to Jerry Brown?" *New York Times Biographical Service* (March, 1980), p. 321.
[73]*Ibid.*, p. 324.
[74]Charles Krauthammer, "Brownian Motion," *The New Republic* (August 1 and 8, 1981), pp. 10-11.
[75]Harris, "Whatever Happened to Jerry Brown?" p. 324.
[76]*Ibid.*, p. 321.

[77]Representative Olympia Snowe, as quoted in "Political Humor Is a Serious Commodity in Washington," *Los Angeles Times,* as reprinted in the *The Arizona Republic* (September 23, 1979).
[78]Jimmy Carter, quoted in *ibid.*
[79]Neal R. Peirce, "California Governor Leaves Legacy for Other States to Follow," *The Arizona Republic* (December 5, 1982).
[80]Allen P. Sindler, *Huey Long's Louisiana: State Politics, 1920-52* (Baltimore: Johns Hopkins, 1956), p. 45.
[81]Quoted in *ibid.,* p. 67.
[82]*Ibid.,* p. 70.
[83]*Ibid.,* p. 83.
[84]*Ibid.,* p. 83.
[85]*Ibid.,* p. 99.

7

THE POLITICS OF JUSTICE

As formulators of public policy, the courts use the murkiest of processes. Even so, "State courts are not less political than state legislatures or state executive agencies, but they are usually less openly partisan. They are more the captive of a single profession than any other major institution of government, but they nevertheless participate in almost all major conflicts that occur within the state political arena."[1]

THE JUDICIAL SCENE

That "single profession" is law. In an extensive analysis of all 50 states, it was found that the legal profession indeed has a major policy impact on the workings of the state court system.[2] Although the depth of judicial professionalism in any one state varied, the large industrial urban states had higher levels of court professionalism. The Southern states tended to have less professional court systems. The only major exception was Indiana, which, although it is a large industrial urban state, ranked low in judicial professionalism. Table 7-1 indicates the level of judicial professionalism in the American states. As we shall see, any public institution whose behavior is formed by a single profession has characteristics that relate peculiarly to that profession, particularly in the institution's decision-making process.

Decisions, of course, are what courts are all about, and the courts in the states make an enormous number of decisions. State courts try more than 98 percent of all cases in the nation, or some 90 million cases a year. Moreover, the increase in the judiciary's work load has been enormous. Although the country's

Table 7-1 Judicial Professionalism in the American States

	Rank of States	*Composite Score*
1	California	21.7
2	New Jersey	18.0
3	Illinois	17.7
4–5	Massachusetts, New York	16.7
6–7	Alaska, Michigan	16.3
8–9	Maryland, Hawaii	15.3
10	Pennsylvania	15.0
11–13	Colorado, Washington, Wisconsin	14.3
14	Ohio	14.0
15	North Carolina	13.7
16	New Hampshire	13.4
17–19	Arizona, Oregon, Rhode Island	13.3
20	Nevada	13.0
21	Connecticut	12.6
22–24	Idaho, Minnesota, Oklahoma	12.0
25	North Dakota	11.3
26	Kentucky	11.0
27	Iowa	10.9
28–29	Maine, Wyoming	10.7
30	Vermont	10.3
31–33	Florida, Montana, Virginia	10.0
34–36	Delaware, Louisiana, Missouri	9.6
37–38	New Mexico, Utah	9.3
39–40	Nebraska, South Dakota	9.0
41	South Carolina	8.7
42–45	Georgia, Kansas, Tennessee, Texas	8.0
46	Indiana	7.6
47	West Virginia	7.3
48	Alabama	6.0
49	Arkansas	5.3
50	Mississippi	3.4

Source: Henry Robert Glick and Kenneth N. Vines, *State Court Systems* (Englewood Cliffs, N.J.: Prentice-Hall, 1973), p. 12.

population grew by only 36 percent between 1955 and 1979, the court's case load exploded by 1,000 percent! Comparative data for these years are unavailable, but we do know that between 1971 and 1975, the number of judicial employees increased by 29 percent, while expenditures burgeoned by 52 percent.[3] Still, as a percentage of overall state and local budgets, the public's investment in the court system remains small. The judiciary receives less than 1 percent, on the average, of all state and local expenditures, or about 12 percent of all state and local expenditures for criminal justice—that is, prisons, police, prosecutors, public defenders, as well as courts.[4]

The courts are organized along the lines sketched in the box on page 193, "Structure of State Court Systems." As it shows, all courts within a state, including city courts, traffic courts, and justices of the peace, are part of the same system. Local governments cannot create their own courts. The courts are generally organized in three tiers: *state appellate courts,* whose primary function is to review the decision of lower courts; *state trial courts,* which have general jurisdiction and the broadest authority; and a number of *specialized local trial courts* of relatively limited jurisdiction, primarily over minor cases. Of course, the structure of each state's court system varies to a significant degree, ranging from the simple and modern to the complicated and traditional. Table 7-2 indicates these differences by state.

Structure of State Court Systems

SUPREME COURT

All states have one supreme court. In some states this court is termed the Supreme Judicial Court or Court of Appeals.

INTERMEDIATE APPELLATE COURTS

Twenty-three states have intermediate courts of appeals. Oklahoma, Tennessee, and Texas have two intermediate courts of appeals, one each for civil and criminal cases. Intermediate appellate courts have various names: Superior Court, Court of Appeals, Appellate Division of the Supreme Court, or Appellate Division of the Superior Court.

TRIAL COURTS OF GENERAL JURISDICTION

Thirty-eight states have one type of trial court of general jurisdiction, nine states have two, two states have three, and one state has four. The names of these courts vary widely: Circuit Court, Superior Court, District Court, Court of Common Pleas, and in New York, the Supreme Court.

TRIAL COURTS OF LIMITED JURISDICTION

Eight states have only one or two of these kinds of trial courts; ten states have different kinds; twenty states have four or five; twelve states have six or more different kinds. The names and functions of these courts vary widely. They include probate courts, justice courts, police courts, small claims courts, city and town courts, juvenile courts, orphan's courts, courts of oyer and terminer, and courts of chancery.

State Court Systems (Chicago: The Council of State Governments, 1966); *Martindale-Hubbell Law Dictionary, 1970; Intermediate Appellate Courts* (Chicago: American Judicature Society, 1967), as derived by Henry Robert Glick and Kenneth N. Vines, *State Court Systems* (Englewood Cliffs, N.J.: Prentice-Hall, 1973), p. 28.

Certainly the most famous (or infamous) segment of the state court structure is the lowest level, referred to in the box above as the *trial courts of limited jurisdiction.* Frequently, judges in these courts have little or no legal training, but they have a great deal of political experience. The most exemplary in this dubious regard are those judges who are known as justices of the peace.

In the next tier of the court structure are the major *trial courts of general jurisdiction,* which deal with criminal felonies (serious crimes) and civil cases (noncriminal offenses). Normally their scope of jurisdiction is the county or city. There are about 1,500 major trial courts in the country. Juries usually decide cases at this level.

Every state has a court of last resort, generally called the *supreme court.* These courts range in size from three to nine justices and hear cases on appeal from the major trial courts. In a few states, however, the supreme courts have the right of *original jurisdiction* in certain types of cases (that is, they may try a case before it is heard by another court). They do not rely upon a jury for rendering

Table 7-2 Differences in State Court Organization[1]

SIMPLE AND MODERN		*COMPLEX AND TRADITIONAL*	
Group 1 (6 states)	*Group 2 (20 states)*	*Group 3 (20 states)*	*Group 4 (4 states)*
*Arizona	*Alabama	Connecticut	*Arkansas
*California	*Alaska	Idaho	Delaware
*Illinois	*Colorado	Iowa	Mississippi
*North Carolina	*Florida	Kansas	Virginia
*Oklahoma	*Georgia	Kentucky	
*Washington	Hawaii	Maine	
	*Indiana	Massachusetts	
	Louisiana	Minnesota	
	*Maryland	Montana	
	*Michigan	Nebraska	
	*Missouri	New Hampshire	
	Nevada	North Dakota	
	*New Jersey	Rhode Island	
	*New Mexico	South Carolina	
	*New York	South Dakota	
	*Ohio	*Tennessee	
	*Oregon	Utah	
	*Pennsylvania	Vermont	
	*Texas	West Virginia	
	Wyoming	Wisconsin	

* States marked with an asterisk have intermediate appellate courts.

[1] In order to place the states in one of the four groups distributed along the continuum, they were given a weighted score according to the specific characteristics of the court system. The higher the score, the more simplified and modern the court system. The score was computed as follows:

A. A court system is considered simplified and modern if it has one intermediate appellate court, but more complex if it has two or more types of intermediate appellate courts. It is considered much less modern, however, if it has no intermediate appellate court. Therefore, each state received:

4 points for having one intermediate appellate court
3 points for having two or more types of intermediate appellate courts
0 points for having no intermediate appellate court

B. The fewer types of trial courts of general jurisdiction which a state has, the more modern and simplified its court system is considered to be. Therefore, each state received:

2 points for having one trial court of general jurisdiction
1 point for having two types of trial courts of general jurisdiction
0 points for having more than two types of trial courts of general jurisdiction

C. The fewer types of trial courts of limited jurisdiction that a state has, the more modern and simplified its court system is considered to be. Therefore, each state received:

3 points for having one trial court of limited jurisdiction
2 points for having two types of trial courts of limited jurisdiction
1 point for having three types of trial courts of limited jurisdiction
0 points for having more than three types of trial courts of limited jurisdiction

The score for each state is the sum of its scores in sections A, B, and C. Scores ranged from 1 to 9. The scores included in each group are Group 1: 7, 8, 9; Group 2: 4, 5, 6; Group 3: 2, 3; Group 4: 1.

Source: Henry Robert Glick and Kenneth N. Vines, *State Court Systems* (Englewood Cliffs, N.J.: Prentice-Hall, 1973), p. 30.

judgments, since they are considering questions of law rather than questions of fact.

Finally, many states have *special courts,* and, as their title indicates, they handle such special problems as wills, small claims, and juvenile delinquency. These courts are usually found in the more urban and industrialized states with large populations.

THE JUDICIAL STYLE

The courts determine and resolve issues of public policy differently from the other two branches of government. These differences are ones of style, access, procedures specificity, and apparent objectivity.[5]

In *style* the courts are passive; they hardly ever initiate policy decisions. Decorum, dignity, and unanimity are highly valued styles of judicial decision making. Some have contended that laziness also is a part of the judicial style. A spot survey of judges in Chicago found that the average judge spent fewer than four hours a day on the bench.[6]

Access to the courts is also established by peculiar procedures. Courts must agree that they have proper jurisdiction in particular cases, and litigants must have a fair amount of cash available to acquire a ruling from the courts. People also must be able to demonstrate to the court's satisfaction that they have a real case to argue. In other words, a litigant must show personal damage; he or she cannot bring a suit solely as a matter of principle.

Procedures in the courts also differ from procedures in other branches of government. Communication between all parties involved in litigation is extremely formalized, and propriety is the rule of the day in all courtroom proceedings.

Courts also must direct themselves to *specific cases.* Normally, courts refrain from addressing themselves to general policy issues, and almost always have opted instead to deal only with a particular situation. For example, the U.S. Supreme Court in *Topeka* v. *Brown* said in effect that the Topeka school system ought to be desegregated. It did not say that *all* school systems ought to be desegregated, although such was the actual impact of that "specific" decision.

Finally, the *appearance of objectivity* in the courts is highly valued; partisanship and compromises are eschewed in all judicial decision making. An objective appearance in courtroom decision making is enhanced by the judiciary's reliance on the technique of *stare decisis,* or precedent. What was done previously often forms a basis for current decisions.

These distinctive aspects of policymaking accord the courts an unusual amount of legitimacy in the political sphere, particularly in contrast to the legislature and the bureaucracy. Their unique stature aids the courts in achieving popular acceptance of their decisions.

HOW AND WHY JUDGES MAKE PUBLIC POLICY

Each one of the 90 million cases considered by the state and local courts every year represents a public policy decision. In state supreme courts, criminal appeals make up nearly one-third of the work load; civil liberty issues are involved in only 2 percent of the cases, because such cases are often shifted to the federal courts. Most state supreme court decision making concerns contentions between economic interests.

What factors influence the judges as they make decisions about these important issues? There are a number of significant variables, most of which are included in Figure 7-1. They include the socioeconomic status of the states in

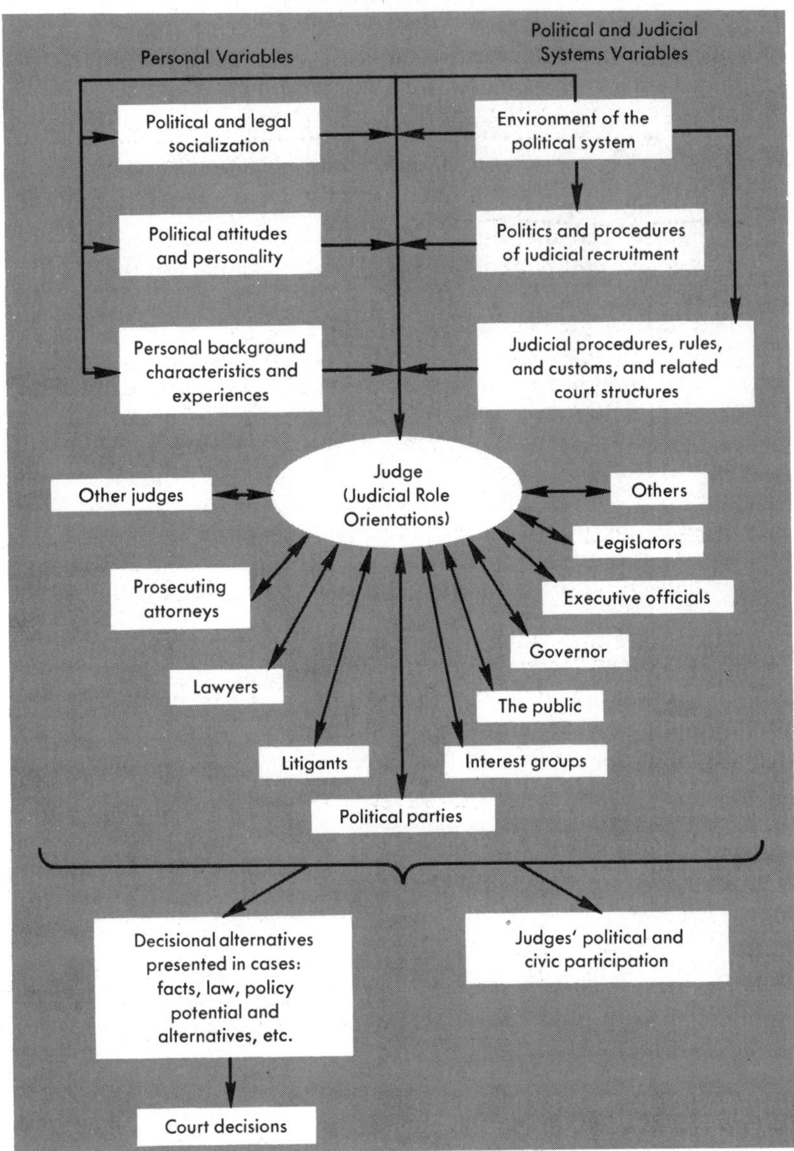

Figure 7-1 Variables affecting judicial role orientations and a description of judges' role relationships. (*Source:* Henry Robert Glick and Kenneth N. Vines, *State Court Systems* (Englewood Cliffs, N.J.: Prentice-Hall, 1973, p. 55. ©1973, reprinted by permission of Prentice-Hall.)

which the courts must function, the personal backgrounds of judges, the unique roles of dissent and conflict in judicial decision making, the influence of political parties, the role of ethnic identification among judges, ideological considerations, and the way judges view their own roles and places in the policymaking process. We consider these in turn.

The Polity of the State

There is a relationship between the kinds of economic litigation (which is the largest single kind of case considered by state courts) and the social and economic characteristics of the state. Supreme courts in rural, Southern, and relatively poor states spend considerably more time on the litigation of private economic disputes (such as wills, estates, contracts, titles, and trusts) while courts in the more urban, industrial, and Northern states are more involved with issues of governmental regulation of big economic interests and corporate law.[7] Such a finding, of course, appeals to common sense. A poor state has fewer large economic interests with which the courts are going to be concerned; court-resolved economic conflicts would center instead on disputes between individuals and relatively small-scale matters.

Who Are the Judges?

A second consideration is the shared experiences the judiciary had before its members donned the black robes of justice. In an extensive study of 306 state supreme court judges, it was found that they shared certain characteristics to an almost awesome degree. Nearly 90 percent of this population spent their childhoods in the same state where they were appointed to the bench; an additional 6 percent spent their childhoods in the same region, if not the same state. Ninety-two percent had a law degree (not terribly surprising), but almost 73 percent had held at least one nonjudicial political office, and only 31 percent had held a previous state or local judgeship (somewhat less expected). Table 7-3 outlines these characteristics.

Judges are something less than the cream of the legal profession. Among judges in urban areas, few have entered the bench from the larger, more prestigious law firms, and few were among the top graduates of the better law schools. "Most judges of city courts come from local, middle-ranking law schools

Table 7-3 Selected Background Characteristics of State Supreme Court Judges

Characteristics	*Percentage of Judges (Nu = 306)*
Spent childhood in same state as court.	89.0%
Spent childhood in same region but not same state as court.	6.1
Attended law school in same state as court.	60.4
Attended law school in same region but not same state as court.	20.5
Held a law degree.	92.4
Held previous state or local judgeship.	31.2
Held at least one nonjudicial political office.	72.5

Source: Various volumes of *Who's Who* and other state publications, as derived by Henry Robert Glick and Kenneth N. Vines, *State Court Systems* (Englewood Cliffs, N.J.: Prentice-Hall, 1973), p. 55.

and middle-ranking careers."[8] They are also middle-aged men who received their judgeships in their forties or fifties while practicing law. Once on the bench, they almost invariably remain there for the remainders of their careers. Only 3 percent of the judges on all major state appellate courts and trial courts are women.[9]

Dissent, Conflict, and Suppression

The role of dissent and conflict in courtroom decision making is another important variable and is perhaps the most distinctive aspect of how the judiciary resolves public policy issues. The suppression of dissent is a byword in terms of the courts' role in society and, even more important, in many respects is vital to its carefully cultivated image in society. As Table 7-4 indicates, the number of dissenting opinions in the state supreme courts is moderate at best, and unanimous decisions are the rule. "No where else in the American political process (not even in the federal courts) is conflict so well suppressed or disguised."[10] The rate of dissent in the state supreme courts is less than 10 percent in more than half the states, and in only a handful of states (California, New York, Ohio, Michigan, and Pennsylvania) is the dissent rate more than 20 percent on any regular basis.[11]

This relative lack of open disagreement among the members of one of

Table 7-4 Percentage of Dissenting Opinions in State Supreme Courts, 1966 and 1972

State	*1966*	*1972*
Highest-dissent courts (in 1966)		
Michigan	46.5%	56.2%
Pennsylvania	41.0	29.7
New York	41.0	38.4
Ohio	34.9	29.7
California	32.3	37.5
Florida	28.2	39.9
Oklahoma	26.5	26.2
South Dakota	24.3	22.9
Lowest-dissent courts (in 1966)		
Massachusetts	1.2	5.1
Rhode Island	1.4	2.1
North Carolina	2.4	10.7
South Carolina	3.4	11.6
Maryland	5.4	3.4
Arizona	6.1	3.2
Minnesota	6.8	4.4
New Jersey	7.1	11.0
Illinois	7.2	17.6
Alabama	7.4	17.0
Average dissent rate for all 50 states	12.6	15.1

Source: State reporters, 1966 and 1972, as compiled by Kenneth N. Vines and Herbert Jacob, "State Courts and Public Policy," in Herbert Jacob and Kenneth N. Vines, eds., *Politics in the American States: A Comparative Analysis*, 3rd ed. (Boston: Little, Brown, 1976), p. 261.

the nation's foremost political institutions can be attributed to several factors. One is *legal tradition,* which long has placed a strong stress on erudite unanimity and on judicial decisions that are not confused by opposing opinions. Another is the *heavy case load* of the state supreme courts. This situation has resulted in the assigning of cases to only one judge, who becomes responsible for both researching and writing the ensuing opinion that ultimately is endorsed by the court at large. Because the other judges are busy writing their own opinions on other cases assigned to them, they seldom bother to check the opinions of their colleagues.

There also is considerably *less diversity among the personalities* that constitute supreme courts than among other branches of government, such as the legislature and the bureaucracy. People of similar backgrounds, as we have noted, often tend to agree on policy issues.

Beyond these factors that work to suppress overt conflict in state supreme courts, there are techniques that are used to settle disputes and reduce dissent. These techniques include persuasion, compromise, and a judicial form of logrolling among justices. Social and economic characteristics of the states do not seem important as determinants of dissent rates among the state supreme courts.[12]

The Omnipresent Party

Political party affiliation also has considerable influence on how judges make decisions. Although people do not like to think of judges as making decisions on the basis of partisan affiliation, at least a couple of studies have found that, nonetheless, judges tend to do so. For example, in competitive party states, judges are more apt to air their disagreements and dissents with each other in public; judges in states without competitive party systems are less apt to.[13] This generalization holds, of course, only when judges of both parties are represented on the court.

Republicans are far more successful than Democrats in capturing judgeships; they outnumber Democrats almost 2 to 1 in judicial positions. Although this varies with the type of state (for example, Republicans do not fare as well in seeking judgeships in states controlled by the Democrats), they are very competitive in winning judgeships in two-party states and do considerably better than Republican candidates for the legislature or governorship in such states.[14]

Although a judge's party affiliation has little importance in the decision-making process on the lower trial court level (a level that has little to do with public policymaking), political party membership does seem to be a factor in the upper echelons of the court hierarchy. Stuart Nagel found that Democratic judges were different from their Republican counterparts in that the former decided for the defense measurably more frequently in criminal cases, for the administrative agency in business regulation cases, for the claimant in unemployment compensation cases, for finding a constitutional violation in criminal cases, for the government in tax cases, for the tenant in landlord-tenant cases, for the consumer in sales-of-goods cases, for the injured party in motor vehicle cases, and for the employee in employee injury cases. Nagel concluded that Democratic judges basically were more in sympathy with the working person, the defendant (at least in criminal cases), and the consumer. Democratic judges were less sympathetic than Republican judges with utilities and businesses.[15]

Race and Religion

Ethnicity and religion also play vital parts in the decision-making process of judges. Judges generally come from higher income groups, and White Anglo-Saxon Protestants (WASPs) are overrepresented among state judges. In contrast to judges who were WASPs, Nagel found that judges from minority groups were prone to decide for the defense in criminal cases, for finding a constitutional violation in criminal cases, and for the wife in divorce cases. Catholic judges tended to decide for the defense in criminal cases, for the administrative agency in business regulation cases, for the wife in divorce settlement cases, for the debtor in cases between debtors and creditors, and for the employee in employee injury cases.[16]

World Views and Ideologies

The ideology of judges is also important when judges make decisions and is closely related to that of political party affiliation. One clear conclusion may be drawn: the bench is conservative, although there are liberal and conservative dimensions within this framework. Judges with more liberal attitudes decide more frequently for the defense in criminal cases, for the administrative agency in business regulation cases, for the injured person in automobile accident cases, and for the employee in employee injury cases. The more conservative judges exhibit a propensity to find in favor of the state prosecutor in criminal cases, against the state in business regulation cases, and in favor of insurance companies and employers.[17]

In an interesting analysis of the Louisiana Supreme Court under Governor Huey Long in the 1930s, the political ideology of the judges appears to be the central determinant of how cases were decided. In the Louisiana instance, ideology meant a judge's personal allegiance to Huey Long; from 1928 to 1935 the state supreme court was crucial in maintaining the "Kingfish" in office. Similarly, another investigation found that between 1954 and 1960, judges in New Orleans sentenced blacks with considerably more harshness than whites. As racial tensions grew during those six years, the severity of sentencing for blacks by white judges increased as well.[18]

Roles Judges Play

A final source of important influence on how judges make decisions is how judges view their role in the judicial process, and indeed, in the policymaking process itself. A study of supreme court justices in four states found that judges define their duties according to five distinct roles: the ritualist, the adjudicator, the lawmaker, the administrator, and the constitutional defender.

The *ritualist* focuses on the clerical and day-to-day routines of the judge's job, such as supervising secretaries and law clerks. A majority of the justices were ritualists.

The *adjudicators* center their activities on the weighing of arguments among attorneys, focusing on the imperativeness of deciding cases, or concerning themselves primarily with whether the decisions made in the lower courts should be reversed or upheld.

The *lawmaker* sees the overriding orientation of his role as one of literally "making law." He or she realizes that "Judges make decisions that have the potential of substantially altering the interpretation of state law and its application to numerous economic, social, and political relationships."[19]

The *administrator* focuses on two forms of control that state supreme courts can wield over the lower courts. One is that the supreme court can review the decisions of lower courts and, in effect, change the procedures of the lower courts in certain cases if it so wishes. The other is that the supreme court can also regulate the personal conduct of personnel in the lower courts and of lawyers practicing throughout the state.

Finally, the *constitutional defender* sees himself or herself as a guardian of "the American form of government by protecting the Constitution against various political enemies."[20]

The clear majority of judges viewed their role as one of ritualism and adjudication. This is less than astounding, since both roles are vital to the basic functions of the courts in society. Most of those few judges who saw themselves as lawmakers opted for a conservative interpretation of that role; the administrator and constitutional defender roles were not especially important to most judges.

THE COURTROOM WORK GROUP

There are more people inhabiting courtrooms than defendants, plaintiffs, and judges. James Eisenstein and Herbert Jacob have developed the useful notion of the "courtroom work group," or the legal professionals who must work together every day in the attempt to execute criminal justice.[21] Besides judges themselves, prosecutors, defense counsels, and clerks are constantly interacting.

Prosecutors, also known as state's attorneys or district attorneys, are lawyers who are responsible for pressing the public's prosecution in criminal cases. They are almost always elected officials who serve four-year terms. In large cities, the "D.A.'s" job is often competitively sought, since it brings substantial political visibility and frequently provides an entree to higher elective office; in the smaller towns, the prosecutor's position more commonly provides a path to more lucrative private law firms. Unlike judges, virtually no prosecutor makes a lifetime career of the job, and the same pattern holds true even for appointed assistant prosecutors.[22]

Regardless of the type or size of jurisdiction in which they serve, prosecutors are surprisingly apolitical. Typically, they view the public as being misinformed about legal issues and tend to follow their own opinions about the complexities of the law.[23]

Perhaps the lowest status and least "plugged-in" politically of the principal participants in the courtroom work group (aside from the clerks) are the defense attorneys.[24] Most comprise the entire staff of their law firm, or belong to a small partnership that shares a secretary. In those jurisdictions where a public defender's office exists (i.e., a full-time lawyer hired by the government to defend the accused), most defendants in criminal cases are represented by it; if such an office is not present, the court assigns indigent defendants to a private attorney.[25] Most big cities fund a public defender, and public defenders seem to be a bit more professionally successful as lawyers than are the court-appointed private attorneys for the indigent.[26] Unlike public prosecutors, public defenders are almost always appointed, although a few are elected. How well public defenders and court-appointed attorneys represent their clients is open to speculation; the complaints from defendants about the professional competence of their publicly provided counsels has been stringent, vocal, and long-lasting.[27] An assistant attorney general of the United States has stated that public defenders are "warm bodies with law degrees" and that "too often the courthouse lawyers who will represent the poor are simply walking violations of the Sixth Amendment," which guarantees the right to counsel.[28]

The courtroom work group of judges, prosecutors, and defenders obviously pertains only to criminal, as opposed to civil, cases. Nevertheless, it is an integral component of the institution of the judiciary, and the human combinations found in these work groups affect the process of "blind justice." In fact, the process of justice can be seen as a type of political process, in which the policy outputs can range from the traditional to the innovative.

STATE COURTS AS POLICY INNOVATORS: THE CASE OF CALIFORNIA

Although judges tend to take the more conservative view of their role in society as policymakers, a significant proportion of them are quite willing to act as a full and vibrant branch of government and make new and innovative public policies through their judicial decision making. Moreover, it is important to realize that the social impact of the decisions made by judges is not confined to the cases they decide: "Although court decisions are usually directed only at litigants directly involved, they generally have a ripple effect. . . . Thus, although in form court actions are particular, their effect is general."[29] An example is provided by the U.S. Supreme Court's ruling on abortions; as a result of that decision, it was not necessary for every patient to file her own court action in order to have an abortion.

This ripple effect is amplified when the courts are innovative, and courts are more innovative as policymakers than often is realized. A study of state supreme court cases found that the courts were most innovative as policymakers in the areas of constitutional rights of defendants and criminals, civil rights, taxation, governmental regulation of business, elections, legislative apportionment, and various other types of suits against the government. Table 7-5 indicates the results of the analysis.

The California Supreme Court is among the most innovative of all the state supreme courts and, indeed, has recently shown itself to be more innovative than the U.S. Supreme Court. For example, it was the California Supreme Court that ruled in the famous case of *Serrano* v. *Priest* that discrimination on the basis of wealth was not constitutional. This ruling had and is having a major impact on the distribution of education budgets in the states, because the California court ruled that students from less wealthy school districts were being denied a civil right by not acquiring an education comparable to that received by students from wealthier districts. Twenty other state courts soon were hearing similar cases after *Serrano* v. *Priest* was decided by the California Supreme Court.

Table 7-5 Innovative Policies in State Supreme Courts, 1964–1969

Number	*Policies pertaining to*
16	Constitutional rights of defendants and criminals
7	Civil rights
7	Taxation
5	Governmental regulation of business
5	Elections
4	Legislative apportionment
8	Other suits against government

Source: Henry Robert Glick and Kenneth N. Vines, *State Court Systems* (Englewood Cliffs, N.J.: Prentice-Hall, 1973) p. 95, as derived from *State Government News, 1964–1969.* In constructing this table, Glick and Vines borrowed Walker's concept of policy innovation. See Jack L. Walker, "The Diffusion of Innovations Among the American States," *American Political Science Review,* 63 (December, 1969), pp. 880–889.

Another area of policy innovation is that of class action suits, and, again, California has expanded the concept significantly. In the 1970s the California Supreme Court ruled that consumers may bring a class action suit against a company, even though each consumer was treated as an individual, rather than as a "class," when he or she did business with that company. Prior to California's state supreme court ruling to this effect, consumers were treated by the law as individuals, not as a class that could take action. The expansion of class action to incorporate this concept is a great boon to consumer protection.

Finally, the California Supreme Court has led the way in confronting the death penalty and calling for its elimination on the grounds that the death penalty is cruel and unusual punishment, an act prohibited by the U.S. Constitution.

In short, although the innovativeness of the state courts often is obscured by the legalistic and unemotional language that the courts use in announcing their decisions, the policies nonetheless are creative and have a major impact on the social fabric of the country. In the examples just listed, for instance, the supreme court of the nation's most populous state has redistributed educational opportunity among all income groups, has given consumer interests a major new tool for defending themselves against unscrupulous corporations, and has eliminated the ultimate penalty for crime. These are not minor public policies.

REFORMING THE COURTS

Because they are such basic makers of policy and, relatively, are so removed from popular control, the courts are especially prone to reformist pressures. Chief among the proposals for reform are acquiring and retiring judges, court administration, and revamping the criminal code, which we shall consider in turn.

Getting Judges

One of the great dilemmas of the American judiciary is how to select judges. How judges have been and are chosen in the American states has varied with modes of social thinking throughout our history. For a time, the original 13 states continued the method used by their Colonial governors, which was simply gubernatorial appointment. Of the 9 states that still use this method to select some or all of their judges of major courts, 8 were among the original 13. Election of judges by legislators came into favor in some states immediately following the Revolution, and 5 states still use this device; all 5 were among the original 13 colonies. In 30 states, some or all of the judges are elected by the people. Fourteen of these states use partisan elections, and these are located mostly in the East and Southeast—areas that were "most affected by the Jacksonian movement" that touted government based on partisan patronage.[30] Sixteen states, mostly in the West and Midwest, use nonpartisan elections. These states were heavily influenced by the Progressive Reform Movement and related antiparty sympathies that were politically stylish around the time when they were admitted to the Union.

The newest method for the selection of judges, called the Missouri Plan, is gaining widespread popularity. During the past 25 years, in fact, no state has changed to any method other than the Missouri Plan. Missouri and California adopted the Missouri Plan in 1940, and currently 15 states have switched to it as a means of choosing some or all of their judges. The Missouri Plan, which boasts the trappings of reform in judicial selection, states that the governor may appoint all (or the more important) judges, but that after a two-year interim in office the judges are put up for popular election. Voters may cast a vote, "Yes" or "No," for each judge's retention after his or her performance is on the record. The idea is to acquire both judicial expertise and popular responsiveness in judges through this combination of appointive selection and voter ratification.

Table 7-6 indicates which states use which form of selecting judges for their major courts, and also shows which methods are more likely to be employed according to the relative influence by parties or by professional interests, notably, the American Bar Association. A number of states use mixes of various types of selection procedures, as shown in the lower part of the table.

What are the consequences of these various selection plans? What impact will they have on public policy? Insofar as most studies can determine, not much. For example, gubernatorial appointment of judges does not actually seem to remove the judge from politics, as some people contend it should. In one significant study, it was concluded that "governors have used their appointments to reward friends or past political supporters and have implemented the plan very largely from a personal and political viewpoint."[31]

Governors, in fact, have a surprising amount of influence on the selection of judges even in those states where judges are elected by the people. In Minnesota, for example, one study found that only 7 percent of the judges had actually been elected to their first judgeship; the remaining 93 percent had been appointed by the governor. Such ratios often reflect local political customs that promote the practice of judges resigning shortly before their terms expire so that the governor may appoint a successor. Governors seem to have more influence in this respect in states that use nonpartisan elections of judges. In these states, the proportion of judges elected to their first judicial office ranges from 7 percent (in Minnesota) to almost 66 percent (in Michigan). In states that elect judges by partisan ballots, however, the proportion of judges elected to their first judicial seat ranges from more than 94 percent (in Arkansas) to almost 32 percent (in North Carolina).[32] Such patterns make it all the more difficult to ascertain if the different methods of selecting judges result in different kinds of

Table 7-6 Judicial Selection in the States (Appellate and Major Trial Courts: Initial Selection Only)

MUCH PARTY INFLUENCE AND LITTLE BAR INFLUENCE			*LITTLE PARTY INFLUENCE AND MUCH BAR INFLUENCE*	
Partisan Election	*Election by Legislature*	*Gubernatorial Appointment*	*Nonpartisan Election*	*Missouri (or "Merit" Plan)*
Alabama Arkansas Georgia Illinois Mississippi New Mexico Pennsylvania Texas West Virginia	Connecticut South Carolina Vermont Virginia	Delaware Hawaii Maine Maryland New Hampshire New Jersey	Kentucky Michigan Minnesota Montana North Dakota Ohio Oregon South Dakota Washington Wisconsin	Alaska Colorado Idaho Iowa Nebraska Utah Wyoming
The Following States Use One System for Selecting Judges for Some Courts and Another System for Selecting Judges for the Remaining Courts:				
Indiana New York North Carolina Tennessee	Rhode Island	New York Rhode Island	Arizona California Florida Kansas Oklahoma	Arizona California Florida Indiana Kansas Oklahoma Tennessee North Carolina

Source: Derived from *Book of the States*,1980–81 (Lexington, Ky.: Council of State Governments, 1980). pp. 156–157.

judges. However, one investigation found that "merit plan" judges (gubernatorial appointees) did not have noticeably better legal qualifications or other attributes of consequence than judges who were elected to office.[33] In fact, the majority of judges who seek reelection are generally unopposed, and less than 10 percent of the judges seeking reelection are ever defeated.[34]

Use of the Missouri Plan has not changed these kinds of patterns. In a study of the Missouri Plan, it was found that only one judge out of 179 appointed under the plan had ever been defeated by election of the people. This seems to be the case because it is quite easy to win an election when you are running against no one.[35]

In summary, it appears that whatever method of selecting judges is used—popular nonpartisan election, partisan election, gubernatorial appointment, legislative appointment, or the Missouri Plan—there is little difference in results. How judges are placed on the bench appears to be more a result of passing social fancy than of matching a selection process with preferred judicial behavior.

Getting Rid of Judges

Another area of concern to judicial reformers is how long judges may stay in office and how the people can rid themselves of incompetent judges. As Table 7-7 indicates, judges, as compared to legislators and governors, stay in office for quite some time. In most states governors hold office for four years, state representatives are elected to two-year terms, and state senators are elected to four-year terms. But judges serve for periods ranging from a minimum of two years to the remainder of their life, up to the age of 70. The reason given for lengthy tenure is that many states have adopted the view that if a judge's job cannot be threatened by outside political pressures, then he or she is more likely to exercise independence and good conscience in making decisions. It also can be argued, of course, that the judge is just as likely to exercise bad judgment or dependence on particular sources of power. Recall, in this respect, the courts of the 1930s in Louisiana, in which the primary criteria for decisions made by the Louisiana judiciary seemed to be the Kingfish's political needs or simple racism.

Table 7-7 Length of Tenure of State Judges[1]

Tenure	*Courts of Last Resort*	*Intermediate Appellate Courts*	*Major Trial Courts*
Life (or to age 70)	4	1	3
14–15 years	3	1	3
10–12 years	15	6	4
5–8 years	27	15	26
4 years	0	0	16
2 years	1	0	0
Total	50	23	52[2]

[1] Figures indicate number of states.

[2] The total is greater than 50 because some states have several major trial courts with different lengths of tenure in each.

Source: Book of the States, 1974–75 (Lexington, Ky.: Council of State Governments), pp. 122–123.

This takes us to another area of concern to reformers, that of the removal of judges. In comparison with other state officeholders, judges are generally subject to broader and less defined criteria for removal. For example, judges have been removed from office for showing lascivious movies at a social gathering, consorting with criminals, or not cooperating with other state officials. In 32 states, judges are removed by impeachment or by vote of the legislature. A few states are empowered to use the recall; a few permit removal by the state supreme court. Forty-nine states have adopted clearly reformist ideas on how to remove judges.[36] Many states have *judicial tenure commissions* that hold hearings and make recommendations (for the most part, directly to the state supreme court) for the removal or retention of lower-court judges, while the other states use *judicial courts* and, in instances where these courts find for judicial misconduct, they may remove the judges.

Despite a spate of devices for doing so, precious few judges are removed for reasons of incompetence, and those who are have often diminished the dignity of the courts by making public spectacles of themselves. Consider some examples:[37] William Perry was relieved of his position as judge in a Long Island traffic court in 1975 for ordering a coffee vendor arrested and hauled into his courtroom in handcuffs, where he was berated by Perry over the quality of the coffee that the vendor had sold him. An 82-year-old justice of the California Supreme Court was fired in 1977 by that state's Commission on Judicial Performance on grounds of senility—the venerable justice would occasionally doze off while presiding over trials, and then reinvigorate himself by doing exercises in the courtroom. But perhaps the most notorious instance of judicial incompetence resulted in the popular recall in 1977 (Wisconsin's first) of County Judge Archie Simonson, who released into custody two teenaged rapists on the interesting logic that women in Madison were guilty of wearing "provocative" clothing. (Evidently, the judge considered sweat shirts and jeans to be seductive, since those were what the victim had worn.) Judge Simonson was challenged by no less than five candidates for his seat, which was won by a young woman running as an independent, who became the first woman elected to that office in Dane County (Madison).

Managing the Courts

A third area of interest to judicial reformers is that of administration. Courts, like the other branches of government, have bureaucrats, too, and it is becoming increasingly evident that all branches of government, including the courts, could use higher-quality administrators than currently seem to be available. Indeed, efficient administration is particularly important in the courts, since justice itself is defined by the speed with which it is executed. A major reform of this facet of the judiciary has been the establishment of the office of *court administrator*. By 1980, all states had created such an office (in 1965, only half the states had one) to assist the chief justice of the state supreme court in the management of the overall state court system.

Related suggestions for administrative reform focus on the need for reorganizing the court structure. Reformers generally feel that all court systems should be unified under the supervision of the chief justice of the state supreme court and that judges should be subject to assignment throughout the state by the chief justice. At least thirty-four states have reorganized their court systems and have attained a moderate level of unification since 1970.[38]

The Law Itself

A final area of reform concerns the criminal code itself. It is argued that certain kinds of cases, such as victimless crimes, automobile accidents, and traffic violations, should be handled by some means other than that of a full-blown jury trial. In this light, "no-fault" insurance programs can be interpreted as a step toward the modernization of the court systems in that they reduce the pressure on the courts to handle a burgeoning case load of insurance claims stemming from automobile accidents. Similarly, half the people in prison and half the trials in the states involve people accused of victimless crimes. Decriminalizing certain crimes (such as public drunkenness) could substantially reduce the case load of the courts.[39]

RESISTING REFORM

Reforming the courts has not been and will not be an easy task. Although a number of "heavies" support the kinds of court reforms just reviewed, notably the National Center for State Courts, the American Bar Association, the Conference of Chief Justices, the Institution for Judicial Administration, and the American Judicator Society, the system itself often works against reform.

Courts are major dispensers of political patronage as well as makers of public policy. Both political parties and economic interests will fight to preserve the existing structure of the courts if the proposed reform seems threatening. By way of example, in Chicago the Democrats succeeded in forcing the acceptance of a compromise state court reform proposal that did not affect the selection procedures in Cook County. Although the proposals did not win voter approval in a statewide referendum, the proposal itself was designed to preserve Democratic dominance in recruiting judges in Chicago. Similarly, minority groups and labor unions have been known to oppose the appointment of judges through a commission system because they feel that they will be excluded from more judgeships than they would be if judges were elected by the populace at large. Rural interests occasionally block reform, and sometimes for sensible reasons; county court dockets are often not as loaded as urban court dockets, and the proposed reforms are superfluous. Indeed, those states that have been most influenced by proposals for reform uniformly have a high degree of urbanization and industrialization. California, New Jersey, Illinois, Massachusetts, and Michigan are perhaps among the most responsive to professional calls for modernization of the court system. The three lowest-ranking states in this regard are Alabama, Arkansas, and Mississippi; indeed, most of the Southern states are resistant to changing their courts.[40] Finally, even as legal professional groups vociferously propose court reforms, lawyers are among those who are the most vocal in opposing selected reforms, because lawyers may feel that the existing system works to their best economic advantage.

It also has been contended that the reformist drive is tragically misdirected because it fails to comprehend how the courts really work and often is largely motivated by "a law-business ideology which [mistakenly] glorifies the importance of formal rules."[41] One review of analyses of recent reforms in the judiciary concluded that most of the reforms had not attained their stated objectives:

> There is no support for the belief that the backgrounds of judges, including formal training and experience, are affected by merit selection or that decision making and judicial conduct have been altered. . . . Comparative research on large numbers of courts and studies of individual courts over time reveal that there is no connection between the amount of work to be done and the time it takes to do it, and that more judges do not necessarily decide more cases. . . . Many factual studies show, however, that as many as 90 percent of all cases are settled through informal negotiation. . . . Delay often is caused, not by the crush of judicial business, but by judges who permit lawyers to draw out litigation through repeated continuances.[42]

Nevertheless, when all is said and done, the states are generally responsive to proposals for court reform. The people, it seems, are interested in the politics of justice and, in spite of the arcane aspects of courtroom procedures, participate in judicial politics and wish to make it better.

NOTES

[1]Kenneth N. Vines and Herbert Jacob, "State Courts and Public Policy," in Herbert Jacob and Kenneth M. Vines, eds., *Politics in the American States,* 3rd ed. (Boston: Little, Brown, 1976), p. 265.

[2]Henry Robert Glick and Kenneth N. Vines, *State Court Systems* (Englewood Cliffs, N.J.: Prentice-Hall, 1973), p. 60.

[3]Jay C. Uppal, "The State of the Judiciary," *Book of the States, 1980-81* (Lexington, Ky.: Council of State Governments, 1980), p. 143.

[4]As derived from Table 4, *Book of the States, 1980-81,* pp. 448-449. Figures are for fiscal year 1977.

[5]Thomas R. Dye, *Politics in States and Communities,* 4th ed. (Englewood Cliffs, N.J.: Prentice-Hall, 1981), pp. 184-186.

[6]Patrick F. Healy, executive director of the Chicago Crime Commission, as cited in John Leo, "Why the Justice System Fails," *Time* (March 23, 1981), p. 23. The survey was taken in 1980.

[7]Burton M. Atkins and Henry Glick, "Determinants of Issues in State Courts of Last Resort," *American Journal of Political Science,* 20 (February, 1976), pp. 27-74.

[8]Herbert Jacob, *Crime and Justice in Urban America* (Englewood Cliffs, N.J.: Prentice-Hall, 1980), p. 74.

[9]*Ibid.,* pp. 74-75; and Bureau of the Census, *Statistical Abstract of the United States, 1980* (Washington, D.C.: U.S. Government Printing Office), p. 515. Percentage is for 1979.

[10]Vines and Jacob, "State Courts and Public Policy," p. 261.

[11]Council of State Governments, *Workload of State Courts of Last Resort* (Chicago: Council of State Governments, 1962).

[12]Vines and Jacob, "State Courts and Public Policy," p. 263.

[13]Dye, *Politics in States and Communities,* p. 196.

[14]Stuart Nagel, "Unequal Party Representation in State Supreme Courts," *Journal of the American Judicature Society,* 44 (1961), pp. 62-65.

[15]Stuart Nagel, "Political Party Affiliation and Judges' Decisions," *American Political Science Review,* 55 (June, 1961), pp. 843-851.

[16]Stuart Nagel, "Ethnic Affiliation and Judicial Propensities," *Journal of Politics,* 24 (February, 1962), pp. 92-110.

[17]Stuart Nagel, "Off the Bench Judicial Attitudes," in Glendon Schubert, ed., *Judicial Decision-Making* (Glencoe, Ill.: The Free Press, 1963).

[18]Both studies are in Herbert Jacob and Kenneth N. Vines, *Studies in Judicial Politics,* Vol. XIII (New Orleans: Tulane Studies in Political Science, 1963).

[19]Glick and Vines, *State Court Systems,* p. 60.
[20]*Ibid.,* p. 60.
[21]James Eisenstein and Herbert Jacob, *Felony Justice* (Boston: Little, Brown, 1977), pp. 19-64.
[22]Jacob, *Crime and Justice,* pp. 76-78.
[23]David W. Neubauer, *Criminal Justice in Middle America* (Morristown, N.J.: General Learning Press, 1974), p. 45.
[24]Edward O. Laumann and John P. Heinz, "Specialization and Prestige in the Legal Profession: The Structure of Deference," *American Bar Foundation Research Journal* (1977), pp. 155-216; Neubauer, *Criminal Justice,* pp. 68-71; and Joel Handler, *The Lawyer and His Community* (Madison: University of Wisconsin Press, 1967), pp. 39-42.
[25]Jacob, *Crime and Justice,* p. 78.
[26]Michael R. Gottfredson, Michael J. Hindelang, and Nicolette Parisi, *Sourcebook of Criminal Justice Statistics, 1977* (Washington, D.C.: Law Enforcement Assistance Administration, 1978), p. 35; and Jacob, *Crime and Justice,* p. 78.
[27]Jonathan Casper, *American Criminal Justice* (Englewood Cliffs, N.J.: Prentice-Hall, 1972), pp. 106-115.
[28]Barbara Babcock, address before the Twenty-fourth Annual National Institute on Crime and Delinquency, as quoted by United Press International, *The Arizona Republic* (June 20, 1977).
[29]Vines and Jacob, "State Courts and Public Policy," p. 243. The following discussion of California's judiciary is drawn from *ibid.,* pp. 244-246.
[30]Glick and Vines, *State Court Systems,* p. 40.
[31]Richard A. Watson and Rondal G. Downing, *The Politics of Bench and the Bar: Judicial Selection Under the Missouri Nonpartisan Court Plan* (New York: John Wiley, 1969), pp. 338-339.
[32]John Paul Ryan, Allen Ashman, and Bruce D. Sales, "Judicial Selection and Its Impact on Trial Judges' Background, Perceptions, and Performance," paper presented to the Annual Conference of the Western Political Science Association, Los Angeles, March, 1978, p. 26. See also James Herndon, "Appointment as a Means of Initial Accession to Elective State Courts of Last Resort," *North Dakota Law Review,* 38 (1962), pp. 60-73.
[33]Council of State Governments, *State Court Systems* (Lexington, Ky.: Council of State Governments, 1974), pp. 53-68.
[34]Jack Ladinsky and Alan Silver, "Popular Democracy and Judicial Independence," *Wisconsin Law Review* (1966), pp. 132-133.
[35]Watson and Downing, *Politics of Bench and the Bar.*
[36]Advisory Commission on Intergovernmental Relations, *The Question of State Government Capability* (Washington, D.C.: U.S. Government Printing Office, 1985), p. 185.
[37]Uppal, "The State of the Judiciary," p. 147.
[38]The following examples are drawn from *The New York Times* Syndicate, "Tirade About Bad Coffee Costs Judge His Job and a Small Fortune," *The Arizona Republic* (July 21, 1977); Associated Press, *The Arizona Republic* (March 28, 1977) and (January 8, 1977); and *The New York Times* Syndicate, "Independent Woman Lawyer Trounces Recalled Judge," *The Arizona Republic* (September 12, 1977).
[39]Alan V. Sokolow, "The State of the Judiciary," *Book of the States, 1974-75* (Lexington, Ky.: Council of State Governments, 1974), pp. 115-119.
[40]Kenneth N. Vines and Judson B. Fisher, "Legal Professionalism in the American States," mimeographed paper, State University of New York at Buffalo, 1971, as cited in Vines and Jacob, "State Courts and Public Policy," p. 256.
[41]Mark W. Cannon, "Innovation in the Administration of Justice, 1969-1981: An Overview," *Policy Studies Journal* (June, 1982), p. 687.
[42]*Ibid.,* pp. 686-687.

8

A ZOO OF GOVERNMENTS:

cities, counties, and other oddities

In Part Three we consider the politics of the 82,290 "creatures" of the states: cities, counties, special districts, towns, townships, suburbs, and other communities. These are the species that make up America's governmental "zoo." We begin with the biggest: cities.

GOVERNING CITIES

Municipalities use two major kinds of government, the "weak executive" model and the "strong executive" model. Within these two categories are various forms of municipal government, notably, the mayor-council form, which may rely on either a "weak mayor" or a "strong mayor" system, the commission form, and the council-manager plan. A discussion of each of these forms follows, and they are illustrated in Figure 8-1; you may wish to refer to Figure 8-1 as you read about them.

The "Weak Executive" Form of Urban Governance

The two principal models of the "weak executive" form of municipal administration are the "weak mayor" government and the commission plan. Both are characterized by their integration of the executive and legislative functions.

The *weak mayor form of government* is usually associated with a *mayor-and-council arrangement* in city hall, a form of municipal government favored by 56 percent of all cities with more than 2,500 people.[1] The mayor has inconsequential powers, and most of the managerial prerogatives are parceled out to the many elected officials or are already vested in the members of the city council. Council members are generally elected at large. The long ballot of municipal elections, characteristic of weak mayor governments, assures that administrative powers are splintered among council members and other elected officers. The mayor is little more than a chairperson of the city council.

The problems of a weak mayor form of government are the classic problems of any overly decentralized administrative system. Comprehensive planning, especially comprehensive financial planning, becomes virtually impossible. Compounding this is the areal decentralization prevalent in most Metropolitan Statistical Areas—a plethora of districts and jurisdictions, each with its own powers and administrative responsibilities.

"Weak Executive" Forms

1. Weak Mayor-Council Form

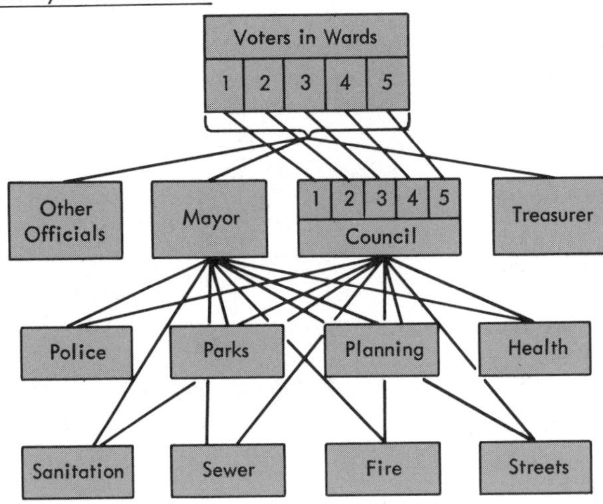

2. Commission Form

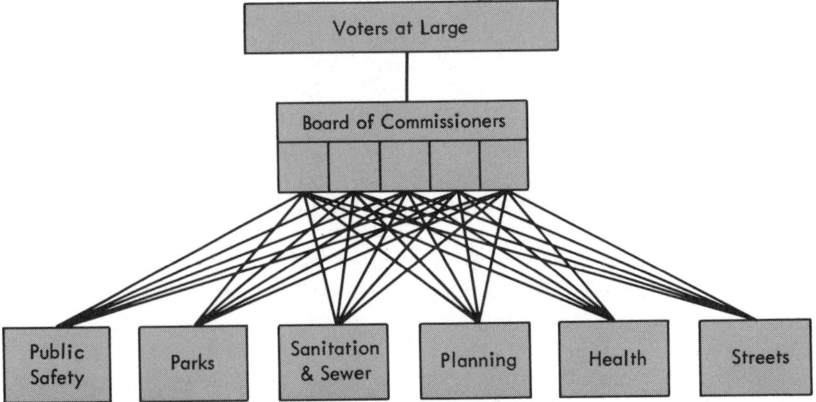

Figure 8-1 Forms of urban government.

"Strong Executive" Forms

1. Strong Mayor-Council Form

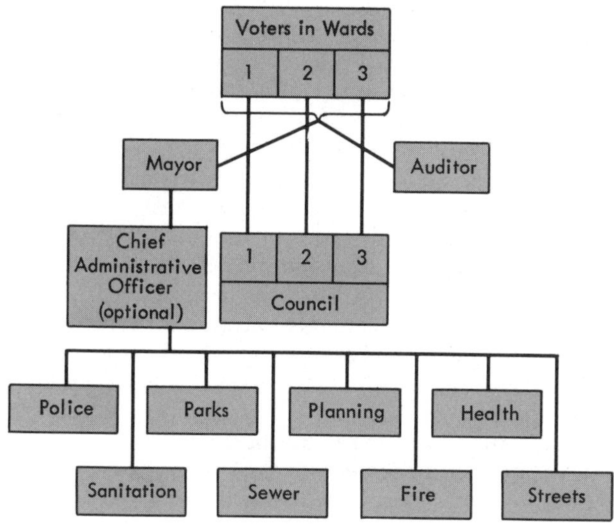

2. Council-Manager Form

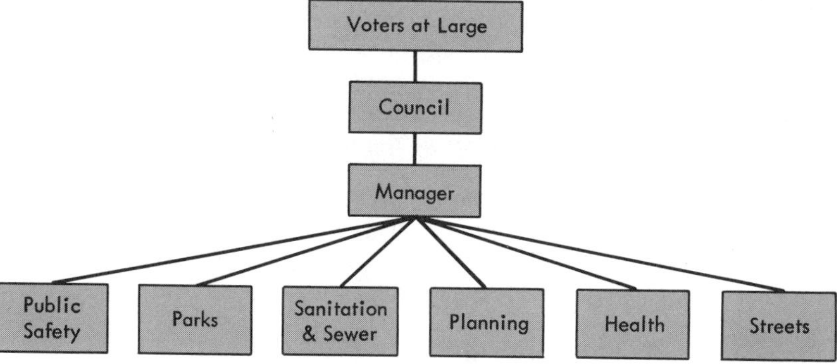

Figure 8-1 (Continued)

It is often difficult to adjudge whether or not a city government uses a weak mayor or strong mayor form (although clearly Los Angeles and Minneapolis are examples of the former). Perhaps the classic example is the late Richard Daley's Chicago. Mayor Daley inherited a weak mayor form of municipal government and, at least on paper, that remains the structure of Chicago's government. Daley "reported" to a city council of 50 members; the city had numerous independent boards (including those that dealt with such important areas as education and housing) and had other features that make a weak mayor form of government. Nevertheless, there is no question that Mayor Daley was a strong mayor and that he implemented, in practice if not on paper, a strong mayor form of government.

The *commission plan,* initially created as a reaction against the weak mayor form of government, ironically shares many of its underlying disadvantages. It came about because of a local disaster. In 1900 Galveston, Texas, was flooded by a raging Gulf of Mexico. Within 24 hours, one-sixth of the population was dead or injured, fresh water supplies were gone, food was dwindling, sanitation was nonexistent, and looting was rampant. The mayor called together Galveston's leading citizens—the city's "real" leaders—and from their ranks formed a Central Relief Committee, which became Galveston's operational government. Each member of the committee was "commissioned" to accomplish a particular task and to make policy on how that task was to be accomplished. Thus, the committee possessed both an executive and a legislative function, and, in terms of restoring order out of chaos, the committee worked.

Galvestonians were convinced that they had discovered a revolutionary form of municipal government; they petitioned the Texas legislature to legitimate it, which it did, and the commission form of government was inaugurated.

Under the commission plan, city commissioners are generally elected at large in an attempt to reduce parochialism, and the short ballot predominates (i.e., comparatively few officeholders are elected). Each member of the council is formally both a legislator and administrator. Policy is set collectively and is executed individually, and the mayor is little more than an important commissioner. Indeed, in some cities commissioners rotate the office of mayor among themselves. The initiative, referendum, and recall generally are features of the commission plan, and nonpartisan elections are the norm. Unfortunately, because each commissioner is both legislator and administrator, he or she is often predisposed to protect his or her individual "barony," and to do so, he or she must "go along to get along" with his or her fellow commissioners. Were the commissioner to do otherwise, he or she would be singled out, and his or her power base would necessarily be undercut. The commissioner would become a minority player in a game that can be won only by a majority.

Ten years after the Galveston flood, the commission plan was in use in 108 cities, but now only 16 cities of more than 50,000 people, plus a number of smaller towns, mostly in the South, are using it; currently, less than 3 percent of the nation's cities with more than 2,500 people use the form.[2] The lack of administrative integration and the belief of many citizens that the commission plan amounted to government by amateurs has led to its decline.

The "Strong Executive" Form of Urban Governance

While the mayor-and-council form of urban governance can employ a weak mayor variant, more frequently the form favors the use of the *strong mayor-and-council government.* Six of the ten largest cities in the United States have a strong mayor form of government. That larger cities would choose a strong mayor form of government is predictable: the media tend to focus on the mayor as the representative of power in city hall; the size and complexity of big cities mandate a political executive who is more than a figurehead; and, because of the city's legal subservience to the state, a strong mayor option helps attract able persons to municipal service, persons who can deal effectively with the governor and state.

Political patterns in strong mayor cities are similar to the basic patterns of the national and state governments. Under a strong mayor form, a skilled mayor can become both chief legislator and chief executive, just as an adept president or governor can. The city council usually is small, elected by wards, and relatively "pure" in its legislative function. The partisan short ballot is common; often only the mayor, council members, and auditor are subject to election. The mayor has the sole power to form budgets, administer municipal departments, and make most of the policy decisions. The council, of course, must approve budgets, appointments, and policies, and it has the power to launch potentially embarrassing investigations of the mayor's administration.

Besides being associated with big cities, strong mayor-council forms of government are also associated with cities that have relatively older citizens, more blue-collar workers, a less well-educated population, and slower economic growth rates. The obverse of these characteristics in a city tends to be associated with the council-manager form of government. Strong mayor-council governments are also clearly associated with the Eastern and Midwestern cities.[3]

The third major form of urban government is the *council-manager form.* Like the commission form, it has an unusual history. In 1908 the city council members of Staunton, Virginia, became frustrated with the welter of "administrivia" of city government that tends to crop up under any weak executive model. They decided to hire a professional manager—the council would decide policy, the city manager would execute it. Although the commission plan was then the national rage, Staunton's idea gradually began taking root. In 1913 the influential National Municipal League approved the plan in its model city charter. But the decision in 1914 of Dayton, Ohio (which, like Galveston, had been badly damaged by flood), to alter its governmental form and switch to a council-manager system provided the real impetus for the novel plan. With its new city manager, Dayton centralized, economized, and enlarged a number of municipal functions, rebuilding and improving a largely destroyed town in record time.

The essence of the council-manager form is that while legislative (city council) and executive (city manager) powers are clearly separate, administrative powers are highly unified under the aegis of a professional city manager. The council controls only the manager—it hires and may fire him or her—while the manager controls the administrative apparatus of the city. Elections in council-manager municipalities usually are nonpartisan (unlike strong mayor governments) and have a short ballot; the electorate usually has the initiative, referendum, and recall.

Since 1914, the council-manager plan has been growing in popularity among municipalities. Almost 35 percent of all American cities with more than 2,500 people and more than half of American cities of more than 25,000 population use the plan.[4] The council-manager plan governs more than 100 million Americans, and it is encroaching on big cities, which traditionally have favored a mayor-council form of government; Dallas, Phoenix, San Antonio, San Diego, and Kansas City are all council-manager metropolises. In fact, 44 of the 100 largest cities use the council-manager plan.[5] Although this form of urban government is closely associated with at-large electoral systems, this combination appears less often among the nation's 44 biggest council-manager cities: only 16 of them use multimember electoral systems, and 16 employ a combination of the two.[6]

Just as the mayor-city council form of government is associated with big cities in the East and Midwest having heterogeneous and working class populations and declining or stable growth rates, the council-manager form of government is associated with medium-sized cities in the West. The use of the council-manager form also is related to cities that have middle-class, white-collar workers, relatively low proportions of foreign-born residents, and people with comparatively high educational attainment. In other words, council-manager government normally walks hand-in-hand with middle-class values, while mayor-council forms are associated with working-class values. Hence, council-manager forms of government are found mostly in the suburbs. Politically, council-manager governments usually rule in cities with nonpartisan elections, with one dominant party, or with weak political parties. Mayor-council forms of government tend to be associated with competitive party systems.

The form of government in the cities also reflects its state's political system. Mayor-council plans are found most frequently in states with competitive two-party systems; council-manager forms are found most frequently in states with either one dominant party or with relatively weak party organizations. To quote one observer, "Whatever the case, manager government appears incompatible with strong partisan politics in a community."[7]

In some ways the council-manager and the mayor-council variants of urban government appear to be blending into a new office, the *chief administrative officer,* which is rising in popularity in the cities. It is held by a professional administrator (such as a city manager) who is accountable only to the mayor rather than responsible to the city council.

COUNTIES, OR THE FADING FIGURE OF THE COURTHOUSE GANG

Counties govern close to 190 million Americans directly. There are 3,043 counties, or an average of 61 counties per state. Each county serves slightly more than 62,000 people on the average.

With the exception of Connecticut and Rhode Island, all states have county governments, and they are among the oldest form of government in the country. Those who read the book (or saw the television series) *Roots,* which dealt with the black experience in the United States, could draw the conclusion from that series alone that the counties were the most viable of all forms of governments, at least in the early days of our nationhood. And, indeed, counties have been governing in the United States for more than 350 years.

The United States adopted counties from England, where they had existed for six centuries as "shires" administered by sheriffs before the first European settlers arrived in America. Virginia created the first American counties in 1634, followed by Massachusetts nine years later. The kinds of counties established by Virginia and Massachusetts were quite different. In Virginia, the counties were strong governments, with distinct electoral, managerial, judicial, and even military responsibilities; "county home rule," an idea arguing that counties should be autonomous units of government with their own elected officials, got its start in Virginia. But in Massachusetts, the original counties were run by officials appointed by the governor; as with England's shires, the Massachusetts counties were perceived as being administrative arms of the king—or, in the case of Massachusetts, the king's designate, the governor.[8]

Virginia's model of county government spread throughout the South, and even today Southern counties seem to be more significant jurisdictions in their states than elsewhere. The Virginia model, by and large, spread westward, with permutations added by Pennsylvania, which originated the concept of a governing body for counties—the county board of commissioners, or supervisors—elected by each county's citizens. The Massachusetts model was heavily influential in the Northeast; because counties were simply extensions of the state governments in the Northeast, self-governing towns and townships became the predominant units of local governments.[9]

Even though the Virginia model, which espoused the notion that counties should be independent local governments, was clearly gaining in popularity as the nation moved West, the early court decisions on the place of counties in the federal framework advocated the traditional Massachusetts model, which conceived of counties as administrative arms of the state. In 1845, the U.S. Supreme Court ruled in *Maryland* v. *Baltimore and Ohio Railroad* that the "counties are nothing more than certain portions of the territory into which the state is divided for more convenient exercise of the powers of government." This and later rulings by the courts sharply constricted the services that counties would be able to provide their citizens as independent governments.

But if counties could not provide their own services, they could—and did—provide their own elected officials, who were duly paid out of their states' treasuries. As new states were admitted to the Union, they adopted—kind of—the Virginia model. By that we mean that the symbols of county independence were touted, but not the reality. The symbols were the counties' elected "row officers," a term covering county sheriffs, prosecuting attorneys, clerks, auditors, recorders, assessors, treasurers, coroners, and commissioners. While some of these row officers have authority, notably, those associated with the criminal justice system, not all do because the state governments have not granted them any policymaking responsibilities. For example, the county commissioners in most counties—supposedly the policymaking bodies of county government—have little if any policy to make because the state legislature calls the tune, and then simply orders the counties to play it. Similarly, most of the other county row officers have responsibilities that are purely clerical in nature, responsibilities that hardly warrant their election to office by county voters. Thus, most counties appear to combine the worst of both worlds: little authority, but lots of responsibility, at least in the eyes of the counties' residents.

The Commission Plan

Nowhere is this dilemma better expressed than in the mode of government favored by most counties: the *commission plan,* also known as the *plural executive plan.* Indeed, about 2,300 of the 3,043 county governments still use the commission form of government, and the majority of boards consist of three to five members who are elected for two- to four-year terms.[10] These county boards of commissioners are responsible for appointing advisory boards and commissions, adopting the county budget, and enacting various ordinances. But, "With no single person recognized as overall county administrator in this form, the governing board shares the administrative responsibilities with officials elected to perform specific county operations."[11] Traditionally, however, the chair of the county board is often in effect the chief executive officer for the county.

Figure 8-2 illustrates the county commission form of government. The figure also sketches the other two forms of government that counties use, and you may wish to refer to Figure 8-2 as our discussion continues.

The commission plan is perhaps the purest expression of England's 900-year-old shires (the American counties' parentage) that can still be found in this nation's governmental menagerie. Royal thinking in the Middle Ages, when the English shires were founded, did not distinguish between administration and policy; those who made policy (kings, dukes, and sheriffs, for instance) also implemented it, and those who administered policy (again, kings, dukes, and sheriffs) also made it. When we examine the role of the American county commissioner under the commission plan, we see a replication of the medieval royalist mind-set: those who are privileged to reign must also personally deliver.

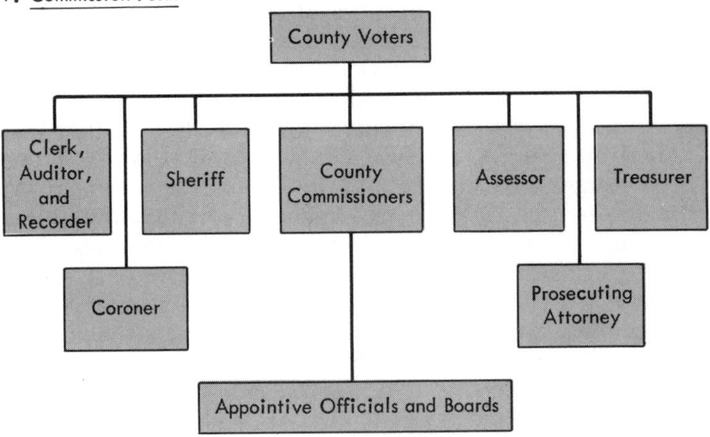

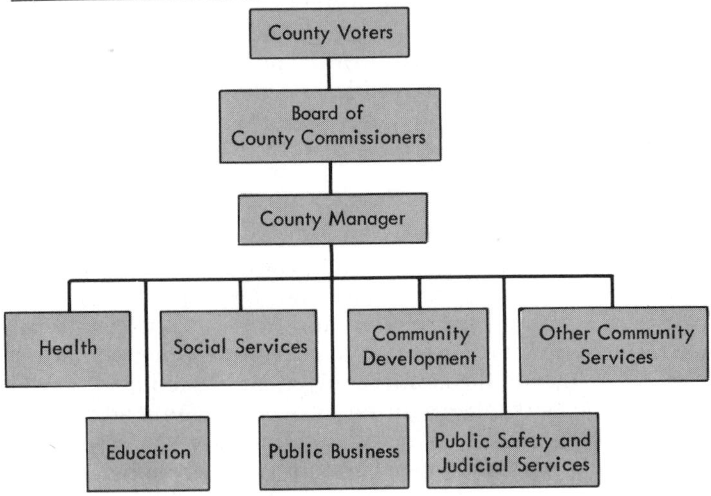

Figure 8-2 Forms of county government.

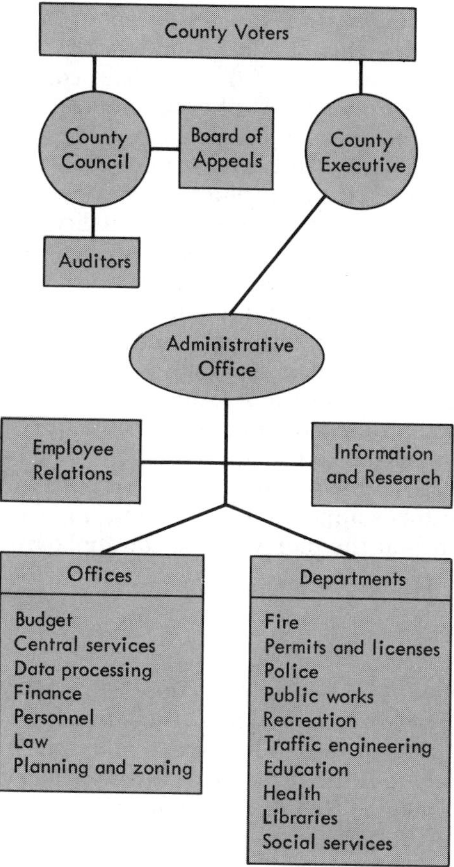

Figure 8-2 (Continued)

There are advantages to the traditional commission form of county government: it brings government closer to the people and is, in that sense, democratic; it promotes a unified system of administration and policymaking, since this form of government does not distinguish between politics and administration; and it has a widespread system of checks and balances that results from the individual election of officials. The disadvantages are perhaps more obvious: it is an antiquated form of government that may no longer be suitable for the twentieth century; the lack of a chief executive officer can lead to inefficiency in delivering services to county residents; administration by the "citizen-legislator" no longer is feasible in a society as highly technological as ours; and voters are seldom sufficiently familiar with the myriad—often powerless—row officers whom they must elect, an unfamiliarity that can give certain, shrewder county officials a concentration of power, since no one really knows who they are nor what they do.[12]

The Council-Administrator Plan

In many respects, the commission plan, which is favored by about three quarters of the counties, is analogous to the commission plan used by cities and shares many of its deficiencies. As a consequence, one of the trends in county government is the adoption of the *council-administrator form* of government. This is the counties' counterpart to the council-manager plan used by cities. The first county to adopt this plan was Iredell County in North Carolina in 1927.

Like the council-manager plan for cities, the council-administrator plan for counties gives a county administrator chief administrative responsibility and policymaking responsibility; the county administrator reports to the county board. The plan is clearly the coming trend in county government; and today about a fifth, or 644 counties, of all counties have a county administrator; all counties with more than 250,000 people (or 244 counties) hire adminstrators.[13] The advantage of the council-administrator plan is that it separates policymaking and administration, supposedly removing the administrator from political influence. Appointed administrators often are recruited on a national basis, unlike locally elected county officials, and thus are likelier to provide professional management skills. Criticisms brought against the council-administrator plan include the argument that because the administrator is appointed he or she cannot be responsive to the needs of the people and is at the mercy of the county board, particularly when the board is politically split.

The Council-Elected Executive Plan

The third type of county government is used in 146 counties[14] and is perhaps the most complex of all governmental versions. The *council-elected executive plan* provides legislative and executive branches. The executive branch is headed by a strong, elected administrator who is the formal executive officer of the county and often has a veto power similar to that of a state governor. The power of the county administrative officer under the council-elected executive form is greater than that of the other forms of county government, although the relationship between the county council and the county executive is similar to that of the council-administrator form. The disadvantages of the council-elected executive form center on the possibility of political bossism emerging in the form of the elected administrative officer. There are talent problems, since the position does require at least as much political skill as administrative abilities. Other disadvantages include risks of fostering a legislative conflict and high cost, since this represents a relatively professional form of county government. The advantages of the elected executive form of government include the visibility of the policymaking process in the community; the development of strong political leadership, which is particularly advantageous in large urban areas; political responsiveness, since the elected executive is responsible to the public; greater public visibility of the county government; and a desirable system of checks and balances provided by the separation of powers.

Trends in county government have favored the council-elected executive plan, and, during the past 15 years, counties have opted for hiring full-time, professionally qualified administrators. Very few counties have voluntarily chosen the commission plan in recent years.

Perhaps, in some ways, counties represent the most significant but least recognized innovation in American government. Counties have been with us longer than our portion of the continent has been a nation, yet their very traditionalism permits counties to be more innovative than other governments, simply because governmental innovation in counties is not as noticeable. To quote the National Research Council,

> Already in existence, the county does not raise the fear of a new unit government. Recognition of the fact that counties can provide services over a wider area has led to efforts to modernize county governments, which in many places are archaic.[15]

TOWNS AND TOWNSHIPS: THE TINIER GOVERNMENTS

Closely related to both the notion and the reality of county government in the United States are the New England towns and townships, the "two important regional exceptions to the commonly established systems of local government."[16] Both can trace their origins, as can counties, to prerevolutionary America; both have deep roots in the American tradition of self-government; and it is in the town or township that the original "town meeting," a device so praised in texts on democracy, got its start. The first town meeting was authorized by the Pilgrims of Plymouth Colony (now Massachusetts) in 1636 to a single town, Scituate, and eventually was permitted by the colony in all its towns.[17]

About 48 million people, or 20 percent of the American population, are directly governed by the 16,734 towns or townships, although fewer than half the states (only 20) have towns or townships as entities of government. Most towns are found in New England; townships are generally found in the Middle Atlantic states and the Midwest.

The New England town clearly is the more viable and dynamic of the two forms. In Colonial times, the townspeople "selected" selectmen at their town meetings to run the day-to-day affairs of government between meetings. This tradition carries on today, although it has evolved in some New England areas from a direct democratic form of government to a representative form, as the New England towns have grown in size from hundreds to thousands of people. More important, New England towns function as counties, and virtually all of New England (the exceptions are largely in Maine) is governed by towns.

Townships, however, are clearly on the decline politically. The township, like counties or some small villages, is governed by a board of supervisors or trustees that is elected directly by the people. But the township shares powers with county governments and other types of governments, so it does not have the independent status or the dynamism of the New England town. Indeed, it is often seen more as an anachronistic hindrance than a facilitator of the policies of the people.

Figure 8-3 illustrates how this form of government—the town meeting—is organized. As it shows, there are two kinds of town meetings: the representative type, in which a large number of representatives are elected to represent the townspeople at the meeting, and the classic, open meeting, at which all the town's or township's citizens vote. Both representative and open town meetings are the form of governance used by a fraction of 1 percent of municipalities with more than 2,500 people, although the open town meeting is favored over the representative town meeting by these towns and townships by nearly 5 to 1.[18]

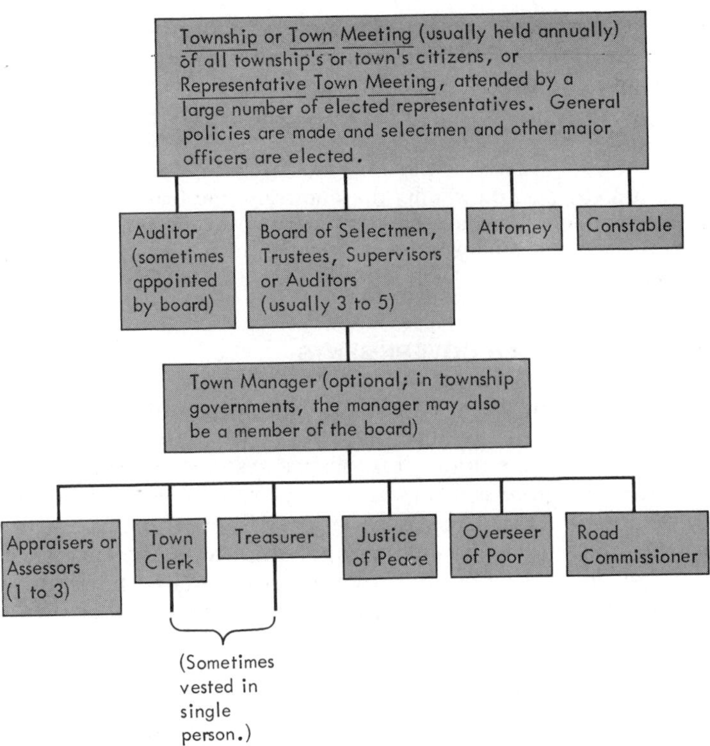

Figure 8-3 Township Meeting, Town Meeting, and Representative Town Meeting government.

An examination of the town meeting in five New England states uncovered mixed results about the efficacy of direct democracy as practiced in town meetings. Average attendance at annual open town meetings was highest in the smallest towns (occasionally exceeding a fourth of the townspeople) and lowest in the largest ones (never topping 5 percent of the populace). Town clerks (the effective city managers in these jurisdictions) generally rated the quality of debate during both open and representative town meetings as good to exceptional. "Sentiment alone is not responsible for the tenacity of the open town meeting. . . . Local lawmaking appears to be functioning adequately in most open meeting towns . . . and no evidence has been presented that alternative lawmakers would exercise greater sagacity in choosing solutions for town problems."[19]

MULTIPURPOSE DISTRICTS: PROMISE VERSUS PRACTICE

In considering municipalities, counties, towns, and townships, we have been talking about political and administrative units that share at least one commonality: they usually have relatively comprehensive political and administrative authority over a particular geographic area. For example, a county has control over a number of public functions, such as transportation, health, and road maintenance, not just one special function, such as education. Although the concept of multipurpose functions of a governmental unit is a good one, a problem is that no matter how many functions a government is empowered to perform, frequently the problems go beyond that government's territorial boundaries. To counteract this condition, a number of governments have cooperated in what is known as the multipurpose district, which is a type of special district. What a multipurpose district does depends upon the nature of the district itself, but through these districts local governments have tried to match governmental power with the public's problems on an areawide scale.

Multipurpose districts are a fairly new idea. They are authorized to make policy and administer it within a considerable range of different governmental functions. The multipurpose district is a government unto itself, virtually like a county or a municipality. It can be created in one of three ways: by giving existing metropolitan districts more functions, by consolidating those functions in existence, or by passing broad new state legislation that basically forms whole new agencies or permits their formation in the future. Although there has been some progress in forming multipurpose districts, their adoption has been quite limited. Of the nation's 28,588 special districts, fewer than 1,750 are responsible for more than one function.

SPECIAL DISTRICTS: SEMIGOVERNMENTS OF SPECIALIZATION

Far more common units of government are the remaining special districts that have only a single function. If we count school districts as special districts (which they are), there are 43,439 special districts in the country. America's 14,851 school districts are considered more thoroughly in Chapter 17, but other kinds of special districts warrant a description here.

Special districts continued to increase during the 1970s, although not as rapidly as in the 1950s and 1960s. Special districts are favored in the Metropolitan Statistical Areas and make up about one-third of all types of governments found in the MSAs.

The 28,588 special districts concern themselves with a wide variety of functions. For example, 42 states have 3,296 special districts responsible solely for housing and community development; 47 have 6,232 special districts responsible for natural resources, such as water; 30 states have 4,560 fire protection districts.[20] Special districts are also assigned responsibility for such functions as airports, sewage disposal, bridges, housing, public transportation, tunnels, terminals, water supplies, parks, and recreation, among other single functions. Figure 8-4 indicates the kinds of services that special districts provide.

The National Research Council concluded that the proliferation of special districts is a political by-product of the fact that metropolitan areas have been unable to obtain voter approval of proposed reorganization plans, but that the public's needs that these plans are designed to meet nonetheless remain. Hence, politically expeditious special districts continue to multiply because local governments seem unable to create more administratively rational multipurpose districts.[21]

These, then, constitute our zoo of governments: strong mayor-council cities; weak mayor-council cities; commission plans; the council-manager form; the commission, or plural-executive, form of county government; council-administrator counties; council-elected executive counties; townships; towns;

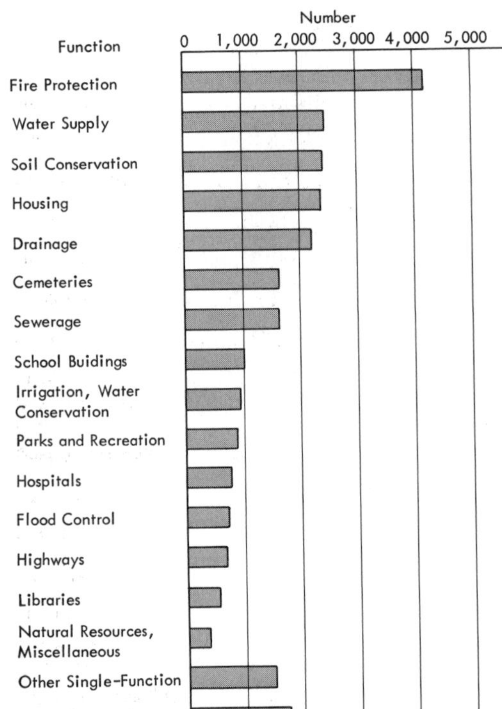

Figure 8-4
Special districts, by function, 1977. (*Source:* U.S. Bureau of the Census, 1977.)

open town meetings; representative town meetings; multipurpose districts; and special districts. Whew! America's menagerie of local governance encompasses many species; it is a singularly rich political ecology.

NOTES

[1]As derived from Table 3, *Municipal Year Book, 1985* (Washington, D.C.: International City Management Association, 1985), p. xv. Of the 19,076 municipalities in the United States, only 6,627 have more than 2,500 people.
[2]*Ibid.* Figures are for 1985.
[3]Leo Schnore and Robert Alford, "Forms of Government and Socioeconomic Characteristics of Suburbs," *Administrative Science Quarterly* (June, 1963), pp. 1-17.
[4]*Municipal Year Book, 1985,* p. xv.
[5]Frank Turco, "Leadership of Most Big Cities Picked Through Some Type of Ward System," *The Arizona Republic* (November 27, 1982). Figures are for 1982. The article is based on a survey conducted by the Phoenix Citizen Charter Review Committee.
[6]*Ibid.*
[7]Thomas R. Dye, *Politics in States and Communities,* 4th ed. (Englewood Cliffs, N.J.: Prentice-Hall, 1981), p. 240.
[8]Robert Sydney Duncombe, *County Government in America* (Washington, D.C.: National Association of Counties, 1966), pp. 20-23.
[9]*Ibid.*
[10]U.S. Bureau of the Census, *Governing Boards of County Governments* (Washington, D.C.: U.S. Government Printing Office, 1973), p. 4, as updated using data in Table 4, *Municipal Year Book, 1985,* p. xv.
[11]Florence Zeller, "Forms of County Government," *County Year Book, 1975* (Washington,

D.C.: National Association of Counties and International City Management Association, 1975), p. 28.

[12]*Ibid.*

[13]As derived from Table 4, *Municipal Year Book, 1985,* p. xvii.

[14]Patrick J. Chase, "A Profile of Elected County Executives," *Urban Data Service Reports,* 12 (November, 1980), p. 1.

[15]National Research Council, *Toward an Understanding of Metropolitan America* (San Francisco: Canfield, 1975), pp. 110-117.

[16]John C. Bollens and Henry J. Schmandt, *The Metropolis,* 3rd ed. (New York: Harper & Row, 1975), p. 48.

[17]Joseph F. Zimmerman, "The New England Town Meeting: Pure Democracy in Action?" *Municipal Year Book, 1984* (Washington, D.C.: International City Management Association, 1984), p. 102.

[18]As derived from Table 3, *Municipal Year Book, 1985,* p. xv.

[19]Zimmerman, "The New England Town Meeting," p. 106. The states studied were Connecticut, Maine, Massachusetts, New Hampshire, and Vermont.

[20]Bureau of the Census, *Statistical Abstract of the United States, 1985* (Washington, D.C.: U.S. Government Printing Office, 1984), Table 461, p. 283. Figures are for 1982.

[21]National Research Council, *Toward an Understanding of Metropolitan America,* pp. 115–116.

9

THE FACES OF FEDERALISM

Political science calls the relationships that governments maintain with each other *intergovernmental relations,* or *federalism.* Intergovernmental relations is more formally defined as the series of legal, political, and administrative relationships established among units of government that possess varying degrees of authority and jurisdictional autonomy.

FEDERALISM IN TURMOIL

The concept, structure, and practice of federal relations in the United States have been in turmoil for the last decade. Authorities differ on the effects of new forms of federalism on the public and its interests. Theodore J. Lowi has attacked new variations of federalism, particularly those of the Johnson administration, as overly decentralized, inducing a "crisis of public authority" antithetical to the national interest, and indicative of "the end of liberalism."[1] Lowi's attack is devastating, particularly in his real-life account of urban renewal in "Iron City," where federal administrations knowingly permitted and financed what amounted to a "Negro removal" program by local officials. On the other hand, Vincent Ostrom has applauded the decentralizing overtones of new ventures in federal relations as beneficial to the assurance of a "compound republic"—that is, one where multiple and jurisdictionally overlapping administrative units are most responsive to the needs of the individual citizen.[2]

Considering how opinions differ among both politicians and political scientists on the nature of intergovernmental relations, it is not surprising to learn that we are dealing with an extraordinarily complex system.

Given the complexity of the federal system, the crises of federalism, not surprisingly, are many. These crises are administrative, jurisdictional, political, and financial. Political and financial problems are of such importance that they are considered in separate chapters. In this chapter we will concentrate instead on the administrative and jurisdictional problems of intergovernmental relations. Table 9-1 shows the 82,341 governments in the United States by type and indicates their fluctuations between 1942, 1962, and 1982.

Table 9-1 indicates that American governmental units are many. The U.S. Task Force on Land Use and Urban Growth in its report *The Use of Land* noted that much of this fragmentation goes back to "a long American tradition of localism in land use control, dating at least to the issuance of the Standard State Zoning Enabling Act of 1924, an act which most states copied and which viewed land use controls as a matter of local rather than state control."[3] Much of the proliferation of units of local government occurred in the years following World War II, particularly around the fringes of big cities. It was largely due to white flight from the inner cities and unplanned metropolitan growth. The lack of prior planning for urban regions is particularly noticeable when we consider these examples of growth: 44 new suburban governments were created between 1945 and 1950 around St. Louis by builders desirous of escaping strict municipal building codes. New towns were formed around Minneapolis solely as a means of taxing a newly arrived industry, and one village was incorporated for the single purpose of issuing a liquor license. Bryan City, California, was created so that a circus owner could zone for animal populations as he saw fit. The town of New Square, New York, was established so that a kosher slaughterhouse could be operated. Gardenia, California, was incorporated so that its residents might play poker legally.[4] Yet, eager as Americans appear to be to set up small towns, they are wary of creating large ones. Community efforts to merge urban and suburban governments (considered later in this chapter) have generally failed, despite frequently intensive efforts by urban political elites. With the exceptions of school districts, which have been diminishing in number since the 1930s, and special districts, which have been slowly multiplying, the numbers of governmental units in all categories have remained essentially the same since 1960.

Jurisdictional crises of federalism are real and severe, yet at most levels governments have been making genuine strides during the last 20 years to reduce the adverse effects of governmental fragmentation. We shall consider

Table 9-1 Number of Governmental Units, by Type of Government: 1942, 1962, and 1982

Type of Government	*1942*	*1962*	*1982*
Total	155,116	91,237	82,341
U.S. Government	1	1	1
State governments	48	50	50
Local governments	155,067	91,186	82,290
County	3,050	3,043	3,041
Municipal	16,220	18,000	19,076
Township and town	18,919	17,142	16,734
School district	108,579	34,678	14,851
Special district	8,299	18,323	28,588

Source: Bureau of the Census, *Statistical Abstract of the United States, 1985* (Washington, D.C.: U.S. Government Printing Office, 1984), Table 433, p. 261.

some of these efforts in turn, first approaching the federal government's role in intergovernmental relations, then moving to the states' role, then considering some aspects of the local scene.

THE CONSTITUTION AND COURTS

The federal government interacts in major ways with both state and local governments. We shall consider federal interaction first with states, then with localities.

Much of the federal government's cooperation with state governments is specified by the Constitution, which organized the federal system around three basic ideas: (1) drawing of boundaries between governmental activities of the states and the nation, (2) establishing and maintaining the identity of state and national governments, and (3) politically integrating the nation and the states.[5]

Section 8 of Article I of the Constitution was instrumental in making distinctions between state and national functions. It delegated 17 specific powers to the national government, including defense, general welfare, and commerce, and left the remaining powers to the states. These remaining powers are now known as "reserved powers," a phrase taken from the Tenth Amendment, which was added rather hastily by the founders in response to such populist rabble-rousers as Patrick Henry. The Tenth Amendment was designed to grant the states a more visible and defined territory for exercising their powers. Section 9 of Article I also dealt with states' boundaries by preventing the national government from doing certain things, such as suspending the writ of *habeus corpus,* and also forbidding the states from doing certain things, such as entering into treaties with foreign nations and coining money.

The second area of constitutional federalism deals with establishing and maintaining the identities between state and nation. The most important clause here is Section 2, Article IV, which stipulates that "no new States shall be Formed or Erected within the jurisdiction of any other State; nor any State be formed by the junction of two or more States, or Parts of States, without the Consent of the Legislature of the States concerned."

Finally, the Constitution dealt with the integration of national and state governments, primarily by providing for cooperation among them in the performance of certain functions. For example, the states and the nation cooperate in amending the Constitution and electing a president. As Kenneth Vines observes, "Perhaps the most important factor in making possible political integration between the two levels is the scarcity of officials with a clearly defined identification with the states, resulting in the creation of a group of national officeholders who also have links to the states."[6] This arrangement, of course, was designed by the founders. As Madison noted in the *Federalist* papers, "a local spirit will infallibly prevail much more in the members of Congress than a national spirit will prevail in the Legislatures of the particular states."[7]

These three major features of the relations between the state governments and the national government—boundary settlement, separate identities, and national and state integration—were refined by the courts over time. Without question, the most influential single case in this process of refinement was *McCulloch* v. *Maryland,* which was settled by the Supreme Court under Chief Justice John Marshall in 1819. Marshall and his colleagues supported the expansion of national powers under the commerce clause of the Constitution, which gave the national government a powerful ability to interpret what was necessary and proper in the way of policy under the Constitution. The case involved the state of Maryland's attempt to tax the second United States Bank, which was located in Maryland. Alexander Hamilton, as secretary of the Treasury, had proposed a national bank and argued that it could be established under a strong national government, which could and should adopt such measures because they were "implied powers" under the Constitution, even though the Constitution did not specifically authorize such policies as the establishment of the bank. The Marshall Court agreed with Hamilton's argument, stating that, although a bank was not explicitly authorized as a power granted to Congress under the Constitution, it nonetheless was implied under Congress's abilities to establish and collect taxes, regulate commerce, raise and support armies, and so on. Hence, Congress had the ability to adopt appropriate measures for the realization of the powers granted to it by the Constitution to do whatever is "necessary and proper to implement its specified functions." This notion of implied powers as an interpretation of the "necessary and proper" clause of the Constitution is with us today, and (with the exception of the Civil War) remains the strongest statement of national power as opposed to state power. Table 9-2 lists the principal powers of the federal government and the implied powers of the states.

THE EVOLUTION OF INTERGOVERNMENTAL RELATIONS

Operating within the formal rules of the game established by the Constitution and by subsequent judicial interpretation, localities, states, and the federal government have gone through a number of phases in their relationships. During the twentieth century, we can discern at least six such phases, often overlapping in time, but each possessing its own set of unique characteristics.[8]

The first of these phases occurred from the late nineteenth century to 1930 and was characterized by the conflict among states, localities, and Washington. The major problems centered on defining the boundaries and proper spheres of influence among various governmental jurisdictions, and intergovernmental actors (i.e., relevant public officials at all governmental levels) saw themselves in an adversary and antagonistic relationship with each other. The mechanisms of intergovernmental relationships prior to 1930 were relatively simple and relied largely on legislative statutes, judicial rulings, and federal regulations. What Deil S. Wright calls the "federalism metaphor"—that is, how intergovernmental relations were perceived and described in metaphorical terms—during this period was "layer cake federalism." In other words, people saw the relationships between governments as a series of layers: localities on the bottom, states in the middle, and the federal government on top.

The next federal phase occurred during the 1930s and the 1950s and represented quite an opposite composite of relationships from the previous period of intergovernmental conflict. The 1930s, 1940s, and 1950s were decades of "cooperative federalism" in which everyone faced up, essentially as an intergovernmental team, to common problems of the Great Depression, World War II, and the rise of international Communism. In stark contrast to the pre-1930s, officials involved in intergovernmental relations stressed collaboration

Table 9-2 The Constitution's Federal Divisions of Power

Major Powers of the Federal Government	*Major Implied Powers of the States*
Tax for federal purposes.	Tax for local purposes.
Borrow on the nation's credit.	Borrow on the state's credit.
Regulate foreign and interstate commerce.	Regulate trade within the state.
Provide currency and coinage.	Make and enforce civil and criminal law.
Conduct foreign relations and make treaties.	Maintain a police force.
Provide an army and navy.	Furnish public education.
Establish and maintain a postal service.	Control local government.
Protect patent and copyrights.	Regulate charities.
Regulate weight and measures.	Establish voting and election laws.
Admit new states.	Plus all "powers not delegated to the United States by the Constitution, nor prohibited by it to the States are reserved to the States respectively, or to the people."
"Make all laws which shall be necessary and proper" for the execution of all powers vested in the U. S. Government.	

and supportive relationships. The mechanisms of working relationships among governments moved from simple statutes and court orders to a national planning mode involving the introduction of formula grants and more sophisticated versions of intergovernmental tax credits. The federalism metaphor changed from "layer cake federalism" to "marble cake federalism"; increasingly, it was difficult to separate the governmental activities of localities, states, and nation.

The next phase, which occurred during the 1940s through the 1960s, has been called "concentrated federalism." During this period, the shape of intergovernmental relations was increasingly functional, focused, and specific. The federal government attempted to meet the public service obligations and the physical development needs of states and localities. In terms of the working styles of officials who participated in intergovernmental relations during this period, "politics" were largely "out" and "professionalism" was largely "in"; a kind of engineering mentality predominated. The new mechanisms of intergovernmental relations evolved from a national planning format to an emphasis on detailed and targeted categorical grants and the monitoring of certain service standards. The federalism metaphor changed from a "marble cake" to "water taps," stressing the focused and channeled nature of the concentrated federalism phase; that is, federal grants, released by Congress from the federal spigot, flowed from Washington to the states and from the states to the localities.

The 1950s and 1960s saw the emergence of "creative federalism." Here the emphasis was on meeting the problems of urban America, the poor, the dispossessed, and the minorities. The apolitical, engineering mentality held by officials who were involved in intergovernmental relationships during the concentrated period of federalism gave way to a more political view, focusing on the achievement of national goals as they pertained to President Lyndon Johnson's Great Society programs. The mechanisms for achieving all this largely were participation by the citizenry, program planning, and an increasing emphasis on project grants—that is, aid given by the federal government to states and localities for the completion of specific projects. The federal metaphor that had relied on plumbing ("water taps") was replaced with one that focused on botany; suddenly there was a "flowering" of federalism, a metaphor that emphasized the verdant proliferation of various intergovernmental programs.

The 1960s and 1970s saw the emergence of a new phase of federalism that stressed competition among governmental jurisdictions. After federalism's flowering phase, new problems emerged involving coordination, program effectiveness, the competency of delivery systems, and the accessibility of citizens to the policymaking process. As in the conflictually oriented phase of intergovernmental relations, a renewed emphasis was seen on disagreement, tension, and rivalry among competitors for federal grants. The mechanisms of intergovernmental relations shifted from project grants and participation to the consolidation of federal grants through such devices as block grants, revenue sharing, and the reorganization of categorical grants. The operative metaphor of federalism's competitive phase became "picket fence federalism," which stressed the fragmented, discrete nature of the hundreds of different kinds of categorical and project grants that developed during this phase.

Finally, the 1970s and the 1980s have seen the emergence of "calculative federalism." Calculative federalism amounts to the intergovernmental system's way of coping with an age of limits. The main problems are ones of accountability, monetary constraints, fiscal dependency, diminishing public confidence in the institutions of government, and the rising rate of governmental bankruptcies. The public officials who participate in intergovernmental relations perceive the shape of federalism to be one of gamesmanship and concentrate their energies on such endeavors as using federal grants for the attainment of local goals that were not necessarily envisioned by federal policymakers, and of coping with an overload of demands for governmental services while functioning under severe budgetary constraints. Increasingly, the mechanisms of dealing with the relationships among governments stress loans, entitlements, Washington's bypassing of state governments and working directly with localities, and a variety of crosscutting regulations. The current metaphor of federalism has been called one of "facade." In other words, federalism, as it has been traditionally understood, no longer exists; so powerful has the federal government become that the powers of states and localities, at least in relative terms, are no longer of consequence. However, as Washington withdraws its assistance dollars from subnational governments (as it is doing), "facade" takes on a new meaning, and facade refers less to the overwhelming dominance to the federal government in the intergovernmental system and more to the sharp decline in federal dollars that long have supported that system.

In describing these phases of federalism, we have relied on hyperbole and caricature as methods of getting the main points across. Nevertheless, characterizing federalism along these six phases is useful as a background in gaining a more complete understanding of the relations among America's governments. As we see next, one of the results of the evolution of federalism has been the emergence of states and localities as special interests within the intergovernmental system.

GOVERNMENTS AS PRESSURE GROUPS

The States as Special Interests

Foremost among America's subnational governments, the states have become increasingly active lobbyists to the national government. Much of their lobbying stems from the states' interest in acquiring more money from the national government to pursue their own policies, a point which we shall consider in greater detail in Chapter 12. Suffice it to note for now that national aid contributes about a fourth of the states' service delivery budgets, and how this money is granted means a great deal to the states.[9]

Also, in recent years the national government has taken some unprecedented steps in intervening with policies made by the states. Although none of this intervention approaches the magnitude of the Civil War in terms of the national government establishing its supremacy over state political systems, various public problems have involved the national government in the management of state governments in new and different ways. The action of the governor of Arkansas in the 1950s to block school desegregation in Little Rock, the efforts of the governor of Mississippi to block desegregation of the University of Mississippi, when the governor of Alabama "stood in the school house door" to stop the representative of the U.S. attorney general, Nicholas Katzenbach, from enrolling a black student in his state's major university—all represent major interventions by the national government in state governments. Hence, the states have assumed an increasingly active role as lobbyists in Washington for both financial and political reasons.

It is not too surprising that, while only 1 state had a Washington liaison office in 1960, and only 5 states had such offices by 1970, there were 31 by 1980.[10] Whether these Washington offices maintained by the states actually help their states is an open question. One investigation found that "states with Washington offices tend to receive lower levels of federal outlays per capita than others"![11] However, a more detailed study suggests that when the governor's party, the power of the state's congressional delegation, and the levels of a state's urbanization and wealth are accounted for, then a Washington office can make a positive difference in a state's share of federal funds.[12]

The major lobbying organization for the states is the National Governors Association (NGA), formerly called the National Governors Conference. Ironically, the NGA was initiated by President Theodore Roosevelt in 1908 as a device for pressuring Congress to pass more legislation dealing with natural resources. The NGA had fallen into dormancy until, in 1966, it established a full-time Washington office called the National Governors Conference for Federal-State Relations. The National Governors Association has increasingly taken outspoken policy positions on various issues. Perhaps most notable has been the NGA's consistent position that the national government should take over all social welfare policies in the United States rather than let these policies reside with the states.

The NGA's lobbying function is bolstered through such related state lobbies as the National Conference of State Legislatures, the Council of State Governments, the National Association of State Budget Officials, the American Association of State Highway Officials, and the National Association of Attornies General. Most of these are more specific lobbies, but nevertheless they work in conjunction with the NGA on state-related national legislation.

Urban Lobbying

Just as the National Governors Association has evolved into a powerful tool for states lobbying the federal government, the major urban areas have also become increasingly active in pressuring the federal government for relief. The major lobbying organizations for cities are the United States Conference of Mayors, the National League of Cities, and the International City Management Association. They often are joined by such groups as the Urban Coalition, the National Association of Counties, the National Housing Conference, the National Association for Housing and Redevelopment Officials, and similar groups.

The United States Conference of Mayors brings together the chief executives of the 840 cities with more than 30,000 people (or 110 million citizens) and "is the fulcrum of collective urban lobbying"; nearly 15,000 smaller cities tend to work through the National League of Cities.[13] The Conference of Mayors was quite successful during the 1930s in its national lobbying efforts. Its success was attributable to the desperation of the Great Depression of the 1930s and shrewd tactics, but primarily to Franklin Delano Roosevelt's need for political support, which was based in the big cities. The National League of Cities has had good relationships with the Republicans and the Conference of Mayors with the Democrats; together, they work as an effective coalition for urban interests. Often, they work with the powerful, but nonpartisan, National Association of

Counties, representing about 1,500 of the more metropolitan counties, and the International City Management Association, which speaks for more than 7,000 professional administrators in local governments. In addition, about two dozen counties and 100 cities maintain their own Washington offices.[14]

Getting Theirs: When Governments Go to Washington

The dramatic expansion of professional Washington lobbyists representing state and local governments signifies more than these governments' concerns over participating in the formulation of national policy and getting their cut of federal grants; it also implies that senators and congress members may represent their people, but not their governments in the national capitol. As one representative of a state government has put it, "A Congressman has a mental checklist when he votes. He says, 'Where are my five biggest contributors on this issue? Where are the Jews, the Catholics, the women, the chamber of commerce?' But the state government, as an institution, usually isn't on that list. My job is to put it there."[15] Subnational governments have chosen to put themselves on that list like any other special interest—by hiring lobbyists to do it.

The states' lobbying organizations and the cities' lobbying organizations can often be in conflict when presenting their cases to the national government. An example of this is the dispute between "dirty cities" and "clean states" in the effort to renew the nation's clean air laws. Representatives from the less industrialized states have tended to resist clean air legislation on the grounds that such laws discourage industrial development of less developed states.

Senator Jake Garn of Utah, for example, killed a compromise clean air bill in 1976 with a personal filibuster because he felt it would hamper industrialization in his state. The nonindustrialized states often have congressional allies with industrial interests. It is the representatives from the "dirty cities" that are pushing clean air legislation, because they can feel and see the effects of air pollution on the health of their citizens more readily than can the representatives of the less industrialized states. Clean air legislation is but one example among several at the federal level where the tensions between states and cities are evident when lobbying is at its sharpest.

THE STATES: SOVEREIGNTY WITHIN LIMITS

So far we have been discussing federalism from the viewpoint of the government in Washington. But the states also have active governments. In this section we review the states' relations with Washington and each other and their involvement (or lack of it) in the business of their cities, counties, and towns.

Capitols to Capitol: The States and Washington

As we explain in Chapter 12, the percentage of federal aid that comprises a typical state's budget has risen from less than 15 percent in 1960 to roughly 25 percent in the 1980s,[16] and, just as state governments have felt they had to increase their lobbying activities in Washington to assure that they got their slice of the federal pie, state officials have had to devote increasing blocks of their time to administer federal dollars (and their accompanying rules and regulations) within their states. Governors in the 1960s devoted less of their time to state-federal business than did governors in the 1970s, and today the typical governor spends almost a full working day in a six-day working week to these concerns.[17] The impact of Washington on the states is clearly apparent, and only 3 percent of more than 100 former governors responding to one survey stated that they would advise new governors to spend less time than they did on state-federal relations.[18]

Despite the demands on their time that relations with Washington require, the governors believe that the time is worth it. Only 6 percent of the governors in the poll just mentioned believed that state-federal relationships were not significant to their overall programs to improve the quality of life for their states' citizens.[19]

Yet, there are frustrations. Washington has grown (at least until 1981, with the advent of the administration of Ronald Reagan) more intrusive in the affairs of state government, and federal regulations over how states (and localities) must conduct their intergovernmental programs have proliferated. One study found that Washington imposed nearly 1,300 mandates on subnational governments in its intergovernmental programs; the average number of federal regulations affecting the jurisdictions examined was 570 regulations per government![20]

Federal intergovernmental regulations come in four types:[21]

Crosscutting requirements. These are the most numerous and have been around the longest; they apply to virtually all federal assistance programs and are used to further national objectives. For example, nondiscrimination clauses are in all federal intergovernmental programs, and if a state violates the clause, Washington can withdraw the program—or never grant it.

Partial preemptions. The subnational governments are partially preempted from their traditional prerogatives in this kind of regulation because the federal government demands that the states adopt and administer program standards set by Washington, rather than by the states, if the states want federal aid.

Crossover sanctions. These permit the federal government to punish a state by reducing or withdrawing federal aid in one or more programs if its standards are not being satisfied in another program.

Direct orders. An eyeball-to-eyeball standoff between a state capitol and the national capitol is the last occurrence federal officials want, so these are the least used; to pit Congress against the states raises serious constitutional questions. Nevertheless, Congress began mandating direct orders to subnational governments in the 1970s, such as its direct order in 1977 prohibiting cities from dumping sewerage at sea.

Figure 9-1 shows the dramatic proliferation of all four types of regulations in federal intergovernmental programs since the 1930s. This expansion has been felt by the states. Governors who served their states in the 1960s and 1970s believe strongly that these kinds of regulations have encroached on states' rights and responsibilities. More than 88 percent said that the federal government has assumed many of the responsibilities that appropriately belong to the

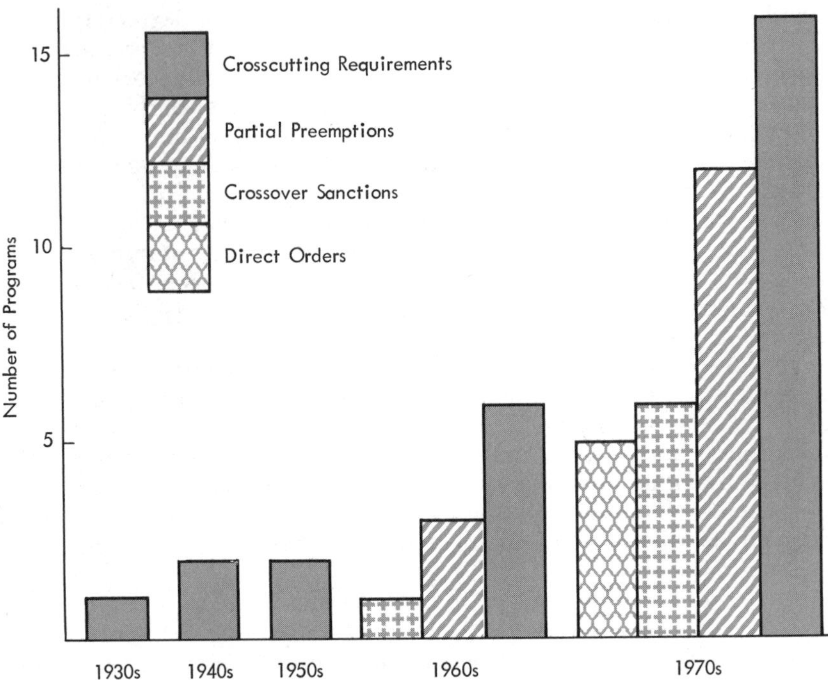

Figure 9-1 The growth of major programs of intergovernmental regulation, by type of instrument, by decade, 1930–1980. (*Source:* Advisory Commission on Intergovernmental Relations, *Regulatory Federalism: Policy, Process, Impact and Reform,* A-95. Washington, D.C.: U.S. Government Printing Office, 1984, p. 97.)

states, and more than 86 percent thought that the intergovernmental system needed a "major overhaul."[22]

State administrators share these views, and go a step farther: they believe that federal governmental programs have distorted policymaking itself in their states. Surveys indicate that some three quarters of state agency heads believe that federal aid has led to national interference in state affairs. Eighty-three percent believed that there should be more decentralization of authority from the national government to the state. Even more significantly, 70 percent of state administrators in 1978 (up from 52 percent in 1964) felt that they would use federal assistance grants for different purposes if the "strings" attached to those grants were relaxed, indicating the distorting effect that federal aid may have on state priorities.[23]

There is a more subtle, but potentially equally harmful, impact of federal assistance on state governments. Because federal aid flows directly to state agency heads—federal intergovernmental funds for environmental improvements, for example, go directly from Washington to state environmental protection agencies—rather than to the states' chief executive officers, the governors, it has been suggested that those state agencies that are heavily funded by Washington are also more autonomous because they are less dependent upon their governors and legislatures for their budgets. Hence, Washington, through its intergovernmental programs, has made the governors' management task more difficult. And, despite the fact that virtually all governors believe that Washington's dollars helped them implement their programs for their states, there is some reason to believe that the conjecture is valid: surveys of state administrators taken since 1964 have found that from 44 percent to 48 percent of state administrators admit they are less subject to supervision by the governor and the legislature because of federal aid.[24]

Interstate Cooperation—and Conflict

States have been known to cooperate and not cooperate with each other, although the Constitution requires that "full faith and credit shall be given in each state to the public acts, records, and judicial proceedings of every state." Since the clause applies only to civil matters and not necessarily to criminal violations, we occasionally witness states harboring fugitives from other states if public officials feel that the fugitive has been treated unjustly in the state from which he or she fled. States also cooperate to create interstate compacts and interstate agencies.

There are 179 interstate compacts in operation, the great majority of which had been entered into during the past three decades. As Table 9-3 shows, only 57 interstate compacts were agreed to between 1789 and 1940, but during the next four decades, an additional 122 of these agreements emerged.

Interstate compacts normally require congressional approval to be set into motion, and many have evolved into ongoing interstate agencies. There are more than 60 such agencies dealing with educational concerns, river basin management, transportation, water fronts, fisheries, and energy. Perhaps the most notable example of an interstate agency is the Port Authority of New York and New Jersey. Established in 1921 and headed by six commissioners appointed by the governor of each member state, the Port Authority is in charge of virtually all transportation in the New York and New Jersey areas. It has 8,000 employees, more employees than any other interstate agency (few interstate agencies exceed 50 employees and a number have none).

Although most textbooks on state and local government delineate the kinds of cooperative activity between states, few discuss the kinds of conflict in which states engage. The most obvious example occurred in 1861 when the

Table 9-3 Frequency of Interstate Compacts

Years	*Frequency*
1789–1900	25
1901–1920	9
1921–1930	7
1931–1940	16
1941–1950	24
1951–1960	32
1961–1970	48
1971–1979	18

Source: Benjamin J. Jones, "Interstate Compacts and Agreements: 1978–79," *Book of the States, 1980–81* (Lexington, KY.: Council of State Governments, 1980), p. 598.

nation went to war with itself, an event that in the North is called the Civil War, but in the South is still referred to as the War Between the States.

A more recent example concerns the gradually developing shortage of water in the nation.[25] Although this shortage is more pronounced in the West than in other parts of the country, some researchers have estimated that by the year 2000 only 3 of the nation's 19 water regions will be able to live even close to comfortably within their water supplies. (The three exceptions are New England, the Ohio Basin, and the South Atlantic-Eastern Gulf areas.)

This possible serious shortage in the nation's water is already straining relationships among states. Montana and Idaho threatened to sue the state of Washington if that state seeded clouds over the Pacific Ocean, thereby "stealing" water that might have fallen as rain farther inland. Oregon and Washington have resisted attempts to divert water to areas in the western Sunbelt states. When Boston embarked on a program to divert water from the Connecticut River, Connecticut objected because it did not wish to give up water rights that it might need in the future. The eight states and two Canadian provinces that surround the Great Lakes—the world's largest reservoir of fresh water—agreed in 1982 to block attempts to divert their water unless all ten governments agreed. Iowa, Nebraska, and Missouri filed suit opposing South Dakota's efforts to divert part of the Missouri River to Wyoming, and El Paso, Texas, challenged New Mexico's law that forbids all out-of-staters from using its groundwater.

Although water wars long have erupted among the states, and will continue to do so as long as water supplies deplete, hydraulic technology innovates, and rivers meander, interstate antagonism is surfacing in other fields as well. Thirty-three states use some sort of severance tax—that is, a tariff on natural resources exported to other states—and some states have been using the device, according to some regional analysts, as a weapon against other states to recruit new industry by lowering taxes. One estimate contends that the dozen states that export energy to other states (such as Montana, which has a 30 percent severance tax on coal) will gain close to $200 billion over ten years through their severance taxes on their energy supplies.[26] Some states have threatened reciprocity; for example, the governor of Iowa floated the notion of introducing a severance tax on corn.

Other statewide "exports" are free of severance taxes, such as pollution spawned in one state but that ends up in another state. Northeastern states long have argued that they are the primary recipients of Midwestern air pollutants that produce acid rain. Other states export other kinds of undesirable items. Between 1978 and 1982, South Dakota gave 93 people charged with burglary, forgery, theft, and other felonies the choice of facing prosecution or moving to California; all 93 moved to the Golden State, whose officials promptly dubbed South Dakota's actions as outrageous. In 1984, Oregon hiked by up to $400 the income tax that it levies on some 40,000 Washington State residents who work in Oregon; Washington retaliated with a $30-a-month tax on Oregonians who work in Washington. Texan welfare officials take pains to inform their clients that benefits are higher in every other state except Mississippi and that welfare payments in Texas show no prospects of rising, while Florida officials have carefully explained to their Haitian refugees that ten other states might offer better relief aid.

All is not happy in the realm of the American states.

The States Tame Their "Creatures"

The states can cooperate with each other as equals, but their relationships with their own local governments are quite different. Indeed, the title of Part Three of this book, "Creatures of the States," is drawn from a statement made by Judge John F. Dillon in 1868 that is now known as "Dillon's rule." "Creatures of the state," a concept upheld by the U.S. Supreme Court in 1923, simply means that such units of government as counties, towns, townships, special districts, multipurpose districts, cities, and villages have no independence beyond what the state grants them. The state government determines the area of political and administrative discretion its subunits of government may or may not have. "This means that a city cannot operate a peanut stand at the city zoo without first getting the state legislature to pass an enabling law, unless, perchance, the city's charter or some previously enacted law unmistakably covers the sale of peanuts."[27]

State legislatures achieve this kind of control through the type of charter that they grant a city. Most city charters are quite long (New York City's, for example, fills several hundred pages) because the states often want to retain minute degrees of control. There are four general types of charters: special act charters, general act charters, optional charter laws, and home rule charters.

The *special act charters* are charters that have been drawn specifically for a particular city. Such cities remain completely under state legislative control; often these charters help state legislatures to pass laws that are written specifically for a particular city. Edward Banfield and James Q. Wilson quote by way of example an ordinance stating that "Fall River be authorized to appropriate money for the purchase of uniforms for the park police and watershed guards of said city."[28]

General act charters tend to categorize cities by population and then apply state legislation to all cities in each size category. Usual divisions are cities with less than 10,000 people, with 10,000 to 25,000 people, and so on.

Optional charter laws give city governments relatively more free choice. They offer optional forms of government that a city may wish to adopt, such as council-manager, commission, or whatever.

Finally, *home rule charters* provide cities with the greatest degree of self-governance. Still, home rule charters are furnished by the state legislature or the state constitution and may be taken away as easily as they are granted. Home rule got its start in 1875 in Missouri; today more than half of the states have constitutional clauses that provide for home rule charters. Roughly two-thirds of the cities in this country with populations of more than 200,000 people have some form of home rule. Political battles over acquiring urban home rule often are bloody, with good-government groups, city mayors, and city managers usually pitted against rural legislators and large municipal taxpayer groups.

Regardless of the type of charter a city may have, the point remains that these charters are granted according to the discretion of the state polity; Judge Dillon's rule stands in that all cities and other units of government remain the creatures of the state.

Table 9-4 Discretionary Authority of Cities and Counties by State and Function

	CITY				*COUNTY*			
	Structure of Government	*Functional Areas*	*Finance*	*Personnel*	*Structure of Government*	*Functional Areas*	*Finance*	*Personnel*
United States[1]	2.05	2.02	3.16	2.10	3.30	3.24	3.69	2.87
Alabama	4.50	2.50	2.00	1.75	4.50	4.00	4.75	2.25
Alaska	1.00	2.00	2.00	2.00	1.00	2.00	2.00	2.00
Arizona	2.50	2.00	1.75	1.75	4.00	4.00	4.00	4.00
Arkansas	5.00	3.00	3.00	1.50	1.00	3.00	3.00	1.50
California	2.00	2.00	2.00	2.00	3.00	3.00	3.00	3.00
Colorado	2.50	3.00	3.50	2.00	4.50	5.00	4.50	3.00
Connecticut	1.00	1.00	2.00	2.00	—[2]	—[2]	—[2]	—[2]
Delaware	1.50	2.00	3.00	2.50	3.00	2.00	2.00	2.00
Florida	1.00	1.30	4.50	2.50	1.00	1.30	4.50	2.75
Georgia	5.00	1.00	3.00	1.00	5.00	5.00	3.00	3.00
Hawaii	—[3]	—[3]	—[3]	—[3]	1.00	3.20	4.00	3.50
Idaho	3.00	2.00	5.00	4.00	5.00	3.00	5.00	4.00
Illinois	1.10	2.00	1.50	2.60	2.10	3.30	2.80	3.80
Indiana	5.00	2.50	4.00	2.00	4.00	3.50	4.00	2.00
Iowa	1.80	1.90	4.50	3.30	4.00	2.50	4.50	3.60
Kansas	1.00	1.00	3.00	1.50	2.50	2.50	3.00	3.00
Kentucky	1.50	3.50	2.60	3.50	3.50	3.50	2.60	2.50
Louisiana	1.00	1.50	3.00	1.00	2.00	2.00	3.50	2.00
Maine	1.00	1.00	1.50	1.50	1.75	4.00	3.50	2.00
Maryland	1.00	1.50	2.25	1.25	2.60	2.33	3.20	2.20
Massachusetts	1.00	2.00	5.00	3.00	5.00	5.00	5.00	5.00
Michigan	1.00	1.00	2.00	1.00	4.50	3.50	3.50	3.50
Minnesota	1.00	1.00	4.00	1.00	3.00	3.00	3.00	2.00
Mississippi	2.00	2.00	4.00	2.00	5.00	4.00	4.00	3.00
Missouri	1.00	1.00	3.00	1.00	5.00	5.00	5.00	4.00
Montana	1.00	2.00	5.00	2.00	1.00	2.00	4.00	3.50

Nebraska	1.50	2.00	3.50	1.00	3.00	4.00	5.00	3.00
Nevada	2.50	3.50	4.00	3.00	2.00	4.00	4.00	4.00
New Hampshire	2.00	1.50	4.00	1.00	5.00	4.00	5.00	1.00
New Jersey	3.00	2.00	4.00	2.00	3.00	3.50	4.50	3.00
New Mexico	3.00	5.00	3.00	5.00	3.00	3.00	3.00	5.00
New York	1.50	3.00	4.00	4.00	1.50	3.00	4.00	4.00
North Carolina	1.00	1.00	2.50	1.00	1.00	1.25	2.50	2.50
North Dakota	1.80	1.50	3.50	2.00	3.00	3.00	4.00	2.00
Ohio	1.00	1.50	2.50	1.50	4.00	4.00	4.00	4.50
Oklahoma	1.00	1.50	2.50	1.50	4.00	3.50	3.50	3.50
Oregon	1.00	1.50	2.00	1.50	1.00	1.50	2.00	1.50
Pennsylvania	2.00	2.00	2.50	2.00	2.00	2.00	2.00	2.00
Rhode Island	1.00	2.00	5.00	3.00	—[2]	—[2]	—[2]	—[2]
South Carolina	4.00	2.00	2.00	2.00	4.00	3.00	2.00	2.00
South Dakota	3.00	4.00	3.00	3.00	5.00	3.00	5.00	3.00
Tennessee	3.00	3.00	3.00	2.00	5.00	3.00	5.00	2.00
Texas	1.00	1.20	1.50	1.00	5.00	4.80	4.50	2.00
Utah	2.50	2.00	3.50	2.00	3.50	3.00	3.00	1.50
Vermont	5.00	2.00	5.00	3.00	5.00	5.00	5.00	3.00
Virginia	3.00	1.50	2.00	1.25	4.00	2.50	3.00	2.25
Washington	1.30	2.50	3.50	3.00	3.00	2.80	4.00	4.50
West Virginia	4.00	2.00	5.00	3.00	5.00	3.00	5.00	3.00
Wisconsin	1.00	2.00	3.00	2.00	2.50	3.00	3.00	2.50
Wyoming	1.00	3.00	3.00	2.50	5.00	4.00	3.00	3.00

Key: A score of 1 indicates the greatest amount of freedom from state control, a score of 5 indicates the least.

[1] Unweighted average

[2] There are no organized county governments in Connecticut or Rhode Island.

[3] There are only four local governments in Hawaii; County of Hawaii, County of Kauai, County of Maui, and City and County of Honolulu.

Source: Joseph F. Zimmerman, *The Discretionary Authority of Local Governments*, Urban Data Services Reports, Vol. 13, No. 11 (Washington, D.C.: International City Management Association, November, 1981), p. 11. Data printed with the permission of the U.S. Advisory Commission on Intergovernmental Relations.

State Urban Policy: A New Responsiveness

As the foregoing review of city charters implies, states can treat their creatures with severity or laxity. Joseph Zimmerman has observed that states may play the role of inhibitor, facilitator, or initiator in their relations with their own local governments, and the role the most frequently played in Zimmerman's view is, unfortunately, the first.[29] Nonetheless, the states have made strides in contributing constructively to urban government.

Table 9-4 presents an overview of how free from restraints local governments are from their states. Nationally, counties tend to have less freedom than do cities; cities enjoy their greatest freedoms from state controls in functional areas, such as sanitation, and have the least liberty in the area of finance; and counties have the most freedom in personnel matters but, like municipalities, are most restricted by their states in the finance area. States clearly seem concerned with the fiscal health of their local governments.[30]

All states have established offices specifically endowed with responsibilities pertaining to local affairs, although only five existed prior to 1966.[31] These offices provide advisory services and assist the state in coordinating local administrative functions. Most are concerned primarily with regional planning; relatively few have responsibility for specific programs such as urban renewal, housing, and poverty.

The states have taken a variety of managerial and policy steps in dealing with their local governments. Ten states have created their own Advisory Commissions on Intergovernmental Relations patterned after the federal model, and another 21 have created similar advisory panels of local officials. Forty-three states have commissions on intergovernmental cooperation, and all states have departments of community affairs.[32]

Research indicates that those state commissions that focus on local governments tend to stress the desirability of fiscal reforms, of reducing functional fragmentation among local governments, and of providing greater authority and more home rule for local jurisdictions.[33] In a few states, these and related bodies are beginning to take on a genuine policymaking role for their urban and local governments. Texas, for example, has been active in discouraging the separate incorporation of satellite cities, as have Indiana and Minnesota, although to lesser degrees. In 1968 Connecticut abolished counties as a unit of government and, as a result, "state government may in effect become the metropolitan government unit in Connecticut, since Connecticut transferred county functions to the state."[34]

What of the larger panorama of relationships between the states and their local governments? Is the role of the states declining, or is it actually increasing?

The typical answer to these questions, at least in the past, has been that the states have often proven to be more of a hindrance than a facilitator in resolving the problems of local governments. Consider, in this regard, the following conclusions from several studies: "Despite the increasing amount of effort that they have devoted to urban affairs, the states have continued to evidence little desire to intervene in metropolitan governmental reorganization—with the important exception of school districts."[35] Or "Although states have increased their aid to local governments, such aid generally has not gone to the areas of greatest need."[36] Or "If one were to use the past as the basis of forecasting the future role of the state and local government reorganization, the prospects for a new, affirmative role would be exceedingly dim."[37]

By the 1970s, however, such views were beginning to change. In part, this change resulted from the simple fact that more empirical and systematic investigations were being conducted on the relationships between states and their local governments. Some of the results of one of these investigations are shown in Table 9-5, which displays an inventory of state actions that provide assistance to poor and otherwise distressed communities. The study covered five broad program areas: housing, economic development, community development, fiscal reform, and the enhancement of local capabilities, such as state aid and the local creation of redevelopment agencies. The research findings summarized in Table 9-5 are supported by other studies that have indicated that the states tend to emphasize four policy areas when they deal with local governments: physical development, such as upgrading industrial and residential infrastructures; the enhancement of cooperation between the public and private sectors; fiscal incentives to help local development patterns; and citizen participation in the development of local objectives.[38]

Related research has concluded that states are really rather sensitive to the needs of their more depressed cities, at least when this sensitivity is measured by the amounts of money that states transfer to their needier urban areas. Localities receive grants from other governments in three forms: direct aid from their states, direct aid from the federal government, and aid from state governments that combine state funds with federal funds received by the states (or what are known as "passthrough" funds, since federal money is being passed through state governments to local governments). One analysis found that depressed cities benefited most favorably when they received intergovernmental grants through this final method, indicating an awareness by states of their more pressing urban problems. In fact, the state capitols may be more concerned with these issues than is Washington:

> a state-federal partnership in allocating aid to local jurisdictions has produced greater responsiveness to distressed cities than has federal aid alone. Among plausible explanations for this finding are the substantial management difficulties inherent in the federal attempt to deal directly with local governments, the perceived need for direct federal aid programs to include a sufficient number of local jurisdictions to assure majority votes in the Congress, and the inability of federal grant programs to take account of differing fiscal relationships among levels of government. . . . In contrast, individual states deal with smaller numbers of local governments, have a clearer understanding of their problems, and therefore can deal with those problems in a more responsive and flexible manner.[39]

Just as research has indicated the deepening and increasingly sensitive state interest in local problems, the apparent withdrawal of federal interest in the affairs of both state and local governments has led some observers to conclude that the states will, by necessity, assume a new and more aggressive posture relative to their local communities. As we discuss in Chapter 12, President Ronald Reagan's call in 1982 for massive cuts in the federal government's assistance to state and local governments has, at least potentially, placed a burden on state governments to become more directly concerned with the fiscal and social health of their localities. But even before Republican Reagan's call for a "New Feder-

Table 9-5 Targeted State Programs To Aid Distressed Communities

	INDICATOR	NUMBER OF STATES WITH PROGRAM	NORTHEAST											NORTH CENTRAL/MIDWEST											
			CONNECTICUT	MAINE	MASSACHUSETTS	NEW HAMPSHIRE	RHODE ISLAND	VERMONT	DELAWARE	MARYLAND	NEW JERSEY	NEW YORK	PENNSYLVANIA	ILLINOIS	INDIANA	MICHIGAN	OHIO	WISCONSIN	IOWA	KANSAS	MINNESOTA	MISSOURI	NEBRASKA	NORTH DAKOTA	SOUTH DAKOTA
	HOUSING																								
1	Single-family home construction	41	●	●	●	●	●	●	●	●	●		●	●	●	●		●	●		●	●	●		●
2	Multi-family home construction	31	●	●	●	●	●	●	●	●	●	●	●	●		●		●				●			●
3	Housing rehabilitation grant or loan	19	●	●	●					●	●	●	●	●		●		●	●				●		●
4	Housing rehabilitation tax incentive	16	●		●		●				●	●	●		●		●	●	●		●	●			
	ECONOMIC DEVELOPMENT																								
5	Industrial or commercial site development	13	●								●	●	●		●					●	●		●		
6	State financial aid for industrial or commercial development	12	●		●						●	●	●	●			●				●				
7	Customized job training	42	●	●	●			●	●	●	●	●	●	●	●	●	●	●	●		●	●	●	●	●
8	Small business development	8	●							●	●			●											
9	Industrial revenue bonds	5	●		●		●				●								●						
	COMMUNITY DEVELOPMENT																								
10	Capital improvements	20	●		●						●						●							●	
11	Local neighborhood improvement efforts	14			●				●		●	●	●		●	●		●			●	●			
	FISCAL REFORM																								
12	State revenue sharing	23		●	●	●						●		●		●		●			●				
13	Education finance reform	18	●											●	●	●		●	●	●		●		●	
14	Assumption of local public welfare	27	●		●		●	●	●	●				●		●				●		●			
15	Reimbursement of state-mandated programs	12					●							●		●									
16	Improving local government' access to credit markets	16	●	●		●		●			●	●	●		●		●			●	●			●	
	ENHANCING LOCAL CAPABILITIES																								
17	Local use of tax increment financing	20	●		●									●			●	●	●	●	●			●	
18	Local creation of redevelopment agencies	49	●	●	●	●	●	●	●	●	●	●	●	●	●	●	●	●	●	●	●	●	●	●	●
19	Local sales or income taxing authority	34							●	●	●	●	●	●	●	●	●		●	●	●	●	●		
20	Local discretionary authority	11		●									●	●		●									

	INDICATOR	NUMBER OF STATES WITH PROGRAM	SOUTH																WEST										
			ALABAMA	ARKANSAS	FLORIDA	GEORGIA	KENTUCKY	LOUISIANA	MISSISSIPPI	NORTH CAROLINA	SOUTH CAROLINA	TENNESSEE	VIRGINIA	WEST VIRGINIA	ARIZONA	NEW MEXICO	OKLAHOMA	TEXAS	COLORADO	IDAHO	MONTANA	UTAH	WYOMING	CALIFORNIA	NEVADA	OREGON	WASHINGTON	ALASKA	HAWAII
	HOUSING																												
1	Single-family home construction	41		●	●	●	●		●	●	●	●	●	●		●		●	●	●	●	●	●	●	●	●		●	●
2	Multi-family home construction	31			●		●				●	●	●	●				●	●	●	●	●		●	●	●			●
3	Housing rehabilitation grant or loan	19			●									●		●			●							●			●
4	Housing rehabilitation tax incentive	16			●																●			●		●			
	ECONOMIC DEVELOPMENT																												
5	Industrial or commercial site development	13	●	●		●			●			●																	
6	State financial aid for industrial or commercial development	12					●					●						●							●				
7	Customized job training	42	●	●		●	●	●	●	●	●	●		●	●		●	●	●			●	●	●	●	●	●	●	●
8	Small business development	8			●			●																●			●		
9	Industrial revenue bonds	5																											
	COMMUNITY DEVELOPMENT																												
10	Capital improvements	20		●	●	●						●	●	●	●	●			●		●	●	●				●	●	
11	Local neighborhood improvement efforts	14			●	●													●					●					
	FISCAL REFORM																												
12	State revenue sharing	23		●		●		●			●	●	●		●		●					●	●		●	●	●	●	●
13	Education finance reform	18			●						●	●			●	●		●	●		●			●					
14	Assumption of local public welfare	27	●	●		●	●	●			●			●		●	●	●		●		●				●	●	●	●
15	Reimbursement of state-mandated programs	12				●						●	●		●					●	●			●			●		●
16	Improving local government access to credit markets	16				●				●	●																●		
	ENHANCING LOCAL CAPABILITIES																												
17	Local use of tax increment financing	20			●		●								●			●	●			●	●	●		●		●	
18	Local creation of redevelopment agencies	49	●	●	●	●	●	●	●	●	●	●	●	●	●	●	●	●	●	●	●	●	●	●	●	●	●		●
19	Local sales or income taxing authority	34	●	●		●	●	●		●		●	●		●	●	●	●	●			●	●	●	●		●	●	
20	Local discretionary authority	11						●			●		●		●			●						●				●	

Source: Advisory Commission on Intergovernmental Relations, *The States and Distressed Communities: 1980 Annual Report,* M-125. Washington, D.C.: U.S. Government Printing Office, 1981, p. 3.)

alism," there were prior indications that Washington was losing interest in the affairs of its subnational governments. In terms of constant dollars, for example, federal aid to state and local governments peaked in 1978 (when Democrats controlled the White House and both houses of Congress) and has been in decline ever since. President Jimmy Carter's Commission for a National Agenda for the '80s also displayed a growing disinclination by a Democratic administration to further its involvement in state and local matters. In its *Report on Urban America,* the Commission advocated that a number of state and local issues be removed as matters of national concern: "The purpose and orientation of a 'national urban policy' should be reconsidered. There are no 'national urban problems,' only an endless variety of local ones. Consequently, a centrally administered national urban policy that legitimizes activities inconsistent with a revitalization of the larger national economy may be ill-advised."[40]

As a consequence of these kinds of shifts at the national level, plus a growing body of information about state and local governmental relationships, the overall scholarly assessment of the states' role in local affairs is showing indication of change. As a leading scholar of intergovernmental relations has observed, "The states have been roundly and soundly chastised for their neglect of urban distress and decline. The criticisms are not without foundation. Yet a balanced view, particularly taking into account developments of the 1970s, shows the states on record as taking numerous and varied urban-oriented policy initiatives."[41]

CITIES AND OTHER URBAN CREATURES

Direct Federalism: The Feds and Cities

If anything, the federal government has a greater political impact on localities than on states. The formal linkage between local and national government often has been called "direct federalism," indicating that state governments are frequently bypassed. Nevertheless, the major impact of the federal government on local governments is more accidental than planned. For example, Rand Corporation studies have shown that federal officials may often have more control than local officeholders over the shape of the economy in a particular locality. The Rand studies indicated the following: in St. Louis, federal housing and highway policies attracted many central-city residents to the suburbs; in San Jose, federal military procurement procedures accelerated the local growth rate; in Seattle, Federal Civil Aviation policies were probably detrimental to the area's major employer.[42] There is, in fact, substantial evidence to warrant the conclusion that "federal stimulation produced independent housing authorities, a type of special district, and federal encouragement of the growth of suburbia through underwriting liberal mortgage arrangements indirectly led to the creation of many new suburban governments," and that the creation of the federal Department of Housing and Urban Development and Department of Transportation are "both institutional examples of recognition by the national government of its deep involvement in metropolitan affairs."[43]

Since 1960, this "deep involvement" by the federal government in local affairs has increased. Although local governments received only 10 percent of the total federal aid package in 1965, by 1980 the figure had hit 30 percent.[44] By

1980 there were 39 separate federal grants programs in which Washington dealt directly with community officials, bypassing, in the process, state administrators altogether. Federal regulations on the conduct of local governments have accompanied these programs with a vengeance. Of the nearly 1,300 federal mandates built into the intergovernmental grant system, a surprising number, 911, applied only to local governments or directly affected local governments through the states.[45]

How federal concerns with local matters affect local governments depends upon a variety of factors. Consider one example in this regard that occurred in San Antonio, Texas. In 1977 San Antonians voted to stop electing their city council members at large and instead to elect them by a ward system. This in itself is not unusual; what is unique is that the U.S. Justice Department pressured for this basic change in the political structure of the city. The Justice Department contended that the city's land annexations, which were completed in 1972, effectively reduced the voting power of the city's Mexican-American population from 53.1 percent to 51.1 percent. As a consequence, the city had to change its electoral procedures along lines mandated by the department. The Voting Rights Act Extension of 1975 enables the Justice Department to disallow certain types of municipal policies, including changing a city's boundaries. In San Antonio's case, the department said it would disallow the 1972 annexations unless the city dropped its at-large electoral system. The city fathers were concerned that, if they attempted to challenge the Justice Department's position in court, the city would be forbidden to hold its scheduled City Council elections, to annex land, or to float bond issues until the suit was settled. In any event, the San Antonio example illustrates the impact that the federal government has on a city's basic political system.[46]

Because of incidents such as these, it is not too surprising, perhaps, that local officials have a less than trusting attitude concerning the federal government. A national study of cities found that pluralities or majorities of local officeholders believed in most cases that federal regulations on local governments resulted from Washington playing an inappropriate role in urban affairs (40 percent); that their cities did not have the resources to comply with federal regulations (39 percent); that inefficient federal management made compliance difficult (65 percent); that Washington went too far in stipulating how its requirements should be met (51 percent); and that the mandates themselves were unrealistic (50 percent).[47]

One examination of the economic impact of federal regulations on seven localities in only five grant programs concluded that the cost borne by these local governments in complying with them was about $25 per citizen! Compliance costs in these five programs alone equaled 19 percent of the total federal aid received by the seven local governments, effectively canceling out what they received from Washington under general revenue sharing![48]

Quite aside from concerns about management and money, federal intergovernmental programs may, in the view of local officials, also distort local policy. A survey of local administrators in all cities and counties that had received federal aid during the past year found that officials in about two-thirds of these cities, and roughly 80 percent of the counties, stated that they would have made different budgetary allocations had they been permitted to do so. Seventy-five percent of both city and county administrators would have made moderate to substantial changes. More than two-thirds of the city administrators, and more than three quarters of the county administrators believed that their governments would shift their local funds to other efforts if their federal grants were cut off. Such a finding implies that local officials are making policy decisions to a large extent based on what federal money is available rather than on the basis of what their genuine local needs are.[49]

Interlocal Agreements

If there is tension between Washington and local governments, local governments themselves seem to be getting on famously with each other. Cities and counties have devised a number of ways of working together as a means of providing more, better, and cheaper services to their citizens, and they are cooperating with each other enthusiastically.[50] One method is the *intergovernmental service contract,* as when one jurisdiction pays another to deliver certain services to its residents. More than half—52 percent—of cities and counties have entered into intergovernmental service contracts. Cities and counties contract most frequently with each other for jails, sewage disposal, animal control, and tax assessing.

Another form of interlocal agreement is the *joint service agreement,* or agreements between two or more governments for the joint planning, financing, and delivering of certain services to the residents of all participating jurisdictions. Sixty percent of cities and 54 percent of counties have entered into joint service agreements. The services most frequently provided under these agreements are libraries, communications among police and fire departments, fire control, and sewage disposal.

Cities have moved away (albeit marginally) from entering into intergovernmental service contracts since 1972 (when the first national survey on the practice was conducted) and have shown an increasing preference for contracting with private firms and negotiating joint service agreements with other local governments. Joint service agreements in particular are experiencing an upsurge in popularity, from 35 percent of cities that were involved in them in 1972 to 55 percent in 1983.[51]

A third type of interlocal agreement is the *intergovernmental service transfer,* or the permanent transfer of a responsibility from a jurisdiction to another entity, another government, a private corporation, or a nonprofit agency. Transferring a responsibility permanently is a serious matter for any government because it is a sacrifice of authority and power, so it is perhaps surprising that 40 percent of cities and counties executed such transfers between 1976 and 1983. Favored areas of transfer were public works and utilities, health and welfare, and general government and finance.[52]

Regardless of the type of interlocal agreement, patterns emerge. Larger jurisdictions are far more willing to enter into them than are smaller ones. Council-manager cities and counties with a county administrator tend to favor them, as do inner cities over suburbs and metropolitan counties more than nonmetropolitan ones. The motivation of local officials to enter into interlocal agreements is usually "economies of scale"—they believe that some services can be delivered more effectively and efficiently over larger tracts of territory, or by larger jurisdictions.[53]

BOUNDARIES AND REFORM: THE PROBLEMS OF MATCHING PEOPLE, POLICIES, AND POWER

The popularity of interlocal agreements among local officials points to a problem unique to American federalism: matching people, politics, and political boundaries best to meet the needs of the citizens is one of the overriding dilemmas of American government. Reorganizing the structure of local governments and redrawing jurisdictions are not easy tasks. Political boundaries can be matched with the needs of the citizenry in many ways. Which ways political scientists would choose to bring boundaries and people together depend very much on the values the particular political scientists hold. There are at least three different approaches to the boundary question in metropolitan affairs: (1) ultralocalism, (2) gargantua, and (3) compromise.

Ultralocalism: The *Status Quo* and the *Status Quo Ante*

A large and growing circle of political scientists argue that what really is needed is the current state of fragmentation of local governments—or perhaps even more fragmentation of local governments. This school of thought is called "public choice" or "political economy." Not too long ago it was called the "no-name school of public administration" because its main theorists, who are associated largely with public administration, had not fully defined what they were doing. Since then, these theorists have formed the Public Choice Society.

Perhaps the classic expression of public choice as it is applied to urban affairs is an article that appeared some years ago entitled, "The Organization of Government in Metropolitan Areas: A Theoretical Inquiry," by Vincent Ostrom, Charles M. Tiebout, and Robert Warren. The authors argued for what they termed "polycentric or multinucleated political systems" as the most responsive to the citizenry's needs. The view is that many units of government, units that often overlap jurisdictionally and are perhaps inefficient economically, will be most responsive to a citizen's demands.

To offer a hypothetical example, suppose you were a resident of an urban area and your house were being broken into by a very mean-looking burglar. Your first inclination would be to lock the bedroom door and call the police. The public choice theorists would say that, under the normal system of government, you would have only one option: to call your metropolitan police. Your city's finest might not respond because they would have an effective monopoly on the delivery of safety services to you as a citizen. Or a squad car might be at your door in 30 seconds. Or the sergeant answering your call might chuckle at your plight. Under public choice theory, however, you could call (1) your metropolitan police, (2) the county sheriff's office, (3) the state troopers, or (4) perhaps even a private firm offering security protection against burglars. Under the public choice school, all these crime prevention agencies and perhaps even others not yet conceived would have overlapping jurisdictions. Hence, if one police department is not up to snuff or is unresponsive, another police department can fill the gap. Free market competition thus equals government responsiveness. To quote Ostrom, Tiebout, and Warren,

By analogy, the formal units of government in a metropolitan area might be viewed as organizations similar to individual firms in an industry. Individual firms may constitute the basic legal entities in an industry, but their conduct in relation to one another may be conceived as having a particular structure and behavior as an industry. Collaboration among the separate units of local government may be such that their activities supplement or complement each other, as in the automobile industry's patent pool. Competition among them may produce desirable self-regulating tendencies similar in effect to the "invisible hand" of the market.[54]

Perhaps it is because of this kind of analogy that critics of the public choice school argue that it is a highly conservative political theory that can work against the dispossessed. Members of the political economy camp argue that it is just the opposite. Many proponents of public choice seem to come from Los Angeles and its environs, where interlocal cooperation is perhaps more extensive than it is in many major metropolitan areas.

Regardless of criticism, however, it seems apparent that "minigovs" are required for urban governance for much the same reasons as are "unigovs." In 1968, the National Commission on Urban Problems reported that "the psychological distance from the neighborhood to City Hall has grown from blocks, to miles, to light-years. With decreasing communication and sense of identification by the low-income resident with his government have come first apathy, then disaffection, and now—insurrection."[55] Similarly, middle-class residents of "bedroom" suburban communities have become disaffected with town councils controlled by local construction interests that zone the town for their maximal profit and ensure that questions of public concern are placed on the agenda of council meetings for consideration during the wee hours on weekdays. It is an unusual town meeting that is attended by a significant portion of the town's people.

From a practical viewpoint, the adoption of a public choice concept in the real governance of metropolises probably is best expressed in the movement begun in the mid-1960s toward neighborhood governments. Much of this movement is a reaction against what is perceived as the condescension of "professional managers" in the urban bureaucracy, and the very existence of the movement—which advocates a limited disannexation of neighborhood communities rather than outright secession from city hall—does not do credit to public officials in big cities.[56]

Two practical consequences of the neighborhood government movement have been the rise of "neighborhood corporations" and the now dormant drive for community control of public schools in municipalities. Neighborhood corporations are nonprofit organizations, chartered by the state and managed for the public benefit of specified urban areas by its residents. Many received their initial funding in 1966 under the the provisions of the Economic Opportunity Act of 1964, and later under the Model Cities program. An analysis of these groups concluded that, although their record of success had been spotty, neighborhood corporations had established a genuine rapport with residents. Nevertheless, just how representative the corporations are is open to question when it is realized that resident turnout to elect the directors of these organizations has been less than 5 percent of the eligible voters,[57] and it appears that more informal neighborhood associations, which we discuss in Chapter 10, have filled this role in recent years.

Gargantua

The term *gargantua* is used in the same sense that Robert C. Wood used it several years ago: "the invention of a single metropolitan government or at least the establishment of a regional superstructure which points in that direction."[58] A number of political scientists, in complete contrast to the public choice school, argue that the many splinters of metropolitan government must be consolidated if the public is to acquire effective and efficient public services. The emphasis is not on "responsiveness"; it is on "efficiency." Often, of course, responsiveness and efficiency are synonymous—most taxpayers prefer getting the biggest bang for their buck—but they are not always the same. For example, if your house is being burglarized, getting a police car there quickly may be very important to you at the time of the burglary. But when you are filling out your local property tax form, you may object vociferously to the "waste" engendered by many overlapping units of government, even though this so-called waste may have facilitated that police car speeding to your house when you needed it.

It is efficiency that has been valued by such groups as the Committee for Economic Development, a business-dominated organization that in 1966 recommended reducing the number of the nation's local governments by a whopping 80 percent (to 16,000) and consolidating the country's 2,700 nonmetropolitan counties into no more than 500. Four years later, however, the Committee modified its view and recommended what amounted to a compromise reorganization of metropolitan governments.[59] Similarly, in 1968 the National Commission on Urban Problems urged governmental consolidation, but less for the sake of fiscal economies and more to encourage the construction of new housing and greater responsiveness to other kinds of urban crises.

Consolidation for efficiency. Economic waste is commonplace and unavoidable in overly small governments.[60] For example, in the opinion of a study team in Illinois, the liquidation of *all* town governments in the state and consolidation of its 102 counties into 24 would save Illinois taxpayers as much as 40 percent. The 80,000 governments in the United States, many of which are of Lilliputian dimensions, support nearly 500,000 elected officials. Consider, for instance, Blue Earth County, Minnesota, whose 44,000 residents were governed a few years ago by 155 units of local government, 105 state bureaus, and 38 federal agencies. Or consider Allegheny County, Pennsylvania, with 129 municipalities, 78 boroughs, 23 first-class townships, 24 second-class townships, 116 school districts, as well as the governments of the city of Pittsburgh and Allegheny County. Then there is the awesomely bureaucratized community of Wilton, New Hampshire, whose 60 officials administer a total of 1,724 citizens. Bayfield County, Wisconsin, has fewer than 12,000 people but is governed by 100 elected legislators in various legislatures, assemblies, and councils and nearly 200 additional elected officials, including 29 treasurers, 29 assessors, and 29 tax collectors. More than 85 percent of all local governments in the United States have less than 5,000 people, and less than 50 percent even contain 1,000 constituents.

Delivering public services to the citizenry can be obstructed to the point of absurdity in jurisdictionally fragmented regions. For example, a few years ago there was a fire in a house less than three blocks from a fire station in Las Vegas, Nevada, but just beyond the city limits. The Las Vegas fire fighters watched the house burn until county fire engines arrived. The city fire fighters had been instructed by their superior to prevent the fire from reaching city property. Angry neighborhood residents hurled rocks at the immobile city fire engines, causing substantial damage. To take another example, the 40,000 independent police jurisdictions in the United States render coordinated law enforcement action difficult. In 1965, St. Louis County plainclothes detectives conducting a gambling raid were arrested by police from the town of Wellston, who were staging their own raid. Coordinated and effective programs in air and water pollution control, public health, and highways also are impeded or prevented by the irresponsibility, diseconomies, and buck-passing brought about by a plethora of tiny governments.

The argument for gargantua is not as unsophisticated as it might appear at first glance. One review of much of the research on economies and diseconomies of scale concluded that only in the smaller cities, those with less than 25,000 people, could economies of scale be attained by broadening the scope of government. Size was not a factor in cities populated by between 25,000 and 250,000 people. In cities with more than 250,000 people, expanding the scope of government further seemed to produce *dis*economy of scale and lower levels of service to the public when calculated on a per capita basis. Although it is doubtful that such findings will hold true for every city, the point is aptly made that economies of scale can work two ways.[61]

It has been contended that the argument for governmental consolidation is the product of an "efficiency mentality," which prefers dictatorial efficiency to democratic due process, participation, and representativeness. But making certain government services more effective and less costly through administratively rational consolidation does not necessarily mandate the establishment of a supercentralized bureaucracy unhindered by popular preferences and insensitive to the subtleties of neighborhood values. Nor is the implicit argument of the defenders of ultralocalism adequate—that is, that the *status quo* assures governmental responsiveness to local needs.

Recall from our discussion in Chapter 2 that less than 30 percent of Americans typically vote in local elections, and, as we explain in Chapter 10, 85 percent of cities elect all or some of their council members in at-large electoral districts, a practice that tends to limit minority representation on city councils; generally speaking, the smaller the jurisdiction, the more likely it is to have lower voter turnout in local elections and to elect its legislators at large rather than in single-member districts. The long ballot used in many localities is also of questionable value to democratic ideals because it diverts voter attention from the policymaking offices. For example, a woman obtained the nomination for the coroner's office in a New Jersey primary by persuading nine of her friends to write in her name on the ballot. Although she publicly proclaimed herself totally unfit for the office, she won the election by 80,000 votes because she was the candidate of the dominant party. The voters of Milton, Washington, elected (to their subsequent embarrassment) a mule to the Town Board. Smallness of size, in short, does not necessarily equate with democratic control.

Consolidation by annexation. In practice, the cities have attempted to swallow their surrounding local governments politically. The efforts of major metropolises to annex their environs can be seen as having three historical phases. Phase one occurred before the turn of this century and had three major characteristics. Municipalities absorbed great hunks of territory, the land they annexed was largely rural when the cities grabbed it, and often with annexation came a reorganization of government, such as the separation of a city from a county. Phase two occurred after 1900. The character of municipal annexation changed dramatically, and until World War II, annexation was very seldom used by cities.

After the war, however, phase three was initiated, and it displayed a resounding reversal of the trends shown in phase two. In 1945 alone, 152 cities with populations of 5,000 or more annexed outlying territory. The total exceeded by substantial margins the number of annexations that had been accomplished during the 1930s, and this trend has yet to be stopped; during the 1970s, about two-thirds of all cities with more than 2,500 people annexed more than 8,000 square miles and 3.2 million people.[62]

This resurgence in annexation can be traced to two factors. One is continued metropolitan growth; the other is the almost universal reluctance of the public to accept comprehensive governmental reorganization. Usually this reluctance emerges politically in the form of outlying suburbs resisting annexation; it is the tax-hungry central cities that generally want it. Small suburban governments tend to resist annexations most strongly when the metropolitan area is older, as are areas in the East or the South; when there are wide status differences between the inner city and the outer suburb; and when the form of city government is something other than the council-manager system.[63]

A major variant of annexation, and one that may represent a breakthrough in comprehensive governmental services, is that of *city-county consolidation;* 26 consolidations have occurred since the first, in 1805. Prior to the early 1900s, all city-county consolidations were brought about by state legislation, not by the approval of local voters, and usually a vestigial county government was permitted to remain in some fashion; 8 city-county mergers occurred in this way. In this century, however, proposals for city-county consolidations must be placed before the voters. After World War II, a relative spate of city-county consolidations took place. The city of Baton Rouge merged with East Baton Rouge Parish in 1947; Nashville merged in 1962 with Davidson County; Jacksonville merged in 1967 with Duval County; and Indianapolis joined with Marion County in 1969. These 4 are the major city-county consolidations that have occurred since World War II, although a total of 18 city-county consolidations of consequence have since taken place since 1945. It seems probable that annexation will continue as a technique of making metropolitan government more managerially rational, but it is dubious that city-county consolidations will occur as rapidly as they have in the last few years.[64]

It also seems likely that school districts will continue their remarkable consolidation, and in this respect they too can be included in the gargantuan tradition of political reform. School districts have been reduced from roughly 127,000 (or nearly 75 percent of all governmental units) in the 1930s to less than 15,000, and we will consider this trend more thoroughly in Chapter 17. Suffice it to note, however, that the gargantuan "approach to area-wide problems has in general seen its heyday [and] with some exceptions will almost certainly be bypassed in favor of other techniques."[65]

The Compromise Approach

The third and final approach to questions of boundaries and power is the compromise approach, which is of course the classic one of the American polity. This accommodation recognizes that efficiency and responsiveness are both beneficial values. On the one hand, responsiveness can be obtained in areas where it ought to be retained, such as planning, community-police relations, complaint systems, recreational activities, schools, public health clinics, building and housing code inspections, and other operations that call for quick, responsive, and personal reactions by governments. On the other hand, certain other kinds of functions that governments perform can be centralized for greater economy. These functions that belong in the gargantuan category of metropolitan government include, at least potentially, environmental planning, pollution control, tax collection, sanitation, fire protection, computer services, and crime control and a variety of operations that are subject to economies of scale that can be standardized and that require coordination. Hence, both fragmentation and gargantua are reconciled in the compromise approach.

In practice, the compromise approach to urban governance has taken two major tacks: metropolitan districts and comprehensive urban county plans. Let us consider them in turn.

The metropolitan district. Metropolitan districts are certainly the less controversial version of the compromise approach. A metropolitan district generally encompasses the entire metropolitan region, or at least a major portion of it; some, in fact, have waxed into regional governments. We have reviewed a number of their variations in the discussion of special districts in Chapter 8, and, as noted, most metropolitan districts are relegated to a single service or to a very limited area of activities. Roughly 125 metropolitan districts are now functioning in more than a quarter of the Metropolitan Statistical Areas, and they are particularly popular in cities of more than 500,000 people. They administer such services as port facilities, transportation, parks, public housing, and water supplies. The Port Authority of New York and New Jersey and the Bay Area Rapid Transit (BART) District in San Francisco are among the better known examples of metropolitan districts. State legal provisions permit them to flourish, at least in comparison to other forms of metropolitan governmental innovation, but they have been criticized as not being politically accountable to the citizenry and, thus, not responsive to the people. When it is realized that we are talking about a governmental form that generally is responsible for only a single function of government, and one that often requires a good deal of expertise, the problem of popular representation in metropolitan districts becomes a particularly difficult one. Metropolitan districts have also been criticized because of their single-purpose organization and the ensuing lack of policy and administrative coordination that often results.

The comprehensive urban county plan. A second variation of the compromise approach is the *comprehensive urban county plan.* The only metropolitan area in the nation that uses this is Miami and Dade County. This fact need not detract from its potential utility, particularly when it is realized that a number of artificial barriers prevent its widespread use. Cleveland, Dayton, Houston, and Pittburgh, for example, have all tried to establish such a plan and have failed because of these barriers. The barriers include the lack of legal authorization by states to use this concept; entrenched local officials who may resist what they often regard as a sweeping renovation of local government; the difficulty in selecting criteria for structuring the new governmental body of the county; the new duties to be assigned to county government; and inadequate funds to finance the new authority of county governments under such a plan.

That comprehensive urban county plans are useful has been testified to by the Miami-Dade County experience. In that metropolitan region a countywide land-use plan that includes tough regulations on air and water pollution control has been adopted. Such functions as traffic laws and traffic courts, tax assessment and collection, zoning regulations and enforcement, youth services, and mass transit all have been coordinated and standardized throughout the region.

Efficiency or Responsiveness? A Problem of Balance

Matching political boundaries with political functions has always been difficult for American government. Ultralocalism brings with it inefficiencies and ineffectiveness, but the American populace has tolerated these fiscal and administrative inefficiencies as the price of responsiveness. Indeed, it can be argued that the American people prefer these inefficiencies in that the governmental fragmentation that spawns them is the price of the most effective defense possible against tyranny.

Yet, when the price of ultralocalist government soars too high, the citizens respond accordingly. We have witnessed this response in taxpayer revolts against school bond issues. Indeed, as school district consolidations have increased dramatically, the number of taxpayer revolts against school bond elections also has gone up; in the 1970s more than 90 percent of the school bond issues went down in defeat, despite radical consolidations of school districts for the sake of economy and efficiency. There are exceptions to this rule—some citizens revolt against school districts on political rather than economic grounds—but it is the exception that proves the rule. An example is Kanawha County, West Virginia, whose citizens banned certain books from the school system because they felt these books were depraved, anti-Christ, and immoral. But if the data are to be read dispassionately, it seems that most Americans will let their children read anything the school assigns and will let the school bureaucracy distance itself from accountability to parents, so long as educational costs can be kept down. Only in the schools (which consume nearly half of state and local budgets) do Americans seem to prefer efficiency over responsiveness; this preference has not yet made itself felt in the counties, cities, and towns.

FEDERALISM AND THE PYRAMIDING OF POWER

A final summing up on the nature of relations between governments in the United States points to one conclusion: that governmental power in this country is centralizing despite Americans' ultralocalist leanings.

Perhaps the clearest indication of this can be seen by examining measures of financial resources, services, and worker availability. The nation's 80,000 local governments raise less money today than do the nation's 50 state governments and considerably fewer dollars than does the national government.

Although money is paid to the national government by citizens and part of these revenues are sent back to the state and local governments through revenue sharing and federal grants, this practice connotes, at least in the view of some, a centralization of governmental power at the national level.

But such centralization also may be happening at the state level. By ranking the local proportions of financial resources, services, and worker availability by state, G. Ross Stephens found that certain states were quite centralized in relation to their local governments, while others were relatively decentralized. Stephens concluded that larger states tend to be decentralized governmentally, whereas smaller states are more centralized.[66] Other studies by and large confirm Stephens's findings.[67]

There is additional evidence that governments are centralizing. Not only is centralization occurring at the state level, but at the local level, too. In national studies conducted since 1972, it has been found that, generally speaking, larger local governments are taking over the responsibilities of smaller ones.[68] Fifty-six percent of the intergovernmental service contracts let by cities, for example, are given to counties.[69] A plurality (48 percent) of all joint service agreements are entered into with counties, and counties are the principal service providers for more than half of all services provided through these agreements.[70] Most significantly, however, counties and regional organizations receive most of the intergovernmental service transfers; in other words, these relatively large units of local government are permanently taking over the traditional duties of cities and towns, and at the request of those cities and towns. Fifty-four percent of all intergovernmental service transfers go to counties, and 14 percent (the next highest) go to regional organizations, such as councils of governments.[71]

Whatever the cause and whatever the outcome, it appears that subnational governments are moving power not only *up* the intergovernmental pyramid, to higher levels of government, but *out* of smaller jurisdictions and into larger ones. If, it seems, the American people like ultralocalist government, the people whom Americans elect and appoint to run their governments do not. State and local officials have been engaged in a slow but steady process of centralizing and shifting responsibilities for service deliveries both upward and outward for many years in an effort to meet the needs of their citizens more effectively and efficiently. It is a process that shows no signs of reversing. Thus, we are increasingly faced with batteries of small local governments that may symbolically satisfy their people's psychic needs for "community," but which have, by their own volition, less and less to really do for their citizens.

Only in America.

NOTES

[1]Theodore J. Lowi, *The End of Liberalism* (New York: W. W. Norton, 1969), pp. 250-266.
[2]Vincent Ostrom, *The Intellectual Crisis in American Public Administration* (University: University of Alabama Press, 1973), pp. 10-11.
[3]Task Force on Land Use and Urban Growth, *The Use of Land* (New York: Thomas Y. Crowell, 1973), p. 16.
[4]Henry S. Reuss, *Revenue Sharing: Crutch or Catalyst for State and Local Governments?* (New York: Praeger, 1970), pp. 53-56.
[5]Kenneth N. Vines, "The Federal Setting of State Politics," in Herbert Jacob and Kenneth N. Vines, eds., *Politics in the American States,* 3rd ed. (Boston: Little, Brown, 1976), p. 4.
[6]*Ibid.,* p. 7.

[7]Alexander Hamilton, John Jay, and James Madison, *The Federalist* (New York: Random House, 1937), p. 347.

[8]The following discussion is drawn from Deil S. Wright, *Understanding Intergovernmental Relations,* 2nd ed. (Monterey, Calif.: Brooks/Cole, 1982), pp. 43-82.

[9]Advisory Commission on Intergovernmental Relations, *The Federal Role in the Federal System: The Dynamics of Growth* (Washington, D.C.: U.S. Government Printing Office, 1981), p. 159.

[10]Vines, "Federal Setting of State Politics," p. 38; and Lisa B. Belkin, "For State and Local Governments, Washington Is the Place to Be," *National Journal* (September 6, 1980), p. 1485.

[11]David L. Cingranelli, "State Government Lobbies in the National Political Process," *State Government,* 56, No. 4 (1983), p. 126.

[12]David L. Cingranelli, "A Political Model for the Determinants of State Fiscal Success During the Fiscal Crisis of the 1980s," paper presented at the 1981 Annual Meeting of the American Political Science Association, New York, September 3-6, 1981.

[13]Suzanne Farkas, *Urban Lobbying* (New York: City University of New York Press, 1971), p. 67.

[14]Belkin, "For State and Local Governments," p. 1485. Figures are for 1980.

[15]Unidentified state lobbyist, as quoted in Eugene Carlson, "State Lobbyists in Washington Emphasize 'Damage Control'," *The Wall Street Journal* (June 8, 1982).

[16]Advisory Commission on Intergovernmental Relations, *The Federal Role in the Federal System,* p. 159.

[17]Dennis O. Grady, "American Governors and State-Federal Relations: Attitudes and Activities, 1960-1980," *State Government,* 57, No. 3 (1984), pp. 110-111.

[18]*Ibid.,* p. 109.

[19]*Ibid.*

[20]Catherine H. Lovell et al., *Federal and State Mandating on Local Governments: An Exploration of Issues and Impacts* (Riverside: Graduate School of Administration, University of California, 1979), p. 82. Lovell and her colleagues found 1,259 federal mandates affecting state and local governments.

[21]The following typology is described more fully in Advisory Commission on Intergovernmental Relations, *Regulatory Federalism: Policy, Process, Impact and Reform,* A-95 (Washington, D.C.: U.S. Government Printing Office, 1984), pp. 7-10.

[22]Grady, "American Governors and State-Federal Relations," p. 107.

[23]Advisory Commission on Intergovernmental Relations, *State Administrators' Opinions on Administrative Change, Federal Aid, Federal Relationships,* M-120 (Washington, D.C.: U.S. Government Printing Office, 1980), pp. 39-59.

[24]*Ibid.,* p. 51.

[25]Much of the following discussion on interstate conflict is drawn from Joanne Omang, "In This Economic Slump, It's a State-Eat-State Nation," *Washington Post* (June 14, 1982); and Richard Benedetto, "States Skirmish in 'Border War'," *USA Today* (February 24, 1984).

[26]The 12 energy exporting states were projected to reap $193 billion in severance taxes between 1982 and 1992 by the Northeast-Midwest Economic Advancement Coalition, as cited in Omang, "In This Economic Slump."

[27]Edward C. Banfield and James Q. Wilson, *City Politics* (Cambridge, Mass.: Harvard University Press, 1963), p. 65.

[28]*Ibid.,* p. 66.

[29]Joseph F. Zimmerman, "The Role of the States in Metropolitan Governance," paper presented at Conference at Temple University, Philadelphia, August 17, 1973. Cited in John C. Bollens and Henry J. Schmandt, *The Metropolis,* 3rd ed. (New York: Harper & Row, 1975), p. 58.

[30]Carl W. Stenberg, "The New Federalism: Early Readings," *Public Management* (March, 1982), p. 5.

[31]National Research Council, *Toward an Understanding of Metropolitan America* (San Francisco: Canfield, 1975), p. 109.

[32]Advisory Commission on Intergovernmental Relations, *State-Local Relations Bodies: State ACIRs and Other Approaches* (Washington, D.C.: U.S. Government Printing Office, 1981), p. 3; and Jane Roberts, Jerry Fensterman, and Donald Lief, "States, Localities Continue to Adopt Strategic Policies," *Intergovernmental Perspective,* 11 (Winter, 1985), p. 29.

[33]Patricia S. Florestano and Vincent L. Marando, "Urban Problems from State Commissions: A Research Note," *Urban Affairs Quarterly,* 15 (March, 1980), pp. 337-338.

[34]National Research Council, *Toward an Understanding of Metropolitan America,* p. 109.
[35]Bollens and Schmandt, *The Metropolis,* p. 58.
[36]National Research Council, *Toward an Understanding of Metropolitan America,* p. 108.
[37]Daniel R. Grant, "Urban Needs and States Response: Local Government Reorganization," in Alan Campbell, ed., *The States and the Urban Crisis* (Englewood Cliffs, N.J.: Prentice-Hall, 1970), pp. 59 and 83.
[38]Advisory Commission on Intergovernmental Relations, *State Community Assistance Initiatives: Innovations of the Late 1970s* (Washington, D.C.: U.S. Government Printing Office, 1979), pp. 15-36.
[39]Fred Teitelbaum, "The Relative Responsiveness of State and Federal Aid to Distressed Cities," *Policy Studies Review* (November, 1981), p. 320. "Distressed cities" in this study referred to those municipalities identified as in severe hardship by the Brookings Institution's "central city hardship" index. See Richard P. Nathan and Charles Adams, "Understanding Central City Hardship," *Political Science Quarterly,* 91 (Spring, 1976), pp. 44-52.
[40]President's Commission for a National Agenda for the Eighties, *Urban America in the Eighties: Perspectives and Prospects* (Washington, D.C.: U.S. Government Printing Office, 1980), p. 99.
[41]Wright, *Understanding Intergovernmental Relations,* p. 389.
[42]R. B. Rainey et al., *Seattle: Adaptation to Recession;* Barbara R. Williams, *St. Louis: A City and Its Suburbs;* Daniel Atesch and Robert Arvine, *Growth in San Jose: A Summary Policy Statement* (all published in Santa Monica, Calif.: Rand Corporation, 1973).
[43]Bollens and Schmandt, *The Metropolis,* p. 60.
[44]Carl W. Stenberg, "Federalism in Transition, 1959-79," *Intergovernmental Perspective,* 6 (Winter, 1980), pp. 6-7.
[45]Lovell, *Federal and State Mandating on Local Governments,* p. 82.
[46]"San Antonio Under the Gun," *The Wall Street Journal* (January 20, 1977).
[47]National League of Cities, *Municipal Policy and Program Survey* (Washington, D.C.: National League of Cities, 1981), as cited in Advisory Commission on Intergovernmental Relations, *Regulatory Federalism,* p. 175. But see also Jeffrey L. Pressman, *Federal Programs and City Politics: The Dynamics of the Aid Process in Oakland* (Berkeley: University of California Press, 1975), p. 85.
[48]Thomas Muller and Michael Fix, "The Impact of Selected Federal Actions on Municipal Outlays," in *Government Regulation: Achieving Social and Economic Balance,* Vol. 5 of *Special Study on Economic Change,* Joint Economic Committee, U.S. Congress (Washington, D.C.: U.S. Government Printing Office, 1980), pp. 327, 330, and 368.
[49]Albert J. Richter, "Federal Grants Management: The City and County View," *Municipal Year Book, 1977* (Washington, D.C.: International City Management Association, 1977), pp. 183-184.
[50]The following typology is drawn from Lori M. Henderson, "Intergovernmental Service Arrangements and the Transfer of Functions," *Municipal Year Book, 1985* (Washington, D.C.: International City Management Association, 1985), p. 194.
[51]*Ibid.,* p. 201. The 1972 survey is in Advisory Commission on Intergovernmental Relations, *The Challenge of Local Government Reorganization,* A-44 (Washington, D.C.: U.S. Government Printing Office, 1976).
[52]Henderson, "Intergovernmental Service Arrangements," pp. 199-200.
[53]*Ibid.,* pp. 196-198, 201.
[54]Vincent Ostrom, Charles M. Tiebout, and Robert Warren, "The Organization of Government in Metropolitan Areas: Theoretical Inquiry," *American Political Science Review,* 55 (December, 1961), pp. 831-842, as reprinted in Jay S. Goodman, ed., *Perspectives on Urban Politics* (Boston: Allyn & Bacon, 1970), pp. 100-101.
[55]National Commission on Urban Problems, *Building the American City* (Washington, D.C.: U.S. Government Printing Office, 1968), p. 11.
[56]See Joseph F. Zimmerman, *The Federated City: Community Control in Large Cities* (New York: St. Martin's, 1972); Milton Kotler, *Neighborhood Government* (Indianapolis: Bobbs-Merrill, 1969); and Alan A. Altshuer, *Community Control: The Black Demand for Participation in Large American Cities* (New York: Pegasus, 1970).
[57]Howard W. Hallman, "Guidelines for Neighborhood Management," *Public Management* (January, 1971), pp. 3-5.
[58]Robert C. Wood, "The New Metropolis: Greenbelt, Grass Roots versus Garguantua," *American Political Science Review,* 52 (March, 1958), pp. 108-122.
[59]Committee for Economic Development, *Modernizing Local Government* (New York: Com-

mittee for Economic Development, 1966); and Committee for Economic Development, *Reshaping Government in Metropolitan Areas* (New York: Committee for Economic Development, 1970).

[60]The following examples of governmental fragmentation at the local level are drawn from Reuss, *Revenue Sharing*. While the statistics are somewhat dated (most are from the 1960s), the facts of fragmentation still remain.

[61]Elinor Ostrom, "Metropolitan Reform: Propositions Denied from Two Traditions," *Social Science Quarterly*, 53 (December, 1972), pp. 474-493.

[62]Joel C. Miller and Richard L. Forstall, "Annexations and Corporate Changes: 1970-79 and 1980-83," *Municipal Year Book, 1984* (Washington, D.C.: International City Management Association, 1984), p. 96.

[63]Thomas R. Dye, "Urban Political Integration: Conditions Associated with Annexations in American Cities," *Midwest Journal of Political Science*, 8 (November, 1964), p. 446.

[64]National Association of Counties and International City Management Association, "Consolidated County-Type Governments in the United States," mimeo, 1980; and Miller and Forstall, "Annexations and Corporate Changes," p. 101.

[65]Bollens and Schmandt, *The Metropolis*, p. 264.

[66]G. Ross Stephens, "State Centralization and the Erosion of Local Autonomy," *Journal of Politics*, 36 (February, 1974), p. 67.

[67]See, for example, Advisory Commission on Intergovernmental Relations, *The Condition of Contemporary Federalism: Conflicting Theories and Collapsing Constraints* (Washington, D.C.: U.S. Government Printing Office, 1981), pp. 68-70; and Jeffrey M. Stonecash, "Fiscal Centralization in the American States: Increasing Similarity and Persisting Diversity," *Publius*, 13 (Fall, 1983), pp. 123-137.

[68]Henderson, "Intergovernmental Service Arrangements," pp. 194-202, for 1983 data; Advisory Commission on Intergovernmental Relations, *Pragmatic Federalism: The Reassignment of Functional Responsibility* (Washington, D.C.: U.S. Government Printing Office, 1976) for 1975 data; and Advisory Commission on Intergovernmental Relations, *The Challenge of Local Government Reorganization*, for 1972 data.

[69]Henderson, "Intergovernmental Service Arrangements," p. 196. All information in this paragraph is for 1983.

[70]*Ibid.*, p. 198.

[71]*Ibid.*, p. 202.

10

POWER IN COMMUNITIES:

who plays, wins, loses

"Community power" long has been an object of research. In this chapter we sample the traditional literature on community power, but with a difference. Instead of dwelling on elitist versus pluralist interpretations of community power, we emphasize the role of Washington and its intervention in the local politics of cities and suburbs; further, we shall review how the feds have, in the 1980s, withdrawn their support of activist local groups and the subsequent patterns of lobbying and legislating at the grassroots.

COMMUNITY: QUARRELS OVER A CONCEPT

The Community as a Village

Before getting to the nitty-gritty of grassroots politics and power, we first must define *community*. John C. Bollens and Henry J. Schmandt observe that "two core definitions" emerge from the literature on communities: "One refers to the modes of relationships in which the individuals and families involved share common values and objectives and closely identify themselves with the aggregate population; the other indicates a spatially defined social unit that has functional significance and relates to the interdependence of individuals and groups."[1] The first definition is the classic one, and we refer to it as the "village" model; it applies to such groupings as a neighborhood or New England town.

The Community as Class and Profession

The second definition refers to the interdependence that arises among groups as a result of large-scale specialization, or professionalization. "The strong interest of communion and shared values characteristic of the first meaning [i.e., the village] may no longer be present, but the high degree of interdependence in daily activities that the urban system imposes on the aggregation creates a social group with strong ties of mutual interest and concern." The community, in this sense then, is a "mosaic of subareas whose inhabitants are highly interdependent on a daily basis in terms of needs, communication, and commutation to and from work."[2] This definition we refer to as the "class/professional" model.

The National Research Council perhaps puts the foregoing—and rather arcane—concepts into perspective when it notes that, if the ideal of "community" is to be attained, then "metropolitan people and their leaders must somehow gain a clearer appreciation of their actual interdependence and their potential common interest. This is what community in the most useful sense means."[3]

In this book, we accept the "class/professional" model—that *community* refers to economic, social, and political interdependence among people who fall into broad social categories, as opposed to the "village" idea. This is a fairly important point. We are saying that the traditional definition of community no longer applies. We are contending that not only is "the melting pot" (that is, ethnic groups intermarrying, homogenizing, and "Americanizing" over time) a fallacy, but that the ethnic neighborhood increasingly is becoming a memory rather than a reality. For example, although there is a "Little Italy" in Chicago, about half of the Italian immigrants did not settle in Italian neighborhoods, but dispersed themselves throughout the metropolitan area. In arguing against the "community-as-village" thesis, research repeatedly finds that as urban units increase in size, their populations become less traditional and less conservative. "This is true for various aspects of life, including race relations, sexual behavior, the family, religion, and law and politics . . . consequently, cities historically have been the scenes of scientific, economic, social and political innovation as well as turbulence and dislocation."[4]

Another conventional wisdom concerning the idea of community is the image of neighbors talking to neighbors, residents knowing each other (and keeping tabs on each other), and the whole *Gestalt* of folksy neighborliness. Nevertheless, little if any of this exists in metropolitan areas. One study found that in six metropolitan areas, only one-third of suburban residents had any contact at all with their immediate neighbors, and in the inner cities, the percentage was even less.[5] It seems that people do not really interact with other people in the suburbs and cities on a neighborhood basis; they interact instead on a social and economic basis. That is, lawyers talk to lawyers, the poor talk to the poor, but neighbors rarely talk to neighbors.

Like most of the findings in social science, this conclusion is not without its exceptions, but it does seem that the local neighborhood has become substantially less significant either as a "community" or as a force in forming individual personality. The neighborhood survives primarily as a means of control over the immediate physical environment, and people in it tend to work together only when challenged by some outside force.

COMMUNITY POWER: VIEWS AND COUNTERVIEWS

Both the "village" and the "class/professional" definitions of community have held sway over researchers in their attempts to discern how power politics is played in cities and towns. Some scholars appear to accept implicitly the "village" definition by engaging in *reputational analyses* of community power: they simply ask notable people in a community who they think has power and proceed from that point. Those who have local reputations for "getting things moving" are seen as being powerful in this kind of an analysis. The classic example of reputational analysis is Floyd Hunter's 1954 study, *Community Power Structure,* in which he concluded that Atlanta, Georgia, was ruled by a handful of powerful men.

At the other end of the continuum is what is known as *event analysis,* which appears more suited to a "class/professional" definition of community. Event analysis traces patterns of interaction among policymakers rather than the opinions of community residents about who is powerful. The best known exponent of event analysis is Robert Dahl. His work, *Who Governs,* used event analysis to examine how 16 decisions were made on urban redevelopment, public education, and mayoral nominations in both political parties for a period that extended through seven elections in New Haven, Connecticut.

POWER: PLURALIST OR ELITIST?

Regardless of the methods used to study community power, at least two major points of view have emerged in the literature over time: the pluralist view and the elitist view.

Pluralism assumes that while a community may have some powerful individuals, power nonetheless is accessible to virtually anyone who becomes interested in acquiring it. Power is dispersed. Elites are not monolithic power elites that can start or stop any project at anytime, anywhere, but rather there are many elites that specialize in many issues. Although these elites may be powerful in terms of a particular issue, they are not powerful on all issues. Dahl, who represents the pluralist view, states that no one elite is a "ruling group, but is simply one of many groups out of which individuals sporadically emerge to influence the politics and acts of city officials."[6]

The elitist model, on the other hand, assumes that there is indeed an all-powerful ruling elite in a community, and change can be accomplished only with the consent of this power elite. Without that consent, change is not accomplished. Moreover, this elite is commercial rather than political—that is, it is economically powerful, but not elected or appointed to office.

Of course, it should be noted that *pluralist* and *elitist* are highly relative terms: "No matter what methodology is employed and no matter what the type or size of town examined, the results invariably show that only a small minority of the citizen body, actually less than 1 percent, are active and direct participants in the community decision-making process (other than voting on referenda)."[7]

Another major factor in community power studies is the physical size of the community to be analyzed. Researchers have studied cities from the size of Atlanta and New York to cities the size of Muncie, Indiana, which at the time of the study had a population of 35,000. Taken together, size of the community and elitist or pluralist conclusions about the type of power structure found in those communities are perhaps the two most significant variables pertaining to all the community power literature. We consider some of these studies in turn.

The Power Elite in Big Cities

Hunter found that a small elite of businessmen pretty much ran Atlanta in the early 1950s.[8] Peter B. Clark, however, approached the same idea from quite a different point of view.[9] He studied businesspersons rather than communities and found America's people of commerce to be extraordinarily uncreative in suggesting new civic policies. Generally, business people were used as prestigious front persons for ideas that were thought up by professional staffs of civic organizations or the city government itself. Once a well-thought-out innovation for a community had received the public backing of prestigious business people, the innovation almost always became a city policy.

Edward C. Banfield came up with a variation on the same idea.[10] In the early 1960s Banfield found that the ruling elite of Chicago, while not a ruling elite in the classical sense, nevertheless tended to be concentrated in the city government itself, principally in the form of the late Mayor Daley's political machine. Although there was no economic or business-oriented ruling elite of Chicago, wealthy individuals played prominent political roles. Nevertheless, because business leaders do not always agree on all issues, because they do not communicate effectively among themselves, and because they do not have their own political organization, they in effect had to defer to the Daley machine to implement any kind of policy, and even to reconcile their own differences. Therefore, the Chicago power elite was clearly political, not economic.

The Power Elite in Small Towns

A classic study of community power was conducted by Robert Lynd and Helen Lynd. Known as the "Middletown" studies, they were conducted over a period beginning with the mid-1920s and continuing through the mid-1930s. The Lynds used an anthropological approach and focused on one "Family X," which, in their view controlled the destiny of most "Middle-towners" (actually, residents of Munice, Indiana). The Lynds concluded, "The lines of leadership and the related controls are highly concentrated today in Middletown"; they added that they felt the control had centralized over time.[11]

A fascinating variation on the Lynds's conclusions about Muncie is contained in Robert O. Schultze's study of "Cibola," which was actually Ypsilanti, Michigan. Schultze found that as Ypsilanti's local commerce integrated with the national economy, the "old families" of Ypsilanti gave way to a new management class—that is, highly paid employees who worked for absentee corporate landlords.[12] He found that the new managerial elite did not have the same interest in local issues and in the local community as did the traditional, locally based industrialists. The managers were mainly concerned with what those in their national company headquarters were thinking, although the headquarters were often located several thousand miles away.

The Big City as a Pluralist System

Quite the opposite of the elitist model is the pluralist model. Pluralism accepts the idea that all organized groups can become actively involved in the community's political process. As we observed in Chapter 3, this view represents "the hydraulic theory of power," in which countervailing interest groups are at loggerheads with each other. Those groups with the greater skill or power tend to garner policies from "the system" that are more favorable to them than to others.[13] The conventional wisdom in political science circles is that this system represents a good and just policy. Pluralism sees an interest in politics and a willingness to be involved in a piece of the action as the keys to influence, whereas the elitist concept puts mere economic wealth as the cornerstone of community power.

Frank J. Munger studied patterns of political power in Syracuse, New York, and came up with a pluralist conclusion about how politics were structured in that city. Munger's conclusion was that "in reality, there appear to be many kinds of community power with one differing from another in so many fundamental ways as to make virtually impossible a meaningful comparison." He goes on to note that there were "as many decision centers as there are important decision areas, which means that the decision-making power is fragmented among institutions, agencies and individuals."[14]

Similarly, Wallace B. Sayre and Herbert Kaufman in their enormous work, *Governing New York City,* concluded that "no single ruling elite dominates the political and governmental system of New York City" and added that "New York was governed by ceaseless bargaining and fluctuating alliances among the major categories of participants in each center, and in which the centers are partially but strikingly isolated from one another."[15] Thus in Sayre and Kaufman's view, New York is run through a process that they call "decisions as accommodation." In this light, "building temporary or lasting alliances, working out immediate or enduring settlements between allies or competitors, and bargaining for an improved position in the decision centers are the continuing preoccupations of all leaders—whether party leaders, public officials, leaders of organized bureaucracies, or leaders of nongovernmental groups."[16]

Pluralism in Small Towns

The final category in this discussion of community power structure concerns those small towns that have been seen by some analysts as pluralist systems. Overall, the literature tends to regard big cities as composites of many competing forces (in other words, a pluralist system) and small towns as dominated by powerful economic elites. Of course, there are exceptions to this rule. Perhaps the best known exception to the conventional wisdom that small towns are run by powerful rich folks is the study conducted by Aaron Wildavsky of Oberlin, Ohio. He found a number of different power bases and all kinds of controversies. Although Wildavsky's investigations do not disprove the findings of those many analysts who have found significant economic elites dominating small towns in America, they do indicate that there is no preset pattern of political power that necessarily will dominate in a small town setting. As Wildavsky concluded, "the roads to influence . . . are more than one; elites and nonelites can travel them, and the toll can be paid with energy and initiative as well as wealth."[17]

Conclusions About Community Power

The findings of the literature on community power are considerably more sophisticated than the preceding overview indicates. Thomas R. Dye, in a useful summarization, notes the following conclusions, or hypotheses, on community power that have been drawn from this voluminous body of writing:[18]

1. Communities without substantial class or racial cleavages have more concentrated power structures; social differences and community conflicts tend to be associated with a pluralist political system.
2. An upswing in many different kinds of industrialization tends to increase political pluralism, whereas elite power structures tend to be found in communities with a single dominant industry.
3. Metropolitan central cities tend to be pluralist in nature; suburbs in those same metropolitan areas are usually more elitist.
4. The bigger the city, the greater the likelihood of a pluralist power structure.
5. The older a community, the greater the likelihood of an elitist structure.
6. Southern cities tend to be more elitist than Northern cities.
7. Cities with nonpartisan elections, council-manager governments, and highly professional bureaucracies (a fairly common combination in suburbs) tend to be associated with elitist power structures, whereas cities with partisan elections, a mayor-council form of government, and relatively more patronage positions available in city government normally are associated with pluralism.
8. Community power tends to destabilize over time, so that communities with elitist power structures tend to evolve into pluralist systems.

The bulk of research indicates that although power in small towns often is held by business leaders who are not formally elected or appointed to office or by alliances of economic interest groups and formal officeholders, in big cities, at least, the power largely is where it is supposed to be. In other words, political power in major cities is held by those who are formally elected or appointed to office, and these officials serve as brokers between competing interest groups in the community.

In support of this contention, Claire Gilbert, in her review of 167 studies of community power, found that in towns with 20,000 to 50,000 people, business leaders who did not hold public office did indeed tend to dominate the local power structure. But the studies also indicated that in the big cities there was no covert power elite that manipulated the formal officeholders. The power was held by those who were elected or appointed to public office;[19] indeed, Banfield's study of Chicago, Sayre and Kaufman's study of New York, and Munger's study of Syracuse all confirmed this. Hence, it seems to follow that the larger a community is, the more likely it is that the people who are in a position to control and filter information that they receive from various interest groups become the effective decision makers in communities. In large cities, power is less in the hands of a privileged elite and increasingly in the hands of the "brokers," whether elected or appointed, who can bring together the various components of decision making in the community. Nevertheless, this conclusion is less valid for the smaller towns, where a local elite can indeed dominate the elected and appointed officials of the community—at least most of the time.

Brokers, local elites, and even pluralistic systems of interest groups headed by their own elites, somehow do not strike us as "democratic." And it appears in retrospect that particularly in the 1960s the federal government made an effort to reach down to the grassroots of local polities, nourish those roots, and thereby change and "democratize" community power structures. In some ways this federal effort (supplemented, to be sure, by spontaneous, homegrown organizations) represented a somewhat nostalgic attempt to reinstate the "village" concept of community at the expense of the "class/professional" model.

As Frank X. Steggert has observed, there was, especially during the 1960s and 1970s, a heavy federal emphasis on citizen participation in the policymaking process of local government and "a broad range of attempts to institutionalize new channels for such citizen expression. The thrust of this new movement toward institutionalization has derived from action at the federal level."[20] Washington has stipulated that local citizens participate in no fewer than 155 separate policy areas, if local and state governments want its money.[21] The federal government has called for neighborhood action task forces, more effective methods for processing citizen grievances, and hearings by local legislative bodies on inner city problems. It has encouraged the setting up of neighborhood city halls to act as informal channels for complaints and grievances and called for more effective community participation through neighborhood self-determination or control by the community.

The principal rationale that federal policymakers and politically liberal local elites have used to justify this activity is usually called *community development.* Community development assumes that, while there is enough indigenous leadership in communities, some help from the outside nonetheless is needed. Conflict between the power elite in a city and the grassroots is discouraged; instead, learning to "work with" the power elite is promoted. Occasionally, this emphasis of the community development approach alienates local citizens. For example, "Even organizations such as the Urban League that have long worked within the established structure were compelled to assume more militant stands to avoid losing the support of blacks altogether." This occurred when blacks felt that they were not being accorded their full rights in local government; thus, "the community development model is more compatible with the American myth of 'pulling oneself up by his own bootstraps,' and this arouses less hostility."[22]

What does community development mean precisely? At the federal level, it is seen as a particular kind of public policy through which government improves the living conditions of its people. This is how Richard M. Nixon defined it as president in 1971, when he proposed to Congress the creation of a new Department of Community Development. The federal government has at least four basic concerns relating to community development:

1. The physical improvement of the urban environment.
2. The improvement of the social aspects of urban areas.
3. The improvement of the performance of local governmental institutions.
4. The increased participation by local citizens in making decisions that affect their own communities.

The Roots of Community Development

Congress first became concerned with community development in 1892 when it appropriated $20,000 for a study of slum conditions. In 1908 President Theodore Roosevelt established a commission to survey slums. Neither study resulted in any federal action that benefited cities.[23] It was not until Theodore's cousin, Franklin, became president in the 1930s that the federal government again took an interest in community development. FDR pushed the National Housing Act through Congress in 1934, which created the Federal Housing Administration and, in so doing, amounted to a political legitimization of Washington's role in community development. The Housing Act of 1937 linked, for the first time, the provision of public housing for Americans with slum clearance and, thus, set the stage for the federal government's initial, large-scale involvement in community development.

Urban Renewal: Community Development for the Middle Class

This involvement was cemented in 1949 with the passage of the Housing Act of that year, especially as it was amended in 1954. Title I of the Housing Act of 1949 began to displace the concept of providing decent public housing to the poor with the far broader vision of renewing the entire urban scene. And it did so in a highly revolutionary manner: it redefined the doctrine of eminent domain.

Eminent domain means that a government may purchase, at a price it deems to be fair, a person's property for the public good, such as a right-of-way for a new road. But the Housing Act of 1949 said that, while a government could still force a person to sell his or her property to it, the government no longer was completely in charge of deciding how that property should be used for the public good. Instead, the government turned the property over to a private developer, who could do with it (within certain broad guidelines) as he or she saw fit. In other words, under the Housing Act of 1949, eminent domain now meant that government could force the transfer of private property to private interests for private profit.

The reasoning behind this somewhat radical public policy was not, at first glance, as sleazy as it might appear. It was never the goal (at least, not the preeminent goal) of federal policymakers to redefine eminent domain so that private investors might profit; such profits were seen as only an additional (and secondary) bonus of a policy designed paramountly to revitalize inner cities.

To do this, Urban Renewal blended conservative and liberal belief sets and was supposed to work in the following way: by exercising their rights of eminent domain, local governments would purchase tenements in the slums, evict the tenants (but only after finding them comparable or better shelter elsewhere), clear the land, offer it to local real estate developers at a bargain-basement price, and voila!—the city would be renewed by the creativity of the private sector. To get this sequence going, the federal government would absorb two-thirds (or, on occasion, even three-fourths) of the net project costs, and the local government would pick up the remaining costs, usually on highly favorable terms.

On the face of it, this was a no-lose deal for developers. But developers soon discovered a hitch. The Housing Act of 1949 specified that any redevelopment projects they undertook had to be "predominantly residential" (i.e., more than half residential), and often, they argued, that clause meant lower profits, particularly when such housing was built for the poor. Local government officials also were concerned, contending that "the mix"—that elusive combination of residential, commercial, cultural, and governmental functions—should be the central goal and ultimately would be the most beneficial objective, of urban renewal projects. Even graver, from the perspective of local policymakers, was the fact that public housing for the poor was exempt from the property tax and, hence, did not help generate local revenues.

Thus it was that Congress in 1954 amended the 1949 Act to say that nonresidential uses could be considered in urban renewal projects—indeed, up to 10 percent of the buildings could be used for nonresidential purposes; the 1954 Housing Act also was the first legislation to use the phrase "urban renewal." In 1959, this ratio was upped to 20 percent; in 1961, to 30 percent; and in 1965, to 35 percent. Sheltering people was becoming less important than was "renewing" the downtown.

And if providing urban shelter as such gradually was becoming less consequential to local governments, then sheltering the urban poor was becoming even less so to local developers. Building new apartments for poor people simply was less lucrative than building housing for the wealthy and the middle class. When developers could find ways to avoid building new houses for the poor in Urban Renewal projects, they often did so. And if developers did not have confidence in the profit potential of a particular project, no matter how heavily subsidized it might be by federal and local governments, they simply did not involve themselves in developing land that had already been cleared by optimistic and overconfident local officials, leaving tracts resembling moonscapes around some inner cities for years.

These grim realities had a lasting impact on local public planners, who began granting developers significant concessions in redesigning urban areas and then using their governments' power of eminent domain to facilitate the developers' plans.[24]

The upshot of these simultaneous pushes to rehouse the poor, renew downtowns, and clear slums resulted in some mixed urban blessings. On the one hand, it appears that, by and large, most cities that initiated Urban Renewal projects gained an expanded tax base. The Urban Renewal Administration has claimed that local tax bases in renewed areas almost quadruple after a project is completed, although such claims may well be exaggerated.[25] In any event, Urban Renewal seems to have stimulated more economic activity in formerly depressed areas and thereby has added to local tax revenues.

But Urban Renewal has by no means added to the national housing supply. Under its auspices, 538,044 housing units were razed between 1967 and 1971, but only 200,687 were built; of these, only 101,461 units were built as public housing or for people with low to moderate incomes.[26]

A related, and even starker, irony of Urban Renewal has been its apparent effect on downtown business enterprises. Although Urban Renewal originally was perceived as a deliverance for urban commercial interests, it appears that it may be the final blight of the small businessperson. Investigations by the federal government indicate that approximately one-third of the businesses relocated by Urban Renewal projects across the nation never reopened their doors.[27]

Although the number of people displaced and relocated by Urban Renewal is difficult to cull from available data, we do know that, between 1964 and 1972, 825,000 families and 136,000 businesses—perhaps 3 million people over eight years—were forced to move at least once by either the Urban Renewal or federal highway programs, and that almost 300,000 more people were relocated by these same programs between 1973 and 1982.[28] Most of these people—more than 60 percent—were black or brown, and many were elderly. The Urban Renewal Administration states that nine out of ten of these people are moved to standard housing, but such claims have been questioned and, in any event, do not consider the frequent increase in housing costs that relocatees must bear.[29] More to the point, these people suffer. One study of relocatees in Boston's West End found that the reaction of displaced residents to being removed from old, familiar neighborhoods could be best described as simple "grief," followed by a deep and bitter anger at government authorities.[30] This resentment can be far from helpful in attaining the avowed objective of federal officials to "develop communities."

Making War on Poverty: Community Action versus Model Cities

The 1960s saw a resurgence of federal interest in community development, largely through President Lyndon Johnson's "War on Poverty." The two major community development programs initiated by Johnson were the Economic Opportunity Act of 1964, which set up the U.S. Office of Economic Opportunity (OEO) and Community Action Agencies in most of the nation's cities, and the Demonstration Cities and Metropolitan Development Act of 1966, which established City Demonstration Agencies in 66 cities to administer the Model Cities Program.

The Economic Opportunity Act was designed ultimately to redistribute urban political power through a broadly based antipoverty program. Although Community Action Agencies could be set up to operate within city hall, most (70 to 80 percent) chose to remain outside. Significantly in this respect, the act mandated "maximum feasible participation" by the poor in any programs conducted through Community Action Agencies.

Big-city mayors in particular were not at all happy with the Community Action Agencies. They viewed the agencies as being staffed by "radicals" and often felt that the agencies constituted a threat to their own political machines. As a result of pressure from big city mayors, in 1966 Congress passed the Demonstration Cities and Metropolitan Development Act. Rather than requiring "maximum feasible participation" by the poor, this act merely noted that "widespread citizen participation" would be nice. Consequently, City Demonstration Agencies were set squarely within city hall, and often became hemmed in politically by the urban bureaucracy. A "technical board" was required to review all programs proposed by City Demonstration Agencies; a citizen's board was also required. Many observers objected that the required technical boards gave effective veto power to the urban bureaucracy, but, beyond that, final approval of all programs developed by City Demonstration Agencies lay with the mayor or the city council, or both, not with neighborhood citizen groups.

If the 1966 act was not adequately discouraging to the development of citizen action groups, in 1967 Congress passed the "Green Amendment" to the Economic Opportunity Act of 1964. Named in honor of Representative Edith Green of Oregon, the amendment was enacted at the behest of a number of big-city mayors. It deleted the clause calling for "maximum feasible participation" of the poor and prohibited Community Action Agency personnel from clashing with city hall through protest marches, voter registration drives, and similar activities. Congress also broadened the Political Activities Act of 1939 (the Hatch Act), which prohibits political activity by federal employees in the civil service, to cover state and local employees working in federally funded projects and personnel in private organizations working in community action programs. This extension of the Hatch Act also effectively dampened conflicts between neighborhood organizations and city hall.

By the late 1960s Community Action Agencies had evolved into an "outside," contention-oriented program, but their budgets and programs had already been seriously slashed as a result of congressional reaction to pressure from the big cities. Meanwhile, City Demonstration Agencies had developed into "inside," work-within-the-system groups that were restricted in their political clout by administrative and political checks brought on by being located within city hall itself. In 1975 OEO became the much-reduced Community Services Administration, and in 1981 the agency was abolished altogether. Nevertheless, the two programs—the more liberal Community Action Agencies and the more conservative City Demonstration Agencies—have provided excellent examples of federal involvement in "developing" communities. Indeed, some urban observers argue that the programs' real goals—that of raising the political consciousness of the poor and the dispossessed—have effectively been achieved and that official instigation of community development no longer is necessary.

Conservatizing Community Development: The Housing and Community Development Acts

The most recent major pieces of federal legislation dealing with community development are the Housing and Community Development Acts of 1974 and 1977. Between 1974 and 1982, Congress appropriated almost $27 billion that was expended through this legislation by the Department of Housing and Urban Development (HUD). These payments are in the form of broad, flexible block grants to local governments. Included within these Community Development Block Grants are the programs of Urban Renewal, Model Cities, water and sewer facilities, open spaces, neighborhood facilities, rehabilitation loans, and public facility loans. Localities are required to give priority to programs that benefit urban families with low or moderate incomes, and the secretary of HUD may disapprove an application if he or she believes that proposed local use would be plainly inappropriate. Thus, the main features of the Housing and Community Development Act are that it (1) supplants the seven existing grants-in-aid programs just mentioned; (2) introduces a very simplified application procedure requiring HUD to act speedily on applications from large cities; (3) establishes a statutory formula for allocating community development funds instead of relying on competitive, "grantsmanship" procedures; (4) sets up a direct linkage between community development and housing policies; and finally, (5) contains no requirement that a locality has to match any funds received from the feds. The act is a truly innovative community development policy.

Congress was sufficiently pleased with the Housing and Community Development Act that it enacted a second one three years later. This law continued the innovations of the 1974 legislation, increased funding levels for community development, and initiated an innovative, Urban Development Action Grant Program targeted at 2,100 decaying cities, largely in the Snowbelt. The Action Grant Program, designed primarily to upgrade cities physically and economically by "leveraging in" the private sector, was central to the Carter administration's efforts to develop a comprehensive urban policy. Between 1977 and 1982, Congress spent more than $2 billion through its Urban Development Action Grants Program. HUD stated that these funds created almost 300,000 permanent jobs in distressed cities, saved another 100,000 jobs, produced nearly 60,000 new or rehabilitated housing units, and generated more than $220 million in annual property taxes; for $2 billion in public funds, the private sector channeled in more than $12 billion to urban projects that were sponsored by the Action Grant Program.[31]

Despite the fact that the Urban Development Action Grant Program represented a return to the business-oriented tenets of urban renewal, President Ronald Reagan significantly undermined the relatively conservative, private sector-emphatic Urban Development Action Grant Program in 1981 by folding it into the Community Development Block Grant Program. This was part of the administration's concentrated effort to deregulate in as many spheres as possible, and the federal regulations pertaining to Community Development Block Grants were reduced by half as a result of legislation contained in the Omnibus Budget Reconciliation Act of 1981. No longer are applicants for Urban Development Action Grants (which were broadened in 1981 to include Indian tribes as "cities") required to submit plans for citizen participation, community development, and housing assistance, among other simplifications that have virtually eliminated the distinctive features of the program.

The trend of federal involvement in community development has been increasingly conservative. When we look at the Economic Opportunity Act of 1964, an act that originally required the "maximum feasible participation" by local citizens in all federally sponsored community development programs, we can perceive quite a change. Although the Housing and Community Development Act of ten years later was flexible and innovative, it nonetheless was directed more toward the needs of public bureaucrats and local politicians rather than the citizenry. This is not to say that local public administrators are not able to meet the needs of their citizenries more readily than federal administrators, but rather that federal public policy for community development is increasingly aimed at the public official rather than the people.

Whether or not this change will benefit local citizens more than past federal policies have remains a moot point, but the relationship between the federal government and American communities is increasingly one between Washington and city hall rather than between Washington and individual citizens. And, as the federal government cuts back on domestic expenditures, as is the case in the 1980s, even this relationship is beginning to wither.

LOCAL LOBBYING: CITIZENS AND CITY HALL

The federal government has pushed localities into providing a variety of formats designed to encourage its citizens access to the grassroots decision-making process. Perhaps the most critical of these is the effort made by the feds to assure that the people participate in the formulation of that most critical of policies, the budget. When Congress extended revenue sharing in 1976—a policy that transfers billions of federal dollars to some 39,000 local governments every year and with few strings—it stipulated that provisions must be made for citizen involvement in the local budgetary process—a critical area in any public policy. Localities responded with alacrity; although most local governments already provided various ways in which citizens could participate in the budgetary process, virtually all cities and counties increased the mechanisms—for example, holding hearings, facilitating citizen inspection of the budget—through which local people could involve themselves in fiscal decision making.

Lobbying the Local Budget

How frequently citizens avail themselves of their expanded opportunities for participation varies, however, and public attendance at local budget hearings ranges, depending on the locality, from an average of 1,250 people to 1; the typical city holds two hearings on the budget, and average attendance is from 17 to 31 people.[32]

Table 10-1 indicates the kinds of urban interests that are represented at local budget hearings. The table shows high levels of attendance by a wide spectrum of local interest groups, from reform-minded associations to more narrowly defined and self-interested groups. Senior citizen organizations attend budget hearings in force, as do social service organizations. Organized groups are the most active at the budget hearings held by central cities—especially racial and ethnic groups—in contrast to independent municipalities and suburbs. In the suburbs, homeowners organize and turn out more than any other kind of group.[33]

The Representativeness Question: People or Pressure Groups?

It is at least an open question whether more citizen participation means more representativeness at the local level. In any case, the mandate by the federal government that citizen participation must occur in local decision making about some major federal assistance programs does not appear to have resulted in a more representative policymaking process in local governments. One analysis concluded that, despite the

> rapid expansion of [federally] mandated citizen participation in the urban policymaking process . . . it would appear that mandated citizen participation did *not* consistently represent public perceptions and preferences as the various federal statutes intended. Instead, mandated citizen participation seemed to represent additional special . . . interests in the community.[34]

City officials seem to share this perspective, and are not always impressed by the community representativeness of the citizens attending these hearings.

Table 10-1 Citizen Organizations Attending Various Types of Municipal Budget Hearings

	TYPE OF HEARING							
	Combined Hearing on Revenue Sharing and Local Budget		*Separate Hearing on Revenue Sharing*		*Separate Hearing on Local Budget*		*Community Development Block Grant Hearing*	
Type of Citizen Organization	*No.*	*% of Total*	*No.*	*% of Total*	*No.*	*% of Total*	*No.*	*% of Total*
League of Women Voters	413	48.5%	291	41.0%	247	44.2%	324	37.8%
Social service	438	51.5	346	48.7	252	45.1	494	57.6
Business and/or industry	401	47.1	253	35.6	254	45.4	326	38.0
Taxpayer	293	34.4	192	27.0	208	37.2	203	23.7
Senior citizen	523	61.5	428	60.3	291	52.1	557	65.0
Racial and/or ethnic	240	28.2	189	26.6	121	21.6	382	44.6
Homeowner	249	29.3	148	20.8	144	25.8	255	29.8
Neighborhood	318	37.4	216	30.4	166	29.7	450	52.5
Other	82	9.6	53	7.5	56	10.0	81	9.5
Total number of cities reporting	851		710		559		857	

Source: John Rehfuss, "Citizen Participation in Urban Fiscal Decisions," *Municipal Year Book, 1979* (Washington, D.C.: International City Management Association, 1979), p. 90.

According to one "Citizen participation appears to be generally in the form of special interest groups and/or official city committees or commissions. Rarely do 'public hearings' involve the general public."[35]

Local Pressure and Public Priorities

Representative or not, lobbying in the fiscal affairs of communities can produce policy results. Public officials in cities and counties report that citizen participation clearly affects, for example, local decisions about what kinds of federal grant opportunities their governments should pursue; in other words, is it worth a community's time, effort, and expenditure to endure the complex process of applying for a federal grant in work force planning? Or should it apply instead for federal funds in transportation, housing, or law enforcement? With few exceptions, substantially more than half of local governments hold public hearings and use citizen advisory committees to deal with these questions.[36] Moreover, these methods seem to be effective. More than 60 percent of city and county officials report that their governments developed new grant proposals and sent them to Washington because of citizen participation![37]

In general, local lobbying produces fiscal results, at least in the opinions of local officials. More than four out of every ten of them, for example, believe that public participation in the budget process has a measurable effect on the setting of local priorities. There are a number of additional indications of this impact as well, and Table 10-2 lists how local officials perceive the effectiveness of local lobbies. As it shows, important policy decisions are made and changed because of the power of participation.

Table 10-2 Local Officials' Opinions About the Impact of Public Participation in the Local Budgetary and Policymaking Processes

	OPINION	
Question	*Cities % Yes*	*Counties % Yes*
Have grant proposals developed by local government staff been dropped because of citizen participation?	16.8%	11.8%
Have new grant proposals been developed as a result of citizen suggestions?	60.9	63.3
Has your local government transferred funding for a service or program from its general budget to a grant because of citizen participation?	19.7	26.9
Has your local government assumed the costs in its general budget for continuing a service or program funded through an expired grant because of citizen participation?	40.7	58.8
Has your local government dropped a service or program funded through a grant when the grant expired because of citizen participation?	12.2	18.6
Has citizen participation had a measurable effect on the setting of priorities within your local government's general budget?	42.9	43.8

Source: John Rehfuss, "Citizen Participation in Urban Fiscal Decisions," *Municipal Year Book, 1979* (Washington, D.C.: International City Management Association, 1979), p. 92.

Other studies also indicate a pronounced awareness by community policymakers of the power of local interest groups. Research conducted in the San Francisco Bay Area found that only 16 percent of 115 council members did not perceive any groups whatever as "influential" in their city; 68 percent identified at least two groups as influential, and some 17 percent were able to name five or more as influential.[38] The recognition of the roles that interest groups play is considerably higher among city council persons than among state legislators—indeed, more than twice as high.[39]

It appears that interest groups at the local level have a very different style than at the state level. Most lobbies in communities take such forms as citizen groups and improvement associations rather than groups with economic interests. In the California study, 94 percent of the council members saw interest groups as largely a civic association phenomenon; only 28 percent identified economic interests as major pressure groups in their cities. This is not because economic interests are not concerned with local government, but because interest groups assume a different form at the local level than at the state and national level.[40]

Urban interest groups are not paper tigers. Once formed, they do in fact play a powerful role when relevant issues arise. In one city it was found that, of the roughly 200 groups with an expressed interest in influencing local government, most of them were politically active during the year. "A city's community action grouping may represent a minimum potential for organized political action. Most community organizations—including many that may appear to be only peripherally related to local government—can be politicized when the occasion requires.[41]

A study by The Urban Observatories of ten major cities found that most of these community action groups concerned themselves with the issues of planning and development, usually involving housing, freeway construction, race relations, taxation and revenue, and education. Generally speaking, the larger the minority population, the more race relations became a major theme in the politics of all issues.[42]

One reason why local lobbies are powerful relates to the kinds (and numbers) of people who are in them. These people are both articulate and numerous. Surveys of the ten cities found that the membership figures for groups concerned with local problems ranged between 6 and 19 percent of the adult urban population. High-income citizens were the most likely to belong to organized groups with an interest in city problems. Interestingly, the studies as a whole found that whether a person was white or black was negligible in accounting for participation in community action groups. However, upper-class blacks were much more likely than were upper-class whites to belong to these kinds of organizations.[43]

How do the people in power feel about community action groups? Most elected representatives and appointed bureaucrats pay lip service to the concept of community involvement in the policymaking process, but express reservations about the ability of central-city residents to run their own programs, and usually insist that elected officials must have final decision responsibility. Those groups with which elected and appointed officials do choose to work generally represent a higher than average income level in the community and are perceived as being more conservative than other segments of the local population. "City officials did develop expectations about how citizen groups should act. To a degree, this involved the absence of conflict. . . . Group effectiveness may depend to a considerable degree on the ability to meet expectations of local government officials. . . . 'Successful' community action groups are cooperative rather than conflict oriented. . . . Such successful groups used their problem-related information in simple and forthright ways; they made the kind of demands that could be politically acceded to."[44] In brief, those who go along, get along.

Increasingly, however, this ancient maxim of politics may apply more to the denizens of city hall (who now may have to be more cooperative) and less to local organizations of citizens, particularly neighborhood groups. In part because of Washington's encouragement, but in even larger part because of a growing grassroots distrust over the "big-government" solution of local problems, neighborhood associations have become new centers of community power. These mostly nonpartisan, multiracial, decentralized, and, above all, persistent local groups have waxed into a national (if rarely nationally coordinated) political force. They go by many titles—for example, Brooklyn's AID (Against Investment Discrimination), the North West Bronx Community and Clergy Coalition, Cleveland's Citizens to Bring Broadway Back, and the Dallas Bois d'Arc Patriots—and there are at least 200 of them across the country. Occasionally they will band together to achieve national legislative goals, but their norm is to do their own things in their own cities. For example, to convince the Dallas city fathers that East Dallas needed a greater share of federal community development funds, the Bois d'Arc Patriots made a presentation to the city council that featured a model of a typical house in their neighborhood. At the end of their presentation, they smashed the model, releasing thousands of cockroaches that scuttled furiously around the council chambers. These neighborhood associations are the new wave of local lobbying. As a federal housing official has put it, "Twenty neighborhood groups have accomplished more . . . than all of the federal programs."[45]

The Urban Group Process: A Caveat

Although the bulk of research on the topic tilts in favor of stating that local interest groups are influential and effective forces in local policymaking, some caveats are in order. In a careful analysis of neighborhood organizations' behavior in 47 cities, Edward G. Goetz concluded that among those city governments that were the most receptive to participation in the policy process by neighborhood groups, there was "no strong evidence" that formal recognition of the groups as legitimate interests and their inclusion in the local policy process by the city actually enhanced "the access of these groups."[46] In other words, even though their recognition and participation were accepted (and even encouraged) by city governments, the power of neighborhood groups in making policy did not seem to increase. Yet the level of conflict in the policymaking process did go up significantly in those cities whose governments recognized and welcomed (at least relative to other cities) the participation of neighborhood organizations.

What we may have, then, is the worst of all worlds: "progressive" urban governments that actively promote "the group process"; interest groups that experience no enhancement in their influence in the making of urban policy, despite official promotion of their participation in the policy process; and rising levels of conflict among interest groups and local officials, signifying largely nothing in terms of tangible policy outcomes. This is symbolic politics at their least productive.

LOCAL LEGISLATING: COUNCIL MEMBERS AND CITY HALL

Among the more significant local policymakers with whom citizens, organized or otherwise, must deal are the elected members of the city councils and county boards. And there are a lot of them: 158,527, to be precise. Counties elect 21,160 supervisors and commissioners to their governing boards, municipalities elect 99,993 council members and aldermen to their councils, and towns and townships elect 37,374 selectmen and trustees to their boards.[47] Virtually all these officials—95 percent of them—are part-time elected officeholders and are paid accordingly.[48]

Cities and the Wary Welcoming of Ward Elections

Most local lawmakers are elected "at-large," that is, in multimember district systems. As Table 10-3 shows, more than two-thirds of municipalities with more than 2,500 people use an at-large system, another sixth use a combination of an at-large and a ward system, and not quite 15 percent use a straight ward, or single-member district, system. Although smaller, Western, council-manager cities favor at-large systems more than do larger, Eastern mayor-council cities, local governments nonetheless show a decided preference for electing their representatives at-large. By contrast, as we noted in Chapter 5, fewer than 17 percent of the electoral districts of the state houses of representatives, and less than 6 percent of state senate electoral districts use an at-large system.

Table 10-3 Types of Electoral Systems

Classification	*TOTAL NO. OF CITIES REPORTING (N)*	*AT-LARGE SYSTEM*		*WARD OR DISTRICT SYSTEM*		*COMBINATION SYSTEM*	
		No.	*% of Total*	*No.*	*% of Total*	*No.*	*% of Total*
Total, all cities	4,089	2,721	66.5	595	14.6	773	18.9
Population group							
Over 1,000,000	3	0	0.0	1	33.3	2	66.7
100,000–249,999	95	48	50.5	15	15.8	32	33.7
2,500–4,999	1,205	860	71.4	220	18.3	125	10.4
Form of government							
Mayor-council	2,111	1,199	56.8	438	20.7	474	22.5
Council-manager	1,878	1,422	75.7	157	8.4	299	15.9
Commission	100	100	100.0	0	0.0	0	0.0

Source: Adapted from Heywood T. Sanders, "The Government of American Cities: Continuity and Change in Structure," *Municipal Year Book, 1982* (Washington D.C.: International City Management Association, 1982), p. 180.

The 100 largest cities tend to prefer a district system; fewer than a third (31) of these cities elect their council members at-large. Another 31 of the biggest cities use a pure ward system, and 38 employ electoral systems that intermix elements of multimember and single-member systems. Table 10-4 lists these cities by type of electoral system.

As we discussed in Chapter 5, and address again later in this chapter, at-large electoral systems tend to work against the interests of minorities, and it is perhaps for this reason that the U.S. Supreme Court in 1968 ruled in *Avery* v. *Midland* that the "one person, one vote" principle first annunciated by the Court for the states in 1962 also applied to local legislative bodies that elect some or all of their members from single-member districts, or wards. The Court held that the "actions of local governments are the actions of the State," and, therefore, whenever a state delegates authority to its localities to establish electoral districts for the election of local legislators, then the state "must insure that those

Table 10-4 Election Systems Used in the 100 Largest U.S. Cities, 1982

At-Large	*Districts*
These 31 cities elect all council members at-large:	These 31 cities elect all council members by district:
Anaheim, Calif.	Albuquerque, N.M.
Arlington, Texas	Anchorage, Alaska
Austin, Texas	Baltimore, Md.
Boston, Mass.	Baton Rouge, La.
Birmingham, Ala.	Chicago, Ill.
Chattanooga, Tenn.	Cleveland, Ohio
Cincinnati, Ohio	El Paso, Texas
Columbus, Ohio	Flint, Mich.
Dayton, Ohio	Fort Worth, Texas
Detroit, Mich.	Fresno, Calif.
Greensboro, N.C.	Grand Rapids, Mich.
Huntington Beach, Calif.	Honolulu, Hawaii
Jackson, Mich.	Las Vegas, Nev.
Kansas City, Kan.	Long Beach, Calif.
Little Rock, Ark.	Los Angeles, Calif.
Lubbock, Texas	Madison, Wis.
Miami, Fla.	Milwaukee, Wis.
Mobile, Ala.	Minneapolis, Minn.
Norfolk, Va.	Montgomery, Ala.
Phoenix, Ariz.	Oklahoma City, Okla.
Pittsburgh, Pa.	Omaha, Neb.
Portland, Ore.	Providence, R.I.
San Francisco, Calif.	Richmond, Va.
Seattle, Wash.	Riverside, Calif.
Spokane, Wash.	Sacramento, Calif.
Tampa, Fla.	St. Paul, Minn.
Toledo, Ohio	Salt Lake City, Utah
Tulsa, Okla.	San Antonio, Texas
Warren, Mich.	San Jose, Calif.
Wichita, Kan.	Shreveport, La.
Worcester, Mass.	Yonkers, N.Y.

Table 10-4 (Continued)

Mixed	*Mixed*
These 27 cities elect some council members at-large and others by district:	These 5 cities nominate all council members by district but elect them at-large:
Aurora, Colo.	Louisville, Ky.
Akron, Ohio	San Diego, Calif.
Buffalo, N.Y.	Santa Ana, Calif.
Charlotte, N.C.	St. Petersburg, Fla.
Colorado Springs, Colo.	Tucson, Ariz.
Columbus, Ga.	
Dallas, Texas	These 4 cities nominate some council members by district and some at-large but elect all of them at-large:
Denver, Colo.	
Des Moines, Iowa	
Fort Wayne, Ind.	
Houston, Texas	Corpus Christi, Texas
Indianapolis, Ind.	Knoxville, Tenn.
Jacksonville, Fla.	Tacoma, Wash.
Jersey City, N.J.	Virginia Beach, Va.
Lexington, Ky.	
Lincoln, Neb.	
Memphis, Tenn.	These 2 cities nominate and elect some council members by district but nominate others by district and elect them at-large:
Nashville, Tenn.	
Newark, N.J.	
New Orleans, La.	
New York, N.Y.	
Oakland, Calif.	Atlanta, Ga.
Philadelphia, Pa.	Kansas City, Mo.
Rochester, N.Y.	
St. Louis, Mo.	
Syracuse, N.Y.	
Washington, D.C.	

Listing based on responses to survey by Phoenix city staff for Citizens Charter Review Committee.

qualified to vote have the right to an equally effective vote in the election process."

The judiciary has never said that at-large electoral systems are unacceptable, but they do seem to be an object of judicial suspicion (although in 1980 the Court ruled in *City of Mobile* v. *Bolden* that at-large systems were unacceptable only if it could be proven that they were used purposely to discriminate against minorities). Hence, local governments have been slowly moving away from at-large systems and toward the establishment of single-member wards in cities and counties. In a unique survey of all 172 cities with populations ranging between 50,000 and 1 million that elect some or all of their council members from single-member wards, it was found that about 40 percent of these cities had adopted the ward system since 1965, or the period when the courts initiated their intervention in state and local legislative apportionments. Most of these new (post-1965) adoptions occurred in the South and West.[49]

Approximately three quarters of all cities using single-member electoral districts rely on their city councils to redistrict; the remainder use independent redistricting councils, the local planning commission, or other local or state agencies. This practice contrasts with the redistricting arrangements used by the state legislatures, none of which has ever released ultimate authority to redistrict to any body other than itself. Most cities that use wards redistrict following each decennial census (although smaller cities are somewhat more casual about this), and the principal criteria that cities attempt to meet in redistricting include the formation of wards that have roughly equal homogeneous populations, and that are compact, contiguous, and representative of the minority populations in the city. Southern cities, large cities, and cities with populations that are more than a fourth black or that have stable black populations are the most sensitive to the final criterion of redistricting: assuring minority representation.[50]

Council Members, Incumbency, and Autonomy

The typical city has between six and seven members on its council, although council size is very much a product of city size; cities with a million people or more have an average of 22 members serving on their councils. A majority of cities have council members who serve four-year terms, and cities that use a multimember district system favor longer terms than do municipalities that elect council members by wards. Less than 30 percent of at-large municipalities elect council members for two-year terms, compared to more than 40 percent of cities using a single-member district electoral system. More than three quarters of all cities arrange their elections so that their council members' terms overlap, in an effort to gain some political continuity and stability over time.[51] An unusual number of council members are appointed to office. The study undertaken of Bay Area cities found that almost 25 percent of the council members interviewed were initially appointed to office rather than elected.[52]

Once in office, incumbency (or being an elected officeholder) is a major advantage in running for city councils. As Table 10-5 shows, 78 percent of the council incumbents in 1975 who ran for reelection won. Moreover, more incumbents are campaigning for reelection and are winning than ever before. In 1962, 61 percent of the incumbent city council members decided to run for reelection; by 1975, this proportion had risen to 72 percent. Consequently, the percentage of council seats filled by reelected incumbents rose, too, from 46 percent in 1962 to 56 percent 13 years later. Only in cities with a commission form of government did incumbents' election victories decline, and incumbents in partisan elections stood a better chance for reelection than did their counterparts in nonpartisan elections. With the exception of the very biggest cities, incumbents tended to be retained in office "regardless of population size, governmental form, and electoral form."[53]

Of all elected lawmakers—members of Congress, state legislators, county commissioners, and city council members—the council members are perhaps the most autonomous. When we realize that perhaps a quarter of all council members are appointed rather than elected to their first term in office, that nearly three-fourths of incumbent council members stand for reelection and that almost eight in ten of these win, that the median number of citizens voting for their council members is less than 30 percent and falling and, finally, that most council members are never thrown out of office by a disaffected electorate but simply retire voluntarily[54]—then "electoral stability" seems a modest term in-

Table 10-5 Council Incumbency and Turnover, 1962 and 1975

Classification	NO. OF CITIES REPORTING		INCUMBENTS SEEKING REELECTION (%)		INCUMBENTS REELECTED (%)		OFFICES FILLED BY INCUMBENTS (%)	
	1962	*1975*	*1962*	*1975*	*1962*	*1975*	*1962*	*1975*
Total, all cities	574	778	61	72	76	78	46	58
Population group								
Over 500,000	19	23	77	76	88	88	67	68
100,000–249,999	72	91	59	70	78	82	46	58
25,000–49,999	307	430	61	73	76	75	46	54
Form of government								
Mayor-council	186	280	63	73	78	80	49	59
Council-manager	322	446	63	69	73	77	46	53
Commission	58	52	71	81	74	70	52	57
Unknown	8		—		—		—	
Form of election								
Partisan	157	210	62	73	76	82	47	59
Nonpartisan	414	568	61	72	75	76	46	55
Unknown	3		—		—		—	

Source: Albert K. Karnig and B. Oliver Walter, "Municipal Elections: Registration, Incumbent Success, and Voter Participation," *Municipal Year Book, 1977* (Washington, D.C.: International City Management Association, 1977), p. 66. Reproduced by permission of the publisher.

deed as a description of the extraordinarily solid job security enjoyed by city council members.

Who Are the Council Members?

Members of city councils are, with few exceptions, white, middle-class males in their mid-forties who probably have not completed college.[55] Most have served four years or fewer on their councils, although a greater longevity in office is evidenced among council members in cities with mayor-council forms of government.[56] Few council members are women. Eight percent of county commissioners are women, and 10 percent of municipal council members and town board members are women.[57] Although precise figures are unavailable, it appears that considerably less than 4 percent of city and county council members are blacks.[58] One study found that only 19 percent of America's city councils had one or more nonwhite members, and these tended to be the larger cities, which generally have high concentrations of black and brown people anyway.[59]

One reason why minorities are so underrepresented on city councils is the heavy use by municipalities of the at-large electoral system; as we observed earlier, approximately two-thirds of all municipalities use a pure multimember district system, and less than 15 percent use a pure single-member district system. An investigation of 139 cities that compared black representation on city councils with the proportion of blacks in the cities' population concluded that blacks had only half of their fair share of the council seats as determined by their percentage of the municipal population. In Southern cities with at-large elections, black representation on the council amounted to only a third of their ratio in the population, but in Northern cities with ward elections, black representation on the council was virtually equal to their share of the population.[60]

As we stated earlier, an at-large electoral system works against minority representation because even if every minority voted for members of their race, they could still be outvoted by the white majority, and this dynamic is accelerated in Southern cities. In a ward system that creates some predominantly minority electoral districts, however, minority candidates have a much better chance of being elected.

The data derived from the intensive studies of the San Francisco Bay Area tend to support national surveys about the characteristics of council members, but with some interesting variations. Bay Area council members were likely to represent such economic interests as manufacturing and utilities (22 percent); banking, insurance, and accounting (21 percent); business and real estate (13 percent); law (10 percent); construction and trucking (16 percent); civil service and public administration (a somewhat surprisingly high 14 percent); and agriculture (4 percent). A number of members of city councils in the area were retired or were housewives. In the cities with nonpartisan elections, Republican council members outnumbered Democrats by an 11 percent margin, even in the relatively liberal Bay Area; in recent years, the party registration rates for the Bay Area electorate have favored the Democratic Party by almost a 3-to-2 ratio.[61] Such data correspond to other findings concerning the edge that Republicans seem to have when campaigning in nonpartisan elections.

Games Council Members Play

City council members are remarkably similar—they are middle aged, middle class, and have midlevel educations—but the roles that they play once they enter the city council can be quite varied. Betty H. Zisk has given us a particularly useful categorization of these roles. She observes that there are the *pluralists,* or those who value interest groups, who perceive many groups, and who are "relatively sophisticated in regard to the group universe."[62] Then there are the *tolerants,* who may be one of three types: those who are neutral toward groups; those who have strong feelings one way or the other about groups, but demonstrate both low levels of perception of how many groups exist and low levels of sophistication about how they work; and third, those who esteem groups but are either unsophisticated in their views or perceive relatively few groups. Finally, there are the *antagonists,* who are sophisticated in their view of groups and demonstrate a high perception of how many groups there are, but who reject groups as not being legitimate.

These types of roles also correspond to how council members interact with each other and their colleagues in city hall, notably the mayor or city manager. Pluralists, like those in the other roles, seek out city officials as their main source of advice when making policy, but they are less likely than other types of council members to depend on the expertise of the city manager and his or her staff. The pluralist prefers to interact with representatives of interest groups. Antagonists are relatively oblivious to requests or contacts from groups, and they rarely seek advice from groups. Antagonists get their advice in making policy from city officials and "influential individuals." Tolerants, as might be expected, are in a midway position; they are less likely than the pluralists but

Table 10-6 Relation Between Interest Group Role Orientation of City Council Members and Seeking of Group Support*

	INTEREST GROUP ROLE ORIENTATION		
	Pluralist (*N* = 100)	*Tolerant* (*N* = 252)	*Antagonist* (*N* = 30)
Percentage of Council Members Who Seek Group Support	57%	27%	10%
Type of Groups from Whom Support Is Sought		Percentage of Total Responses (*N* = 196)	
Chamber of Commerce, Jaycees	21%	25%	**
Homeowners groups, taxpayers	25	23	
Service clubs	17	8	
Merchants' group	7	8	
Women's groups	5	5	
All other, including *ad hoc* organizations (no category was mentioned by more than 4% of the respondents)	25	31	
	100%	100%	
Kinds of Support Sought		(*N* = 131)	
Help at hearings or in trying to sell councilmember's position to others	61%	55%	**
Information on public attitudes, on potential impact of proposal on groups	19	12	
Facts, expertise, background information	6	9	
Effort to convince group of correctness of councilman's position	14	24	
	100%	100%	

* The question: "Before a Council decision is made, do you ever actively seek support from any of the groups you have mentioned? (IF YES): What kind of support do you seek? May I ask from which groups you have sought support?"

** We have not computed percentages for the responses of the three antagonists who seek support, since figures computed on such a small base are misleading and meaningless.

Source: Betty H. Zisk, *Local Interest Politics: A One-Way Street* (Indianapolis: Bobbs-Merrill, 1973), p. 57.

more likely than the antagonists to look for help or advice from groups. Interestingly, tolerants are the least likely of all council members to identify representatives of special economic interests as influential people when they are making their decisions, and they are the most likely to base their decisions on advice from the public and the city staff. Zisk concludes that while tolerants "believe in general terms of accessibility to the public, their conception of local politics appears the very antithesis of an interest based bargaining process or 'group struggle.' "[63]

Table 10-6 summarizes Zisk's findings in terms of how council members perceive pressures at city hall. Community action groups would seem to be most welcomed by the pluralist type of city council member. Antagonists and tolerants, according to Zisk's research, would not be particularly receptive to learning anything about community action groups (or, for that matter, any other kind of groups) in their own communities.

PATERNALISM, POWER, AND POLITICS: AN ASSESSMENT

Power in communities rarely is monopolized for long by a single player; instead, power rolls and bounces like a ball around the town, from player to player, and "ball hogs" in the game emerge only occasionally. The federal government has attempted to become a kind of paternalistic, Super Referee in the community power game, applying its own rules, goals, and values at the grassroots, and trying to assure that "ball hogs" are not allowed to play.

But, judging its performance by its own criteria, Washington may have fallen short in "developing" communities along the lines of its original vision that we described earlier in this chapter. Has the urban environment been physically improved over the past 30 years? Have the social aspects of cities been bettered? Have local governments been rendered more effective and efficient? Has the quality of citizen participation in local decision making been raised?

Assessing the success or failure of such value-heavy and broadly based federal objectives is not possible in a single chapter. But as citizens, each one of us can draw his or her own conclusions.

Has the Super Ref on the Potomac really changed the rules and the scores of the many political games being played on local sandlots across the nation?

NOTES

[1]John C. Bollens and Henry J. Schmandt, *The Metropolis,* 3rd ed. (New York: Harper & Row, 1975), p. 7.
[2]*Ibid.*
[3]National Research Council, *Toward an Understanding of Metropolitan America* (San Francisco: Canfield, 1975), p. 45.
[4]*Ibid.*
[5]A. H. Hawley and B. B. Zimmer, *The Metropolitan Community: Its People and Government* (Beverly Hills, Calif.: Sage, 1970).
[6]Robert Dahl, *Who Governs?* (New Haven, Conn.: Yale University Press, 1961), p. 72.
[7]Bollens and Schmandt, *The Metropolis,* p. 112.
[8]Floyd Hunter, *Community Power Structure* (Chapel Hill: University of North Carolina Press, 1953).
[9]Peter B. Clark, *The Businessman as a Civic Leader* (New York: Glencoe Free Press, 1964).
[10]Edward C. Banfield, *Political Influence* (New York: Glencoe Free Press, 1961), p. 263.
[11]Robert S. Lynd and Helen M. Lynd, *Middletown in Transition* (New York: Harcourt Brace Jovanovich, 1927 and 1965). Reprinted in Willis D. Hawley and Frederick M. Wirt, eds., *The Search for Community Power* (Englewood Cliffs, N.J.: Prentice-Hall, 1974), p. 50.
[12]Robert D. Schultze, "The Role of Economic Dominants in a Community Power Structure," *American Sociological Review,* 23 (February, 1958), pp. 3-9.
[13]L. Harmon Zeigler and G. Wayne Peak, *Interest Groups in American Society,* 2nd ed. (Englewood Cliffs, N.J.: Prentice-Hall, 1972).
[14]Frank J. Munger, *Decisions in Syracuse* (Bloomington: Indiana University Press, 1962), p. 119.

[15]Wallace B. Sayre and Herbert Kaufman, *Governing New York City* (New York: W. W. Norton, 1965), pp. 710 and 716.
[16]*Ibid.*
[17]Aaron Wildavsky, *Leadership in a Small Town* (Totowa, N.J.: Bedminister Press, 1964), p. 214.
[18]Thomas R. Dye, *Politics in States and Communities,* 3rd ed. (Englewood Cliffs, N.J.: Prentice-Hall, 1977), pp. 58-59.
[19]Claire Gilbert, "Community Power and Decision-Making: A Quantitative Examination of Previous Research," in Terry N. Clark, ed., *Community Structure and Decision-Making: Comparative Analyses* (San Francisco: Chandler, 1968), pp. 139-158.
[20]Frank X. Steggert, *Community Action Groups and City Government* (Cambridge, Mass.: Ballinger, 1975), pp. 1-2.
[21]Catherine Lovell and Charles Tobin, "The Mandate Issue," *Public Administration Review,* 41 (May/June, 1981), pp. 318-339.
[22]Bollens and Schmandt, *The Metropolis,* pp. 122-123.
[23]National Research Council, *Toward an Understanding of Metropolitan America,* pp. 81-82.
[24]Harold Kaplan cites the case of Newark, New Jersey, in which large areas of tenements were razed, only to result in a keen lack of interest by developers in replacing them with anything. In Newark, the operative planning maxim became, "Find a redeveloper first, and then see what interests him." See Kaplan's *Urban Renewal Politics* (New York: Columbia University Press, 1963), p. 24.
[25]For 768 urban renewal projects, estimated property values soared from $468 million to $1.7 billion. See Department of Housing and Urban Development, *HUD Statistical Yearbook* (Washington, D.C.: U.S. Government Printing Office, 1971), p. 55. Nevertheless, when one accounts for such factors as the likelihood of similar projects being initiated with or without urban renewal, tax losses suffered during the razing and construction period, and inflation, these figures take a considerable downturn. See Martin Anderson, *The Federal Bulldozer* (Cambridge, Mass.: M.I.T. Press, 1964). Overall, however, it appears that local tax bases generally benefit from urban renewal projects.
[26]John A. Weicher, *Urban Renewal: National Program for Local Problems* (Washington, D.C.: American Enterprise Institute, 1972), p. 6.
[27]Study conducted by the Renewal Assistance Administration, as cited in Advisory Commission on Intergovernmental Relations, *Metropolitan America* (Washington, D.C.: U.S. Government Printing Office, 1966), p. 69.
[28]Congressional study as cited in Robert L. Lineberry and Ira Sharkansky, *Urban Politics and Public Policy,* 3rd ed. (New York: Harper & Row, 1978), p. 381; and Felicity Barringer, "Relocation Law Faulted on Equitable Treatment," *Washington Post* (February 14, 1985).
[29]*Ibid.,* pp. 381-382; Chester Hartman, "The Housing of Relocated Families," *Journal of the American Institute of Planners,* 30 (November, 1964), pp. 266-286; and Weicher, *Urban Renewal,* p. 47.
[30]Marc Fried, "Grieving for a Lost Home," in Leonard J. Duhl, ed., *The Urban Condition* (New York: Basic Books, 1965), p. 151.
[31]Department of Housing and Urban Development, Office of Community Planning and Development, *Consolidated Annual Report to Congress on Community Development Programs, 1982* (Washington, D.C.: U.S. Government Printing Office, 1982), p. 60.
[32]John Rehfuss, "Citizen Participation in Urban Fiscal Decisions," *Municipal Year Book, 1979* (Washington, D.C.: International City Management Association, 1979), p. 87. Rehfuss surveyed all municipalities with more than 10,000 people and all counties with populations of 50,000 or more; he obtained responses from 1,817 governments, or a response rate of 57 percent.
[33]*Ibid.,* p. 89.
[34]Steve Redburn, Terry F. Buss, Steven K. Foster, and William C. Binning, "How Representative Are Mandated Citizen Participation Processes?" *Urban Affairs Quarterly,* 15 (March, 1980), p. 350.
[35]Unidentified "official in a Southern California city," as quoted in Rehfuss, "Citizen Participation in Urban Fiscal Decisions," p. 89.
[36]*Ibid.,* p. 91.
[37]*Ibid.,* p. 92.
[38]Betty A. Zisk, Heinz Eulau, and Kenneth Prewitt, "City Councilmen and the Group Struggle," *Journal of Politics,* 27 (August, 1965), p. 633.

[39]Dye, *Politics in States and Communities,* p. 300.
[40]Zisk, Eulau, and Prewitt, "City Councilmen and the Group Struggle," p. 635.
[41]Steggert, *Community Action Groups and City Government,* p. 6.
[42]*Ibid.,* pp. 7-8.
[43]*Ibid.,* pp. 4-8.
[44]*Ibid.,* pp. 7-8.
[45]Monsignor Geno Baroni, assistant secretary for the Office of Neighborhoods, Department of Housing and Urban Development, as quoted in John Herbers, "Neighborhood Activists Are Gaining Credence as Political Force," *The New York Times,* as reprinted in *The Arizona Republic* (August 12, 1979).
[46]Edward G. Goetz, "Beyond Pluralism: A Look at the Formal Linkages Between Urban Governments and Neighborhood Interests," paper presented at the 1984 Annual Meeting of the American Political Science Association, Washington, D.C., August 30-September 2, 1984, p. 19.
[47]Bureau of the Census, *1977 Census of Governments: Popularly Elected Officials* (Washington, D.C.: U.S. Government Printing Office, 1979), pp. 2-3. Figures are for 1977.
[48]Raymond Bancroft, *America's Mayors and Councilmen: Their Problems and Frustrations* (Washington, D.C.: National League of Cities, 1974), p. 29.
[49]W. E. Lyons and Malcolm E. Jewell, "Redrawing Council Districts in American Cities," paper presented at the 1985 American Political Science Association, August 19 - September 1, 1985, New Orleans, p. 6. Sixty-eight percent (117 cities) of the cities responded.
[50]*Ibid.,* pp. 4-6.
[51]Heywood T. Sanders, "The Government of American Cities: Continuity and Change in Structures," *Municipal Year Book, 1982* (Washington, D.C.: International City Management Association, 1982), pp. 182-183. Sanders surveyed all municipalities with more than 2,500 people (plus 385 villages with fewer than 2,500 residents) and obtained responses from 4,659, for a response rate of 69 percent. He eliminated from his analysis those responding municipalities with fewer than 2,500 people.
[52]Kenneth Prewitt, *The Recruitment of Political Leaders: A Study of Citizen-Politicians* (Indianapolis: Bobbs-Merrill, 1970), p. 148.
[53]Albert K. Karnig and B. Oliver Walter, "Municipal Elections: Registration, Incumbent Success, and Voter Participation," *Municipal Year Book, 1977* (Washington, D.C.: International City Management Association, 1977), p. 66.
[54]Prewitt, *Recruitment of Political Leaders,* p. 148.
[55]Allan Klevit, "City Councils and Their Function in Local Government," *Municipal Year Book, 1972* (Washington, D.C.: International City Management Association, 1972), pp. 15-19.
[56]*Ibid.*
[57]Figures are for 1982. See Bureau of the Census, *Statistical Abstract of the United States, 1985* (Washington, D.C.: U.S. Government Printing Office, 1984), p. 251, Table 420.
[58]As estimated from data presented in *ibid.,* p. 250, Table 418; and Bureau of the Census, *Popularly Elected Officials,* pp. 2-3. In 1984 there were 3,259 blacks holding elected city and county offices (including mayors, vice mayors, and regional officials). Data are not available on Hispanics.
[59]Klevit, "City Councils and Their Function," p. 19.
[60]Albert K. Karnig, "Black Representation on City Councils: The Impact of Reform and Socio-Economic Factors," *Urban Affairs Quarterly,* 12 (December, 1976), pp. 223-242.
[61]Heinz Eulau and Kenneth Prewitt, *Labyrinths of Democracy* (Indianapolis: Bobbs-Merrill, 1973), pp. 626-628.
[62]Betty H. Zisk, *Local Interest Politics: A One-Way Street* (Indianapolis: Bobbs-Merrill, 1973), p. 19.
[63]*Ibid.,* p. 58.

11

THE URBAN EXECUTIVES

mayors and managers

Urban politicians are among the more colorful in the country, and in this chapter we sample some of the more vivid varieties of local politics, as well as describing the political patterns and styles of the urban chief executive.

"HIZZONER DA MARE"

The typical American mayor is a white male in his forties or fifties and has served in office approximately four-and-a-half years.[1]

Only an infinitesimal proportion of mayors are black. Although there are more than a thousand American cities with more than 25,000 people, only about two dozen of them have black mayors.[2] In a majority of these cities, there are large black populations, although black mayors have been elected in cities with relatively small numbers of black residents. Only 6 percent of American mayors are women.[3]

Compared to governors, mayors are not well educated; not much more than a third have completed four or more years of college, although slightly more than half of all mayors have attended at least some college classes. Not quite a third like the job well enough that they intend to run for an additional term. Almost half (47 percent) come to the mayor's office from the business world, a ratio more than double that of governors, who predominantly are lawyers.

A few counties (146 in 20 states) elect county executives, who are the functional equivalents of mayors. As a group, elected county executives are very similar to mayors, although they tend to be more educated and somewhat less likely to be businesspersons. Elected county executives also have considerably greater decision-making authority than most mayors.[4]

The Mayoral Career

The best known, and often most glamorous, mayors are those who are mayors of the big cities. Do these mayors move up in electoral politics? Do they have a political future?

By and large, they do not. As Boston's James Michael Curley put it, "Being mayor is fun and exciting, but there's no future in it."[5] A study of 164 contemporary mayors of big cities found that less than 10 percent went on to higher elected offices.[6] Table 11-1 indicates these patterns.

Other investigations arrive at comparable conclusions. One study observed that only one big city mayor has ever been elected president (Grover Cleveland, who had been mayor of Buffalo) and few ever get to the governor's mansion.[7]

Nevertheless, two caveats are in order concerning just how "dead end" a job big-city mayors have. One is that few occupants of any high political office—governors, congressional representatives, and senators, as well as big-city mayors—later get elected to a higher office. In fact, a comparison of mayors with these other officeholders concluded that "the advancement rates [of big-city mayors] are neither significantly better nor worse than those of other major offices."[8]

The second caveat is more interesting and deals with the kinds of people who become big-city mayors: it may be that big-city mayors are people who have no aspirations for "higher" office, because the office of big-city mayor requires skills, personalities, and interests that differ radically from those of governors, congressional representatives, senators, and presidents. Some analysts have contended that these differences between mayors and other kinds of elected politicos boil down to simple mayoral stupidity: "The rewards of [the mayor's] office are so slight that no one of intelligence would want it"[9] and that therefore "men of inferior calibre are attracted to it."[10] But a less arch viewpoint holds that people attracted to high urban office are not "inferior," but they are different. This difference stems from the nature of the mayoral office itself, which, when compared to governors and other major elected positions, demands a highly personal political style, involves constituencies that possess an unusual intimacy with their elected chief executive, and electorates that feel the impact of mayorally sponsored public policies quickly and react accordingly. The mayor

Table 11-1 Subsequent Careers of Big-City Mayors, 1940–1976

	Number	*Percent of Total*
Higher office		
Elected	15	9.1
Appointed	13	7.9
Minor office	22	13.4
No office	114	69.5
Total	164	100.0

Source: Russell D. Murphy, "Whither the Mayors? A Note on Mayoral Careers," *The Journal of Politics,* 42 (February, 1980), p. 280.

> is expected to be more accessible personally, and such accessibility means that he is more likely to encounter single-issue, short-term activists. . . . As a group, these participants . . . are probably less amenable . . . to bargaining and compromise. . . . It may be . . . that distinct personality traits and political skills are attracted to the executive office at different levels of government, that mayors, more so than presidents or governors, must be equipped to deal more directly with street-level politics. If so, then even if one assumes that most mayors lack the qualities for presidential or gubernatorial leadership, most presidents and governors may in turn lack the stuff of which mayors are made. In brief, it is as difficult to envision Richard Nixon as mayor of Los Angeles . . . as it is to picture Richard Daley as President.[11]

Mayoral Campaigning: Portraits in Black and White

Mayoral political campaigns can be as seamy as they come. Two cases in point were the basically racist campaigns that occurred in Los Angeles in the late 1960s and early 1970s and the Chicago race for mayor in 1983.

"Mayor Sam" versus "Bradley Power." Mayor Sam Yorty, known to most Angelinos as "the Little Giant" and self-proclaimed as "America's Greatest Mayor," had served as mayor of Los Angeles since 1961. "Mayor Sam's" initial politics were ultraliberal, and he espoused a number of share-the-wealth plans that were popular in the 1930s. But, by 1939, his tune had changed substantially and, by the time he was mayor, a favorite device of his was to call everyone in sight a Communist. Municipal-level communism is a ridiculous charge on its face, and, when one probes deeper, it is still ridiculous. Nevertheless, it seemed to work for Mayor Sam, at least most of the time.

> Sam Yorty's favorite campaign issue has been anti-communism. . . . If an opponent is more liberal than he is, Yorty can credibly paint him as backed by radicals. If the opponent is more conservative, then Yorty responds that he is a victim of a communist smear attack.[12]

Yorty also established a reputation for launching personal attacks during a campaign, calling former Governor Pat Brown, first, "minor league" then a "machine" politician. Governor (later President) Ronald Reagan became an "amateur," and Senator George McGovern was "anti-American" and he "spoke like Hanoi."[13]

These kinds of campaign tactics reached full flower in the mayoral campaigns of 1969 and 1973 in Los Angeles, when Tom Bradley, a black, ran for mayor. Bradley had served as an officer in the Los Angeles Police Department for 21 years before he ran for mayor. By studying at night he received a law degree from Southwestern University, and, in 1963, with Yorty's endorsement, Bradley ran for the Los Angeles City Council and won easily in his largely black district. He and two others were the first black men in Los Angeles's history to be elected to serve on that city's council.

In 1969, Yorty ran an insipid campaign for mayor and, much to everyone's surprise, Bradley garnered nearly 42 percent of the vote (Yorty received 26 percent, the other votes were divided among some minor contenders). A runoff election was required, and Yorty, seeing these results, stiffened his resolve and his organization for the second try. Bradley was and is a moderate who had stated, "I believe the way that you change the system is from the inside.

Separatism won't work."[14] Nevertheless, Yorty launched a consciously racist campaign, stating that Bradley was backed by "extremist militants." Ludicrously, but effectively, Yorty charged that Bradley, despite his 21 years on the L.A. police force, was "antipolice" because he favored citizen review of police actions. In spite of the fact that Yorty was a Democrat, he based most of his campaign organization on talented campaign managers furnished by conservative Republican Ronald Reagan, then governor of California. Bumper stickers mysteriously appeared during the campaign printed with the upraised black fist, and proclaiming "Bradley power"; pamphlets were distributed in largely white neighborhoods urging voters to make Los Angeles "a black city."[15] Bradley evidently had no connection with any of these distributions, and Yorty took no public credit for them. Yorty did take credit, however, for putting up posters inquiring, "Will your family be safe?" and "Will your city be safe with this man?" "Sam wanted to make sure that whites were universally aware of Bradley's blackness."[16]

Yorty won—in part because of his smear tactics, but also because of a seasoned and tough campaign organization. Also Bradley unwisely dwelt on such issues as corruption in city hall and environmental pollution, when the "real" issues in Los Angeles that year were, according to the polls, street crime and school-related issues such as busing. And one must recall that the late 1960s was a period of racial disturbances across the country. This fact could not have been lost on the white voters of Los Angeles, who were being exhorted by Yorty troops not to vote for an "extremist group that put up a black man for the purpose of polarizing the community."[17] Still, Bradley did all right, winning nearly 47 percent of the vote to Yorty's 53 percent.

In 1973, Bradley tried for the mayor's office again, but Bradley had spent the four intervening years softening up the L.A. voters, emphasizing his moderate racial position and his experience in fighting crime. While he still spoke about smog and mass transit, crime and his law-and-order position became a major theme. Yorty resurrected his smear tactics, but this time Bradley was both better organized and better financed, with money coming in from national contributors. Bradley trounced Yorty in 1973 with 56 percent of the vote. Most estimates agree that he won almost one-half of the white vote and virtually all of the black vote in the city.

Bradley established himself as a competent and low-key chief executive. In 1974 he was elected president of the National League of Cities, was easily reelected as mayor in subsequent elections, and in 1982 ran for governor of California; he was narrowly defeated by a conservative Republican who was closely identified with President Ronald Reagan.

By 1985, the politics of race had radically abated in Los Angeles. Not only was there a marked disinterest in the election (only about 35 percent of Los Angeles's nearly 1.4 million voters, the lowest turnout in years, cast votes in 1985), but Bradley defeated his opposition handily, outdistancing his Republican contender by 68 percent of the vote to 30 percent.[18]

"It's our turn now" or "Before it's too late"? But if the racial question seems to have diminished in Los Angeles, the nation's most racially diverse city, such is not the case in Chicago.

Nineteen eighty-three was an unusual year in Chicago's already unusual politics. Three major politicians wanted the job of mayor: the incumbent, Jane

Byrne; Richard M. Daley, the state's attorney general for Cook County and son of the late Richard J. Daley, who had ruled Chicago for more than two decades; and Harold Washington, a black congressman. To become mayor, the successful candidate had to win the city's Democratic primary; no Republican had ever won any of the 16 mayoral elections held since 1931.

Byrne and Daley split the white vote in Chicago's Democratic primary, and Washington narrowly won his party's nomination for mayor. Shortly after his win, Washington proclaimed before a black rally, "It's our turn now!" thus sending a discomfiting message to the white voters in the city.[19] Washington attempted to ameliorate the impact of his candidacy by stressing a citywide program that would enable "all Chicago to move forward," but white Chicagoans by this time were not listening, if, indeed, they ever were.[20]

Washington committed a second gaffe that also eroded his support, but in this instance, it was less the support of whites as such, and more the support of Chicago's Democratic machine, one of the very last party organizations that remains effective in urban politics. Washington told reporters that there would be "no deals made" between him and party committeemen, and further stated that Chicago's deep running patronage system had "to end. . . . It's costly. It's wasteful. It's a shutout mechanism that keeps people out of government rather than bringing them in."[21]

The upshot of these remarks and the attendant fears engendered among white Chicagoans concerning issues of race and the Democratic machine was that the Republican Party got a significant boost. The Republicans' nominee for mayor in 1983 was Bernard Epton, a wealthy businessman from Chicago's Lakeshore district and former state senator, who, like his 16 Republican predecessors since 1931, had entered the race with no real hope of winning. Suddenly, there was hope. Volunteers overflowed Epton's campaign offices. Buttons and banners appeared with such slogans as "Democrats for Epton," "Polish for Epton-ski," and "Italians for Epton-ini." "The reaction was the same wherever Epton appeared: Polish, Italian, Lithuanian, Greek, and Irish audiences received him warmly, rhythmically chanting, 'Ber-nie, Ber-nie.' It was a spontaneous uprising at the grass roots, a ground swell unlike anything I've seen . . . in thirty years in politics," his deputy campaign manager observed.[22]

The Democratic committeemen—the backbone of Chicago's Democratic Party and Chicago's government—soon began deserting their party's nominee for mayor. The first was Alderman Aloysius Majerczyk of Chicago's twelfth ward, who, in announcing his support for the Republican nominee, stated that his constituents were "giving me a message of racial pride. . . . We're against open housing in my ward and they always have been."[23] Ultimately, only 6 of the 35 white Democratic committeemen supported Washington, 8 opposed him openly, and most of the others were aiding Epton's campaign covertly.[24]

The open opposition of the Democratic Party committeemen was largely the result of their concern for their personal futures. Epton posed essentially no threat to their control of city government because there were no Republicans and only a handful of independents in the city council. Hence, Epton would never be able to build a coalition, or even to control the council's override of his vetoes; the ward barons would still run the city. On the other hand, Washington was a far more serious threat to their control because he had a strong base of support in the black community (which comprised 40 percent of Chicago's population) and, thus, would have solid support in the city council—if not, perhaps, the majority. But in any event, Washington clearly could disrupt the Democratic machine and thus restrain the power of the committeemen.

Epton chose to capitalize on Washington's weaknesses by, like Yorty in Los Angeles, conducting a barely hidden racist campaign. His campaign theme became "Epton, before it's too late," and his supporters sang songs with such lyrics as "your record, Bernie, shows you're tough/and as for us, we've been pushed enough" to the tune of "Bye-Bye Blackbird."[25] As a campaign strategy, unfortunately, such an approach was about the only one that Epton could use if he wished to win. "While Epton expressly disavowed racial appeals and racist support, the only electoral strategy opened to him involved mobilizing white voters, which gave its campaign the aura of a white movement from its outset."[26]

Epton and his supporters were able to veil thinly the more racist aspects of the campaign by focusing on Washington's character. Washington had been sent to jail in 1972 for failing to file income tax returns, and his law license had been suspended for not delivering legal services for which clients had paid. There were other examples of unpaid bills brought up by the Republicans, plus the fact that Washington was a part owner in a slum building in the black community whose tenants had been evicted by the city due to its unsafe conditions.[27] Epton and his supporters made full and lurid exposures of these incidents in Washington's past a major part of their campaign.

The Republicans' tactics eventually assured their loss of control of their own campaign. Epton's white ethnic supporters grew increasingly racist. As one of his campaign managers noted, "the campaign was out of control," and as the candidate's daughter explained after the election, it "was mass hysteria. . . . we tried to ignore it because we couldn't do anything about it. Nobody could."[28]

Nevertheless, these tactics were bringing success. Washington's citywide lead shortly after winning the Democratic primary had placed him 28 points ahead of Epton, but soon the distance between the two candidates was diminishing almost daily, and some polls toward the end of the campaign showed Washington losing to Epton.[29]

But as the campaign grew more racist on the part of whites, blacks began coalescing as never before. This, of course, greatly assisted Washington, who knew that he needed unprecedented support in the black community, and no less than 15 percent of the city's white vote, to win. So Washington courted Chicago's black vote as it had never been courted before, and black voters had never been more responsive. Consider the following description of the candidate speaking before an all-black audience from Chicago's Robert Taylor Homes, one of the country's grimmer public housing projects:

> "We've talked to everybody in this great big city," Washington began, "and some of them are not going to vote for us." Washington paused. "You know why," he added quietly.
>
> There was silence. The thought carried itself over the crowd in the approaching darkness. . . .
>
> "We tried to reach out to them," Washington said sadly, "but we failed. So we're just gonna have to do the job ourselves. . . ."
>
> Then something happened. . . . As Washington continued speaking, his inflections lost their cultured edges. He began talking in the language of the black people standing there before him, to show them how truly he was one of them.

"If you don't vote," he said, "I don't make it. Momma, don't let anybody stay home on Tuesday.

"If that man don't vote, don't let him put his foot under that table. And you young people . . . you know Momma's tired. But remind her, too. . . . Do it firmly, but gently. Get out there and vote."[30]

Ultimately, Washington won, but by the narrowest margin since Chicago's mayoral race of 1919. Washington polled less than 52 percent of the votes cast to Epton's 48 percent. Washington won more than 9 out of 10 black votes, nearly 3 out of 4 Hispanic votes, and less than 2 out of 10 white votes.

Never had Chicagoans displayed a greater civic consciousness in an election. During the Democratic primary, blacks and whites had turned out to vote at a rate of about 65 percent each. But in the general election, black turnout reached more than 73 percent, or almost 6 percentage points higher than white turnout rates. In the past, black turnout in Chicago trailed that of whites, typically by about 15 percentage points.[31]

Mayors and race. What are the implications of Bradley's experiences in Los Angeles and Washington's experiences in Chicago for the future of black mayoral candidates? An interesting comparison has been made between Philadelphia and Chicago in this regard. One month after Chicago's general election in 1983, Philadelphia held its Democratic primary for mayor and the city's black managing director, W. Wilson Goode, trounced Philadelphia's white former mayor, Frank Rizzo.

The Philadelphia election contained little of the raw drama that Chicago had shown the nation. Indeed, its tone was markedly civil. But beyond that, there were some notable similarities. Quite aside from the fact that a black beat a white in the Democratic primary in a predominately Democratic city, both Chicago and Philadelphia have voting-age populations that are approximately 40 percent black; neither Washington nor Goode had been elected to an executive office in the past, and both were running against whites who had held significant positions as elected chief executives; finally, both elections were highly partisan.

In an analysis of the Philadelphia and Chicago elections, it was found that more than 9 out of 10 blacks supported the black candidates in both cities, while only about 2 out of 10 whites voted for the black candidate. After controlling for such variables as party, liberal and conservative attitudes, youth, and income, it was nonetheless found that race was "the pivotal variable" and explained more than 70 percent of the vote in both the Chicago and Philadelphia experiences.[32] "The tone and character of the Chicago and Philadelphia elections differed greatly, but the impact of race and the patterns of white voting in both places were strikingly similar."[33] In urban politics, it appears that race counts.

Money and the mayoral campaign. It also appears that, increasingly, money counts as well in mayoral races. Chicago's 1983 mayoral campaign, for example, was the most costly municipal campaign in the nation's history. Some $18 million were expended by both sides, or about $10 per voter.[34] In the 1985 campaign in Los Angeles, nearly $4 million were spent in an election that was considerably less competitive.[35] Even in such towns as Fresno, California, the winner of the mayoral race spent more than $300,000 in 1985.[36] As one observer put it, "from its start in Big City, U.S.A., highpowered campaigning—the mother's milk of a growing army of pollsters, media consultants, and direct mail specialists—is seeping into mayoral and city council races in smaller towns."[37]

An analysis of the 1985 mayoral election in Los Angeles[38] found that 42 percent of the contributors to the mayor's race were doing business with the city or were seeking city permits for themselves or their clients; 25 percent were in real estate; 14 percent were in the financial industry (which sells municipal bonds, among other services provided to cities for handsome fees); and 13 percent were from political action committees (in other words, the financial arms of special interests). Only a fraction of 1 percent of the contributions were under $100, implying that small donations by individual citizens are not funding races for mayor: special interests are.

Very little is known about contributions to local candidates on a systemic scale; 17 states do not require even the most minimal reporting of contributions to these races, and only 1 city, Seattle, has placed caps on contributions and limited spending in mayoral campaigns. Seattle, in fact, contributes matching funds for campaign gifts to candidates of up to fifty dollars.[39] But the sole city of Seattle is the exception that proves the rule; local campaigning is becoming an expensive proposition.

A Mayoral Typology: Brokers, Entrepreneurs, Reformers, and Managers

Regardless of how they get there, once in office mayors find themselves facing a Gordian's knot of urban ills. To begin unraveling the municipal tangles confronting them, mayors have had to change with their society. One researcher has argued, for example, that a more complex metropolitan society has resulted in mayors who are increasingly "managerial" in their political styles. This notion identifies four "types" of big-city mayors. One is the *broker,* which refers to mayors who use the more traditional political methods in establishing their political bases, such as ethnic groups, parties, political machines, and personal relationships. They maintain a low public profile, accommodate existing power relationships in that they consciously decline to redistribute resources and political values within their cities, and rely principally on patronage and logrolling to obtain their goals.

Another type is the *entrepreneur,* who seeks high visibility, maintains an active stance regarding his or her responsibility for municipal problem solving, and employs managerial and bureaucratic methods to achieve his or her goals. However, entrepreneurs resemble brokers in that they are very conservative in their policy orientation and decline to redistribute resources and political values within the system.

The *social reformer* mayor resembles the entrepreneur in that such mayors seek higher visibility of their leadership role, assume an active political stance toward local problem solving, and use managerial and impersonal techniques to obtain policy objectives. However, unlike any of the other three types, social reformers want to redress past neglects and open up political opportunities for new groups that have been neglected in the past. In this sense, they adopt a redistributive policy orientation.

Finally, *managers* constitute a type of mayoral style that, in many ways, resembles the most traditional mayoral type of all, that of the broker. Their leadership role has a low public visibility, their problem-solving stance is highly passive, and their policy orientation is quite conservative, concentrating on the provision of basic municipal services. They differ from the broker, however, in that their methods of achieving political and administrative ends, like the methods of the social reformers and the entrepreneurs, are impersonal and bureaucratic.[40]

Informed observers suggest that the managerial style is the prescription of the future and that brokers are slowly wending the way of the dinosaur. Both entrepreneurs and social reformers, if they stay in office for any length of time, eventually transform their political styles into that of a manager, or are quickly replaced by the management minded—or what some have called the "New Fiscal Populists," or mayors who are socially liberal and fiscally conservative and who favor the individual citizen over the organized interest groups as a legitimate source of influence on urban policy formation.[41]

Mayoral Style: "King Richard" and "the White Knight"

To gain a flavor of what these mayoral types mean in a living political context, let us consider two examples. Since it is difficult to find any one "pure" mayoral type in the real world, we shall focus on two mayors whose leadership styles combine elements of two closely related types. One is the late Richard Daley of Chicago, whose style represents elements of the broker and entrepreneurial types, and the other is John Lindsay of New York, who moved from a clear social reformer mode to a managerial one.

"King Richard": The mayor as entrepreneurial broker. As we noted in Chapter 8, the late Mayor Richard Daley of Chicago assumed "power" under a weak executive form of government. Yet, from 1953, when he was elected chair of the Cook County Democratic Party (he was not elected mayor of Chicago until 1955) until his death in 1976, no one questioned his absolute authority in Chicago.[42] Many have said that Daley was a "throwback," and, indeed, he paralleled remarkably the characteristics of the turn-of-the-century big-city bosses. He was born of first-generation Irish parents, was a Roman Catholic, went to work in the stockyards, and only 20 years later took over the Chicago City Council.

"King Richard," as he was called in Chicago, often played political kingmaker. In 1960, Daley scrounged enough votes from his machine-dominated "river wards" to deliver Illinois and the presidency to John Kennedy. In the mid-1960s, the Reverend Martin Luther King, Jr., called Chicago "the most segregated city in the North" and roused the Boss's ire. When King was murdered, and riots by blacks erupted in Chicago as a result, Daley ordered police to kill arsonists and to shoot "to maim or cripple" looters. As one black noted about Richard Daley, "I think that one of the real problems he has with Negroes is understanding that the Irish are no longer the out-ethnic group," and this assessment certainly seemed to apply on occasion.[43] During the infamous 1968 National Convention of the Democratic Party held in Chicago, Daley, fighting both liberal Democrats and "Yippies" in his home city, stood up in the convention hall, shook his fist at Connecticut Senator Abraham Ribicoff, and ordered all power cut off to the delegates' microphones. He then turned his police on the antiwar demonstrators in the streets and staged what appeared to be one of the least spontaneous political demonstrations in American political history—which was, of course, pro-Daley, with neatly printed placards stating "I Love Mayor Daley" being carried around the convention hall by members of his organization.

Daley also had some endearing qualities, the most notable being his almost uncanny ability to mangle the English language. For example, "We will reach greater and greater platitudes of achievement"; or "They have vilified me, they have crucified me, yes, they have even criticized me!" or "The policeman is here to preserve disorder"; or "I resent these insinuendos." The press loved it.[44]

Was Daley "good" or "bad" for Chicago? That question perhaps will never be answered. He does not seem to have been personally corrupt, and lived modestly in the neighborhood where he grew up. Although many of his close aides were convicted of corruption, Daley never was. When pressed by reporters on such improprieties, Daley replied that his mother once told him that, in such situations, he should "pin the mistletoe on my coattails."[45]

Some have argued that Daley was successful where social reformers may have failed, that he made Chicago "work." And no doubt Daley had a hand, and a creative one, in his extensive urban renewal of Chicago, which resulted in some of the most magnificent architecture in the country today. Although Chicago unlike New York was in relatively sound fiscal shape, Chicago in fact paid no welfare bills, supported no schools, and paid only a small portion of the cost of its own mass transit system; the Transit Authority and the Board of Education of Chicago, both controlled by the Daley machine, were always under severe fiscal restraints.

King Richard was a pragmatist who understood power and humanity's corruptibility. He was unique as a mayor, boss, and party chair. His 50-member city council, which occasionally had a political spread of 49 Democrats and 1 Republican, was "frequently described as a trained dog act," and Daley was not above turning off an alderman's microphone when he disagreed with his statement during city council meetings. "In sharing the power that fueled his political organization, he resembled a shark with a chunk of meat."[46] But even Daley recognized that the day of the big-city boss was gone or going fast.

In retrospect, Daley combined elements of both the broker and entrepreneur styles of mayoral leadership. Although he preferred to maintain a low political profile, the press often succeeded in raising it despite Daley's best intentions. He assumed an active stance in terms of his willingness to assume responsibility for problem solving in Chicago, but also was extremely conservative in his political beliefs. Not only did he accommodate the existing power patterns of Chicago, but, in a true entrepreneurial fashion, he developed a close working relationship with the business elite in the community. Unlike an entrepreneurial mayor, however, "King Richard" was solidly a broker in his political and administrative methods. The Daley machine, above all, was a highly personal one that relied on patronage, reciprocity, and logrolling.

"The White Knight": The mayor as reformist manager. Representing quite the opposite of Boss Daley in virtually every conceivable way was Mayor John V. Lindsay of New York.[47] While Daley was a Democrat and a machine politician who was less than elegant in his appearance and manner, Lindsay was a Republican, a reformer, a manager, and, above all, a sophisticate. As a resident of

Chicago who was a transplanted New Yorker once observed, "We think of reform as being an effete Easterner idea."[48]

During his first administration, John Lindsay as mayor was a reformer to his very soles. The son of a wealthy lawyer, an Episcopalian educated at Yale, he was pure WASP. He grew up as a great admirer of Mayor Fiorello LaGuardia, one of New York's most vigorous reform mayors.

Between 1958 and 1966, Lindsay was a congressman from Manhattan's "silk stocking" district, and in his last congressional race in 1964, he received an incredible 71 percent of the vote, despite the presence of Barry Goldwater on the ballot as the national candidate for president, against whom his district voted. As a Republican reform mayor in a city, where at the time of his election, registered Democrats outnumbered Republicans 2,400,000 to 700,000, he was known as "Pretty Boy," "The White Knight," "Destiny's Tot," or "Mr. Clean"—perhaps fitting appellations for one who called New York "Fun City."

Fun City was never that much fun. As Lindsay testified in 1966 before a congressional subcommittee, 2 million white residents, mostly in middle- and high-income groups, had moved away from New York during the 20 years prior to his administration. And 750,000 blacks and Puerto Ricans, who for the most part were very poor people, had moved in, expanding their ratios in the city's population from 10 percent in 1945 to 25 percent two decades later. Almost 15 percent of the entire city budget was devoted to welfare alone; 2 million people in New York were living below the poverty line when Lindsay became mayor.

Lindsay's outstanding characteristics as mayor were his style and his desire to get out in the streets and mingle with the people, particularly poor people. As a leader of a black organization called the Harlem Mau-Maus stated, "Lindsay helps. He'll leave Gracie Mansion on five minutes' notice and he'll talk to the bottom of the barrel."

In contrast to Boss Daley of Chicago, Lindsay argued that "We are not going to shoot children in New York City," but also was aware that "New York or Chicago or any other big city could ignite tomorrow. There are incidents that could act as a trigger every day. If New York blows first, the press will charge that my 'soft' policies failed. If it happens in Chicago first, they'll write Daley's 'hard line' tactics were at fault. In either case, it will be an over-simplification and unfair."

Integral to Lindsay's reformist drives was his belief in "modern management." Lindsay would complain bitterly about the managerial problems that he had inherited from "thirty years of simple indifference to the *ad hoc,* unplanned growth of municipal bureaucracy,"[49] and would point to the lack of coordination and planning in city government, referring to it as "all Scotch-taped together."[50] Given his belief in management as the primary means to political ends, Lindsay did accomplish quite a bit in reforming city government. He reduced 51 municipal departments to 10. He broke up what was known as the "Irish Mafia" that had long ruled police precinct houses, and he substantially increased the size of the police force. He enacted the nation's strongest air pollution law up to that time, closed Central Park to Sunday traffic, and initiated tough towing programs for illegally parked vehicles. He established "Little City Halls" in various neighborhoods (a program that got him into some trouble with his own city council, since it was seen as a ploy to establish his own personal political organization). He introduced new budgeting procedures for the city, designed to improve efficiency, and he simultaneously pushed for more sophisticated information management in New York's government.

Lindsay, in short, combined both the managerial and social reformer styles of mayoral leadership. The high visibility of his leadership as mayor of the nation's largest city, his active posture in grasping responsibility for the moral leadership of the community, and his redistributive policy orientation, all mark him as a social reformer. On the other hand, his high commitment to the techniques of modern management also place him in the manager camp. Indeed, toward the end of his mayoral career, his overall style began to change to a more managerial mode as his political profile became distinctly lower than in his earlier years.

ON THE PLEASURES OF BEING MAYOR

Yes, mayors of big cities do have tough jobs. Crime, recession, dilapidation, poverty, racism, and more are policy problems that eventually wind up, in some form, on the mayors' desks. But the office also has rewards. Consider the following example, drawn from the life of Jimmy "Beau James" Walker, who was the elegant mayor of New York during the depression-wracked 1930s. As it indicates, all mayors have style, but few mayors have style like New York mayors.

Queen Marie of Romania was the first "crowned head" greeted by Walker. Whether or not Her Majesty was charmed by Walker's speech of welcome or by two incidents which happened more or less off the record, the still beautiful queen did not say. One of these occurred while Jim was attempting to pin a medal upon her coat. The lady from the Balkans owned a splendid, although somewhat buxom figure, and the place where the medal properly belonged—high up, and a bit to the left—suggested, among other things, a delicate target for a carelessly directed pin.

"Your Majesty," Jim said, "I've never stuck a queen, and I hesitate to do so now."

"Proceed, Your Honor," replied the Queen. "The risk is mine."

"And such a beautiful risk it is, Your Majesty," Jim said in a low voice.

The Queen and her royal party left New York for Washington at the conclusion of the City Hall ceremonies. Although it was a raw October day, Marie was seated in an open-top automobile so that citizens along the way from City Hall to Pennsylvania Station might look upon a reigning monarch.

Jim sat at Her Majesty's left in the touring car. As the royal automobile was passing a newly begun skyscraper on Seventh Avenue, her lap robe slipped from her knees. Walker leaned over to adjust the robe. At this one of the riveters perched on a girder of the partly completed steel framework of the building cupped his hands and called out, "Hey, Jimmy! Have you made her yet?"

Just how much slang Queen Marie understood I am not prepared to say. She turned an inquiring glance upon her host and said sweetly, "You Americans are quite droll, don't you think?"

"When you travel across our great country," Jim hedged, "you will come upon many interesting evidences of our democracy."

"Everyone seems to know you in this great city," she observed.

"Yes, Madam," Walker replied, "and some of them know me very well indeed."

Source: From *Beau James: The Life and Times of Jimmy Walker* by Gene Fowler.

The Mayor and the Politics of Proscribed Power

Both Richard Daley and John Lindsay were exceptional mayors. But they were exceptional for more reasons than simply their distinctive styles and dramatic impact on the national political scene. Unlike the bulk of American mayors, "King Richard" and the "White Knight" had genuine authority in their municipal governments. In contrast to the mayors of the very largest cities (and even among these, there are notable exceptions), most mayors are sharply proscribed in the powers they may exercise in forming urban policy.

Significant numbers of American mayors are not elected in their own right as mayors (and thus have no constituents that they can call their own), have brief terms of office, and may exercise few formal powers of office (and often have no duties beyond ceremonial ones), such as the power to veto actions taken by the council or the power to appoint important municipal officials. Let us consider some of these limitations in turn.

The mayor as a not-quite-elected executive. Perhaps most significantly, the mayors in more than a fifth of American cities are not elected directly by the voters of their own municipalities, but instead are selected by their city councils. In these cities, the mayors are elected at large by the people, but only as a member of the city council. In those cities with a council-manager form of government (or about 35 percent of American cities with more than 2,500 people), this figure doubles to 40 percent; in other words, in council-manager municipalities, two-fifths of the mayors are selected by the council from among its members. Obviously, this form of selection does not endow mayors with a political base that they can call their own. In reality, they are simply chairs of their city councils. By contrast, 96 percent of the mayors in mayor-council cities run publicly for the mayor's office and are elected directly by all the city's voters.[51]

Short tenures. Once elected to office, by whatever means, mayors tend to have shorter terms of office than their counterparts at the state and national levels. One survey of all communities with more than 2,500 people found that 41 percent of all cities limited their mayors' terms to two years and another 11 percent to only one year. Forty-five percent of all cities permit their mayors four-year terms, and fewer than 3 percent give them three-year terms. The shorter terms are favored by smaller cities in the West and on the East Coast, and by cities having a council-manager form of government.[52]

The very limited veto. Besides relatively short terms of office, most mayors have relatively few legal powers that they can exercise. A study of cities with 2,500 people or more found that only 35 percent of all municipalities permitted their mayors to veto, in even a limited way, measures passed by their councils; and in only 47 percent of *these* cities (or less than 17 percent of all municipalities) could the mayors veto all actions passed by their city councils. Small cities constrain their mayors' veto powers more than larger ones (although only 21 percent of cities with more than 500,000 people allow their mayors to veto all actions of the council) and council-manager cities more than mayor-council cities; only 13 percent of council-manager cities permit their mayors to veto anything, compared to 59 percent of mayor-council cities.[53]

The very limited vote. The power to veto is central to the authority of any political chief executive, and America's urban governments clearly have taken great pains to erect barriers against this basic executive power. But even more remarkable is the fact that, in a number of American cities, the mayor, even though he or she may be elected as a member of the city council, does not even have the right to vote as a member of the city council! Almost 55 percent of cities with more than 25,000 people permit their mayors to vote on all issues before the city council. Beyond this overall datum, however, the voting rights of mayors in mayor-council cities differ radically from those of mayors in council-manager cities. In mayor-council cities, the mayor is generally elected by the entire municipality as mayor, and does not serve as a member of the city council. Therefore, it follows that in fewer than 10 percent of these cities may the mayor vote on all issues before the council, since almost all of these mayors hold some sort of veto authority. By contrast, mayors of council-manager cities frequently are simply the council member receiving the greatest number of votes in the at-large election, or are selected by the council members themselves, and serve as chairs of the councils. The mayors in almost 90 percent of these cities may vote on all issues confronting the council.[54]

The proscribed power of appointment. The mayors of mayor-council cities tend to have relatively more authority than their counterparts in council-manager governments. Other data confirm this. Almost 46 percent of the mayors in mayor-council cities have substantial appointment authority; that is, they may personally appoint persons of their choosing to no fewer than four major municipal positions—police chief, fire chief, city attorney, and chief personnel officer. Often they may appoint additional municipal officials as well. In only 13 percent of all mayor-council governments are mayors denied the power to appoint any of these major officials.[55]

Mayor-council versus council-manager government: The crucial question of governmental form. Table 11-2 indicates the kinds of cities in which mayors of mayor-council municipalities have the least and most authority. The table is a summary of the mayors' powers to veto and the extent of their appointment authority. Thus, at the highest end of the scale, we find that almost 19 percent of the mayors in mayor-council cities have the ability to veto all acts passed by the city council and to appoint no fewer than four major administrative officers. At the lowest end of the scale, at least some of the mayors have limited powers of veto or appointment. Although regional data are not shown on the table, mayor-council cities on the West Coast and with more than 500,000 people tend to grant their mayors the least amount of authority, while cities located in the Rocky Mountain states and that have between 250,000 and 500,000 people tend to grant their mayors the most authority.

Even though mayors in mayor-council cities with more than 25,000 people are notably circumscribed in their authority, mayors in council-manager municipalities are even more severely constrained. Only 10 percent of these mayors have any veto power at all, and this power includes the authority to veto all acts passed by the council in only about a fourth of these municipalities. The mayors are almost always part time, with only 4 percent of the mayors in council-manager communities having a full-time mayoral job. Mayors of council-manager cities have virtually no powers of appointment, beyond the largely honorific

Table 11-2 Mayoral Power in Mayor-Council Municipalities

		POWER OF MAYOR[1]													
	TOTAL NO. OF CITIES	2		3		4		5		6		7		8	
Classification	*REPORTING*	*No.*	*% of Total*[2]	*No.*	*% of Total*[2]	*No.*	*% of Total*[2]	*No.*	*% of Total*[2]	*No.*	*% of Total*[2]	*No.*	*% of Total*[2]	*No.*	*% of Total*[2]
Total, all cities	123	6	4.9%	6	4.9%	28	22.8%	12	9.8%	39	31.7%	9	7.3%	23	18.7%
500,000 and over	7	1	14.3	0	0.0	3	42.9	2	28.6	0	0.0	0	0.0	1	14.3
100,000–249,999	18	0	0.0	1	5.6	2	11.1	2	11.1	9	50.0	1	5.6	3	16.7
25,000–49,999	58	3	5.2	1	1.7	14	24.1	5	8.6	17	29.3	4	6.9	14	24.1
Appointed chief Administrative officer															
Cities	30	3	10.0	5	16.7	6	20.0	4	13.3	8	26.7	1	3.3	3	10.0
Cities without	91	3	3.3	0	0.0	22	24.2	8	8.8	30	33.0	8	8.8	20	22.0
Unknown	2	—[3]	—[3]	—[3]	—[3]	—[3]	—[3]	—[3]	—[3]	—[3]	—[3]	—[3]	—[3]	—[3]	—[3]

[1] This index of mayoral power is the sum of veto power (yes = 1, no = 0), the ability to veto all acts (yes = 2, no = 0) and the mayor's appointment authority (on a scale of 0 to 4). The index ranges from 0 to 8, the higher the number, the greater the power. The index shown in the table begins with 2 as no municipalities were classified lower on the index.

[2] Percentages may not total 100% because of rounding.

[3] Dashes indicate data not applicable or not reported

Source: Adapted from Heywood T. Sanders, "Governmental Structure in American Cities," *Municipal Yearbook, 1979* (Washington D.C.: International City Management Association, 1979), p. 10.

authority to appoint members of certain citizen advisory boards and commissions, since this capacity resides with the council and the city manager in council-manager governments.[56]

In short, mayors have the most circumscribed powers of all elected political chief executives—that is, governors and the president—in the nation.

Although mayors of mayor-council cities exercise greater authority than their counterparts in council-manager cities, their power in both forms is limited. The normal authorities that one expects to find in the province of the political executive—the powers of the veto, appointment, and even a distinctive and recognized constituency—are rarely present among America's mayors.

If mayors in most cities have such diluted strength, then who, or what, provides executive capacities among local governments? Increasingly, it is the urban bureaucrats.

THE POLITICS OF SMOOTH: THE URBAN MANAGER

Because city managers, or chief administrative officers, in cities and towns are appointed rather than elected, they have a relatively unusual way of achieving policy goals. City management is a quiet profession in a chaotic urban world, and only comparatively recently have political scientists begun to appreciate the policy impact that the city manager has. Indeed, it has been argued that city managers and their bureaucracies are the real policymakers in urban areas, and the magnitude of the manager's purview is impressive, with more than a third of all American cities, including some of the nation's largest, using the council-manager plan exclusively. In addition, slightly more than 30 percent of mayor-council cities have employed a chief administrative officer. Chief administrative officers differ from city managers in that they report to the mayor rather than to the city council. Nevertheless, the growing popularity of chief administrative officers among mayor-council municipalities indicates the increasing dependency of mayor-council cities on the concept of professional management.[57]

Who Are the Managers?

The typical local public manager is an unusually well-educated (most have a graduate degree) white male in his early forties who perceives himself to be a dedicated professional working in the public service. Approximately 3 percent of local public managers are minorities, more than half of whom are Hispanics; the remainder are blacks, native Americans, or Asian-Americans. Despite these fractional proportions, it appears that the numbers of minority local managers are growing. In 1971, there were virtually no minority managers in local government. About 5 percent of local public managers are women, and this figure also represents gains for this group. In 1974, barely 1 percent were women.[58]

Local public managers are also more conservative and politically independent than is the population at large. Only 28 percent of local managers identify themselves as Democrats (compared to 40 percent of all Americans), 26 percent say they are Republicans (compared to 24 percent of the populace), and 46 percent state they are Independent or have no political affiliation (compared to 37 percent of the population).[59]

A Professionalization of Politics?

During the 1960s, the role of the professional city manager came under fire. When cities exploded in race riots, the thrust of the criticism was that the profession of city management was overly technical, and, in its intellectual thrust, it had defined out vital political variables. "Technocrats," as exemplified by city managers, had little sensitivity to the human problems of cities and little understanding of the plight of minority groups, unlike such mayors as John Lindsay of New York. The National Advisory Commission on Civil Disorders stated in the late 1960s that "city manager government has eliminated an important political link between city government and low-income residents."[60] The argument continued that city managers were more likely than a lifelong "pol" to have a technocratic "engineering mentality" and that, if true, this mental set could exacerbate political tensions in cities.

This line of thinking assumes that administrators do only "administration" and politicians do only "politics." Such an assumption is rarely accurate. The field of public administration long ago recognized that it is difficult if not impossible to distinguish what is administration and what is politics. It accepts as legitimate the concept that public administrators do political things and make political decisions.

Empirical investigation seems to indicate that although city managers are certainly involved in both politics and administration, their political style is very different from that of an elected chief executive. A study of Florida city managers found that in cities where politics maintained a relatively low profile and low levels of conflict, city managers lasted longer in their jobs; where political conflict was high and factions were obvious, city managers lasted less long. A major reason for this was that members of city councils tended to use city managers as their scapegoats when their own policies proved to be unpopular.[61]

The primary reason that managers are fired, in fact, deal with their relationships with the city council; only 6 percent leave their position by choice, even though 57 percent of all local public managers have considered leaving their jobs because of job-related pressures.[62] And job tenure is not long; on the average, city managers have been in their jobs for a little more than five years.[63]

Making Cities Work: "Politics" or "Administration"?

City managers have always been aware that being sensitive to politics is necessary to survive, and in fact, more recent investigations indicate that the city manager is evolving into a conscious political force in metropolises.

A comprehensive study of San Francisco Bay Area city managers found that a high portion of the city managers responding in that study perceived clear political roles for themselves. Interestingly, education appeared to affect whether city managers saw themselves as "politicians" or as "administrators." Those managers who saw themselves in a highly political role tended to have majored in the social sciences or public administration. Those who viewed themselves as relatively managerial in nature were less likely to have a college degree and displayed career patterns that often started with such jobs as director of public works, building inspector, city engineer, and so on, and from these jobs they moved to the top position after several years of working for the city. Nevertheless, all managers believed that they should participate in the initiation, formulation, and presentation of policy proposals to their councils. By contrast, city council members tend to perceive the city manager as no more than a staff administrator, a servant to the council, and they thought this only proper.[64]

Table 11-3 indicates this quiet conflict between managers and council members. For example, 78 percent of the city managers disagree with the proposition that managers "should act as administrators and leave policy matters to the council," but only 12 percent of the council members disagree with that notion.

Most studies consistently indicate that city managers generally tend to see their roles as more political than administrative; city councils tend to view the managers as more administrative than political. Shrewd city managers can deal with this difference in viewpoint and avoid conflict while still getting their way. A major study of 1,744 responding cities found that almost 90 percent of the city managers and chief administrative officers indicated that they always, or nearly always, participate in formulating municipal policy; the percentage was even higher in the larger cities. More than 60 percent of the managers responding felt they always, or nearly always, played a leading role in making policy, and more than 94 percent took some responsibility for setting the policy agenda of cities. Interestingly, more than 12 percent reported that they always, or nearly always, gave political help to incumbent candidates for the city council; under most city

Table 11-3 Disagreements About Policy Expectations Between City Managers and City Council Members

	MANAGERS		*COUNCIL MEMBERS*	
	% Agree	*% Disagree*	*% Agree*	*% Disagree*
1. City managers should act as administrators and leave policy matters to the council.	22%	78%	88%	12%
2. City managers should work through the most powerful members of the community to achieve their policy goals.	88	12	42	58
3. City managers should give a helping hand to good council members who are coming up for reelection.	53	47	12	88
4. City managers should maintain a neutral stance on issues that may divide the community.	24	76	64	36
5. City managers should encourage people whom they respect to run for the council.	44	56	23	77
6. City managers should consult with their councils before drafting their own budget proposals.	31	69	49	51
7. City managers should advocate policies even if important parts of the community seem hostile to them.	55	45	46	54

Source: Adapted from Ronald O. Loveridge, "The City Manager in Legislative Politics: A Collision of Role Conception," *Polity*, I (Winter 1968), pp. 212–236. Reproduced by permission of *Polity*.

charters, this would be in clear violation of the nominal role that the city manager is expected to play.[65]

Another study of local public managers found that significant numbers of them perceived their political influence to be increasing over time. Forty-seven percent of local public managers anticipated that their policy recommendations and their role in the formulation of local policy would gain greater influence over time, in contrast to only 10 percent who thought that they would lose influence as policymakers. Relatedly, 44 percent saw themselves as taking a greater leadership position in the formulation of public opinion in the future, compared to only 11 percent of local managers who thought that their leadership of public opinion would decline.[66]

Urban Politics and the Control of Information

How is it that local public managers see themselves as being so politically active and influential? The major reason appears to be that local managers are extremely aware of their ability to control critical information in the local political system. The most consistent finding of one major study was that more than 60 percent of the city managers voiced strong opposition to a full-time paid city council and that "this item evoked the strongest expression of opinion in the entire series of questions."[67] Moreover, a majority of city managers in the study opposed the provision of a full-time separate staff for the mayor, and 77 percent of the respondents reported that they always, or nearly always, resisted council involvement in management issues.

These opinions on the part of city managers indicate that the appointed urban chief executive officer is well aware that one of his or her major political bases is the control of information. A full-time professional staff for the mayor and a full-time hard-working city council that is interested in management issues are anathema to the typical city manager. Theirs is an example of the politics of expertise, an area that provides city managers with an ability to have their policies adopted by the city council primarily because they control a major source of information, the city bureaucracy itself.

A similar study conducted of 645 city managers concluded that the more professional and the more highly educated the manager was, the more the manager tended to resist public participation in city decision making, particularly in fiscal matters. Additionally, the more professionally oriented city managers tended to see themselves in a more positive policymaking role than the more locally oriented city managers.[68]

If educational trends are any indication, it appears that the power of the local public managers will increase at the long-term expense of the local city councils. One reason for this pertains to the concept that knowledge is power, and the educational levels of local managers are increasing dramatically, even though these levels have always been relatively high. In 1971, for example, 27 percent of local public managers had a master's degree, but by 1984, this had increased to 58 percent. The proportion of local public managers who had not completed college shrank by considerably more than half between 1971 and 1984.[69]

In addition, city and county managers evidence a burgeoning preference for government and management degrees as opposed to engineering degrees. In 1971, one-third of the bachelors degrees held by local managers who had completed college were in engineering; by 1980, this proportion had been reduced to 13 percent. By contrast, 65 percent of city managers who had completed college in 1971 held degrees in management or government, but by 1980 this ratio had increased to 76 percent.[70]

The implications of the more recent studies on city managers have an intriguing corollary for higher education. The studies, taken whole, indicate that the more educated and professional a city manager is, the more likely he or she is to assume a greater personal policymaking role in cities. Moreover, education in the social sciences and public administration seems to correlate more heavily with city managers who are oriented toward the political sphere than does an education in engineering, or simply less education. Education may, after all, have an impact on the way people see themselves, at least if the surveys on city managers are any indication.

The data also indicate that city managers are experts in the politics of being smooth. While they often seem to get their way in forming urban policies, they do so by maintaining a low profile, by using finesse rather than clout and anonymity instead of notoriety. In this regard they are very different from governors, mayors, or other elected officials. They play the same games, but more quietly, sometimes safely, and above all, effectively.

City managers also are responsible for hiring, firing, and using the vast urban bureaucracy; we consider the state and local bureaucracy, and public policies concerning it, in the following chapters.

NOTES

[1]Raymond Bancroft, *America's Mayors and Councilmen: Their Problems and Frustrations* (Washington, D.C.: National League of Cities, 1974). Unless noted otherwise, the discussion in the following three paragraphs is drawn from this volume.

[2]Robert L. Lineberry and Ira Sharakansky, *Urban Politics and Public Policy,* 3rd ed. (New York: Harper & Row, 1978), p. 197. Figures are for 1974.

[3]Bureau of the Census, *Statistical Abstract of the United States, 1985* (Washington, D.C.: U.S. Government Printing Office, 1984), Table 420, p. 251. Figure is for 1982.

[4]Patrick J. Chase, "A Profile of Elected County Executives," *Urban Data Service Reports,* 12 (November, 1980), pp. 1-5.

[5]As quoted in John T. Galvin, *Twelve Mayors of Boston, 1900-1970* (Boston: The Boston Public Library, 1970), n.p.

[6]Russell D. Murphy, "Whither the Mayors? A Note on Mayoral Politics," *Journal of Politics,* 42 (February 1980), pp. 278-279, 280-281.

[7]Marilyn Gittell, "Metropolitan Mayors: Dead End," *Public Administration Review,* 23 (March, 1963), p. 21. Gittell studied 96 mayors elected in big cities between 1940 and 1960, of whom only 10 went on to higher office.

[8]Murphy, "Whither the Mayors?" p. 280.

[9]Joseph Dineen, *The Purple Shamrock* (New York: W. W. Norton, 1949), p. 313.

[10]Gittell, "Metropolitan Mayors," p. 23.

[11]Murphy, "Whither the Mayors?" p. 288.

[12]John C. Bollens and Grant B. Geyer, *Yorty: Politics of a Constant Candidate* (Pacific Palisades, Calif.: Palisades, 1973), p. 214.

[13]*Ibid.,* p. 138.

[14]*Ibid.,* p. 165.

[15]*Ibid.*

[16]*Ibid.,* p. 166.

[17]*Ibid.,* p. 167.

[18]"Governor Bid Not Ruled Out by L.A. Mayor," *Los Angeles Times,* as reprinted in *The Arizona Republic* (April 11, 1985).

[19]Quoted in Nicholas Henry and John Stuart Hall, *Reconsidering American Politics* (Boston: Allyn & Bacon, 1985), p. 55.
[20]Quoted in Stephen C. Baker and Paul Kleppner, "Race War, Chicago Style: The Election of a Black Mayor, 1983," paper presented at the 1984 Annual Meeting of the American Political Science Association, Washington, D.C., August 30-September 2, 1984, p. 2.
[21]Quoted in *ibid.*
[22]Quoted in *ibid.*
[23]Quoted in *ibid.,* p. 3.
[24]Quoted in *ibid.,* p. 3.
[25]Henry and Hall, *Reconsidering American Politics,* p. 56.
[26]Baker and Kleppner, "Race War, Chicago Style," p. 3.
[27]*Ibid.,* p. 4. As Baker and Kleppner note on p. 14, however, the federal government had regularly been deducting its tax claims from Washington's paycheck, even though he had neglected to file his annual return, and a federal audit had revealed that his total unpaid tax bill was around $500. Washington had been sentenced to jail for this $500 debt in 1972 during the peak of President Richard Nixon's use of the Internal Revenue Service to harass those people whom the White House regarded as "political enemies."
[28]*Ibid.,* p. 4.
[29]*Ibid.,* p. 5.
[30]Tom Fitzpatrick, "Racist Mudslinging Grows Filthier in the Vicious Brawl for Helm of Windy City," *The Arizona Republic* (April 9, 1983).
[31]Baker and Kleppner, "Race War, Chicago Style," pp. 6-7.
[32]*Ibid.,* p. 10.
[33]*Ibid.,* p. 11.
[34]Henry and Hall, *Reconsidering American Politics,* p. 56.
[35]Neal Peirce, "Ad-Vantage: Slick Campaigning Hits Cities," *The Arizona Republic* (April 12, 1985).
[36]*Ibid.*
[37]*Ibid.*
[38]*Ibid.*
[39]*Ibid.* Seattle's campaign regulations became effective in 1987.
[40]Clarence N. Stone, "Complexity and the Changing Character of Executive Leadership: An Interpretation of the Lindsay Administration in New York City," paper presented at the 1981 annual meeting of the American Political Science Association, September 3-6, 1981.
[41]*Ibid.,* pp. 16-19; Terry Nichols Clark, *City Money* (New York: Columbia University Press, 1983); and Terry Nichols Clark, "A New Breed of Cost-Conscious Mayors," *The Wall Street Journal* (June 10, 1985).
[42]Unless noted otherwise, the discussion of Daley is drawn from David Halberstam, "Daley of Chicago," *Harper's Magazine,* 237, No. 1419, pp. 25-36.
[43]Associated Press, *The Arizona Republic* (December 21, 1976).
[44]United Press International, *The Arizona Republic* (December 21, 1976).
[45]Associated Press, *The Arizona Republic* (December 21, 1976).
[46]*Ibid.*
[47]Unless noted otherwise, the discussion of Lindsay is drawn from Larry L. King, "Lindsay of New York," *Harper's Magazine,* 237 No. 1419, pp. 37-44.
[48]Quoted in Halberstam, "Daley of Chicago," p. 27.
[49]John V. Lindsay, *The City* (New York: W. W. Norton, 1970), p. 84.
[50]Nat Hentoff, *A Political Life: The Education of John Lindsay* (New York: Alfred A. Knopf, 1969), p. 82.
[51]Heywood T. Sanders, "The Government of American Cities: Continuity and Change in Structure," *Municipal Year Book, 1982* (Washington, D.C.: International City Management Association, 1982), p. 181.
[52]*Ibid.*
[53]Robert P. Boynton, "City Councils: Their Role in the Legislative System," *Municipal Year Book, 1976* (Washington, D.C.: International City Management Association, 1976), p. 73.
[54]As derived from data in Heywood T. Sanders, "Governmental Structure in American Cities," *Municipal Year Book, 1979* (Washington, D.C.: International City Management Association, 1979) p. 103.
[55]*Ibid.,* p. 104.
[56]*Ibid.*

[57] *Ibid.*, p. 102.
[58] Mary A. Schellinger, "Local Government Managers: Profile of the Professionals in a Maturing Profession," *Municipal Year Book, 1985* (Washington, D.C.: International City Management Association, 1985), pp. 182-183. Figures are for 1984. The term "local public managers" includes the top appointed executive officers of cities, counties, and councils of governments. The survey polled 3,315 cities, 238 counties, and 144 councils of governments that used a council-manager-type plan. Not quite two-thirds of these governments responded.
[59] *Ibid.*, p. 184. Figures are for 1984. The figures on national party identification are from "Opinion Roundup," *Public Opinion* (October/November, 1983), p. 25.
[60] The National Advisory Commission on Civil Disorders, *Report* (New York: Bantam Books, 1968), p. 287.
[61] Gladys M. Kammerer and John M. DeGrove, *Florida City Managers: Profile in Tenure* (Gainesville: Public Administration Clearing Service, University of Florida, 1961), pp. 34-35.
[62] Richard J. Stillman II, "Local Public Management in Transition: A Report on the Current State of the Profession," *Municipal Year Book, 1982* (Washington, D.C.: International City Management Association, 1982), pp. 166, 170.
[63] Schellinger, "Local Government Managers," p. 185.
[64] Ronald A. Loveridge, *The City Manager and Legislative Policy* (Indianapolis: Bobbs-Merrill, 1971).
[65] Robert J. Huntley and Robert J. McDonald, "Urban Managers: Managerial Styles and Social Roles," *Municipal Year Book, 1975* (Washington, D.C.: International City Management Association, 1975), pp. 149-159.
[66] Stillman, "Local Public Management in Transition," p. 171.
[67] Huntley and McDonald, "Urban Managers," p. 150.
[68] Timothy A. Almy, "City Managers: Public Avoidance and Revenue Sharing," *Public Administration Review*, 37 (January-February, 1977), pp. 19-27.
[69] Schellinger, "Local Government Managers," p. 184.
[70] Stillman, "Local Public Management in Transition," p. 163.

12

GRASSROOTS FINANCE

the many pockets of the public purse

Only one thing is more important to government than the people's trust, and that is money. Money, it is said, makes the world go around, and governments are very much a part of that world.

THE GROWTH OF GOVERNMENT: THE MONEY MEASURE

Government expenditures at all levels handily surpass a trillion dollars a year—a phenomenal sum by any reckoning—and government spending at all levels exceeds one-third of the gross national product. But only a portion of these vast expenditures is spent on the domestic needs of the citizenry. Less than 62 percent of all federal expenditures are spent on domestic programs, including Social Security payments and all federal aid to state and local governments. State and local governments account for about 30 percent of all public expenditures, virtually all of which goes to domestic programs.[1]

The revenues that governments collect also have gone up, but not nearly as rapidly as expenditures. Government revenues, like government expenditures, amount to more than a trillion dollars per year, with state and local governments accounting for 38 percent of those revenues from their own sources. When federal intergovernmental grants are added to state and local revenues, their revenue share jumps to 46 percent.[2]

These are very substantial increases in both expenditures and revenues by governments, and the public clout in the nation's economy is substantial. In this chapter, we consider some of the ramifications of that clout, focusing on the rise of the federal government since the early part of this century as the dominant fiscal actor in intergovernmental finance; the impact that Washington has had on states and communities, especially in terms of the deepening dependency of subnational jurisdictions on Washington; the emergence of "direct federalism" and the growing "grants war" among regions of the country for Washington's dollars; President Reagan's proposal for a new set of federal relationships; how states and localities finance themselves with property, sales, and income taxes, and the fairness of these taxes; and finally, the burgeoning public debt.

THE INTERGOVERNMENTAL MONEY GAME

The Rise of the Feds

The old question in politics of who gets what, when, where, and how is nowhere more evident than in the intergovernmental money game. During the twentieth century, these political patterns have changed radically, as Figure 12-1 indicates.[3]

From 1913, the year that the Sixteenth Amendment, which initiated a tax on income, was enacted, to 1929, when the Great Depression struck, the federal government spent less than 3 percent of the gross national product and accounted for about 30 percent of all governmental outlays at all levels. Federal aid to state and local governments was essentially nonexistent.

But by 1948, the national government was spending almost two-thirds of all government outlays—a ratio that more or less holds to this day (federal spending has since crept up to 70 percent of all public outlays). Nevertheless, federal aid to state and local governments as a proportion of federal outlays still had not increased by very much; in 1948, federal aid accounted for less than 3 percent of the federal budget.

From 1948 to 1984 these relationships again altered radically, but in different ways. The role of the federal government in relation to the total economy almost doubled—from less than 14 percent to 24 percent of the gross national product. Equally significant is the fact that federal aid to subnational governments grew from less than $2 billion to almost $93 billion during that 36-year period. Federal assistance to states and communities accounted for almost 11 percent of the federal budget (although its share had peaked in 1978, when it hit nearly 17 percent). Most of this increase occurred since 1960. Figure 12-2 traces the amount of federal aid to state and local governments from 1900 through 1980.

The fiscal scene at the subnational levels also has displayed some dramatic changes during this century. In 1913, state government expenditures accounted for less than 1 percent of the gross national product, but by 1984 expenditures by state governments contributed from their own sources of revenues (i.e., not counting federal aid to states) amounted to 6 percent of the gross national product. State government spending increased its proportion of total public expenditures from not quite 12 percent in 1913 to nearly 18 percent in 1984. State fiscal assistance to their local governments also grew enormously during the century, from less than $100 *million* in 1913 to nearly $100 *billion* in 1983 (not counting federal grants passed on to local governments by the states). State aid to local government now accounts for more than half of local revenues.[4]

The enormous monetary growth of the state and national governments

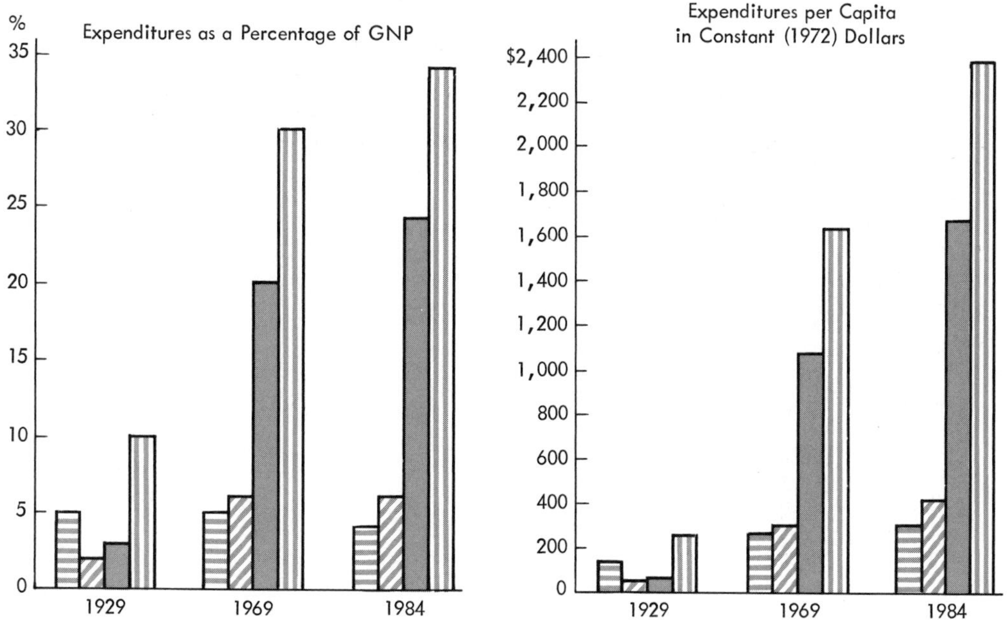

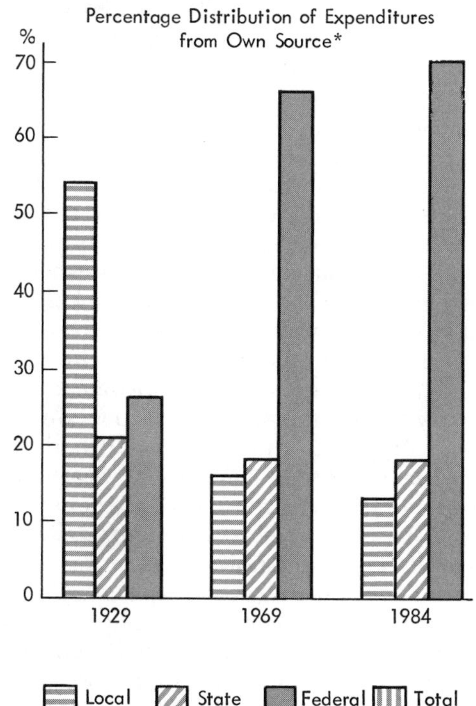

*Does not include transfer payments from other governments.

Figure 12-1. Government expenditures as a percentage of gross national product, per capita in constant (1972) dollars, and percentage distribution of expenditures from own sources by level of government, 1929, 1969, and 1984. (*Source:* Advisory Commission on Intergovernmental Relations, *Significant Features of Fiscal Federalism, 1984.* Washington, D.C.: U.S. Government Printing Office, 1985, pp. 10–11.)

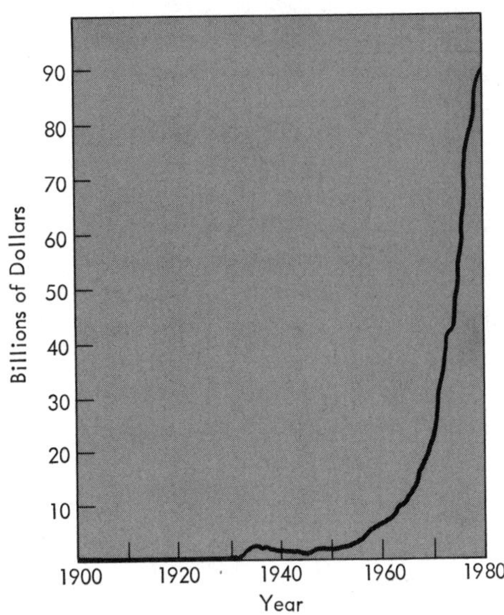

Figure 12-2
Amount of federal aid to state and local governments, 1900–1980. (*Source:* Advisory Commission on Intergovernmental Relations, *The Federal Role in the Federal System: The Dynamics of Growth,* A-77. Washington, D.C.: ACIR, 1980, p. 48.)

had to come at someone's expense, and that "someone," as Figure 12-1 makes clear, was the local governments. In 1929, local governments expended nearly 60 percent of all public outlays, virtually all of it from their own sources of revenues, and accounted for almost 5 percent of the gross national product; they were the dominant governmental actors in the American economy until the depression. But by 1984, and in spite of the fact that the expenditure rates of local governments expanded more rapidly than did the national economy, spending by local governments from their own revenue sources fell to less than 13 percent of total public outlays and about 4 percent of the GNP.

The reasons why the federal government in particular expanded at the expense of both state and local governments, but especially local governments, was the introduction in 1913 of the federal tax on income. Figure 12-3 shows the incredible productivity of the income tax by all levels of government and explains, at least in part, why the federal government became the dominant tax collector over the century. Prior to 1913, the income tax was the least productive tax, while the property tax was the most productive. But well before midcentury, the property tax had slipped to third place, and had been far outstripped by both the income and sales taxes as a source of governmental revenues.

The productivity of the income tax as a generator of government revenues had, of course, its effects on governments as revenue collectors. Figure 12-4 illustrates these effects. As it shows, local and state governments were displaced by the federal government as the major tax collector.

Because the federal government, through its predominant use of the income tax, had become the major fiscal source for governments, ways had to be found to pass governmental revenues back to those levels that could meet the peoples' needs most directly. These ways are what we call "fiscal federalism," a form of intergovernmental relations that grew to dominate the field around 1960. Prior to 1960, federal grants were used to help state and local governments to achieve their own policy objectives, but following that year an increasing tendency was evident for the federal government to use the

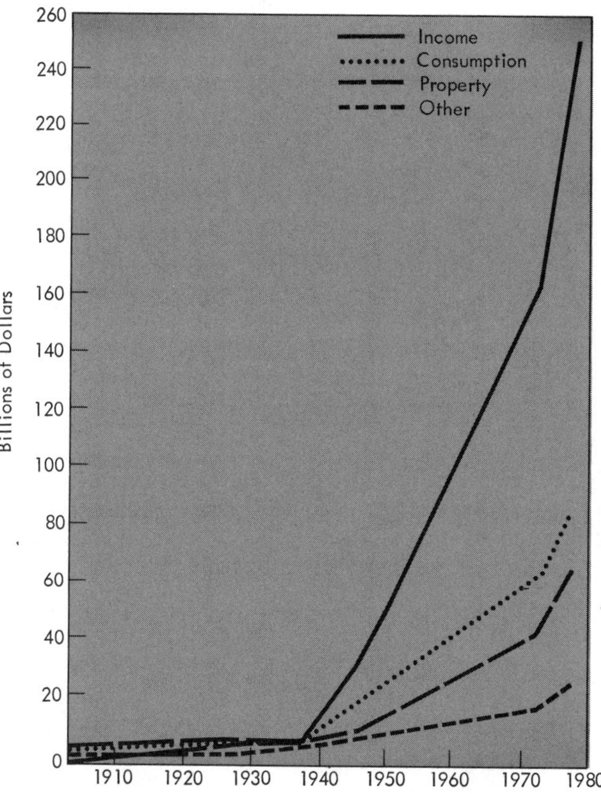

Figure 12-3
Tax collection by type of tax for all levels of government, 1910–1980. (*Source:* John S. Hall and Albert K. Karnig, *The Impact of the New Federalism on Arizona.* Tempe, Ariz.: Arizona State University, 1982, p. 11.)

intergovernmental grants system to, in effect, bribe state and local governments to accomplish national objectives.[5] Between 1960 and 1980, the number of federal grants programs grew from 150 to more than 500, indicating the new reliance that the federal government was placing on the grants system to achieve its ends.

The Politics of Grants: Categoricals, Blocks, and Revenue Sharing

Washington uses three major types of grants to pass money to the state and local governments: categorical grants, block grants, and revenue sharing. *Categorical grants* are highly specific and rather rigid programs that address narrow policy issues. The typical categorical grant has a number of strings attached, and each qualification must be met by the recipient in order to receive the grant. Categorical grants account for approximately four-fifths of the money that the state and local governments receive from the federal government. Washington obviously favors these categorical grants since they offer the most opportunity for retaining control over the expenditures of its money on the policy objectives for which federal dollars are spent.[6]

Block grants account for less than 15 percent of the money that Washington expends. A *block grant* is more general than a categorical grant, but still attaches some strings. Its major difference is that it allows the recipient to exer-

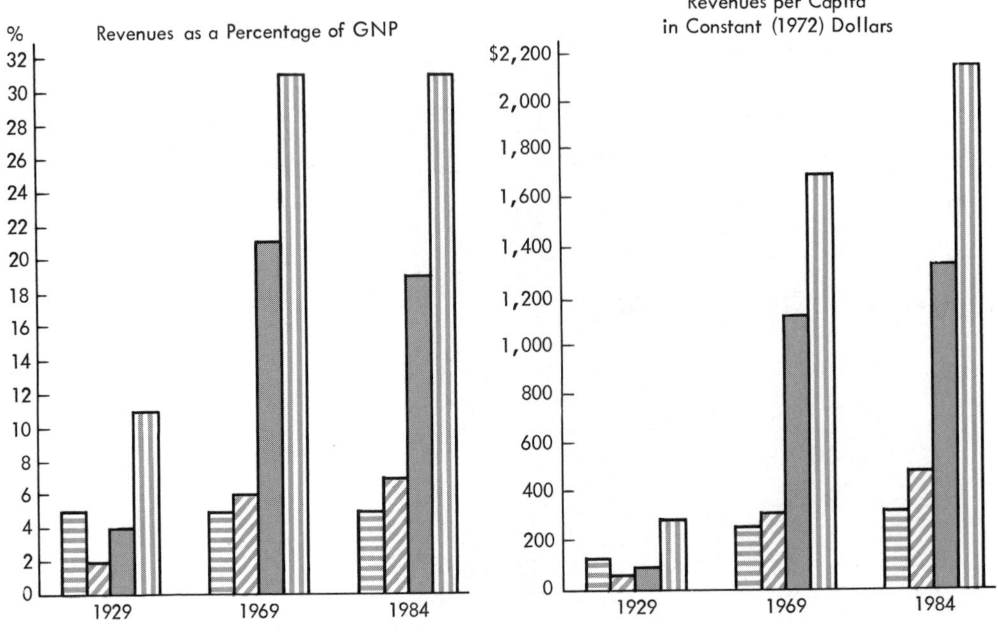

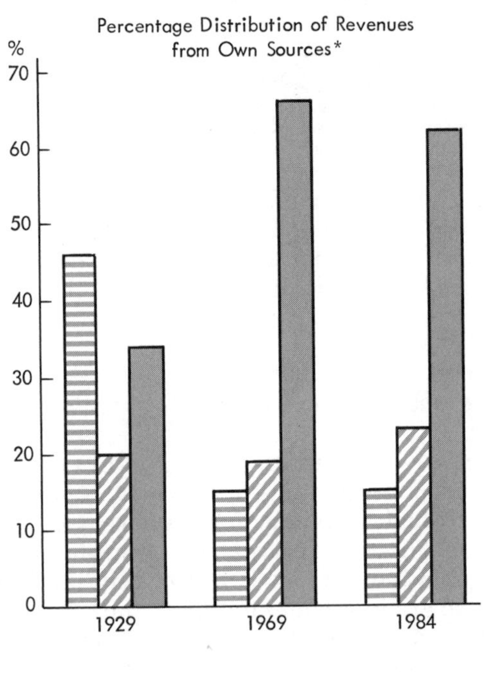

Local State Federal Total

*Does not include transfer payments from other governments.

Figure 12-4. Government revenues as a percentage of gross national product, per capita in constant (1972) dollars, and percentage distribution of revenues from own sources by level of government, 1929, 1969, and 1984. (*Source:* Advisory Commission on Intergovernmental Relations, *Significant Features of Fiscal Federalism, 1984.* Washington, D.C.: U.S. Government Printing Office, 1985, pp. 12–13.)

cise more discretion in the way that federal dollars granted to it are expended.

Block grants generate substantial political heat. At the center of the argument is the level of trust that one has in state and local officials, as opposed to national officials, and the kinds of programs that each level of government would fund with block grant money. Those who favor focusing federal dollars toward the needs of the poor and the deprived tend to favor the use of categorical grants to achieve these ends, while those who favor letting state and local governments—or those governments that are somehow "closer to the needs of the people"—decide how money should be spent and in what areas favor the use of block grants.

Investigations do indicate that when state and local governments receive block grants, they tend to use the money for programs other than those related to the impoverished. For example, when Congress, at President Richard Nixon's urging, consolidated seven basic national programs under the Housing and Community Development Act of 1974, essentially converting them from categorical to block grants, and thereby giving local leaders more control over how the funds underwriting these programs were to be used, the Brookings Institution found that poverty programs had fared better under the old Model Cities program initiated during the 1960s than under the new Community Development programs. (Model Cities was one of those programs that were subsumed by the Housing and Community Development acts.) There had been a shift, both in funding and decision making, away from the poorest people in the neighborhoods to more mixed patterns, and programs had changed from an emphasis on social services, such as health and education, to short term capital spending for projects such as parking lots and downtown renewal. Social services spending was found to be low under the Community Development program.[7]

Nixon's halting steps toward decentralization of the intergovernmental grants system, which he took by increasing the stature of block grants, were accelerated by the Reagan administration. In 1981, Congress enacted the Omnibus Budget Reconciliation Act, which consolidated 77 categorical grants and 2 block grants, with authority to spend $7.5 billion, into 9 new or modified block grants. In addition, 62 categorical grant programs were eliminated altogether.

The effects of these consolidations and eliminations were dramatic, at least if we use the number of federal assistance programs as a measure. In 1981, Congress had funded 534 categorical grant programs and 4 block grants; in 1984, 394 categorical grants and 12 block grants were funded.[8] But if we use money as a measure, the effects are less visible; block grants still account for less than 15 percent of the federal funds granted to states and localities.

The growing (but still marginal) use of block grants as opposed to categorical grants by Washington in the 1980s has been accompanied by important changes in the federal system. First, states rather than local governments are now the prime recipients of federal block grants; the states, particularly during the 1960s and 1970s, often had been bypassed in the federal grant system. A second difference is that the states have even broader discretion in terms of how money channeled to them through block grants might be spent than they did under the block grant programs of the 1960s and 1970s. Finally, and of greatest significance insofar as the recipients of grants from Washington are concerned, the total funding for the new block grant programs under Reagan indicates a large and overall reduction in funds for programs that they are designed to implement. Unlike the Nixon block grant programs of the early 1970s, there was no "sweetened pot" to make the displacement of categorical grants by block grants more palatable to the more liberal members of Congress.

The third major form of intergovernmental assistance from Washington is known as *revenue sharing,* and it accounts for about 7 percent of the federal aid package. Revenue sharing was enacted by Congress in 1972 when it passed the State and Local Fiscal Assistance Act and has been renewed by Congress for intervals of three to four years ever since. As a form of federal assistance to states and localities, revenue sharing has, by far, the fewest strings attached and disburses funds to subnational governments by formula. Revenue sharing is the most direct kind of federal aid insofar as local governments are concerned; revenue sharing funds go to 39,000 state governments, special districts, counties, cities, towns, townships, and Indian tribes.

Revenue sharing funds are distributed according to the proportion of federal personal income tax funds provided by state and local units of government; thus, richer units of governments as defined by their tax bases, tend to be favored. New York, California, Pennsylvania, Illinois, Texas, Michigan, and Ohio generally are the leading recipients of revenue sharing funds in any given year. About a third of the revenue sharing funds go to the states; the other two-thirds go to local governments.

More politics than fiscal rationality went into the complex formula that Congress devised to disburse revenue sharing funds, and full consideration was given to whose district would get what. As a consequence, financially marginal units of government are supported, and more viable governments that are in desperate need of additional cash, notably, big cities, often are underfunded. This situation arose because of two basic and opposing themes within Congress. One group in Congress insisted that revenue sharing be computed on the basis of need. Only a reading of the poverty levels and the number of people at or below the poverty level would be necessary to develop the formula. But another large group within Congress believed that revenue sharing would be an incentive to state and local governments to do more for themselves. This group reasoned that those governments that did more for themselves, by deriving greater revenues from their people, should be rewarded by receiving federal money through general revenue sharing. Obviously, the two points of view were contradictory.

The result was a compromise. Consequently, the formula finally adopted, though very complex, nevertheless did resolve the problem by accommodating both the "need" and the "incentive" factors. In other words, the formula considered "need" by determining the number of families at or below the poverty level, but it also recognized that state and local governments that taxed more and did more for themselves would be rewarded. State and local governments may use revenue sharing dollars for capital expenditures, maintenance, and operating costs in areas including public safety, environmental protection, transportation, health, recreation, libraries, social services for the old and the poor, and financial administration.

But how the grassroots governments may use shared revenues, and how they do use them, comprise quite different stories. Analyses of revenue sharing that have been conducted since 1972 conclude that, while small cities and towns use about three quarters of their revenue sharing funds for new spending programs (mostly for capital projects), bigger urban areas with 100,000 people or more use only half of the money for new spending programs; the remaining half goes to keep taxes down or to avoid borrowing. Among the states, only a third of shared revenues is used for new programs, and the tendency of both state and local governments to use revenue sharing funds for keeping a muzzle on the tax bite rather than initiating new spending programs appears to be growing. One reason for this trend is that, especially during the 1970s, inflation slashed the real purchasing power of revenue sharing dollars. Thus, state and larger local governments frequently use shared revenues mainly to keep their fiscal heads above water by maintaining existing services without raising taxes; merge revenue sharing funds with other revenue sources, thus reducing the political visibility of revenue sharing; retain traditional patterns of political power and enhance the clout of entrenched special interests; and, contrary to widespread speculation (and hope), reinforce the existing inefficiencies of public management systems.[9]

THE IMPACTS OF WASHINGTON

The Feds' Fiscal Hook in States and Communities

The dramatic expansion of the federal government's role in fiscal federalism has had an equally dramatic impact on state and local governments. Perhaps the most visible effect of Washington's growing influence in intergovernmental relations has been the sinking of its fiscal hook into the affairs of states and localities. Federal grants in 1954 accounted for about 11 cents in every dollar that states and localities collected in 1954, and for approximately 22 cents in each dollar by 1983, although this was down from its peak in 1976 when Washington's grants accounted for more than 34 cents of each dollar of state and local revenues![10]

Direct Federalism

It is the local governments that are the most dependent upon both state and national governments for their fiscal survival. State governments provide most of the revenue sources for their localities, and have for a number of years. State contributions to their local governments as a percentage of general revenue from the local governments' own sources peaked in 1980, when the states provided nearly 64 percent of their localities' general revenues; in 1983, state aid to local governments had declined to around 55 percent of their total revenues. Direct federal aid as a revenue source of local government revenues peaked in 1978, when Washington was providing almost 18 percent of the local government budget; today, it is around 12 percent.[11]

These figures do not tell the entire story about the level of local dependency on the federal government. If we count federal aid to local governments that is passed through the state governments, as well as direct federal aid to local governments, we find that the amounts of federal aid retained by state governments are only slightly in excess of the amounts received by local governments both directly and indirectly by passing those funds through the states.[12]

Table 12-1 clarifies the extent of local government dependency that developed between 1962 and 1983. In 1962, for example, federal and state aid as a percentage of local governments' own sources of general revenue, amounted to 44 cents in every dollar. By 1983, this percentage had increased to 67 cents. Direct federal aid to local governments increased from 3 percent in 1962 to 12

Table 12-1 Local Government Dependency Index,[1] Fiscal Years 1962, 1978, 1983

Unit of Government	*1983*	*1978*	*1962*
Federal and State Aid[1] per $1 of Own Source General Revenue			
All local governments	$0.67	$0.76	$0.44
Counties	0.63	0.80	0.60
Cities	0.46	0.62	0.26
Townships	0.40	0.41	0.28
School districts	1.13	1.01	0.65
Special districts	0.36	0.44	0.15
Federal Aid[1] per $1 of Own Source General Revenue			
All local governments	$0.12	$0.18	$0.03
Counties	0.09	0.19	0.01
Cities	0.15	0.26	0.05
Townships	0.09	0.13	0.01
School districts	0.02	0.04	0.02
Special districts	0.27	0.34	0.11
State Aid[1] per $1 of Own Source General Revenue			
All local governments	$0.55	$0.58	$0.41
Counties	0.53	0.61	0.59
Cities	0.31	0.37	0.21
Townships	0.32	0.28	0.27
School districts	1.11	0.97	0.63
Special districts	0.08	0.10	0.04

[1] Intergovernmental revenue from state and/or governments. Interpretation: A figure of $0.50 means that for each $1.00 of local own source revenue, $0.50 is received from the federal and/or state governments.

Source: Advisory Commission on Intergovernmental Relations, *Significant Features of Fiscal Federalism, 1984* (Washington, D.C.: U.S. Government Printing Office, 1985), p. 65.

percent in 1983 (although it peaked in 1978 at 18 percent). State aid to local governments has more or less steadily increased as well.

The emergence of "direct federalism"—that is, the federal government dealing directly with local governments and bypassing the state governments in the process—emerged largely under the aegis of the Nixon administration. Between 1968, when Richard Nixon assumed office, and 1976, at the close of the Nixon administration (counting the year and a half occupied by President Gerald Ford), the federal aid package to state and local governments tripled. In 1968, federal grants-in-aid as a percentage of state and local revenues from their own sources amounted to slightly more than 22 percent. By 1976, however, this had sharply increased to more than 31 percent. Through his initiation of revenue sharing alone, Nixon increased the number of local governments directly participating in federal grants programs from approximately 4,000 under President Lyndon Johnson to more than 39,000.

The Grants War

If two of the major effects of the dramatic growth of fiscal federalism during the 1960s and 1970s were the development of state and local financial dependency on the federal government and the emergence of direct federalism between Washington and localities, a third impact was the fostering of an increasingly cutthroat competitiveness among state and local governments for federal dollars. This competitiveness in turn led to a growing regional rivalry that has continued unabated. Although among the wealthiest of the nation's regions, the Northeast and Midwest, beginning in the 1970s, have complained that they are losing industry and jobs to other sections of the country, especially to the Far West and the Sunbelt states. These regions argue that, since they have supported other regions in the country over the years through a variety of federal grants programs that have favored those regions that have been traditionally less wealthy, it is now time for the federal government to tilt its grants programs toward the Northeast and Midwest.

The contention that certain regions are favored by the federal grants system more than others is a controversial one. Figure 12-5 illustrates regional and federal fiscal relationships over time. As the figure indicates, there has been a dramatic narrowing of regional gaps since 1952 in terms of the tax revenue-federal expenditure ratio. Today, New England, the Mideast, and the Far West generally gain more in federal grants and other kinds of federal expenditures than they pay in taxes, while states in all the other regions (except the Plains states, which break dead even) generally pay more in taxes than they gain in federal expenditures.[13]

At least one analysis of regional spending patterns by Washington indicates that "any lessening of the [regional] inequalities has been almost entirely accidental," and the federal government "has not intentionally adjusted spending and tax policies to help one region or punish another."[14]

Nevertheless, these equalizing trends, however unplanned, have not reduced the growing tension between regions of the country and the competition

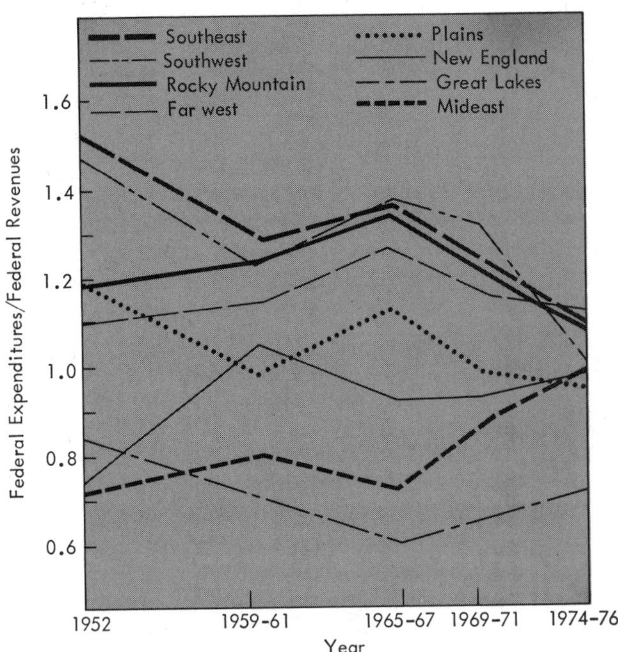

Figure 12-5
Ratio of federal expenditures to federal revenues, by region, 1952–1976. (*Source:* Advisory Commission on Intergovernmental Relations, *Regional Growth: Flows of Federal Funds, 1952–1976.* Washington, D.C.: U.S. Government Printing Office, June, 1980, p.55.)

for federal dollars, and increasingly a variety of regional organizations have cropped up in an effort to gain a competitive edge for those dollars. For example, in 1977, the 13 Western states formed the Western Governors' Policy Office (WESTPO) with a fully staffed office in Denver to conduct regional analyses of sensitive issues, but primarily energy policy. Similarly, in 1976, 7 states in the Northeast (Connecticut, Massachusetts, New Jersey, New York, Pennsylvania, Rhode Island, and Vermont) formed a Coalition of Northeastern Governors and stated as one of its principal objectives the presentation of "a united front before the Congress and the national administration in an effort to redress the current federal expenditure imbalances."[15] The founding of WESTPO and the Coalition of Northeastern Governors was in part a reaction to the founding in 1972 of the Southern Growth Policies Board, a 13-state organization that conducts research on economic growth management in the South and has a well-staffed office in Washington. In Congress, regions have banded together in a variety of formats including the New England Congressional Caucus, the Northeast-Midwest Economic Advancement Coalition, the Great Lakes Conference, the Sunbelt Conference, and the Western States Coalition (not to mention a Suburban Caucus, a Rural Caucus, and a Metropolitan Area Caucus), all of which symbolize a growing regional rivalry that has been promoted at least in part by the intergovernmental grants system.[16]

The Reagan Revolution

It was these conditions—the growing fiscal dominance of the federal government over state and local governments, the undercutting of state governments via direct "direct federalism" between Washington and localities, and the increasingly hot "grants war" between subnational governments competing for Washington's dollars—that led to the far-reaching proposals of President Ronald Reagan in 1982, calling for the reform of the federal structure. At the heart of his proposal is the notion that the federal government should not be involved in the business of state and local governments. This differs from the assumptions that have been held by federal policymakers since at least 1960, which hold that the federal government should pay the governments of states and communities to implement national policies and federal goals. In his 1982 "State of the Union" address, President Reagan proposed his own version of "new federalism." Under the first phase of this proposal, Washington would take over the Medicaid program in its entirety; Medicaid is a joint federal-state program that provides medical assistance to the indigent, and by assuming responsibility for Medicaid, the federal government would save states and localities more than $19 billion in annual expenditures.[17] In return, states and communities would absorb two significant welfare programs that are also run jointly by the state and federal governments: Aid to Families with Dependent Children (AFDC) and food stamps. This move would cost the states $16.5 billion each year. Moreover, Washington would "turn back" to the states from 60 to 70 categorical grant and block grant programs in education, revenue sharing, transportation, community development, and social services amounting to more than $30 billion every year. It would be up to the states if they wanted to accept any or all of these programs. Washington would compensate for this voluntary "turn back component" by setting up a trust fund of an estimated $28 billion to be funded by federal excise taxes, and that would be used to offset the roughly $30 billion in annual cost that the states would be absorbing by taking over those 60 to 70 federal programs. Ultimately, the trust fund would be phased out, as would be the federal excise taxes that financed it. If the states wished to continue any of the various programs that were eliminated by the federal government, they would have to enact their own versions of these programs, and in all likelihood, their own taxes to finance them, since the only federal excise tax left would be a 2-cents-per-gallon tax on gasoline, which would be earmarked for the interstate highway system. Hence, the states would be fully responsible for providing a wide variety of social programs currently provided by Washington, including such items as school lunches, water and sewer system assistance, local roads, energy assistance for the poor, mass transit, and a variety of others. But the states would not be required by Washington or anyone else to provide these and any other programs that had been returned to them.

Objections to President Reagan's proposals came from two very different sources. One was a national source and was related to the level of trust that national policymakers have in the motivations and capabilities of state and local administrators and legislators. Liberal members of Congress in particular were suspicious that the states would not favor the continuance of federal programs aimed at the poor, but instead would use the money received from the federal government to finance programs more acceptable to the middle class, such as a tax reduction or road improvements.

A similar concern held by national policymakers related to the level of competency found in subnational governments. Some federal officials were openly worried about the abilities of state and local administrators to administer welfare programs. As one congressman put it, "There has been no showing that the states do a fairer, more humane job in administering welfare. And problems won't go away just because Mr. Reagan shifts responsibility for solving them to the states. They'll still be there."[18] Or, as a congressional staffer noted, "Don't forget, many congressmen served in state legislatures before they got [to Washington]. They know that if you lined up all the jerks in the world, the first twenty would be state legislators."[19]

The other source of objections to the Reagan proposals came from state and local officials themselves and, unsurprisingly, did not relate to qualms held about their own competence that some national policymakers had. Here the issues dealt with fiscal equalization and balance. Could Washington turn back more and more responsibility to the states, while ignoring the fact that some states were rich and others poor? Would Washington, in a period of increasing fiscal limitations, still accept the notion that the federal government was obliged to distribute a monetary dividend to states and localities in the form of intergovernmental assistance? As a consequence of these concerns, the National Governors Association (which was the leading articulator of the viewpoints held by subnational governments), the National League of Cities, the National Conference of State Legislatures, and other state and local government lobbies resisted the Reagan proposals in a way quite different from that of liberal members of Congress. While the Reagan White House had proposed that food stamps, Aid to Families with Dependent Children, and some 60 to 70 categorical grant and block grant programs be turned back to the states, the National Governors Association and its allies recommended that food stamps and AFDC be retained by the federal government, and that only 50 to 60 grant programs be turned back, because they wanted transportation grants to be retained by Washington. The National Governors Association also proposed that the trust fund of $28 billion proposed by the federal government be limited to only $13 billion, since there would be no AFDC or food stamp burdens to be placed on the states, and it had some counterproposals regarding the timing of the various phases of the turnback program.

Although Reagan's revolutionary proposals for reforming fiscal federalism have stalled, they remain on the public agenda, and they represent an admirable attempt to "sort out" intergovernmental relations. Less admirable, in the view of some, is the parallel effort by the Reagan administration to cut back federal support of those social programs that are implemented through the intergovernmental structure.

OF DEATH AND TAXES

We have been discussing the ways in which governments help each other to cope with the pressing needs of their citizens, and the growing gravity of the fiscal condition of states and localities despite that help. But how do states and communities help themselves through their own tax revenues?[20] Despite the fiscal hook amounting to more than a fifth of state and local revenues that the federal government has sunk into America's subnational governments, the fact is that 39 cents of each tax dollar paid by Americans nonetheless goes to their state and local governments, and more than half of that amount (which is more than $400 billion a year) goes to the states. Perhaps no single policy reflects the differences in state and local political cultures more than their tax systems. Some states prefer taxing the poor, and other states (though precious few) prefer taxing the rich. Some states favor taxing everyone less, and other states favor taxing everyone more. Some states put a great deal more effort into supporting themselves than do other states. Table 12-2 ranks the states by how highly they tax their citizens as measured by the percentage of state personal income the state takes. For example, Alaska taxes its people the most by this measure and takes more than 45 percent of its citizens' personal incomes in taxes; Arizona is the median state, and Missouri is the lowest.

To a degree, these patterns reflect the ability of states to tax their citizens; after all, some states are poorer than are others, and states can differ significantly in their ability to raise revenues. Table 12-2 also ranks the varying abilities of states to raise taxes. The "tax capacity index" featured in the table was developed by the Advisory Commission on Intergovernmental Relations as a reflection of each state's ability to raise revenues from all sources. For example, Alaska's ability to raise revenues is indexed at 313, or 213 points greater than the national average of 100. This is more than four times the ability of Mississippi, the nation's poorest state, which has a tax capacity index of 71.

Some states, as the table shows, are in a position to tax their citizens more than they do, such as Connecticut, which ranks thirty-first in terms of the tax bite it places on its citizens but seventh in terms of its capacity to tax more. Others tax their people more than their relative ability to do so, such as Mississippi, which ranks last in terms of its tax capacity but thirty-seventh in terms of its take from its people's personal incomes.

Regardless of tax capacity, all state and local governments acquire their revenues essentially from the same sources, primarily property, income, and sales taxes. States rely disproportionately on the income tax and the sales tax; localities have developed the property tax as their major revenue source. Figure 12-6 indicates the major source of tax revenues by level of government.

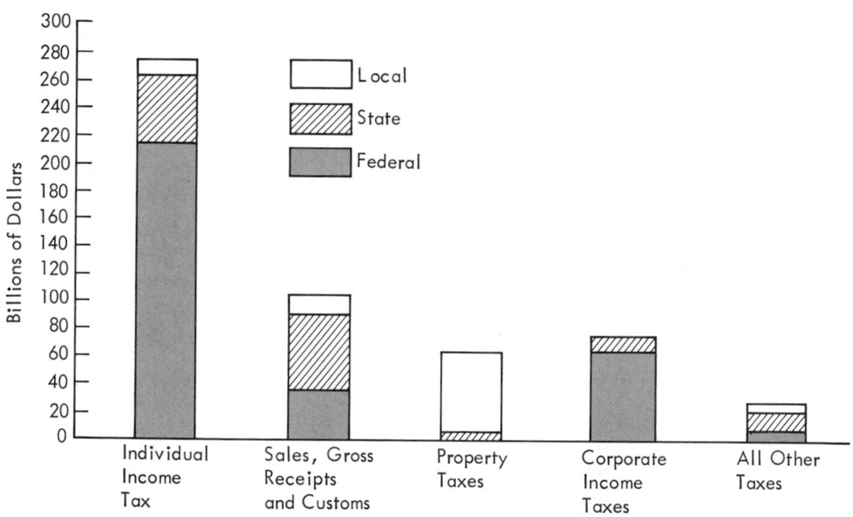

Figure 12-6. Tax revenue by type of tax and level of government. (*Source:* Bureau of the Census, *Governmental Finances in 1978–1979.* Washington, D.C.: U.S. Government Printing Office, 1980, p. 4.)

Table 12-2 States Ranked by State and Local Taxes as a Percentage of State Personal Income and by Tax Capacity, 1982

				U.S. Average	*100*
Rank	*State*	*State and Local Taxes as a Percentage of State Personal Income*	*Rank*	*State*	*Tax Capacity Index*
1	Alaska	45.42%	1	Alaska	313
2	Wyoming	19.98	2	Wyoming	201
3	New York	15.57	3	Nevada	151
4	Washington, D.C.	14.17	4	Texas	130
5	Montana	13.12	5	Oklahoma	126
6	New Mexico	12.82	6	Colorado	121
7	Hawaii	12.75	7	Connecticut	117
8	Vermont	12.36	7	Hawaii	117
9	Wisconsin	12.23	9	California	116
10	Maine	11.98	10	Delaware	115
11	Rhode Island	11.97	10	New Mexico	115
12	Minnesota	11.96	10	North Dakota	115
12	Massachusetts	11.95	10	Washington, D.C.	115
14	Michigan	11.64	14	Louisiana	113
15	Utah	11.50	15	Montana	110
15	West Virginia	11.47	16	Kansas	106
17	California	11.12	16	New Jersey	106
17	Oklahoma	11.12	18	Florida	104
19	Oregon	11.08	19	Washington	102
20	Louisiana	11.03	20	Massachusetts	101
21	New Jersey	10.98	21	Maryland	100
22	Delaware	10.97	21	New Hampshire	100
23	Maryland	10.94	23	Illinois	99

24	Pennsylvania	10.70	23	Minnesota	99
25	Iowa	10.51	23	Oregon	99
26	Arizona	10.45	26	Nebraska	97
27	Georgia	10.30	27	Arizona	96
28	Illinois	10.29	27	Iowa	96
29	Washington	10.28	29	Virginia	94
30	North Dakota	10.25	30	Michigan	93
31	Connecticut	10.22	31	New York	92
32	South Carolina	10.20	31	Ohio	92
33	Nevada	10.14	31	West Virginia	92
34	Colorado	10.13	34	Missouri	91
35	North Carolina	10.11	35	Indiana	89
36	Nebraska	10.10	35	Pennsylvania	89
37	Mississippi	10.07	35	Vermont	89
38	Kentucky	9.97	38	South Dakota	87
39	South Dakota	9.93	38	Wisconsin	87
40	Virginia	9.72	40	Idaho	86
41	Idaho	9,53	40	Utah	86
42	Texas	9.52	42	Georgia	84
43	Ohio	9.47	42	Maine	84
44	Kansas	9.44	44	Kentucky	82
45	Alabama	9.16	44	North Carolina	82
46	New Hampshire	9.05	46	Rhode Island	81
47	Indiana	9.00	47	Arkansas	79
47	Tennessee	9.00	48	Tennessee	77
49	Arkansas	8.90	49	Alabama	74
50	Florida	8.71	49	South Carolina	74
51	Missouri	8.59	51	Mississippi	71

Source: Advisory Commission of Intergovernmental Relations, *Significant Features of Fiscal Federalism, 1984* (Washington, D.C.: U.S. Government Printing Office, 1985), pp. 129–131.

The Income Tax

The states have been the primary users of income taxes and sales taxes. States and, to some degree, localities, got into the income tax business shortly after a national income tax was enacted as the Sixteenth Amendment to the Constitution in 1913. Since then, 41 states have enacted individual income taxes. Only Connecticut, Florida, Nevada, New Hampshire, South Dakota, Tennessee, Texas, Washington, and Wyoming do not collect individual income taxes, although Connecticut, New Hampshire, and Tennessee do collect taxes on income from interest dividends and capital gains, but not income derived from wages. Nevada, Texas, Washington, and Wyoming are the only states that do not tax the income of corporations.

The state income tax has been a steadily rising source of state revenues, and has moved from less than 20 percent of state revenue in 1960 to more than 38 percent as a source for state revenues. Of course, the amount of revenues that the income tax pays into state coffers varies widely from state to state; Oregon, at one extreme, collects about half of its revenues through its income tax, while Louisiana, at the other, collects less than 10 percent through this tax. Local income taxes are used in 11 of the states, but they generate less than 6 percent of all local tax revenues.[21]

The Sales Tax

Another major source of revenues favored by state governments is the sales tax. The most common types of sales, or excise, taxes are those on gasoline, liquor, tobacco, and parimutuels, though there are others. Taxes on gasoline and related products are the cornerstone sales tax for all states, accounting for almost half of all sales tax collections. Oregon passed the first gasoline tax in 1919, and every state in the union had one within the decade.

The next largest source in sales tax revenues for a specific item is the tax on tobacco, which accounts for approximately a fifth of all sales tax revenues. Iowa, in 1921, enacted the first cigarette tax, and 40 years later, all the states and the District of Columbia were taxing tobacco in some form.

The biggest sales tax of all is the general retail sales tax. With the stock market crash of 1929, states saw virtually all their sources of income drying up and turned to the sales tax as a means of financial salvation. Mississippi was the first state to adopt such a tax in 1932, and within only a dozen years, the general retail sales tax had become the most important tax source of all for state governments. Only Alaska, Delaware, Montana, New Hampshire, and Oregon do not have a general sales or gross receipts tax. Yet, it accounts for 48 percent of the tax revenues collected by state governments. Nevertheless, the sales tax as a percentage of state revenues is in decline; in 1960 it accounted for 58 percent of state tax revenues.

Local governments also soon proved to be enthusiastic developers of local sales taxes. New York City set the example for establishing a local sales tax in 1934, and currently more than 5,000 local governments in 26 states, but particularly in California, Illinois, Texas, and Washington, use a general retail sales tax. The local sales tax as a percentage of local tax revenues has essentially doubled since 1960 and accounts for nearly 15 percent of all local tax revenues. Cities use it significantly more than do other forms of local government.

The Property Tax

The property tax is used by most local governments as the major source of tax revenues. Historically, the property tax has been the nation's fiscal heavyweight. In 1902, the property tax provided more than half of total federal, state, and local tax collections, but with the rise of taxes on income and sales, this position quickly slipped. Today the property tax provides around 13 percent of all federal, state, and local tax revenues, although the federal government no longer is in the property tax collecting business. In the 1930s, state governments began moving away from the property tax (largely because the depression had raised the specter of mass tax defaults by property owners), leaving it to the purview of local governments, and today the general property tax provides less than 3 percent of the tax revenues of state governments.

The general property tax is essentially the only local tax of consequence, and it provides 75 percent of the total tax revenues for local governments (down from about 86 percent in 1960). Cities rely on the property tax considerably less than does any other type of local government. New England relies on it most, the Far West the least.

Although the property tax as a percentage of tax revenues for local governments is in decline, it still remains extremely important to these jurisdictions. And the reason is clear: local governments have very few other options. Levying local taxes on personal income, sales, or businesses could potentially reduce the local tax base, and it often does. People and businesses can and do move out of the city; land cannot.

The property tax has an enormous administrative problem associated with it, that of assessment. By *assessment* is meant how governments evaluate the worth of the property to be taxed, and the rule of thumb is to assess property well below its true market value. If all property is assessed at the same percentage of true value, this practice is, of itself, not necessarily unfair; but such uniform assessment is rare, and assessments vary widely from jurisdiction to jurisdiction.

Other Sources of State and Local Revenues

Other than transfers of funds between governments themselves, taxes on income, sales, and property are the major sources of revenues for state and local governments. Nevertheless, there are other sources of revenues, and these account for almost 20 percent of total state and local revenues from their own sources.[22] Among these other revenue sources are death and gift taxes. All the states levy inheritance and estate taxes and 16 tax gifts. Increasingly popular are "user charges," which levy charges for water, electric power, and highway tolls. These kinds of charges appear to be growing, particularly in states that have suffered tax revolts. Public lotteries are one of the newer and more exotic sources of state and local revenues. Introduced in 1964 in New Hampshire, these games of chance are offered to the citizens of 20 states and are becoming an increasingly important source of tax revenues for the states, earning more than $2 billion for state coffers every year.[23] Finally, interest earnings comprise a growing source of general revenues for states and communities.

THE EQUITY QUESTION: TAXES AND FAIRNESS

Before continuing our discussion of the public purse, let us address here the question of fairness and tax policy. *Fairness,* or *equity,* means that a tax system does not cut more deeply into the incomes of poor people than rich people in terms of real purchasing power. In this light, taxes may be progressive, regressive, and proportional. Taxes are *progressive* when the ratio of tax to income rises as income rises; they are *regressive* when the ratio of tax to income falls as income rises; and they are *proportional* when the ratio of taxes to income is the same for all classes of income.

It is generally believed that a progressive income tax is fairest to all taxpayers. The federal income tax, for example, does not tax the very poor at all, and it taxes the very rich at 27 percent. At the state and local levels, however, taxes are not always necessarily progressive.

States that impose high taxes on their citizens tend to be relatively progressive in their tax policies, with the upper and middle classes bearing most of the tax burden. Table 12-3, which is a composite of state taxes on sales and personal and corporate incomes, ranks the states according to the progressivity of their tax policies. As it shows, the more progressive states are found in the West and Midwest, while the more regressive states are largely in the South.

Table 12-3 State Tax Burdens and Progressivity

	Rank in tax progressivity		*Rank in tax progressivity*
Oregon	1	Ohio	26
Michigan	2	Delaware	27
Wisconsin	3	New Hampshire	28
California	4	Kansas	29
Minnesota	5	Virginia	30
Idaho	6	Florida	31
Hawaii	7	Nevada	32
Colorado	8	Connecticut	33
Alaska	9	Pennsylvania	34
Massachusetts	10	Maine	35
Nebraska	11	Oklahoma	36
Georgia	12	Washington	37
Vermont	13	Missouri	38
North Carolina	14	South Carolina	39
Iowa	15	West Virginia	40
North Dakota	16	Illinois	41
New York	17	Kentucky	42
Montana	18	Indiana	43
New Mexico	19	Rhode Island	44
Arizona	20	Louisiana	45
Maryland	21	Texas	46
South Dakota	22	Tennessee	47
Utah	23	Wyoming	48
New Jersey	24	Mississippi	49
Arkansas	25	Alabama	50

Source: Virginia Gray, Herbert Jacob, and Kenneth Vines, eds., *Politics in the American States,* 4th ed. (Boston: Little, Brown and Co., 1983), pp. 426–427. Copyright © 1979 by The New York Times Company. Reprinted by permission.

Both state and local tax policies are regressive in comparison to national policies. Regardless of which theory of economics is applied to the data, federal taxes are progressive tax policies, but state and local taxes clearly are regressive for virtually all income groups.[24] Perhaps the major cause for inequitable state and local tax systems is the predominance of the sales and property taxes at these levels, both of which are highly regressive. Let us examine these in greater detail.

The Sales Tax and the Income Tax: A Marriage of Fiscal Convenience

A tax on sales taxes what people consume, and since, by definition, poor people must consume the necessities of life (such as food and shelter) approximately as much as rich people, they pay an unfair share of the sales tax relative to their incomes. Table 12-4 indicates clearly the regressive aspects of the state and local general sales tax for a family of four, by income. For example, a family of four with an annual income of $5,000 is going to pay nearly 2 percent of that $5,000 in sales taxes; by contrast, a family earning $50,000, or ten times as much, is going to pay less than 1 percent of its income in sales taxes. Given the nature of the sales tax, this regressivity cannot be avoided, and this fact of tax life is one of the main arguments against relying on the sales tax for state and local revenues.

It is quite unlikely, however, that states that rely primarily on both the income tax *and* the sales tax as their sources of revenue will abandon the sales tax, or use one in favor of the other. Because the sales tax is relatively "hidden," at least in comparison to the income tax, raising it is less likely to result in voter opposition. Moreover, if state income taxes were truly progressive and cut relatively deeply into the incomes of high earners, the rich might move from the state, thereby further diminishing the state's tax base.

Trends also indicate that the states will rely on both the sales tax and the income tax in the future. Figures 12-7 and 12-8 indicate the growth in popularity of both the general sales tax and the personal income tax among the states, particularly as the states' use of those taxes has grown since 1950. As shown in Figure 12-7, the number of states using a general sales tax grew from 29 in 1950 to 45 today, and the number of states using a personal income tax grew from 31 in 1950 to 41. Similarly (see Figure 12-8), the number of states using *both* an income and general sales tax more than doubled from 17 in 1950 to 36 cur-

Table 12-4 Estimated Burden of State and Local General Sales Taxes for a Family of Four, by Income Group, 1972

Family Income (in dollars)	*Rate (in %)*
$ 5,000	1.8%
7,500	1.6
10,000	1.4
20,000	1.1
25,000	0.9
50,000	0.7

Source: Advisory Commission on Intergovernmental Relations, *Significant Features of Fiscal Federalism, 1973–74* (Washington, D.C.: U.S. Government Printing Office, 1974), p. 53.

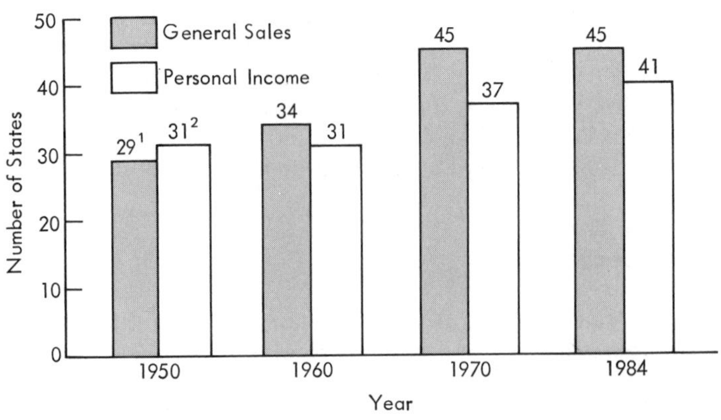

¹ Includes Hawaii
² Includes Alaska and Hawaii

Figure 12-7
State use of general sales and broad-based personal income taxes, selected years, 1950–1984. (*Source:* Advisory Commission on Intergovernmental Relations, *Significant Features of Fiscal Federalism,* 1980–1981, p. 36; and Council of State Governments, *Book of the States, 1984–1985,* pp. 320–321.)

rently, but states with *neither* an income nor a sales tax slipped from 7 in 1950 to only 2. The states have long favored the use of the sales tax, if for no other reason than because the federal government, by not employing it to any great extent, has made the sales tax more available for their use. Nevertheless, the states' reliance on this tax has about topped out, and it appears that the personal income tax will become the next major revenue-generating tax source for state governments.

The Property Tax: Unfair or Misunderstood?

Many people believe that the property tax is the most regressive and unfair tax in America. A family of four with an income of $2,000 or less pays almost 17 percent of its income in residential property taxes, but a family with an income of $25,000 or more pays only 2 percent of its income in residential property taxes.[25] Moreover, the property tax seldom adjusts to the changing fortunes of the individual. For example, if a family purchased and paid for a house in their thirties, and retired in the same house in their late sixties, the property tax would not adjust to their declining income; indeed, it would probably go up as the value of the property went up.

In this light, it also has been charged that the property tax actually promotes the deterioration of cities. If a homeowner improves his or her residence and makes it worth more in the open market, the property is consequently assessed at a higher value and the homeowner must pay a higher property tax, despite the money and effort that he or she may have poured into the house. Thus, in a peculiar kind of way, it "pays" to let one's house fall into disrepair, at least insofar as the property tax system is concerned.

Finally, large tracts of land in cities and states are not taxed at all—for example, land belonging to another government, such as the national government, to churches, and to various kinds of charitable institutions. These exemptions have increasingly become sore points with people who pay residential property taxes, and the logic justifying them is that such institutions work for the public welfare and therefore should not be subject to tax. Nevertheless, exempting them from the property tax has contributed to the erosion of the local tax

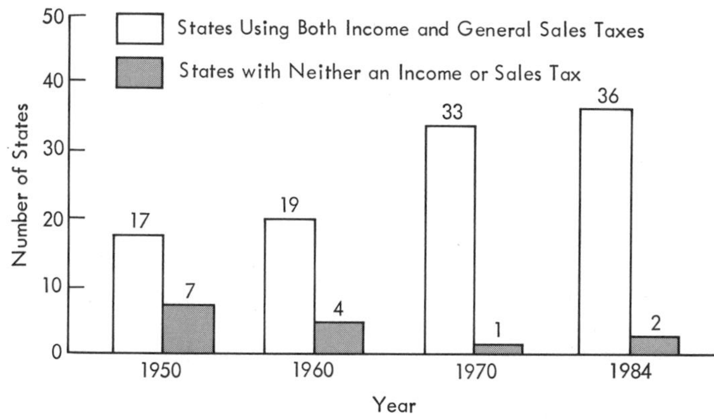

Figure 12-8
Number of states with both general sales and personal income taxes, and number with neither tax, selected years, 1950–1984. (*Source:* Advisory Commission on Intergovernmental Relations, *Significant Features of Fiscal Federalism, 1980–1981,* p. 36; and Council of State Governments, *Book of the States, 1984–1985,* pp. 320–321.)

base. Although the total value of all such excluded property nationally is not known, it appears to be substantial. Most of the exemptions, nearly 60 percent, apply to government buildings, followed by educational, religious, and charitable properties.[26]

There are still other types of property tax exemptions. In many localities, industries are exempted, at least for a period of time, in order to lure these employers to the locality. Eleven states permit exemptions from the local property tax to farmers, and many states also grant exemption of some sort to veterans.

The "circuit breaker" on the property tax also reduces revenues to state and local governments. A *circuit breaker* goes into effect when the property tax exceeds a predetermined percentage of the personal income of an individual. It relieves the excess financial pressure by reducing or eliminating the homeowner's property tax. This device is intended to make the property tax somewhat more equitable, and 31 states and the District of Columbia have circuit-breaker programs.[27]

Although most people would agree with the intention of rendering the property tax more progressive, not everyone agrees that circuit breakers work as they are supposed to. Henry J. Aaron, for example, contends that circuit-breaker laws are unfair because they give the most tax relief to those in each income class who possess the greatest net worth in the first place—that is, those who own a house and property, as opposed to those who have never been wealthy enough to purchase a house and property. Aaron argues that the real problem is not the nature of the property tax itself, but the administration of it that causes inequities.[28] In this contention, Aaron is at least partially correct, and among the administrative reforms that should be undertaken are the reorganization of local assessment districts and state supervision of the administration of local property assessment and taxation.

THE PEOPLE'S CHOICE: TAXES AND TAXPAYERS

We have seen how state and local tax systems work, and what some of the experts think about how they should work. But how do the taxpayers themselves view the tax system and the kinds of taxes that they pay? A number of opinion polls have attempted to assess how people feel about various types of taxes.[29] Table

12-5 summarizes some of these surveys taken since 1972. As it indicates, there has been a relatively steady rise in popular dissatisfaction with the federal income tax; in 1972, 19 percent of Americans thought that the federal income tax was the least fair, but by 1980 this had almost doubled to 36 percent and has stayed essentially constant since then. By contrast, there has been a decline in popular dissatisfaction with the local property tax—from 45 percent of Americans who thought that this tax was the least fair in 1972 to 29 percent in 1984.

The growing dissatisfaction with the federal income tax appears to be squarely rooted in reality. Figure 12-9 compares the direct tax burdens borne by average- and upper-income families for selected years. Not only does it indicate a steady growth in federal, state, and local tax takes, but it also shows that the federal government has taken an increasingly disproportionate share of average- and upper-income families' incomes.

The decline in popular hostility toward the local property tax correlates with the grassroots tax revolts that began in the 1970s and which rendered the tax less onerous. Between 1972 and 1980, the property tax as a percentage of state and local tax revenues declined from almost 40 percent to about 30 percent (where it has since remained), or a decrease of roughly one-fourth.[30] As with the federal income tax, popular perceptions of the property tax appear to be based on fiscal reality.

What if a community needs to raise more money? Which taxes are the least likely to cause public outcry if they are newly imposed or significantly raised? Could the tax system be altered better to accommodate the people's wishes? Respondents to various surveys on these questions believed, for the most part, that at least some of the services and facilities that were usually supported from general city taxes could be put on a break-even, fee-for-service basis (in other words, a user charge). A majority of the respondents in nine of ten major cities surveyed in one poll were willing to start taxing private schools as a new means of raising revenues, and in seven cities most people were willing to start taxing church property.

The sales tax is by far the most popular way of raising revenues, the income tax is next, and the property tax is clearly the least popular method of taxation among all respondents. Of course, there are some variations; the wealthier respondents are more likely to favor increasing the sales tax than are the poor respondents, although even low-income groups would prefer raising the sales tax to any other form of taxation. People who rent their residences are more likely to favor a hike in the property tax than are those who own their own homes, but none of these variations really affects the basic ordering.

Table 12-5 Which Do You Think Is the Worst Tax—That is, the Least Fair? (Percentage of U.S. Public), 1972, 1975, 1977, 1980, and 1984

	1984	*1980*	*1977*	*1975*	*1972*
Federal income tax	36%	36%	28%	28%	19%
Local property tax	29	25	33	29	45
State sales tax	15	19	17	23	13
State income tax	10	10	11	11	13
Don't know	10	10	11	10	11

Source: Advisory Commission on Intergovernmental Relations, *1984 Changing Public Attitudes on Governments and Taxes,* S-13 (Washington, D.C.: U.S. Government Printing Office, 1984), pp. 1–4.

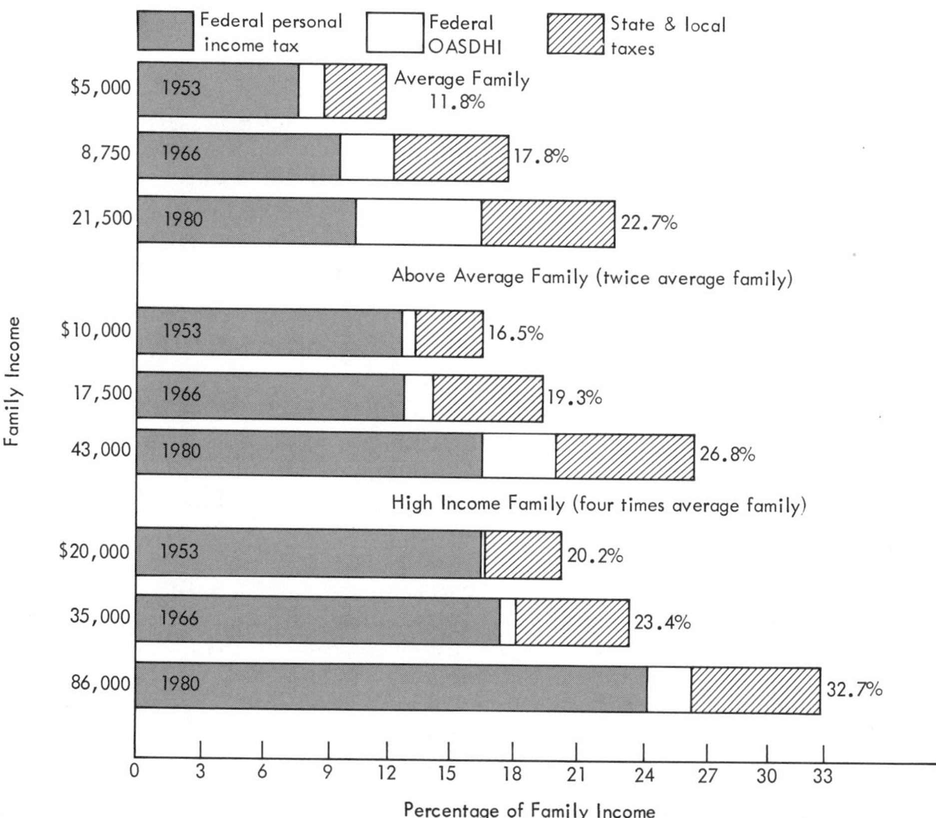

Figure 12-9. A comparison of direct tax burdens borne by average and upper income families, calendar years 1953, 1966, and 1980,* showing the steady growth in the federal-state-local tax take. (*Source:* Advisory Commission on Intergovernmental Relations, *Significant Features of Fiscal Federalism, 1980–1981,* p. 48.)

When all is said and done, however, most Americans would prefer paying the fewest taxes possible, and at no time was this attitude in more evidence than during the grassroots tax revolts that began in the 1970s. The popular disaffection with tax rates began much sooner than most people realize. Although California's Proposition 13, enacted by a 2-to-1 popular vote in 1978, is often cited as the symbol of the grassroots' tax revolt (Proposition 13 mandated a Draconian slash of all residential and commercial property taxes to 1 percent of the properties' 1975-76 market value, and these taxes were allowed to increase by no more than 2 percent a year until the property was resold, amounting to a 57 percent decrease in property tax revenues), the actual turnaround in state and local revenue collections began first at the local level, and considerably earlier than the advent of Proposition 13. In 1975, "real" spending (i.e., eliminating the inflation factor) first began to decline at the local level. In 1977, this same phenomenon occurred at the state level, and in 1978 real federal assistance to state and local governments peaked and began a long-term decline that has yet to be reversed.

These pinches in state and local treasuries are largely the people's doing. Of the 108 tax and expenditure restrictions that state governments have imposed upon themselves or their local governments—restrictions ranging from limits on taxes, revenues, and expenditures to full disclosure requirements—24 percent were enacted, often by popular vote, between 1970 and 1977, and another 46 percent between 1978 and 1984.[31]

Increasingly, the grassroots governments are being challenged to deliver more with less.

PAYING THE PIPER: BORROWING AND DEBT

Despite unprecedented revenues, virtually all governments in America are in hock. The total government debt is about $2 trillion, or more than $3,600 for every man, woman, and child in the nation. Figure 12-10 provides some basic measures of the public debt.

Governments have borrowed money to finance projects of various kinds and, occasionally, to pay for day-to-day operations. Governments borrow this money from the people. The interest on municipal bonds, for example, is tax exempt, and such bonds normally earn a higher than usual rate. While this indebtedness is not necessarily dangerous in and of itself, there is a danger when government borrows to meet current expenses or to finance programs that are not of an emergency nature. Mortgaging future revenues in this way creates a mounting debt, which ultimately requires additional borrowing to make up the old debt, and it takes from the money marketplace capital that is needed for the development of private industry.

As Figure 12-10 shows, the federal government is by far the leading debtor among American governments, accounting for three quarters of all public debt. State debt (at least technically, as we explain in Chapter 14) has been controlled throughout this century, largely because all state constitutions (except in Vermont) require balanced budgets each year. Local debt as a proportion of all government debt has fallen significantly, largely because the federal government has gone so deeply into hock, but also because state governments and Washington have taken over (or at least pay for) many local responsibilities.

Have state and local governments overextended themselves? That is a difficult question to answer. (In fact, it is sufficiently complex that part of our response is contained in Chapter 14.) Although the state and local debt has tripled since 1960, the "debt service payments" (or interest) in relation to state and local revenues have remained relatively constant at about 20 percent. Similarly, the percentage of total debt outstanding in relation to the total personal income in states and localities also has remained at around 20 percent.[32]

Experts generally think that these figures indicate an ability by most state and local governments to pay their debts without going under. Nevertheless, some spectacular fiscal crises have erupted during the last few years, such as Cleveland's default on $15.5 million in short-term bank notes, which occurred in 1978, and the extraordinarily serious fiscal situation that occurred in New York beginning in 1975. Although New York City had more or less gained financial stability by 1980, the process involved pain for many citizens. Investors in New York City municipal bonds lost 45 percent of their bonds' face value when New

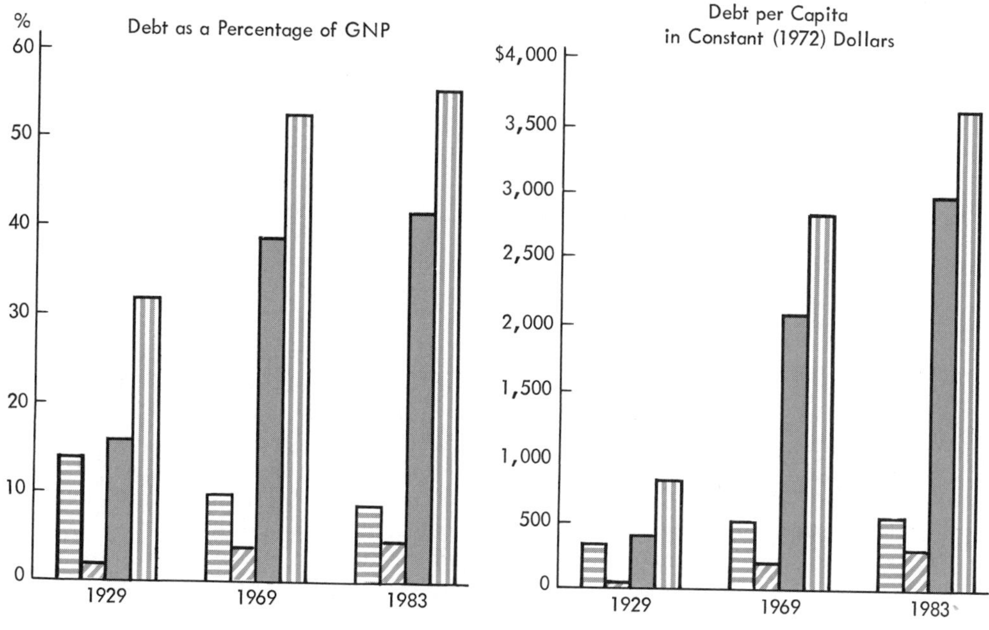

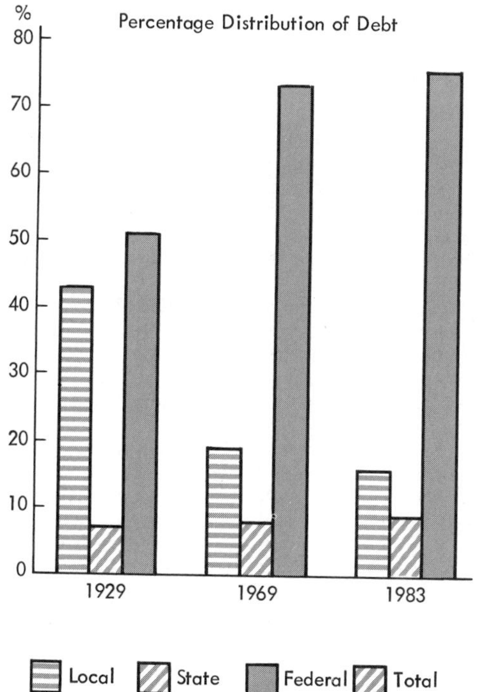

Figure 12-10. Government debt as a percentage of gross national product, per capita in constant (1972) dollars, and percentage distribution, by level of government, 1929, 1969, and 1983. (*Source:* Advisory Commission on Intergovernmental Relations, *Significant Features of Fiscal Federalism, 1984*. Washington, D.C.: U.S. Government Printing Office, 1985, pp. 15–16.)

York's monetary plight was exposed; the U.S. Securities and Exchange Commission charged that the city's financial practices and the activities of six major banks participating in New York's municipal bonds sales had verged on fraud; campaigns for bond sales in other states lost by large margins at the polls during New York City's financial duress—a development that was attributed directly to its fiscal crisis—and larger, older cities were forced to pay abnormally high interest rates on their debts; New York's bond rating sank from "A" to "B," thus further discouraging investment in the city; and the municipal income tax for New Yorkers was increased by an average of 25 percent, while the city's work force was reduced by some 55,000 people, and the wages of most remaining workers were frozen or deferred.[33]

Despite increasingly tight times for cities, defaulting on loans is a rare occurrence among municipalities. In 1838, Mobile, Alabama, became the first to hold that dubious distinction. Most municipal defaults on obligations occurred right after the Civil War, and again during the depression of the 1930s. After World War II, 431 American cities defaulted on obligations (as of 1980), but at least 306 of these were technical and temporary defaults. Defaults total less than one-half of 1 percent of all municipal debts outstanding.

In this chapter, we have reviewed some of the major trends in state and local finance. Public finance is a central concept of public administration at the grassroots, but it takes people as well as dollars for governments to function. In the following two chapters, we examine how governments use their people to expend public dollars.

NOTES

[1]Advisory Commission on Intergovernmental Relations, *Significant Features of Fiscal Federalism, 1984* (Washington, D.C.: U.S. Government Printing Office, 1985), p. 13. Figures are for 1984. In that year, all governments spent $1,258 billion; 70 percent of that sum, or $880 billion, was spent by the federal government.

[2]*Ibid.*, p. 64. Figures are for 1984. In that year, all governments collected $1,134 billion, or $124 billion less than they spent; virtually all the overage was incurred by the federal government.

[3]Unless noted otherwise, the following discussion is based on Deil S. Wright, *Understanding Intergovernmental Relations,* 2nd ed. (Monterey, Calif.: Brooks/Cole, 1982), pp. 83-86; and Advisory Commission on Intergovernmental Relations, *Significant Features of Fiscal Federalism, 1984,* pp. 1-4.

[4]Advisory Commission on Intergovernmental Relations, *Significant Features of Fiscal Federalism, 1984,* p. 64.

[5]James L. Sundquist and David W. Davis, *Making Federalism Work* (Washington, D.C.: Brookings Institution, 1969).

[6]David B. Walker, Albert J. Richter, and Cynthia Cates Colella, "The First Ten Months: Grant-in-Aid, Regulatory, and Other Changes," *Intergovernmental Perspective,* 8 (Winter, 1982), p. 6; and "Dimensions of the Federal Grant-in-Aid System: 1981-84," *Intergovernmental Perspective* (Winter, 1985), p. 13.

[7]Paul R. Dommel et al., *Decentralizing Community Development: Second Report of the Brookings Institution Monitoring Study of the Community Development Block Grant Program* (Washington D.C.: Brookings Institution, 1978).

[8]"Dimensions of the Federal Grant-in-Aid System," p. 13.

[9]Richard P. Nathan et al., *Monitoring Revenue Sharing* (Washington, D.C.: Brookings Institution, 1975); and Richard P. Nathan and Charles F. Adams, Jr., *Revenue Sharing: The Second Round* (Washington, D.C.: Brookings Institution, 1977).

[10]Advisory Commission on Intergovernmental Relations, *Significant Features of Fiscal Federalism, 1984,* p. 63.

[11]*Ibid.*, p. 62.
[12]Advisory Commission on Intergovernmental Relations, *Recent Trends in Federal and State Aid to Local Governments* (Washington, D.C.: U.S. Government Printing Office, 1980), p. 1. Data are for 1977.
[13]Advisory Commission on Intergovernmental Relations, *Significant Features of Fiscal Federalism, 1984,* p. 22.
[14]Joel Havemann and Rochelle L. Stanfield, "'Neutral' Federal Policies Are Reducing Frostbelt-Sunbelt Spending Imbalances," *National Journal* (February 7, 1981), p. 233. This analysis covered the years 1975 and 1979.
[15]Spokesperson for the Coalition of Northeastern Governors, as quoted in Bernard L. Weinstein and John Rees, "Sunbelt/Frostbelt Confrontation?" *Transaction* (May/June 1980), p. 17.
[16]David P. Mullhollan, Susan Webb Hammond, and Arthur G. Stevens, Jr., "Informal Groups and Agenda Setting," paper delivered at the annual meeting of Midwest Political Science Association, Cincinnati, Ohio, April 16-18, 1980.
[17]Figures in this and the ensuing discussion of Reagan's proposal are for fiscal 1984.
[18]Congressman Jack Brooks, as quoted in Dennis Farney, " 'New Federalism' Gets Icy Reception from Many Democrats in Congress," *The Wall Street Journal* (February 23, 1982).
[19]An unidentified "committee staff member," quoted in *ibid.*
[20]The following discussion on various types of taxes, unless noted otherwise, is drawn largely from James A. Maxwell and J. Richard Aaronson, *Financing State and Local Governments,* 3rd ed. (Washington, D.C.: Brookings Institution, 1977), pp. 92-168; and Advisory Commission on Intergovernmental Relations, *Significant Features of Fiscal Federalism, 1984,* p. 51. The reader should be aware that percentages refer to percentages of all state or local *tax* revenues, and do not include intergovernmental transfer payments and other nontax sources of revenues, such as user charges, lotteries, and interest. All current figures refer to 1984.
[21]Advisory Commission on Intergovernmental Relations, *Significant Features of Fiscal Federalism, 1984,* pp. 51 and 81.
[22]"State and Local Government Finances in 1979-80," *The Book of the States, 1982-83* (Lexington, Ky.: Council of State Governments, 1982), p. 355. Figure is for 1980.
[23]Advisory Commission on Intergovernmental Relations, *Significant Features of Fiscal Federalism, 1984,* p. 5. Number of states refers to 1985; dollars generated refer to 1983.
[24]Joseph A. Pechman and Benjamin A. Okner, *Who Bears the Tax Burden* (Washington, D.C.: Brookings Institution, 1974), pp. 61-64.
[25]Advisory Commission on Intergovernmental Relations, *Financing Schools and Property Tax Relief: A State Responsibility* (Washington, D.C.: U.S. Government Printing Office, 1973), p. 36. Figures are for 1970.
[26]Bureau of the Census, *Census of Governments, 1977,* No. 2 (Washington, D.C.: U.S. Government Printing Office, 1978), p. 6.
[27]Advisory Commission in Intergovernmental Relations, *Significant Features of Fiscal Federalism, 1984,* p. 108.
[28]Henry J. Aaron, *Who Pays the Property Tax? The New View* (Washington, D.C.: Brookings Institution, 1975).
[29]The following discussion is drawn from Advisory Commission on Intergovernmental Relations, *Changing Public Attitudes on Governments and Taxes, 1972* through *1984* (Washington, D.C.: U.S. Government Printing Office, 1972-1984); and Floyd J. Fowler, Jr., *Citizens' Attitudes Toward Local Government Services and Taxes* (Cambridge, Mass.: Ballinger, 1974), pp. 57-86.
[30]Advisory Commission on Intergovernmental Relations, *Significant Features of Fiscal Federalism, 1984,* p. 51.
[31]*Ibid.*, p. 146.
[32]Maxwell and Aaronson, *Financing State and Local Governments,* p. 196.
[33]For a review of New York City's financial crisis that occurred during the late 1970s, see Nicholas Henry, *Governing at the Grassroots,* 2nd ed. (Englewood Cliffs, N.J.: Prentice-Hall, 1980), pp. 321-328.

13

GRASSROOTS BUREAUCRATS

In the preceding chapter, we observed that few things are more important to governments than money. But it takes people to expend that money and to conduct public programs in efficient and effective ways.

The people who disburse public revenues are called, depending on one's point of view, "bureaucrats" or "public servants," but whatever the perspective, both appellations refer to public employees. And there are a lot of public employees—more than 16 million of them. Of these, only 2.9 million are federal civilian employees (or 117 federal employees per 10,000 Americans); more than 3.8 million are state employees (or 24 percent of all public employees), and more than 9.3 million (58 percent) are employees of local governments. There are 465 state and local government employees per 10,000 people in the country.[1]

The number of governmental employees has almost doubled since 1960. The rate of expansion was particularly rapid at the subnational levels. The number of state employees (of whom about a third are in education) grew by about 250 percent, and the number of local employees (more than half of whom are educators) more than doubled.[2]

Although the reasons underlying the dramatic growth in the number of government employees are myriad, at least one of the reasons is that government has become a reasonably attractive place to work. The average wage and salary level of government workers is 96 percent of the average wage and salary level of workers in all domestic industries.[3] When this earning level is combined with the high job security offered by the public sector, government employment becomes a more attractive option.

One reason that government employers have become more competitive with private industry has been the introduction of the "merit principle" in state and local governments, or the idea that public employees are hired, promoted, demoted, or fired on the basis of their professional competence. The federal government has had a major impact on how civil service systems, which use the merit principle, have evolved in state and local governments. The single law that had the most influence was the Civil Service Act of 1883. Known as the Pendleton Act, it was designed to make government administration a profession, and it served as the operative civil service policy at the national level until 1978, when the Civil Service Reform Act was passed. Over time, state and local governments slowly began adopting the basic principle (at least on paper) that was set forth in the original Civil Service Act. These governments no doubt were strongly encouraged to do so by the passage of the Social Security Act of 1940, which was instrumental in encouraging states and localities to adopt merit systems since federal funding for welfare, health, and a variety of other grant programs was tied to such adoption. In any event, 36 states now have statewide merit systems, and the remaining states have partial merit systems. Urban civil service systems protect an estimated 95 percent of all municipal employees (excluding educators, who are protected by academic tenure).[4]

The reasons behind the expanding adoption of state and local merit systems are reasonably clear. With public employment at the grassroots steadily growing, it is not surprising that party patronage slowly would be displaced by people demanding "fairer" access to government jobs. Technical credentials for employment also have proliferated as society and its governments become more complex.

Regardless of why the merit system has burgeoned in state and local governments, one should realize that

> all statistics concerning merit system coverage are inherently deceptive. While such figures may be numerically accurate, they merely indicate that merit systems are "on the books," not that they exist in practice. . . . Consequently, while the arithmetic of these surveys [on state and local merit systems] may be impeccable the resulting summaries frequently belie the true extent of merit systems coverage. Remember, the City of Chicago has an excellent merit system on the books, yet it manages to retain its well-earned reputation as the large American city most famous for its patronage abuses.[5]

THE POWER OF PUBLIC PERSONNEL ADMINISTRATION

"Merit," as a concept, is quintessentially middle class. It is designed to displace the machine bosses whose primary constituency were the poor, the immigrants, and the dispossessed. Given this premise, does the merit system work as it is supposed to? Does it assure more responsive government? Perhaps it does, but not necessarily. Although the merit system may assure "cleaner"—that is, more efficient and less corrupt—government, at least by middle-class standards, a major criticism of the whole concept of merit is that it establishes a vast bureaucracy over which elected officeholders have little control. "Political" appointees are indeed inept on occasion, but it does not necessarily follow that appointments made according to civil service criteria are necessarily any better, at least in terms of assuring more responsive government. Many politicians believe that the "civil service thwarts government progress. Civil servants, considered by some to be human paperweights, can sabotage an administration through laziness or inefficiency or by being just plain ornery. Unaccountable to anyone, they can easily thwart those who are accountable to the electorate."[6]

Frank J. Thompson, in his study of public personnel policy and politics, traces how this lack of control by elected officials occurred in Oakland, California, one of the most "reformed" of city governments. Council-manager, or reformed, governments tend to shift the center of personnel decision making to the urban bureaucracy: "Reformed government strips power resources from elected officials and emphasizes that professionally trained experts should conduct much of government's business."[7] Hence, the person with the real power in Oakland's personnel decisions was the personnel director. With more than 98 percent of the city's personnel classified under civil service, the personnel director had (and has) far-reaching power. Moreover, having "imbibed the good government, anti-party culture so much a part of Oakland's local government tradition, [the mayor and the city council] have little desire to influence bureaucratic appointments and removals."[8] This means, in effect, that bureaucrats control the bureaucracy.

HOW THE MERIT SYSTEM WORKS: THE POLITICS OF COMPLEXITY

If public bureaucrats were to manage by the rules and regulations set down by their civil service commissions, it is unlikely, some observers suggest, that they could accomplish anything of consequence in terms of transferring, hiring, and firing of public personnel. Frequently, finding ways to get around the regulations of their own system becomes the objective of civil servants. Whether this bypassing is intended to maintain the spirit of good government or is designed to further political patronage depends upon the situation. But it has been contended that, "The perversion of most civil service merit systems for private, administrative, and especially partisan ends is one of the worst kept, yet least written about, secrets in government."[9]

In council-manager cities where the impact of the merit principle in public personnel administration thinking is the most profound, the city manager ultimately reigns supreme in personnel decisions. Contrary to conventional wisdom, the city manager is not an empire builder—indeed, quite the reverse. "The manager naturally casts a jaundiced eye on any request which will further drain the city treasury. For him, the basic concern is not whether a proposal will enhance organizational efficiency. . . . In his unrelenting war against greater costs, the manager believes that it is particularly important to resist work force expansion."[10] This stands to reason: the manager must report to the council, and the council, in turn, must report to taxpayers. Therefore, it behooves the manager to keep government costs down.

In contrast to the city manager, the heads of municipal agencies usually want to expand the number of people and the areas of authority that they control. But they are seldom able to accomplish this without the approval of the city manager. While Thompson found that most of Oakland's top bureaucrats were "at least latent manpower imperialists," these bureaucrats found it difficult actually to act on such an expansionist disposition without the approval of the city manager.

HIRING AND (SELDOM) FIRING PUBLIC BUREAUCRATS

Governmental Recruiting

How does one get a job in government? According to merit principles, all one should need are the "right" educational and professional credentials and a high score on a test. But more is involved, particularly when a personal interview is required. Employers in government (and presumably in private enterprise as well) sometimes would rather hire someone who is less able according to technical criteria and more amiable according to personal criteria. Consider the following passage from Thompson's Oakland study:

> The attitudes of the statistical service officer show how important amiability can be. He would rather hire a mediocre programmer who is easy-going and pleasant, than a very able one who is abrasive—who "makes waves and stirs up trouble." On one occasion, he served on an oral board which was interviewing a young lady. In terms of the applicant's computer knowledge, she was clearly superior to all the other applicants. But he and the other board members felt that she was too "aggressive and dynamic." There was too much "hostility" in her replies and, consequently, they flunked her.[11]

So much for merit principles in hiring.

There is some evidence to suggest that the test-based merit system does not work even when judged by its own standards. In a study conducted of the New York City civil service, which had roughly 250,000 out of a total of 400,000 employees who were considered "competitive class" employees (that is, they were hired and advanced on the basis of competitive tests), it was found that the "merit system discriminated *against those applicants who are most qualified according to its own standards.* Candidates with low passing grades are actually *more* likely to be hired than those with high passing grades! Furthermore, this perverse result seems to hold true for all skill levels."[12]

How so? The investigators found that the city had a lengthy waiting period between the date that an applicant took the examination and the date of hire—a median of seven months—and that, during this period, the best qualified were skimmed off by other employers. Conclusion: *"New York City's civil service system functions as an inverse merit system* (something the public at large has cynically assumed for years)."[13]

Trial by Fire: Firing Public Employees

One of the major arguments against civil service systems is that they provide a sinecure for life to public bureaucrats. Since their jobs cannot be threatened, they are responsible and responsive to no one. Nevertheless, it is unclear how firmly ensconced in their positions public bureaucrats really are. Although it is difficult to compare the proportionate number of dismissals between the public and private sectors, it nonetheless appears that, "There is every reason to believe that the annual rate of removal, ranging from a little less than 1 to about 1 1/2 percent of public jurisdictions in the United States as a whole, is exceeded, if at all, in certain categories of private employment, such as a few areas of manufacturing."[14] In other words, the proportionate numbers of people fired in both private enterprise and in government are about the same.

If these figures are accurate, then it is surprising that the rate of dismissal in the public sector is as high as it is. It is inordinately difficult to fire a public employee. In California, for example, a teacher may demand a hearing upon receiving notice of dismissal, and, unless the school board rescinds its action, it must file a complaint in Superior Court requesting the court to make an inquiry and to determine if the basis of dismissal is supportable. Then court-appointed referees hold hearings and report back to the court, a trial is held by the court itself, and a decision is made on whether the board may, in fact, dismiss the teacher. In effect, any contested dismissal of a California teacher brings the judiciary into the act.[15]

But even getting to the point of firing a public employee is difficult, and it is much more difficult to adjudge an employee's performance in some types of jobs than in others. In local government, the standards used to evaluate performance can themselves be unclear, and the visibility of a subordinate to his or her supervisor can vary from agency to agency. For example, it is relatively clear whether or not a secretary is turning out typing (the usual standard of performance for a secretary), and a secretary is relatively visible to his or her supervisor. But in such agencies as police departments, patrol officers are not very visible to their supervisors, nor is their standard of performance particularly clear.[16]

To compensate for these problems of assessing personnel in agencies where employees are relatively on their own, supervisors develop complicated performance forms and rating systems. These forms seldom follow function, and the presumption that the form is actually evaluating the performance of an employee is likely to be wrong. Nevertheless, bureaucrats are not spending their time ritualistically filling out useless pieces of paper; the forms actually are used to prevent problems from arising and to justify to outsiders a disciplinary action or decision to remove an employee.[17]

Public administrators using past personnel records as a political defense is not as cautionary as it may seem. Employees who are fired often attempt to bring in outsiders and apply public pressure to be reinstated. The ploy of expanding the scope of conflict between the employee and the employer, either in the courts or with the public, is a classic one in public employment circles. For example, while dismissals of the Oakland work force averaged less than 1 percent a year, almost two-thirds of those fired were on probation and therefore had no right of appeal to the city's civil service commission, but at least one-third of those persons who were dismissed as regular, nonprobationary employees appealed their dismissals to the commission.[18] In short, a supervisor can expect problems if he or she fires someone in the public bureaucracy.

Although state and local civil service systems may be both perverse and perverted by bureaucrats and elected officials alike, the presence of the system makes a difference in terms of how the politics of patronage is conducted. For example, in Oakland, a city that is virtually the archetype of reformed governments and council-manager rule, we have seen that the city manager and various appointed bureaucrats conduct the politics of personnel, but in boss-rule cities, the mayor takes over. For instance, the late Mayor Daley of Chicago was known to review the applications for even the lowest-level positions throughout the city.[19] Daley's chief concern was loyalty to himself and the Democratic Party, but even he could not totally ignore minimal professional competence as a requisite for an appointment. Similarly, we may expect state legislators and city council members to be much more interested in public appointments in states and cities where civil service traditions are not strong than in states and cities where a civil service system has been entrenched for some years.

THE CHALLENGES TO "MERIT"

The politics of public personnel administration, whether conducted according to the principles of merit or the boodle of patronage, can be complicated and arcane. Public personnel administration is a political phenomenon, and none the less so because of the rise of the civil service. In recent years, the civil service personnel system has received a series of major challenges to its principle of merit. Among these challenges are (1) the question of hiring and promoting greater numbers of citizens from deprived groups such as minorities, women, and the physically handicapped; and (2) the rise of unionism, collective bargaining, and strikes among public employees. These issues constitute the major challenges to the concept of merit in public employment.

RACE, SEX, AND JOBS: THE CHALLENGE OF AFFIRMATIVE ACTION

One of the myths of American democracy is that jobs, especially public jobs, are open to all. They are not. Prejudice is still with us, and it works against both women and members of minority groups. As a result, the public bureaucracy has witnessed the rise of "affirmative action." Affirmative action is a policy that argues for the hiring of members of disadvantaged groups on the grounds that government positions should be open to as many people as possible.

Affirmative Action: Pro and Con

Affirmative action is a highly sensitive issue in state and local public administration today. Those who favor affirmative action argue that government should make special efforts, including the reduction of entrance standards, to hire members of those segments of American society that have endured various forms of racial, religious, ethnic, or sexual discrimination. They reason that, because of cultural bias in testing, lack of educational opportunity, and general social prejudice, government owes those people who have suffered these injustices a special chance to get ahead. If this issue entails some bending of the civil service regulations, as often is done for veterans, so be it. Such rule-bending will, after all, only balance the social equities for those applicants who have had to suffer bigotry in the past. This is as it should be, since government is the single institution most responsible for assuring equality of opportunity in society.

Those who argue against affirmative action claim that no "lowering of standards" should be tolerated, regardless of the applicant's past tribulations. The logic for this viewpoint is that government owes the best possible governance to all the governed. To hire applicants who do not score as well on tests as other applicants, or who do not have comparable educational attainments, or who are just somehow less qualified, irrespective of the tough breaks in their backgrounds, is to do a disservice to the populace generally, deprived groups included. The economy, efficiency, effectiveness, and responsiveness of government will deteriorate to the detriment of all, unless only the top applicants are hired and promoted.

The Federal Impact

The federal government has adopted the first position. It favors hiring members of deprived groups, and consequently, it has implemented affirmative action policies that have had and are having a profound effect on state and local governments. The major legislation in this regard is the Civil Rights Act of 1964, which paved the way in a general fashion for the more specific efforts that followed. These included tougher executive orders by the president, prohibition of discrimination in federal agencies and by private contractors on the federal payroll, and some significant court decisions.

An especially important law in this light is the Equal Employment Opportunity Act of 1972. This brought state and local governments under the provisions of the Civil Rights Act for the first time. The act prohibits discrimination based on race, religion, sex, and national origin and directly affects roughly 13 million state and local government employees. The U.S. Equal Employment Opportunity Commission (EEOC), which the act established, may investigate charges of employment discrimination in state and local governments, and, if no conciliation is achieved, the U.S. Department of Justice may bring suit against the alleged offender. On top of that, the person in question may also initiate his or her own private litigation. It is this kind of federal legislation, plus significant court cases, that have made state and local governments extremely aware of the demands of minority groups and women.

Quotas or "Quality"?

These realities of national policy bring us quickly to the question of quotas. The term *quota* refers to the argument that the traditional entry and promotion qualifications of the civil service should be reduced or waived for women and minority group members until their numbers in government, at all ranks, equal their proportion of the population at large. In brief, each group would have a quota, or a percentage, of the public jobs allotted to it and that percentage would be equal to the group's percentage in the state's or city's population. If a city had 10 percent blacks in its population, then blacks would be allocated 10 percent of the city's jobs.

Pressure to establish quota systems in state and local governments has met with some success. In 1972, for example, a federal district court ordered that one black be hired for every newly hired white until the all-white Alabama state police force was 25 percent black, a figure corresponding to the percentage of blacks in Alabama according to the 1970 census. Although in another 1972 decision the federal court denied the legitimacy of an outright quota system, it nonetheless ordered the Minneapolis Fire Department to hire at least 1 minority applicant for every 2 whites in its next 60 openings. In 1973, the federal court ordered the San Francisco Civil Service Department to establish two separate lists of candidates for entry-level positions and promotions, one list for minorities and one for nonminorities, and to hire 3 minority candidates for every 2 nonminority candidates until the number of minority police patrol officers was brought up to at least 30 percent of the total. The court also ordered the department to promote one minority and one nonminority candidate until the total number of minority sergeants in the department also equaled at least 30 percent of the total number of sergeants. Similarly, openings in the Chicago police force were ordered to be filled in groups of 200, with 100 positions to be filled by blacks and Spanish-surnamed males, 33 to be filled by women, and 67 to be filled by other men.[20] Victor A. Thompson contends that the Chicago police department had more than 600 vacancies in 1974 "as a result" of such court orders.[21]

Minorities and Public Employment: Testing for What?

A landmark court case that has had a major impact on state and local public personnel practices as they applied to minorities was the 1971 U.S. Supreme Court case, *Griggs* v. *Duke Power Company*. On the face of it, the *Griggs* decision had nothing whatever to do with governments. The Court ruled that the Civil Rights Act banned discriminatory employment practices against blacks in a private company. Nevertheless, this decision has had considerable relevance for public personnel administration because it effectively bars those employment practices (notably intelligence tests and minimum education requirements) that operate to exclude members of disadvantaged groups when those practices cannot be shown to relate to job performance. The ruling did not demand the institution of flat quota systems in the employment of minority group members, nor did it preclude the use of tests in performance measurements. It did require that any such device actually indicate levels of employee performance and individual potential objectively.

The Supreme Court's decision in *Griggs* leads directly to the issue of test validity. *Test validity* means, "Do the several kinds of tests administered by the public bureaucracy for determining entry and promotion really indicate how well qualified an employee is for a job?" Test validity is determined by comparing "successful" employees with their scores on tests that are thought to be job related. High job performance should correlate with high test scores.

The growing controversy over test validity relates to another problem of public personnel examinations, that of cultural bias in testing. *Cultural bias* refers to the tendency of those highly educated people who write examinations to unwittingly slant the phrasing and nuances of their test questions in a way that reflects their own culture. Thus, people taking an examination who are not members of the dominant culture (i.e., who are not white) are unfairly handicapped in their chances to score as well as those examinees who have been reared in the prevailing culture. After investigating the phenomenon of cultural bias in testing, the California State Personnel Board concluded that "written tests were more of a barrier to employment of minorities than any other phase of the selection process." Accordingly, the board instituted greater use of nonverbal aptitude tests, tried to root out culturally biased language in written examinations, and placed more members of minority groups on oral examination boards.[22]

Reflecting this concern over cultural bias in testing is a spate of recent court cases. In 1975, a federal court held (in *David* v. *Washington*) that the fact that black applicants failed a written test given to all applicants to a local police force at a rate of more than four times that of whites was adequate evidence to prove that the examination had a "racially disproportionate" impact and that blacks were therefore being discriminated against in police force hiring.

A second significant case is that of *Albemarle Paper Company* v. *Moody,* which was decided by the Supreme Court in 1975. In its decision, the Court stated that back pay could be awarded to an employee who had been denied a promotion as a consequence of discriminatory testing procedures, even though the employer was not intentionally discriminating. The decision also held that a promotion system based on supervisory ratings was questionable because subjective human judgments were involved. The case reified the importance of developing valid testing procedures for promotions and other personnel decisions.

In 1982, the Supreme Court again addressed the problem of cultural bias in testing in the public service in the case of *State of Connecticut et al.* v. *Winnie Teal Adele.* Black state employees who had been serving as provisional welfare eligibility supervisors in Connecticut had failed a written examination. The passing rate for blacks was approximately two-thirds of that for white applicants. But the state of Connecticut argued that it had promoted more minorities than it had promoted whites, and so the "bottom line" was not discriminatory against blacks or other minorities. Thus, the use of the test that had discriminatory effects was irrelevant, since more blacks nonetheless were being promoted than whites.

The Court disagreed with the state's arguments, and held that merely because the "bottom line" was that more blacks were being promoted than whites, the state still could not allow racial discrimination against those black employees who were failing a test that was itself discriminatory. The Court held quite clearly that cultural bias in testing is against the law.

State and local governments have taken the problem of cultural bias and discrimination in testing fairly seriously. A survey conducted by the National Civil Service League of every major state and local public personnel system (outside of education) in 1970 indicated that only 54 percent of them validated any tests in any way regardless of type—written, oral, or whatever.[23] But a second survey taken about five years later by the National Civil Service League found that 87 percent had initiated test validation procedures.[24]

Women and Public Employment: The Curious Question of "Comparable Worth"

A somewhat newer wrinkle in the fabric of affirmative action is that of comparable worth. *Comparable worth* means that employees should be paid the same rate of pay for performing tasks that involve roughly the same levels of importance, knowledge, stress, skills, and responsibilities, even though the tasks themselves may be quite different. For example, a secretary may be performing a task that compares favorably to that of a highway repair worker in terms of its importance to society, the knowledge and skills it requires, the mental demands it makes, the stress it induces, and its level of responsibility.

As a practical matter, comparable worth is being used to pressure state and local employers to pay women as much as men. American women, on the average, earn about a third less than do men.[25] Although this margin is significantly narrower in the public sector, as we detail later, the difference nonetheless remains dramatic for public employees, too.

An important point is that the unit of analysis used in comparable worth is not individual positions, such as a secretary, but whole position classifications, such as all secretaries. Comparable worth as a concept relies on comparing different job classifications; when one job classification is judged to be of comparable worth to another job classification (for example, if secretaries are deemed to be comparable to highway repair workers), then both classifications must be paid at a comparable rate.

Questions of comparable worth are especially likely to rise when an entire position category is female dominated, as secretarial and clerical categories usually are. These female-dominated classes are compared to job categories of comparable worth that are dominated by men, and if the female-dominated job class is found to be paid less than the male-dominated class, it is assumed that the pay differential is attributable to systematic discrimination against women, and all employees in that class (including men) must be paid at a rate comparable to that of the male-dominated class. Since female-dominated and male-dominated position classes are considerably more evident than are minority-dominated and white-dominated classes, women are favored in most efforts to attain comparable worth.

Comparable worth relies on the idea that the social value of occupations can be compared, and this can be a tricky business. Is, for example, a city's symphony conductor worth "more" to society than the head of the municipal waterworks? The contributions of the conductor may elevate and inspire our souls, but we need potable water. Because the theory of comparable worth leads to these kinds of questions, the chair of the U.S. Commission on Civil Rights (a black male) called the concept "the looniest idea since Looney Tunes came on the screen," and in 1985 the Civil Rights Commission itself formally rejected comparable worth as a legitimate idea in assuring civil rights.[26] Women's rights groups immediately took sharp issue.

Controversial or not, comparable worth is making headway among the grassroots governments. At least 30 states have established various kinds of commissions to study and make recommendations to their legislatures about adjusting state government salaries for purposes of achieving comparable worth between male- and female-dominated jobs.[27] Four states have gone farther. Minnesota, New Mexico, and Washington adopted comparable worth plans in 1983, and began the process of raising the salaries of numerous female-dominated job classes; Iowa initiated its comparable worth adjustments in 1984.

Much of the interest in comparable worth associated with the case of *American Federation of State, County, and Municipal Employees (AFSCME)* v. *State of Washington.* A federal district court ruled in 1983 that Washington's state government had violated Title VII of the Civil Rights Act by discriminating against its employees on the basis of sex (despite the fact that the state already had initiated its own comparable worth plan) and ordered Washington to award back pay (possibly as much as $1 billion) to 15,500 employees in female-dominated position classifications and to speed up the implementation of the state's comparable worth plan.

But the judiciary appears to be ambivalent on the issue of comparable worth. In 1984, the Ninth Circuit Court of Appeals upheld the decision of the lower court by ruling in *Spaulding* v. *University of Washington* that the University was not in violation of Title VII, even though it paid its nursing faculty (who are mostly women) less than faculty in male-dominated departments.

More significant was the decision rendered in 1985 by the same court in the appeal by Washington State over the case it had lost in 1983, *American Federation of State, County, and Municipal Employees (AFSCME)* v. *State of Washington.* The court overruled the lower court and held that Washington did not have to award back pay to 15,500 employees in position classifications dominated by women. "Neither law nor logic deems the free market a suspect enterprise," said the court, adding that the Civil Rights Act did not obligate Washington "to eliminate an economic inequality which it did not create." Women's rights groups reacted to the decision immediately, vociferously, and hostilely. Ultimately, the case was settled out of court.

If the courts are undecided about comparable worth, so are the grassroots governments. Although four states have taken the initiative in introducing comparable worth plans (and, in the case of Minnesota, extending the concept to its local governments as well), another four (Colorado, Florida, Missouri, and Nebraska) have explicitly rejected comparable worth. Whether comparable worth is "looney" or progressive, it will be an issue for some time to come.

And What About White Males? The "Reverse Discrimination" Dilemma

The court orders and public policies that we have reviewed have resulted in the accusation of "reverse discrimination," a charge usually leveled by organizations made up largely of white males. White police officers in Dayton, Ohio, for example, sued that city in 1973 charging racial discrimination in promotions. The most famous reverse discrimination case is *Regents of the University of California* v. *Bakke,* in which Allan Bakke, a white male, was denied admission to the University of California's Medical School at Davis because that institution had set aside a portion (16 percent) of each entering class for blacks and other minorities.

In 1978, the Supreme Court, in a 5-to-4 decision, ruled against the university. Importantly, the Court did not rule that racial quotas were unconstitutional. If the majority had held that the University of California had violated the Constitution, then affirmative action programs across the country would probably have faced dismantling. Fortunately for these programs, however, all nine justices agreed that affirmative action programs per se were neither unconstitutional nor illegal and that being from a minority group could "be deemed a 'plus' in a particular applicant's file," although it would "not insulate the individual from comparison with all other candidates."

A year following the *Bakke* ruling, the Supreme Court heard a second case that came to be known as the "blue-collar Bakke" decision. In *Weber* v. *Kaiser Aluminum and Steel Corporation and United Steel Workers Union,* Brian Weber, a white lab technician, charged that both his employer and his union were discriminating against whites by mandating that a joint union and company training program for skilled craft jobs must have half of its available positions filled by whites and the other half filled by blacks. Weber had been denied entrance into the program, even though he had more seniority than two blacks who were admitted. The Court, in a 5-to-2 decision, held that Kaiser as well as other employers could consider race as a factor in hiring and promotion policies. The Court argued that Title VII of the Civil Rights Act had been passed for the purpose of improving the economic status of blacks, and so a voluntary program in the private sector that gave special preferences to blacks was not in violation of the statute.

In 1984, the Supreme Court altered the direction of its moderately pro-affirmative action decisions in the area of reverse discrimination by overturning two lower courts and ruling in a 6-to-3 opinion that layoffs based on seniority did not violate Title VII of the Civil Rights Act. *Firefighters Local Union No. 1784 et al.* v. *Carl W. Stotts et al.* involved the city of Memphis's decision in 1981 to lay off fire fighters on the basis of seniority (i.e., last hired, first fired), a standard practice among unionized workers, and a resultant temporary restraining order by a federal district court forbidding the city to lay off any black fire fighters in the process. The reasoning of the district court in issuing its order was that Memphis had entered earlier into a consent decree, approved by the district court in 1980, that held in part that the city would try to attain a goal of a fire department that was 20 percent black. In the district court's view, to lay off fire fighters by seniority would not only violate the consent decree, but would disproportionately affect blacks, who had been hired later than whites. Thus, the city was ordered by the district court to lay off whites who had more seniority than blacks. This ruling was upheld by the U.S. Court of Appeals.

The Supreme Court took a different perspective, however, and stated that "there was no finding that any of the blacks protected from layoffs had been a victim of discrimination and no award of competitive seniority to any of them." Hence, the Civil Rights Act had not been violated by Memphis's decision to lay off its fire fighters on the basis of seniority because the intent of Congress in the act is to "provide make-whole relief only to those who have been victims of illegal discrimination." In other words, black fire fighters in Memphis, according to the Court, had not been discriminated against in the past, and therefore a policy of last hired, first fired was an appropriate way to decide who was going to be laid off.

The likely effects of this decision is to make it more difficult for minorities and women to keep their jobs in unionized government agencies and industries because minorities and women tend to have less seniority than do white males. The Court's opinion—an important one for blue-collar public employees—was not greeted with favor by the nation's civil rights groups.

Regardless of how reverse discrimination suits will be decided in the courtroom, it is clear that the problem is both real and divisive, not only for public administrators, but for the citizenry. A review of public opinion polls on the topic concluded that "Americans are sensitive to the distinction between *compensatory action* and *preferential treatment*" in the hiring and promotion of minorities and women.[28] Vast majorities of whites in various surveys conducted from 1972 on respond that they approve of such actions as government job-training programs for minorities, but draw the line in suspending normal merit standards as a means of hiring and promoting minorities. Indeed, blacks and women also respond in this way; in a Gallup poll, for example, blacks endorsed promoting minorities on the basis of "ability" over "preferential treatment" by 64 to 27 percent, and 71 percent of the women respondents favored the same distinction.[29] Nevertheless, whose ox is gored remains a valid political principle, and the discrimination issue is no exception. College faculty members, for example, heavily favor using affirmative action criteria in deciding the admission of undergraduates to college (62 percent), but when it comes to deciding their own careers, they are not nearly so positively disposed toward the notion; less than 35 percent of the nation's professors favor giving preferential treatment to women and minority applicants for faculty positions.[30]

In responding to the dilemma of reverse discrimination, some state and local governments seem to have gone overboard—perhaps in part because of the wiliness of their employees. Consider these examples.[31] In 1977, 53 San Francisco police officers claiming that they were American Indians were hauled before the Equal Opportunity Commission, and all were officially reclassified as white.

In Los Angeles, a city long under federal pressure to desegregate its schools, the school board was attempting to attain faculties in each school that were at least 30 percent minorities. Both white and minority teachers began claiming they were of a different race to avoid being sent to another school district. To counter this ploy, Los Angeles established "ethnic review committees" that investigated "ethnic discrepancies" among teachers.

In New York, both teachers and pupils are "visually confirmed" by the Board of Education for racial identification purposes—and the subsequent assignment to a school.

All this may sound like springtime in Hitler's Germany. Racial certification, regardless of motivation, is unpalatable to most Americans. Nevertheless, racial review boards may become a standard component in the state and local governments of the future as public employees of all races try to "pass" for the sake of enhancing their work location and promotion prospects.

The Politics of Affirmative Action: The Oakland Experience

How local governments respond to the question of affirmative action has been detailed in Thompson's case study of Oakland. In 1969, spokespersons for minority job hunters challenged Oakland's personnel director over his affirmative action policies. The challenge came as the result of a report issued by the U.S. Commission on Civil Rights, which observed that Oakland was the only major jurisdiction among seven metropolitan areas studied in which the three main minority groups were substantially underrepresented in the city's job rosters. With a minority population of almost 50 percent in Oakland, only 15.3 percent of its city hall employees were black, 1.5 percent had Spanish surnames, and 1.6 percent were Oriental.

Oakland's minority leaders focused on two strategies. They attempted to "bang Oakland officials over the head" with the city's dismal record of minority employment, and they also tried to involve themselves in the recruitment structures of the city. A major target of the minorities was the police force; minority leaders felt that its written tests were culturally biased, and a suit was duly filed. Minorities also pressured for a Citizen's Advisory Committee for the force; the police chief and the personnel director resisted, seeing it as a front for a community control board.

Oakland city officials were quick to construct their own version of a domino theory on affirmative action: if one department "fell" to minority pressure, then all the departments would become more susceptible to affirmative action demands. Although Oakland officials had the legal and actual power to deny flatly the demands of minorities, they chose not to be so direct and thus avoided an image of unresponsiveness. Delay was a major tactic in this strategy. Because recruitment authority in Oakland's city hall was widely dispersed, officials had a great deal of opportunity to pass the buck. One frustrated minority spokesperson compared the bureaucracy of Oakland to a "monolithic multi-headed hydra—when we approach one head, it always tells us that the other head is responsible." Or, as another minority member stated, "In Oakland the buck never stops."[32]

Meanwhile, city officials marshalled a variety of tactics designed to justify their own positions and throw the blame on the minorities. For example, the personnel director warned, "The city is responsible to the taxpayer and can't afford to hire people not capable of doing their jobs."[33]

Not all of Oakland's officials were so recalcitrant on the issue. Some procedures were changed to encourage minority applicants, and the use of oral examinations was expanded to facilitate the entrance of minorities into city government. As Thompson observes, "Orals make favoritism feasible both in structuring the mechanism and scoring applicant responses. Furthermore, racial preference in the oral is not as visible within the bureaucracy as are other adjustments aimed at helping minorities (for example, lowering credential requirements). Consequently, manipulation of the oral is less likely to precipitate organized opposition."[34] Thompson concludes that, in the face of demands from minorities to expand minority representation in the city, a personnel director generally will put more pressure on those city departments that have hired few minorities, that have made little effort to recruit them, and that have a substantial number of open slots.

The Effects of the Efforts

The city of Oakland is a microcosm of the problem of representation of deprived groups in state and local governments across the country. But despite the political problems that are inherent in hiring members of deprived groups in state and local governments, some progress has been made. More than a fifth of full-time state and local employees (excluding educators) are from minority groups, but most minorities are found at the bottom rungs of the state and local employment ladders. However, it should be noted that state and local governments are substantially ahead of their federal counterpart in that significantly greater proportions of minorities are at the the top of the state and local employment ladder.[35] Nine percent of minorities are officials and administrators in state and local governments and 16 percent are professionals of other kinds. Table 13-1 shows these relationships.

Minority groups also are paid less (14 percent less, on the average) than are their white counterparts for doing similar jobs. This is true in every occupational category displayed in the table. However, when we look at data for the nation as a whole, minorities are paid about 20 percent less than are whites, on the average.[36]

Table 13-1 also displays data for women. As it shows, 41 percent of all state and local employees (again excluding educators) are women. As with minorities, most women employees in state and local governments tend to be found on the lower rungs of the ladder, particularly in the paraprofessional and office clerical categories. However, unlike the federal government, a significantly greater number of women are found in the upper rungs of the occupational ladder.[37] Twenty-three percent are officials or administrators in states and lo-

Table 13-1 Full-time Employment and Salaries in State and Local Governments by Sex and Minority Groups, 1980

	Total[1]	*Officials admin-istrators*	*Profes-sionals*	*Techni-cians*	*Protec-tive service*	*Para-profes-sionals*	*Office/ clerical*	*Skilled craft*	*Service/ mainte-nance*
Percentage Employed[2]									
Male	59%	77%	66%	61%	93%	30%	11%	96%	73%
Female	41	23	44	39	7	70	89	4	27
White	79	91	84	83	86	53	79	82	62
Minority groups, total[3]	21	9	16	17	14	47	21	18	37
Black	16	6	9	12	10	28	14	12	30
Hispanic	4	2	3	4	3	3	5	5	7
Median Annual Salary ($1,000)									
Total	$13.3	$21.8	$18.2	$13.9	$16.0	$10.4	$10.6	$14.1	$11.1
Male	15.2	23.2	20.0	15.6	16.3	11.5	11.9	14.2	11.6
Female	11.4	17.5	15.7	11.8	13.0	9.9	10.4	13.6	9.2
White	13.8	21.8	18.3	14.2	16.2	10.6	10.6	14.1	11.4
Minority groups, total[3]	11.8	20.6	17.0	12.6	15.0	10.9	10.5	13.6	14.4
Black	11.5	20.9	16.0	12.1	14.6	9.9	10.4	13.4	10.2
Hispanic	12.3	20.4	17.6	13.5	15.8	12.3	10.4	13.8	10.9

[1] Excludes educators.
[2] Percentages have been rounded.
[3] Includes other minority groups, not shown separately.

Source: As derived from U.S. Bureau of the Census, *Statistical Abstract of the United States, 1982–83* (Washington, D.C.: U.S. Government Printing Office, 1982), Table 504, p. 305.

calities and 44 percent are professionals, a percentage higher than the total number of women working for state and local governments.

It is in the area of salaries that genuine disparities are evident. On the average, women earn 25 percent less than do their male colleagues in state and local governments, although, as we noted earlier, this is less of a difference than is found in the private sector.

Although some action has been taken regarding attempts to improve the representation of women and minorities at the grassroots levels of government, the initiative that these governments have shown, especially at the local level, has not been impressive. A survey of more than 2,000 city managers found that 54 percent of the responding managers stated that no action plans had been taken by their jurisdictions concerning affirmative action for women, and of those cities that had taken such action, the initiative had been taken on the city manager's own initiative in more than four-fifths of the cases. In only 52 percent of the cases did the manager have the support of his or her own city council.

In terms of initiating affirmative action plans for minorities, the percentages were a little higher: 55 percent of the cities surveyed had initiated an affirmative action plan for minorities, a significantly higher proportion than that for women. In 84 percent of those cities, the action had been started by the city manager, and, in 56 percent of those cases, the manager had the support of the city council. "While managers and chief administrators exhibit no strong personal commitment to such [equal opportunity] goals, they are far and away the principal initiators of affirmative action in their governments."[38]

Indeed, of all the cities surveyed, council-manager cities tended to be the most positive in establishing employment goals and objectives for minorities and women and in relaxing temporarily civil service requirements to increase minority employment.

Affirmative action, or more properly defined, the giving of an even break to people who have been disadvantaged in society because of their race or sex, is one of the knottier problems of state and local governments. Judging by the available data, state and local governments have made some progress in opening their doors to members of disadvantaged groups. This is as it should be. If government—the institution in society most responsible for according people an equal chance regardless of race, religion, sex, or handicap—is not responsive, then what social institution will be?

BLUE-COLLAR BUREAUCRATS: THE CHALLENGE OF PUBLIC EMPLOYEE UNIONISM

The unionization of public employees is a relatively new and occasionally discomfiting phenomenon in public administration. Nearly 17 percent of all union members are public employees; more than 6 percent of all union members work for the federal government, and more than 10 percent have jobs in state and local governments. Not quite half of all full-time state and local employees are members of unions or closely related organizations.[39]

Table 13-2 breaks down the percentage of state and local full-time employees who are in labor unions by job function. Fire fighters have long led the list as the most heavily organized of public employees, followed by teachers and

Table 13-2 Percentage of State and Local Employees (Full-Time) in Labor Unions by Job Function, 1980[a]

Functions	*State and Local Governments (%)*
Fire fighters	77%
Teachers	70
Police officers	56
Sanitation workers	50
Highway employees	46
Public welfare employees	45
Hospital employees	42
All other functions	39

[a] Percentages have been rounded.

Source: U.S. Bureau of the Census, *Labor Management Relations in State and Local Government, 1981* (Washington, D.C.: U.S. Government Printing Office, 1982.

police. These and other occupational groups are represented by more than 25,000 bargaining units.

The major unions of state and local government workers are the National Education Association with nearly 1.7 million members; the American Federation of State, County and Municipal Employees (AFSCME) with more than 950,000 members; the American Federation of Teachers with more than 450,000 members; the Fraternal Order of Police with more than 150,000 members; and the International Association of Firefighters with approximately 140,000 members.[40]

Among the states, Rhode Island has the greatest proportion of its state and local public employees organized, with 83 percent of them belonging to unions. Rhode Island is followed closely by New York and Connecticut, which both have more than 72 percent of their public employees in unions. At the other end of the scale is Mississippi, with fewer than 9 percent of its state and local employees who are organized. By and large, the most fully organized public employees are found in the Northeast, and the least organized are in the Southeast.[41]

Efforts to organize public employees are not new, and attempts to organize government workers can be traced back to the 1830s.[42] And, in the 1800s, there was much reason for public employees to organize. Police and fire fighters, for example, who are among the most heavily unionized public employees today, have traditionally tolerated among the worst working conditions. In 1907, the New York Health Department condemned 30 of the city's 85 police stations as uninhabitable, and the police worked from 73 to 98 hours a week. Fire fighters, who commonly were paid low salaries, worked 21 hours *a day* and had only one day off in eight![43] Still, despite such conditions, there was considerable resistance to the unionization of public employees. The reasons were mostly ideological, but also economic. As merit systems developed in state and local governments, job security became more assured and working conditions did improve. There were (and are) also a spate of state and local laws forbidding or discouraging any kind of union activity by government workers (the constitutionality of which is at least questionable). White-collar workers, as a class, had never really identified with unionization, and, finally, there was a considerable weight of public opinion against the notion of government workers being allowed to disrupt vital public services by resorting to the strike.

Big Labor and Public Management

The indications that attitudes on the issue of organizing public workers were shifting came first at the state and local levels. In 1959 Wisconsin passed the first law requiring its local governments to bargain collectively, and 41 of the states and more than 16 percent of the nation's local governments now have some sort of a labor relations policy. Among the local governments, school districts clearly lead the way, with almost 55 percent of the nation's school districts reporting some sort of labor relations policy.[44]

State and local governments are only beginning to become sophisticated in their dealings with organized employees. Generally, state and local policies on government negotiations with organized employees are of two types. The *collective bargaining* approach permits decisions on salaries, hours, and working conditions to be made jointly between employees and employer representatives. Thirty-five states use collective bargaining as their primary method of dealing with labor unions, although only six of these use collective bargaining exclusively. Of the 13,053 local governments that have some sort of labor relations policy, 82 percent use collective bargaining in their dealings with organized public employees.[45]

The *meet-and-confer* tack says only that both sides must meet and confer over these issues but that management has the final decision. Only six states use a meet-and-confer approach exclusively, and only 18 percent of the local governments that have an explicit labor relations policy use it. Presumably, however, those states and localities that do not have any stated labor relations policy rely informally on a meet-and-confer approach.

State and local governments are becoming increasingly innovative in bargaining with their employees. Englewood, Colorado, for example, has passed a city ordinance stipulating that an impartial fact-finders' recommendation will be put on the ballot with the best last offer of the union and management alongside it; then Englewood lets the voters decide the issues.[46] Englewood reflects the increasing use of "goldfish bowl bargaining," or "sunshine bargaining," in which the public is being brought increasingly into the negotiation process, a process that traditionally, particularly in the private sector, has gone on behind closed doors. This protects the public's right to know and opens up the bargaining at a time when the public's knowledge can affect the outcome of the negotiation process. About a dozen states have enacted sunshine bargaining statutes.[47]

Collective Bargaining: The Record in Dollars

The basic dilemma of collective bargaining in the public sector is the fact that, unlike the private sector, neither side is bargaining with its own money. Public labor is demanding tax monies that may or may not be in the public till, and public management is negotiating with tax money that likewise may not be in the public till. The person who pays is the taxpayer. With this reality in mind, it is not too surprising that public labor unions have made considerable gains financially in their negotiations with public management. Personnel costs account for between 50 to 80 percent of a typical city budget, and at least part of that percentage stems from the gains that workers have won in collective bargaining.[48]

An important negotiating area between public employers and employees is that of pensions. In police departments, for example, the national tendency has been to permit retirement at half-pay after 20 years' service. Such arrangements, of course, aggravate urban financial problems, as happened in New York City. In New York, transit workers, police, fire fighters, and other workers are allowed early retirement with generous benefits, and "the pension specialist" of the American Federation of State, County, and Municipal Employees has been quoted as saying that its "members are just beginning to realize that pensions can be negotiated." When queried where the money for higher pensions is coming from, the pension specialist for AFSCME replied, "That's government's problem. Just because there is a pinch for money, it's no excuse to make the employees do without."[49]

Collective bargaining has given public employees a relatively good deal. For example, a study by the Institute of Labor Relations of 12 Michigan school districts concluded that collective bargaining appeared to have given teachers 10 to 20 percent more in wage increases than unilateral school board action would have furnished.[50]

The Public Strike: The Public Record

Because of the potential fiscal impacts that collective bargaining can have on state and local governments, states and cities often are reluctant to "come across" to union demands. The result of such reluctance can be, and occasionally is, a strike. At one time sanitation workers were the most frequent public employees to walk picket lines, but more recently, it has been teachers who are most inclined to strike. Table 13-3 indicates the kinds of public workers who tend to strike and the dimensions of their strikes. As it shows, the vast bulk of public employee strikes are conducted at the local level, and the great majority are conducted by educators. Wages are the chief issues in these strikes, followed closely by pensions. Since 1979, strikes have been in decline, and it appears that their duration is growing briefer.[51]

Regardless of whether or not there are laws permitting or prohibiting strikes in the public sector, strikes are realities. The emotional issue of the public employee's right to strike nonetheless runs deep. One viewpoint holds that a strike by public employees amounts to an act of insurrection because such strikes are directed against the people themselves. The opposing view contends that the right of government workers to strike is a basic freedom protected under the Constitution. To deny public employees a right granted to workers in private corporations is to treat public personnel as second-class citizens. The courts thus far have held that there is no constitutional right of public workers to strike, but neither has the judiciary prohibited the enactment of laws permitting government employees to strike.

Table 13-3 Work Stoppages in State and Local Governments, 1980

Item	Total[1]	EDUCATION Total	EDUCATION Instructional	EDUCATION Other	Highways	Hospitals	Police and fire protection	Public welfare
Work stoppages (number)[2, 3]								
Total	502	287	225	62	45	20	63	14
State	22	7	4	3	0	4	1	1
Local	480	280	221	59	45	16	62	13
Employees involved in work stoppages (1,000)[3]								
Total	233	126	99	27	3	7	10	3
State	16	4	2	2	0	1	Fewer than 500	Fewer than 500
Local	217	122	97	25	3	6	10	3
Days of idleness (1,000)[2]								
Total	2,407	1,534	1,235	298	26	32	92	23
State	90	37	18	20	0	2	Fewer than 500	Fewer than 500
Local	2,317	1,496	1,218	278	26	30	92	23

[1] Includes other functions, not shown separately.

[2] Represents period from October 16 of previous year to October 15 of year stated.

[3] Contains duplication; each work stoppage is counted separately for each function affected, but only once in total work stoppages.

Source: Derived from Bureau of the Census, *Statistical Abstract of the United States, 1985* (Washington, D.C.: U.S. Government Printing Office, 1984), Table 711, p. 425.

Unions versus "Merit": The Basic Differences

The future of collective bargaining, unionization, and the right to strike bodes ill for the traditional merit standards of the civil service personnel system. At root, the differences between the "collective system" and the "civil service system" are two. One difference concerns the notion of *sovereignty*. The civil service systems holds that a public position is a privilege, not a right, and that each public servant is obliged to uphold the public trust accorded to him or her by a paternalistic government. Conversely, the union system holds that employees are on an equal footing with employers and that they have a right to use their collective powers as a means of improving their conditions of employment. The civil service system, by contrast, sees this contention as a threat to the sovereignty of the state, whereas the union system views the traditions of the civil service as smacking of worker exploitation.

The second difference concerns the concept of *individualism*. The American civil service system long has valued the ideal that the individual worker should be judged for a position on the basis of his or her unique merits for performing the duties of a particular job. The union system, on the other hand, argues that the identity of the individual should be absorbed in a collective effort to better the conditions of all workers. Hence, the relations of the individual with his or her government employer are replaced by a new set of relations that exist between the government employer and a collective "class" of employees. Among the conflicts over sovereignty and individualism that result from these fundamental differences between the two systems are disputes over employee participation and rights (equal treatment versus union shop), recruitment (competitive test versus union membership), promotion (performance versus seniority), position classification and pay (objective analysis versus negotiation), working conditions (determination by legislatures and managements versus settlement by negotiations), and grievances (determination by civil service commissioners versus union representation to third-party arbitrators).

THE RISE OF THE PROFESSIONAL PUBLIC ADMINISTRATOR

In the face of the manifold problems challenging the grassroots bureaucrats, it is encouraging that our state and local governments are blessed with public managers who are likely more capable and professional than ever before. State administrators, for example, have been surveyed since 1964, and the data indicate that, at the top levels, they are becoming an increasingly professional "administrative class." One indication is their consistently improving educational levels. In 1964, more than a third of state agency heads had not completed college, 15 percent had not attended college, and 40 percent held a graduate degree; by 1978, 11 percent had not completed college, only 3 percent had not attended college, and 58 percent had earned a graduate degree, mostly in management and public administration.[52] These are impressive figures, and they indicate that state governments are moving away from "good ol' boy bureaucracies" and toward administrative organizations that are based on technical expertise and managerial competence. Table 13-4 indicates these trends.

A second mark of growing professionalism among state administrators is the deepening commitment that these men and women appear to have to careers in the state public service. One indication of this commitment is the career patterns of state administrators. Increasingly, state agency heads are entering the state service at an earlier age and are pursuing long-term careers in it. In 1964, 35 percent of state agency heads held their first position in state government before they were 30 years old, and their median age when they first entered state government was 33. By 1978, nearly 50 percent of top state administrators had entered state public service before they were 30, and their median age at that time had slipped to 30. The proportion of state agency heads whose job immediately prior to taking their present position was an elected office declined by half between 1964 and 1978, indicating that out-of-work politicians are being less cared for at the expense of state government than they once were. By contrast, the proportion of top state administrators who have moved up the agency ladder to the top spot has burgeoned from 28 percent in 1964 to 41 percent in 1978.[53]

As levels of education and professionalism have increased among state agency heads, so has the quality of representativeness. As Table 13-4 shows, although the numbers still leave much to be desired, the percentage of top state administrators who are women has quadrupled in the 14 years between 1964 and 1978, and the proportion of blacks has tripled.

Within these general trends, the professionalism of state bureaucracies varies widely. Table 13-5 is an effort to compare the states' bureaucracies on the basis of professional criteria—that is, level of training for personnel, salaries of administrators, information processing capacities, "innovativeness" as determined by the states' adoption of advanced budgeting techniques, and political

Table 13-4 Personal and Background Characteristics of State Agency Heads (in percentages, unless otherwise indicated)

Characteristics	COMPARED AGENCIES (27 COMMON AGENCIES) 1964	1968	1974	1978	All Agencies 1978 (75 agency types)
Age					
Under 40	13%	14%	17%	22%	26%
40–49	28	29	31	33	31
50–59	35	38	33	31	31
60 and over	24	19	19	14	12
Mean age (years)	52	50	50	48	47
Median age (years)	52	51	50	49	48
Sex					
Male	98	95	96	93	92
Female	2	5	4	7	8
Ethnic background					
White	98	97	96	92	93
Black	1	1	2	2	3
American Indian			0.1	1	1
Oriental	1	2	2	4	2
Spanish	NA	NA	NA	1	1
Educational attainment					
High school or less	15	7	4	3	3
Some college	19	18	13	11	8
Bachelor's degree	25[a]	15	18	15	15
Some graduate study		16	17	14	15
Graduate degree	40	45	47	56	58
Highest college degree					
None	34	24	17	14	11
Bachelor's	25	31	36	29	31
MA or MS	8	10	13	18	24
Professional master's	3	4	5	11	11
Doctorate (except JD)	9	13	12	13	12
Law (includes JD)	21	18	17	15	11
Major areas of specialization[1]					
Accounting	15	21	23	21	18
Business	19	20	34	32	30
Legal	30	23	20	22	18
Management	NA	NA	46	53	52
Public administration	14	19	46	45	44

[a] This figure includes some graduate study.

[1] From 1964 and 1968, areas of specialization included any training beyond high school. The data for 1974 and 1978 include training in addition to degree specialties.

NA – Not available.

Source: State Government, Vol. 55, No. 1 (Lexington, Ky.: Council of State Governments, 1982.

neutrality. Using these measures, the wealthier, industrial states fare well, notably, California, Michigan, New York, Pennsylvania, and Wisconsin, but the poorer, rural states do not, particularly Alabama, Arkansas, Mississippi, Montana, Nebraska, North Dakota, and Wyoming. But if the data on state agency heads are any indication, the professionalism of state administration is improving across the board over time.

Table 13-5 The "Quality" of State Administration

State	EXPERTISE		INFORMATION-PROCESSING CAPACITY		INNOVATIVENESS	PARTISAN NEUTRALITY
	Professional training	Administrative salaries	Publications	EDP equipment	Performance budgeting	Merit system
Alabama	0.36[a]	32[b]	150[c]	6[d]	0[e]	100.0%[f]
Alaska	1.65	—	356	0	2	87.5
Arizona	1.46	37	195	0	0	14.4
Arkansas	0.00	33	173	4	—	10.5
California	5.73	2	1,282	30	3	100.0
Colorado	2.11	15	177	5	4	75.0
Connecticut	1.62	10	275	9	4	77.9
Delaware	0.00	45	103	3	0	6.2
Florida	0.33	13	499	6	1	33.3
Georgia	0.00	9	753	11	1	53.0
Hawaii	0.00	—	490	3	3	41.4
Idaho	0.00	46	217	1	0	100.0
Illinois	0.73	6	839	—	3	40.4
Indiana	0.15	22	539	5	1	64.4
Iowa	0.23	24	156	6	0	7.4
Kansas	1.99	27.5	425	—	4	66.7
Kentucky	0.00	29	362	—	1	82.7
Louisiana	0.00	44	543	7	3	79.4
Maine	0.00	35	225	1	0	94.7
Maryland	4.66	14	323	—	4	90.1
Massachusetts	2.49	16	1,040	10	2	—
Michigan	1.36	4	476	10	0	97.6
Minnesota	1.41	17	364	4	1	85.1
Mississippi	0.28	47	330	1	0	—
Missouri	6.74	23	457	9	3	45.0
Montana	0.00	43	309	4	2	10.0
Nebraska	0.22	42	150	—	0	10.0
Nevada	0.00	26	324	2	1	70.0
New Hampshire	0.00	38	61	0	—	100.0
New Jersey	1.91	11	537	7	3	84.5
New Mexico	0.00	36	255	4	1	95.2
New York	4.54	1	1,415	24	3	89.4
North Carolina	2.05	21	659	2	4	5.0
North Dakota	0.00	40	107	3	0	—
Ohio	0.52	3	630	8	0	90.9
Oklahoma	7.82	19	342	4	4	56.2
Oregon	0.00	18	701	6	3	88.5
Pennsylvania	3.74	5	693	5	3	54.3
Rhode Island	1.77	25	95	0	2	81.9
South Carolina	0.00	20	226	6	0	—
South Dakota	0.49	41	251	2	—	7.6
Tennessee	0.91	34	445	2	0	18.1
Texas	0.35	8	903	9	1	8.6
Utah	5.98	31	245	7	2	50.5
Vermont	0.00	30	69	1	2	93.9

Table 13-5 (Continued)

State	EXPERTISE		INFORMATION-PROCESSING CAPACITY		INNOVA-TIVENESS	PARTISAN NEUTRALITY
	Profes-sional training	*Admin-istrative salaries*	*Publi-cations*	*EDP equip-ment*	*Performance bud-geting*	*Merit system*
Virginia	0.44	27.5	760	6	1	11.9
Washington	1.61	7	690	—	4	85.7
West Virginia	0.00	39	283	—	1	—
Wisconsin	0.80	12	444	7	3	78.2
Wyoming	0.00	48	144	0	0	100.0

[a] This is a weighted measure of full- and part-time graduate students in advanced degree programs in public affairs and administration in a state per 1,000 state employees.
[b] The administrative salaries indicator focuses on the ability of state bureaucracies to attract expert personnel. It is a measure first devised by Ira Sharkansky, "State Administrators in the Political Process," in Herbert Jacob and Kennet Vines, eds., *Politics in the American States* (Boston: Little, Brown, 1971), pp. 238–271. The table entry is the state rank.
[c] Number of publications issued by each state government in 1970.
[d] Number of computers available for state government use.
[e]Table entry reports the extent to which a state has adopted one or more of four types of performance data in its budget documents.
[f] Percentage of state government employees covered by a comprehensive merit civil service system.

Source: Lee Sigelman, "The Quality of Administration: An Exploration in the American States," *Administration and Society,* 8 (March 1976), pp. 107–144.

TURMOIL IN THE PUBLIC SERVICE

The problems that we have reviewed here dealing with "the administrative class" in state and local governments are complex and massive. Public personnel administration, like any other form of public administration, has large dollops of politics as part and parcel of it. The historic efforts of "good government" reformers to rid public personnel systems of "politics" traditionally have been based on the introduction of "merit principles" in the management of the public bureaucracy. Merit principles, as they normally have been understood, are now under considerable attack. The efforts to include more minorities and women in government, the attempts to expand freedom of political expression for government employees, and the reality of strikes, unionism, and collective bargaining, all lead one to wonder what "merit" in public personnel administration really means.

These problems of the public bureaucracy have, in the view of some, rendered it a helpless giant in dealing with the public's problems. But if public servants do not deal effectively with public problems (and it is our contention that in fact they do), then how do such vital public services as road construction, recreation facilities, hospitals, health services, environmental controls, and a variety of other programs get accomplished? We consider how these and other policies are implemented in the following and concluding chapter of this section on grassroots bureaucracy, and in so doing we explore an area of state and local politics that amounts to *terra incognita* for most citizens: the contracting out of public services to private interests and public corporations.

NOTES

[1]Advisory Commission on Intergovernmental Relations, *Significant Features of Fiscal Federalism, 1984* (Washington, D.C.: U.S. Government Printing Office, 1985), p. 133. Figures are for 1983.
[2]*Ibid.*, p. 134; and Bureau of the Census, *Statistical Abstract of the United States, 1985* (Washington, D.C.: U.S. Government Printing Office, 1984), Table 474, p. 293.
[3]Advisory Commission on Intergovernmental Relations, *Significant Features of Fiscal Federalism, 1980-81* (Washington, D.C.: U.S. Government Printing Office, 1981), p. 71. Figure is for 1979.
[4]O. Glenn Stahl, *Public Personnel Administration*, 8th ed. (New York: Harper & Row, 1983), pp. 42-43. Figures are for 1980.
[5]Jay M. Shafritz et al., *Personnel Management in Government: Politics and Process* (New York: Marcel Dekker, 1978), p. 45.
[6]Martin Tolchin and Susan Tolchin, *To the Victor—Political Patronage from the Clubhouse to the White House* (New York: Vintage, 1971), p. 102.
[7]Frank J. Thompson, *Personnel Policy in the City: The Politics of Jobs in Oakland* (Berkeley: University of California Press, 1975), pp. 15-16.
[8]*Ibid.*, p. 76.
[9]Shafritz et al., *Personnel Management in Government*, p. 52.
[10]Thompson, *Personnel Policy in the City*, pp. 21-22.
[11]*Ibid.*, p. 106.
[12]E. S. Savas and Sigmund G. Ginsburg, "The Civil Service: A Meritless System?" *The Public Interest*, 32 (Summer, 1973), p. 76. Emphasis is original.
[13]*Ibid.*, p. 77.
[14]O. Glenn Stahl, *Public Personnel Administration*, 7th ed. (New York: Harper & Row, 1975), p. 309. All other references to Stahl pertain to the eighth (1983) edition of this work.
[15]Stahl, *Public Personnel Administration*, p. 158.
[16]Thompson, *Personnel Policy in the City*, pp. 142-143.
[17]Herbert Kaufman, *The Forest Ranger* (Baltimore, Md.: Johns Hopkins, 1960), p. 158.
[18]Thompson, *Personnel Policy in the City*, p. 156.
[19]Mike Royko, *Boss* (New York: Signet, 1971), pp. 22-23.
[20]Charles S. Rhyne, "The Letter of the Law," *Public Management*, 57 (November, 1975), pp. 9-11.
[21]Victor A. Thompson, *Without Sympathy or Enthusiasm: The Problem of Administrative Compassion* (University: The University of Alabama Press, 1975), p. 79.
[22]Vernon R. Taylor, "Cultural Bias in Testing: An Action Program," *Public Personnel Review*, 29 (July, 1968), p. 170.
[23]Jean Couturier, "Court Attacks on Testing: Death Knell or Salvation for the Civil Service System," *Good Government*, 88 (Winter, 1971), p. 12.
[24]Jean J. Couturier, "The Quiet Revolution in Public Personnel Laws," *Public Personnel Management*, (May/June, 1976), pp. 150-159.
[25]In 1983, the median weekly earnings of all full-time wage and salary workers who were women were 66 percent of the mean earnings of men. See Bureau of the Census, *Statistical Abstract of the United States, 1985*, Table 700, p. 419.
[26]Judy Mann, "Pay Discrimination," *Washington Post* (April 17, 1985). Mann is quoting Clarence M. Pendleton, Jr.
[27]The following discussion is drawn from Keon S. Chi, "Comparable Worth: Implications of the Washington Case," *State Government*, 57, No. 2 (1984), pp. 34-45; and Keon S. Chi, "Comparable Worth in State Governments," *State Government News*, 27 (November, 1984), pp. 4-6.
[28]Seymour Martin Lipset and William Schneider, "An Emerging National Consensus," *The New Republic*, 8 (October 15, 1977), p. 9. Emphasis is original.
[29]*Ibid.* The survey was taken in 1977.
[30]*Ibid.* Figures are for 1975.
[31]The examples of "reverse passing" are in "Disadvantaged Groups, Individual Rights," *The New Republic*, 7 (October 15, 1977); and Eliot Marshall, "Race Certification," *ibid.*, p. 19.
[32]Quoted in Thompson, *Personnel Policy in the City*, p. 120.
[33]*Ibid.*, p. 121.
[34]*Ibid.*, p. 136.

[35]In 1982, only 0.3 percent of top-level federal executives were black, and only 0.1 percent were Hispanic. See Bureau of the Census, *Statistical Abstract of the United States, 1985*, Table 532, p. 326.
[36]In 1983, the median weekly earnings of all full-time wage and salary workers who were black averaged 19 percent less than that of whites. Hispanics earned 22 percent less than did whites, on the average. See *ibid.*, Table 700, p. 419.
[37]In 1981, 24 percent of federal professional employees, and 19 percent of federal administrators, were women. See *ibid.*, Table 529, p. 325.
[38]Robert J. Huntley and Robert J. McDonald, "Urban Managers: Organizational Preferences, Managerial Styles, and Social Policy Roles," *The Municipal Year Book: 1975* (Washington, D.C.: International City Management Association, 1975), p. 157.
[39]Bureau of the Census, *Statistical Abstract of the United States, 1985,* Table 711, p. 425.
[40]*Ibid.,* Table 708, p. 423. All figures are for 1983, except for the Fraternal Order of Police, which is for 1980.
[41]Bureau of the Census, *Census of Governments 1977: Labor Management Relations in State and Local Governments,* Vol. 3, *Public Employment,* No. 3 (Washington, D.C.: U.S. Government Printing Office, 1979), pp. 9-21.
[42]This paragraph is drawn from Sterling Spero and John M. Capozolla, *The Urban Community and its Unionized Bureaucracies* (New York: Dunellen, 1973), p. 15; and Lawrence D. Mankin, "Public Employee Organizations: The Quest for Legitimacy," *Public Personnel Management,* 6 (September-October, 1977), pp. 334-340.
[43]Hugh O'Neill, "The Growth of Municipal Employee Unions," in Robert H. Connery and William V. Farr, eds., *Unionization of Municipal Employees* (New York: Academy of Political Science, 1970), pp. 3-4.
[44]Bureau of the Census, *Census of Governments 1977: Labor Management Relations in State and Local Governments,* p. 2.
[45]*Ibid.,* p. 22.
[46]Sam Zagoria, "Attitudes Harden in Government Labor Relations," *ASPA News and Views,* 26 (December, 1976), pp. 1, 21-22.
[47]Marvin J. Levine, "The Status of State 'Sunshine Bargaining' Laws," *Labor Law Journal* (November, 1980), p. 713.
[48]Spero and Capozolla, *The Urban Community,* p. 218.
[49]*Ibid.,* p. 219.
[50]Charles N. Rehmus and Evan Wilner, *The Economic Results of Teacher Bargaining: Michigan's First Two Years* (Ann Arbor, Mich.: Institute of Labor and Industrial Relations, 1968).
[51]"Bureau Notes Decline in Public Sector Strikes," *Public Administration Times* (February 15, 1982), p. 3.
[52]F. Ted Hebert and Deil S. Wright, "State Administrators: How Representative? How Professional?" *State Government,* 55, No. 1 (1982), pp. 23-25. The figures cited here and in the rest of this section refer to 27 different kinds of state agencies in 1968 and 75 "agency types" in 1978.
[53]*Ibid.,* pp. 24-25.

14

IMPLEMENTING PUBLIC POLICY

beyond grassroots bureaucracy

We learned in the last chapter that the 13 million bureaucrats and laborers who toil in the grassroots governments are responsible for a wide spectrum of public policies. However, what is less known is how many of these policies are implemented by administrators who do not work directly for governments. These people work, instead, either for private companies that have contracted with state or local governments to provide services to their citizens or for public corporations that have been chartered (but are not controlled) by state or local governments. In this chapter we consider some of the implications of both means of implementing public policies at the grassroots.

THE PRIVATIZATION OF PUBLIC POLICY

When a state or local government contracts out a public program for implementation by a private corporation, it is often called "privatization." Although contracting out at the state and local levels has never attained the proportions achieved by the federal government, it nonetheless represents a significant way that state and local governments implement their public programs.

Table 14-1 lists the major services that cities contract out to private firms as a percentage of all the contracts they let, that is, contracts to other governments and private firms combined. Of the 23 services listed, contracting to private companies increased in all but 4 from 1972 to 1982. These increases occurred primarily at the expense of intergovernmental service contracting by cities, which we discussed in Chapter 9.[1] The data in Table 14-1 are supported by other measures of the growth in privatization at the grassroots. State and local

Table 14-1 Cities' Use of Private Contracting as Percentage of Their Use of All (Public Plus Private) Contracting: 23 Selected Services, 1972 and 1982

	1972 survey, 2,375 cities responding	*1982 survey, 1,439 cities responding*
Services with similar names in both surveys		
Solid waste disposal	44%	46%
Street lighting	80	66
Utility billing	56	61
Ambulance services	57	60
Animal control	31	26
Housing	5	23
Hospitals	38	61
Recreational facilities	4	33
Parks	3	68
Museums	20	20
Legal services	84	90
Payroll	56	85
Tax assessing	14	15
Personnel services	8	73
Public relations	67	89
Services with slightly different names in both surveys		
Snow plowing	30%	85%
Crime prevention/patrol	2	42
Traffic control	4	20
Insect control	8	33
Public health	2	19
Drug/alcohol treatment	7	15
Mental health	18	14

Source: Lori M. Henderson, "Intergovernmental Service Arrangements and Transfer of Functions," *Municipal Year Book, 1985* (Washington, D.C.: International City Management Association, 1985), p. 201.

spending for services provided by the private sector nearly tripled between 1975 and 1982, when it hit $81 billion.[2] The privatization option clearly is an increasingly popular one among state and local officials.

The kinds of services that local governments contract out to private corporations are surprisingly broad. Contracts are let for construction; purchasing equipment, supplies, concessions, and franchises; as well as services such as garbage collection. There have been a number of studies on the kinds of services that local governments privatize, and most of them agree that garbage collection is among the most commonly privatized service.[3] The problems of privatization revolve around competitive bidding and program evaluations, neither of which is done as much as it should be; adequate government controls; and occasionally corruption. Consider the case of the largest service contract area that applies to direct citizen delivery: municipal garbage collection.

Collecting urban garbage is a big business. More than 10,000 companies do it, but the business is dominated by relatively few firms; the 1,500 largest companies serve about 70 percent of the nation's private clientele and drive 60 percent of the industry's trucks.[4] The "Big Three" in the garbage collection trade are Browning-Ferris, Waste Management, Inc., and SCA Services. Of these major national operations (the Houston-based Browning-Ferris operation, for example, does $300 million worth of business a year across the country), two of them have been involved in bribery cases concerning local officials. In 1976, Browning-Ferris admitted it had made approximately $100,000 in bribes to local officials during the preceding four years, while Waste Management, Inc., admitted to charges by the Securities and Exchange Commission (SEC) of making an illegal $35,000 payment to an unidentified political party in a foreign country, as well as maintaining a secret slush fund. SCA Services, the remaining third member of the Big Three, was under SEC investigation during the same period.

The garbage collection industry as a whole has long been under federal investigation concerning its ties with organized crime, and it has been alleged that the Mafia dominates the industry in New York, portions of Connecticut, Florida, New Jersey, and other areas. As early as 1960, the late Robert F. Kennedy, then U.S. attorney general, wrote that "garbage removal is used by gangsters as a vehicle of extortion . . . because it is comparatively easy to gain and maintain, gangsters and racketeers have been attracted to the multimillion dollar industry."[5] The participation of organized crime in the garbage collection industry can be very rough. For example, when one retailer canceled his contract with a private firm and began taking his own trash to the dump, he found the next morning that his trash had been returned to his doorstep along with a note stating that he should renew his contract or his business would be blown up.[6] The business can be even rougher, and murder is not unknown.[7]

When a government is corrupt in the first place, its corruption is most evident in the government's relations with private contractors. Consider the city of Albany, New York, which for years had been in the pocket of one of America's last urban political machines.

The New York State Commission of Investigation stated in 1973 that the city of Albany's contracting procedures evidenced a complete lack of governmental supervision. According to the report, "The Commission was unable to ascertain a single instance where a city bureau or department had questioned or contested a claim voucher submitted for payment," by a contractor or vendor. "The situation which prevailed amounted to a complete trust and reliance upon the good faith and integrity of the contractor or vendor to submit true, accurate, and fair claims." There was, by the way, scant evidence that fair claims were being submitted.[8]

According to the chair of the New York State Commission of Investigation,

> It appears quite clear, and indeed startling and shocking, that the City of Albany, in connection with its purchasing practices and procedures . . . has permitted itself to be bilked and fleeced. This is a strong statement, but it certainly describes fairly what has been going on in Albany for a number of years.[9]

Perhaps it is superfluous to add that competitive bidding in Albany was usually avoided, but the city's strategy for short-circuiting the bidding process was (and is) typical of that used by local governments when they wish to award a contract to a chosen firm. Often a city council will pass special ordinances that declare a particular service to be of an "emergency" or "impractical nature" and will thus award a contract without competitive bidding. Albany, of course, went to extremes; the Albany City Council passed 101 such special ordinances involving $2.25 million in a single six-month period.[10]

When all is said and done, however, state and local governments appear to have a reasonably firm, if occasionally tenuous, grip on their private contractors. One reason why is that privatization is relatively restricted among the grassroots governments, and so the supervisory chore is more manageable. The total contracting expenditures by state and local governments amount to about a fifth of their expenditures.[11] Even though privatization is growing in popularity among state and local governments, one review of the literature on the topic concluded that subnational contracting of all types with private firms was "limited" and that privatizing public services by local governments ran a distant third to governments providing the services themselves or via intergovernmental agreements. "Even in the case of the two governmental services most frequently contracted to private firms, refuse collection and engineering tasks, many more jurisdictions provide these two services themselves than contract with private firms or other governments."[12]

A second reason is that public controls over certain categories of contracting are relatively thorough at the subnational levels. Virtually all state and local governments have detailed regulations governing construction contracts with private builders; they maintain sizable building inspection operations and central purchasing units that are normally responsible and well run and have considerable experience in using the contract (in the form of letting franchises, leases, concessions, and arranging sales) as a device that actually makes money for governments rather than as a mechanism for spending it.

Third, competitive bidding, while not as common a practice as it perhaps should be, seems to be used frequently by subnational governments. One national study found that the proportion of local contracts let to the private sector on a competitive basis was about equal to the proportion that were negotiated.[13]

Finally, oversight of a company's performance by state and local officials, while less than systematic, at least seems to be a matter of concern. One survey found a surprising propensity among these officials to take "the fairly dramatic step" of changing from private supplier to public provider, or vice versa, indicating an interest by state and local governments in determining whether the private sphere or the public one was the most efficient deliverer of services.[14]

Privatization as Politics

Why does government privatize? There are several motivations (including the as-yet-unproven possibility that privatization really is cheaper), but most of these motivations relate to political flexibility. Political debts can be paid off, the size of governments can, at least on paper, be reduced, and genuine and responsible political responsiveness can, on occasion, be attained by maneuvering around a cumbersome public bureaucracy. Let us consider some of these incentives in turn.

1. Contracting out, as opposed to using government personnel, permits the government to experiment with policies. The government can always terminate a contract if the experiment fails, with little or no objection by an affected public.
2. Privatizing permits the government to hire specialists and people of unusual

talent, without paying as much attention to such "affirmative action" items as sex, ethnicity, or veteran's status, which can affect government hiring.

3. Contracting out permits government agencies to benefit from the existence of voluntary or charitable organizations that already may be doing what the government wishes to do.
4. Certain short-term savings often can be realized. For example, civil service rules on pay scales and fringe benefits may be skirted by using contractors who pay only minimum wages to their employees, and by leasing rather than purchasing new buildings, since the resultant government budget will show only the annual cost of the rent, as opposed to the expense of a capital project.
5. The personnel working for government can be expanded through contracts, even though the official size of the civil service remains the same or is actually reduced. This final point is especially pertinent when we consider the burgeoning pension programs for government employees. The actual cost of the pension programs to taxpayers is not completely known, but it is known that these programs are unusually (and perhaps unrealistically) generous.

Most state and local retirement plans are Lilliputian in size and of questionable soundness. There are more than 6,500 subnational plans covering more than 13 million workers, and some four-fifths of the plans have fewer than 100 members.[15] The overall costs of pension plans for state and local workers has increased by more than 300 percent since 1965. About one quarter of these costs are drawn from the paychecks of the workers themselves, another quarter come from earnings on investments, and roughly half are contributed by governments.[16] The governmental contributions to the retirement pensions of state and local employees is especially worrisome, since these plans are consuming ever-larger bites of state and local government budgets. Currently, these governments spend substantially more on their retirement systems than they spend on police protection for their citizens, and their costs to governments continue to spiral: in 1967, pension plan contributions by governments accounted for less than 7 percent of total state and local government payroll costs; a decade later the figure was almost 10 percent.[17]

The prospects are that the tax burden of these pensions will grow heavier. Not only are the salaries of all government workers growing, but the entire federal retirement system and at least four out of five state pension plans have built-in provisions for increasing benefits after retirement; usually, these formulas are pegged to inflation rates.[18] Unfortunately, however, several studies have concluded that a number of cities and some states may face insolvency and thus never be able to deliver their promised pensions to their retirees.[19] One detailed study of state and local retirement systems by the U.S. General Accounting Office found that about two-thirds of the plans received contributions that were insufficient to meet the standards imposed on their counterparts in private sector by the Employee Retirement Income Security Act of 1974. Many of the plans examined would have had to double their funding levels to meet these standards.[20]

The result of this dismal situation is that one of the potential advantages of contracting out services by government to the private sector lies in keeping the number of government employees stable or even reduced, and thus may reduce the ultimate cost of these pension policies to the public.[21]

To Privatize or Not to Privatize?

Although we have considered some of the benefits of contracting out public programs to the private sector, what do local officials themselves think about the privatization option? Table 14-2 indicates these opinions. By and large local officials think that they get both efficient and effective service by privatization, although there are some substantial minority opinions to the contrary. But it should be noted that local officials have approached the contracting alternative with some caution. One study found that local governments contracted out no less than 33 services to private contractors but that the average number of services contracted out by cities and counties averaged fewer than 8. "With such a large number of possible services, an average of less than eight does not indicate a substantial movement from public to private service delivery."[22]

The reluctance of local officials to privatize extensively is rooted in certain political realities. One is the relatively vibrant role of unions of state and local employees. Between 1960 and 1980, membership in these unions more than tripled, and organized state and local public employees currently account for nearly half of all people who work for the grassroots governments. Organized labor can and does exert considerable pressure against state and local administrators not to "contract away" the jobs of their members to the private sector, and in some states such restrictions are written into the civil service statutes themselves.

Table 14-2 Local Public Administrators' Opinions on Contracting Out Local Services to Private Firms

	COUNTY		*MUNICIPALITY*		*All Responses*	
Statement	*Number*	*% of Total*	*Number*	*% of Total*	*Number*	*% of Total*
Contracting out costs *less* than government provision	31	56%	66	39%	97	43%
Contracting out costs *the same* as government provision	3	5	26	15	29	13
Contracting out costs *more* than government provision	14	26	46	27	60	27
No answer	7	13	32	19	39	17
Total	55	100	170	100%	225	100%
Contracting out results in quality *poorer* than government provision	4	7%	13	8%	17	7%
Contracting out results in quality *the same* as government provision	21	38	50	29	71	32
Contracting out results in quality *better* than government provision	12	22	59	35	71	32
No answer	18	33	48	28	66	29
Total	55	100%	170	100%	225	100%

Source: Patricia S. Florestano and Stephen B. Gordon, "A Survey of City and County Use of Private Contracting," *The Urban Interest*, 3 (Spring, 1981), p. 25.

A second political reality is the antiquated state constitutions, particularly as they apply to state finances. As we noted in Chapter 12, only one state (Vermont) permits its legislatures to submit unbalanced budgets, and most states are saddled with moribund constitutional limitation on public debt and cumbersome financing procedures. Nevertheless, state and local governments have borne the brunt of public demands for greater services over the last few decades and have, as a result, been forced to find ways to accommodate those demands. The answer that most states and local jurisdictions have found is the creation of the public corporation, a mysterious, veiled, and secretive entity that works at the fringes of the public domain.

The government corporation, also known as the special authority or public authority, is an independent, legislatively created monopoly empowered to build, maintain, and manage public services such as hospitals, bridges, university dormitories, tunnels, roads, senior citizen centers, public housing, seaports, mental health facilities, airports, pollution control programs, water and sewage plants, electrical power utilities, and a variety of other projects. The great bulk of these special authorities have been created by state and local governments, and only until comparatively recently have they really been scrutinized.

THE SECRET WORLD OF THE GOVERNMENT CORPORATION

But government corporations are not easily examined. Careful investigators vary widely on even how many public authorities exist at the subnational level, and the estimates range from 5,000 to 18,000.[23] Table 14-3 indicates the 15 major government corporations in states and localities. As the table implies, the numbers that public authorities produce are impressive. Government corporations employ 3 percent of the nation's labor force and account for 15 percent of the national fixed investment. Public authorities control three quarters of the market shares of the country's water systems, a fourth of its electrical plants and railways, and 80 percent of local transit.[24] The enormity of these quasi-public operations can be placed in perspective when we realize that the Port Authority of New York and New Jersey (which ranks fourth on the table) had more outstanding debt than that of 39 state governments combined and more operating revenues than all but 9 of the nation's biggest cities.[25]

New York and Pennsylvania are the major states that use the public authority and, between them, have developed the two basic models for setting them up. New York has more than 230 public authorities, all of which are individually chartered by the state legislature. In Pennsylvania, however, local governments (cities, counties, and school districts) can create government corporations through a number of different devices, and with little or no interference from the state. As a consequence, there are close to 2,000 municipal corporations and 10 state public authorities in Pennsylvania, the most in any state. Most states, more than two-thirds, use variants of the Pennsylvanian approach, and only Maine and New York actually require that the state legislature enact specific legislation to set up a public authority.

Public authorities support themselves by borrowing money in the nation's money markets, by grants from their sponsoring governments, and by charging user fees to customers who use the facilities they build—such as toll charges levied on toll road drivers. Most of their budgets, however, are bor-

Table 14-3 Functional and Financial Activity of Major State and Local Public Enterprise, 1976–1977

Public Enterprise	*Function(s)*	*Revenues[1] (millions)*	*Outstanding Debt (millions)*
New York State Housing Finance Agency (1977)	Housing, health and human welfare projects	$309	$4,792
Washington (State) Public Power Supply System (1977)	Electric power	28[2]	2,803
New York State Power Authority (1977)	Electric power	439	2,299
Port Authority of New York–New Jersey (1977)	Terminal and transportation facilites	524	1,821
Salt River Project (Arizona) (1977)	Electric power, water	311	1,583
Nebraska Public Power District (1977)	Electric power	188	1,406
Puerto Rico Water Resource Authority (1977)	Electric power	606	1,115
Washington Metropolitan Area Transit Authority (1976–77)	Transportation	625	1,024
New Jersey Turnpike Authority (1977)	Roads (transportation)	105	829
South Carolina Public Service Authority (1977)	Electric power	126	810
San Francisco Bay Area Transit District No. 2 (1976–77)	Transportation	144	749
Omaha Public Power District (1976–77)	Electric power	141	729
Metropolitan Water District of So. Calif. (1976–77)	Water, electric power	168	671
Washington Suburban Sanitary Commission (1976–77)	Water, sewage	174	615
Dallas–Fort Worth Regional Airport Authority (1976–77)	Transportation	57	591

[1] 1977 data are operating revenues; 1976–77 data are total revenues.

[2] Revenues reported are small because authority does not actually sell power; it simply owns and operates projects.

Source: Michael Denning and David J. Olson, "Public Enterprise and Emerging Character of State Service Provisions: Application to Public Ports," paper presented at the 1981 Annual Meeting of American Political Science Association, New York, September 3–6, 1981.

rowed, and special authorities have been consuming increasingly vast amounts of borrowed money. State and local public authorities spend more than $14 billion a year on operations. They invest more than $10 billion annually in new capital facilities—more than all state and municipal governments combined![26]

"WHOOPS!"

A recent incident illuminates the growing economic role that government corporations are playing in the nation.

The Washington Public Power Supply System (WPPSS), known as "Whoops!" to some critics, is a consortium of 23 public utilities in Washington State and 88 additional public utilities in the Northwest. Created in 1957 by 19 public utility districts and 4 Washington cities to construct a small hydroelectric project, WPPSS bumped along for years as a typical government corporation, thriving with ease in a monopolistic market. Then, in the early 1970s, after reading that demand for electricity in the Northwest was expected to increase by 7 percent a year for the foreseeable future, the directors of WPPSS decided to build three nuclear power generators, and later expanded the project to five.

By 1983, as a result of borrowing to finance the five plants, "Whoops" was more than $8.3 billion in debt. Like governments, government corporations such as WPPSS are free to raise revenues by selling "municipal" (even though they are not municipalities) bonds in the bond market. Investors in municipal bonds—nearly 90 percent of whom are private citizens—find municipal bonds attractive because the interest that the bonds earn is not subject to the income tax; they are tax free. And, at a 12.5 percent interest rate for some of its bond issues, the WPPSS consortium was selling a lot of bonds. In fact, WPPSS was the largest issuer of tax-exempt municipal bonds ever!

WPPSS was issuing a particular type of long-term municipal bond, the revenue bond, to underwrite its nuclear plants. Revenue bonds repay their buyers through fees collected from users of the project that they finance; in the case of "Whoops," for example, the bonds' purchasers would be paid back in the form of tax-exempt interest with the profits WPPSS made on selling electricity generated by its new nuclear facilities.

The other kind of municipal bond is the general obligation bond. General obligation bonds are backed by the full faith and credit of the government that issues them. In other words, a government is legally compelled to raise taxes, if necessary, to meet its "general obligations." For this reason, all issues of general obligation bonds must be first approved in a referendum by the voters. Not so, however, with revenue bonds, and that is why governments (and government corporations) increasingly like them. In the face of tax revolts at the grassroots, state and local governments have been squeezed into issuing more and more revenue bonds. In 1970, 33 percent of all long-term tax-exempt bonds were revenue bonds; in 1983, 75 percent of these issues were revenue bonds.

Governments feel constrained to issue revenue bonds to meet basic service demands, but also to finance projects that may not be so basic. States and localities now issue revenue bonds to underwrite all kinds of "private uses," such as building factories and housing and buying pollution control equipment, that would not have been contemplated before the tax revolt. The reasoning behind this maneuver is that the government is enhancing the public interest by making more jobs available, "leveraging in" private sector dollars to strengthen the tax base, assuring public health, or whatever. But while revenue bonds may be in the best interest of a local jurisdiction's citizenry, they may not be in the best interest of their investors, who can lose their investments if the jurisdiction defaults.

In 1983, WPPSS defaulted. It was not a small default. In fact, it was a national record: $2.25 billion was defaulted on revenue bonds that had been issued for plants 4 and 5.

What happens when a public authority, or a government, defaults? It does not necessarily declare bankruptcy and go out of business (as WPPSS did not); it merely declines to pay its investors—about 100,000 individual investors in the case of the "Whoops" default, such as the retired Tulsa policeman who had invested $45,000 in plants 4 and 5. In fact, more than half of the investors in plants 4 and 5 were retirees, and nearly 9 out of 10 of these retirees were counting on their investments in WPPSS for a significant portion of their retirement income. Although the bond issuer must sell the holdings it has acquired under the bond issue and turn over the proceeds to its investors, these returns typically amount to pennies on the dollar. Who, for example, would be in the market for two partially constructed nuclear plants and the roads leading to them?

Another effect of default, but especially the largest municipal bond default in the nation's history, is that it hurts others besides investors. The governor of Washington released a study concluding that the WPPSS default would cost the state 20,000 jobs.

Finally, the viability, competence, and ethics of the bond market, Wall Street, and government come under question. In the case of WPPSS, perhaps with reason. Even after the board of WPPSS was well aware that the Northwest's projected electricity consumption rate was never likely to attain 7 percent a year, and in fact was increasing by closer to 1 percent annually, plants 4 and 5 were begun anyway. Because "Whoops" wanted to spread the wealth (and reap the resultant political support), 45 to 65 contractors were employed on each job site, where 9 to 10 were the norm, resulting in a sixfold hike in the system's original cost estimates.

"Wall Street was intimately involved every step of the way, and kept the spigot wide open until belated investor skepticism forced it closed," according to *Business Week* magazine. An open fiscal spigot apparently was irresistible to the small-town business leaders who largely made up the WPPSS board. According to their own chairman of the board, the WPPSS directors "had unlimited money. That was the worst of it." As one director put it, "Whenever cash was low, we'd just toddle down to Wall Street."

Wall Street was so pleased to sell the increasingly questionable "Whoops" bonds (pleased, possibly, to the point of "bond dumping" WPPSS issues on unsuspecting investors) that the Securities and Exchange Commission launched an investigation similar to the one that it conducted in 1977 of New York banks, after the city had nearly defaulted in 1975. The SEC's 1,000-page report in that case alleged that in 1975 the six banks sold $4 billion in city bonds when they knew a possible default was imminent and simultaneously dumped their own New York City bonds before the roof fell in.

The Washington Public Power Supply System expresses many of the dilemmas of government corporations. They are controlled neither by public institutions nor economic competition, yet they are increasingly important political and fiscal forces. *Caveat emptor.*

The preceding discussion is drawn from "The Fallout from 'Whoops,' " *Business Week* (July 11, 1983), pp. 80-87; James Bennett and Thomas DiLorenzo, "Utility Bond's Default: Iceberg's Tip?" *Washington Times* (October 26, 1983); "Learning from Whoops," *The Wall Street Journal* (July 27, 1983); "WPPSS Default Investigated," *Washington Post* (November 30, 1983); Andy Logan, "Around City Hall," *The New Yorker* (January 23, 1978), pp. 98-103; and Carrie Dolan, "Several WPPSS Issues Still Unresolved," *The Wall Street Journal* (October 24, 1985).

Most of us have heard about these public authorities in the context of the notorious "tax-exempt municipal bonds." In fact, government corporations are able to raise more money for investment than are either all-state or all-municipal governments precisely because the formers' bonds are, like those issued by states and localities, tax exempt. Public authorities are the largest single category of borrowers in the tax-exempt municipal bond market and borrow more money than all state and local governments combined![27] "This corporate investment exerts a massive influence on the patterns of development in the nation, an influence that is largely insulated from public debate."[28]

The extent of borrowing by state and local government corporations has begun to reach ominous proportions—ominous because the debts incurred by public authorities are "nonguaranteed," which means that they are not technically obligated to pay off creditors in the event that they go under. The concept of permitting public authorities to acquire nonguaranteed debts allowed state and local governments to evade their own archaic constitutional restrictions on borrowing and thus meet rising demands for services. But it is possible that the concept has been stretched too far. By 1979, nonguaranteed debt had hit 50 percent (up from 28 percent in 1955) of all state and local long-term debt, which accounts for about 95 percent of all state and local debt,[29] or 15 percent of all federal, state, and local outstanding debt, and all of it had been acquired by public authorities.[30] All states allow the use of nonguaranteed debt (only 31 did in 1931), and today more than half of all municipal long-term debt is nonguaranteed.[31]

Just how free of the mounting "nonguaranteed" debts that are being incurred by special authorities state and local governments really are is eminently debatable. Should a public authority default, the courts could easily find that the government that created it nonetheless owes its creditors—and, in fact, the courts have so ruled in such cases.[32] Moreover, many government corporations are empowered by their creators to issue "moral obligation bonds," which means that, although a state or locality may not technically be responsible for an authority's debts, it nonetheless has a legally recognized "moral obligation" to back them. In short, it appears that if the typical government corporation goes bust, it is the taxpayer who ultimately will pay its "nonguaranteed" debt.

Two Centuries of Fiscal Experiments

Fiscally speaking (and, as we shall shortly see, politically speaking, too), the relationship of government corporations to the subnational governments is not merely one of the tail wagging the proverbial dog, but of figuring out which end of this moving and shaking mass is the tail and which is the dog! This disturbing situation is in part the result of fiscal experimentation by the federal, state, and local governments over the past two centuries. The first government corporations were banks chartered by the states; the federal government often held significant portions of the stock of these banks. Later in the nineteenth century, when all kinds of private companies in nearly all the states were required to have a special state charter to set up business, a relationship frequently would develop between individual legislators and corporate interests to expedite the applications of business charters. Over time, these relationships reached such an intimacy that major scandals erupted in many states, and both states and municipalities often would default on their debts because of the financial collapse of speculative business projects in which they had invested. These defaults occurred from the late nineteenth century throughout the 1920s, usually in the form of investments involving real estate development.

As a consequence of these statewide and local defaults on debt, and also as a result of the public administration reform movement that was sweeping state and local governments around the turn of the century, virtually all state constitutions to this day have prohibitions not only on debt, but against lending or granting state or local money or credit to individuals or firms as well, and these clauses have inhibited the development of public ownership and investment in private corporations. As an alternative, state and local statutes and constitutions have encouraged the development of the quasi-governmental public authority and its revenue bond method of financing for funding state and local capital projects.

In the twentieth century, the development of public authorities can be viewed as a series of adaptations to meet governmental needs through private devices that maximize profits for individuals and groups. Because of a near-moratorium on capital improvements during World War II, the resultant pressures for new capital ventures resulted in a dramatic proliferation of public authorities, which have the political advantage of being able to secure funds for building faster than governments. In fact, between 1947 and 1957, the number of government corporations quadrupled across the country; most were created to build schools, sewers, reservoirs, and other major installations needed by suddenly expanding municipalities.

During the 1950s and 1960s, new pressures began pushing for the development of public authorities. Policymakers felt that local political boundaries of long standing were obsolete, and indeed dysfunctional, to the development of comprehensive regional policies designed to meet new public problems. Thus, this period witnessed the creation of additional special districts managed by public authorities designed to relieve regional difficulties, such as environmental programs, health programs, and so forth, which span political boundaries. During the 1970s, this concept was continued, particularly in the form of municipal bond sales designed to pay for pollution control equipment of private firms faced with new environmental restrictions mandated by federal, state, and local governments.[33]

Born Free: The Autonomy of Government Corporations

Political control over a public authority is a supremely difficult achievement. The available tools for controlling public authorities are quite limited, usually involving powers of appointment, occasional supervision by an executive agency, legislative actions, court reviews, and local voter approval. The government corporation is, in theory, responsible to those who appoint its board members, and normally this is the governor. Although political patronage often dominates the initial appointments of members of the boards of directors of public authorities, the staggered terms of board membership inhibit any kind of effective political control by the governor.

The supervision of government corporations typically is assigned to an executive agency or several executive agencies of the government, but very few states and localities have emulated the kinds of rigorous controls exercised over the roughly 100 federal public corporations.[34] In most state governments, no single department even maintains an accurate listing of active public corporations, who their officers are, and even what their addresses might be. Data on financial transactions, not surprisingly, are negligible at the state and local level. Somewhat incredibly, the Securities Industries Association has no more information than do state governments on the financial transactions of government corporations.[35]

State legislatures and city councils also have very limited control, if any, over their own public authorities. Although the statutes that establish public authorities can be and frequently are very specific and detailed, once the authority is established, legislative control often becomes a mockery. In fact, legislators ritualistically carp that they have very little control over their own bureaucracies, much less the independent public authority, and even "sunset legislation," which has been enacted in a number of states, has not been effective in implementing any kind of meaningful legislative review and control over either the bureaucracy or the government corporation. Thus, while elected bodies may have a rather impressive array of sanctions with which to threaten public corporations, they do not have any realistic means of enforcing those sanctions. This problem is compounded by the intergovernmental system that exists in virtually all states for establishing public authorities, and that permits counties and municipalities to create public corporations essentially on their own, and often these local charters are vague and unstandardized.[36]

Suing government corporations in court has not provided consistent public control over government corporations. Although the courts have chipped away, on occasion, at the more arbitrary actions of certain public corporations, this process has been piecemeal at best, and the judiciary has not produced any guidelines of consequence for the control of public authorities.

These realities have contributed to an independence of economic and political action that any company executive or politician would envy. Public authorities, although chartered by governments, are rarely controlled by them. The career-oriented professional managers of government corporations are casually supervised by politically appointed boards that do not spend an inordinate amount of time at such chores. Public authorities have at their disposal vast sums of capital to invest and contracts to let, but they are free from review by the Securities and Exchange Commission. Tax-exempt bondholders have even less interest in scrutinizing the day-to-day activities of the government corporation than do the stockholders of private corporations. As long as the public corporation meets the minimum revenue producing requirements, its management does not have to show increasing profits, dividends, or stock prices. Marketplace competition for most public corporations is minimal because they operate in monopolistic economic conditions, and revenues, as a consequence, rarely decrease. Moreover, management of public corporations can operate at a much higher level of secrecy than can private firms, which must report their finances to the Securities and Exchange Commission.

In short, the managers of the public corporations have all the powers and autonomy of management that are shared by their counterparts in the private corporation, and which the on-line, government bureaucrat does not have; yet, the manager of the public corporation does not have to be responsive or responsible to the stockholders, bondholders, boards of directors, or even the public. As a result of this uniquely independent position in the marketplaces of both commerce and politics, public authorities have waxed more powerful at the expense of the subnational governments that chartered them, but especially local governments. But this power has brought its inevitable backlash. As Annmarie Hauk Walsh observes, "the successes of public authorities have, in fact, motivated much of the criticism of them. Critics on the left seek a more purposeful, dynamic, and democratically controlled public sector. Those on the right seek to reduce the scope of government enterprise, or at least check its growth, and to limit its activities to those that aid private endeavors, . . . public authorities have withstood such assaults practically unscathed and continue to claim rights of independent management."[37]

THE NEW YORK EXPERIENCE: MOSES VERSUS ROCKY

Well, "practically unscathed" until recently. As we enter our new "age of limits," public authorities have come under increasingly severe criticism. An example of this process but, more important, a case study of all the manifold strengths and weaknesses of the government corporation, is provided by the state of New York, particularly the rise of Robert Moses and his Triborough "empire," and Moses's ultimate conquest by the late Governor Nelson A. Rockefeller, who was unique in his own use (and abuse) of the government corporation. Few, if any, examples can furnish as rich a study of what the special authority means in American politics than New York's experiences with it.

Moses: "Masterbuilder" or Mass Destroyer?

The late Robert Moses held an unbelievable quantum of power in New York State for 44 years (1924-1968) and in New York City for 34 years (1934-1968). It is not hyperbolic to dub him America's greatest builder. He changed the face of New York by raising and spending $27 billion (in 1968 dollars) for public works.

Through shore line projects, he added 15,000 acres to the city and changed its physical configuration. With one exception (East River Drive), Moses built every major expressway in the metropolitan region. Nine enormous bridges link the island city of New York; Moses built seven of them. Lincoln Center, the New York Coliseum; the campuses of Pratt Institute and Fordham and Long Island universities; the headquarters of the United Nations; 416 miles of landscaped parkways; Jones Beach; more than 1,000 apartment buildings housing more people than live in Minneapolis; 658 playgrounds; 673 baseball diamonds; 288 tennis courts—all these and more are his. Beyond the city, Moses built huge power dams on the St. Lawrence and at Niagara, Massens, and elsewhere; more parkways, more public beaches; and more parks. Especially parks. By the time Moses had finished, New York owned 45 percent of *all* the nation's acreage devoted to state parks![38]

To build, Moses destroyed. A quarter-million people—the equivalent population of Chattanooga—were dispossessed for his highways. Perhaps another quarter-million saw their homes razed for other kinds of projects.[39] His apartment buildings, parks, and playgrounds, with few exceptions were built for the white and the wealthy. His expressways slash through a region of 14 million people, carving the metropolis into separate and often mutually hostile enclaves of rich, poor, white, black, and brown.[40]

Moses entered the New York scene in 1924, when Governor Alfred E. Smith asked him to design the State Council on Parks, and he quickly assigned himself as chair with a tenure that extended beyond that of the governor's term. He also exempted the new State Council on Parks from the state civil service system, granted it independent bonding and land acquisition powers, and used the Council to further his own ambitions. When Franklin D. Roosevelt succeeded Smith as governor of New York in 1929, Moses's power in state government began to wane. Nevertheless, he was able to keep his position in the State Council on Parks and began seeking bureaucratic allies in the federal government.

In 1932, FDR was elected president, and in the same year Moses made his alliance with Jesse Jones, who had been appointed by Herbert Hoover as head of the newly created federal Reconstruction Finance Corporation (RFC). Both staunch Republicans, Jones and Moses disliked Roosevelt, an antipathy that likely cemented their bond. With Jones and his Reconstruction Finance Corporation as his newly found ally in Washington, Moses worked himself into the position of heading up New York State's efforts to put depression-wracked New Yorkers back to work through the creation of capital projects that were financed with federal funds provided by Jones's RFC; and Moses immediately began building the Triborough Bridge with RFC grants.

In 1936, Moses was appointed by the mayor of New York City as chair of the Triborough Bridge Authority, and he served in that capacity until 1966. Using as his power base his position as the state's liaison with the federal public works funding programs, Moses moved forcefully to enhance his chairmanship of the Triborough Bridge Authority by setting up two additional authorities that were approved for federal funding, the Henry Hudson Parkway Authority and the Marine Parkway Authority. To solidify his position, Moses created a board for each authority, but appointed himself as the only board member. In 1938, both authorities were absorbed in the newly created New York City Parkway Authority, and, once again, Moses wrote himself in as the only member of the board.

During this period, Moses was consolidating his power with considerable speed. In 1934 alone, he became president of the Long Island Parkways Commission, commissioner of the New York City Parks System (which he remained until 1960), and chair of the New York State Council on Parks (a position he held until 1963), and he established the Beth Page and Jones Beach park authorities.

Moses was capitalizing on national trends of the time. As one analyst points out, "Moses used building blocks typical of public authority structures: independent financial power, corporate leadership, business patronage, civic reputation, and freedom from the encumbrances of democracy."[41] Thus, Moses consolidated his power position and political independence by drafting legislation, graciously enacted by the New York State legislature in 1946, that merged the Triborough Bridge Authority, the New York City Parkway Authority (which only eight years earlier had merged the Henry Hudson Parkway Authority and the Marine Parkway Authority under its auspices), and the New York City Tunnel Authority (which had been created in 1945 with Moses as its chief executive officer) into the Triborough Bridge and Tunnel Authority (TBTA). The effect of this exercise in bureaucratic imperialism was to enhance Moses's already considerable influence in New York; ultimately, Moses headed 14 state and city agencies at the same time.

Significantly, the legislation that Moses had drafted gave TBTA the right to refinance any of its outstanding debt at any time, thus granting Moses an extraordinarily solid power base; as soon as profits were amassed, but just before debts were about to be paid off, Moses could issue new bonds and start a new project. This, in fact, was precisely what Moses did since new projects could be financed with ease in the tax-exempt and laxly regulated municipal bond market.

Triborough's regulations and bonding powers cannot be changed by federal, state, or local governments; its army of Bridge and Tunnel officers and Parkway police reported only to Moses; and its toll booths provide a cornucopia of self-renewing treasure. At its peak (attained in 1960), Triborough controlled a land mass half the size of New York City itself, and annual revenues have neared a quarter-billion dollars.

Those who believe that men and women who dedicate their careers to public service face a life of genteel economic modesty should explore the world of government corporations. Moses maintained a yacht for his personal use that was skippered by three captains. Four dining rooms scattered around the city, each with its own full-time staff and chefs, served only Moses and his guests. Triborough secretaries not only were paid higher salaries than were New York City commissioners, but were given bigger cars and their own chauffeurs, who were on call 24 hours a day. The group of Triborough managers known as "Moses Men"—his closest allies—were made millionaires and multimillionaires by Moses.

Moses's period of greatest power and building occurred from 1946 through 1953. During this period, essentially no construction of consequence was even attempted in Gotham without his approval. "For thirty-four years, Moses played an important role in establishing the city's priorities, and for seven years, he established *all* the city's priorities."[42]

Moses was powerful far beyond the boundaries of the country's most important city. He changed the nation, too. In the fields of parks, highways, and urban renewal, Moses was a formative force in the country.

In parks, it was Moses who conceived the notion of state and urban recreational complexes linked by landscaped parkways. Prior to Moses, 29 states did not even have a single park, and 6 had only one. The parks system he bulldozed in New York was widely copied across the nation.

In highways, Moses had completed half a dozen urban expressways in metropolitan New York before Congress passed the Interstate Highway Act of 1956, which funneled federal money into the construction of urban freeways across the country. Prior to the act—which Moses was instrumental in drafting—metropolitan highways were virtually nonexistent except in New York.

Moses also was critical in drafting the Housing Act of 1949, which inaugurated the nation's controversial Urban Renewal program (described in Chapter 10), and Moses was quick to use the federal program that he himself had helped form. Eight years after the passage of the Housing Act, Moses, who controlled all Urban Renewal projects in New York, had spent more than twice the amount of federal urban renewal dollars than all American cities combined! His contracts were used as the model for Urban Renewal administrators across the country.

There was a fourth field in which Moses shaped America: urban planning. He was against it. Although he served on the New York City Planning Commission for 18 years (1942-1960), he blocked all attempts to establish a rational, comprehensive plan for the city at every turn. The lack of urban planning that is worthy of the name in all major American cities reflects the policy biases of the special authorities that Moses directed. As the urban scholar Lewis Mumford, one of Moses's most tenacious foes, has written, "In the twentieth century, the influence of Robert Moses on the cities of America was greater than that of any other person."[43]

Was his influence good or ill for New York and the nation? Moses's special authorities built needed public works that, in all probability, would never have been built without the bold concepts he originated. But the human costs of his Herculean projects, and the physical devastation that highways and urban renewal have wrought in America's cities in the absence of local planning, may not have been worth the price.

How did a man, initially dismissed as a "Goo Goo" (for "Good Government" reformer) by New York's Tammany Hall, come to wield such power? Moses built his power on an adoring media, the greed of others, tight secrecy (few have ever seen Triborough's detailed financial records), and political savvy that occasionally degenerated into personal vindictiveness. Much of his empire was built on deceptions, the most notable being that the government corporation was "above politics" (an assertion bought with slathering eagerness by the press) and was economically efficient. Through the nickels and dimes collected at his tollbooths, Moses bankrolled huge economic interests in New York and paid off individuals (perfectly legally) who were important to him. The retainers that

Triborough granted to public relations firms alone hit about $250,000 a year; legal fees amounted to another quarter-million dollars, and insurance commissions were half-a-million dollars annually. Moses was giving out a million dollars a year to those who played ball in a game he umpired in a modern-day equivalent of Tammany Hall's Christmas turkey baskets.[44]

But a million dollars a year in Tammany turkeys does not compare to the real plums Moses could distribute. Because Moses did not have to be particularly cost conscious, he could let very fat contracts to banks, labor unions, and the private sector. As a consequence, his union and business support was almost unprecedented in the New York metropolitan area. They, like the media, could always be depended upon for support when summoned—a loyalty that was enhanced considerably by the fact that, for 20 years (1948-1968), Moses maintained a secret agreement with the State Department of Public Works that gave him a personal veto over all contracts awarded by the department in metropolitan New York.[45]

Moses gave a new meaning to political pressure, boasting that "nothing I have ever done has been tinged with legality."[46] Moreover, he could use political pressure with a savagery that made old-time pols look like Goldilocks. Moses kept on his payroll men whom he called "bloodhounds." Moses's bloodhounds were charged with, among other unpleasantries, building embarrassing dossiers on persons of influence. If a man's past was inadequately juicy, he would visit the sins of their fathers upon him. A well-known and esteemed financier once rose during a City Planning Commission hearing to oppose a zoning change sponsored by Moses, only to hear Moses reply by reading into the hearing transcript newspaper accounts of a scandal, which had no connection whatever with zoning, in which the financier's father had been implicated 40 years earlier, when the financier was a child.[47] Moses ruined the careers of at least a dozen public officials with these tactics.

If all else failed, Moses would innovate. Although municipal-level communism is ludicrous on the face of it, two "Red scares" and ensuing witch hunts erupted in New York City in 1938 and 1958; both were largely fueled by gossip and misinformation leaked to the press by Moses. For example, when New York City Council member Stanley Isaacs opposed Moses on the grounds that he was razing, on a vast scale, low-income housing in the city, Moses was vicious in his counterattack. Isaacs wanted to reduce the demolition and add antidiscrimination clauses for public housing that was being built. Moses steamrollered Isaacs, citing, among other points, the fact that "Isaacs runs as a Republican among conservatives and is a pinko among radicals."[48] Similarly, the Tuscarora Indians objected to the prospective flooding of their land by the construction of Niagara Dam, a pet Moses project. Moses subsequently described the tribal leaders as "utterly incredible and clownish."[49] Another opponent was described by Moses as being "the infant prodigy who continued to be an infant long after he had finished being a prodigy."[50] As one observer has noted, "Moses was probably ruder, more manipulative, and more powerful than other authority managers . . . but regardless of the merits of the results, Moses spoke and acted as can only an authority manager—who will never face election himself or require direct support from community groups and other politicians, and who is not accountable to stockholders, competitors, or questioning board members."[51]

As noted, efficient management, while hardly a watchword in the Triborough empire, nonetheless was a widely accepted Moses myth that was critical to his political success. But the extent of the mismanagement, quite aside from the personal luxury that the unending flow of silver from the tollbooths provided Triborough's administrators, is nonetheless startling; for example, Moses paid $40 million in interest that he did not need to pay on a single bridge, and the state secretly underwrote Triborough to the tune of hundreds of millions of dollars. The city purchased much of the land on which Moses's projects were built; by turning the property over to Moses, Gotham also exempted this valuable land from its own tax rolls.[52]

Although Moses touted the supremacy of business efficiency, his first real venture into the free enterprise marketplace was a total failure. In 1962, Moses took over the second New York World's Fair project and raised funds by promising investors that he could turn the World's Fair into a profit-making event. In fact, Moses was so keen on turning a profit, that he initially opposed cut-rate tickets for schoolchildren. Nevertheless, when the project was completed, Moses defaulted on almost two-thirds of the Fair's debts. Moses failed his first real test of the marketplace.[53]

The myth of government corporations as just another competitor in the marketplace, and its unwarranted image of managerial efficiency, was beginning to fade in the 1960s, and this change in public attitude may have been encouraged by the behavior of Moses. In 1965, a number of bankers (after discovering that Moses, as president of the New York World's Fair, had guaranteed himself $100,000 in salary and annual expenses) resigned from the World's Fair Finance Committee on the grounds that Moses would not give them adequate financial information on how he was running the Fair's operations.

A Rocky Conquest: Rockefeller and His Follies

Robert Moses continued his remarkable successes throughout the 1950s. But in 1958, Nelson A. Rockefeller was elected governor of New York and began to challenge Moses's heretofore undisputed preeminence over the region's public corporations.

Rockefeller's challenge was made easier by the fact that in 1959 Moses had received his first "bad press" as a result of his chairmanship of New York City's Slum Clearance Committee. Scandals erupted in the program that were widely publicized, and, since slum clearance contract records were open to the public (unlike most financial records of the enterprises that Moses headed), the opportunities for media criticism were relatively ample.

The essence of Rockefeller's attack on Moses was his aggressive development of his own public authorities at the state level; by so doing, he was creating competition for Moses. In 1963, Rockefeller asked Moses to retire as head of the State Council on Parks, a position he had held since 1934. Rockefeller wished to appoint his brother Lawrence to the position, and Moses objected. Characteristically, Moses relied on a political device that had served him well in the past; he threatened to resign, not only from the State Council on Parks, but from the chairmanship of the New York Power Authority and several other state posts as well. His decision to escalate the conflict was ill advised. Rockefeller happily accepted Moses's departures from all the state posts for which he had tendered resignations!

While Rockefeller had won a battle, his real objective was to reduce Moses's power in the transportation field. To do this, Rockefeller had to gain control over transit finance in the state, and in 1967 he successfully pushed a huge, $2.5 billion, general obligation transportation bond issue. Rockefeller was accorded this bond issue by a statewide referendum, and it gave him the freedom to build transportation facilities that formerly had been controlled almost exclusively by Moses. Rockefeller then went to the state legislature and broadly reorganized New York's transportation policy machinery by creating the Metropolitan Transportation Authority. Central to this reorganization was the inclusion of Moses's Triborough Bridge and Tunnel Authority into Rockefeller's new Metropolitan Transportation Authority. Moses fought this merger on every front, including the courts, and lost on all of them. In 1968, the merger was achieved, and Moses was edged out of regional transportation policymaking. The merger also marked the downfall of the world's greatest builder.

The experiences of Robert Moses illustrate (if on a somewhat larger than life scale) the problems inherent to the operation of government corporations in a democracy: freedom from accountability, both political and financial. The decline of Moses' prestige and power was at least the partial result of a series of direct challenges to Robert Moses by Governor Nelson Rockefeller. The bitter war waged between Rockefeller and Moses illuminates how public authorities can weaken not only the powers of local governments but of state governments as well. As with government corporations at the local level, public authorities at the state level function in a political atmosphere of virtual nonaccountability to the public and its elected and appointed representatives. But Rockefeller's experience with public corporations deviated from this pattern. Although the device of the state government corporation is used more extensively in New York than in any other state, public authorities created by Rockefeller were unique in that he, as governor, controlled them absolutely. While this is not to say that these corporations were publicly accountable, at least an elected governor actually governed them—and with a rare thoroughness.

Nelson A. Rockefeller served as governor of New York from 1958 through 1974, and his ambitions to redevelop the physical plant and appearance of the state were rivaled only by Robert Moses and possibly the pharaohs of Egypt. Included in Rockefeller's plans were the redevelopment of Manhattan, for which he committed more than $6 billion to build, among other edifices, the World Trade Center, renovate docks, and renew the face of the city; the creation, virtually out of whole cloth, of a major state university system, which ultimately became the second largest in the country; the construction of massive public housing and public health facilities; the reconstruction and redesign of the capital city of Albany, rendering it, in the words of one observer, "architecturally respectable."[54] (Those who have seen Albany before and after the Rockefeller regime could reasonably conclude that what Rockefeller accomplished there is analogous to building the Great Pyramid in the middle of Altoona, Pennsylvania.) For fillers, Rockefeller built new mental health facilities, established a thoroughbred horse breeding program for the state, and raised private capital for the construction of new nursing homes, colleges, dormitories, hospitals, prisons, and a variety of other projects. All these enormous undertakings were accomplished through public authorities.

Why did Rockefeller rely so extensively on the government corporation to achieve his ends? The reasons are typical of why public authorities have proliferated in recent years. One is that Rockefeller had little regard for the desultory pace of his own state bureaucracy, particularly the hide-bound Department of Public Works. Nor, as an art connoisseur of considerable note, did he care for the kind of architectural design that all too frequently emanated from that department. So Rockefeller turned to the public corporation as a means of building both faster and better, since his public authorities could pay higher architectural fees and avoid reams of red tape.

The government corporation also enabled Rockefeller to bypass voter disapproval of many of his projects. Just two years prior to Rockefeller's taking office, the voters, for example, had voted for a third time to limit a housing bond issue. When Rockefeller became governor in 1958, he quickly created a Housing Finance Agency as a government corporation that built low-income housing. In 1961, New Yorkers defeated for a fourth time a major bond issue for higher education, so Rockefeller created the State University Construction Fund as a public authority designed to raise money for the same purpose that the voters had denied it. In 1965, voters rejected for a fifth time a low-income housing bond proposal, which Rockefeller answered with his creation of the Urban Development Corporation. Through these and other authorities, Rocky could borrow, veil his borrowing from the public eye, and make the legislature pay later.

Finally, Rockefeller found that, in an accounting sense, he could at least convey the appearance of balancing his state budget by creating public authorities, and this had political benefits. In 1962 Rockefeller pushed through a law that changed state accounting methods by striking the requirement that money granted by the state to public authorities be listed in the state budget. The effect of this change was to grant Rockefeller a major political boon because his budgets looked considerably leaner by not listing the costs of his public corporations in them, and such "fiscal responsibility" was in harmony with his "pay as you go" motto that characterized his four gubernatorial campaigns.

We have noted that Rockefeller was unique in that he was a governor who really controlled his own government corporations. How did he accomplish this?

One method was Rockefeller's connections with the New York financial community. Few governors have the fiscal background of a Rockefeller, and, as governor, Rocky capitalized on his network within the limited world of high finance. Rockefeller was able to raise more than $6 billion from Wall Street simply because the bankers trusted him.

Rockefeller also freed his public authorities from the fetters of the state. Although the state of New York was legally responsible for paying off the vast bulk of the public debt that Rockefeller's government corporations incurred, Rocky was adroit in assuring that the legislature and bureaucracy had virtually no control over their policies and operations. Of the 22 state corporations that Rockefeller created during his administration, 14 (including such major ones as the Urban Development Corporation) were completely beyond the scope of New York's public authorities law. This meant that almost two-thirds of the public authorities Rockefeller founded had boards appointed exclusively by Rockefeller, were exempt from state budgetary controls, did not have to submit their policy decisions to the governor for approval, and, in the case of the Urban Development Corporation, not even its own board of directors could review its budget! Moreover, those remaining government corporations created by Rockefeller that did fall under the state's public authorities law often were able to avoid any close supervision. For example, the Metropolitan Transportation Authority (MTA), a Rockefeller creation, submitted such jurisdictionally complex and fiscally convoluted budget reports to the legislature that the legislative staff was understandably confused and effectively gave up trying to conduct responsible oversight of the agency.

But the most spectacular method that Rockefeller used to control his public authorities were his personal administrative appointments to those authorities. Unlike other governors in other states, Rockefeller, using his almost unlimited wealth and a rare political ruthlessness, appointed directors of his various government corporations who were personally committed and loyal only to him. For example, Rockefeller hired Edward J. Logue to head his Urban Development Corporation (UDC) and went to extraordinary lengths to protect Logue politically, including threatening legislators to "take away their judgeships" if they failed to support Logue. Logue was appointed directly by the governor; in fact, not only did the board of directors of the Urban Development Corporation have no legal voice in the hiring of its own executive director, but the chair of the UDC had no managerial control whatever over its own executive director, who reported directly to Rockefeller. Similarly, Rockefeller appointed his long-time executive secretary, Alton Marshall, as a member of the Urban Development Corporation Board and as a board member of the New York Sports Authority.

While there are many examples of appointees to the boards of public corporations who had a total loyalty to Rockefeller, perhaps the most remarkable is William J. Ronan, who, under Rockefeller, was both chair of the board and chief executive officer of the Metropolitan Transportation Authority, and later served on the boards of the New York Port Authority (as chair) and the New York Power Authority. So extensive was Ronan's influence, thanks to Rockefeller's unstinting support, that he became known as the "Holy Ronan Empire." Ronan paralleled Robert Moses in that he had been a student of public administration and had conducted some outstanding research on the concept of the public authority; in fact, prior to his first appointment in the state government in 1959, Ronan had been dean of the Graduate School of Public Administration at New York University.

One of the major reasons that Rockefeller was able to retain the loyalty of people like Logue, Marshall, and Ronan was his generosity. Rocky made them all rich. Ronan received his first gift of $75,000 from Governor Rockefeller in 1958, and it was estimated that, during his 16 years as governor, Rockefeller eventually gave Ronan as much as $650,000. Logue, as chair of the UDC, received gifts and loans from Rockefeller that totaled more than $175,000, while Marshall was loaned more than $300,000 in 1970 alone.[55] There are many other examples.

Perhaps because Rockefeller's chief appointees were not working in a world of personal fiscal reality, none of them was terribly skilled in financial management and cost control. When Rockefeller turned the state house over to the Democrats in 1974, many of his public corporations were in deep financial trouble. For example, very soon after Ronan left as chair of the board of the MTA in 1973, virtually all projects under construction (including partially dug tunnels) had to be halted by his successor because there were no funds left to complete them. The Urban Development Corporation, headed by Logue, was spending $1 million a day in the same year[56] and was in such serious financial difficulty that Logue was forced to resign in 1975, shortly after a new governor assumed office.

Rockefeller's government corporations had, among other things, overestimated student housing needs, set up a situation in which private developers could manipulate mental health facilities for their own profit, and imposed a highly questionable financial system for state transportation. In 16 years, Rockefeller had created so many public authorities of such enormous scope that they currently account for more than a third of all revenue bonds issued across the country! Public authorities still are the single most important sector of public finance in the state of New York. When a Democratic governor took over in 1975, he was confronted with a debt incurred by the state's public authorities of more than $12 billion (in 1962, the outstanding debt of New York's public authorities was only $129 million), or almost four times the amount of debt incurred by the state government itself! Moreover the state had been obligated to pay off two-thirds of this $12 billion, and the state's public authorities still were planning to embark on projects that would involve legislative appropriations of an additional $1.9 billion during the next five years.[57]

For better or worse, New York symbolizes the rise of the public corporation and its relationships with state and local governments. Public authorities, which are beginning to dominate the financial structures of subnational governments, now largely control critical public programs, particularly in energy, water, communication, and transportation; as some observers have put it, the American experience with government authorities has been one of extending "the public's credit, rather than the public's control"[58] in these and a wide spectrum of other policy areas.

But other public programs have remained the preserve of the on-line government agencies, notably, welfare, criminal justice, education, public planning, and land use. Still other policies, such as transportation, remain in a twilight zone between government corporation and government agency. We consider the more significant of these policies—and their effects on people—in the next and final part of this book.

NOTES

[1]Lori M. Henderson, "Intergovernmental Service Arrangements and Transfer of Functions," *Municipal Year Book, 1985* (Washington, D.C.: International City Management Association, 1985), p. 201.

[2]Keon S. Chi, "Privatization: A Public Option?" *State Government News* (June, 1985), p. 6.

[3]E. S. Savas, *Evaluating the Organization of Service Delivery: Solid Waste Collection and Disposal* (New York: Center for Government Studies, Graduate School of Business, Columbia University, 1976). Savas found that 62 percent of all American cities use private companies for garbage collection.

[4]Donald Fisk, Herbert Kiesling, and Thomas Muller, *Private Provision of Public Services: An Overview* (Washington, D.C.: The Urban Institute, 1978), p. 20.

[5]Robert F. Kennedy, *The Enemy Within* (New York: Popular Library, 1960), pp. 230-234.

[6]John D. Hanrahan, *Government for Sale* (Washington, D.C.: American Federation of State, County and Municipal Employees, 1977), p. 47.

[7]*Ibid.*, p. 52.

[8]New York State Commission of Investigation, "An Investigation of the Purchases Practices and Procedures and Other Related Matters of the City of Albany, New York" (Albany: N.Y.S.C.I., 1973), as cited in *ibid.*, p. 16.

[9]Paul J. Curran, chair of the New York State Commission of Investigation, transcript of statement of Albany investigation, December 22, 1972, as cited in *ibid.*, p. 13.

[10]*Ibid.*, p. 15.

[11]See Chi, "Privatization," p. 6; and Advisory Commission on Intergovernmental Relations, *Significant Features of Fiscal Federalism, 1984* (Washington, D.C.: U.S. Government Printing Office, 1985), p. 10. Figure is for 1982.
[12]See Fisk et al., *Private Provision of Public Services,* p. 89.
[13]*Ibid.* Another survey found that 97 percent of American cities (1,350 cities responded) required sealed bids on purchasing contracts. On the other hand, nearly 87 percent of these same cities permitted bidding to be waived under certain circumstances. See Dan H. Davidson and Solon G. Bennett, "Municipal Purchasing Practices," *Municipal Year Book, 1980* (Washington, D.C.: International City Management Association, 1980), Tables 3/10 and 3/12, pp. 236-237.
[14]Fisk et al., *Private Provision of Public Services,* p. 92.
[15]Advisory Commission on Intergovernmental Relations, "State and Local Pension Reforms," *Information Bulletin No. 79-2* (March, 1979), p. 3.
[16]Tax Foundation, *Employee Pension Systems in State and Local Government* (New York: Tax Foundation, 1976), p. 1.
[17]Advisory Council on Intergovernmental Relations, *Information Bulletin No. 79-2,* p. 3. In 1977, state and local governments paid out $12.4 billion to worker retirement plans (in addition to Social Security payments), or about 7 percent of their overall tax revenues. This amounted to about $2 billion more than these governments expended on their police forces.
[18]Tax Foundation, *Employee Pension Systems,* p. 1.
[19]Advisory Commission on Intergovernmental Relations, *Information Bulletin No. 79-2*; Tax Foundation, *Employee Pension Systems;* Comptroller General of the United States, *Report to the Congress Funding of State and Local Government Pension Plans: A National Problem,* HRD-79-66 (Washington, D.C.: U.S. General Accounting Office, 1979), pp. i-v; and Pension Task Force, Committee on Education and Labor, U.S. House of Representatives, *Task Force Report on Public Employee Retirement Systems,* 95th Cong., 2d sess. (Washington, D.C.: U.S. Government Printing Office, 1978).
[20]Comptroller General, *Report,* pp. i-v.
[21]The sources for these points are Ira Sharkansky, "Government Contracting," *State Government,* 53 (Winter, 1980), p. 23; and James W. Fesler, *Public Administration: Theory and Practice* (Englewood Cliffs, N.J.: Prentice-Hall, 1980), pp. 293-294.
[22]Patricia S. Florestano and Stephen B. Gordon, "A Survey of City and County Use of Private Contracting," *The Urban Interest,* 3 (Spring 1981), p. 27.
[23]Annmarie Hauk Walsh concludes that there are about 5,000 to 7,000 public authorities, a number that excludes authorities that are not organizationally independent of government agencies. But Charles E. Lindblom contends that if the count included public corporations that are authorized to issue general obligation bonds, the number would jump to 18,000. See Annmarie Hauk Walsh, *The Public's Business: The Politics and Practices of Government Corporations* (Cambridge, Mass.: M.I.T. Press, 1978), p. 5; and Charles E. Lindblom, *Politics and Markets: The World's Political Economic Systems* (New York: Basic Books, 1977), p. 114.
[24]Michael Denning and David J. Olson, "Public Enterprise and the Emerging Character of State Service Provisions: Applications to Public Ports," paper presented at the 1981 annual meeting of the American Political Science Association, New York, September 3-6, 1981, p. 6.
[25]*Ibid.,* p. 9.
[26]Walsh, *The Public's Business,* p. 6.
[27]In 1983, according to the Public Securities Association, 58 percent of all bond issues were let by "special districts and statutory authority," the category that includes primarily government corporations. The remainder were issued by state and local governments, including school districts. In 1970, only 33 percent of bond issues were released by special districts and statutory authority. See Bureau of the Census, *Statistical Abstract of the United States, 1985* (Washington, D.C.: U.S. Government Printing Office, 1984), Table 450, p. 274.
[28]Walsh, *The Public's Business,* p. 6.
[29]Bureau of the Census, *Statistical Abstract of the United States, 1985,* Table 451, p. 274.
[30]Denning and Olson, "Public Enterprise," pp. 10, 42.
[31]Kathryn E. Newcomer, Deborah L. Trent, and Natalie Flores-Kelly, "Municipal Debt and the Impact of Sound Fiscal Decision Making," *Municipal Year Book, 1983* (Washington, D.C.: International City Management Association, 1983), pp. 218-219.

[32]For example, *Williamsburg Savings Bank* v. *State of New York* (1928) and *Robertson* v. *Zimmerman* (1935).
[33]Walsh, *The Public's Business,* pp. 118-119.
[34]Denning and Olson, "Public Enterprise," Table III.
[35]Walsh, *The Public's Business,* p. 289.
[36]Nathanial S. Preston, "The Use and Control of Public Authorities in American State and Local Government," Ph.D. dissertation, Princeton University, Princeton, N.J., 1960.
[37]Walsh, *The Public's Business,* p. 4.
[38]Robert A. Caro, *The Power Broker: Robert Moses and the Fall of New York* (New York: Alfred A. Knopf, 1974), pp. 5-10.
[39]*Ibid.,* pp. 19-20.
[40]*Ibid.*
[41]Walsh, *The Public's Business,* p. 213.
[42]Caro, *The Power Broker,* p. 38.
[43]Quoted in *ibid.,* p. 12.
[44]*Ibid.,* p. 18.
[45]*Ibid.,* p. 15.
[46]United Press International, " 'Master Builder' Robert Moses, 92, Dies," *The Arizona Republic* (July 30, 1981).
[47]Caro, *The Power Broker,* p. 15.
[48]Robert Moses, *Public Works: A Dangerous Trade* (New York: McGraw-Hill, 1970), p. 438.
[49]*Ibid.,* p. 394.
[50]United Press International, " 'Master Builder'."
[51]Walsh, *The Public's Business,* p. 221.
[52]Caro, *The Power Broker,* p. 17.
[53]Walsh, *The Public's Business,* p. 220.
[54]*Ibid.,* p. 265.
[55]*Ibid.,* pp. 271-272.
[56]*Ibid.,* p. 275.
[57]*Ibid.,* pp. 263-264 and 276.
[58]Denning and Olson, "Public Enterprise," p. 6.

15
THE WELFARE MESS

In Part Five we consider the major political issues that state and local governments must face: welfare, crime, education, planning, land use, transportation, and corruption.

Public policies for people inevitably are directed at social classes. The issues of poverty, welfare, and crime are all interrelated and affect predominantly society's underdogs; these are public policies designed largely for the poor and the deviant. On the other hand, planning, land-use, transportation, and education policies are designed primarily for the middle class, which always has taken a peculiar interest in these problems. The issue of political corruption, one not normally covered in books on state and local governments, approaches political corruption as the politics of the rich. Political corruption can, of course, occur at all levels of society, but the people who reap the greatest benefits from it are often among the wealthier classes.

A class-based approach to the study of public policy is hardly new (Karl Marx, for one, was vaguely aware of it), but class is often overlooked as a central variable in understanding how and why public policies are made. It is worth recalling that public policies are made for groups (and classes) of people at least as much as they are formed for "all the people." Charles Reich has castigated public policy in America as an "inhuman medium" largely on the grounds that, since the New Deal of the 1930s, laws have been written for groups and categories of people (for example, farmers, old people, young people, the poor, students, veterans, and so forth) and not for the individual citizens, who once stood as equals before the law simply as persons rather than as "farmers" or "students." By addressing groups rather than individuals, public policy has waxed into something that the lone citizen no longer can understand, but that groups of citizens *must* understand if they are to be a part of the larger society.[1]

Whether or not Reich's analysis is correct, it is provocative enough to warrant approaching public policy issues as class issues in this and the succeeding chapters of this book.

We begin at the bottom, with the underclass.

UNDERSTANDING THE UNDERCLASS

The idea of an underclass is a relatively new one, and it includes people who are both below and above the official poverty line. Estimates on the size of the underclass vary, but typically range from 7 million to 10 million people.[2] The underclass includes approximately 1 million "discouraged" unemployed who have ceased to seek employment because their efforts have come to naught; roughly 10 million people (or from a third to a half of the indigent population) who are the long-term poor; unemployed youth; segments of the physically and mentally handicapped; and criminals and other deviants. The underclass represents a minority of the poor.[3]

In part, this is because many members of the underclass participate in an "underground economy" of increasingly vast proportions, possibly reaching as large an amount as $300 billion per year.[4] The underground economy is largely illegal but not entirely. It refers to monetary transfers that are not reported to the Internal Revenue Service, and hence are never taxed, and includes all those expenses that are incurred "off the books," such as tax avoidance, tips, and cash for services. The underground economy also encompasses revenues never reported to the Internal Revenue Service for quite obvious reasons, such as those derived from drug dealing, prostitution, and street crimes. Thus, although the underclass associates to some degree with the underground economy, that economy is hardly the exclusive preserve of the underclass.

Among the characteristics shared by the underclass are a lack of family stability, a lack of any kind of job skills, and a lack of ability to function normally in society. Whether members of the underclass live in the inner city or in rural America, they share a lack of exposure to the working world, a background of excessive violence in the home, the absence of an admirable role model, and a dependency on the welfare system.[5]

Being a minor in a home without an adult male seems to be a predominant characteristic of the underclass. A national survey of teenagers who could be reasonably identified as being members of the underclass (i.e., they had histories of difficulties with law enforcement officials and drug addiction) found that nearly 40 percent of the white youths lived with just their mothers, 48 percent of the Hispanics lived with only their mothers, and more than 61 percent of the blacks lived only with their mothers. Only a quarter of these teenagers lived with both parents.

A lack of job skills also characterizes the underclass. The largest private employer in New York City, the New York Telephone Company, reports that 60 percent of its applicants fail the competency test it gives to prospective employees, while the Carnegie Council on Policy Studies in Higher Education has stated that one-third of American teenagers are "ill-educated, ill-employed, and ill-equipped to make their way in American society."[6] Most studies also conclude that people in the underclass "often exhibit abnormal behavior—hostility, poor work habits, passivity, low self-confidence, alcoholism, drug addiction."[7]

Perhaps the most worrisome aspect of the underclass is that it appears to be becoming permanent. Moreover, "solutions" seem increasingly difficult to find. As one official of the Department of Housing and Urban Development has observed, "The underclass presents our most dangerous crisis, more dangerous than the Depression of 1929, and more complex."[8]

DEFINING POVERTY

The poor, whether in the underclass or not, always will be with us. One reason is because *poverty* must be defined in relative terms. Poverty, by definition, means that someone is getting much less money than someone else, and when the discrepancy between income levels becomes intense, the lower portion of the scale becomes the impoverished.

In 1955 the federal government defined poverty in more quantitative terms; a federal survey of that year revealed that the poor spent 30 percent of their after-tax income for food. Using this finding, the "poverty line" was invented and established by federal statisticians at a point slightly more than three times the price of an "adequate" diet. How realistic this kind of "poverty line" is is a matter of conjecture but, in any case, the poverty line uses a grim measure of indigence: eating or starving.

In 1964, the federal government refined its measurement of poverty by devising the "cash-income" method of determining impoverishment. The cash-income method simply means that the poverty line is determined exclusively by how much dollar income a family or an individual receives during the year. In 1983, the "poverty line" for an urban family of four was almost $10,200; by contrast, the average income for American families of four that year was more than $21,400.[9]

In 1980, Congress began questioning the cash-income method as the principal definition of poverty, and ordered the Census Bureau to study what the effects would be if "noncash income" (also known as "in-kind benefits") were calculated as part of an individual's or family's income. These "noncash" benefits include such federal, state, and local programs as Medicare, Medicaid, food stamps, public housing, school lunch subsidies, and related government programs aimed at alleviating poverty. Congress wanted to learn more about the effects of these programs on people's living standards because these noncash benefits have risen substantially since 1964, when the cash-income–only measurement was originated. In 1965, noncash benefits accounted for $2.2 billion, but by 1980 this figure had risen to $72 billion. (When inflation is held constant in this increase, the 1980 figure becomes $27.8 billion in "real" dollars, still a sizable increase in noncash benefits.)[10]

Obviously there are some real problems in attempting to interpret noncash benefits to the poor in ways that reflect real cash income. These problems include the difficulty of counting medical benefits, estimating the actual cash value of the benefit to the recipient, and determining how much an average poor person would spend on food, housing, and medical care if all that person's income were in cash.[11] Despite these difficulties, in 1982 the Census Bureau responded to Congress's request, and its study found that including noncash benefits in the measurement of poverty would reduce official poverty rates in the nation by substantial margins. Under the broadest interpretation of noncash benefits, the Census Bureau found that the poverty rate would decrease by almost half, or 42 percent. Under the narrowest interpretation, which, among other aspects, would exclude medical benefits because of the difficulty in assigning values to such benefits, the reduction would be 12 percent.[12]

WHO IS POOR?

Irrespective of the method used in calculating how many people are poor (and the official method still remains that of measuring cash income only), the fact remains that some 35 million Americans, or 15 percent of the population, including more than 12 million children under the age of 16, are officially categorized as poor people.[13] Table 15-1 lists some of the characteristics of people who have incomes below the official poverty line.

Although blacks account for only 12 percent of the American population, 36 percent of blacks live in poverty; 28 percent of Hispanics, who comprise approximately 5 percent of the population, are in poverty. The number of blacks who are impoverished has been in decline since 1959 (when statistics on black and white indigence were first collected). More than 55 percent of blacks in that year were considered to be below the poverty line, compared to more than 18 percent of whites. Data on Hispanic impoverishment have been collected

Table 15-1 Kinds of People Below the Poverty Line, 1983

Selected Characteristics	*Poverty Rate (%)*[a]
White	12%
Black	36
Hispanic	28
Under 17 years	23
65 years and over	14
Northeast	13
South	17
Midwest	15
West	15
Families in metropolitan areas	11
In central cities	16
Suburbs	8
Families in rural/nonmetropolitan areas	15
In families with female householder, no husband present	36[b]
All other families	10[b]
Householders with less than eight years of school	28
Householders with one year or more of college	5
Overall poverty rate (1983)	15

[a] Percentages have been rounded.
[b] Percentages are for 1982.

Source: Bureau of the Census, *Statistical Abstract of the United States, 1985* (Washington, D.C.: U.S. Government Printing Office, 1984), Tables 758–760, pp. 454–456; and Table 764, p. 458.

only since 1972 and have remained more or less stable over the years for which we have data. Typically, Hispanic indigence ranges from a fifth to a quarter of the Latino population.[14]

The Feminization of Poverty

Perhaps the most striking trend that is occurring among the indigent has been the feminization and "youthification" of poverty. A disproportionate share of the poor in this country have always been women (and, for that matter, their children). Mothers and their children comprise approximately two-fifths of the American population, but more than one-half of all people living below the official poverty line.

There are approximately 31 million women with children in this country, of whom 3.9 million are below the poverty level. Of these 3.9 million poor women with children, approximately two-thirds are female householders with no husband present. In fact, the single greatest demographic characteristic of the indigent population is that it is female and heads a family. Forty percent of female heads of households who have children live in poverty; by contrast, the poverty rate for wives of heads of family households who have their own children is only 6 percent. The number of families headed by women increased by 62 percent between 1970 and 1980. Families headed by women are *five times* more likely to be poor than are two-parent families. As one observer has put it, "Increasingly, the division between those who rise into the middle class and those who are poor can be viewed in terms of two-parent families versus families maintained by women."[15]

The Youthification of Poverty

Of course, the children in these families are poor, too. Children under 18 years of age make up 27 percent of the national population and 39 percent of all poor people. Even though the total number of children decreased by 9 million from 1968 to 1983, the number of poor children increased by 3 million. Yet, welfare benefits for poor children fell by about a fifth in terms of real spending power between 1976 and 1983.[16]

The United States may be unique among all nations in that more children live in poverty than do older people. In one of the world's wealthiest countries, a third of its children will be living on welfare before they are 14.[17]

Table 15-2 indicates some characteristics of poor children. As it shows, being in a family headed by a woman, particularly if the woman never married, is the likeliest place to find a poor child.

BEING POOR AND BEING DESPISED

To be poor in America is to be disproportionately ill schooled, female, black, brown, Southern, a resident of central cities or rural areas, old, and young. But demographics do not tell the whole story.

Thomas Gladwin, an anthropologist, states in succinct terms that poverty in America means being not only poor, but also powerless, incompetent (insofar as the employer is concerned), and despised. Significantly, being loathed

Table 15-2 Poverty Among Children, 1983

Children	*White*	*Black*	*Hispanic*	*All Children Under 18 Years*
Total	17%	47%	38%	22%
In female-headed families (total)	48	69	71	56
Mothers never married	71	77	86	75
Mothers separated or divorced	47	67	70	54
Mothers widowed	28	61	39	41
In male-present families	12	24	27	14

Source: Congressional Research Service and Congressional Budget Office, *Children in Poverty* (Washington, D.C.: U.S. Government Printing Office, 1985).

does not necessarily associate with being a member of a minority race, but being poor does:

> It is obvious that poverty and discrimination are closely and complexly interrelated. For example, putting the relationship the other way around, it is hard to think of any large group of really poor people about whom stereotypes and prejudices have *not* developed. In the 1930s numbers of small independent farmers, in other times idealized as staunch repositories of the American pioneering spirit, were stripped of their farms and their money. They became almost overnight the most stigmatized population of the Depression years, the Okies. Similarly, the purest descendents of the early days of White Anglo-Saxon Protestants have now become in their poverty the Appalachian hillbillies, probably as ruthlessly plundered of their property and power as any of our minorities, except the decimated Indians, and the butts of a special school of American belittling humor which extends back over several generations. The little child in eastern Kentucky, hiding and peeking out in wide-eyed fright at the stranger, knows as well as any child in an urban ghetto that he is powerless to protect himself against a world which has judged him worthless. Under these circumstances, what good would it do him to be told that he is a blond blue-eyed Anglo-Saxon and therefore potentially heir to all the privileges of the land?[18]

Welfare policies have exacerbated the middle class's loathing of the poor. In part, this is because welfare "is a system replete with anomalies—intended to reduce dependency, it requires dependency as a condition of receiving welfare benefits; encouraging recipients to find gainful employment, it penalizes their success by withdrawing benefits so that a former client is often in worse straits while employed than while receiving welfare."[19] Facts support this description. In Oregon and New York, for example, the cash payments available to a family of four under just two welfare programs—Aid to Families with Dependent Children and food stamps—exceed the earnings of a full-time worker at the minimum wage in 22 states![20] In the opinion of most Americans, former President Richard M. Nixon was correct when he spoke of welfare as a "monstrous, consuming outrage."[21]

The fires of this "consuming outrage" are stoked by other facets of welfare policy. Encouraged by federal legislation, state welfare administrators, beginning in the 1960s, began to admit larger numbers of fatherless families to their welfare rolls on the logic that families without a breadwinner needed help more than most; today, four-fifths of the recipients of Aid to Families with Dependent Children (AFDC), the nation's principal welfare program, are families headed by women.

The middle class and, for that matter, the "working poor," were particularly sensitive to this feminization of the welfare rolls (if, perhaps, less so to the feminization of poverty itself). Middle America no longer (if it ever did) saw "the dole" going to God-fearing, upright widow ladies who scrubbed floors to get their children through college, but instead being funneled by Big Government to insatiable "welfare queens," who kept having babies to increase their welfare payments, and to shiftless, male "welfare bums," who were happy to slop at the public trough for the remainder of their idle days. Not too long ago, an Illinois legislator consistently called the Aid to Families with Dependent Children Program the "aid to bastard children program."[22] Similarly, the mayor of Hondo, Texas, wrote the president and requested a list of 181 "loafers" he could import to Hondo to increase the city's unemployment rate and thereby qualify it for federal funds. The mayor argued that because 24 percent of Hondo's 8,000 residents earned salaries below the national poverty level, he needed 181 people who would not work to raise Hondo's unemployment levels to the federal minimum. Federal administrators treated the mayor's request as a joke, which it evidently was not.[23]

Such are the stereotypes. Are they valid? No.

Do poor women who head families (i.e., the archtypical welfare recipient) want to work? They want to work more than most, at least if we are to answer this question by using available data. Poor women who head families are more likely to have jobs than are poor women who have husbands. Forty-three percent of poor women who have children and head their own families hold down jobs, compared to 36 percent of indigent women with husbands and children.[24]

Are these women "baby machines"? Again, facts run counter to the stereotype that poor women who head families are having children out of wedlock more frequently than the rest of the population. Between 1967 and 1977, the proportion of children receiving AFDC benefits because their parents were unwed increased by seven percentage points (from less than 27 percent to nearly 34 percent).[25] But, during this same ten-year period, the national rate of illegitimate births swelled by 40 percent, or by a substantially higher rate than that of the welfare population.[26] Thus, when we place the "aid to bastard children program" in a national context, the welfare mothers are, relatively speaking, paragons of virtue resisting a rising tide of promiscuity.

Are welfare mothers being abandoned by irresponsible men who leave their indiscretions on the taxpayers' doorstep? Again, the facts belie the stereotype. Most of the increase between 1973 and 1977 in AFDC recipients who were women that maintained families were women who were divorced rather than deserted. In fact, the number of families added to the AFDC rolls as a result of desertion by a man during this period declined from 28.8 percent to 25.5 percent.[27]

Finally, and perhaps most importantly, does welfare trap indigent mothers in a "cycle of dependency" on welfare from which there is no escape (except the withdrawal of welfare benefits)? Contrary to popular impressions, apparently not. A study of 300 teenagers—nearly all of them poor, all of them black, and all of them pregnant—begun in the 1960s, found that they did surprisingly well in breaking out of poverty.[28] Some 16 years after they had had their babies, Frank Furstenberg found that the group of poor pregnant teenagers had matured into contributing, productive members of society: the women's average annual income was marginal but well above the poverty line (and a fourth of them had incomes exceeding $25,000); more than two-thirds had jobs; only a quarter were on welfare, although more than two-thirds had been on welfare at some point in their lives; 70 percent had earned their high school diplomas, a fourth had attended college, and 5 percent had graduated from college. Marriage, getting an education, and making a decision to limit childbearing (none had more than three children and the vast majority stopped at two) were the most significant factors in breaking out of poverty. Of these, the most important was the final one; 56 percent of the women had had themselves sterilized and many more had had abortions—strong indications of their determination to get off welfare.

Furstenberg's research is unique because it provides the longest view of welfare mothers ever taken. Other credible studies arrive at different conclusions, usually implying that it is virtually impossible for indigent, single mothers to break poverty's cycle, but these investigations typically were conducted shortly after the mothers had given birth. Even Furstenberg's data support the contention that, in the relatively short term, welfare mothers are trapped in a cycle of dependency; Furstenberg also interviewed the 300 black mothers about five years after they had had their babies and found that virtually all of them were still mired in the welfare system. But not so a decade later; welfare mothers can—and do—get out.

There are the facts. But facts seldom alter opinions in such emotionally charged fields as welfare. Indeed, as we detail later in this chapter, perhaps the most astounding fact of all is that, for all the heat generated by welfare payments and the people who get them, most of the poor do not even receive welfare!

WELFARE FOR WHOM?

It should be stated early and clearly that welfare in America is not something provided only to the poor. Farm price supports, "corporate welfare" (such as is occasionally supplied to giant aircraft corporations), subsidies to the railroad and trucking industries, tax write-offs for interest incurred on home mortgages, and tax preferences for families and people over 65—all are forms of welfare, and most of the time such welfare provides benefits to people who are not poor at all. One in 3 households in America receives some sort of welfare, quite aside from Social Security payments;[29] 1 in every 12 individuals receives some form of welfare, and 1 in every 4 households receives income from Social Security.[30]

But if most of governments' welfare payments do not go to the poor, it is the poor who nonetheless are the most dependent on them. More than 68 percent of the incomes of the poorest households—those with incomes of less than $600 a month—comes from the government. By contrast, less than 3 percent of the incomes of the wealthiest households—those that earn $5,000 a month—comes from government. Most of the government assistance that the poor households receive is in the form of Social Security checks, followed by

AFDC payments.[31] The poor, in short, are deeply dependent on government for their survival.

WELFARE POLICIES: THE POLITICS OF COMPLEXITY

The Social Security Act of 1935: Welfare's Cornerstone

If there is a single act of legislation that is the bedrock of welfare policy in the United States, it is the Social Security Act of 1935, enacted as a major response to the Great Depression, and its subsequent amendments. "Social security" as a policy has two broad thrusts: one is social insurance and the other is public assistance.

Social insurance benefits are paid for by compulsory payroll taxes; the category entitled FICA (Federal Insurance Contributions Act) on a paycheck stub notes how much of one's check is deducted for "social security." *Public assistance* spending for "welfare" is funded from general tax revenues, and, unlike social insurance, this money is not earmarked. Thus, when money is spent for welfare policies, it is being spent at the potential expense of some other policy. Social insurance is a national policy that covers the vast majority of all Americans, and it is uniform in its distribution of benefits throughout the states. By contrast, public assistance is a decentralized system predicated on the premise that state governments can better judge the needs of their people and the resources of their taxpayers than Washington bureaucrats can, and is administered on the basis of federal grants to state governments. Public assistance is handled in one of two ways—either by direct formula grants to states, based on certain categories of need, or by categorical grants to the states, which permit the states to retain greater discretion on how those federal funds are used.

Social Insurance: Three Major Programs

"Social Security." Within these two broad thrusts of social insurance and public welfare are a number of specific programs. The first, pertaining only to social insurance, is Old Age, Survivors, Disability, and Health Insurance, or OASDHI. This program, commonly known as Social Security, is designed to reduce the loss of a person's income because of unemployment resulting from old age, disability, or death of the head of the family. A major component of OASDHI is Medicare, and we consider Medicare later. About a fifth of the federal budget is spent through OASDHI each year and goes to one-seventh of the population. It is no small social insurance program.

Unemployment benefits. A second program initiated by the Social Security Act is unemployment insurance. Although benefits are actually provided by the federal government through a tax on all employers who employ four employees or more, states have a greater say in determining how unemployment benefits should be paid.

Unemployment tends to hit all skill levels in the work force, but it concentrates on particular age groups and women. Those who are 45 to 54 and the young, particularly teenagers, are statistically the hardest hit by unemployment, and black teenagers are especially hard hit. This tendency for the young to be unemployed more frequently than most other age groups strikes blacks especially hard, since nearly half of all black Americans are under age 25. In other words, although unemployment insurance as a welfare policy is applicable to all groups in society, it tends to focus on women, minority groups, the young, the middle-aged, and people who have little or no work experience.

General health care and Medicare. A third component is health insurance. Health care is the nation's third largest industry: Americans spend almost 10 percent of the gross national product on their health, more than any other nationality, but, unlike many Western democracies, less than half this sum is expended by governments.[32] Federal expenditures account for most of the public spending on health (about 70 percent).[33] The remaining money dedicated to public health is spent by 57 state and territorial agencies, plus the District of Columbia, and more than 3,000 local health agencies located in 46 states. State health agencies spend more than $5 billion a year, most of it on personal health programs that serve almost a third of Americans directly. More than half this money is drawn from state revenues, about a third comes from federal grants, and the remaining tenth or so is derived from local fees. Local health agencies spend more than $2 billion a year, virtually all of it on personal health programs.[34]

In 1965 Congress enacted two important pieces of legislation designed to enhance health in America: Medicare and Medicaid. Medicare provides comprehensive medical care for people over age 65 and is part of the Social Security Insurance program. Medicare also provides low-cost voluntary medical insurance for the aged, and it is financed through payroll taxes collected under FICA. Medicare accounts for more than a fifth of the total federal benefits package for the elderly, including Social Security payments.

Public Assistance: Four Major Programs

Medicaid. Unlike Medicare, which is a social insurance program for the elderly, Medicaid is a public assistance program designed for the needy, and its beneficiaries generally are welfare recipients. Of the 22 million people receiving Medicaid benefits (including 11 million children), more than 5 million of these adults also receive welfare in the form of Aid to Families with Dependent Children, and more than 6 million adults receive Supplemental Security Income assistance (SSI). All the states except Arizona (which began an experimental pilot program in 1982) participate in the program, and 30 states extend Medicaid's benefits beyond the indigent to the "medically needy," or those whose incomes are higher than the eligibility standards for AFDC or SSI. The costs of Medicaid have burgeoned by almost seven times since 1970, and the states, which typically pay 45 percent of the Medicaid bill from their own coffers, are feeling the pinch; the states' share of the Medicaid bill amounts to nearly 6 percent of state expenditures from their own sources.[35]

Supplemental Security Income assistance. Federal formula grants to states for welfare are used to assist three categories of the needy: the aged, the blind, and the disabled. Old Age Assistance, Aid to the Blind, and Aid to Permanently and Totally Disabled have remained relatively stable in terms of their cost to the states since the 1960s, although Aid to the Permanently and Totally Disabled has increased, largely as a result of a more flexible application of eligibility requirements.

In 1974 a new national program called Supplemental Security Income assistance, or SSI, went into effect. Before the enactment of SSI, each state could calculate its own minimum income standards for its poor, and the determination of cash assistance levels and eligibility were entirely matters of state policy. Under SSI, however, national minimum standards for eligibility and for cash assistance were established. It was further stipulated that, if one category of need was receiving higher monthly benefits than another (for instance, the blind have traditionally received more than the elderly), then the other two categories had to be brought up to the same level. Thus the Supplemental Security Income programs have had two effects. First, all categories of "the needy" have been equalized in terms of level of cash assistance; the blind, for example, are not receiving more money than the elderly simply because they are blind. Second, state policymakers have been displaced by national policymakers in the degree of discretion that they may wield over these areas of welfare. Although the states have the option of going beyond the levels of assistance mandated by SSI—and only Texas has refused to provide supplements to the program[36]—it nonetheless stands that the states have had their authority reduced substantially in this area of welfare policymaking.

Supplemental Security Income pays out nearly $8 billion in federal funds to more than 4 million people. But the states add more than $2 billion from their own revenues in payments to the blind, the old, and the disabled.

Aid to Families with Dependent Children. Finally, there are two forms of public assistance that have grown extremely controversial in recent years: the Aid to Families with Dependent Children program and the food stamp program. Both programs are administered almost entirely by state governments, but in some states local governments are also involved.

AFDC is the largest federally assisted program for state public welfare. Originally it was meant to provide a minimum standard of existence for orphans, children cared for by a widowed mother, or families where the father was unavoidably absent. Over time the kinds of family units receiving AFDC payments has changed. Since 1962, for example, AFDC payments can go to two parents in the same home if one parent is incapacitated or unemployed, if the state agrees; 21 states and Washington, D.C., use this option. The federal government contributes, on the average, slightly more than half (54 percent) of the AFDC payments to beneficiaries; the states (and, in a dozen states, localities) make up the rest. But these federal contributions vary widely among the states because they are keyed to a formula that is based on each state's per capita income. Hence, Washington provides anywhere from half to three quarters of the states' AFDC payments. But the states determine the eligibility requirements. Almost $14 billion is expended by federal, state, and local governments in Aid to Families with Dependent Children and goes to more than 10 million people.[37] Four-fifths of the people who receive AFDC benefits live in metropolitan areas; four-fifths of all the families receiving these payments are headed by women; 40 percent of the families on AFDC are white, 43 percent are black, and 13 percent are Hispanic; blacks, especially black children, are increasingly dependent on the program, with nearly one in five of all blacks receiving AFDC payments.[38]

Food stamps. Supplementing AFDC payments are food stamps, and the two assistance programs are closely interrelated; in a typical year, more than 40 percent of the households that receive AFDC payments also use food stamps. The food stamp program was enacted in 1964 with the passage of the Food Stamp Act, which is intended to improve nutrition in low-income families. It is a unique form of public assistance in that it is the only program that helps all poor people simply because they are poor. The federal government administers the program through the U.S. Department of Agriculture's Food and Nutrition Service, but state and local welfare agencies are empowered to establish eligibility for the program, issue the stamps, and maintain quality control; the program has been operating nationwide only since 1974. The program allows a family of four to pay about 25 to 30 percent of its net income for a specified dollar value in food stamps. The food stamps are redeemed at a grocery store for a fraction of the true value of the food that food stamp recipients purchase, and, in this fashion, the needy have their diets supplemented. More than half the recipients of food stamps are children.

Because the food stamp program is so controversial (who, after all, has not heard of the proverbial, mink-draped "welfare queen" purchasing top-grade tenderloin at the neighborhood grocery store with food stamps and driving away in her Cadillac?), Congress has attempted to crack down on alleged fraud in the program and curtail its spiraling costs. The Food Stamp Act of 1977 and the Budget Reconciliation Act of 1981 represent serious efforts in this direction.

Nevertheless, it can be argued that food stamps are among the more successful welfare programs in the country. Nutritionists state that some 20 million to 30 million Americans ate inadequately during the 1960s, before food stamps were distributed nationally. In 1967, a team of medical experts sponsored by the Field Foundation surveyed Americans' diets and concluded that malnutrition existed in all regions of the country, in rural areas, suburbs, and inner cities, and among all racial groups. Ten years later, after the food stamp program was well established, the Field Foundation sent out a second medical team, and found that, while poverty was still with us, malnutrition was not, and ascribed this change to the food stamp program.[39]

Do State and Local Governments Care? The Role of "General Assistance"

In addition to administering much of the national welfare program, the states have also implemented their own *general assistance programs* for their citizens. General assistance is entirely a state and local responsibility, and about 1 million people in 40 states receive roughly $1.4 billion in general assistance from their state and local governments each year.[40] Usually the recipients are people who do not qualify for AFDC and SSI, but general assistance benefits vary hugely from state to state. Mississippi, Oklahoma, and West Virginia allocate less than $15 per month per recipient, while California, Hawaii, New York, and Wyoming each disburse monthly benefits of more than $160 per recipient. The average payment is less than $130.[41] Most states count on their local governments to provide general assistance, and fewer than half the states make a significant contribution to support local general assistance programs. Recall, in this regard, that federal welfare accounts for only four categories of people: the blind, the old, the disabled, and the impoverished. It is up to state and local governments—and primarily local governments—to take care of other kinds of needy people.[42]

Welfare as an Intergovernmental Policy

Food stamps, Aid to Families with Dependent Children, Supplemental Security Income, and Medicaid comprise the four cornerstones of national welfare policy. But, in reality, these programs are "national" in funding only—and, even in the financial arena, states and localities play a highly significant role. Administratively and politically, state and local governments loom larger than Washington. Table 15-3 lays out the complex program designs of AFDC, SSI, and food stamps. As it indicates, welfare "policy" in the United States is less than united; it is, rather, fragmented, localist, and intensely intergovernmental.

Table 15-4 indicates how each state has responded to intergovernmental welfare. Some, such as Alaska, Illinois, and Washington, are quite forthcoming in assuming their responsibilities and pay more than half the costs themselves. Other states, such as Arizona, New Hampshire, and Minnesota, shift significant welfare costs to their local governments; nevertheless, the federal contribution still amounts to less than half of welfare expenditures in these states. In 42 states, the feds pick up more than half the tab.

WELFARE POLICY IN THE STATES: VARIATIONS ON A VERY BROAD THEME

One should not conclude from Table 15-4 that, simply because a state or local government is paying a relatively high amount in welfare from its own coffers, it is somehow more sensitive to the needs of the down and out. States set their own standards of need, and the variations range widely. Texas, for example, has determined that $187 per month is "adequate" to maintain a family of four receiving AFDC, while Vermont (at the other end of the scale) has stipulated that $753 is closer to the mark.[43]

But benefit amounts are not the half of it. Consider some additional examples of how the states determine need:[44] In Washington State, no welfare recipient can possess a car that is worth more than $1,500; in Arkansas, the figure is $300; and in Georgia, the rule is that the car cannot be less than four years old. In New York, a family of two was eligible for welfare with a monthly income of $309 in 1977, but in Texas the same family with an income over $115 was not eligible. In many states, possessing life insurance renders people ineligible for welfare, and it is possible for a divorced woman with two children and a home or car worth more than is allowed by the state to be ineligible for welfare assistance even though she has no income whatever. Thirty-eight states have done away with placing a maximum value on a home as a condition for receiving welfare, so that a family does not have to dispossess itself to be eligible. But some states still retain such a rule. In Alabama, for example, a person with more than $2,500 equity in a house cannot qualify for aid. Hawaii, with a higher cost of living, stipulates that the tax-appraised value of a home cannot exceed $25,000 for its owners to be eligible for welfare. In Minnesota, a family may have no more than $500 cash value in life insurance to qualify for welfare, but in Delaware the cash value per person of life insurance can be as high as $1,500.

Table 15-3 Program Design of AFDC, SSI, and Food Stamps

	Aid to Families with Dependent Children (AFDC)	*Supplemental Security Income*	*Food Stamps*
Accounting period	State discretion; usually monthly, prospective.	Quarterly, prospective.	Monthly, prospective.
Filing unit	Single-parent families families with children; incapacitated parent (with spouse in all but three states) and children; unemployed father with spouse and children in 21 states, Washington, D.C., and Guam in 1983.	Eligible individual or eligible spouse.	Household.
Assets test	Home value at state discretion. Other assets at state discretion up to $2,000 per family member.	Value of home is excluded.	$1,750 per household, $3,000 for households with elderly persons.
Work requirement	Able-bodied recipients must register for work. Exempt are mothers of children under age 6 and certain other persons.	No provision.	Able-bodied persons must register for work, fulfill "job search" requirements, and accept suitable job offers. Exempt are persons caring for children under age 12 and certain others. Separate work rules for college students. Persons who voluntarily quit a job are ineligible for 60 days.
Financing	Open-ended federal appropriations for 50% to 78% of each state's payments. Federal funds pay 50% of cost of state-local administration.	Federal general revenues. State supplementary payments are state financed and administrative costs are federally funded if the state supplement is federally administered.	Open-ended federal appropriation. States and localities pay 50% of their administrative costs.
Administration	State administration or (18 states) local administration under state supervision.	Federal administration through Social Security Administration regional and field offices.	USDA administers through state and local welfare offices.
Benefit reduction rate for earnings	Disregarded: first $30 plus one-third of the rest plus work-related expenses.	Disregarded: first $65 plus one-half of the rest.	Benefits are reduced by 30% of net income after deductions.[1] A flat 20% of earned income is deductible.

Table 15-3 (Continued)

	Aid to Families with Dependent Children (AFDC)	*Supplemental Security Income*	*Food Stamps*
Maximum benefit level	State discretion. Range (July 1976) $60 in Mississippi per four-person family to $514 in Hawaii and $476 in New York.	Maximum federal benefits in July 1977, $177.80 per individual and $266.70 per eligible couple. States may supplement.	Varies by family size (July 1977): 1 person $52, 2 person $94, 3 person $134, 4 person $170.
Form of benefit	Cash grants.	Cash grants.	Monthly food stamps allotment.

[1] Each household receives a standard $60 monthly deduction. In addition, up to $75 monthly may be deducted for each excess shelter costs and/or dependent care expenses.

Source: Advisory Commission on Intergovernmental Relations, *The Federal Role in the Federal System: The Dynamics of Growth,* A-79 (Washington, D.C.: U.S. Government Printing Office, July, 1980), pp. 94–95.

Delaware and New Jersey both insist that a potential welfare recipient have too little cash to provide groceries and shelter for one month. For a child to qualify for public aid in 21 states, his or her father must be unemployed. There may be a trend toward a uniform welfare policy for the poor in America, but it is by no means the rule.

Within this welter of regulations, the states vary substantially on how well they respond to the needs of their impoverished. Table 15-5 displays various ways to determine the sensitivity of state governments to their welfare recipients. The first column of the table ranks the states by welfare expenditures (i.e., AFDC, Medicaid, and SSI) per $1,000 of personal income. By this measure, Rhode Island leads, and Arizona falls in last. Another measure is the percentage of a state's budget allocated to welfare (shown in the second column). By this standard, Massachusetts ranks first, and Arizona (again) is last.

Another question that might be asked as an indicator of state welfare policy is how many people in a state get welfare? The third column indicates this measure. Here, Mississippi leads, with more than 70 AFDC recipients per 1,000 population; Nevada and Wyoming are last, with only 14 per 1,000 people. The measurement is an important one, because some states will restrict entry to their AFDC rolls as a means of containing welfare costs.

How adequate are the benefits that welfare recipients garner from the states? Inflation has badly eroded the real benefits in even the most generous states, but, within that constraint, some states treat their recipients considerably better than others. Table 15-5's fourth and fifth columns indicate this measure. The measure of "adequacy" itself warrants some explanation. It refers to the ratio of AFDC grants (with and without food stamps) per family to median family income in each state. The AFDC grant to a New York family, for example, is the most generous of all by this standard, because it amounts to more than 20 percent of the median family income in New York; when food stamps are added, New York slips to third place. Mississippi ranks fiftieth by this measure; its AFDC grants amount to less than 6 percent of Mississippi's median family

Table 15-4 Percentage of Federal, State, and Local Expenditures for Welfare by Contributing Levels of Government, Ranked by Order of Reliance on State and Local Funding, 1983

		PERCENTAGE FINANCED BY[1]		
Rank	*State*	*Federal*	*State*	*Local*
	United States	57%	38%	5%
1	Arizona	26	36	38
2	Alaska	35	62	4
3	New Hampshire	42	27	30
4	Ohio	45	49	2
5	Iowa	46	45	9
6	Connecticut	47	48	5
6	Illinois	47	52	2
7	Michigan	48	48	4
7	Washington	48	51	0
8	Minnesota	49	31	20
9	California	51	47	1
9	Kansas	51	46	3
10	Colorado	52	49	0
10	Wyoming	52	46	3
11	Maryland	53	47	0
12	Florida	55	38	6
12	Georgia	55	38	6
12	Maine	55	44	2
12	Nevada	55	35	9
12	New Jersey	55	43	2
13	Massachusetts	56	42	2
14	Delaware	57	43	0
14	Pennsylvania	57	42	1
15	Hawaii	58	40	2
15	Wisconsin	58	42[a]	NA
16	Montana	59	27	14
16	Virginia	59	33	8
17	Indiana	61	27	13
17	Washington, D.C.	61	NA	39
18	Nebraska	62	28	9
18	New York	62	20	18
19	Kentucky	63	35	2
20	Missouri	64	35	1
20	West Virginia	64	35	1
21	Texas	65	33	3
22	Oregon	66	26	8
23	New Mexico	67	30	3
23	Oklahoma	67	33	0
24	North Dakota	68	24	9
24	Tennessee	68	27	5
25	Louisiana	69	30	2
25	Vermont	69	31[a]	NA
26	Georgia	70	29	1
26	Mississippi	70	27	3
26	Utah	70	29	1
27	North Carolina	71	15	15

Table 15-4 (Continued)

Rank	State	PERCENTAGE FINANCED BY[1] Federal	State	Local
28	Arkansas	72	28[a]	NA
28	Idaho	72	22	6
29	South Carolina	74	27	5
30	Alabama	76	22	1

[1] Percentages have been rounded.
[a] Includes local contribution.
N.A.–not available.

Source: Advisory Commission on Intergovernmental Relations, *Significant Features of Fiscal Federalism, 1984* (Washington, D.C.: U.S. Government Printing Office, 1985), p. 36.

income. But when food stamps are added to this calculus, Mississippi shoots up to thirty-seventh among the states, with its welfare grants to families amounting to more than 17 percent of median family income. Adding food stamps makes a considerable difference in the states' ranking on the "adequacy" dimension because food stamps have a substantial impact on the very poor states, which have modest budgets, low median incomes, and lots of indigent people. "Poverty is not simply a condition of poor persons in a society; to some degree it is a condition of poor governments as well."[45]

Beyond this fact, however, lie some intriguing variations of state policy. Some state governments, for example, seem more prone to redistribute their wealth to their poor regardless of how wealthy they, as states, may be. Why?

Research has indicated that neither voting turnout nor party competition associates with the way state welfare policies are made,[46] but that the patterns of income distribution among a state's population do correlate with how sensitive state welfare policies are to the needs of the indigent. In a careful analysis, David Jacobs matched four measures of economic inequality in the states (for example, the income gap between a state's richest and poorest people was one such measure) with seven welfare policies that were relatively free of federal influence (such as funding levels for social insurance programs). The most striking finding was that relatively parsimonious welfare policies in the states associated most closely with economic relationships between lower- and middle-income groups, as opposed simply to the presence of poor people or wealthy people or the income gap between the middle class and the affluent.[47] Thus, at least one determinant of state welfare policies may be the relations between economic classes in a state, particularly between those who have "made it" (if just barely so) and those directly underneath who want to make it.

THE ANOMALY CALLED WELFARE

The following items are drawn from press reports about welfare policies as they are implemented in America. As the randomness of the reports themselves indicates, welfare is a "system" replete with contradictions. Designed to help the poor, it has been accused of breaking up families and rendering the impoverished dependent upon a faceless welfare bureaucracy. To gain a flavor of what the welfare system in America means to the individual citizen and to the public, read on.

In 1982, an unemployed mother with two children saw her child support payments cut off by the Texas Department of Human Resources for the next four and one-half months because she had been given a $500 reward for helping the police find a murder suspect. The Omnibus Budget Reconciliation Act of 1981 prohibits anyone on welfare from receiving income from outside sources. The unemployed mother stated: "Now, I don't even think I'm gonna be able to get my kids anything for Christmas. I was only helping out the police, and I don't think I ought to be punished for that."[a]

A study of 148 poor single parents who were denied help under the Aid to Families with Dependent Children program in four states found that these people frequently were denied welfare benefits illegally, were eliminated from the welfare roles for the wrong reasons, and often were forced to wait unduly long periods of time for their benefits. Welfare case workers often made illegal decisions on welfare rules or treated welfare clients capriciously. One welfare case worker, for example, denied AFDC payments to four Cleveland mothers on the grounds that they were too young to qualify when, in fact, no age minimum applies. Another woman who had only one leg was told to get a doctor's letter saying she was disabled.[b]

In 1982, a woman in San Jose, California, purchased a fake identification card for five dollars; the cards were offered through an advertisement in *True Story* magazine. The woman used the card to get a welfare check on the same day that she applied for benefits. Eventually, she purchased ten phony identification cards, using ten different names, and eventually ended up on ten different welfare rolls in ten different welfare application offices. Almost a year later she had collected nearly $12,000 in welfare payments and food stamp benefits under her ten assumed names; she was apprehended by what had amounted to a fluke.[c]

In 1982, a 40-year-old woman committed suicide because she apparently misread a letter from the Social Security Office that her disability benefits under the Supplemental Security Income program would be cut off. The woman was a schizophrenic, and her case was only under review.[d]

Wanda Taylor, the celebrated Chicago "welfare queen," eventually was convicted in 1977 for receiving illegally welfare checks that amounted to more than $150,000 a year.[e]

A 67-year-old woman who had been crippled since infancy, was confined to a wheelchair, and sold newspapers on a street corner for a living was denied her Medicaid benefits on the grounds that she had bought a $1,000 funeral certificate, thus making her ineligible for benefits under the Supplemental Security Income program. To preserve her benefits under SSI, she had to give up Medicaid. Even though she transferred the funeral certificate to a friend, who promised to bury her according to her wishes, the benefits were still denied because she had not sold the certificate and used the money to purchase necessities as mandated under Medicaid.[f]

The editor of the newsletter of the Council on Welfare Fraud, an organization formed in 1978 of local administrators of cash assistance, food stamp and Medicaid programs, estimates that fraud, abuse, and error rates range from 10 percent to 30 percent of the total public welfare bill. The Council has cited examples of food stamps used to purchase cars, stereos, shotguns, marijuana, liquor, prostitutes, and even a funeral.[g]

[a] *Source:* Associated Press, "Welfare Mom Loses Kids' Aid Due to Reward," *The Arizona Republic* (November 6, 1982).

[b] *Source:* Iver Peterson, "Inequity Reported in Welfare Survey," *The New York Times* (September 21, 1981).

[c] *Source:* Jeff Kaye, " 'So Easy': She Got Welfare with Ten Fake IDs Obtained Through Magazine Ad," *Philadelphia Inquirer* (August 29, 1982).

[d] *Source:* Mary Jane Fine, "In Death, She Raises Questions About Cuts in Disability Benefits," *Philadelphia Inquirer* (June 13, 1982).

[e] *Source:* Eric Pianin, "Welfare Fraud Crackdown Here Getting Results," *Washington Post* (December 3, 1981).

[f] *Source:* James Kilpatrick, "The Rules: Burial Certificate Costs Disabled Virginia Woman Her Medicaid Coverage," *The Arizona Republic* (August 4, 1982).

[g] *Source:* Helen Leavitt, "Council Tackling Welfare Abuse," *Los Angeles Times* (December 8, 1981).

Table 15-5 State Scores and Ranks for Five Indicators of State Welfare Efforts, 1978 (ranked by state expenditure per $1,000 personal income)

	STATE WELFARE EXPENDITURE PER $1,000 PERSONAL INCOME		*WELFARE EXPENDITURE AS A PERCENTAGE OF TOTAL STATE GENERAL EXPENDITURE*		*NUMBER OF AFDC RECIPIENTS PER 1,000 POPULATION*		*ADEQUACY OF AFDC GRANTS*		*ADEQUACY OF AFDC GRANTS WITH FOOD STAMPS*	
	Score	*Rank*	*Score*	*Rank*	*Score*	*Rank*	*Score*	*Rank*	*Score*	*Rank*
Rhode Island	$33.79	1	26.2%	4	52.7	12	18.1%	7	21.9	8
Massachusetts	33.35	2	29.1	1	63.0	5	18.4	5	22.2	6
California	31.45	3	29.0	2	61.6	7	17.2	11	20.3	21
Pennsylvania	30.37	4	28.7	3	52.7	11	17.8	8	22.0	7
New York	29.78	5	24.4	7	63.4	4	22.1	1	25.2	3
Maine	29.71	6	21.6	9	54.7	9	15.8	19	22.4	5
Hawaii	28.53	7	15.6	25	65.9	3	20.7	2	25.7	1
Vermont	27.21	8	17.2	18	40.2	24	20.4	3	25.3	2
Michigan	26.71	9	24.9	5	67.5	2	19.3	4	22.6	4
Wisconsin	26.42	10	21.1	10	40.4	23	18.4	6	21.6	10
Minnesota	22.68	11	17.1	19	32.0	31	16.8	12	20.3	20
Mississippi	21.75	12	15.4	26	70.2	1	5.8	50	17.3	37
Illinois	21.69	13	24.8	6	60.9	8	14.9	21	19.8	25
Oregon	21.44	14	19.0	13	48.6	16	15.3	20	18.7	27
Arkansas	20.92	15	17.4	17	40.1	25	11.0	36	20.9	14
Kentucky	19.94	16	15.4	27	47.1	17	11.1	35	18.6	31
Oklahoma	19.60	17	19.0	12	30.2	35	13.6	27	18.9	26
New Jersey	19.52	18	21.7	8	62.5	6	15.9	18	20.2	23
Utah	18.40	19	13.4	35	28.0	38	16.2	15	20.3	22
Washington	18.15	20	16.3	21	36.5	28	17.8	9	21.5	11
Louisiana	17.91	21	13.4	33	13.4	13	8.4	44	16.9	40
Connecticut	17.85	22	20.1	11	43.8	20	17.7	10	21.6	9
Maryland	17.14	23	15.9	22	49.6	14	10.1	41	15.1	48
Georgia	16.60	24	15.6	24	41.1	22	6.6	47	14.7	49
Alaska	16.53	25	6.3	49	31.6	33	14.4	23	20.2	24
Delaware	16.49	26	12.5	38	52.9	10	21.1	31	16.9	41

Table 15-5 (Continued)

	STATE WELFARE EXPENDITURE PER $1,000 PERSONAL INCOME		*WELFARE EXPENDITURE AS A PERCENTAGE OF TOTAL STATE GENERAL EXPENDITURE*		*NUMBER OF AFDC RECIPIENTS PER 1,000 POPULATION*		*ADEQUACY OF AFDC GRANTS*		*ADEQUACY OF AFDC GRANTS WITH FOOD STAMPS*	
	Score	*Rank*	*Score*	*Rank*	*Score*	*Rank*	*Score*	*Rank*	*Score*	*Rank*
South Dakota	16.48	27	14.0	32	29.8	36	14.8	22	20.1	17
West Virginia	16.48	28	11.7	41	36.0	29	12.1	30	20.8	15
Tennessee	16.41	29	16.4	20	36.8	27	7.6	45	16.5	43
Iowa	16.06	30	15.0	29	31.7	32	16.8	13	21.0	13
Kansas	15.94	31	18.1	15	27.0	40	14.3	24	18.6	30
Alabama	15.89	32	12.8	36	46.8	18	7.3	46	16.6	42
Ohio	15.75	33	18.5	14	30.2	35	12.9	28	18.5	32
Colorado	15.15	34	15.7	23	28.8	37	12.2	29	17.1	38
South Carolina	15.10	35	12.6	37	49.1	15	5.8	49	15.2	47
Montana	14.53	36	10.3	43	22.6	44	14.0	25	20.6	16
North Carolina	14.34	37	12.0	40	34.3	30	10.4	39	18.3	33
Idaho	13.81	38	11.4	42	22.1	45	16.3	14	20.5	18
New Mexico	13.80	39	8.7	47	41.7	21	10.3	40	17.7	35
North Dakota	13.68	40	10.0	44	20.4	48	16.2	16	21.3	12
New Hampshire	13.57	41	15.1	28	24.4	42	13.9	26	18.7	28
Virginia	13.34	42	13.4	34	31.1	34	11.9	34	17.4	36
Nebraska	13.31	43	14.3	31	22.6	43	16.0	17	20.4	19
Texas	11.58	44	14.4	30	22.1	46	6.3	48	14.2	50
Indiana	10.39	45	12.4	39	27.4	39	11.0	37	16.0	45
Missouri	8.86	46	17.9	16	39.9	26	12.0	32	18.6	29
Nevada	8.67	47	8.9	46	14.0	50	10.5	38	16.2	44
Wyoming	7.93	48	6.4	48	14.0	49	11.9	33	17.1	39
Florida	7.41	49	9.0	45	26.7	41	9.9	42	18.3	34
Arizona	6.28	50	5.7	50	21.1	47	8.6	43	15.5	46

Source: U.S. Bureau of the Census, *Statistical Abstract of the United States* (Washington, D.C.: Government Printing Office, 1979), pp. 14, 444; (1980), pp. 355, 356, 446, 455.

THE FADING "EXPLOSION" IN WELFARE

Certainly the most obvious feature of the welfare system is its explosively growing cost. Figure 15-1 indicates this growth in welfare recipients and welfare dollars.

Another indicator of the rapid rise in welfare expenditures is the fact that, in 1970, welfare expenditures at all levels of government accounted for less than 15 percent of the gross national product (state and local expenditures for welfare accounted for less than 7 percent of the GNP) and 48 percent of all government outlays (but 64 percent of state and local outlays). By 1982, welfare expenditures at all levels of government surpassed 19 percent of the GNP (still about 7 percent for the state and local share) and constituted nearly 56 percent of total government outlays (and 62 percent of state and local outlays).[48]

These increases in expenditures for social insurance and public assistance programs become all the more puzzling when we realize that the number of recipients of major welfare programs has not increased by comparable rates. Between 1970 and 1983, public assistance programs grew by relatively nominal increments in terms of recipients, while social insurance programs, whose recipients are often elderly, expanded their rolls rather substantially, although even here, the rate of increase among recipients was considerably less than the growth in expenditures. In addition, although the dollars spent on public assistance increased at somewhat faster rates than did the expenditures channeled to social insurance between 1970 and 1983, the expansion patterns for the recipients of the two programs was precisely the opposite: the social insurance rolls grew markedly faster than did the public assistance rolls. In fact, beginning in 1975, the rolls of AFDC, the nation's central welfare program, actually declined by about a half million recipients.[49]

The welfare "explosion" so often viewed with alarm was largely a phenomenon of the 1960s—not the 1970s. This is not to say that welfare expenditures and recipients did not continue to grow during the 1970s. They did. But they grew at a considerably slower rate than in the 1960s. In the 1960s, virtually every state witnessed ballooning numbers of people seeking and obtaining welfare (during the 1960s, the number of welfare recipients burgeoned by a factor of three), dramatically expanding federal subsidies for state welfare budgets, and an increasingly important role for the large urban states in the welfare system. In the 1970s, most of these patterns altered. With the exception of Medicaid, the rate of state expenditures for welfare in the 1970s—unlike the 1960s—fell below the rate of total state spending.[50]

WHY THE GROWTH?

Although the explosive growth in welfare rolls and expenditures of the 1960s slackened in the 1970s and 1980s, increases in costs and in the case loads of some programs nonetheless have continued. Why? There are several theories, and we review the principal ones here.

Moving North?

One rationale for the rise in welfare rolls argues that poor blacks have moved from the states in the Deep South that grant low welfare payments to more generous states in the North. Facts refute this interpretation. Black migration from the South into the northern industrial states peaked during the 1950s, yet

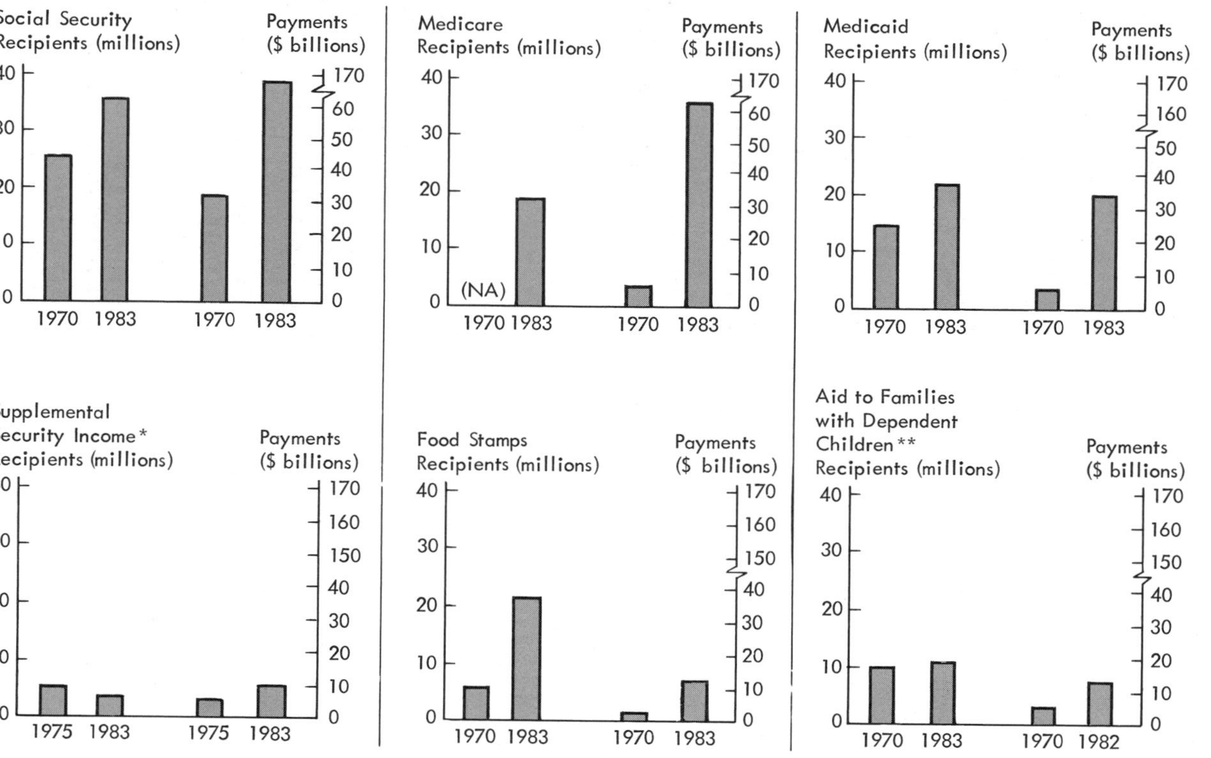

*Supplemental Security Income data begin with 1975, when the program went into effect.

**Fiscal data on Aid to Families with Dependent Children are not available for 1983, and the 1982 figure is provided.

Figure 15-1. Growth in major public assistance and social insurance programs, payments and recipients, 1970–1983.* (*Source:* Bureau of the Census, *Statistical Abstract of the United States, 1985.* Washington, D.C.: U.S. Government Printing Office, 1984, p. xxii.)

AFDC case loads increased only moderately during this period. In the 1960s, when black migration rates to the North actually declined, AFDC case loads were increasing by a factor of three to seven times in the large urban states.[51]

The 1970s witnessed parallel patterns. Between 1975 and 1980, AFDC case loads went up in 25 states, but in only 13 of these states was there a net in-migration of blacks, and in the remaining dozen states, blacks, as a percentage of the population, did not fluctuate. In fact, in New York, which experienced a dramatic decline in its AFDC case loads during this period, there was an upswing of black in-migration of almost 3 percent![52] "The data clearly indicate that migration for purposes of obtaining higher welfare payments is not a factor in determining welfare case loads."[53]

Unemployment Equals Welfare?

A second explanation for the increase in welfare recipients is that as unemployment increases, welfare rolls go up. This is, of course, true up to a point. But unemployment does not seem to explain adequately the increase in AFDC case loads. For example, among the 21 states that have adopted an "unemployed parent" component in their AFDC policies (a national program optional for the states), the recipients under this program account for only 7 percent of all AFDC recipients. Consequently, unemployment is "hardly a significant factor in explaining sharp rises in welfare spending or case loads, even in participating states."[54]

Black Power?

A third, and one of the more romantic explanations for the rise in welfare case loads, contends that state and local governments did become more generous to the poor during the 1960s, but purely in response to governmental confrontations with blacks and other minorities in the form of race riots and greater voting participation by minorities. Nervous state and local officials, the argument continues, "bought off" the poor by expanding their welfare rolls as a means of preventing a social revolution.[55]

The facts do not support this thesis, either. The obvious test of the "keep-the-lid-on-the-revolution" hypothesis is whether or not a rise in welfare rolls in particular cities coincides with large urban riots in those same localities. Welfare case loads did increase in most of the large urban areas that experienced racial disturbances during the 1960s, but case loads increased at a *declining rate,* which would seem to argue against the black power theory. Moreover, when real spending power is measured, the relative economic condition of the poor actually declined during the 1960s, because welfare payments did not keep up with the rise in the cost of living.[56]

The "Moynihan Thesis"?

A fourth, and increasingly debated, explanation for the increase in welfare rolls has been expounded by Daniel Patrick Moynihan.[57] Moynihan argued, first, that discrimination against blacks throughout society amounted to a major reason for the disproportionate dependency of blacks on welfare (not especially a surprising thesis in itself). But then Moynihan extended this view, arguing that the black family was essentially matriarchal (i.e., mother dominated) and that black males did not play a large role in keeping the family together; indeed, black males frequently did not remain with the family. Hence, matriarchal black families were increasingly dependent upon welfare, and this "cultural" factor explained the increasing numbers of blacks on the welfare rolls even in times of prosperity.

Data collected during the 1960s appeared to deny the Moynihan thesis. Between 1959 and 1966 neither the desertion by males of either black or white families nor illegitimacy rates were factors in the increasing number of families receiving AFDC assistance.[58] Similarly, surveys conducted in 1961 and 1967 found, "While the absolute number of deserted families increased during this period, they actually represented a slightly smaller percentage of the national regular AFDC case load in 1967 than in 1961."[59] Thus, while more families headed by women (both black and white) were receiving AFDC, their proportionate representation on the welfare rolls seemed to be declining.

Such data, plus accusations leveled against Moynihan that his argument was implicitly racist, sexist, or both, deflected discussion throughout the 1970s of the notion that unstable families, especially among poor blacks, was a root cause of poverty and a growing dependency on welfare. But more recent analyses indicate that broken families and indigence not only correlate, but that the combination is a particularly vicious one among blacks; the late Martin Luther King, Jr., called this combination a "social catastrophe."[60]

Analyses conducted by the National Advisory Council on Economic Opportunity and the Department of Health and Human Services indicate that a black household headed by a woman earns a median income of about one-third of that of a two-parent black family. (Comparable proportions hold for Hispanic and white families, since, in a majority of two-parent households, regardless of race, both adults work.) Yet, when the median incomes of two-parent white families and two-parent black families are compared, the average difference in incomes is only 10 percent (with blacks earning the lesser amount). Figure 15-2 indicates how family situation relates to the incomes of both races.

These patterns conform to the fact that the segment of the indigent population that has made the greatest strides out of the swamp of poverty since 1970 is the two-parent family, whether black, white, or Hispanic. In fact, two-parent black families have made more progress than have two-parent white families; in 1967, 31 percent of two-parent black families were poor, but by 1984, 19 percent were.[61] On the other hand, the group that continues to be sucked into that swamp is the family headed by a woman. Between 1969 and 1978, the number of poor households of all races headed by women increased by two-thirds—from 1.8 million families to 2.7 million families. (By contrast, the number of poor households headed by men declined during the same period.)[62] Most of these indigent families headed by women were and are black; almost three quarters of all poor black households are, in fact, maintained by women, compared to slightly more than half of all indigent families of all races that are headed by women.[63] Since black families are nearly four times more likely to be headed by a woman than are white families, it follows that the nation's welfare rolls are largely black and female.

It is the prevalence of households headed by women among blacks that appears to be most responsible for maintaining the economic gulf between the races. (Blacks as individuals typically earn two-thirds of what whites earn in a given year.) According to one investigator, "The single most important reason

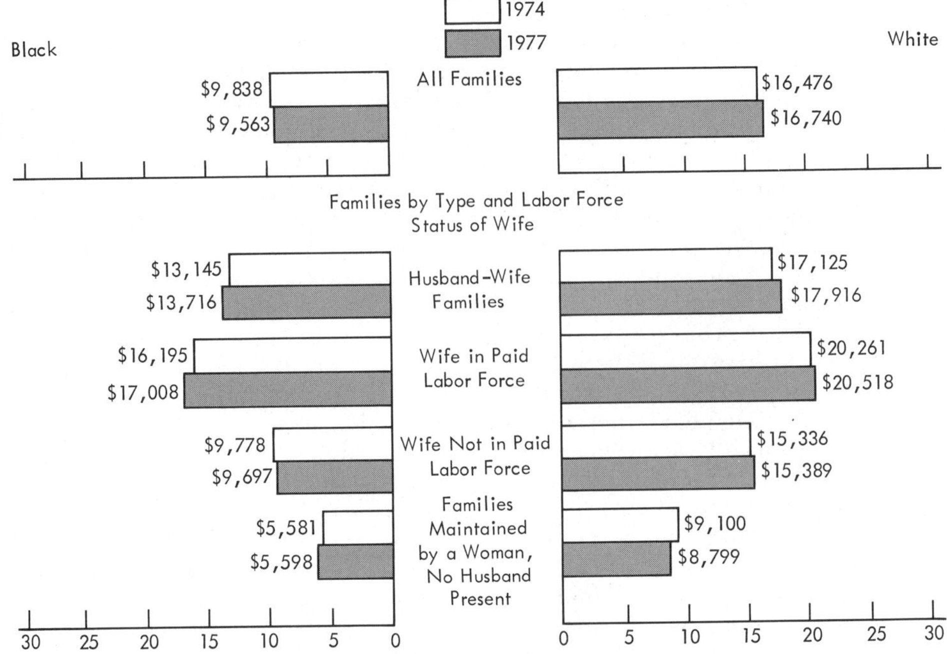

Figure 15-2. Median income of families by selected characteristics, 1974 (revised) and 1977 (adjusted in 1977 dollars). (*Source:* U.S. Department of Commerce, Bureau of the Census, "Economic Characteristics," *The Social and Economic Status of the Black Population in the United States: A Historical View, 1790–1978.* Washington, D.C.: U.S. Government Printing Office, June, 1979, p. 184.)

for the deterioration in the black-white income ratio between 1970 and 1978 is the substantially faster growth of female-headed families for blacks than whites. . . . In fact, if the pattern of family composition that existed in 1970 were present in 1978, the black-white income gap would have narrowed by six percentage points," going on to note that about a third of the income gap between blacks and whites is attributable to the considerably larger proportion of black families supported by women.[64]

The point is this: Moynihan likely was wrong in singling out the black family as his central explanation of the problems of the impoverished. Instead, he should have singled out the family headed by a single woman as his core definition of poverty, because this is the essence of the issue. Poverty is less a matter of race and more a matter of family.

The Impact of Washington?

Although the growth in families headed by women appears to be an increasingly significant factor in the *growth of poverty,* it seems that the single most important reason underlying the *growth of welfare* has been the changing policies of the federal government. As Tables 15-4 and 15-5 imply, Washington has simply made more numerous, more liberal, and more lucrative welfare programs available to the states. In 1965 Congress adopted a series of amendments to the Social Security Act, notably, Medicaid, which rapidly rose to become the largest single item in state public assistance budgets. The degree to which the federal government matched categorical assistance programs was increased. These federal incentives to the states to increase their welfare rolls succeeded beyond the expectations of a number of policymakers. The rise in case loads clearly correlates with these innovations in federal welfare policy. As Albritton concludes,

> The pattern of welfare spending for medical care is clearly consistent with an explanation of the general rise in state welfare spending as a response to innovations in legislation at the federal level. . . . Interpreted in this light, the course of welfare activity does not warrant characterization as an explosion; rather it simply records the abrupt change in the welfare policy system due to federal legislation and returns it to normal growth patterns or even lesser levels of growth, albeit at a notably higher level.[65]

HAS WELFARE WORKED?

Assessing welfare's effectiveness is relatively simple: Are there more or are there fewer poor in America after the inauguration of welfare policies?

Measured by historical time, the indicators are encouraging. In 1960, just prior to Lyndon Baines Johnson's "War on Poverty," about one-third of all families earned less than $10,000; only 20 percent had incomes of more than $25,000 a year. By 1983, and holding dollars constant for inflation, not quite 23 percent of all families took in less than $10,000, and more than 41 percent earned $25,000 or more.[66] Because inflation is factored into these figures, it appears that real strides have been made in raising the real spending power of most Americans during the past three decades. Figure 15-3 illustrates these gains since 1960 by race. Although black families obviously lag whites, an economic betterment and a redistribution of incomes have occurred even among these segments of the population. Other figures reveal similar gains against poverty. In 1960, 22 percent of the population had cash incomes that placed them under the official poverty line; by 1983, even at the height of a major economic recession, that ratio had been reduced to 15 percent.

Such data, of course, reflect some very broad economic trends that may or may not be influenced by welfare policies. Although these policies have alleviated poverty, their impact has been scattered. This becomes especially evident when we realize that two-fifths of the poor do not receive Medicaid, food stamps, subsidized school lunches, or subsidized housing. Conversely, a majority of the households that do receive these noncash benefits are above the poverty line![67]

Obviously, not all these welfare recipients could be "officially poor." A major reason why many of the nation's poor do not receive public assistance is because they work for a living. They are ineligible for welfare assistance simply because they hold jobs, despite the fact that these jobs pay very little. The average welfare payment to families on AFDC is less than 60 percent of the poverty level, and the average food stamp benefits account for only another 9 percent, bringing the national average of welfare assistance to less than 70 percent of the poverty level. In 30 states, however, AFDC families receive even less than the national average monthly payment.[68] Overall, then, welfare policy in America has not alleviated poverty to the degree it might have.

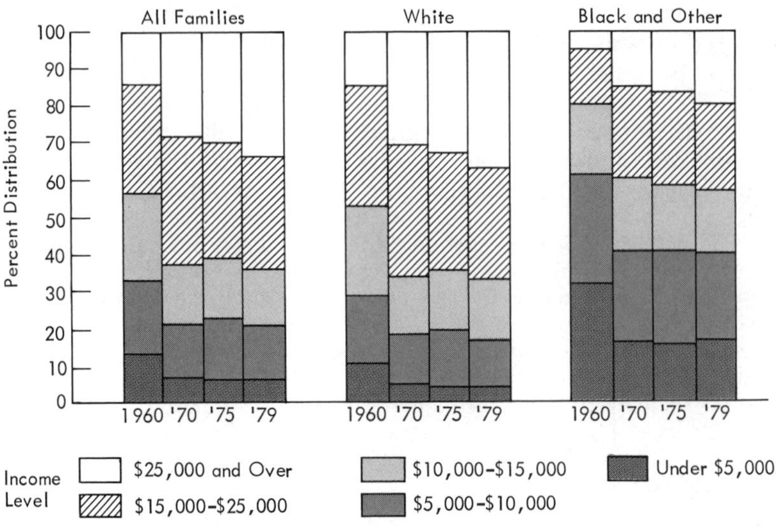

Figure 15-3. Money income of families in constant (1979) dollars—percent distribution by income level and by race: 1960 to 1979. (*Source:* U.S. Department of Commerce, Bureau of the Census, *Statistical Abstract of the United States, 1981.* Washington, D.C.: U.S. Government Printing Office, 1981, p. 420.)

REAGANOMICS AND THE POOR: DECLARING A TRUCE ON WARS ON POVERTY

Yet, the costs of welfare programs have soared, and this anomaly was not lost on the American voters when they elected Ronald Reagan, a Republican conservative, as president in 1980. A year following his election, Reagan had initiated significant reductions in the incomes of the poor. His Omnibus Budget Reconciliation Act of 1981 reduced the incomes of almost half of America's indigent.[69] Sixty percent of the cuts that President Reagan and Congress made in entitlement programs in 1981 came from welfare programs designed for the poor.[70] The president cut the number of food stamp recipients by 300,000 people, the number of AFDC recipients by 600,000, and the number of Medicaid beneficiaries by 400,000.[71] Conservative Republican Senator Robert Dole, no enemy of the president, after reviewing the impact of these federal budgetary cuts on the poor, stated, "I do believe, and I think with some accuracy, there is this perception that somehow the [Reagan] programs are impacting most severely on low-income Americans."[72]

The irony in all this, especially in light of the traditional GOP's declared faith in the "work ethic," is that those indigents who are hurt most by Reaganomics are not the notorious "welfare queens" so frequently chastised by Republicans, but the working poor who, more often than not, are not eligible for such welfare programs as food stamps or Aid to Families with Dependent Children simply because they work. Separate studies conducted out of Princeton University and the University of Chicago on the impact of Reaganomics both found that poor people who worked suffered most under Reagan's budgetary cuts, but that poor people who did not have jobs had suffered "little impact" from the changes in federal benefit programs.[73] This conclusion may not hold true, however, in the basic area of nutrition. Surveys conducted since 1983 by the Food Research and Action Center have found that the demands on "emergency food providers," such as urban soup kitchens, have increased by as much as 22 percent a year across the nation. The Center blames these increases on cuts in the food stamp program.[74]

Reagan's cutbacks in federal poverty programs symbolized not only a desire to cut spiraling federal deficits, but perhaps a basic attitudinal change among Americans about the efficacy of federally sponsored "Wars on Poverty" as they had been initiated by President Lyndon B. Johnson during the 1960s. Whether, however, Reaganomics represented a social improvement is another matter.

Welfare is designed to alleviate poverty and, as such, it obviously applies to the underclass. Other major public policies that affect the underclass more directly are various policies against crime. This is not to argue that these policies were designed specifically for the poor or that only the poor are criminals. But statistics clearly indicate it is the poor who are found most frequently in prisons for robbery and acts of violence—in other words, "street crime." We consider this area next.

NOTES

[1]Charles Reich, *The Greening of America* (New York: Random House, 1970).

[2]"The American Underclass," *Time* (August 29, 1977), pp. 14-27.

[3]Ken Auletta, "The Underclass—III," *The New Yorker* (November 30, 1981), p. 132.

[4]Ken Auletta, "The Underclass—II," *The New Yorker* (November 23, 1981), p. 156; and Alfred L. Malabre, Jr., "'Thanks to Off-the-Books Income, Consumers Save More than Meets the Eye,' Economists Say," *The Wall Street Journal* (June 11, 1982).

[5]Auletta, "The Underclass—II," p. 156.

[6]Both studies are cited in *ibid.,* p. 157.

[7]Auletta, "The Underclass—III," p. 134.

[8]Monsignor Geno Baroni, quoted in "The American Underclass," p. 15.

[9]Bureau of the Census, *Statistical Abstract of the United States, 1985* (Washington, D.C.: U.S. Government Printing Office, 1984), Table 758, p. 454; and Table 737, p. 444.

[10]Bureau of the Census, *Current Population Reports,* Series P-60, No. 131, *Characteristics of Households and Persons Receiving Selected Noncash Benefits: 1980* (Washington, D.C.: U.S. Government Printing Office, 1982). See also Spencer Rich, "Fewer Are 'Poor' If Benefits Counted," *Washington Post* (April 15, 1982); and John Herbers, "Measuring Poverty: Perplexing Tasks Ensures a Debate," *The New York Times* (April 15, 1982).

[11]Rich, "Fewer Are 'Poor' If Benefits Counted."

[12]*Ibid.* In 1983, 15.2 percent of the population was considered to be below the poverty line. Under the broadest interpretation of noncash benefits, this figure would be reduced to 10.2 percent of the population. Under the narrowest interpretation, it would be reduced to 14 percent. Bureau of the Census, *Statistical Abstract of the United States,* 1985, Table 767, p. 458.

[13]Figures are for 1983. These were the highest poverty rates since the early 1960s.

[14]Bureau of the Census, *Statistical Abstract of the United States, 1985,* Table 758, p. 454.

[15]Auletta, "The Underclass—III," p. 132. Figures are for 1980.

[16]Congressional Research Office and Congressional Budget Office, *Children in Poverty* (Washington, D.C.: U.S. Government Printing Office, 1985), as cited in Robert Pear, "Study Finds Poverty Among Children Is Increasing," *The New York Times* (May 23, 1985).

[17]Gilbert A. Lewthwaite, "20 Years After Controversial Report, Moynihan Says All Families Face Crisis," *Baltimore Sun* (April 10, 1985).

[18]Thomas Gladwin, *Poverty, U.S.A.* (Boston: Little, Brown, 1967), pp. 83-84.

[19]Robert Albritton, "Welfare Policy," in Herbert Jacob and Kenneth N. Vines, eds., *Politics in the American States: A Comparative Analysis,* 3rd ed. (Boston: Little, Brown, 1976), pp. 349-350.

[20]Donald C. Bacon, "Another Go at the Welfare Mess: Will It Work?" *U.S. News & World Report* (August 8, 1977), p. 47.

[21]Richard M. Nixon, State of the Union Address, 1971, quoted in Albritton, "Welfare Policy," p. 350.

[22]As quoted in Robert B. Albritton, "Subsidies: Welfare and Transportation," in Virginia Gray, Herbert Jacob, and Kenneth N. Vines, eds., *Politics in the American States: A Comparative Analysis,* 4th ed. (Boston: Little, Brown, 1983), p. 384.

[23]United Press International, "Hondo Wants 'Loafers'," *The Arizona Republic* (July 3, 1977).

[24]Bureau of the Census, *Characteristics of the Population Below the Poverty Level: 1979,* (Washington, D.C.: U.S. Government Printing Office, 1981), p. 3. Figures are for 1979.

[25]Social Security Administration, *Recipient Characteristics Study, 1977* (Washington, D.C.: Office of Research and Statistics, 1980).

[26]Bureau of the Census, *Statistical Abstract of the United States, 1980* (Washington, D.C.: U.S. Government Printing Office, 1980), Table 95, p. 66.

[27]Albritton, "Subsidies," p. 400.

[28]Fawn Vrazo, "Study Disputes Stereotype of Black Teen Mothers," *Philadelphia Inquirer* (March 31, 1986). Furstenberg's research, according to the article, was to be published as a book, *Adolescent Mothers in Later Life.*

[29]Bureau of the Census, as cited in United Press International, "Federal Aid Went to 1 in 3 Families," *The Arizona Republic* (March 14, 1981). The Census Bureau's study was the first of its kind, and did not cover many additional programs, such as Aid to Families with Dependent Children, Social Security, unemployment insurance, and Supplemental Security Income. Nevertheless, virtually every household that received benefits through one or more of the programs studied in 1980 would also be receiving benefits from one or more of the more broadly gauged welfare programs as well. Of the 79.1 million households in 1980, 27.2 million received some sort of federal assistance.

[30]U.S. Bureau of the Census Regional Office, "Mountain/Plains Census Data Highlights" (July/August 1982). In 1982, the federal government shelled out nearly $367 billion and the state and local governments another $226 billion in welfare benefits. See Bureau of the Census, *Statistical Abstract of the United States: 1985,* Table 592, p. 356. This was the total value of federal outlays for Social Security, federal employee benefits, veterans' benefits, public assistance, unemployment insurance, railroad retirement, food stamps, child nutrition, and health care and housing, as well as some minor programs.

[31]Census Bureau survey, as cited in Spencer Rich, "68% of Income for Poor Comes from Government," *Washington Post* (June 7, 1985).

[32]Spencer Rich, "Cost of Health Care Rose to $287 Billion in 1981," *Washington Post* (July 27, 1981).

[33]Gary J. Clarke, "State Health and Mental Health Programs," *The Book of the States, 1976-77* (Lexington, Ky.: Council of State Governments, 1976), pp. 367-378.

[34]Jeffrey L. Lake and James T. Dimas, "State Health Agency Programs," *The Book of the States, 1984-85* (Lexington, Ky.: Council of State Governments, 1984), pp. 403-406. Figures are for 1982.

[35]"Health and Human Services," in *ibid.,* p. 392. Figures are for 1982.

[36]*Ibid.,* p. 391. Figures are for 1982.

[37]*Ibid.,* p. 390. Figures are for 1982.

[38]Henrietta J. Duvall, Karen W. Goudreau, and Robert E. Marsh, "Aid to Families with Dependent Children: Characteristics of Recipients in 1979," *Social Security Bulletin,* 45 (April, 1982), pp. 3-9, 19.

[39]Jean Mayer, "The Food Stamp Dilemma," *Washington Post* (February 18, 1982).

[40]"Health and Human Services," *The Book of the States, 1984-85,* p. 391. Figures are for 1982.

[41]As derived from Table 1, "Public Welfare," *The Book of the States, 1982-83* (Lexington, Ky.: Council of State Governments, 1982), p. 50.

[42]Committee for Economic Development, *Welfare Reform and Its Financing* (New York: Committee for Economic Development, 1976), p. 13.

[43]Albritton, "Subsidies," p. 389. Figures are for 1980.

[44]The following examples are drawn from Myra McPherson, "The Crazy Quilt Called Welfare," syndicated column of July 21, 1977, *The Arizona Republic,* as reprinted from the *Washington Post.*

[45]Albritton, "Welfare Policy," p. 368.

[46]See, for example, Richard E. Dawson and James A. Robinson, "Interparty Competition, Economic Variables and Welfare Policies in the American States," *Journal of Politics* (May,

1963), pp. 265-289; Richard L. Hofferbert, "The Relation Between Public Policy and Some Structural and Environmental Variables in the American States," *American Political Science Review,* 60 (March, 1966), pp. 73-82; and Thomas R. Dye, "Income Inequality and American State Politics," *American Political Science Review,* 63 (March, 1969), pp. 157-162.

[47]David Jacobs, "Dimensions of Inequality and Public Policy in the States," *Journal of Politics,* 42 (May, 1980), pp. 291-306.

[48]Bureau of the Census, *Statistical Abstract of United States: 1985,* Table 590, p. 355. It should be noted that "welfare expenditures" are comprised of more programs than are listed in Table 15-5. In addition to social insurance and public assistance programs, education, veterans' programs, housing, and other welfare programs are also included in this category.

[49]*Ibid.,* p. xxii. Between 1975 and 1983, AFDC recipients declined from 11.4 million to 10.9 million.

[50]Albritton, "Subsidies," p. 397.

[51]Albritton, "Welfare Policy," pp. 378-379.

[52]Bureau of the Census, *Statistical Abstract of the United States, 1981,* Table 25, p. 24.

[53]Albritton, "Subsidies," p. 399.

[54]Albritton, "Welfare Policy," p. 381.

[55]Frances Fox Piven and Richard Cloward, *Regulating the Poor: The Functions of Public Welfare* (New York: Random House, 1971).

[56]Albritton, "Welfare Policy," pp. 381-383.

[57]See, for example, Daniel Moynihan, *The Negro Family: The Case for National Action* (Washington, D.C.: U.S. Department of Labor, 1965).

[58]Irene Lurie, *An Economic Evaluation of Aid to Families with Dependent Children* (Washington, D.C.: The Brookings Institution, 1968).

[59]Gilbert Steiner, *Social Insecurity: The Politics of Welfare* (Chicago: Rand McNally, 1966), p. 30.

[60]As quoted in Auletta, "The Underclass—III," p. 130.

[61]U.S. Congress Joint Economic Committee study as cited in Jane Seaberry, "Poverty Rises in Families with Children," *Washington Post* (December 26, 1985).

[62]National Advisory Council on Economic Opportunity, *Women and Children: Alone and in Poverty* (Washington, D.C.: U.S. Government Printing Office, 1982).

[63]Auletta, "The Underclass—III," p. 132. Figures are for 1980.

[64]Steven Sandell, as quoted in Auletta, "The Underclass—III," p. 128.

[65]Albritton, "Welfare Policy," p. 385.

[66]Bureau of the Census, *Statistical Abstract of the United States, 1985,* Table 734, p. 442; and *1981,* Table 725, p. 442.

[67]Figures are for 1982. In that year, 14.3 million households received the noncash benefits listed in the text, of which 7.9 million (or 55 percent) were above the poverty line. Most of these 7.9 million households were "near poor." Also, most (8 million) received only one of the four benefits. See Spencer Rich, "Two-Fifths of U.S. Poor Get No In-Kind Benefits, Census Bureau Reports," *Washington Post* (July 7, 1982). See also Bureau of the Census, *Statistical Abstract of the United States: 1985,* Table 595, p. 359.

[68]Committee for Economic Development, *Welfare Reform,* p. 12.

[69]Ann Crittenden, "Economic Scene: Rich and Poor in U.S. Today," *The New York Times* (December 16, 1981).

[70]Tom Morganthau et al., "Reagan's Polarized America," *Newsweek* (April 5, 1982), p. 17.

[71]Robert Pear, "Reagan's Social Impact," *The New York Times* (August 25, 1982).

[72]As quoted in Herbert Rowen, "A Widening Gap Between Rich and Poor," *Washington Post* (March 11, 1982).

[73]Richard P. Nathan et al., *Initial Effects of Fiscal Year 1982 Reductions in Federal Spending,* and Thomas C. W. Joe, Center for the Study of Social Policy, University of Chicago, as cited in Robert Pear, "Incentive for Not Working Is Found in Study of Budget," *The New York Times* (February 25, 1982). The Princeton study by Nathan analyzed the impact of Reagan administration policies in 14 representative states; the Chicago study by Joe covered 10 major states.

[74]Food Research and Action Center, *Bitter Harvest I* and *II,* as cited in Mark Matthews, "Hunger Rising Despite Drop in Poverty Rate, Group Says," *Baltimore Sun* (December 17, 1985). In 1984-85, the Center surveyed 1,000 emergency food providers, of whom 370 responded in 47 states and Washington, D.C., and found that demand for food had increased by 17 percent; in 1983-84, the increase was 22 percent.

16

CRIME IN THE STREETS

CRIME AND THE UNDERCLASS

Like public welfare, policies concerning street crime do not apply only to the poor, but there is, in fact, a high degree of correlation between people who are in prison for committing street crimes and people who come from poverty-stricken backgrounds. No less a personage than former President Jimmy Carter recognized this grim fact of life when he stated to a Western audience, "I have inspected many prisons, and I know that nearly all inmates are drawn from the ranks of the powerless and poor. A child of privilege frequently receives the benefit of the doubt; a child of poverty seldom does."[1]

Facts confirm the perceptions of the former president. The majority of criminals come from the underclass. They were born poor, they often had neglected childhoods, they frequently dropped out of high school, and they had few opportunities to advance upward. They often have a fatalistic outlook and are unable to support themselves or their families. "Machismo," or an artificial manliness, is frequently characteristic of criminals, and "these traits also lead some of these men to take implausible risks while committing burglaries, thefts, or robberies. . . . The knowledge that they might (and probably will eventually) be caught does not deter them because they feel that they have no control over their fate. Fatalism dulls their caution."[2]

Available data concerning the inmate populations in the nation's local jails underline the underclass aspects of the criminal population. More than 40 percent of these inmates are black; they are young (their median age is approximately 25); they are poorly educated (their average educational attainment is

10.2 years in school); approximately 43 percent were not employed at the time of their arrest.[3]

The poor have fewer resources and less ability to defend themselves in court; therefore, they are more subject to arrest. Historically, societies have always hassled those less able to defend themselves, and American society is no exception. For example, the President's Commission on Law Enforcement and Administration of Justice observed some years ago that a survey of several hundred skid-row residents in Philadelphia concluded that 71 percent had been arrested sometime during their lifetime; one does not find these kinds of proportions in the more affluent areas of cities, and one reason why this is so is that, according to the same survey, skid-row residents showed a low verbal facility, thus making them "extremely vulnerable to dubious police and magistrate practices."[4]

Data reinforcing the common view that policies for criminal justice generally affect the poor more than other classes were found in an analysis of distribution patterns of crime in big cities. A study of the nation's 32 largest cities concluded that patterns of metropolitan suburbanization are linked to rapidly increasing rates of reported crime in the central cities. In other words, the central cities are populated by lower-class whites, blacks, and browns who cannot get out of the inner city, while the middle class has fled to the suburbs. Thus, in this thesis, the poor feed upon themselves and victimize each other; therefore, the more extensive the suburbanization around the central city, the higher the crime rates within the central city.[5]

Also in keeping with the vulnerability-of-the-poor theory, it is relatively easy for police to arrest the poor, because the impoverished have fewer means of defending themselves. To quote the President's Commission on Law Enforcement and Administration of Justice, "Dubious police practices like the investigative arrest fall heaviest in the slums. Slum residents bring few suits for false arrest, and the police are aware of this. A New York City newspaper reported the case of two young Puerto Ricans, picked up by the police on their 119th Street stoop and held eight months in jail for murder before a ballistics test, in another case, implicated a different suspect."[6]

Similarly, access to legal resources can make a difference in how cases are decided. In one investigation, for example, 1,590 poor, homeless men were arraigned over a one-month period in New York City's criminal court for disorderly conduct. Of these, 1,259 pleaded guilty, 325 were acquitted, and 6 were convicted after trial. One year later, after legal aid representation had been introduced into the court, 1,326 homeless men were arraigned over the period of one month, 45 pleaded guilty, 1,280 were acquitted, and 1 was convicted after trial.[7]

WHO ARE THE CRIMINALS?

Beyond certain generalized, underclass characteristics that are shared by most criminals, there are variations. Among the more important of these differences are the motivation of some citizens to commit crimes, and the degree of their commitment to a life of crime. Crime, like most kinds of work, may be full time or part time, while the motivation to commit crimes may be economic or emotional. Full-time criminals often are professionals and tend to concentrate on property crimes, such as burglaries, auto theft, or fraud. Part-time criminals also are economically motivated, but more often than not, they are people from the underclass who live in a twilight zone between the world of crime and law-abiding society. This latter category encompasses a number of juvenile delinquents and those who commit crimes against the person, such as assault and rape.[8]

Particular groups show an alarming propensity for both committing crimes and being the victims of crimes. As the study of professional armed robbers implied, young people are particularly prone to commit crimes. More than 40 percent of all arrests for arson, assault, auto theft, burglary, larceny, murder, rape, and robbery are of youths who are less than 18 years old.[9] The arrest rate for people under 18 is about two-thirds greater than is that for adults.[10] The typical perpetrator of urban robberies, rapes, and murders in America is under 25, poorly educated, deprived economically, unemployed, unmarried, reared in a broken home, and likely to have a prior criminal record.[11]

THE FEAR OF CRIME

If the typical criminal is a born loser, then his or her problems have elicited few sympathies from most Americans. In part this is because of a spreading and pervasive fear of crime among Americans, and this fear is intensifying.[12] In 1949, the Gallup poll found that only 4 percent of big-city residents saw crime as their community's worst problem; by 1965, crime had emerged as a vital issue; and by 1981, more than half of Americans—a record 53 percent—were afraid to walk in certain areas of their own neighborhoods at night. Almost two-thirds (64 percent) of Americans try to avoid going out at night, almost four-fifths never carry very much cash when they do go out, 60 percent avoid certain areas of the city even during the day, 64 percent avoid wearing expensive jewelry, 31 percent keep a gun or other weapon for their personal protection, and another 44 percent keep a dog for protection. Fifty-eight percent of Americans believe that there was more crime in their own area than there was a year ago, and three quarters of the people believe that criminals are more violent than they were five years ago.

The overall fear of crime as measured by such polls has remained essentially constant since 1972, but there have been some radical attitude changes among segments of the population. Poor people are more afraid of crime than are those with higher incomes, blacks are more frightened of violent crimes than are whites, women are more afraid than are men, and the old are more fearful than are the young. Quite aside from the reality of crime, the point stands that all people, and particularly women, old people, poor people, and black people are afraid of it.

THE REALITY OF CRIME

Fears of the citizenry about crime against their persons and their property, especially among the poor and minorities, are well founded. Figure 16-1 indicates the rate of crime from 1972 to 1983. Although the good news is that the crime rate has been in decline since the early 1980s, the bad news is that the

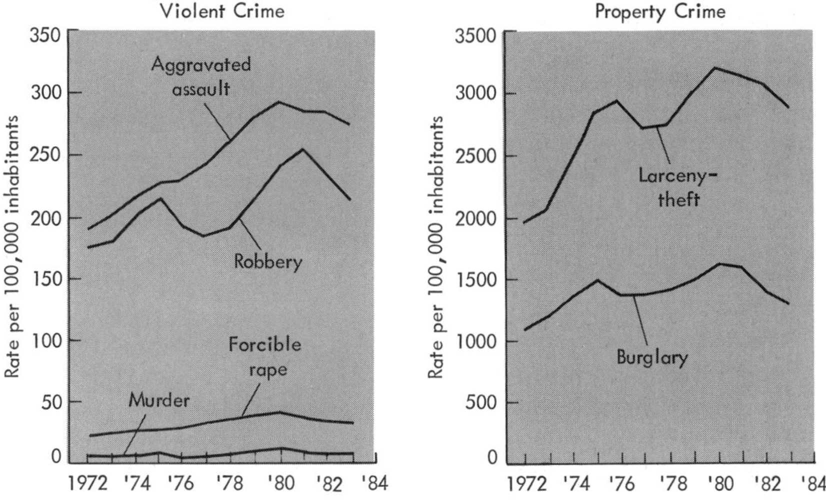

Figure 16-1. Selected crime rates per 100,000 inhabitants, 1972 to 1983. (*Source:* Bureau of the Census, *Statistical Abstract of the United States, 1985.* Washington, D. C.: U.S. Government Printing Office, 1984, p. 162.)

nation is still beset by a lot of violent crime. More people are murdered (more than 10,000 a year) in the United States than in any other country in the world. The homicide rate in America is roughly 10 people per 10,000 population, or approximately the same as the murder rates in Austria, Belgium, Denmark, West Germany, Ireland, Italy, Japan, the Netherlands, Norway, Sweden, Switzerland, and the United Kingdom combined.[13]

These are only the official statistics; the unofficial statistics reveal an even bleaker picture. Surveys of criminal victims in several cities and states indicate that the Federal Bureau of Investigation's (FBI) uniform crime report lists only half, or even a third, of the crimes actually committed. It appears that at least one household in four is hit by some crime in any given year, and in the big cities, those with more than 500,000 people, the ratio appears to be one in every three being struck by some criminal act. Personal victimizations, such as assault, robbery, and rape, are reported to the police less than 40 percent of the time, and household victimization such as theft and burglary, are reported less than half the time.[14]

Approximately 30 percent of American homes, or about 25 million American households, experience some sort of crime, a figure that has held more or less constant since 1975, when such figures were first compiled. About 10 percent of all households in the country are victims of burglary or violent crimes, such as rape, robbery, and assault, although crimes against property outdistance violent crimes against people by about 10 to 1. The most likely people to be victims of crime are people living in cities, and divorced people or people who have never married. Young people are much more likely to be victimized than are the elderly, although the elderly have a much higher fear of crime. Lower-income people and blacks are more likely to be victims of violent crime than are whites or other minority groups. Victims and offenders are of the same race in three out of four violent crimes. By far the most common victims of burglaries are the poorest of the poor households ($3,000 annual income or less), but after that, income level makes little difference in the victimization rate for burglaries.[15]

There are some important local deviations from the national picture. For example, the highest crime rates are found in states and cities that are both rich and urbanized. Thus, California and New York usually rank among the states with the highest reported crime rates, while North Dakota and Mississippi usually have the lowest rates. Recently, crime has been expanding more rapidly in suburbs and rural areas than in cities, and especially in the suburbs. Even so, the greatest volume of crime is found in that heartland of middle America, the average-sized towns and cities.

WHAT IS BEING DONE?

Maintaining law and order is, by definition, essential to the very idea of government. What has government done about both the rise in the fear of crime and the rise of real crime? The evidence indicates that, given the increases in crime, government has not done much. Part of the reason is that the police still rely on very traditional methods of crime control.

The Sheriff, or "You' in a Heap of Trouble, Boy"

Certainly the most traditional of these defenses that society has erected against crime is the office of county sheriff. Analyst after analyst, for more than 50 years, has argued for the abolition of the office of county sheriff as an anachronism in modern society. Alfred Millspaugh wrote more than half a century ago that, "What the sheriff's office has caused society in terms of criminality, insecurity, and highway accidents cannot be computed."[16]

The county sheriff typically is untrained and frequently has no previous law enforcement experience; in every state except Rhode Island, he or she is elected to office. In many states the sheriff is permitted to collect a fee for every warrant, arrest, or order that he or she dispenses. And it is the county sheriff, perhaps more than any other officer, who conjures up in the American mind an image of potbellied, sauntering, sunglassed officialdom, who drawls, "you' in a heap of trouble, boy."

The Local Constabulary: Who Are the Cops?

The towns and cities of America, with their more sophisticated police departments, have been responsive to the dynamic of social change and its relationship to the rise in crime. There are 17,464 local police agencies in America, and most of these are very small—in fact, more than half have fewer than five full-time employees. About one-half of the country's nearly 38,000 counties, cities, and towns have law enforcement agencies, and almost 70 percent of these departments have fewer than ten sworn officers.[17] The National Advisory Council on Criminal Justice Standards and Goals has recommended that police departments with fewer than ten employees be consolidated as a major means of upgrading the war against criminals.[18]

What kinds of people inhabit these almost 17,500 police departments across the country? The typical police officer is from a working class background; very few hail from the middle class. Ninety percent of the nation's police departments require no more education than a high school diploma or the equivalent; only a tenth of 1 percent require a bachelor's degree, and 2 percent of the localities do not have formal education requirements. Nevertheless, the National Advisory Commission on Criminal Justice Standards and Goals recommended that all police departments require four years of college, and roughly a fourth of American cities do provide incentive programs for their officers to further their educations.[19]

Cities and towns get what they pay for in the way of police protection, and, although municipal expenditures for police have been rising steadily since 1970,[20] the typical salary of a municipal police officer still remains under the median income for American households.[21] Even so, police account for more than 16 percent of all municipal employees and almost 19 percent of municipal payrolls. These are the largest slices of the municipal employment pie; even local schools come in with slightly under those figures.[22] Despite sincere efforts by municipal governments to improve the economic lot of their police, it is apparent that police believe they are underpaid. Some experts estimate that from a third to a half of all metropolitan police officers moonlight. Since 97 percent of all American cities permit their police to take on outside employment,[23] it would appear that cities recognize the fact that they underpay their own police officers.

Perhaps it is not surprising, in light of these data, that police are increasingly adopting a siege mentality relative to their own communities. In a poll of the attitudes of experienced police officers in state and local departments across the country, 83 percent felt that most people look down upon a police officer as an "impersonal machine" rather than as a fellow human being. Only half of the officers felt that public support of the police was improving, and almost three quarters felt that they were not receiving enough support from city hall.[24]

On the other hand, half of Americans state that they have not very much or no confidence at all in the ability of police to protect them from violent crime.[25] Such opinions hint at the dangerous job of the police. Nearly 1,400 officers have been killed in the line of duty by felons since 1970, or an average of almost 106 per year.[26] This is a substantial increase from 1960, when fewer than 50 officers were killed in the line of duty.[27] An analysis of police killed in the line of duty in New York City found that, contrary to public opinion, police seldom are killed during domestic disturbances or by deranged lunatics. Typically, the New York police officer was likely to be killed by "rational robbers fleeing the scene of a crime, who routinely used potentially lethal weapons as 'tools of the trade.' "[28]

RACE AND THE POLICE

If the police do indeed feel that they are under siege in their own communities, then this condition may be at least the partial result of their own attitudes. Survey after survey has shown that blacks are far more distrustful of the police than are whites. Almost one-fifth of the whites and four-fifths of the blacks felt that the police discriminated against minority groups. Nearly two-thirds of the white respondents were "deeply skeptical" about the dangers of alleged police brutality, but more than 50 percent of the blacks felt that accusations of police brutality were more likely than not to be true. Whites, in contrast to blacks, tended to accept the idea of a conspiracy afoot to kill police officers.[29] Another survey of citizen attitudes toward police found that blacks' feelings were negative primarily because blacks felt that police did not respond adequately to calls for help.[30]

Traditionally, and regrettably, black perceptions of the police have been largely accurate, although this factor may be changing with the relatively rapid influx of blacks into the nation's police forces. Interviews with police officers in the cities that experienced the major riots of 1967 indicated that police accurately perceived the hostility that was directed toward them by blacks.[31] Police officers felt that very few blacks saw them as friends, but that the great majority of whites did. The survey found that the hostility toward blacks among white police officers was fairly pronounced, with 49 percent of the police not approving of "socializing" between blacks and whites in residential neighborhoods.[32]

It also appears that the private racism of police can emerge in a public context. Data suggest that minorities are, on occasion, arrested in disproportionate numbers in comparison to whites. Table 16-1 indicates that victims perceive their assailants to be members of a minority race less frequently in rape cases (a crime of high emotion for all citizens) than the people whom police arrest. In assaults and robberies, however, this bias does not exist. When we recall that the police depend upon victim reports in all three types of crimes, the question inevitably arises why the police arrest more minority suspects in emotionally charged rape cases than they do in less personal incidents.

The U.S. Commission on Civil Rights has stated that the volume of complaints of police abuse that the Commission receives increases every year. The Commission observed that there seemed to be a linkage between reports of police abuse to the Commission and the lack of effective discipline exercised within the police departments in cases of misconduct and a low level of police training. The Commission also noted that both abuse and ineffectiveness were enhanced by the continuing race and sex bias of police departments in the hiring of officers.[33]

THE POLICING STYLE

Within this general context—a distrustful and fearful citizenry, a frustrated, undertrained, and underpaid police force that may still retain elements of racism—police have evolved different styles in different cities. James Q. Wilson has called these the *watchman style*, the *legalistic style*, and the style that emphasizes a *delivery of services* to the citizens. A watchman style is found in cities that still rely on traditional partisan politics. Often, these cities have ethnically heterogeneous

Table 16-1 Victim Perceptions of Assailants and Race of Arrestees for Selected Offenses, 1975

	PERCENT BLACK AND OTHER MINORITY	
	Victim perceptions	*Arrestees*
Rape	34.2%	47.7%
Aggravated assault	49.4	41.8
Robbery	61.5	60.5

Source: Herbert Jacob, *Crime and Justice in Urban America* (Englewood Cliffs, N.J.: Prentice-Hall, 1980), p. 66.

populations as well, and the emphasis is one of keeping order. In these cities, the police are not above maintaining different standards in different neighborhoods; loiterers may be arrested in one area of the city, but not in another. Entrance requirements to the police force are low, and the management of the police departments is somewhat primitive.

On the opposite end of the continuum is the legalistic police style. The police stress law enforcement rather than the maintenance of order. Universal standards are applied throughout the city, regardless of neighborhood. The legalistic style tends to be seen in newer cities, often those that use the city manager plan and that have a more professional civil service.

A third style falls in the middle of the continuum and emphasizes the delivery of services. These police departments respond to all calls for service, and do not avoid, as legalistic departments tend to do, calls involving the maintenance of order in the city. Unlike watchman police departments, police forces that emphasize the delivery of services enforce the same standards throughout the city in a uniform way, and also have relatively well-trained officers. Service delivery departments have found that training is necessary if they are to deliver services of a high quality that their citizens require.[34]

THE COPS AND THE KLAN

The problems of the police are many, complex, and often confusing. An example of all three is contained in the following passage, which has been culled from news stories about the incident.

In late November 1982, the Ku Klux Klan announced that it would hold its first march in Washington, D.C., since 1925. In 1925, some 40,000 Klansmen displayed a strutting show of power down Pennsylvania Avenue. In 1982, however, the Klan was able to muster only 40 marchers to follow the same path that its members had walked 57 years earlier.

Times have changed since 1925. In Washington, perhaps the most notable change is that the city is now predominantly black, and the Klan, which is against blacks, browns, Asian Americans, native Americans, Jews, and Catholics, among other groups, suspected that it would not be as welcome on Pennsylvania Avenue as it had been in 1925. But the breadth of the spectrum of those who opposed the Klan marching down the nation's main thoroughfare was nonetheless surprising. They included the pro-Palestinian November 29th Coalition, the Spartacist League (a Trotskyite group), the All People's Congress, the Labor-Black Mobilization to Stop the KKK, and Citizens Against Hatred and Violence. In terms of ability to mobilize the citizenry, these and other groups far outclassed the Klan. According to the National Coordinator of the All People's Congress, the counter-Klan rally that his organization intended to sponsor while the Klan marched would draw at least 73 busloads of demonstrators from out of town, and the 100,000 leaflets and 9,000 posters his organization had already distributed were expected to bring out a heavy Washington contingent. He added that "we believe that the KKK, which is known as a secret terrorist organization, should not march and demonstrate unopposed, especially in the nation's capital or in a city primarily black."

The November 29th Coalition, which is comprised largely of Arab-Americans and students from Arab countries, on the other hand, had different reasons for opposing the Klan. Its spokesperson stated that the Coalition opposed the Klan because "Klansmen are anti-Semitic, and Arabs are Semites."

Informed of the view of the November 29th Coalition, the Grand Wizard of the Klan (who could not march in Washington himself because he had been convicted of violating the Neutrality Act in a plot to overthrow the government of Dominica) expressed his surprise.

"We're certainly sympathetic to the plight of the Palestinian people in being displaced by the Israelis with American support."

Both sides agreed, however, that the government was trying to block their rallies. In the case of the Klan, it was because their Grand Wizard had been refused permission to attend the march, and in the case of the anti-Klan groups, it was because the police chief of the District of Columbia was urging Washingtonians to stay home when the Klan marched. The chief stated that the march would "evoke a great deal of animosity. I am personally recommending that the people avoid the rally and not show up. Any outside attendance would only serve to draw greater attention to it." In addition, the police chief had prohibited the wearing of masks during the march. This affected both the Klan, which traditionally has favored a mask as well as a hood and robe as part of its members' costume, and Arab groups, whose members occasionally pull the *kaffiyeh,* or the traditional Arab headdress, across the face when demonstrating.

On the day of the march, there were at least 3,000 anti-Klan demonstrators who were sufficiently incensed that the Washington police were forced to bustle the 40 Klansmen off to a secure area so that they were never able to march. Anti-Klan demonstrators, frustrated over their inability to take on the Klan personally, instead turned against the police. For more than two hours, bricks, bottles, and rocks were hurled at police and shops, causing damage estimated in the tens of thousands of dollars. A dozen police officers and 7 demonstrators suffered minor injuries, and police arrested 38 people, including 12 on charges relating to looting. The chief of police in Washington blamed "opportunists" and "misfits" for the violence, which he called "blind, senseless rage. They were frustrated and took out their emotions on police."

Sources: Associated Press, "Washington's Residents Urged to Ignore Protest Rally by Klan," *The Arizona Republic* (November 27, 1982); and United Press International, "Damage Repaired After Anti-Klan Riot," *The Arizona Republic* (November 29, 1982).

ARE THE POLICE EFFECTIVE?

In the light of high crime rates, a burgeoning popular paranoia over crime, and hostility between the police and the community (at least insofar as the poor and minority races often are concerned), how well have the police fared in their war against crime? Consider an example: the Forty-first Precinct in the South Bronx of New York City between 1970 and 1976. In the 1960s the 50 miles of the precinct's streets were occupied by sedate Irish, Italian, and Jewish residents who were stalwartly middle class. In the early 1970s the area literally exploded in crime for reasons that are not entirely clear, and 90,000 people—half of the area's population—left, leaving behind 80,000 who could not. One-third of the apartments and business premises were destroyed during the six-year period, turning the area into what one writer called "a moonscape." The Forty-first Precinct was known nationally in police circles as "Fort Apache," although now it is called the "Little House on the Prairie" because the intense crime has moved elsewhere.[35]

For understandable reasons, the police of Fort Apache were ill equipped to deal with such sustained and prolonged violence against people and property. But when the police are provided with adequate resources, what is the result?

Studies have generally concluded that greater levels of police activity and more police do not result in less crime. For example, a well-known behavioral study was the famous Kansas City Patrol experiment, which was conducted with a particularly rigorous methodology. In this study, the Kansas City Police

Department, with assistance from the Police Foundation, divided certain of its beats into three categories. In one area, no patrols were sent out; police responded only to specific calls for help. In the second area, patrols were strengthened substantially, often to the point of being doubled or tripled. In the third area, the control group, the patrols were maintained at previous levels. The results indicated that there were no statistically significant differences in crime rates among the three types of beats. There also were no differences in citizen attitudes, the number of reports of crimes, citizen behavior, or even in the rate of traffic accidents.[36]

On the other hand, other studies have indicated that additional resources for police departments, when they are creatively used, do correlate with greater numbers of arrests, both in absolute terms and in terms of arrests per police officer. (It does not necessarily follow, however, that greater numbers of arrests equal reduced crime rates.) One study found that cities that employed more than the average number of officers, equipped their police with superior equipment, and used computers more than did the average police department made more arrests in proportion to the crimes reported to them and more arrests in relation to the number of police officers that they employed.[37] Other studies have found that, simply by being present, the police can reduce crime rates. When there are no police, such as during an electrical blackout, crime rises dramatically.[38]

When all is said and done, however, the critical factor in police effectiveness seems to be how police use the resources they have, and here we get to a crucial area of police performance. At least one investigation found that the ordinary patrol officer rarely makes one arrest a week and is more likely to make fewer than one arrest per month.[39] A study of the District of Columbia found that fully one-third of the police who made arrests failed to process a single conviction, and another examination of seven cities found that 15 percent of the police were credited with half of the convictions, while 31 percent of the police had no convictions at all.[40]

Such data imply that the police are less than careful in making their arrests. Although American police officers make more than 10 million arrests every year,[41] it may be that this impressive number represents fewer than 6 percent of the crimes committed in the country. In a study of more than 2,000 incidents that people thought to be crimes, only half were brought to the attention of the police. Of these, the police determined that 29 percent of the original number (or 60 percent of those that had been brought to their attention) were crimes, and they made arrests in only 6 percent of the original 2,000 cases and in only 12 percent of the situations brought to their attention. Figure 16-2 illustrates these findings.

ALTERNATIVES TO THE COPS

If the police are of questionable effectiveness in dealing with criminals, then what, if any, are our alternatives? While no one has proposed the disbandment of the nation's constabulary, at least some suggestions have been made to supplement law enforcement officials: gun control, various kinds of citizen action groups, and assistance from Washington.

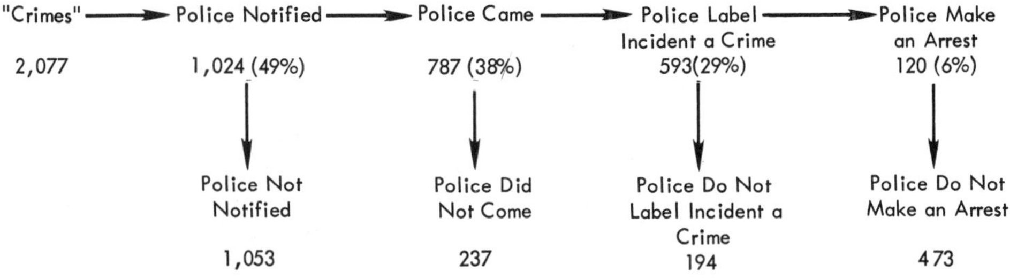

Figure 16-2. Attrition between criminal acts and police arrests, 1967. (*Source:* Philip H. Ennis, *Criminal Victimization in the United States,* Field Surveys II, The President's Commission on Law Enforcement and the Administration of Justice. Washington, D.C.: U.S. Government Printing Office, 1967, p. 48.)

A Mass Movement: Controlling Guns

Perhaps the single most popular movement in America to prevent crime is the gun control movement. Opinion polls conducted since 1967 have found that from approximately two-thirds to three quarters of Americans want gun purchases to be registered.[42] These surveys have found that gun registration is favored by all kinds of citizens, including those who own firearms, city and rural dwellers, and people in all regions of the country.

Almost half of all Americans believe that easy access to guns is a major contributor to criminal violence. And the people should know. Firearms are the weapon used in approximately 60 percent of all murders, a fifth of all aggravated assaults, and approximately 40 percent of all robberies.[43] Studies indicate that an astounding 47 percent of American households own at least one gun. There are some 55 million automatics and revolvers (or one pistol for every four Americans), and this arsenal is being added to at the rate of 2 million handguns per year. It is estimated that a handgun is sold in the United States every 13 seconds.[44]

As a consequence of these kinds of statistics, state and local governments have tried to implement some kind of gun control legislation, and there are almost 25,000 regulations in these jurisdictions dealing with gun controls.[45] These efforts follow three principal approaches: the so-called "crack down" on the criminal use of guns, the registration of handguns, and the virtual banning of handguns.[46]

Seventeen states and the District of Columbia employ the first method and have enacted stricter sentences for crimes committed with a firearm. Typically, these laws provide for additional sentencing of convicted felons when a handgun has been used in a crime, or the imposition of a sentence of no fewer than five years (with no suspension and no probation) for use of a handgun in a felony.

Registration of handguns takes many forms. Eight states make it a crime to possess illegally certain kinds of firearms; a permit to purchase a handgun is required in an additional 8 states; applications to purchase handguns, as well as a waiting period, are required in 12 states so that law enforcement officials may have time to check the criminal backgrounds of applicants; registration of handguns is required in 4 states; and a license to carry a handgun is required in 3 states.

The toughest gun restrictions are imposed in Massachusetts, New York, New York City, and the District of Columbia. These jurisdictions mandate jail sentences for violations of their laws, which generally require a permit to buy a license or carry a handgun. These laws essentially amount to a banning of handguns.

Whether or not gun registration actually reduces crimes is a moot point. One study compared gun control policies in all 50 states with their crime statistics and found no relationship. There was little difference between states with stiff gun controls and those with few or no controls, in terms of their levels of homicide, assault, suicide, or robbery.[47] On the other hand, another study of the gun law in Massachusetts, which imposes a mandatory, one-year jail term for carrying an unlicensed gun, found that, while the level of criminal activity had not declined, the character of the crime seemed to have been affected. There were in Massachusetts fewer gun-related offenses, and those that were committed appeared to be less deadly. In fact, the murder rate declined by 55 percent during a two-year period after the bill became a law.[48]

Citizens: Advising, Supplementing (and Controlling?) the Police

Another way in which citizens are trying to become more involved with crime and the police is the effort to establish "police-community relations organizations," community-based citizen anticrime programs, and "community review boards." As the Advisory Commission on Intergovernmental Relations concluded, "Not only is crime prevention rendered ineffective by the absence of cooperative citizen action, but bad feeling toward the police actually stimulates crime for a number of reasons," going on to note "that suspicious incidents or persons are not reported to the police, witnesses refuse to testify, actions against the police occur, and the police become reluctant to enforce the law in hostile neighborhoods."[49]

Police-community relations programs can significantly reduce tensions between people (especially minorities) and the police. Moreover, both the people and the police like the idea. One poll found that 69 percent of the police felt that community relations programs were important as a means of opening up lines of communication, building respect, and gaining cooperation from citizens; 68 percent of the white civilians and 82 percent of black civilians favored this idea.[50]

The use of police-community relation programs is on the rise. In 1967, 20 percent of the cities responding in a national poll had a police-community relations program; three years later, 44 percent had such a program.[51] Larger cities favored such programs more than did the smaller ones.

A second method that citizens have employed to assist their police forces is more direct. This is the development of community-based, citizen anticrime programs, and they are experiencing a considerable rise in popularity across the country. Typically, these programs involve coordinating neighbors to watch their neighborhoods for suspicious activity, particularly by strangers. The approaches range from volunteers patrolling the streets in golf carts, as in the affluent town of Harlingen, Texas (which reportedly cut the burglary rate to virtually zero), to the Alliance of Guardian Angels in Manhattan, whose 1,000 self-appointed and youthful members wear red berets and patrol New York's subways. Police have expressed concerns that this latter kind of activity verges on vigilantism.[52] Although there are no comprehensive studies of the effectiveness of such "neighborhood watch" programs, the National Sheriffs Association has stated that reductions in burglaries have ranged from 12 percent to 35 percent in some communities that use these programs.[53] Other sources report substantial reductions in crime in major cities that use these programs, such as Oakland, Los Angeles, and Knoxville.[54]

Civilian review boards, which are empowered to review the behavior of police and to check brutality, constitute a third approach. The public generally favors establishing civilian review boards of police action. One poll found that 69 percent of the white respondents and 74 percent of the black respondents felt that "the public has a right to pass judgment on the way the police are doing their jobs." By contrast, 62 percent of the police officers polled opposed establishing such boards.[55] Nevertheless, Chicago, Washington, D.C., Philadelphia, Minneapolis, Rochester, and New York City, among others, had established such boards by the early 1970s, although many of them were later abolished or ignored. Civilian review boards are perhaps the thorniest point of contention between police departments and their communities today.

Washington: The Negligible Impact of Billions

A third movement of significance to help the police was, until recently, provided by the federal government. Traditionally, Washington maintained a "hands-off" policy toward state and local law enforcement; under the Constitution, crime is not a national problem but a state and local one. This is still relatively true, with the federal government employing about 62,000 people in all of its law enforcement agencies compared with 670,000 state and local law enforcement and corrections officials.[56] Nevertheless, Washington, during the 1970s, was paying a greater proportion of the costs for local law enforcement than it did for local primary and secondary education costs, and, by 1980, the Law Enforcement Assistance Administration (LEAA) had disbursed nearly $6 billion to communities to fight crime.

The federal government got into the crime control business in 1965, when Congress passed the Law Enforcement Assistance Act, which established the Office of Law Enforcement Assistance. In 1968, the Omnibus Crime Control and Safe Streets Act was enacted, setting up the Law Enforcement Assistance Administration, which replaced the Office of Law Enforcement Assistance. LEAA was designed to distribute billions of dollars in block grants to state and local governments to help these governments fight their respective wars against crime. But LEAA was coming under increasing fire, with an article in *Time* magazine stating, "The handling of the programs has been extraordinarily inept. The history of the LEAA has been one of waste and mismanagement."[57] Eighty-five percent of the billions distributed under LEAA was given directly to the states, yet the states also were less than effective in using the money to combat crime effectively. Studies by the Brookings Institution and the General Accounting Office concluded that even by 1975 there was not a single model LEAA state operation.[58]

In 1979, at the urging of the Carter administration, the Law Enforcement Assistance Administration was effectively dismantled. The Justice System Improvement Act of 1979 created the Office of Justice Assistance, Research and Statistics within the Department of Justice, and the new Office subsumed the old

LEAA, which remained a skeleton of its former self. The effective elimination of the LEAA by 1980 meant that "the federal role in state criminal justice assistance had all but disappeared."[59] Although federal funds for criminal justice improvements through the Law Enforcement Assistance Administration had never amounted to more than 5 percent of criminal justice expenditures by state and local governments, the loss was nonetheless felt because some of these grants had been used for innovative experimentation.

THE COURTS: PROTECTING THE ACCUSED

We have seen what happens to the criminal justice system in the streets. But what happens in the courts? The courts represent two social goals that must be kept in tension with each other: protecting the rights of the accused and protecting the rights of society. This tension is normally called "justice."

The Overloaded Courts

Certainly an overriding problem in protecting the rights of the accused is that of overloaded courts. The nation's courts have more criminals than they can adequately process. One study found that most felony cases in state courts were disposed within four months—that is, from the arrest to either verdict, dismissal, guilty plea, or some other outcome. In those cases that went to trial, the disposition time usually exceeded six months.[60]

Because many of the people held for trial are poor, they cannot make bail and must stay in jail. A survey of prisoners found that court delays resulted in prisoners being held without trial for an average of 91 days; some had been waiting six months or a year in jail. One prisoner in the survey, who had been charged with murder, had been waiting for his trial for three years.[61]

When these kinds of delays occur, and they all too frequently do, the constitutional rights of the accused to a speedy trial are violated. And the accused are seldom granted a quick trial.

Four Famous Cases

Other items relating to the protection of the accused are the rights guaranteed under the Constitution. With a series of rulings by the U.S. Supreme Court in the early 1960s, the poor (and for that matter, all citizens) have had their rights protected in court more than they might have otherwise. In 1961, the case of *Mapp* v. *Ohio* barred the use of illegally seized evidence under the Fourth Amendment, thus guaranteeing against unreasonable search and seizures. In 1963, the Court ruled in the case of *Gideon* v. *Wainwright* (an important decision) that the Fourteenth Amendment required that free legal counsel be appointed to all poor defendants in all criminal cases. In *Escobedo* v. *Illinois,* decided in 1964, the Court further ruled that a suspect was entitled to confer with his or her counsel as soon as the police investigation changed its focus from "investigatory to accusatory." A final important decision, decided in 1966, was the famous case of *Miranda* v. *Arizona,* which required police to inform a suspect of all constitutional rights before questioning. These controversial decisions probably have gone farther than any other legal development in twentieth-century America to protect the rights of defendants in the courts, in the precinct houses, and in the streets.

How Grand Is the Grand Jury?

A third major component of the court system designed to protect the rights of the accused is the device known as the grand jury.

The grand jury decides whether evidence presented to it by the public prosecutor is adequate to warrant placing a person on trial in a felony case. In theory the grand jury protects the accused from an overly zealous district attorney who may be more motivated by political ambition than by a sense of justice; it also serves as a protection for citizens against harassment by the public prosecutor.

How well the grand juries actually provide this protection is another question. One study found that a typical grand jury spent only five to ten minutes of deliberation per case, and that most of this time was devoted to listening to the prosecutor's recommendations on how the case should be decided. In more than 80 percent of the cases, the grand jury made a decision on the first ballot, without even discussion among jurors, and the votes were virtually always unanimous. An even more significant finding was that the grand juries followed the recommendations of the prosecutors in more than 90 percent of the cases presented to them.[62]

Why are the grand jurors the sheep to the prosecutor's shepherd (or some might say wolf)? Apparently it is because the district attorney controls the information submitted to grand juries; he or she assumes the role of teacher, as opposed to prosecutor, with jurors. In short, the use of the grand jury as a protection for the accused is at best questionable.

THE COURTS: PROTECTING SOCIETY

America is founded on the unique idea that the individual is supreme and that his or her rights must be protected. Nevertheless, protection cannot be extended merely to the accused in a crime; it also must be extended to the victims of the crime and to those citizens who are potentially susceptible to future crimes. Thus, even in America, something called "society" must also be protected.

The Injustice of Plea Bargaining

How well are the courts protecting society? Their record is not outstanding, and one reason is the widespread practice of plea bargaining. *Plea bargaining* is the negotiating that takes place between the accused's lawyer and the public prosecutor. The defense lawyer argues for a reduced charge while the prosecutor pushes for a conviction. A shared desire by prosecutors, defense attorneys, and judges to avoid the uncertain outcome of a jury trial makes it expeditious for all sides that the defendant plead guilty (usually to a lesser crime) since, in this manner, precious court time is not consumed, the defendant receives a minimal sentence, and the district attorney gets his or her sought-after conviction.

While expeditious, the almost total reliance on plea bargaining in state and local courts is hardly just. Considerable pressure is placed on the accused to plead guilty, and many observers feel that judges tend to hand out harsher sentences to guilty defendants who have demanded their constitutional right to a trial; the all-too-frequent, exceptionally long waiting period before a defendant's trial provides additional pressure on the accused to plead guilty so that he or she may at least be released from jail.

It is not surprising, therefore, that most defendants plead guilty. Investigations have found that from nearly half to more than 90 percent of all convicted defendants in state and local courts were never proven guilty because they never went to trial.[63]

Contrary to popular belief, plea bargaining is not the practical consequence of overloaded dockets. Research has shown that guilty pleas were as prevalent in the late nineteenth and early twentieth centuries as they are today.[64] Moreover, plea bargaining and guilty pleas appear with the same regularity in cities where courts have a light case load as in cities where courts have a heavy case load.[65]

Irrespective of its long tradition, however, plea bargaining undermines popular respect for the criminal justice system in two ways. If the accused really is guilty, then the victim of the crime watches the criminal "get off" with an extraordinarily light sentence; thus the victim does not receive justice. Recall, in this regard, the controversy surrounding the dramatically minimized sentence granted to former Vice-President Spiro T. Agnew relative to the bribery and corruption charges against him, or the total pardon of all crimes, past and future, given out by President Gerald Ford to former President Richard Nixon after he resigned the presidency. Many Americans—the effective "victims" of both politicians—wanted far more severe punishments meted to both the vice-president and the president and felt that the Justice Department and President Ford, through some remarkable plea bargaining, had "let off" a couple of crooks.

Conversely, if the accused is not guilty, but succumbs to the pressures brought to bear upon him or her to plead guilty—including pressure from one's own defense lawyer if he or she is appointed by the court—then the innocent citizen is saddled with a criminal record for life; thus, the accused does not receive justice.

It was with these concerns in mind that Alaska in 1975 became the first and only state to ban plea bargaining. A study of Alaska's experience with this ban by the Alaska Judicial Council and the U.S. Department of Justice found some unexpected effects of its elimination. Contrary to some predictions, the trial process did not mire down, but in fact accelerated. Defendants continued to plead guilty at about the same rate as they had in the past. Although the rate of cases that were decided by trials increased substantially—by 97 percent, for example, in Anchorage, the state's largest city—this growth did not overwhelm the court system.

Interestingly, overall conviction rates in Alaska did not change significantly, although prosecutors won a larger proportion of the cases that actually went to trial. Sentencing became more severe, but not for more serious crimes. The conviction and sentencing patterns for people charged with such major crimes as murder, rape, robbery, and assault remained unaltered while first-time offenders and persons convicted of less serious offenses experienced substantially increased sentences. The reason for this disparity appears to stem from the fact that plea bargaining had resulted in substantially stiff sentences for violent offenders prior to its ban in Alaska, and therefore the severity of sentences for these defendants did not increase after its ban.[66]

Sentencing Whimsically and Fixedly

A second problem that the courts face in protecting society against criminals concerns the judges themselves. It is well known that some judges are extremely lenient in the sentences that they give to convicted felons; others are excessively harsh. In a State of the Federal Judiciary address, Chief Justice Warren E. Burger called to account the problem of wide variation in sentencing, noting, "Some judges let defendants off on probation for crimes that would draw five- or ten-year sentences by other judges. While flexibility in sentencing is essential in dealing justly with individuals, perceived inconsistencies damage the image of the courts in the public mind."[67]

How consistent are the courts? Consider some examples.[68] A businessman was convicted of embezzling $100,000 and given a suspended sentence, while a slum dweller was sent to prison for stealing a cheap watch. During one recent year, one federal court in New York dealt bank robbers sentences that averaged 39 months; another federal court in the same state meted out prison terms averaging 130 months! Fifty federal judges in the Northeast were given a hypothetical profile of fictitious criminal defendants by the Federal Judicial Center and were asked what sentences they would give; the sentences were alarmingly varied, with one judge giving one hypothetical defendant seven and one-half years in the "big house" and another giving the same defendant four years—on probation!

In a more systematic study of federal judges, which involved a three-year study of almost 6,000 presentence investigations and interviews with more than 260 judges, it was found that the pattern of sentencing disparity was even wider than had been previously believed. Judges were presented with 16 hypothetical identical bank robbery and fraud cases and asked to pass judgment upon them. Their sentences in these hypothetical cases ranged from releasing the defendants on probation to sentencing them to 25 years in prison.

These disparities resulted more from the mind-set of judges—that is, their tendency toward toughness or leniency—rather than such factors as the defendant's economic status or race. A quarter of the judges considered rehabilitation to be an extremely important factor in sentencing criminals while almost a fifth ranked rehabilitation as no more than slightly important. Another one-fourth of the judges thought it quite important that defendants be given their "just deserts" when sentencing, compared to almost half of the judges who felt that such a goal was only somewhat important. Southern judges recommended sentences systematically more stringent than those recommended by colleagues in other regions.

Interestingly, in the face of the study's findings, almost two-thirds of the judges believed that unwarranted sentence disparity occurred in their jurisdictions either "never" or "only occasionally." Such views stood in sharp contrast to the opinions of more than half of the prosecutors and defense attorneys in these same jurisdictions, who felt that sentencing by the bench was very unsatisfactory.[69]

Fragmentary data indicate similar patterns appearing at the state and local levels as well. For example, the courts in Minneapolis seem to deal much more severely with convicted defendants than do the courts in Pittsburgh.[70] Defendants convicted of armed robbery in Baltimore, according to one study, received an average sentence of 84 months; in Chicago, the sentence averaged 49 months; but in Detroit, the typical sentence for armed robbery was 35 months. As with studies of federal judges, these sentence disparities do not seem to be linked to the race or economic status of the defendants.[71]

Nevertheless, in part because of these disparities in sentencing by judges, the American public has taken an increasingly dim view of how judges make their decisions. Forty-three percent of Americans believe that judges usually allow personal beliefs and political opinions to play too great a part in their decisions, and 38 percent think that judges tend to be biased against minorities and the poor. More than two-thirds of the public disapprove of the way criminal courts are doing their job. Relatedly, 69 percent of Americans believe that the courts should not allow the insanity defense, while 79 percent disapprove of laws that allow someone to be found guilty because of insanity.[72]

In response to possible disparities in sentencing, a number of states have begun to experiment with "fixed sentencing." Fixed sentencing means that, if a person is convicted of a particular type of crime, the law allows the judge very little or no flexibility in determining the felon's sentence. Maine enacted the first fixed sentencing law in 1975, and today 24 states have adopted some kind of mandatory imprisonment or determinant sentence law, particularly for crimes that generate high fear among the citizenry.[73] Relatedly, there has been a spate of new state laws enacted that deal with the insanity plea in criminal cases. Seven states now have made it more difficult for defendants to plead insanity, including Indiana, which permits a verdict of "guilty but mentally ill" when a plea of insanity is made.[74]

Fixed sentencing also calls into question the traditional penal concept of parole since, under the law, paroles simply are not permitted. In Maine, for example, a person convicted of robbery or rape must be sentenced for at least ten years and must actually serve slightly more than six years. Under Maine's former indeterminate sentencing law, a judge could impose any sentence he or she wished for either crime. But the median sentence for armed robbery in Maine in recent years had been five years, and the average time actually served before parole was somewhat more than three years. For rape, the median sentence was seven years, and the average time served was slightly more than four and one-half years.[75] California's fixed sentencing law retains probation but limits it to one-and-a-half years; it also permits some reduction of sentences through proper behavior. But, unlike previous practices, these minimum times are written into the law and are not subject to the whimsey of parole boards or judges.

In some ways fixed sentencing is a return to "the good old days"—fixed sentencing was "standard operating procedure" in all the states until the turn of the century. By the 1920s reformist thinking in penology circles had brought about a complete conversion to indeterminate sentencing and to the parole board system. The reasoning was that once a prisoner was "rehabilitated," he or she should be released from prison, and that this rehabilitation could be determined only by parole boards or penal officials. Society seems no longer to trust such judgments made by judges or prison officials, particularly in light of the failure of prisons to "rehabilitate" criminals and their corresponding recidivism rates (*recidivism rates* are the number of people who are sent back to prison for additional crimes they commit once they are out). Even so, there are those who are critical of the fixed sentence trend. They argue that considerably more prisons will be needed to house all the people forced into them. Others argue that in some cases (notably, in California), too much latitude in sentencing is still permitted to judges even under fixed sentencing. Both sides ignore the fact that no evidence exists linking tougher sentences with more or less crime.[76] But facts have not deterred the trend toward tougher and less flexible sentencing, and between 1965 and 1980—a period of dramatically rising crime rates—the average prison term increased from 18 to 35 months.[77]

Locking Up the Few

A final area of protecting society involves how frequently the courts sentence people who are found guilty to jail. Americans clearly believe that not enough felons are being incarcerated. A majority, 53 percent of Americans, think that permissiveness in the courts constitutes a major cause of the country's problems. The courts rank second out of 12 possible causes; only a "decline in moral values" tops the judiciary as a cause of national problems. Moreover, people have grown increasingly critical of the courts. In 1973, only 39 percent of Americans attributed the country's problems to the permissiveness of the judiciary. Similarly, 83 percent of the public in 1981 thought that the courts had been too easy in dealing with criminals, and only 14 percent thought that the courts had been fair to defendants (compared to only 52 percent in 1967). Also in that year, 79 percent of the people stated that they did not believe the system of law enforcement worked to discourage people from committing crimes (com-

pared to 53 percent in 1967), and 87 percent of Americans favored a harsher prison sentence for those who were convicted of crimes.[78]

Empirical data back up the perceptions of most Americans. Recall, in this regard, that in perhaps only 12 percent of the incidents brought by the public to the attention of the police is an arrest actually made, but once these arrests get to the courts, the percentage of defendants who are convicted is still not large. Table 16-2 indicates these patterns in selected cities. The proportion of felony defendants sent to prison does not attain 30 percent in any of the cities listed; in New York City the percentage of defendants sent to prison is only 5 percent! Although one might expect that more convictions would correlate with a higher crime rate in a city, no correlation seems to exist. In Hartford, for example, there is a comparatively low crime rate, but a rather high conviction rate. In Los Angeles, however, there are both high conviction rates and high crime rates.

Additional data support these figures. In New York State, there are approximately 130,000 felony arrests every year, of which 8,000 defendants go to prison. In the city of New York, there are 94,000 arrests for felonies, but only 5,000 to 6,000 are sent to prison in any given year. A study conducted of the District of Columbia found that of more than 6,000 aggravated assaults that had been reported, 116 people were sent to prison for them. Although almost three quarters of the murders committed in the nation lead to an arrest (not a low arrest rate compared to other crimes), only 1 murder case in 10 results in a conviction. Arrests are made in approximately 25 percent of robbery cases, and in 15 percent of burglary cases, but only 1 arrested robber in 6, and only 1 arrested burglar in 20 received a prison sentence of even one year.[79]

Table 16-2 Crime Rates and Felony Dispositions in Selected Cities

City	*Major crimes Per 100,000 Population*[1]	*Percentage of Felony Defendants Convicted*	*Percentage of Felony Defendants Sent to Prison*
Baltimore, Md.	5,622	43.7%[a]	27.6%[1]
Chicago, Ill.	3,614	25.6[b]	15.0[a]
Detroit, Mich.	7,095	57.5[a]	20.0[a]
New Haven, Conn,	5,193	48.9[b]	NA
Hartford, Conn.	4,175	49.3[b]	NA
Winstead, Conn.	NA	41.5[b]	NA
Prairie City[2]	NA	60.8[c]	30.2[d]
Los Angeles, Calif.	6,257	79.8[d]	10.0[d]
New York, N.Y.	5,501	55.7[e]	5.0[e]

[1] Federal Bureau of Investigation, *Uniform Crime Reports, 1972* (Washington, D.C.: U.S. Government Printing Office, 1973).

[2] Prairie City is a pseudonym for a city studied by several social scientists.

[a] James Eisenstein and Herbert Jacob, *Felony Justice* (Boston: Little, Brown, 1977), pp. 292–293.

[b] Milton Heumann, *Plea Bargaining* (Chicago: University of Chicago Press, 1978), p. 34.

[c] David W. Neubauer, *Criminal Justice in Middle America* (Morristown, N.J.: General Learning Press, 1974), pp. 201–237.

[d] Peter W. Greenwood et al., *Prosecution of Adult Defendants in Los Angeles County: A Policy Perspective* (Santa Monica, Calif.: Rand Corporation, 1973), pp. 38, 149.

[e] Vera Institute of Justice, *Felony Arrests: Their Prosecution and Disposition in New York's City Courts* (New York: Vera Institute of Justice, 1977), p. 1.

Source: Herbert Jacob, *Crime and Justice in Urban America* (Englewood Cliffs, N.J.: Prentice-Hall, 1980), p. 51.

A study by the Rand Corporation indicates that the "juvenile factor" plays a significant role in these dismal statistics. In this investigation, 49 convicted armed robbers who were serving prison terms, and who had spent their careers as professional criminals, had been arrested only once for every 28 times that they had committed a crime as juveniles or young adults, but once every 9 times when they had committed a crime as an adult. Although these people were eventually incarcerated, they were not placed behind bars until they had committed a substantial number of crimes and had been apprehended on several occasions. The 49 men claimed to have committed a total of 10,505 crimes, most of them as juveniles. As they grew up, however, they tended to commit fewer crimes, but to be arrested and imprisoned more frequently.[80]

In summary, the state and local criminal justice system may be understood as one that reconciles the inclination of society to protect itself by "coming down hard"—and occasionally unjustly—on those who have violated its laws, and the constitutional right of the citizen to full and equal protection under the law. How successful the courts have been in reconciling these two social realities is up to the reader to decide.

PRISONS: "FACTORIES OF CRIME"

Perhaps the single most vexing problem of the criminal justice system is the prisons. There are more than 600,000 inmates in federal, state, and local correctional facilities. Almost 400,000 of these prisoners are in nearly 800 state prisons, and another 224,000 are in more than 3,300 local jails.[81]

Prisons Are Less than Pleasant

Prisons, both federal and state, are not pleasant; as a general rule, they are substantially overcrowded and often seem to be run more by the kept than by the keepers. Fifty-eight percent of one-person units in state prisons and 90 percent of multiple person units are overcrowded.[82] In a number of prisons across the country, there are twice as many prisoners as the facilities were designed to hold.

Prisoners have begun to protest their treatment, and to protest in the most violent ways imaginable. In 1971 the state penitentiary at Attica, New York, erupted in a riot that was to plague the governor politically until his death. In 1980, the New Mexico State prison at Santa Fe exploded in riots that resulted in the deaths of 33 prisoners at the hands of fellow inmates, and in 1981, major disorders occurred at three separate Michigan prisons virtually simultaneously.[83] Between 1971 and 1980, at least 150 inmates, guards, and state police officers died in prison outbreaks in 21 states.[84]

As a consequence of these conditions, lawyers have begun questioning whether or not prisons in America constitute "cruel and unusual punishment," in violation of the Eighth Amendment to the Constitution. The courts have become actively engaged in alleviating prison conditions, requiring state and city officials to spend more money and hire better personnel. Though the courts may order away to their hearts' content, however, the states and localities must provide the money. Nevertheless, the judiciary clearly has brought about change in some states and cities. In the Arkansas prison system, for example, which had been described as a "self-supporting slave camp industry" prior to court-ordered reform, the budget of the Arkansas system was raised from $1 million to $6 million by the courts, and the harshest conditions in the state penitentiary were eliminated. Correctional systems in 23 states are under direct court order to improve the living conditions of their prisoners.[85]

These court-ordered improvements in the living conditions of prisoners have been and will be costly. Despite their conditions, the annual cost of keeping each inmate in prison exceeds the student tuition at major public universities, and in some states it surpasses the tuitions charged at Stanford and Harvard.[86] Moreover, these costs went up—by 115 percent in constant dollars from 1960 to 1980. Only public welfare experienced a higher rate of increased expenditures than did corrections during this period.[87]

The "Rehabilitation" Myth

Despite their conditions and their costs, prisons and jails in America are meant to "rehabilitate" their inmates; that is, they are supposed to turn criminals into law-abiding citizens. Regrettably, there is absolutely no evidence whatever that prisons rehabilitate prisoners; in fact there is every reason to believe that they accomplish just the reverse. About a third of the nation's prisoners have been in prison at least once before—a recidivism rate that indicates prisons are hardly rehabilitating their inmates.[88]

Whether or not prisons are equipped to rehabilitate is another matter; in spite of relatively low budgets, prison officials are expected to make inmates acceptable in a highly educated and skilled society. Yet inmates as a group are extraordinarily undereducated and undertrained. Less than 5 percent of federal prisoners, for example, perform at the twelfth grade level or higher, and 85 percent lack any marketable skill.[89]

The Problem of Parole

This population of the prisons is often sent back to society through a parole system of at least questionable effectiveness. Parolees typically have served only a third of their maximum sentence in prison. Four out of five prisoners are paroled out of prison, rather than serving their full sentence, and more than 1 percent of the American population (or 2.4 million people) is under some form of correctional supervision; three quarters of these people are being supervised in the community (either through parole or probation) rather than serving time in prison.[90]

Parole seems to make no particular difference in whether or not a prisoner is likely to commit another crime. Careful studies of paroled prisoners versus nonparoled prisoners indicate "the almost total absence of linkage between correction variables and recidivism."[91]

In short, prisons have failed to rehabilitate their inmates. Former U.S. Attorney General Ramsey Clark has called American correctional institutions "factories of crime"; the former director of the Federal Bureau of Prisons stated that "anyone not a criminal will be one when he gets out of jail."[92]

Thus far, we have examined the criminal justice system in state and local governments and have come close to concluding that it does not work; or, if it does work, it does not work very well. This is a serious matter. As Chief Justice Burger observed, "A sense of confidence in the courts is essential to maintain the fabric of ordered liberty for a free people." He listed three conditions that could destroy that confidence:

> That people will come to believe that inefficiency and delay will drain even a just judgment of its value; that people who have long been exploited in the smaller transactions of daily life come to believe that courts cannot vindicate their legal rights from fraud. . . . That people come to believe the law . . . cannot fulfill its primary function to protect them and their families.[93]

Yet, the police, the courts, and the prisons seem to be incapable of doing their jobs in terms of reducing crime, arresting suspects, convicting criminals, and rehabilitating prisoners. Indeed, 51 percent of Americans believe that their system of justice needs a basic overhaul or many improvements.[94]

Consequently, we must ask what does work. Or at least we should ask what is more likely to work in protecting both the rights of the individual citizen and the rights of society to be free from fear. Most people who have studied the question of what prevents crime are agreed that the most effective deterrence is the *certainty* of punishment, while severity of punishment does not seem to be much of a factor.[95]

Death Row: One Form of Punishment

Of course, a major question in terms of the severity of potential punishment revolves around the death penalty in America. In the 1970s an argument was voiced that the death penalty constitutes "cruel and unusual punishment," and thus was in violation of the Eighth Amendment. Until 1972 the death penalty was the law in 30 states, and only 15 had actually abolished capital punishment. In that year the U.S. Supreme Court ruled in *Furman* v. *Georgia* that capital punishment violated both the Eighth and Fourteenth Amendments, which prohibit cruel and unusual punishment and insure due process of law. But there was a catch in this ruling. The Court stated that the death penalty, only as currently imposed in the states that employed it, was in violation of the Constitution. For four years after the ruling, there was a spate of rewriting of state legislation regarding the death penalty, and in 1976, in *Gregg* v. *Georgia,* the Supreme Court upheld state laws that were written to insure equity and due process, remarking that death itself was not cruel or unusual in the meaning of the Eighth Amendment. So the death penalty still is with us in most states and has been sanctioned by the U.S. Supreme Court. But its use is dwindling. Between 1930 and 1967, more than 3,800 prisoners were executed, but since 1967, only 11 death penalties have been carried out.[96]

Whether or not the prospect of the electric chair, gallows, gas chamber, firing squad, or hypodermic needle deters crime in the 36 states that use them is quite another question, and, as noted, the evidence indicates that it probably does not. But the findings of academic research can be swept aside when it comes to such emotion-charged issues as the death penalty. Consider the instance of a

New York State senator, who objected before the Mohawk Valley Council of Churches (which opposed the death penalty "as a matter of faith") that Christianity would not exist if, instead of crucifixion, "Jesus got eight to fifteen years, with time off for good behavior."[97] By such reasoning the death penalty becomes the cornerstone of Christendom.

Compensating Victims

A related and even more basic reconsideration of criminal justice policy deals not with deterrence but with what to do once a crime happens. Since 1964, two dozen states have adopted the policy of compensating the victims of crime. Most of these states have set up crime compensation boards, composed of lawyers appointed by the governor. The boards' staffs investigate claims, and, if the victim can demonstrate financial hardship (Hawaii is an exception; there no such hardship must be demonstrated), the victim becomes eligible to receive a usually modest award as compensation. Apprehension of the criminal is not a condition for receipt of the award. The logic behind this approach is that the victim deserves at least as much attention as the offender, and financial compensation can cover some of the cost of medical treatment for injury that may have been sustained because of the crime and pay for bills that accumulate as a result of being out of work while recuperating.[98]

Crime compensation boards are a genuinely innovative policy that probably have helped the poor more than any other social group in society, since the poor are not only the more frequent victims of crime, but are also less likely to have any kind of insurance to protect them from the results of crime.

In this and the preceding chapter we have discussed the two major policies that apply to the underclass. While policies for welfare and criminal justice apply to people other than the poor, they tend to focus more on the poor than do other classes in American society, simply because more poor people are on welfare rolls and more poor people are in prisons. In the next three chapters we consider some major policies for the middle class: education, planning, land use, and transportation.

NOTES

[1]President Jimmy Carter, address, May 1978. Quoted in R. Stanton Evans, *The Arizona Republic,* syndicated column (May 17, 1978).
[2]Herbert Jacob, *Crime and Justice in Urban America* (Englewood Cliffs, N.J.: Prentice-Hall, 1980), p. 34; and Walter Miller, "Focal Concerns of Lower-Class Culture" in A. Ferman, Joyce L. Kornbluh, and Allan Haber, eds., *Poverty in America* (Ann Arbor, Michigan: University of Michigan Press, 1965).
[3]Bureau of the Census, *Statistical Abstract of the United States, 1985* (Washington, D.C.: U.S. Government Printing Office, 1984), Table 313, p. 183. Data are for 1978.
[4]President's Commission on Law Enforcement and Administration of Justice, *Task Force Report: The Courts* (Washington, D.C.: U.S. Government Printing Office, 1967), p. 139.
[5]Wesley G. Skogan, "Public Policy and the Fear of Crime in Large American Cities," in John A. Gardiner, ed., *Public Law and Public Policy* (New York: Praeger, 1976), pp. 13-14.
[6]President's Commission on Law Enforcement and Administration of Justice, *Task Force Report,* p. 140.
[7]*Ibid.,* p. 144. The investigations were conducted in March 1965 and March 1966.
[8]John Irwin, *The Felon* (Englewood Cliffs, N.J.: Prentice-Hall, 1970).
[9]Bureau of the Census, *Statistical Abstract of the United States, 1985,* Table 293, p. 173. Figure is for 1983.

[10]National Institute for Juvenile Justice and Delinquency Prevention, as cited in United Press International, "Juvenile Crime Is 'Vicious Circle,' Justice Report Says," *Washington Times* (August 2, 1982).

[11]President's Commission on Law Enforcement and the Administration of Justice, *The Challenge of Crime in a Free Society* (New York: Avon, 1969).

[12]The following data concerning polls on the fear of crime are drawn from Gene A. Fowler, *Citizen Attitudes Toward Local Government Services and Taxes* (Lexington, Mass.: Ballinger, 1974), pp. 147-150; and the Gallup Organization in a poll for *Newsweek* magazine as cited in Aric Press et al., "The Plague of Violent Crime," *Newsweek* (March 23, 1981), p. 47. Unless noted otherwise, percentages are for 1981.

[13]Bureau of the Census, *Social Indicators, III* (Washington, D.C.: U.S. Government Printing Office, 1980), Table 5/20, p. 252. Figures are for 1975.

[14]Michael J. Hindelang et al., *Source Book of Criminal Justice Statistics, 1976* (Washington, D.C.: U.S. Department of Justice, Law Enforcement Assistance Administration, 1977), pp. 404-405. Figures are for 1975 and cover 13 cities.

[15]Bureau of Justice Statistics, *Report to the Nation on Crime and Justice: The Data* (Washington, D.C.: U.S. Government Printing Office, 1983), pp. 19-20.

[16]Alfred Millspaugh, *Local Democracy and Crime Control* (Washington, D.C.: Brookings Institution, 1936), p. 35.

[17]Emphany McCann, "Law Enforcement Agencies in Urban Counties," *County Year Book, 1975* (Washington, D.C.: National Association of Counties and the International City Management Association, 1975), pp. 110-113.

[18]As quoted in *ibid.*, p. 112.

[19]As cited in James R. Mandish and Laurie S. Frankel, "Personnel Practices in the Municipal Police Service: 1976," in *Municipal Year Book, 1977* (Washington, D.C.: International City Management Association, 1977), pp. 160-161.

[20]Law Enforcement Assistance Administration and U.S. Bureau of the Census, *Trends in Expenditure and Employment Data for the Criminal Justice System, 1971-1975* (Washington, D.C.: U.S. Government Printing Office, 1977), p. 24.

[21]In 1983, the minimum wage scale for police in all cities was $17,120, and the maximum scale was $20,811. The median family income in that year for all households was $20,885. See Bureau of the Census, *Statistical Abstract for the United States, 1985,* Table 734, p. 442; and Gerard J. Hoetmer, "Police, Fire, and Refuse Collection and Disposal Departments: Personnel, Compensation, and Expenditures," *Municipal Year Book, 1985* (Washington, D.C.: International City Management Association, 1985), p. 124.

[22]Bureau of the Census, *1977 Census of Government: Compendium of Public Employment,* Vol. 3, No. 2 (Washington, D.C.: U.S. Government Printing Office, 1979), Table 5, p. 15.

[23]Mandish and Frankel, "Personnel Practices," pp. 160-161.

[24]Nelson A. Watson and James W. Sterling, *Police and Their Opinions* (Washington, D.C.: International Association of Chiefs of Police, 1969), p. 55.

[25]Press, "The Plague of Violent Crime," p. 49.

[26]Bureau of the Census, *Statistical Abstract of the United States, 1981* (Washington, D.C.: U.S. Government Printing Office, 1981), Table 306, p. 179; and *1985,* Table 289, p. 172.

[27]*Ibid.* Between 1970 and 1983, 1,380 officers were killed by felons. The number for 1960 includes officers killed in accidents, which the 1970-1983 figures do not. If accidental deaths are included, a total of 152 officers were killed in 1983. See *ibid.*

[28]Mona Margarita, "Killing the Police: Myths and Motives," *Annals of the American Academy of Political and Social Science,* 452 (November, 1980), p. 63.

[29]The surveys are cited in Advisory Commission on Intergovernmental Relations, *State and Local Relations and the Criminal Justice System* (Washington, D.C.: U.S. Government Printing Office, 1971). Reprinted in W. P. Collins, ed., *Perspectives on State and Local Governments* (Englewood Cliffs, N.J.: Prentice-Hall, 1974), pp. 120-121. See also Herbert Jacob, "Black and White Perceptions of Justice in the City," *Law and Society Review,* 6 (1971), p. 76.

[30]Fowler, *Citizen Attitudes Toward Local Government,* p. 170.

[31]National Advisory Commission on Civil Disorders, *Supplemental Studies* (Washington, D.C.: U.S. Government Printing Office, 1968), p. 44.

[32]*Ibid.*

[33]U.S. Commission on Civil Rights, *Who Is Guarding the Guardians: A Report on Police Practices* (Washington, D.C.: U.S. Government Printing Office, 1981).

[34]James Q. Wilson, *Varieties of Police Behavior* (Cambridge, Mass.: Harvard University Press, 1968), pp. 83-277.

[35]Peter Arnett, "Peace in Crime-Devastated South Bronx Would Look Like Chaos Anywhere Else," Associated Press, *The Arizona Republic* (July 3, 1977).
[36]George Kelling et al., *The Kansas City Preventive Patrol Experiment: Summary Report* (Washington, D.C.: The Police Foundation, 1974), pp. v-vi. See also E. Terrence Jones, "Evaluating Everyday Policies: Police Activity and Crime Incidents," *Urban Affairs Quarterly,* 8 (March, 1973), pp. 267-279.
[37]Wesley G. Skogan, "Efficiency and Effectiveness in a Big City Police Department," *Public Administration Review,* 36 (May/June, 1976), pp. 278-286.
[38]Jacob, *Crime and Justice in Urban America,* p. 64. For a review of this literature, see Colin Loftin and David McDowall, "The Police, Crime, and Economic Theory: An Assessment," *American Sociological Review,* 47 (June, 1982), pp. 393-401.
[39]Jonathan Rubinstein, *City Police* (New York: Farrar, Straus, and Giroux, 1973), pp. 66-68.
[40]As cited in John Leo, "Why the Justice System Fails," *Time* (March 23, 1981), p. 22. The District of Columbia study was conducted in 1974; the study of seven American cities, covering 2,418 police officers, was conducted in 1981.
[41]Bureau of the Census, *Statistical Abstract of the United States, 1985,* Table 292, p. 173. In 1983, police made 10.3 million arrests.
[42]Harris poll as cited in Associated Press, *The Arizona Republic* (October 25, 1975); and the Gallup poll as cited in Walter Isaacson et al., "The Duel over Gun Control," *Time* (March 23, 1981), p. 33. In 1967, 66 percent of Americans favored such a policy; in 1975, 73 percent did so; and in 1981, 52 percent favored such a policy.
[43]Bureau of the Census, *Statistical Abstract of the United States, 1985,* Table 288, p. 172.
[44]Isaacson, "The Duel over Gun Control," p. 33.
[45]*Ibid.*
[46]The following discussion of firearm legislation is drawn from Jack B. Foster, "The States and the Criminal Justice System," *The Book of the States, 1982-83* (Lexington, Ky.: Council of State Governments, 1982), pp. 529-530.
[47]Douglas R. Murray, as cited in Kevin Phillips, *The Arizona Republic* (July 10, 1976).
[48]Glenn Pierce, as cited in Isaacson, "The Duel over Gun Control," p. 33.
[49]Advisory Commission on Intergovernmental Relations, *State and Local Relations,* p. 229.
[50]*Ibid.,* p. 122.
[51]International City Management Association, "Recent Trends in Police-Community Relations," *Urban Data Service,* 2 (March, 1970), pp. 10-11.
[52]Orr Kelly, "Neighborhood Patrols Scout the Enemy," *U.S. News & World Report* (July 13, 1981), p. 54; and "Angels and Other Guardians," *Newsweek* (March 23, 1981), pp. 48-49.
[53]*Newsletter-National Neighborhood Watch Programs,* II (Washington, D.C.: National Sheriffs Association, 1972).
[54]George J. Washnis, *Citizen Involvement in Crime Prevention* (Lexington, Mass.: D. C. Heath, 1976), pp. 57-63.
[55]Advisory Commission on Intergovernmental Relations, *State and Local Relations,* p. 122.
[56]Bureau of the Census, *1982 Census of Government: Compendium of Public Employment* (Washington, D.C.: U.S. Government Printing Office, 1984), Table 3, p. 2.
[57]Quoted in Thomas B. Cronin, "The War on Crime and Unsafe Streets, 1960-1976: Policymaking for a Just and Safe Society," in Allen P. Sindler, ed., *America in the '70s: Problems, Policies, and Politics* (Boston: Little, Brown, 1977), p. 240.
[58]*Ibid.,* p. 247.
[59]Foster, "The States and the Criminal Justice System," p. 523.
[60]Bureau of Justice Statistics, *Report to the Nation on Crime and Justice,* p. 66. Another useful study is Mark W. Cannon, "Administrative Change and the Supreme Court," *Judicature: The Journal of the American Judicature Society,* 57 (March, 1974), pp. 1-6.
[61]Henry Robert Glick and Kenneth N. Vines, *State Court Systems* (Englewood Cliffs, N.J.: Prentice-Hall, 1973), p. 26.
[62]Robert A. Carp, "The Behavior of Grand Juries: Acquiescence or Justice?" *Social Science Quarterly,* 55 (March, 1975), pp. 853-870.
[63]See, for example, Bureau of Justice Statistics, *Report to the Nation on Crime and Justice,* p. 65; and President's Commission on Law Enforcement and Administration of Justice, *Task Force Report: The Courts* (Washington, D.C.: U.S. Government Printing Office, 1967), p. 9.
[64]Milton Heumann, *Plea Bargaining* (Chicago: University of Chicago Press, 1978), p. 28.
[65]*Ibid.,* pp. 31-35; and Malcolm Feeley, "The Effect of Heavy Case Loads," in Sheldon Goldman and Austin Sarat, eds., *The Legal System* (San Francisco: W. H. Freeman, 1978).

[66]National Institute of Justice, *Alaska Bans Plea Bargaining* (Washington, D.C.: U.S. Government Printing Office, 1980). New Orleans, El Paso, and four counties also have enacted prohibitions against plea bargaining. See Bureau of Justice Statistics, *Report to the Nation on Crime and Justice,* p. 65.
[67]Warren E. Burger, Address on the State of the Federal Judiciary to the American Bar Association, August 10, 1970.
[68]The following examples are drawn from "Stepped Up Drive to Make Punishment Fit Crime," *U.S. News & World Report* (September 5, 1977), p. 47.
[69]Justice Department study as cited in Ronald J. Ostrow, "U.S. Judges' Sentencing Disparity Found Wider Than Believed," *Los Angeles Times* (March 16, 1982).
[70]Martin A. Levin, *Urban Politics and the Criminal Courts* (Chicago: University of Chicago Press, 1977), pp. 92-93.
[71]James Eisenstein and Herbert Jacob, *Felony Justice* (Boston: Little, Brown, 1977), pp. 280, 282-286; and Levin, *Urban Politics,* pp. 93-95.
[72]"Opinion Roundup," *Public Opinion* (August/September, 1982), pp. 26-27. Figures cover the years 1979, 1981, 1982.
[73]Foster, "The States and the Criminal Justice System," p. 525. Figure is for 1980.
[74]*Ibid.* Figure is for 1980.
[75]Joseph Tybor, "New Trend Favors Fixed Prison Sentences over Indeterminate Terms," *The Arizona Republic* (September 26, 1976).
[76]Jacob, *Crime and Justice in Urban America,* p. 91.
[77]Leo, "Why the Justice System Fails," p. 24.
[78]"Opinion Roundup," pp. 24-26. Unless otherwise noted, figures are for 1982.
[79]Leo, "Why the Justice System Fails," pp. 22-24.
[80]John Petersilia, Peter W. Greenwood, and Marvin Lavin, *Criminal Careers of Habitual Felons* (Santa Monica, Calif.: Rand Corporation, 1977), pp. 13-19.
[81]Bureau of the Census, *Statistical Abstract of the United States, 1985,* Table 312, p. 182, and Table 318, p. 183. Figures are for 1983.
[82]*Ibid.,* Table 314, p. 183. Figures are for 1979.
[83]Foster, "The States and the Criminal Justice System," p. 524.
[84]"Why American Prisons Are Powder Kegs," *U.S. News & World Report* (February 18, 1980), p. 68.
[85]Edward D. Feigenbaum, "Corrections, Courts and Criminal Justice," *Book of the States, 1984-85* (Lexington, Ky.: Council of State Governments, 1984), p. 415. Figure is for 1983.
[86]The annual cost of maintaining an inmate in a federal, maximum security facility handily exceeds $20,000. In the states, correctional costs per inmate vary widely. In Arkansas, for example, annual costs per inmate in 1983 were less than $8,000; in Alaska, the figure was more than $36,000. See "Breaking Up Government's Monopoly in Prison Cells," *The New York Times* (March 3, 1985).
[87]Bureau of Justice Statistics, *Report to the Nation on Crime and Justice,* p. 100.
[88]*Ibid.,* p. 84.
[89]Congressional Quarterly, *Crime and the Law* (Washington, D.C.: Congressional Quarterly, Inc., 1971), p. 11.
[90]Bureau of Justice Statistics, *Report the the Nation on Crime and Justice,* pp. 74-76.
[91]Frank K. Gibson et al., "A Path Analytic Treatment of Corrections Output," *Social Science Quarterly,* 54 (September, 1973), p. 291.
[92]Quoted in Congressional Quarterly, *Crime and the Law,* p. 11.
[93]Burger, Address on the State of the Federal Judiciary.
[94]"Opinion Roundup," p. 24. Figure is for 1982.
[95]Maynard L. Erikson and Jack P. Gibbs, "The Deterrence Question," *Social Science Quarterly,* 54 (December, 1973), pp. 534-551.
[96]As of 1983. See Bureau of the Census, *Statistical Abstract of the United States, 1985,* Table 321, p. 186.
[97]Zodiac News Service, as published in *New Times Weekly* (April 26, 1978).
[98]Gilbert Geis and Herbert Sigurdson, "State Aid to Victims of Violent Crimes," *State Government,* 50 (Winter, 1977), pp. 16-20; Herbert Edelhertz and Gilbert Geis, *Public Compensation to Victims of Crime* (New York: Praeger, 1974); and Barbra McClure, *Crime Compensation for Victims,* Issue Brief IB 74014 (Washington, D.C.: Congressional Research Service, Library of Congress, 1977).

17

THE EDUCATION ESTABLISHMENT

Education is the primary activity of one out of every four Americans. Most of this activity occurs in institutions supported by state and local governments. There are more than 36 million students and some 2.4 million teachers in nearly 86,000 elementary and secondary public schools, and almost 10 million students and close to 640,000 teachers in some 1,500 publicly supported universities, colleges, and technical schools. American taxpayers spend more than $115 billion for their elementary and secondary schools, and more than $26 billion for higher education, or more than 7 percent of the gross national product.[1]

Americans believe in education.

WASHINGTON AND SCHOOLS: THE ROLE OF FISCAL FEDERALISM

Americans also believe that education is the business of the grassroots governments. But, increasingly, education is an intergovernmental matter, and the federal government has become involved in local school districts. Most federal assistance to local school districts is channeled through the Smith-Hughes Vocational Education Act of 1917, which is still providing federal grants and assistance for training in the trades; the National School Lunch and Milk Programs, initiated in 1946; the Federally Impacted Areas Aid Program, inaugurated in 1950, which assists areas in which federal property that is exempt from local taxes creates a financial crunch for the school district; the National Defense Education Act of 1958 (later amended in 1963), which is designed to improve curricula in a number of specific fields, but particularly in the sciences; the

Elementary and Secondary Education Act (ESEA) of 1964, which is designed primarily for schools in poverty areas and to help indigent children; and the Education for All Handicapped Children Act of 1975 (PL 94-142), which is designed to assist schools in educating handicapped children. The Elementary and Secondary Education Act and the Education of All Handicapped Children Act are the two largest federal programs for local schools.

Federal involvement in local schools began earlier than most people realize. Beginning in 1870 federal interest in schools was largely a function of economic necessity and citizen illiteracy. After this century's midpoint, however, new political values came into play, and most notable among these was the concept of equity. The federal government began funding local programs for school construction, redistributing national resources for the benefit of children in all parts of the country, and providing for more research and innovation in education.

The efficacy of federal involvement in local schools, particularly in those schools located in the inner cities where some of the nation's major educational problems are festering, is open to debate. Approximately 10 percent of the public school population attends school in these facilities, but, as a national news magazine has pointed out, "the education these children receive amounts to a national scandal."[2] A Rand Corporation study, which analyzed 11 New York ghetto schools that had received approximately $40 million in federal assistance during a four-year period, concluded that there had been "no improvement at all in the low academic levels and high truancy rates that the federal money was supposed to fight."[3]

On the other hand, schools in small rural districts do not have the problems of the big city schools, and not only are less dependent on federal aid but on occasion do not want it. Consider the example of the one-room schoolhouse with 11 students in the Walnut Grove elementary district of Yavapai County, Arizona. Federal civil rights officials threatened to cut off Walnut Grove's federal aid because the district had failed to complete required paperwork showing compliance with sex discrimination guidelines, an error that evidently was an oversight on the part of school officials. Washington administrators snarled that they would turn off Walnut Grove's federal assistance, but lost interest when school officials showed civil rights officers that federal aid had contributed a total of $16.57 to Walnut Grove's school budget during the preceding year.[4]

The states' relations with the federal government are on a somewhat different order when it comes to education. Although some observers have contended that federal aid to education has resulted in a "federal takeover" of the state's role in education, empirical studies indicate that such an outcome does not necessarily have to happen—and, in fact, rarely does.[5] A study of eight representative states' use of federal funds under ESEA and the Education for All Handicapped Children Act concluded that, with the exception of those states that had very underdeveloped state education agencies, "most states can be independent actors if they choose. There is no question that the federal government, through regulation and its grant-in-aid programs, forces the states to serve children that might not have been served otherwise [and] in this sense, then, the autonomy of all states has been compromised. But within this basic constraint, states can choose to subordinate federal to state goals or to keep federal programs from encroaching on the state's primary responsibility, general education. Junior partner status is by no means inevitable for most states."[6]

In 1981, Congress made the states even more autonomous from potential federal controls of education by enacting the Omnibus Budget Reconciliation Act, which cut federal expenditures for education, ceded to state and local governments as much authority as possible, and deregulated educational policymaking and management. The 37 federal categorical grants dealing with education (28 of which went directly to local governments or local nonprofit agencies) were absorbed into a single block grant program that went only to the states. However, the major elements of the two principal pieces of federal legislation for local schools, the Elementary and Secondary Education Act and the Education for All Handicapped Children Act, were retained, and were largely unaffected by the new block grant program for education.

THE STATES AND SCHOOLS: CENTRALIZING EDUCATIONAL FINANCE

It is worth keeping in perspective that federal grants to local school districts have never comprised a significant share of school budgets; the federal government provides about 9 percent of public elementary and secondary school revenues. The states furnish approximately 47 percent, and the local school districts contribute 43 percent. Both the state and federal governments have taken up much of the financial burden of education that traditionally has been borne by localities. However, it appears that the ensuing years will witness a decline in the federal share (which is relatively nominal in any case) and that the states will be primarily responsible for taking up the resultant slack.

These fiscal relationships were not always the case. In 1900, states contributed only 17 percent to the budgets of the local schools and the remaining funding was provided exclusively by the local school districts. It was only in 1973 that, for the first time, the average local contribution to education budgets dipped below 50 percent because of steadily growing contributions from both the state and federal sectors.[7]

Just as the states vary widely in terms of how much they support education relative to their localities, states and their local governments display considerable disparities in terms of how much they support public education overall. Figure 17-1 ranks the states by per pupil expenditures. The national average of total per pupil expenditures is more than $2,700, but these expenditures range from about $1,700 per pupil to nearly $6,500. Generally, Northeastern and Rocky Mountain states support their schools the most generously, and Southern states the most parsimoniously.[8]

A number of legislatures (notably, in California, Colorado, Florida, Kansas, Maine, Minnesota, Michigan, and Utah) have adopted measures that, in effect, guarantee each school district in their states a minimum level of per pupil expenditures. Some states have gone farther; Maine, Montana, Utah, and Wisconsin, for example, have enacted measures that use "excess" revenue generated in the very wealthy districts to finance the poor school districts. These policies, known as "recapture provisions," are not politically popular, but they are being adopted by increasing numbers of states in a grassroots effort to equalize school finance.

The reformist efforts by some states to equalize school revenues among wealthier and poorer school districts were instigated by California in the case of

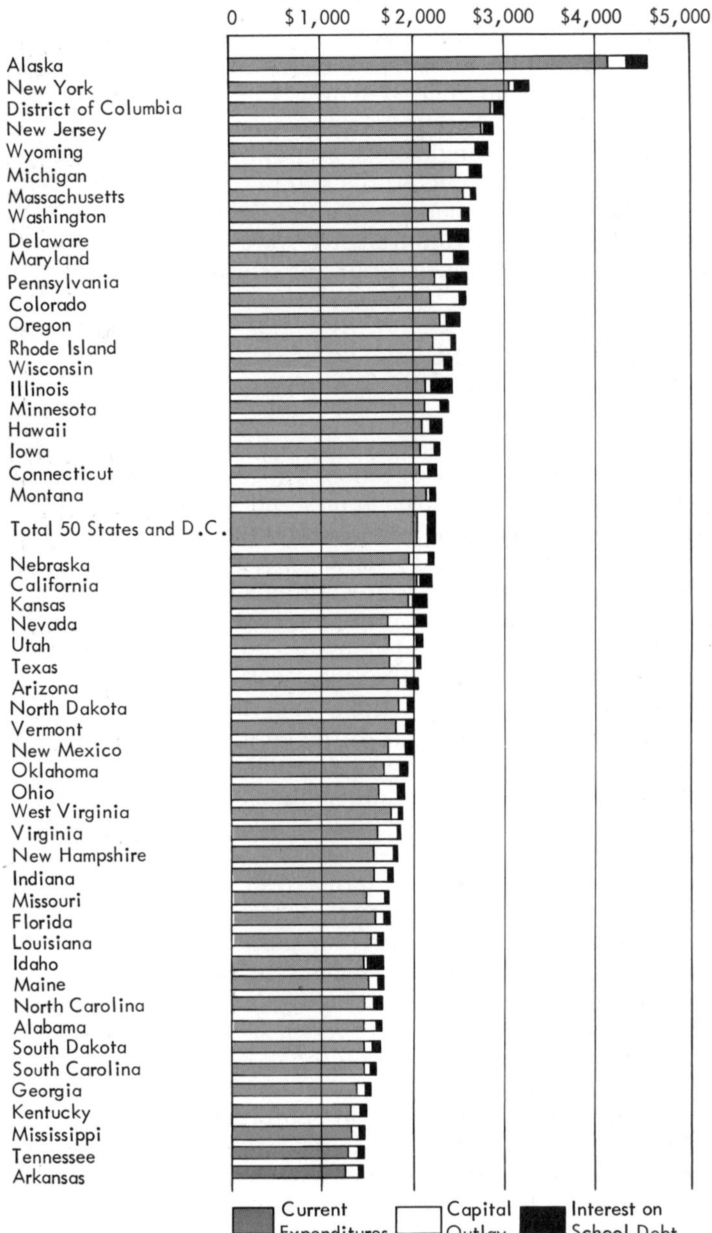

Figure 17-1. Public elementary/secondary school expenditures per student by function. (*Source:* Nancy B. Dearman and Valena White Plesko. *The Condition of Education, 1981,* Washington, D.C.: U.S. Government Printing Office, National Center for Educational Statistics, 1981, p. 103.)

Serrano v. *Priest,* mentioned in Chapter 7. In 1971, the Baldwin Park School District in Los Angeles argued before the California Supreme Court that, because it was a poor district, its students were deprived of their right to an education comparable to that of wealthier districts, even though Baldwin Park's taxpayers tried harder.

Baldwin Park's case hinged on the fact that the property tax is a cornerstone of school finance. Although the states are now the chief financiers of local schools, the 43 percent of school budgets that is raised and provided by local school districts is drawn almost entirely from a single source: the local property tax. Thus (at least until 1971, when Baldwin Park filed its suit), how much a school district's taxable property is worth is critical in determining how much a district is able to spend on its pupils' educations: the higher the property value, the more dollars that the school district can get from the property tax.

This dilemma was particularly vivid in the case of Baldwin Park, which borders another California community called Beverly Hills. The Beverly Hills School District had a per pupil property value that was nearly 14 times greater than that of Baldwin Park's when Baldwin Park brought suit. Thus, even if Baldwin Park set its property tax at a rate more than twice that of Beverly Hills, it would still be spending less than half of what Beverly Hills spent on each pupil. In an unprecedented decision, the California Supreme Court agreed with Baldwin Park's argument, holding that unequal distribution of property tax revenues violated the state's constitution, and state-imposed equalization measures among school districts were soon implemented.

The problem of school finance was brought before the nation in 1973, when the U.S. Supreme Court heard *Rodriguez* v. *San Antonio School District.* The Court, however, neither agreed nor disagreed with the precedent that had been set in California's *Serrano* case. Instead, it ruled that such determinations were matters that should be resolved by each state. At least 20 states soon began initiating significant reforms of their school finance systems.

Among the more intriguing aspects of the school finance reform movement is the favorable impact that it seems to have had on state levels of education expenditures. In the 15 states that enacted the most far-reaching reforms, spending for schools more than doubled, and increased dramatically as a percentage of total state and local expenditures. Overall, state expenditure growth enabled total education expenditures to increase by more than 40 percent faster than inflation, despite large decreases in pupil enrollments.[9] On the other hand, some states have gone in precisely the other direction. Florida, Kansas, Maine, and New Mexico, for example, have set maximum school state tax rates, which, in effect, place limits on total school expenditures. Other states have limited educational expenditures to a fixed percentage of their revenue, but scale limits to the relative wealth of the local school district. This policy protects the state treasury, but still permits poor school districts to catch up with the higher spending areas.[10]

The state reforms in educational finance are significant, and they can be attributed to politically courageous legislators. In the face of voter hostility to the reform of educational finance—statewide referenda on finance reform measures consistently were voted down in the 1970s—legislators in many states nonetheless did what they thought (and what most informed observers think) was right and fair and, in the process, brought more opportunities to be educated better to more people.[11]

THE STATES AND SCHOOLS: CENTRALIZING EDUCATIONAL POLICY

Just as the states are gradually centralizing the financing of the local schools, state centralization of education policymaking is occurring as well. Two-thirds of the states constrain the policymaking autonomy of local school boards in major ways. Table 17-1 ranks the states according to their degree of school centralization. Hawaii, with the highest score on the centralization index (6.00), has no local school districts at all; all education in Hawaii is conducted through the state. At the other end of the scale is Wyoming (with a score of 1.86), which has never become involved in its rural school districts. The average score, according to the study, is 3.56. By and large, states in the Northeast tend to favor a high level of local autonomy, while states in the Deep South have tended to concentrate educational policymaking in their state governments.

There are three primary elements of educational governance at the state level: state boards of education, chief state school officers, and departments of education. If this sounds confusing, it is; although the role of the state as a policymaker for local schools is growing, largely as a function of its expanding fiscal responsibility for elementary and secondary education, statewide policymaking for schooling is not tidy, and often it is not very authoritative, either. One study found that the legislatures have not delegated clear responsi-

Table 17-1 School Centralization Scores and Ranks by States, 1972

State	*Score*	*Rank*	*State*	*Score*	*Rank*
Alabama	4.67	3	Montana	3.47	29
Alaska	3.38	31	Nebraska	3.81	16
Arizona	2.91	41	Nevada	2.84	46
Arkansas	3.57	26	New Hampshire	3.13	40
California	3.65	22	New Jersey	3.87	14
Colorado	3.79	19	New Mexico	3.79	19
Connecticut	2.68	49	New York	3.63	24
Delaware	3.15	39	North Carolina	3.80	27
Florida	4.19	7	North Dakota	2.89	44
Georgia	3.24	35	Ohio	3.65	22
Hawaii	6.00	1	Oklahoma	4.91	2
Idaho	3.26	34	Oregon	4.30	6
Illinois	3.32	33	Pennsylvania	3.75	21
Indiana	3.90	11	Rhode Island	3.21	36
Iowa	3.80	17	South Carolina	4.61	4
Kansas	3.38	31	South Dakota	3.08	42
Kentucky	3.90	11	Tennessee	3.48	28
Louisiana	3.19	37	Texas	2.88	45
Maine	3.09	41	Utah	3.42	30
Maryland	3.56	27	Vermont	3.17	38
Massachusetts	2.73	48	Virginia	3.88	13
Michigan	3.85	15	Washington	4.37	5
Minnesota	4.10	8	West Virginia	3.94	9
Mississippi	3.93	10	Wisconsin	3.62	25
Missouri	2.84	46	Wyoming	1.86	50

Source: Michael W. Kirst, "The States' Role in Education Policy Innovation," *Policy Studies Review* (November, 1981), p. 300.

bility for 40 percent of 148 potentially important educational functions to any board, officer, or department; a quarter of these 148 potentially important functions had been assigned by the legislatures to the state boards, 13 percent to the chief state school officers, and 22 percent to the state departments of education.[12]

State Boards of Education

The nominal state policymakers for education are the state boards of education; 34 states had them before 1900 (typically they amounted to little more than committees of various state officials), and today all the states except Wisconsin do.[13]

The members of state boards of education are elected directly by the people in 13 states (7 of which hold partisan elections), and are elected by representatives of the people in 3 states; in 34 states, the governor appoints all the board's members (in 15 of these states) or a majority of them. In 23 states, boards of education have ex officio members, such as the state superintendent of education. The typical size of a state board of education is nine members.

What do these boards do? In 43 states they serve as policymakers for vocational education, and in 18 as the board of vocational rehabilitation. In 42 states they supervise adult education; in 32 they make policy for educational television; in 25 they approve all textbook adoptions; in 10 they supervise libraries, and in 3 they are in charge of museums. In 45 states, the state boards of education have the authority to issue administrative regulations that have the force of law, and most boards hear grievances about school procedures and their own regulations. State boards of education seldom have any jurisdiction over higher education, although in 14 states they approve teacher training programs in the universities.

Although these responsibilities may appear to be significant, state boards of education are usually hemmed in by the state legislatures, and there often are severe problems of jurisdictional ambiguities and murky lines of administrative authority. These problems include such debilitating arrangements in many states as boards that have more than one executive officer, boards that are given several (and sometimes conflicting) responsibilities, and the appointment of separate boards of education for several specialized (but inevitably overlapping) areas of education.

Chief State School Officers

All states have chief state school officers, although they never use that title; commissioner of education, superintendent of schools, and superintendent of public instruction are the more common monikers. In most states they serve as the head of the state department of education, the chief administrative officer of the state board of education (in these instances he or she reports to the board), and the state's chief administrative officer for education; these roles vary from state to state.[14] In many states, the legislature has authorized the chief state school officer to recommend new policies to the state board of education, propose to the board the annual budget of the state department of education, and manage the personnel system of the department of education. The chief state school officer has never been a particularly prestigious office (although its stature is growing according to some observers), and it is often unclear just what, precisely, the chief state school officer does in some states. Frequently, these individuals serve as a clerk to the state board, which, as we noted, often is itself tightly constrained and splintered in its authority.

Eighteen states choose chief state school officers by popular election (13 of these use partisan elections); state education boards in 27 states select the chief state school officer (a method that is gaining in use—only 3 states did so in 1896); and governors appoint them in 5 states. Minnesota uses a unique appointment process in which the state board of education appoints the chief state school officer jointly with the governor. In most states the chief state school officer serves a four-year term, and in 15 states he or she serves as an ex officio member of the state board of education.

State Departments of Education

Our third leg of the state stool of educational policymaking and administration is the state department of education, found in all the states.[15] If the state board of education is the nominal policymaker for elementary and secondary education, and the chief state school officer its administrator, then the state department of education is its bureaucracy.

Like most bureaucracies, it grew. At the turn of the century, the entire department of education in many states was comprised of one professional employee: the chief state school officer. Today, the average number of professionals in a state department of education is 273.

As the business of education became more complex, departments of education moved from being collectors of statistical data, to becoming school regulators and setters of educational standards, to their present phase of evolving into statewide educational planners and upgraders of educational effectiveness. The departments disburse state funds to the schools; administer federal educational grants; train school administrators; provide a wide variety of materials to school districts, ranging from curricular guides to planning assistance; and establish and enforce educational standards, such as school building codes, accreditation requirements, the length of the school year, and minimum competency and certification standards for teachers.

The federal government, particularly through the Elementary and Secondary Education Act of 1964, has encouraged state departments of education to become more active in the affairs of local schools. ESEA "has, contrary to some popular assumptions, markedly strengthened the role and influence of state education departments" by forcing school districts to turn to state agencies for approval of their proposals and for assistance in meeting their problems, and local school districts have been forced to expand their involvement with other local groups as well.[16]

Although the official state policymaking bodies for education are the state boards of education, they are beset by jurisdictional, political, and managerial problems, and it appears that the state departments of education—headed, usually but not always, by chief state school officers—will evolve into the locus of state educational policymaking in many states. The state departments of education are the liaison between the legislature and the local school districts, and their influence over the local schools likely will wax as legislatures continue to increase their interest in educational affairs.

WHO RUNS THE SCHOOLS? THE ROLE OF THE LOCAL SCHOOL BOARDS

Despite increasing state involvement in education, running the schools still remains largely a local operation. Who runs the schools?

Throughout the country, the fate of local schools is determined by the nation's nearly 15,000 school boards, and school boards have a political process that is uniquely their own. Mark Twain once described fools as God's practice before he created school boards, and perhaps the Lord's wisdom accounts for the oddities of school board politics.[17]

School boards are an ancient and venerable tradition in this country. They originated with the Massachusetts school ordinance of 1647, which instructed every town to choose men to manage the "prudential affairs" of the schools,[18] but perhaps a more legitimate beginning was the law passed by the Massachusetts legislature in 1789, which amounted to the first comprehensive system of public schools in any American state.[19]

By the turn of the century, school boards had become dominated by the political machines of big cities, and schools were used by local party bosses as patronage pools for their loyalists. Teaching positions went to those who were proven party hacks, not to proven, or even trained, teachers; large-scale textbook adoptions by schools often seemed to associate with a handsome donation from the publisher to the local party in power, and similar relationships were evident among building contractors in the cities. Thus, school reformers, who typically were the professional and cultural elites of their communities, launched drives to wrest control of school policymaking and management from city halls. The reformers worked for the establishment of school districts that stood as independent governments in their own right; usually they achieved this by taking referenda and initiatives directly to the people, but occasionally local elites quietly slipped school reform measures through their state legislatures, thereby avoiding popular votes. By the end of the 1920s, the reformers had succeeded, and middle-class WASPs had effectively displaced the representatives of ethnic-based political machines on school boards.[20]

Today, school boards generally are comprised of members who are elected at large in nonpartisan elections by residents of school districts. School districts are created by the states or by municipal governments. School boards are empowered to make school policy, hire and fire school administrators, issue bonds, and impose taxes on district taxpayers to support their schools.

Local school boards remain the core policymaking institution in public education. But, as we have noted, their autonomy has become increasingly constrained. The federal government, particularly in the 1960s, has challenged the powers of local school boards, most notably in the areas of race and busing. The state governments, beginning in the 1970s, have imposed new standards on both teachers and students, and are gradually becoming central planning agencies for statewide education; these developments have come at the expense of the independence of local school boards. And, as we discuss later, education professionals, especially school superintendents and teachers, have grown to be dominant figures in the determination of local education policy, and this has also reduced the power of the school boards.

The Consolidation Movement

Because schooling consumes roughly half of the local tax dollar (a fact not lost on many taxpayers), educational policymakers have attempted to reduce costs where feasible. Certainly the major method that educators have used to cut school costs has been to reduce drastically the number of school districts across the nation. While the number of schools has been slashed, a centralization and enlarging of the neighborhood schools also has occurred. There are 14,851 independent school districts. Such a number may seem like a lot, but consider that some 35 years earlier, there were more than 108,000 local public school systems, and even in 1962 there were approximately 38,000.[21]

The rationale behind this reduction and centralization in school districts has been that of economy. Although the costs of education have certainly not declined with the number of school districts, it has been argued that the costs would be considerably higher if such consolidation had not occurred during the past generation.

Still, the theory that consolidation saves money has been questioned. A study sponsored by the National Institute of Education found that the big, new regional schools cost as much or more to run as the old, decentralized rural school ever did. In 1930 there were 149,000 single-teacher elementary schools in the country; by 1972 there were only 1,475 such schools. During that period, more than 70 percent of all elementary schools were abolished, and the number of four-year high schools was cut in half; at the same time student enrollments in junior high schools and high schools actually tripled. Although there were some savings from improved administrative efficiency, other cost increases may have offset these savings. Most significant were the higher transportation costs of busing students to centrally located regional schools and the increased demand for more specialized teaching skills, which bring with them increased salaries for the teachers. Finally, there was no evidence that consolidation had in any way improved the quality of education.[22]

School Board Politics: A Very Private Affair

School boards, which account for approximately one-sixth of all units of American government, are perhaps the least known and the least understood of any governmental type in America. A Gallup poll found that the general public was largely ignorant of the functions of school boards and school board members.[23] This is not surprising in light of the fact that school boards are perhaps the most politically incestuous of any American institution. About 15 percent of all school boards are appointed rather than elected, and even on those school boards where members are elected by the public, 25 percent of the members had gained membership to the board as appointees to replace board members who had left with unexpired terms.[24]

As with most of the institutions of local government, incumbents rarely are defeated; two-thirds of the board members who leave office do so voluntarily and, adding to this overall appearance of political incest is the fact that board members have a lot of relatives in education; three-fifths have at least one. More than half of the board members have one or both parents or a spouse in education. While the great majority (88 percent) mention relatives who are teachers, 14 percent had relatives who were board members and 10 percent had school administrators among their kin . . . 21 percent have held jobs in education . . ., it is apparent that the occupational involvement of board members in education far exceeds the involvement of the general public.[25]

In short, it should not be surprising that the relationship between teachers and school board members is a particularly cozy one characterized by low profile, a situation that has facilitated a lack of voter concern over school policy; only about one-third of a district's voters turn out for school board elections.

As a result of these conditions, school board members make school policy within an unobserved and isolated political environment. Ironically, however, school boards generally do not govern but merely legitimate the policy recommendations of the professional educational staffs, and this holds true in the most political urban environments. Even in New York City, where interest group politics is extremely pervasive in city government, far-reaching educational decisions nonetheless are made within relatively autonomous professional school staffs.[26]

If a single person typically dominates decisions made about schools in this country, it is the local school superintendent. "School governance has never completely fallen under the sway of the superintendent's office, but there is no question that the first half of the twentieth century saw enormous gains of power for the office."[27] Indeed, in comparison to city managers in council-manager governments, superintendents seem to exercise relatively more power over their boards than do managers over their councils.[28]

Conversely, it should not be surprising that school board members are not particularly responsive to the demands of citizen groups, and most board members candidly admit to qualifying their wholehearted acceptance of requests brought by community groups concerning school board decisions. Oddly, appointed boards, in contrast to elected boards, tend to "overcompensate in their responsive behavior in the absence of being officially 'the people's choice'," and appointed boards actually seem to be more responsive to community requests than do elected ones.[29]

Even so, all this must be cast in relative terms. Americans simply do not display much interest in school politics (other than property tax hikes related to school bond issues), and, while there are some notable exceptions, education politics tend to be a genteel form of good government—and a professionally inbred affair.

RACE AND SCHOOLS

Inbred or otherwise, genteel or not, few battlegrounds in American politics have been as bloodied during the past three decades as have the public schools in their confrontation with the gut issue of race and equality of opportunity.

In terms of providing an equal education to all children, irrespective of their race, most state and local governments have a dreary record. As late as 1954, 17 states mandated the racial segregation of public schools. All were in the Old Confederacy, but there also were some surprising examples (given today's outlook), such as Delaware, Maryland, Missouri, Oklahoma, and West Virginia. Congress required racial segregation of the schools in Washington, D.C., and four additional states—Arizona, Kansas, New Mexico, and Wyoming—permitted local school boards to segregate or not segregate as they saw fit.

The Life and Times of Jim Crow

Racial segregation in the Deep South, of course, went far beyond the schools as a public policy. Blacks and whites, as a matter of law, were not permitted to use each other's elevators, drinking fountains, restaurants, waiting rooms, libraries, restrooms, and even some stores; Southern public policy at midcentury had created a society very similar to what Americans now decry in South Africa. The U.S. Supreme Court had tried to alleviate this situation as far back as 1896 in the case of *Plessy* v. *Ferguson,* in which the Court stated that separating the races as such was not necessarily discrimination, provided that equal accommodations were furnished for all. This rationale became known as the famous "separate-but-equal" doctrine, and soon was used as an excuse for implementing racial segregation policies throughout the nation.

Unfortunately, and as everyone knows, blacks and whites were given separate but not equal facilities. In 1950, for example, in the 17 segregated states, there were 14 medical schools for whites, but not one such school for blacks; there were 16 law schools for whites and only 5 for blacks; there were 15 engineering schools for whites, but there were no engineering schools for blacks; there were 5 schools of dentistry for whites and none for blacks.[30]

In 1954, the Supreme Court committed a very rare act and reversed a previous decision. In the case of *Brown* v. *Board of Education, Topeka, Kansas,* the Court reversed its 1896 *Plessy* ruling as it applied to public schools and stated that segregation *in and of itself* constituted discrimination. A year later, the Court ordered local school boards to move with "all deliberate speed" to integrate public schools.

The Principles of School Desegregation

The Court's decision in 1954, along with the gradual dawning that the federal government intended to enforce that decision, caused bitterness among Southern whites, hope for the nation's blacks, and violence between whites and blacks throughout the South in the years that followed. During those years, the Supreme Court heard a plethora of cases on school desegregation and, in the process, developed the following five basic principles.[31]

1. School segregation is unconstitutional if it results from intentional actions of state and local governments. This principle prevents schools from being constructed on sites that effectively exclude by their locations one race or the other from being taught in them.
2. Busing is an acceptable and, on occasion, necessary solution for attaining desegregated schools. (We shall return later to this point.)
3. Desegregation may not normally be required across jurisdictional boundaries (for example, between cities and their suburbs), but busing can be ordered across jurisdictional lines in special cases—if, for instance, city limits appeared to further segregation by design.

4. Entire school districts must be desegregated if proof can be found of intentional segregation in just a part of the district.
5. Once a school district is desegregated, school officials do not need to take any additional action, even if the schools become resegregated because of changes in housing patterns.

While the judiciary struggled with the desegregation of the public schools, the people's interest in the issue faded. The public's concern with school desegregation has been in decline since 1971 when 21 percent of Americans believed such issues as desegregation and busing to be the major problems confronting the public schools. Today, the number of Americans who feel that desegregation and busing are the major problems confronting the schools has declined to only 10 percent.[32]

Yankee Racism

What have been the results of desegregating the public schools? Minority students represent 27 percent of the total public school enrollment (up from 21 percent in 1970), and, if all minority students were in a desegregated school, then 27 percent of each school's enrollments would be minority students, and all schools in the country would be predominantly white in their enrollments. Nationally, however, such an approximation has yet to be attained. Most minority students are concentrated in schools in which they represent the majority enrollments in those schools. In fact, about 60 percent of minority students across the nation are registered in schools where minorities comprise more than half of the enrollments. Although this situation appears to be improving over time, the figures are not encouraging. Two-thirds of minority students attend classes where minorities make up at least 45 percent of the class roster. One-third attend classes where minorities comprise at least 90 percent of classroom enrollment.[33]

There are, of course, regional variations in school desegregation patterns, and in some of these, the differences are surprising. Despite racial riots and an occasional need to send in federal troops to desegregate the schools, the South has achieved a truly admirable record of integrating the races in their schools. Although much remains to be done, it is a genuine feat of democracy that Southern school desegregation has outstripped that of the North. In 1964, only 8 percent of black pupils in the South attended integrated schools. Only ten years later, however, more than 92 percent of black pupils were attending desegregated schools.

Perhaps the most accurate way of portraying the regional progress of school desegregation is to focus on the racial composition of schools in terms of whether or not they are predominantly white in their enrollments (i.e., minorities comprise up to 50 percent of enrollments) or racially isolated (minorities make up 99 to 100 percent of enrollments). Using these measures, we can trace patterns of segregation or desegregation by region. In the South, for example, 35 percent of the total school enrollment are minority enrollments. Yet 39 percent of Southern schools are predominantly white, and only 14 percent are racially isolated, indicating a relatively high distribution of minorities throughout the Southern school systems. By contrast, 21 percent of the total enrollments in the Northeast are minorities, but 24 percent of these schools are predominantly white, and 27 percent are racially isolated. Similarly, 15 percent of school enrollments in the Midwest are minority enrollments, but 34 percent of these schools are predominantly white, and 28 percent are racially isolated.[34]

Although no region of the country has as many as half of its minority students enrolled in integrated schools, it is clear that the South is among the leaders in terms of school desegregation. Figure 17-2 illustrates these regional variations. The most fully integrated schools are found in the West and in the Border states, and the least integrated are in the Northeast.

The Busing Bungle

In light of the discouraging indications that racial segregation in some quarters of the country may actually be increasing rather than decreasing, how is the nation to assure equality of education between the races? The tentative answer thus far has been: Bus them.

Few political issues have been as controversial as the busing issue. Busing began when a sociologist from the University of Chicago, James S. Coleman (whom *Time* magazine has called a "sort of godfather to busing"),[35] issued a major study that found that black students attending predominantly black schools had lower achievement scores and lower levels of ambition than did blacks from similar social and economic backgrounds who attended predominantly white schools. Indeed, comparisons indicated that the differences in achievement amounted to more than two grade levels.[36] Although Coleman has since questioned his own research, this finding appalled many people in government and angered blacks.

In 1971, the U.S. Supreme Court heard the now famous case of *Swann* v. *Charlotte-Mecklenberg Board of Education,* in which the Court stated that Southern school districts must eliminate all vestiges of dual school systems and that such a responsibility could require the busing of students to and from various schools that were located away from their neighborhoods in an effort to desegregate schools that were segregated because of residential patterns. In 1974 the Supreme Court modified its *Swann* decision and ruled in the case of *Milligan* v. *Bradley* that the Fourteenth Amendment did not require busing across city and suburban school district boundaries to achieve integration. The reasoning underlying this decision was that it was more difficult to prove that Northern governments had purposely established segregated school systems than it was to prove that Southern governments had. While the effect of this decision has been to help keep whites in the suburbs and blacks in the central cities, it did not preclude the Court-ordered desegregation of white and black school districts that are located *within* the same city. Because such intracity desegregation attempts were not precluded, in 1974 and 1975 Judge W. Arthur Garrity, Jr., was able to issue his famous orders in Boston calling for widespread busing, which subsequently caused widespread rioting by Irish-Americans—"the Southies"—in South Boston.

Traditionally, the federal government has been able to keep the pressure on urban governments to desegregate their school systems through busing with the threat of withholding federal funds, but in 1977 Congress removed the executive branch's authority to withhold federal funds from school districts that refused to desegregate by employing busing. This decision, in effect, threw the issue back to the courts, which now must rule on busing plans on a case-by-case basis.

Figure 17-2. Minority enrollment as percent of public elementary/secondary school enrollment, by state, 1980. (*Source:* National Center for Educational Statistics, *The Condition of Education, 1984.* Washington, D.C.: U.S. Government Printing Office, 1984, p. 19.)

Desegregating schools and using a bus to do so has disrupted communities across the country. Has it been worth the effort? The answer is unquestionably, yes! School desegregation does work, according to the U.S. Commission on Civil Rights, but it works best in those cities where community support is the highest.[37] Despite violence in Boston, Chicago, Little Rock, Birmingham, New Orleans, Louisville, Prince George's County, and other places where it has occurred over the years since *Brown* v. *Topeka Board of Education,* state and local governments have achieved one of the world's great accomplishments in the desegregation of their schools. While much remains to be done, particularly in the Snowbelt states, few other nations have been able to give minority kids an equal educational chance—or even to admit they have a problem. Busing may not be the best way of achieving desegregation; integrating neighborhoods would be. But the Supreme Court has not put its prestige behind that option, and the fact remains that state and local governments have made a major effort—and have achieved a fair degree of success—in bringing black, brown, and white children together in the same educational system. The progress made toward desegregating schools has been a major national accomplishment, and, although school desegregation has been mandated by the federal courts, it has been accomplished by state and local governments.

SCHOOLS IN CRISIS

If desegregation and such controversial programs as school busing were not enough to keep school officials and teachers sufficiently harried, then there is a plenitude of other issues that will challenge the public schools well into the 1990s. Among these issues are the continuing rise in educational costs and a corresponding decline in student enrollments; school violence and vandalism, particularly in the inner city schools; evidence that schools are not teaching their students effectively; a decline in public confidence in the nation's school systems; and increasing pressures on school teachers to upgrade their own abilities.

The Double Irony of Educational Finance

Ironically, the costs of schooling have been increasing while fewer students are being schooled. On the one hand, costs continue to go up. It is expected that public expenditures for education will increase by about 3 percent a year for the foreseeable future, even after inflation is discounted.[38] On the other hand, enrollments in public elementary and secondary schools peaked at 46 million in 1971, and have gone into decline since then.[39] Declining enrollments are a relatively new, and unpleasant, phenomenon to educators. Between 1960 and 1969, public school enrollments rose by nearly 23 percent. But from 1970 to 1982, enrollments fell by nearly 14 percent.[40]

The Three Vs: Violence, Vandalism, and Venality

In the face of increasing costs and declining enrollments, schools are also beset by an upswing in violence. A survey of 757 school districts found that violence and vandalism cost the American school as much as it spent on textbooks each year. More than 5,000 teachers and nearly 300,000 students are attacked each month, and more than a fourth of all school buildings are vandalized in any given month. School vandalism costs the American taxpayer an estimated $600 million a year.[41]

The American people are getting increasingly fed up. In fact, polls conducted every year since 1969 have found that the public believes a lack of discipline in the schools to be the number one problem with which schools must contend. Typically, from a fifth to a fourth of the public believes that an absence of discipline is the major problem confronting the schools.[42]

Do Kids Learn?

Another pressure on the schools is the growing public opinion that the educational products being turned out by the schools is increasingly inferior. The number of Americans who believe that schools have a poor curriculum has been increasing, with occasional variations, since 1969. In that year, only 4 percent of the people believed that a poor curriculum was the major problem with which public schools must deal. Today, however, this percentage has increased to 11 percent.[43] Another poll found that 72 percent of the public school parents believed that if the federal government were to focus its resources more heavily on public schools, it should give special attention to basic education, such as reading, writing, and arithmetic. This was the highest response, by far, to any of the possibilities offered in the poll. Sixty-eight percent of adults with no children in school (again the highest single response) also believed that basic education was the most important priority.[44]

There appears to be some substance to the public's perceptions. For 18 years (from 1963 to 1981), student scores on the Scholastic Aptitude Test (SAT), which is taken by roughly 1.5 million high school juniors and seniors every year as part of college entrance requirements, plummeted. An investigation conducted by the College Entrance Examination Board found that the decline in scores measured a real decline in skills, not just a stiffening of the test itself. The Board stated that, "Our firmest conclusion is that the critical factors in the relationships between curriculum change and the SAT scores are that less thoughtful and critical reading is now being demanded and done and that careful writing has apparently about gone out of style."[45]

In 1982, for the first time since 1963, students taking the SAT evidenced some improvement.[46] In response to a growing public concern over the ability of schools to teach effectively (along with suits being brought by parents who have discovered that their high school graduates could not read), more than 30 states have enacted "back to basics" policies,[47] and 40 states since 1970 have established "minimum competency testing"—or the establishment of minimum standards for grade promotion and graduation—for students in their school systems.[48] It is clear that legislatures are increasingly concerned about the educational quality in their states' public schools.

Citizens and Schools: A Deepening Disaffection

Given all the problems faced by the schools, it is perhaps little wonder that the public is increasingly critical of them. Surveys conducted since 1974 have found a growing dissatisfaction among parents who have children in the public schools with the quality of the education that their children are receiving.

In 1974, 22 percent of these parents graded their school with an "A" and 42 percent gave their schools a "B." Today, 13 percent rated their schools with an "A" and 33 percent with a "B," and the average grade was about a "C plus."[49]

Americans do not appear to believe that deteriorating educational quality corresponds with a lack of funds. The number of Americans who think that schools do not receive proper financial support has been in decline since 1971. In that year, 23 percent of Americans thought that the major problem confronting the schools was inadequate financial support, but this figure has sunk to only 10 percent.[50]

The public's apparent beliefs that the public schools are not doing a reasonably competent job by young Americans, and that adequate monetary support for education is not a major problem for the schools, is reflected in school budgets. In 1966, 85 percent of the 1,745 public school bonds proposed were approved by voters,[51] and in the preceding five years (1960 through 1965), an average of more than 70 percent of the school bonds proposed to local voters across the country succeeded. But during the next ten years, this percentage dipped precipitously. Between 1965 and 1975, only half of the school bonds offered were approved by the voters, and by 1977, more than half of the public school bond issues proposed were being turned down by the voters.[52]

These figures become particularly ominous when we place them in the perspective of a growing public dissatisfaction with the conduct of the nation's schools. As we have noted, parents with children in the public schools are increasingly dissatisfied with school performance, yet it is precisely this kind of person who is most likely to vote in school finance elections. Not only are these voters the parents of school children, but they are relatively wealthy, relatively well-educated, middle-aged, homeowners and have a high interest in schools. Research has found that the larger the voter turnout, the smaller the percentage of favorable votes cast in school financial elections; in other words, the more democratic participation there is in school finance elections, the more likely it is that children's educations will suffer.[53]

If, unfortunately, school officials wish to see their bond issues approved by voters, then they should try to reduce voter participation in school finance elections as much as possible. This is not a healthy condition for either the public schools or the democratic process.

Pressure on the Public Schools

In light of rising educational costs, falling student enrollments, vandalism, violence, a growing public concern over the quality of education that pupils are receiving, and a growing public rejection of school bond issues, it is little wonder that teachers are feeling the heat. One survey showed that more than a third of all teachers were dissatisfied with their jobs; 41 percent regretted that they had ever become teachers in the first place.[54] American teachers have, on the average, 14 years of experience in teaching, and more than 45 percent have a master's degree.[55] Yet the median salary of the nation's teachers is less than the median income of the typical urban family.[56] The starting salary for teachers is less than the entry salaries of college graduates entering eight out of nine other major professional fields.[57] Under such circumstances, it is perhaps not surprising that morale among the nation's teachers is low.

New public policies may reduce teacher morale even farther. Increas-

ingly, states are initiating competency tests not only for students, but for teachers as well. Twenty-three states mandate that a test be given to applicants for teaching certificates. Ironically, most of these states are in the South, and it is Southerners who tend to give their schools the highest marks in terms of performance.[58] It appears that there is some reason to force some teachers to take such tests. Florida gave a trial competency test in eighth grade math to 1,200 education majors, and found that one-third of them failed it.[59]

TEACHERS REACT: THE COLLECTIVIZATION AND POLITICIZATION OF EDUCATION

In light of these increasing pressures, it is not surprising that teachers have reacted, and their reactions have taken two tacks: collectivization and politicization.

The collectivization of teachers in the form of teachers' unions has been dramatic. Fifty-five percent of all state and local public school employees are organized, and nearly two-thirds of the teachers are in unions.[60]

Because of this heavy unionization, most states have passed mandatory collective bargaining laws that cover elementary and secondary public school personnel. Twenty-eight states require collective bargaining, and 3 additional states have enacted meet-and-confer legislation. Strikes are permitted in 7 states, and 16 states have enacted provisions for the binding arbitration of contract disputes.[61]

Despite the fact that only a few states permit strikes, teachers are particularly prone to go on strike, regardless of legislation permitting it. Educators are responsible for almost 52 percent of all the work stoppages by state and local government employees; they account for 59 percent of all employees who were involved in work stoppages; and they produce 72 percent of the total days of idleness resulting from strikes by state and local public employees.[62]

The increasing level of strike activity by teachers has not helped them in the general community. As one major news magazine noted, "the unions have . . . provided teachers with bigger pay checks but there have been serious trade-offs. A public that once respected teachers for their long-suffering devotion, now regards them as uppity, assembly line workers."[63]

"Hurricane Al" and the AFT

The most widely known teachers' union is the American Federation of Teachers (AFT), a national union affiliated with the AFL-CIO and boasting more than 450,000 members, mostly from the big Northeastern cities. Headed by Albert ("Hurricane Al") Shanker, the AFT has a reputation for being the most militant of the teachers' unions.

There was a good reason, and there still may be, for Shanker's union to be as militant as it has been. Shanker, who taught in New York City until he moved up in union circles, recounts how the city's starting salary for teachers in 1960 was $4,800, although the then mayor, Robert Wagner, consistently pleaded that the city had no money to raise salaries. During that year, a severe snowstorm and a hurricane forced the city to spend additional millions to clear the streets. Shanker queried how the city suddenly acquired the money and was informed that it was available only for disasters. Shanker has since stated, "That was when we decided to become a disaster."[64] It was also in 1960 that Shanker got his nickname of "Hurricane Al."

The Awakening Giant of the NEA

The most powerful teachers' union, but one that does not have a tradition of militancy, is the National Education Association (NEA). The NEA is the country's second largest union after the Teamsters. The NEA currently is engaged in, according to one observer, "a no-holds-barred, jurisdictional war with the AFL-CIO American Federation of Teachers."[65]

The NEA currently has 1.7 million teachers of the nation's total of 2.4 million public school teachers as members. Until recently, the NEA was a genteel—according to some, even a timid—organization. Between 1952 and 1963 the NEA was not involved in a single work stoppage of teachers. Then something happened. By 1966 the NEA was participating in one-third of all the educational work stoppages. The NEA has initiated about 70 percent of teachers' work stoppages and strikes.[66]

Another facet of the NEA's new-found militancy is its growing political clout. In 1972 the NEA first entered the political arena by investing a modest $30,000 in political contributions. By 1974, the NEA's contributions had increased to $250,000, and in 1976, it donated $579,000 to House and Senate candidates, plus an additional $2 million through its state and local affiliates to candidates for Congress and state offices. In 1972 the NEA sent only 36 delegates to the Democratic National Convention, but four years later, with organized labor sending a record 600 delegates, the NEA provided the biggest single block (135) of labor's delegates to the Democratic convention. The NEA endorsed 323 candidates for the U.S. House of Representatives in 1976, of whom 272 won. It endorsed 26 candidates for the Senate, of whom 19 won—not a bad record for any lobby.[67]

Educators supported Jimmy Carter for the presidency in 1976, and in part because of their assistance, he won the White House. To acquire their support, Carter had promised, and ultimately delivered, a new federal Department of Education. Teachers were grateful. During the 1980 Democratic convention, the NEA had more of its members attending as delegates (302) than did any other state except the nation's largest, California. Of these, virtually all were Carter supporters; only 15 NEA members supported his principal opponent, Senator Edward M. Kennedy.[68] Nevertheless, teachers were not able to wield the political clout necessary for Carter to regain the White House in 1980, and instead a president was elected who had campaigned in part on a platform that advocated abolishing the Department of Education. Despite the fact that the national education lobby was able to forestall the dismantling of its pet federal bureaucracy, federal grants for education were sharply reduced under Reagan. In all, these are grim messages for teachers.

The Education Lobby

Because the message is grim, teachers have begun pressuring legislators in an increasingly well-organized way, but the legislative policies resulting from this pressure have been mixed. A sophisticated study of the education lobby conducted in a dozen states found that teachers, as opposed to administrators and school board members, were by far the most politically active. Teachers directed most of their efforts toward providing information to legislators, although campaign money was also contributed.[69]

The level of political clout of educators in any given state appears to associate with the degree of urbanization and economic mix of a state; the education lobby was seen by legislators as having less influence in those states that had relatively advanced economies, were socially heterogeneous, were more urbanized, and had a high level of legislative professionalism. Interestingly, the amount of money, staff, and membership that the education lobbies had in each state bore no particular relationship to how legislators ranked the power of the state's education lobby.[70]

A NEW INTEREST IN EDUCATION

Although one might reasonably conclude otherwise, the preceding discussion does not necessarily imply that the public interest in good education is an irrelevancy to taxpayers, teachers, and policymakers. In fact, the 1980s are witnessing a renaissance of public interest in improving the public schools; in 1983 alone, more than 20 major reports on elementary and secondary education were published,[71] the most notable being *A Nation at Risk,* which called on Americans to stem the "rising tide of mediocrity" in the country's schools.[72]

As a consequence of such critiques, schools became a major concern of the states in the early 1980s. Nearly 250 high-level task forces in all the states made reports on school improvements to governors or legislatures, and state lawmakers considered more than 7,000 school-related measures in 1984 alone;

according to one survey, public education was the leading issue in more than 60 percent of the state legislatures, outdistancing any runners-up by better than 2-to-1.[73]

Many states are both stiffening standards and investing more heavily in schools. Not only have 23 states implemented minimum competency standards for teachers and 40 states implemented minimum competency test that high school students must pass to graduate, but in the early 1980s, 40 states increased the number of academic courses needed for graduation, 17 raised teachers' salaries, and 12 instituted "master teacher" plans that give good teachers more merit pay.[74] Nevertheless, the states still have some way to go; an analysis of how all state legislatures dealt with educational reforms in the 1980s found that only 15 percent of the reforms recommended by various commissions on educational reform had been adopted by state legislatures.[75]

HIGHER EDUCATION: CRACKS IN THE IVORY TOWER

Politics, pressures, and problems are all tawdry facts of life in the public schools. Are our institutions of higher learning similarly afflicted? The answer, as we shall see, is an unequivocal yes.

The Radicalism of American Higher Education

American higher education is unique. Indeed, one could argue that it is a genuinely radical form of education; only in America has the ideal that all citizens should have an opportunity to go to college been attempted as a matter of public policy. Every country in the world (with the on-again, off-again exception of modern totalitarian states) has predicated its advanced educational system on the notion that higher education is a program reserved for the intellectual and social elites of the nation. (In totalitarian nations, the basic precept often is that education is reserved for the politically trustworthy.)

As a policy meant for "the masses," American public higher education is a policy of some magnitude. Universities and colleges supported by state and local governments account for more than three-fourths of all students in higher education (up from 58 percent in 1960), nearly three-fourths of all instructional staff, and two-thirds of all expenditures on higher education.[76]

The State and Local Patrons

Americans always have had a high level of interest in higher education. The first colleges were founded privately in Massachusetts and Virginia in the seventeenth century, and the first public university to be chartered by a state legislature was in Georgia in 1794. Nevertheless, state involvement in higher education really began with the passage by Congress of the Morrill Land Grant Act of 1862. The Morrill Act encouraged states to set up practically oriented universities emphasizing agricultural education. The West and Midwest were the most affected by the legislation, as students in the South and East continued to attend, by and large, private institutions. Only in the 1960s did the Northeast become truly interested in fostering its own public higher education programs.

Concurrently with the state activity has been a more limited activity at the local level. City governments either have founded or taken over colleges and universities in Akron, Charleston, Cincinnati, Louisville, New York, Omaha, and Toledo, among others. In recent years, a number of these city-run institutions have fallen on hard times and state assistance is increasingly necessary. Perhaps the most spectacular example of this development is the City University of New York, the third largest higher educational system in the country (only California's and New York State's university systems are larger). In 1976 the university was temporarily closed down, shutting out some 250,000 students, 16,000 faculty, and 11,000 other employees because of its inability to meet payrolls. In that year, the university, for the first time since its founding in 1847, began charging students tuition—and a stiff tuition at that.

State institutions of higher education also are suffering under fiscal constraints, and austerity budgets are increasingly the rule. "Real" expenditures (i.e., accounting for inflation) per full-time-equivalent students varied by only 5 percent between 1971 and 1982, and actually were lower in 1982 than 11 years earlier.[77] Although budgets for higher learning seemed to soar upward despite enrollments that have stayed essentially level since 1976, it is important to keep in mind that real per student expenditures for higher education have stayed essentially constant.

More than half of the financial support for four-year public universities comes from governments, and about a quarter from students. It is not well known, but state and local governments contribute almost 3 percent of the revenues of *private* institutions through various sources such as scholarships, grants, and research contracts.[78]

Within these broad parameters, however, the states vary widely in the degree that they support higher education. Table 17-2 ranks the states in selected finance categories. New York, for example, ranks first in its tax effort and second in the tax revenue that it collects per person. But it ranks forty-fifth among the 50 states in terms of the revenue that it spends on higher education. On the other hand, North Dakota ranks forty-fourth among the states in terms of its tax effort, and thirty-second in terms of the tax revenue that it raises per person. Yet it ranks first in terms of the amount of revenue that it devotes to higher education. Alaska ranks first in its appropriations per student, while Vermont comes in last on this measure.

The Federal Patron

Although the federal government has never supported higher education to the degree that state governments have, its financial assistance has often been critical to the development of excellence in a number of universities. Federal funds for all of higher education—student loans, research grants, vocational education funding, public and private—constitute approximately 3 percent of the federal budget, but represent about a fifth of all support for technical schools, colleges, universities, and students.[79] However, the federal contribution to publicly supported four-year institutions has declined from 20 percent in 1971 to less than 13 percent.[80]

Federal involvement in higher education began in 1787, with the endowment of public institutions of higher learning with public lands in what was then called "the Northwest." The primary points of federal assistance to colleges and universities include the first Morrill Act, alluded to earlier, which initiated a federal policy of aid to states for agricultural and industrial education through

Table 17-2 Rank of States in Selected Higher Education Categories

State or Other Jurisdiction	*ENROLLMENT PER 1,000 POPULATION*		*PERCENTAGE OF U.S. AVERAGE TAX EFFORT*		*TAX REVENUE PER CAPITA*		*REVENUE SPENT ON HIGHER EDUCATION*		*APPROPRIATIONS PER STUDENT*	
	Number	*Rank*	*Percent*	*Rank*	*Amount*	*Rank*	*Percent*	*Rank*	*Amount*	*Rank*
United States	29.1	—	100.0%	—	$ 986.50	—	10.7	—	$3,646	—
Alabama	30.8	20	82.8	36	612.90	51	16.1	6	3,205	37
Alaska	24.1	40	166.4	2	3,692.80	1	8.3	42	12,712	1
Arizona	43.5	2	103.3	13	978.20	16	14.2	12	3,193	38
Arkansas	23.4	41	84.4	33	641.50	48	12.6	24	3,441	27
California	39.0	4	95.7	20	1,104.30	8	14.4	10	4,087	12
Colorado	37.8	6	87.6	28	968.30	18	11.2	31	2,874	45
Connecticut	21.7	48	102.3	14	1,059.20	11	7.9	44	3,862	16
Delaware	38.7	5	87.4	29	939.50	21	12.9	20	3,129	40
Florida	23.0	43	69.0	49	708.30	44	11.5	30	3,547	25
Georgia	20.5	49	92.8	21	750,40	38	12.3	26	4,492	6
Hawaii	34.4	11	122.9	4	1,261.20	4	12.7	23	4,662	5
Idaho	28.2	27	81.0	37	735.10	41	14.0	15	3,643	21
Illinois	27.3	30	95.8	19	1,049.00	12	9.6	37	3,676	20
Indiana	26.0	35	78.0	42	738.80	40	11.9	28	3,377	30
Iowa	28.4	26	90.7	23	957.60	19	12.2	27	4,101	11
Kansas	37.2	8	86.1	31	909.30	24	14.7	9	3,587	24
Kentucky	24.4	39	80.4	39	689.60	45	14.1	13	3,975	14
Louisiana	26.7	31	74.5	45	808.80	31	13.3	19	4,017	13
Maine	21.7	46	108.5	9	845.60	27	7.4	47	2,886	44
Maryland	30.1	23	106.0	10	1,024.60	14	9.9	36	3,383	29
Massachusetts	22.4	44	137.1	3	1,230.50	6	5.0	51	2,764	46
Michigan	33.7	12	105.4	11	1,060.80	10	9.5	38	2,993	43
Minnesota	29.8	24	105.2	12	1,079.80	9	9.2	40	3,330	31
Mississippi	30.3	22	90.9	22	637.00	49	18.3	2	3,842	17

Table 17-2 (Continued)

State or Other Jurisdiction	ENROLLMENT PER 1,000 POPULATION		PERCENTAGE OF U.S. AVERAGE TAX EFFORT		TAX REVENUE PER CAPITA		REVENUE SPENT ON HIGHER EDUCATION		APPROPRIATIONS PER STUDENT	
	Number	*Rank*	*Percent*	*Rank*	*Amount*	*Rank*	*Percent*	*Rank*	*Amount*	*Rank*
Missouri	25.4	38	79.3	41	742.90	39	10.3%	33	3,008	42
Montana	33.4	13	88.3	27	984.60	15	11.1	32	3,257	14
Nebraska	34.8	10	100.4	17	940.90	20	14.0	14	3,773	18
Nevada	26.2	33	49.6	51	812.60	30	10.2	34	3,154	39
New Hampshire	22.0	45	72.7	47	688.60	46	6.2	49	1,943	51
New Jersey	21.7	47	113.3	7	1,118.10	7	6.2	48	3,207	36
New Mexico	31.5	17	80.9	38	845.70	26	16.1	7	4,320	8
New York	23.3	42	170.8	1	1,432.50	2	7.8	45	4,795	4
North Carolina	30.5	21	89.6	26	725.10	43	17.5	4	4,156	9
North Dakota	43.0	3	76.0	44	809.30	32	20.7	1	3,890	15
Ohio	25.7	36	83.3	35	797.00	33	8.9	41	2,745	47
Oklahoma	32.0	15	70.0	48	794.60	34	13.7	16	3,406	28
Oregon	36.1	9	90.1	24	933.10	22	12.9	21	3,320	32
Pennsylvania	19.1	50	101.7	15	912.60	23	7.6	46	3,613	22
Rhode Island	26.1	34	119.1	6	975.20	17	9.2	39	3,458	26
South Carolina	27.8	29	89.9	25	682.80	47	16.7	5	4,112	10
South Dakota	29.7	25	83.6	34	758.40	37	10.0	3.5	2,545	40
Tennessee	24.4	37	80.0	40	631.60	50	12.3	25	3,059	41
Texas	31.7	16	62.4	50	763.00	36	18.1	3	4,354	7
Utah	33.0	14	96.4	18	827.30	29	14.4	11	3,609	23
Vermont	27.8	28	101.1	16	838.00	28	8.0	43	2,402	50
Virginia	31.4	18	85.5	32	792.90	35	12.8	22	3,237	35
Washington	44.5	1	86.9	30	891.80	25	13.5	18	2,710	48
West Virginia	26.3	32	76.2	43	728.90	42	13.5	17	3,742	19
Wisconsin	37.4	7	100.7	8	1,048.20	13	11.8	29	3,314	33
Wyoming	30.9	19	74.0	46	1,387.90	3	14.7	8	6,608	2
Dist. of Col.	12.6	51	120.0	5	1,247.30	5	6.1	50	6,072	3

Source: The Book of the States, 1982–83 (Lexington, Ky., Council of State Governments, 1982) p. 462.

land grants for colleges; the Serviceman's Readjustment Act (or what is more popularly known as the G.I. Bill) of 1944, which allocated educational aid to veterans; the National Defense Education Act of 1958, which provided graduate fellowships in science, mathematics, foreign languages, and other areas, and was largely a national political reaction to the Soviets' launch of the earth's first space satellite in that year; the Civil Rights Act of 1964, which desegregated institutions of higher learning; and the Higher Education Act of 1965, which assisted colleges, students, and teachers in a variety of areas. Washington's concern with higher education far exceeds, at least in terms of legislative initiatives, that of federal involvement in elementary and secondary education.

One reason for this involvement by Washington in both public and private higher education is the development of the national higher education lobby. There are six major higher education associations with their own Washington offices, and which claim institutional memberships ranging from 50 to almost 1,400. There are at least another five special-purpose associations, such as the Association of American Medical Colleges and the Council of Graduate Schools, that have Washington offices, and there are, in addition, several smaller associations of higher education institutions that have Washington offices. Many of these associations opened their doors in the capitol in the same year that a federal grants program began for them. Of the 20 major higher education associations, half received a federal grant program in the same year that they established a Washington office. Only 3 of the 20 higher education lobbies with offices in Washington have no grants program oriented specifically toward their needs.[81]

People in Public Higher Education

When all is said and done, higher education is people. But the kinds of people who comprise our colleges and universities are changing rapidly.

Students. There are more minorities, more women, and more older people taking courses in American colleges and universities than ever before. Fourteen percent of students in four-year universities and 21 percent of students in two-year institutions, such as community colleges, are minorities. In four-year universities, 8 percent of the students are blacks, and Hispanics comprise 3 percent; in two-year schools, 10 percent are blacks, and 6 percent are Hispanics.[82] These figures represent huge gains from the 1960s.

Women are increasingly represented among America's students. In 1979, for the first time, the number of women enrolled in higher education exceeded the number of men, and women now comprise 52 percent of the total enrollment as compared to only 45 percent as late as 1976. The reasons for these increases appear to be that women are returning to college after being away for a number of years.[83]

Finally, the student population is older. Almost four out of ten students in colleges and universities are 25 years old or older, compared to three out of ten in 1970. Increasingly, higher education is becoming a lifelong experience.[84]

Are students pleased with their educations? More or less, they are, but in-depth analyses of students and faculty by the Carnegie Foundation for the Advancement of Teaching have found that, although four-fifths of American college students are satisfied with their educations, more than a fourth state that their colleges are much like high school, more than a third are bored in class, 40 percent believe that their professors take no "special personal interest" in their academic progress, 42 percent think that their institutions treat them "like numbers in a book," and 60 percent rate their experiences with academic advisors as merely adequate or worse. "The findings appear to provide strong support to those calling for substantial reform of higher education."[85]

The professoriate. For roughly every 14 students on American campuses, there is a faculty member. Nearly 7 out of every 10 professors in public institutions are tenured, and a quarter of them are women.[86]

The 1970s was a decade of financial belt-tightening for the professoriate. From 1971 to 1980, faculty salaries slipped by nearly 20 percent in real spending power, and the proportion of part-time professors (who are considerably less expensive for universities to hire) rose from 22 percent in 1970 to 31 percent.[87] A study of what had happened to universities during the 1970s concluded that "the financial situation in American higher education has become increasingly tight—and the squeeze has been felt mainly by the faculty," particularly in public universities.[88]

Such trends have not been lost on faculty. One survey found that, by an "overwhelming margin, professors are now of the opinion that their own economic status is eroding in comparison with people employed in nonacademic professions," and there is a feeling among America's college faculty that "they are being singled out for special income discrimination."[89]

One way in which faculty have chosen to arrest their deteriorating economic situation is to unionize. There are 737 campuses where faculty members have chosen collective bargaining agents. (Another 94 campuses, which had been granted this option, have rejected unionization.) Of these, 184 are public, four-year campuses, 458 are public, two-year campuses, 83 are private, four-year campuses, and 12 are private, two-year campuses. The primary collective bargaining agent is the National Education Association, which represents faculty on 324 campuses, although it is followed closely by the American Federation of Teachers, which is found on 246 of the campuses with unionized faculty. Eighty-five campuses work through the American Association of University Professors, and the remaining campuses with unionized faculty have various combinations of the groups mentioned, or use independent bargaining agents.[90]

The drive to organize college faculty has run into unanticipated snags in the courtroom. The National Labor Relations Board of the federal government first supplied the principles of labor relations to university settings in 1970 in a case that had come before it involving Cornell University. But ten years later, the U.S. Supreme Court ruled, in the case of *National Labor Relations Board* v. *Yeshiva University,* that faculty "exercise authority which in any other context unquestionably would be managerial," and thus were not entitled to bargain collectively under the policies established by the National Labor Relations Act. The effect of this 5-to-4 decision by the Court was to reverse the National Labor Relations Board on the issue of college faculty unionism.

Much of *Yeshiva*'s public impact was contained by the fact that more than 70 percent of the colleges and universities that bargained collectively are in the public sector, where bargaining is governed by state enabling legislation or by policies established by boards of trustees. The *Yeshiva* case did not affect these state labor statutes.

Lest it be concluded that professors are more interested in protecting their jobs and their salaries than in being of use to their communities through teaching, research, and public service, it should be noted that at least one study has found that professors are significant contributors to the welfare of their communities. Public administrators in states and localities have often made use of the expertise that resides on their campuses. This expertise frequently comes at a far cheaper price than does that charged by private consultants, and both students and faculty have shown a remarkable willingness to be of use to their state and local governments. A survey of college students indicated that 67 percent of them believed that colleges should have a responsibility for helping solve the social problems of society, and not just through research.[91] The same view was held by 42 percent of 53,000 college faculty members surveyed who engaged in public service professional consulting without pay, and by another 38 percent who consulted off campus for pay.[92]

A unique study of colleges and universities in 14 Southern states found that the 84 institutions surveyed controlled a public service budget of more than $200 million and the region's higher education institutions held contracts and grants with state agencies amounting to almost $33 million, or 16 percent of their overall budgets. A remarkable 95 percent of the state officials surveyed had used or were using the services of the academic community.[93] In short, public universities are attempting to pay back their state governments for their tax dollars by supplying them with the knowledge that their campuses hold in relevant and useful ways.

Administrators. The administrators of academe's groves are a largely white, male lot. At public institutions, women and minorities hold fewer than 20 percent of the top-level administrative jobs. (By contrast, in private institutions, women and minorities hold almost 28 percent of the top-level managerial positions.)[94] At the very top, white males hold at least 94 percent of the chief executive jobs and about 80 percent of the administrative affairs and academic affairs positions.

Despite budget tightening among the states, the chief executive officers of publicly supported colleges and universities are surprisingly optimistic when it comes to the academic future of their institutions. Almost two-thirds of the presidents of public institutions believe that their colleges and universities are gaining ground academically; only 2 percent feel that they are losing ground. By contrast, however, the presidents of public institutions are deeply pessimistic about the financial futures of their colleges and universities. Forty-four percent believe that their institutions are losing ground financially, and only 16 percent believe that they are gaining ground. The presidents of private institutions are substantially more upbeat about their campuses' futures; almost three quarters believe that their colleges and universities are gaining ground academically, and 37 percent think that they are gaining ground financially.[95]

Even though the presidents of public institutions are less optimistic about the future than are their private sector counterparts, it would appear that academic quality can be retained and strengthened, in the view of the chief executive officers of public colleges and universities, even in the face of severe budgetary constraints.

Governing boards. A final group of people in higher education is those who are responsible for making policy for it. Increasingly, these people are the members of boards of trustees, or regents, who govern state universities and colleges. These boards are increasingly important. In 1940, 33 states had no board.[96] Today, only 2 states have none: Delaware and Vermont have planning agencies instead. Twenty-two states have "consolidated governing boards" or a single board that makes policies for all state institutions, although 8 of these states use separate boards for four-year and two-year institutions. The remaining 26 states have separate boards for each institution, although 9 of these are advisory in nature and may only make recommendations to the legislature.[97]

Despite the growth and growing power of these boards, the presidents of public institutions, as well as other observers, are increasingly concerned that the governance of universities is beginning to escape the control of boards of trustees. A number of rivals have emerged to challenge the traditionally exclusive authority of the boards to make policy for university and college campuses. Among these rivals are a proliferating host of academic accrediting associations (there are more than 50 specialized accrediting associations, all demanding that curricula be formed in certain ways), a growing interference by some state agencies in academic governance (although this traditionally has not been a serious problem), an intensifying federal involvement in the affairs of the campus, and a worrisome concern that private corporations may become increasingly involved in the management of universities.[98]

Nevertheless, the center of policymaking for public higher education remains with the states, although within the states, the legislature and the governor often compete with boards for primacy in the policymaking process of higher education. At least 13 legislatures now have separate committees for higher education,[99] and governors are increasingly active in the affairs of their state universities and colleges; governors say they spend about 10 percent of their time on issues of higher education.[100]

The Future of Public Higher Education

It is clear that society is making a burgeoning number of demands on higher education. Only in America has higher education undertaken, as a conscious public policy, the education of as many Americans who wish to receive it. Today, 17 percent of all Americans have completed four years of college, and the typical American has completed an average of 12.5 years of school, indicating at least some exposure by the average citizen to postsecondary education.[101] No other country comes close to these figures, and it is not surprising that higher education in America is an institution that must cope with far more social pressures (because it is far more a part of its society) than do its counterparts in other nations.

Because American higher education is so much a part of its society, the future of publicly supported higher education is of considerable concern to state political officials. A survey of governors, chairs of state legislative education and appropriations committees, higher education executive officers, and state budget chiefs found a surprisingly broad consensus on the future of education in their states. Governors and legislators expected that enrollments would increase and that costs constraints being faced by higher education would be passed on to students. Higher education appropriations were anticipated to lag inflation.

Closings, mergers, and a sharing of resources were all expected to be issues in the foreseeable future, and most thought that the quality of higher education, despite these circumstances, would improve.[102]

Whether it is found in the form of a public school festering in the ghetto or on the rolling lawns of a sprawling state university, education is among the most massive and admirable public policies ever undertaken by the grassroots governments. Education for all the people is a uniquely American notion, and no other nation has attempted to the degree that this one has to offer its citizens as much education as each person wants. Its failures, while ample, are surprisingly few, given the hugely ambitious goals that the public education establishment has set for itself.

NOTES

[1]National Center for Education Statistics, *Digest of Education Statistics, 1983-84* (Washington, D.C.: U.S. Government Printing Office, 1984), pp. 11, 62, 104; National Center for Education Statistics, *The Condition of Education, 1984* (Washington, D.C.: U.S. Government Printing Office, 1984), pp. 6-7; and "Education," *Book of the States, 1984-85* (Lexington, Ky.: Council of State Governments, 1984), pp. 362-363 and 370-371. Figures are for 1982-83. When the statistics for private schools and universities are added to those for public institutions, there were a total of more than 57 million students (12.5 million of whom were in higher education), 3.3 million teachers (865,000 in higher education), 300,000 academic administrators, about 99,000 schools, and more than 3,250 institutions of higher education and vocational schools.

[2]Merrill Sheils et al., "City Schools in Crisis," *Newsweek* (September 12, 1977), p. 62.

[3]*Ibid.*, p. 63.

[4]Cecelia Goodnow, "School Freed from Red Tape," *The Arizona Republic* (May 24, 1977).

[5]Joseph M. Cronin, "The Federal Take-over: Should the Junior Partner Run the Firm?" *Federalism at the Crossroads: Improving Educational Policymaking* (Washington, D.C.: Institute for Educational Leadership, 1976), pp. 1-5.

[6]Lorraine M. McDonell and Milbrey W. McLaughlin, "The State Role in Education: Independent Actor or Junior Partner?" paper presented at the 1981 Annual Meeting of the American Political Science Association, New York, September 3-6, 1981, p. 49.

[7]"Education," *The Book of the States, 1976-77* (Lexington, Ky.: Council of State Governments, 1976), p. 314.

[8]National Center for Educational Statistics, *Condition of Education, 1984,* p. 40. Figures are for 1981-82.

[9]Michael W. Kirst, "The State's Role in Education Policy Innovation," *Policy Studies Review* (November 1981), p. 303.

[10]"Education," *The Book of the States, 1976-77,* pp. 314-315.

[11]Donna Shalala and Mary F. Williams, "State Tax Politics, the Voters, and School Finance Reform," *Phi Delta Kappan,* 56 (September 1974), pp. 10-13.

[12]Dean M. Schweickhard, *The Role and Policymaking Activities of State Boards of Education: Report on a Special Study Project* (Denver: National Association of State Boards of Education, 1967), p. 32. Eleven states were sampled in the study. Though dated, the investigation remains unique.

[13]Unless noted otherwise, the information contained in the following discussion of state boards of education is drawn from Council of Chief State School Officers, *Educational Governance in the States: A Status Report on State Boards of Education, Chief State School Officers, and State Education Agencies* (Washington, D.C.: U.S. Department of Education, 1983), pp. 4-20. Figures are for 1982.

[14]The following discussion of chief state school officers is drawn from *ibid.*, pp. 21-35. Figures are for 1982.

[15]Unless noted otherwise, the following discussion of state departments of education is drawn from *ibid.*, pp. 36-80. Figures are for 1982.

[16]Michael B. Usdan, "The Future Viability of the School Board," in Peter J. Cistone, ed., *Understanding School Boards* (Lexington, Mass.: D. C. Heath, 1971), p. 269.

[17]Mark Twain, cited in *ibid.*, p. 265.
[18]George R. LaNoue and Bruce L.R. Smith, *The Politics of School Decentralization* (Lexington, Mass.: D. C. Heath, 1973), p. 12.
[19]Raymond E. Callahan, "The American Board of Education, 1789-1960," in Cistone, ed., *Understanding School Boards*, p. 19.
[20]Frederick M. Wirt and Michael W. Kirst, *Schools in Conflict* (Berkeley, Calif.: McCutchan, 1982), pp. 2-6.
[21]John O. Behrens, "Financing Public Elementary and Secondary Education," in *Municipal Year Book, 1974* (Washington, D.C.: International City Management Association, 1974), p. 24. Current figure for the number of school boards is for 1982.
[22]Jonathan P. Sher and Rachel B. Tomkins, spokespersons for the National Institute of Education, as quoted by Associated Press, "Consolidation of Schools Not Efficient, Study Finds," *The Arizona Republic* (April 14, 1977).
[23]National School Board Association, *The People Look at Their School Boards: Research Report 1975-1* (Evanston, Ill.: National School Board Association, 1975).
[24]Harmon Zeigler and M. Kent Jennings, with the assistance of G. Wayne Peak, *Governing American Schools: Political Interaction in Local School Districts* (North Scituate, Mass.: Duxbury, 1974), p. 24.
[25]*Ibid.*, p. 27.
[26]Wallace S. Sayre and Herbert Kaufman, *Governing New York City* (New York: Russell Sage Foundation, 1960).
[27]Zeigler and Jennings, *Governing American Schools*, p. 27.
[28]*Ibid.*, p. 251.
[29]*Ibid.*, p. 87.
[30]James MacGregor Burns, J. W. Peltason, and Thomas E. Cronin, *Government by the People*, 9th ed., National, State, and Local Edition (Englewood Cliffs, N.J.: Prentice-Hall, 1975), p. 187.
[31]David E. Rosenbaum, "New Rights Drive Perplexes Nation," *The New York Times* (July 7, 1977), p. 28.
[32]National Center for Education Statistics, *The Condition of Education, 1981* (Washington, D.C.: U.S. Government Printing Office, 1981), p. 40. Figure is for 1980.
[33]*Ibid.*, p. 49; and National Center for Education Statistics, *The Condition of Education, 1984*, p. 4.
[34]*Ibid.*; and Bureau of the Census, *Statistical Abstract of the United States, 1985* (Washington, D.C: U.S. Government Printing Office, 1984), Table 223, p. 139.
[35]"Coleman on the Griddle," *Time* (April 12, 1976), p. 79.
[36]James S. Coleman, *Equality of Educational Opportunity* (Washington, D.C.: U.S. Government Printing Office, 1966).
[37]United States Commission on Civil Rights, *Twenty Years After Brown* (Washington, D.C.: U.S. Government Printing Office, 1975).
[38]National Center for Education Statistics, *Projections of Education Statistics to 1990-91*, Vol. 1 (Washington, D.C.: U.S. Government Printing Office, 1982), p. 104.
[39]National Center for Education Statistics, *The Condition of Education, 1981*, p. 59, and *1984*, p. 16.
[40]*Ibid.*
[41]National Institute of Education, Department of Health, Education, and Welfare, as reported by United Press International, "School Vandalism High," *The Arizona Republic* (January 7, 1978).
[42]Gallup poll as cited in National Center for Education Statistics, *The Condition of Education, 1981*, p. 40; and Dennis A. Williams et al., "Why Public Schools Fail," *Newsweek* (April 20, 1981), p. 64. The polls cover the years 1969-1981.
[43]National Center for Education Statistics, *The Condition of Education, 1981*, p. 40. Figure is for 1980.
[44]*Ibid.*, p. 46. Figure is for 1980.
[45]College Entrance Examination Board spokesperson, as quoted in David Broder, "Reading and Writing: The Principal Failings," *The Arizona Republic* (August 30, 1977).
[46]National Center for Education Statistics, *Digest of Education Statistics, 1983-84*, p. 71.
[47]"Education," *The Book of the States, 1978-79*, (Lexington, Ky.: Council of State Governments, 1978), p. 331.
[48]National Center for Education Statistics, *The Condition of Education, 1984*, p. 179. Figure is for 1983.

[49]National Center for Education Statistics, *The Condition of Education, 1981*, p. 39. Figures are for 1980.
[50]*Ibid.*, p. 40. Figure is for 1980.
[51]As derived from Bureau of the Census, *Statistical Abstract of the United States, 1981* (Washington, D.C.: U.S. Government Printing Office, 1981), Table 254, p. 152.
[52]*Ibid.;* National Center for Education Statistics, *Bond Sales for Public School Purposes, 1957-8 through 1973-4* (Washington, D.C.: U.S. Government Printing Office, 1975); and Lucia Mouat, "Voters Turning Down More School Bond Issues," *The Christian Science Monitor* (October 20, 1976), p. 5.
[53]Philip K. Piele and John Stuart Hall, *Budgets, Bonds, and Ballots* (Lexington, Mass.: D. C. Heath, 1973), pp. 152 and 169.
[54]National Education Association Poll, 1980, as reported in Williams et al., "Why Public Schools Fail," p. 65.
[55]Bureau of the Census, *Statistical Abstract of the United States, 1985*, Table 225, p. 140. Figures are for 1983.
[56]*Ibid.*, Table 226, p. 141. In 1984, teachers earned on the average $22,000.
[57]*Ibid.*, Table 227, p. 141.
[58]"Education," *The Book of the States, 1984-85*, p. 358. Figure is for 1984.
[59]Williams et al., "Why Public Schools Fail," p. 65. The Florida test was given in 1980.
[60]Bureau of the Census, *Statistical Abstract of the United States, 1985*, Table 711, p. 425. Figures are for 1980.
[61]Bureau of the Census, *Census of Governments, 1977: Labor-Management Relations in State and Local Governments*, Vol. 3 (Washington, D.C.: U.S. Government Printing Office, 1979), p. 2.
[62]Bureau of the Census, *Statistical Abstract of the United States, 1985*, Table 711, p. 425. Figures are for 1980.
[63]Williams et al., "Why Public Schools Fail," p. 65.
[64]Thomas Redburn, "Government Unions: The New Bullies on the Block," *The Washington Monthly* (December, 1974), p. 21.
[65]Robert A. Dobkin, "NEA's Militancy Defies Inflation Spiral: They Want Theirs!" *The Arizona Republic* (January 9, 1976).
[66]Ronald G. Corwin, "The Organizational Context of School Board-Teacher Conflict," in Cistone, ed., *Understanding School Boards*, p. 131.
[67]Dobkin, "NEA's Militancy Defies Inflation Spiral."
[68]David Broder, "Democrats: Party Must Deal with Tensions Between Two Factions If It Expects to Regain Power," *The Arizona Republic* (April 3, 1981); and "Periscope," *Newsweek* (June 6, 1980), p. 21.
[69]J. Alan Aufderheide, "Educational Interest Groups and the State Legislature," in Ronald Campbell and Tim L. Mazzoni, Jr., eds., *State Policy Making for the Public Schools: A Comparative Analysis*, (Columbus: Educational Governance Project, Ohio State University, 1974).
[70]Wirt, "Education Politics and Policies," pp. 309-310.
[71]"Education," *The Book of the States, 1984-85*, p. 353.
[72]National Commission on Excellence in Education, *A Nation at Risk* (Washington, D.C.: U.S. Government Printing Office, 1983), p. 10.
[73]Jane Roberts, Jerry Fensterman, and Donald Lief, "States, Localities Continue to Adopt Strategic Strategies," *Intergovernmental Perspective*, 11 (Winter, 1985), pp. 24-25.
[74]*Ibid.*, p. 26.
[75]Doh C. Shinn and Jack R. Van Der Slik, "Legislative Efforts to Improve the Quality of Public Education in the American States: A Comparative Analysis," paper presented at the 1985 Annual Meeting of the American Political Science Association, August 29 - September 1, 1985, New Orleans, p. 19.
[76]National Center for Education Statistics, *Digest of Education Statistics, 1983-84*, pp. 103, 138.
[77]National Center for Education Statistics, *The Condition of Education, 1984*, p. 84. In 1982, public institutions spent $6,816 on each full-time student.
[78]*Ibid.*, p. 80.
[79]Education Commission for the States, *Issuegram* (February, 1981).
[80]National Center for Education Statistics, *The Condition of Education, 1984*, p. 80. Figure is for 1982.
[81]Advisory Commission on Intergovernmental Relations, *The Evolution of a Problematic*

Partnership: The Feds and Higher Ed. The Federal Role in the Federal System: The Dynamics of Growth (Washington, D.C.: U.S. Government Printing Office, 1981), p. 27.
[82]National Center for Education Statistics, *The Condition of Education, 1984,* p. 70.
[83]*Ibid.*
[84]*Ibid.*, p. 76.
[85]Robert L. Jacobson, "Most Students Are Satisfied with Their Education, Survey Indicates, but Frustrations Are Widespread," *Chronicle of Higher Education,* 31 (February 5, 1986), p. 30.
[86]W. John Minter and Howard R. Bowen, "Despite Economic Ills, Colleges Weathered the 70s with Large Enrollments and Stronger Programs," *The Chronicle of Higher Education* (May 12, 1982), p. 5.
[87]*Ibid.* Figure is for 1980.
[88]W. John Minter and Howard R. Bowen, "Colleges' Achievements in Recent Years Came Out of the Hides of Professors," *The Chronicle of Higher Education* (May 19, 1982), p. 8.
[89]Everett Carll Ladd, Jr., and Seymour Martin Lipsett, "The Faculty Mood: Pessimism Is Predominant," *The Chronicle of Higher Education* (October 3, 1977), p. 14.
[90]"Faculty Bargaining Agents on 737 Campuses," *The Chronicle of Higher Education* (September 23, 1981), p. 6. Figures are for 1981.
[91]Carnegie Commission of Higher Education, *Reform on Campus: Changing Students, Changing Academic Programs* (New York: McGraw-Hill, 1972).
[92]American Council on Education, *ACE Faculty and Staff Survey Newsletter* (August, 1973), p. 1.
[93]Nicholas Henry, "State Agencies and Academia," *State Government,* 49 (Spring, 1976), pp. 99-104.
[94]College and University Personnel Association, *Women and Minorities in Administration of Higher Education Institutions* (Washington, D.C.: College and University Personnel Association, 1982). Figures are for 1978-79.
[95]Jack Magarrell, " 'Great Pessimism' Voiced by Chiefs of Public Colleges," *The Chronicle of Higher Education* (December 15, 1982), p. 8.
[96]Madeleine Wing Adler and Frederick S. Lane, "Governors and Higher Education: Politics, Budgeting and Policy Leadership," *State Government,* 58 (Summer, 1985), p. 69.
[97]Aims C. McGuinness, Jr., "State Coordination and Governance of Higher Education: Implications for Governors," *State Government,* 58 (Summer, 1985), p. 77.
[98]Carnegie Foundation for the Advancement of Teaching, as cited in Magarrell, " 'Great Pessimism' Voiced by Chiefs of Public Colleges," p. 8.
[99]Adler and Lane, "Governors and Higher Education," p. 68. Figure is for 1985.
[100]Richard A. Zollinger, "Former Governors Look at Higher Education: Crucial Issues Facing Academe," *State Government,* 58 (Winter, 1985), p. 59.
[101]Bureau of the Census, *Mountain Plains Census Data Highlights* (July/August 1982), p. 7.
[102]Gordon B. Van deWater, *Higher Education in the States,* as cited in Robert L. Jacobson, "Officials See State Funds for Colleges Lagging over the Next Three Years," *The Chronicle of Higher Education* (March 17, 1982), p. 7.

18

THE PLANNING ETHIC

land use and transportation

Planning, like education, affects all people, but it is the middle class that has traditionally chosen the neat rows of picket-fenced houses, tidy boulevards free from pushcarts and litter, and the comfort of knowing that one's residential neighborhood always will be just that—a residential neighborhood. Although the planning profession in recent years has broadened its traditional concerns, it is nonetheless such middle-class values that gave urban planning in particular its beginning. In this chapter, we shall examine the origins of the planning ethic and the evolution of professional planners from ineffectual "do-gooders" to increasingly powerful urban and regional policymakers, focusing especially on the impact that planners are having in forming public policies for land use and transportation.

THE ROOTS OF PUBLIC PLANNING

Early urban planning was part and parcel of what was known around the turn of the century as the "city beautiful movement," and central to this movement was the concept of the physical design of cities. Hence, urban planning was related to the architecture profession, but it was also closely associated with the "good government" reform movement: "A better city (the city beautiful movement), an honestly and ably run city government (municipal reform), and efficient local government (early public administration) were ends to be advanced by city planning. In this sense, early city planning had a moralistic flavor to it, and it was viewed as the means of promoting the good life."[1] Indeed, it was precisely this early moralistic flavor that has led us to base this chapter on the concept that planning is essentially a policy for the middle class.

Nevertheless, planning did bring about some notable early achievements on the American urban scene. It was planners who were responsible for the creation of Pullman in South Chicago and the design and execution of Garden City in Long Island and Shaker Heights in Ohio.[2] More recently, two complete communities—Columbia, Maryland, and Reston, Virginia—have been developed directly from the pens of planners who, particularly in designing Reston, asserted their own values about neighborhoods and living patterns in designing the city that did not necessarily reflect the values of the time.

The Structure of Local Planning

Approximately three quarters of all American communities with more than 5,000 people have some sort of published plan.[3] Almost 11,000 municipalities have planning boards (a figure representing more than half of the local governments that might be expected to have such boards), and virtually all the large cities, those with 50,000 or more people, have planning boards. Ninety percent of cities and towns in the 5,000 to 50,000 population range have planning boards, and all state governments have planning agencies and programs.[4]

Although planning boards are being integrated into the standing city bureaucracy at an increasingly rapid rate, they nonetheless operate somewhat autonomously as governmental units. Members of planning boards are usually appointed or elected for specific terms on a staggered basis. Staggering the terms contributes to the independence of the local planning commission's members since their terms of office do not necessarily coincide with that of the mayor or council members. Boards have an average size of eight to nine members. A highly educated planning staff generally serves the board, and political reality is such that board members usually follow the advice of the professional staff. (Recall, in this light, our discussions of school board members and school superintendents in the last chapter, of legislators and legislative staffs in Chapter 5, and of city managers and city council members in Chapter 11.)

Community planning commissions are generally responsible for revising and updating the comprehensive plan, making rezoning decisions, drawing a zoning map, administering community subdivision regulations, and suggesting changes of the laws in these areas. Planning commissions have particular power in formulating the comprehensive plan and developing land-use controls, the most notable authority here being zoning. Local planning commissions rarely have programs of their own, but they are involved in the programs of a number of other agencies, especially such federally sponsored programs as urban renewal, model cities, community development, and mass transit, and they also are involved in local building and housing code programs.

The actual amount of clout that local planning commissions have in these programs varies. For example, the staff director of Philadelphia's Planning Commission was a "crucial participant in the urban renewal process for years,"[5] while Scott Greer found that the local planning commissions functioned as a "rubber stamp of approval" in urban renewal programs in many communities.[6]

The Uses of the Urban Plan

Although the official plan of a community does not have any legal weight as such, professional planners nonetheless have a variety of tools at their disposal with which to implement their plans. Among these tools are zoning ordinances (perhaps the most significant single tool), regulations concerning subdivisions, the power to draw official maps of the area, building and construction codes, decision-making authority regarding the location of public facilities and buildings, and devising a capital improvement program. Communities increasingly are developing *comprehensive plans,* by which is meant a land-use plan for an urban area that includes all relevant aspects of the system. More commonly used is the *functional plan,* which refers to the specialized planning done by such agencies as urban renewal authorities, health departments, highway departments, and recreation agencies. In this chapter we concentrate on the comprehensive aspect of planning, since comprehensive plans are being used increasingly by local policymakers.

A survey of all cities with more than 150,000 people found that comprehensive planning documents were "frequently" used by city governments to set priorities in the budget process—54 percent of the responding cities reported such a use. On the other hand, about a third of the cities reported that they use their planning document only "to qualify for federal grants." This was particularly true of economic development plans and, to a lesser degree, land-use plans. Such a finding is not too surprising when we recall the negative attitudes of local policymakers concerning the federal government's involvement in local affairs, discussed in Chapter 9.[7]

THE FEDERAL GOVERNMENT AND THE POWER TO PLAN

Planning is an intensely intergovernmental process. As early as the 1920s the federal government assumed the lead in pushing state and local governments into doing more and better planning, but Washington's emphasis has typically been in promoting planning among regions and localities, and less so among states.

Pushing Planning: Washington Wades In

As a partial consequence of Washington's interest in planning, there are more than 600 regional councils of all types, and all are involved in some form of comprehensive or functional planning. About 70 percent are policy councils of various kinds, such as the Economic Development Districts (managed through the U.S. Department of Commerce) and Rural Area Development Committees (administered through the U.S. Department of Agriculture), both of which are controlled almost entirely by the federal government, with only relatively minor concessions to state and local governments. Forty-six percent of these policy councils are regional planning councils, and 30 percent of regional councils of all types are Councils of Governments.[8] The key difference between a Council of Government and a regional planning council is that Councils of Government are voluntary associations of governments while regional planning commissions are generally set up by state legislation, often as a result of pressure from Washington, and they are primarily responsible for comprehensive planning.

National pressure in the development of rational planning among America's plethora of governments can be traced back at least to 1928 with the drafting of the U.S. Department of Commerce's Model Planning Act, known as the Standard City Planning Enabling Act. This act was designed to serve as a guide to state legislatures in permitting their localities to engage in planning, and it was this act that encouraged the establishment of independent planning commissions at the local level.[9]

Since that time, a number of federal laws have encouraged (or even forced) states and localities to engage in more comprehensive and rational public planning. Among the more significant of these acts is the Urban Planning Assistance Act of 1954. Under its Section 701, federal grants were allocated to regional and local planning agencies to promote coordinated planning. Known as the "701" program, these funds were administered by the Department of Housing and Urban Development (HUD). Later the Demonstration Cities and Metropolitan Development Act of 1966 (Model Cities), the Intergovernmental Cooperation Act of 1968, and the National Environmental Policy Act of 1969 were enacted, each of which mandated greater federal involvement in the local planning process.

All these acts and programs were drawn upon when the federal Office of Management and Budget (OMB) wrote its Circular A-95 in 1969, then broadened its scope significantly in 1971. OMB Circular A-95 encouraged a process of review and comment by promoting intergovernmental planning for a variety of federal development programs; it provided a means of coordinating federal development projects with state and local planning agencies; it furnished methods for securing environmental impact statements for federal or federally funded projects. It accomplished all this intergovernmental planning and policy coordination through the establishment of "clearinghouses," to use the term employed in Circular A-95: state clearinghouses designated by the governor or by state legislation; metropolitan clearinghouses or planning agencies recognized by OMB; and nonmetropolitan regional clearinghouses inaugurated by the governor, by state legislation, or through interstate agreements. In addition, federal directives, legislation, and funding have encouraged the development of some 2,000 single-purpose or multipurpose substate (that is, within a state's boundaries) regional associations.

In 1974, the Housing and Community Development Act was passed; Title IV of this act authorizes grants to local and regional governments for planning purposes. Also in 1974, eligibility for "701" comprehensive planning assistance was expanded to include activities leading to the development and carrying out of comprehensive plans, improving management skills to implement such plans, and developing policy planning and evaluation capacities.[10]

Other federal legislation has had a less direct impact on the state and local planning function, but there is a lot of it with which subnational governments must deal. One study found almost 140 federal programs that have a direct impact on state and local land-use policies.[11] Among the more significant of these laws are the Federal Water Pollution Control Act, the Flood Insurance Act, the National Environmental Policy Act, the Coastal Zone Management Act, and the Clean Air Act. Despite Washington's encouragement of state and local planning efforts through its direct planning legislation, these and other federal policies, such as interstate highway systems, federal mortgage policies, and national tax incentives, have had a decentralizing influence on the nation's urban centers.

Between 1970 and 1975, an effort was made at the federal level to correct the effects of fragmented national policies for planning and land use. The intent of a series of bills, sponsored primarily by Representative Morris Udall and the late Senator Henry Jackson during this period, was to assist the states in their attempts to curb urban sprawl, protect the environment, encourage economic development, and provide for orderly land use, but the only significant legislation that emerged was the Coastal Zone Management Act of 1972, which encourages 30 states (including those on the Great Lakes) with federal grants to manage their coastal resources in a comprehensive manner.

The Emergence of State Planning

Until recently, state governments have not been serious planners. Perhaps this was because states tried it in the 1930s and found that planning did not work. In 1933, the administration of Franklin D. Roosevelt offered funds to the states for state planning, stipulating that state planning boards had to be comprised of lay citizen appointed by the governor. The states accepted with alacrity, and by 1938, all the states except Delaware had planning boards. But by the end of the 1940s, virtually all the lay planning boards had died out, probably because they had no real authority and few if any policymakers listened to them.[12]

In 1959, Washington tried again and amended Section 701 of the Urban Planning Assistance Act of 1954 to include states as well as localities as recipients of federal funds for planning purposes. But because this amendment essentially grafted concepts that were originally designed to meet local planning needs onto state governments, the states again found that planning, at least as it was defined by Washington, was really not for them. Although some state planning offices resulted from this federal initiative, the governors generally channeled "701" planning funds into uses that were not clearly related to statewide planning.[13]

Nevertheless, the states were beginning to appreciate the uses of planning, but only on their own terms. In the 1960s, the states began to take a genuine interest in land-use planning, and, by the end of the decade (as we discuss later), a quiet revolution had occurred in statewide planning for the uses of state lands. In the 1970s, the states, particularly the governors, became interested in management planning, notably in the areas of fiscal and budgetary planning; we reviewed this phase in Chapter 6.

Today, although land-use and administrative planning continue to mature in the states, the focus of state planning is on issues of policy development. Forty-five states have state planning and policy development offices. Roughly half of these are located in the governors' offices and 42 percent are in a budget and planning office or a department of administration; in four states planning is a cabinet-level department.[14] Most offices were formed in the 1960s, but have been revitalized, usually by gubernatorial order, since then. The offices identify issues, develop programs to address them, determine the resources needed to deal with the issues, and monitor and evaluate the state's success in resolving the problem.

Pulling Planning: Washington Walks Out

Beginning in 1982, Washington executed a sharp right turn in its long-standing policy of promoting orderly planning among states and localities. Congress started to withdraw its long-standing support of substate regional coordinating associations, such as Councils of Governments, and a few multistate planning commissions began to disappear as well. An estimated 10 percent of the substate regional councils closed their doors, and at least half of them faced severe belt tightening. The ten federal regional councils, which had been established in 1969 and were located in each of the ten federal regions, and were designed to coordinate grant applications from states and localities, were eliminated in 1983 by executive order. In 1982, the "701" program was terminated; after 28 years and more than $200 million expended, the federal government no longer was in the business of granting funds for planning purposes in states and localities.[15]

More significantly, however, the "A-95 process" was effectively dismantled in 1982. The White House first reduced the number of federal grant programs subject to review by regional clearinghouses from approximately 250 to 130, and then President Ronald Reagan signed Executive Order 12372, which revoked Office of Management and Budget Circular A-95 altogether and replaced it with a broader, state-based consultation and program review process. Executive Order 12372 was an effort to give state and local administrators an opportunity to create their own review and planning procedures, to encourage their participation in federal projects that were taking place within their jurisdictions, and to reduce federal regulations. Under the old A-95 process, state and local governments had to follow federally prescribed procedures in reviewing programs; the intent of the president's directive was to eliminate the federal role on the grounds that state and local elected officials should strengthen their authority in the planning process.[16]

The states have been lethargic in responding to Executive Order 12372, perhaps because they are of the view that if it is not broken, do not fix it. Two years after the order went into effect, 48 states were administering it. Of these, only 6 had significantly altered the procedures used under OMB Circular A-95, and at least 40 states still relied on Councils of Governments and similar regional councils as their "review and comment" bodies.[17]

Washington's record in promoting planning among America's communities, regions, and states has been spotty, but not unsuccessful. Local governmental and regional planning associations were created largely because of federal insistence. Yet, now that Washington's pressure has been removed, the grassroots governments seem content to keep the planning structures and procedures that the federal government made them create, and to continue to use them as regional planning vehicles. Even among the states—those governments that were the least responsive to Washington's call for more planning—there has been a renewed interest in planning, and some of that, at least, is attributable to the federal government's initial prodding. Now that Washington appears to have withdrawn from the planning business at the grassroots, it seems that its impact will linger on.

PLANNERS AND THE PEOPLE

While national policies have, until recently, promoted the role of local planners, perhaps an even more significant development has been what appears to be a change of attitude by the public on the role of planning. As Samuel Kaplan has astutely observed, in the past it has been easy to

> put down good government group efforts in support of rational land use by joining with special interests in waving a red flag. Master planning "socialism," and the reputations of some well-intentioned residents were smeared at local hearings by thinly veiled red baiting. The motto of America's suburbs was well stated in the inscription on a wall in the meeting hall of the county supervisors of Los Angeles: "This county is founded on free enterprise. Cherish and preserve it."[18]

And, as Kaplan notes, look what has happened in Los Angeles.

Perhaps because of Los Angeles's example—an example, some contend, of the world's worst case of urban sprawl—planning may be gaining popular acceptance. Studies indicate that the satisfaction of a community's residents correlates with increasing levels of planning and the legal power of local officials to plan. One study of ten communities found that where urban planning was the most extensive, the residents were the most satisfied with the areas in which they lived. Although there was not a 100 percent match, the tendency was that the greater degree of planning, the higher the people's satisfaction.[19]

Who Are the Planners?

While planning has traditionally been quintessentially middle-class in both outlook and action, the planning profession is growing increasingly political and in the process is recognizing the needs of other kinds of people. Planners as professionals are beginning to learn that to get along they must go along. Still, the field's acceptance of politics as legitimate is by no means total, as no professional planner wishes to "prostitute" his or her values for the sake of politics. There are an estimated 20,000 practicing planners in the country, 70 to 80 percent of whom work in the public sector.[20] Public planners are very professionally oriented. More than one-third of the planning directors in big cities come directly from an educational background in planning: most of the remaining two-thirds have educations in engineering, landscape architecture, and public administration, respectively. Seventy percent of all planning directors have planning as their chief work background; of the remainder, most have backgrounds in enforcing zoning and code ordinances, engineering, and public administration. Planning directors are extremely well educated, considerably more so than the typical city council member, with 39 percent holding master's degrees and another 48 percent having bachelor's degrees.[21]

The Politicization of Planners

Given these kinds of educational and professional backgrounds, it is not surprising that some planners elect not to participate in the political process to get their plans implemented. A number of studies have shown that planners adopt three distinctly different professional roles. Francine Rabinowitz has categorized these roles on a professional-political continuum. They range from the *technician,* who develops plans purely on the basis of professional values and who does not get involved in whether or not the plan is accepted by the local government; to the *broker,* who plays the role of a confidential advisor to local officials and is concerned over whether or not a plan is "marketable"; to the *mobilizer,* who goes out and seeks support in the community for the comprehensive plan and solicits the backing of various local interest groups.[22] Corresponding roles are posited by David C. Ranney, who used the same concepts but dubbed them *political agnostic, confidential advisor* and *political activist.*[23]

In the 1960s the planning profession itself began to recognize that politics did play a role in urban planning. An example of this recognition was the rise of "advocacy planning," by which was meant that planners legitimately could be overtly political in getting their plans accepted by the community. Most "advocate planners," as they call themselves, were and are consciously in favor of achieving the goals of the poor, the black, and the dispossessed—advocacy planning clearly was a departure from the normal, staid, middle-class perspective of professional planning.[24]

Although the concept of advocacy planning has declined in recent years, the planning profession nonetheless is becoming increasingly political in its viewpoints and is accepting politics as a legitimate component of the planning process. Increasingly, planning agencies themselves are becoming integrated into the political workings of city hall and the state capital. Moreover, such a trend long has been advocated by scholars of urban affairs. Herbert J. Gans, for example, has urged that planners see themselves as—and become—policymakers, arguing that to remain "technicians" or "political agnostics" will keep planners in ineffectual positions at a time when they are sorely needed if metropolitan growth is to be intelligently managed.[25] As Don Allensworth has observed, "The planning bureaucracy is immeshed in politics, and planning policy can normally be traced to a political base. The planning administrator cannot escape this reality."[26]

It should not be inferred that because planners have refrained from becoming active participants in the rough and tumble political world, they are somehow apolitical. A survey of planners in (mostly suburban) cities with a city-manager form of government found that planners had their own sets of ideologies. Almost 21 percent of these suburban planners were deemed to be "socialists" (the highest percentage for any of the ideological categories), while nearly 8 percent were categorized as "fascists." Most of the planners, however, were nonideological.[27]

THE POLITICS OF THE PLANNING PROCESS: LAND USE

The paramount concern of the grassroots planning process is land use. An estimated 14,000 local governments exercise some form of land-use control.[28] These localities encompass about three quarters of the American population and approximately 2 percent of the nation's land.[29]

The Lobbies of Land-Use Planning

State, regional, and local planning agencies must deal with different interest groups and citizens' associations.[30] The real estate community demands plans that will facilitate development. Builders favor growth, physical revitalization of the downtown, and zoning recommendations that bring more profits for new land uses; they tend to favor increased population density. Construction interests also prefer "flexible" subdivision administration policies. Professional planners (who themselves can be seen as an interest group) generally like seeing their somewhat abstruse models transferred to the world of political and economic realities—a wish that, on occasion, is less than realistic. Then too, the professional planners are public employees, and as such often have their jobs at stake when the planning process gets rough.

Political executives, such as the mayor or city manager, display a desire to control the planning process as a means of building their political bases. Businesspersons obviously tend to favor plans that encourage commerce and that do not introduce new competitors into the community. Commercial interests also favor painting as roseate pictures of their towns as is humanly possible, as in the typical Chamber of Commerce brochures. The state judiciary can be viewed as an interest group in that it may provide standards to which community decision makers must adhere, particularly in the areas of subdivision regulation, administration, and zoning. Other state bureaucracies often act as lobbyists in the planning process. Perhaps the most notorious of these are the state highway commissions. Highway interests can be extremely effective in assuring that the community plan is compatible with their plans for future roads and highways, despite the fact that planning commissions and highway commissions often act separately of each other. Similarly, sewer and water districts, public works agencies, school districts, and public housing authorities may have their own uses for comprehensive plans. Of course, citizens' associations are themselves interest groups and usually call for a plan that preserves the *status quo* and stops land from being developed. In contrast to real estate interests, they favor low residential densities and maintaining the "integrity" of existing neighborhoods.

When planning agencies call public hearings, which often are required by federal law if an agency wishes to keep on getting federal dollars, citizen groups can stage a political drama of the highest order. Consider the following quotation from one such participant:

> Public hearings are unique events, with many bordering on mass hysteria. I have seen at hearings mature professionals transformed into raving demagogues, liberal politicians into fascists, modest laymen into nit-picking self-appointed experts, and loving mothers into shrews. I have heard at hearings clergymen curse, atheists call on God with conviction, and more threats than I care to remember. School auditoriums built and maintained with hard-to-come-by taxpayers' dollars have been wrecked, not by vandals or juvenile delinquents, but by

law-abiding parents out of anger when confronted simply by multi-colored charts and maps of a plan presented "for discussion purposes only." I have witnessed at hearings bloody fights and, despite my bulk, have been pushed and shoved and had my clothes ripped. To stand before a packed auditorium and sense the fear of an audience over a particular plan turn into hate is a frightening feeling.[31]

In other words, citizens can be interest groups, too.

The Zoning Zaniness

Perhaps the single greatest—and most frightening—power that local planners have is the power to zone. Few areas of public policy make suburban homeowners and the Junior Chamber of Commerce angrier than proposed changes in zoning. Zoning policies, believe it or not, are as close as America comes to a comprehensive land-use policy. At root, zoning simply is a plan of how certain sections of the community may be used—for stores, residences, recreation, or whatever. Virtually all American communities have zoning regulations, although Houston stands alone as a major city that not only does not have but has never had zoning. There are sections of Houston where expensive townhouses are located next to topless-bottomless bars, but neither residents nor businesses in that city seem to mind. Such a combination may not be acceptable in other cities, however.

Zoning was not always with us. It got its start in 1916, when New York City passed the nation's first zoning law. As a concept, zoning quickly came under fire as an unconstitutional violation of the right to use one's property as one wished, but in 1926, the constitutional issue was put to rest in the case of *Euclid* v. *Ambler Realty Company,* in which the Supreme Court ruled that municipalities had the right to enact zoning regulations if they were authorized to do so by their state governments. The Court made it clear that the ultimate power to restrict the uses of land lay with the states.

In the years that followed, however, state governments chose to decentralize their zoning powers to their local governments, and the upshot of this devolution was that, in virtually all cities, "zoning was not justified with reference to any clearly articulated public purpose. Zoning, in isolation from planning, became the rather direct tool of private interests. Very few municipalities adopted zoning plans to guide the application of their zoning powers. And even when plans existed, they were ignored. In fact, most cities, even including the largest, did not put together modern planning staffs until the 1960s. Because of its isolation from any planning orientation, zoning did not regulate orderly urban growth so much as it reflected patterns of growth."[32]

Not everyone agrees with this assessment. Some citizens (not only real estate developers, but also some serious urban scholars) argue against the zoning concept. Those urbanists who are against zoning, in the style of Houston, argue that zoning inflates housing costs by limiting the amount of land available for residential building. Moreover, simply by restricting the supply of land on which homes can be built, and then further limiting the number of houses that can be built per acre, zoning forces the construction of dull and dreary housing developments by requiring (as zoning regulations often require) uniform building heights and specification on what houses and apartments may look like. They also argue that zoning contributes to sprawl and a waste of energy since it makes it difficult to convert low-density residential areas in old inner cities into apartments. It fosters the bureaucratization of housing development and thus encourages graft because so much money is at stake in urban development. Finally, they argue, zoning encourages prejudice against the poor and minorities, a point to which we shall return later.[33]

Cities, of course, may enact land-use controls in addition to those that are permitted by traditional zoning ordinances. In a survey of all municipalities with 10,000 people and more, it was found that of nine possible types of land-use controls, only 17 percent of the cities had not enacted any of them.[34] The single most popular land-use control was that of requiring developers to install public facilities (such as sewer lines); 83 percent of the cities responding had enacted such ordinances. Roughly a quarter of all the responding cities had passed ordinances regarding architectural appearance, growth limitations, and historical preservation; from one-third to one-half of the cities had ordinances that zoned for flood plains, open spaces, and natural resources; 12 percent had marsh land controls.

Alternatives to Zoning

Although most municipalities still use the basic zoning ideas that were originated in New York in 1916, many cities and towns (and some states) have begun to incorporate some creative changes in traditional zoning practices. Increasingly, zoning ordinances are becoming more flexible, and local governments are using trade-off techniques to encourage land use that benefits both developers and citizens. How effectively this balance between money making and land using has been attained is a matter of heated debate, but the efforts by localities to do so are diverse. An itemization of some of the new ways that governments are approaching land-use planning follows.[35]

Planned unit development. *Planned unit development* (*PUD*) is by far the most popular of the new zoning techniques. Rather than dividing up subdivisions on a lot-by-lot basis, design standards and performance criteria are established for an entire building site. PUD is used primarily for residential developments, although some commercial uses have been applied as well. Most local governments require a minimum amount of land for a planned unit development and frequently limit the percentage of land in the tract that may be covered by buildings. The advantage of PUD is that design innovations and flexibility are maximized, and development costs are minimized.[36]

Incentive zoning. *Incentive zoning* has a far more commercial bent than does planned unit development. Faced by the increasingly apparent shortcomings of its 1916 zoning law, the New York City Planning Commission in 1961 originated incentive zoning to relieve urban clutter, congestion, and a developing loss of pedestrian space. New York's Planning Commission first "downzoned" the entire city by restricting the size and height of buildings that could be erected, then offered developers a deal. If realtors provided plazas and similar amenities for pedestrians, they could raise the height of their buildings. Congestion would be relieved, pedestrians could walk more freely, and builders could build colossal structures.

Incentive zoning did not work as well as the Planning Commission intended. True, there were more pedestrian walkways available. But buildings continued to reach ever upward, and New York's streets grew ever darker. As the members of one of New York's community boards put it, "We are having unwanted amenities foisted on us at the expense of the best amenities of all—light and air."[37] The reason why incentive zoning created this condition is that the trade-offs established by the New York Planning Commission remain very profitable to developers. One study of all buildings that received bonuses under incentive zoning between 1961 and 1973 found that the extra cost to developers for providing plazas and other amenities amounted to about $4 million. In return, these developers were permitted to erect some 7.5 million square feet of additional floor space worth about $186 million, or a profit of $46 for every $1 expended.[38] Thus, while New York's pedestrians have more "amenities" (plazas, strolling space), they are walking in the dark.

Transferrable development rights. Another innovative concept in local land-use control policies is known as *transferrable development rights,* or *TDR,* which is gaining popularity in the Northeast as well as in Alaska and Colorado.[39] TDR is a compromise between the values of the zoners and the antizoners and, in many ways, is as satisfactory an approach to the problem of urban land use as any. TDR separates the right to improve property from the right to own property, much in the same sense that the right of prospectors to exploit minerals and oil that may be found under the ground can be separated from ownership of the land's surface. Under a TDR program, a community can directly give or withhold development rights in order to restrict development in one area and to encourage development in another. Thus, owners of property in an area where development is banned, such as a street of historic value, are permitted to develop someone else's property in another section, where development is needed. In the event that property owners do not wish to develop property in another portion of the city, they can sell their development rights to another party and thus be compensated. An example is the case of New York's Grand Central Station, where the courts committed the city to preserving the building as a cultural landmark rather than permit it to be replaced by a skyscraper, and compensated its owner, the Penn Central Railroad, by granting it rights to develop other portions of the city.

TDR may appear to be a violation of the traditional property right, but it is in many ways more equitable than zoning. Under zoning, the property owner is not compensated at all if new restrictions are imposed on the use of his or her land. Similarly, when property is condemned for public purposes (such as urban renewal), property owners may be compensated, but urban funds that are available for doing so are often limited. Thus, TDR permits historic and cultural monuments to be preserved while still permitting investment to flourish in a community.

Zoning for limited growth. In recent years, zoning has been used to encourage policies of nongrowth in communities.[40] From an environmental perspective, at least in some cases, *restricting growth through zoning* can be advantageous, but from the perspective of social equity such use of zoning becomes extremely controversial.

The movement to limit municipal growth through zoning can be traced to the town of Ramapo, a suburb of New York City. Between 1960 and 1970 Ramapo grew from 38,000 to 78,000 people, and the land being used by those additional Ramapoans was destroying what many felt was the character of the village. Consequently, Ramapo developed an unusual 18-year, "delayed-growth" model. This permitted the phased development of various service facilities such as water, power lines, and sewers and had the effect of rationing building permits to developers. Ramapo's policy quickly was challenged in the courts (*Golden* v. *Planning Board of Ramapo*); Ramapo lost the first round, but then won in the New York court of appeals. In 1972 the U.S. Supreme Court refused to review the decision, thus upholding the position of Ramapo.

Ramapo was an indirect inspiration to the citizens of Petaluma, a village near San Francisco. Petaluma had grown from 14,000 people in 1960 to 25,000 in 1970, and to 30,000 by the end of 1971. Petaluma was more straightforward in its policy to limit growth than Ramapo and flatly rationed the community's growth to 500 new residential units a year for the next five years. The city council's policy was ratified by Petaluma's voters in 1973. The city's ordinance soon was challenged in the courts (*Construction Industry Association of Sonoma County* v. *City of Petaluma*). Petaluma's lawyers contended that adding more Petalumans would overburden the city's sanitation and school facilities, thus forcing the citizens to vote for increased taxes. The U.S. district court held against Petaluma, ruling that "neither Petaluma's city officials nor the local electorate may use their power to disapprove bonds at the polls as a weapon to define or destroy fundamental constitutional rights," notably, the rights of people to travel and settle.

By this time Petaluma was becoming a symbol, with environmental and urban interests taking the side of the city, and civil rights groups and construction interests banding against Petaluma. Petaluma took its case to the federal appeals court, which reversed the decision of the lower court, stating that Petaluma had a right to use its zoning power "in its own self-interest" by employing zoning as "lawfully delegated to it by the state." The judges observed that "the federal court is not a superzoning board" and "should not be called on to mark the point at which legitimate local interests are outweighed by legitimate regional interests."

Since *Petaluma,* a number of local governments have wrangled over civil rights and *status quo.* In part, this controversy is racial and economic since, by restricting new housing, local governments are limiting the number of new residents that may join their communities and often these policies can amount to *de facto* segregation of whites and blacks, rich and poor. Nevertheless, zoning for no-growth, or for controlled growth, is not the same as "exclusionary zoning," which we consider next.

Exclusionary zoning. To assure that whites, blacks, and browns do not live beside each other, some cities and suburbs have adopted the practice of *exclusionary zoning,* which is an attempt effectively to zone out low-income housing by allowing only relatively expensive homes to be built. Although some would disagree, exclusionary zoning is not quite the same as zoning for controlled growth. In contrast to no-growth, or limited-growth zoning, exclusionary zoning is aimed at discouraging new housing for poor people. This is accomplished by restricting the kinds of residences permitted, by tacking on unreasonable construction requirements to deliberately raise the costs, and through a variety of administrative decisions that effectively limit development, such as minimum floor space requirements for houses, large lot sizes, and so on.[41]

The device of exclusionary zoning has been recognized by a broad spectrum of scholars and legal experts as one that is clearly segregationist. In 1978, a massive, three-year study released by the American Bar Association stated that the practice has helped make new housing prohibitively costly for more than half of all Americans.[42]

The most significant court test of exclusionary zoning involved Mount Laurel, New Jersey, a mostly white township that borders Camden, a community that is largely black and Puerto Rican. In 1975, Mount Laurel's long-standing zoning ordinances were overturned by the New Jersey Supreme Court on the grounds that, "every such municipality must by its land use regulations, presumptively make realistically possible an appropriate variety in choice of housing."[43] Mount Laurel's zoning practices had excluded all dwellings except single-family detached houses that included restrictions on minimum lot sizes, number of bedrooms, building sizes, and a few other items. The *Mount Laurel* decision was hailed as the "most encouraging sign to date that exclusionary suburban zoning practices are being recognized as being discriminatory."[44]

The 1975 decision by the New Jersey Supreme Court became known as *"Mount Laurel I"* because in 1983 a second *Mount Laurel* case (*"Mount Laurel II"*) was heard by the state's supreme court. In its 1983 ruling, the court took a much more aggressive stand against exclusionary zoning and stated that not only did

BOB BUGG. Courtesy of Chicago Tribune—New York News Syndicate, Inc.

a municipality have an obligation to provide housing for its own poor, but that it had a responsibility to furnish a "fair share" of the region's current and projected housing needs for people with low and moderate incomes. Now Mount Laurel had to prove to the satisfaction of the judiciary that it was housing not only its own poor in decent quarters, but some of the indigent residing outside its municipal limits as well. And Mount Laurel's commitment to housing the poor likely would not be easy to prove to the bench. As the court said, even after its invalidation of Mount Laurel's zoning ordinance in *Mount Laurel I*, "Mount Laurel remains afflicted with a blatantly exclusionary ordinance. Papered over with paper studies rationalized by hired experts, the ordinance at its core is true to nothing but Mount Laurel's determination to exclude the poor."[45]

Mount Laurel II was a major victory for the friends of fair housing. As one observer put it, *Mount Laurel II* is the "best thing to happen in civil rights since 1954," when the Supreme Court ruled in favor of desegregating schools.[46]

Inclusionary zoning. Some cities, mostly in the West and particularly in California, have attempted to counter exclusionary zoning practices by developing the concept of inclusionary zoning. *Inclusionary zoning* requires developers to set aside a small portion of newly built homes for occupancy by moderate- and low-income families at reduced rates. For example, the City of Palo Alto, California, requires a developer of ten new condominiums to sell one unit at $60,000 below its market value, or to donate $60,000 in cash to the city's housing fund. The people permitted to buy housing at these reduced rates are chosen by the City Housing Commission.

In California alone, 22 cities and towns have adopted inclusionary zoning and have allocated units to more than 1,000 families. Since local governments never contribute their own funds to help defray the builders' costs, it is a remarkably cheap housing subsidy program insofar as the taxpayers are concerned. But whether inclusionary zoning is fair to those middle-class homebuyers who must absorb the costs that are passed on to them by developers, or even to poor families who are passed over by local housing officials in the allocation of housing units that have been reduced in price by developers to comply with inclusionary zoning ordinances, is another matter. In fact, only 1 family in 50 among those eligible to receive the benefits of inclusionary zoning does so.[47]

Enterprise zoning. Enterprise zones were originated in the United Kingdom in 1980, when the British government established nine enterprise zones in impoverished urban areas around the country. An *enterprise zone* permits businesses that build plants or invest in job-producing activities in a depressed neighborhood to get tax breaks and other advantages that can be granted by government. The idea is that businesses will be more inclined to invest in job-producing activities in poor areas where the jobs are needed most.

Despite White House backing, federally sponsored enterprise zones have not gotten far in Congress. But the states have taken a remarkably bold initiative in their development. Twenty-one states have begun their own variants of enterprise zones. Louisiana has created no fewer than 620 enterprise zones, in which one-eighth of its people live. Louisiana offers businesses five years of exemption from state and local sales and user taxes and, in selected cities, five-year exemptions from the state corporation tax. In Florida, as a result of the Miami race riots of 1980, 186 enterprise zones were created in 26 cities and 4 counties, including Dade County's Liberty City, where much of the rioting occurred. Connecticut has created enterprise zones in 6 cities; the incentives for business include an 80 percent reduction of local property taxes over five years and a 50 percent cut in corporate income taxes for ten years. Arkansas, Illinois, Kansas, and Kentucky also have been aggressive in creating new enterprise zones for their depressed areas. The states, in sum, have been innovative and aggressive in developing enterprise zones and, in effect, are showing the federal government how to do it.[48]

The "Quiet Revolution" in State Land-Use Planning

In 1971, Fred Bosselman and David Callies identified what they called the "quiet revolution in land use control."[49] What they referred to was the virtually unobserved entrance of state governments into the area of land-use planning. Ever since 1916, when New York City passed the nation's first zoning ordinance, the states had effectively ceded their power of land-use planning—a power that had been granted the imprimatur of the U.S. Supreme Court—to their local governments. As a consequence of the plethora of problems that developed from this decentralization of planning power for land use, and the kinds of "zoning zaniness" that evolved at the local levels to cope with these problems, states found that they simply had to get into the land-use planning act.

This renewed interest by the states in land-use planning began in 1961, when Hawaii enacted its exceptionally strong law that preempts Hawaii's local governments in the area of land-use policy. Today, more than 40 states have some kind of significant land-use policy. These policies can be divided into three broad classifications: growth management policies, such as mandatory planning and control of subdivision zoning; siting policies, which pertain to how power plants and surface mining operations are located; and natural areas policies, which govern such areas as wetlands and shore lands.[50]

Table 18-1 displays the complexity of state land-use policies. "Dimension 1" of the table refers to what types of land are regulated by the states, for example, all of the state's lands, such as is done in Oregon and Hawaii; areas of critical concern, such as Connecticut's wetlands and Wisconsin's coast lands; and lands that are regulated for the benefit of a particular region of the state, such as in Minnesota and Florida.

"Dimension 2" refers to how decision making about land use is conducted in each state. Oregon and Hawaii have by far the most authoritative and comprehensive state land-use policies. In those states, planning policy is mandated to local governments, and how local governments implement state land-use policy is reviewed on the states' initiative. Less authoritative in terms of state powers are those states that have enacted their own reviews of local land-use regulations. Nevertheless, these states still have significant powers. They can require permits for certain kinds of development, and they can initiate and review local plans for development and modify those plans when necessary. A variation of this type of land-use planning is called the "double-veto" system. In this version, both state and local approval is required to adopt land-use proposals. The double-veto system preserves quite a bit of power at the local level, but the state still may block development or impose rather stringent conditions on developments that have been approved locally. But the state's role in this system is relatively passive, and states may not approve a development that has been

Table 18-1 Dimensions of State Land-Use Planning

DIMENSION 1: TARGETS OF STATE LAND-USE REGULATION	*DIMENSION 2: PARTICIPANTS IN THE DECISION-MAKING PROCESS AND THE EXTENT OF THEIR AUTHORITY*			
	Mandatory state planning policy, state-initiated review	*Periodic state review of local regulations of state or regional concern*	*Double-veto system: state or regional and local approval*	*State designation guidelines: local implementation may or may not be binding*
All land zoned for planned development	Oregon Hawaii			Wyoming Connecticut[1] Montana
Areas of critical concern				
1. Environmentally sensitive	Connecticut (wetlands) Delaware (coast)	Oregon Florida Wyoming	Vermont California Maine	Colorado[1] Maryland[1] Wyoming
2. Adjacent to public	Wisconsin (coast) Massachusetts (wetlands)	Minnesota	North Carolina New Jersey	
Development of regional impact or benefit	Minnesota	Oregon Minnesota Florida[2] Montana (utilities)	Vermont New York Maryland	Colorado[1]

[1] Not binding.
[2] Florida has a two-tiered system of review.

Source: Alvin H. Mushkatel and Linda Mushkatel, "The Emergence of State Planning and Its Potential Impact on Urban Areas," *State and Local Government Review* (May, 1979), p. 56.)

vetoed by local authorities, such as, for example, a local government's decision not to build low or moderately priced housing. Finally, the weakest statewide land-use planning regulations are those that merely designate guidelines concerning local government policies that may or may not be binding on those governments. When all is said and done, however, the states have moved surprisingly forcefully into the area of land-use planning, and their control of this area is likely to grow.

THE POLITICS OF THE PLANNING PROCESS: TRANSPORTATION

There is at least one other major field of importance to state and local governments in which planners have had a unique impact, and that is transportation. Planning for transportation has its own peculiar politics, and it is a major public policy by any fiscal measure. Americans expend nearly 22 percent of the gross national product on transportation, and about 14 percent of the annual tax take by all levels of government is devoted to transportation.[51]

Financing Highways

The bulk of money for transportation goes to highway systems. America has some 148 million motorists cruising on its 3.9 million miles of roads and highways. Of this, 40,700 miles of tarmac constitute the interstate highway system, which is as yet incomplete; there are still 1,700 miles to construct.[52] Highways in America are financed from five major sources of revenues: toll roads, property taxes, special assessments, user taxes, and federal aid. The most important of these are federal aid and user taxes, particularly state taxes on gasoline and motor vehicle licenses. Roughly half of all state and local highway revenues are derived from user fees levied on vehicle owners.

Federal aid is also a major source of transportation revenues. Until 1982, the federal government collected gasoline taxes to the tune of 4 cents per gallon and generated approximately $7 billion a year. In 1982, however, Congress sharply increased the federal tax on gasoline to 9 cents a gallon, thereby generating an additional $5.5 billion a year. The increase in taxes (which will amount to almost $15 billion a year) is dedicated to highway and bridge projects, with a relatively small amount ($1.1 billion) available for capital assistance to public transit.[53]

Financing, building, and maintaining roads and highways in this country is done through a partnership of state governments and the federal government. Table 18-2 indicates the multiplicity of federal, state, and local arrangements in the financing of highways. Georgia relies most heavily on the federal government to finance its highways, Kentucky pays a greater percentage of its highway costs than does any other state, and New York and Wisconsin lead the other states in terms of shifting the bulk of highway costs to their local governments.

The Feds and Transportation Policy

As Table 18-2 indicates, the federal government long has had an impact on the state and local system of roads. At first, federal policies for transportation emphasized building roads in rural areas, as expressed by the Federal Aid Road

Table 18-2 Percentage of Federal, State, and Local Expenditures for Highways by Contributing Levels of Government, Ranked by Order of Reliance on State and Local Funding, 1983

		PERCENTAGE FINANCED BY[1]		
Rank	*State*	*Federal*	*State*	*Local*
	United States	25%	47%	28%
1	Georgia	49	34	17
2	Montana	47	27	26
3	West Virginia	44	48	8
4	Maryland	43	44	12
5	North Carolina	42	50	8
6	Washington, D.C.	41	NA	59
7	South Carolina	38	62	0
8	Oregon	36	37	27
9	Vermont	35	38	26
10	Hawaii	34	35	30
10	Washington	34	40	26
11	Rhode Island	33	27	40
12	Idaho	32	52	16
13	Alabama	31	49	21
13	Alaska	31	55	14
13	Nevada	31	40	29
14	Arkansas	30	56	14
14	North Dakota	30	49	21
14	South Dakota	30	37	33
15	Delaware	29	58	13
15	Tennessee	29	51	20
15	Utah	29	43	28
16	Illinois	28	42	30
17	Michigan	27	54	20
17	Pennsylvania	27	54	20
18	Missouri	26	45	29
19	Colorado	25	31	44
19	Indiana	25	61	13
19	Kentucky	25	66	9
19	Virginia	25	61	14
20	California	24	46	30
20	Connecticut	24	41	35
20	New Hampshire	24	44	32
21	Arizona	23	58	19
21	Maine	23	48	29
21	Wyoming	23	57	21
22	Kansas	22	33	45
23	Florida	21	48	31
23	Nebraska	21	47	32
23	New Mexico	21	61	18
24	Massachusetts	20	46	34
24	Minnesota	20	39	41
24	Mississippi	20	51	29
25	Texas	19	44	37
26	Iowa	18	51	31
26	Ohio	18	61	20

Table 18-2 (Continued)

Rank	State	PERCENTAGE FINANCED BY[1] Federal	State	Local
27	Louisiana	17	60	23
27	New Jersey	17	46	37
28	New York	16	33	51
28	Wisconsin	16	34	51
29	Oklahoma	15	68	16

[1] Percentages have been rounded.

Source: Advisory Commission on Intergovernmental Relations, *Significant Features of Fiscal Federalism, 1984* (Washington, D.C.: U.S. Government Printing Office, 1985), p. 38.

Act of 1916, which provided the first regular funding for public highway construction. A departure from this rural orientation was signaled in 1944, when the Federal Highway Act was passed. This act helped develop roads designed to assist farmers in getting their goods to the marketplaces, but it also provided for the extension of primary roads in urban areas. This latter innovation, known as "ABC funds," still is continued today, and federal funds are given to the states on a matched basis. The Federal Highway Act of 1944 also promoted development of the national system of highways, using the logic that such highways were necessary for national defense, but it was only in 1956 that a new Federal Highway Act authorized enormous amounts of money to develop the interstate highway system.

The Federal Highway Act of 1956, which stipulated that interstate highways could be developed with 90 percent federal funding and 10 percent state funding, presented an opportunity that the states could not resist. Between 1956 and 1982, the Highway Trust Fund, which had been established by the 1956 act, poured nearly $82 billion into the interstate highway system.[54]

As the nation entered the 1960s, Washington began to take a renewed interest in mass transportation, particularly for urban areas. The first such federal program was contained in the Housing Act of 1961, which authorized somewhat more than $40 million in loans to transit operators and to fund demonstration programs. In 1964, Congress enacted the Urban Mass Transportation Act, which marked the first full-scale entry of the federal government into urban mass transit. This act provided for two-thirds federal and one-third local matching funds for capital programs in metropolitan regions.

By 1972, the year in which the interstate highway system was supposed to be completed, only 87 percent of the goal had been reached, so in 1973 Congress enacted the Federal Aid Highway Act, which extended the authorizations for the interstate highway system, but also contained some funds for mass transit systems. For the first time, funds traditionally earmarked exclusively for highways could be used for urban mass transportation. The act established a ratio of 80 percent federal funds and 20 percent local funds for Urban Mass Transit Administration grants. In 1974, the National Mass Transportation Assistance Act was passed, which expanded state and local opportunities for developing public transit systems, and in 1978 Congress enacted the Surface Transportation Assistance Act, which allocates operating funds to small towns and rural areas. By 1980, federal grants were covering four-fifths of major capital costs for urban mass transit systems and 17 percent of their operating budgets.[55]

In 1982, the federal government sharply reduced its financial assistance to the mass transportation programs of urban governments. In 1981, the federal government had been spending $3.3 billion on capital improvements for urban mass transit; by 1982, this had been reduced by two-thirds to $1.1 billion. By 1981, the federal contribution to the operating costs of urban transits had attained $1.2 billion; by 1982, this was reduced to zero. Increasingly, it was clear that states and localities (especially localities) would be expected to take over the public's transportation programs, and with decreasing help from the federal government.

Some have argued that this federal withdrawal from the transportation field is to the good. There are approximately 1,000 federal transportation programs that are administered by some 64 federal agencies, overseen by 30 congressional committees.[56] The cost to the states of implementing simply the planning mandates of these programs alone is approximately $130 million each year.[57]

Far more serious than these costs, in the view of many, are the heretofore unseen expenses of the 1,000 federal transportation programs. Despite lip service to broad-based planning and "multimodal" (e.g., combined rail, air, water, and road transportation) approaches to transportation policy that is paid by federal transportation officials, several researchers have contended that the continued traditional interest that federal officials have shown in developing highways, working in combination with entrenched state highway department officials, has produced a dismal urban situation. Because state highway departments and federal highway administrators have pursued narrow transit objectives, such as concerning themselves solely with accommodating traffic and studiously ignoring more comprehensive land-use policies in central cities, a number of adverse effects have resulted, including the isolation of minorities in the central cities. Inner-city residents frequently are dependent upon public transit to get to places of employment in the suburbs, and federal and state highway officials are notably insensitive to their problems. "The inertia of this limited purpose highway program has been sustained by massive federal funding, a bureaucratically embedded and technologically intimidating planning methodology, and a system of federal plan and impact reviews whose major effect has been to expedite the approval and construction of highway projects."[58] Thus, the central cities have declined. Highways have slashed through municipal downtowns, accelerating the disintegration process of inner-city neighborhoods, and an underclass population has concentrated in central cities. The President's National Urban Policy Commission stated that, after more than two decades of massive investment in the interstate highway system, the construction of these highways had been "the most powerful direct federal action that has contributed to metropolitan decentralization and central city decline."[59]

The States and Transportation Policy

The states spend nearly $30 billion a year on highways, but less than $2.5 billion on public transit.[60] Following the federal lead, the states have made efforts to systematize their transit programs by eliminating the traditional Bureau of Public Roads and incorporating it into a larger multimodal agency, or the model established by the federal government when it created its Department of Transportation in 1966. Since then, at least 39 states and the District of Columbia have emulated Washington's approach.[61]

The states are directly responsible for close to 930,000 miles of the nation's roads and, like the Federal Highway Trust Fund, state departments of transportation rely on an "ever-normal trough" of earmarked user taxes as their principal means of financing highways and other types of transportation construction.[62]

Like their federal counterpart, states' thinking about transportation typically dwells on highways. Table 18-3 ranks the states along three indicators of state highway policy: per capita expenditure for highways, highway expenditures as a proportion of total state spending, and highway density (or the ratio of highway miles to square miles of land area in the state). As the table indicates, the more industrially developed the state (such as those states in the Northeast), the less emphasis the state will place on the building of highways. The largely agrarian states, such as several in the Midwest and the Rocky Mountain areas, tend to invest heavily in roads and highways. The primary determinant of how much a state commits to roads appears to be highway density. The more rural the state and the more dispersed its people, the more likely that the state will place a high priority on building highways.

By contrast, those states with concentrated populations and that are highly urbanized emphasize urban mass transit systems. Although 32 state government budgets contain an allotment for mass transit planning, capital expenditures, and operating subsidies for their local governments,[63] only 8 states—California, Connecticut, Illinois, Maryland, Massachusetts, New Jersey, New York, and Pennsylvania—account for 87 percent of all state mass transit funds.[64] The bulk of these state grants to local government transportation systems are in the form of capital grants for buses and other kinds of rubber-tired vehicles.

Some states have gone farther than merely financing local transit systems and run the systems directly. Connecticut serves three of the states' largest cities and carries 85 percent of the states' public transit riders. Rhode Island also serves most of the state through a state-operated public transportation system. Maryland operates bus systems in Baltimore and other areas. Nebraska operates Omaha's transit system. West Virginia leases vehicles to regional Councils of Governments, and Delaware operates a system for elderly and handicapped riders.[65]

Mass Transit: A Local Matter

With few exceptions, however, the people who must bear the brunt of state and federal policies for mass transit are the local managers of the nation's 800 public bus and rail systems. Nearly two-thirds of the public transit systems in the country are operated by municipalities, another 20 percent by special districts or public authorities, and 15 percent by counties.[66] Public transit is a local phenomenon, and local governments pay more for it than any other governmental level: 27 percent of the public transit operating budget is paid by local governments.[67]

With the sharp cutbacks in federal support of mass transit, local governments must find new ways of meeting both a rising public demand and grim fiscal realities. This will not be easy. Since the Arab oil embargo of 1973-74,

Table 18-3 State Scores and Ranks for Three Indicators of State Highway Policy, 1978 (ranked by per capita state and local expenditures per $1,000 personal income)

	STATE AND LOCAL HIGHWAY EXPENDITURES PER CAPITA		*HIGHWAY EXPENDITURE AS % OF TOTAL STATE GENERAL EXPENDITURE*		*HIGHWAY DENSITY (HIGHWAY MILES PER SQUARE MILE OF LAND AREA)*	
	Score	*Rank*	*Score*	*Rank*	*Score*	*Rank*
Alaska	$475	1	10.6%	37	0.02	50
Wyoming	284	2	22.0	2	0.35	49
Montana	238	3	17.0	11	0.54	46
North Dakota	218	4	17.7	7	1.54	29
South Dakota	211	5.5	16.8	13	1.09	38
West Virginia	211	5.5	22.8	1	1.56	28
Nevada	204	7	17.4	9	0.45	48
Iowa	195	8	17.4	8	2.18	12
Idaho	182	9	17.2	10	0.77	41
Nebraska	178	10.5	18.4	5	1.26	33
Vermont	178	10.5	11.1	36	1.51	30
New Hampshire	172	12	18.1	6	1.73	21
Minnesota	165	13	10.5	38	1.61	26
Kentucky	162	14	20.6	3	1.74	20
Louisiana	169	15	12.2	30	1.23	35
Maine	155	16.5	13.0	25	0.71	42
New Mexico	155	16.5	14.4	17	0.59	45
Kansas	151	18	15.4	16	1.65	24
Virginia	148	19	18.6	4	1.63	25
Mississippi	140	20	13.6	22	1.45	31
Arizona	139	21	14.1	19	0.51	47
Washington	136	22	13.4	23	1.26	34
Colorado	134	23	11.7	32	0.84	40
Oregon	130	24.5	12.7	27	1.17	36
Wisconsin	130	24.5	8.1	43	1.95	16

Arkansas	127	26	16.9	12	1.42	32
Georgia	126	27	14.1	18	1.77	19
Alabama	125	28	12.9	26	1.72	22
Maryland	120	29	12.4	29	2.73	5
Tennessee	119	30.5	16.1	14	1.99	15
Utah	119	30.5	11.7	33	0.60	44
Hawaii	116	32	6.5	45	0.61	43
Oklahoma	113	33	13.3	24	1.59	27
North Carolina	112	34	12.2	31	1.88	17
Delaware	108	35.5	8.8	41	2.62	8
Missouri	108	35.5	15.9	15	1.70	23
Texas	107	37	13.7	21	1.00	39
Massachusetts	103	38	6.3	46	4.29	3
Illinois	102	39	11.2	35	2.39	10
New York	95	40.5	5.4	48	2.28	11
Pennsylvania	95	40.5	8.2	42	2.64	7
Ohio	94	43	11.5	34	2.71	6
Michigan	94	43	9.2	40	2.10	13
Florida	92	44	12.6	28	1.80	18
Connecticut	90	45.5	8.0	44	3.93	4
Indiana	90	45.5	13.9	20	2.52	9
California	79	47	4.7	49	1.13	37
New Jersey	79	48	6.1	47	4.40	2
South Carolina	71	49	10.0	39	2.04	14
Rhode Island	69	50	4.2	50	5.53	1

Source: U.S. Department of Commerce, Bureau of the Census, *Statistical Abstracts of the United States* (Washington, D.C.: U.S. Government Printing Office, 1980), pp. 12, 209, 300, 643.

approximately one-third of the population, especially people living in suburban and rural areas, has expressed dissatisfaction with public transit services and facilities. By contrast, fewer than 10 percent of Americans are dissatisfied with such public services as schools, shopping facilities, police and fire protection, and hospitals.[68] Those citizens who give up commuting to and from work by private automobile generally prefer switching to a car pool rather than to public transit services.[69]

Such opinions should be kept in perspective; Americans have never been particularly enthusiastic users of public transit. Eighty-four percent of Americans own an automobile, and 37 percent own two or more automobiles.[70] Almost two-thirds of Americans drive to and from work in their own cars, and an additional fifth take the trip by ride sharing with others; only 6 percent of Americans go to work in a bus or commuter train—almost as many people walk to work![71]

Virtually all public transit ridership in the country is concentrated in a few large cities. Fourteen major metropolitan areas, in fact, account for 70 percent of all the nation's public transit passengers. New York City alone accounts for 38 percent.[72] Approximately half of all cities and counties have a bus service, but in 86 percent of those cities, fewer than a fourth of the population uses public transportation on a regular basis. In nearly 13 percent, 26 percent to 50 percent of the population uses public transportation on a regular basis.[73]

Figure 18-1 shows the patterns of passenger ridership carried by local public transportation. The public's use of urban mass transportation began declining after World War II, a decline that continued essentially unabated until 1974, when an all-time low of 5.6 billion passengers were carried. After 1974, ridership began to increase, peaking at more than 8 billion riders in 1980, after which it began a slight decline.

In the face of lethargic public support and cutbacks in federal (and

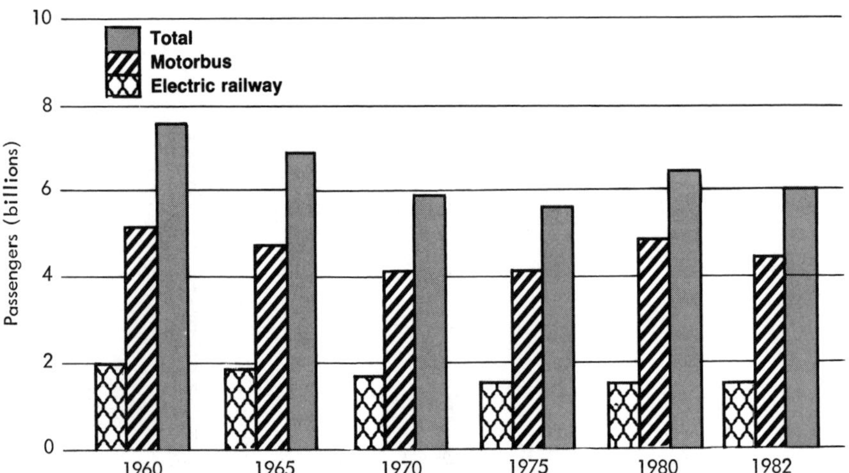

Figure 18-1. Revenue passengers carried by local public transportation, 1960–1982. (*Source:* Bureau of the Census, *Statistical Abstract of the United States, 1985.* Washington, D.C.: U.S. Government Printing Office, 1984, p. 584.

probably state) allocations for urban public transportation, local transit managers are faced with a number of challenges, and local governments have begun financing their own transit systems. Like their federal and state counterparts, most local governments are enacting taxes earmarked for transportation. Methods of financing local transit systems range from a state lottery in Arizona, to commercial bond issues in New York and San Francisco, to a tax on beer in Birmingham, Alabama. Houston in 1982 took the unprecedented step of financing an 18-mile, heavy-rail public transit system, with or without federal funds, relying on a 1 percent sales tax for financing.[74]

A number of cities are also experimenting with public policies that will encourage the development of paratransit services. *Paratransit* refers to such alternative transportation modes as independent car pools, van pools, jitnies, and taxies that are highly decentralized in their approach to meeting urban transportation needs. Approximately 85 percent of cities and counties have taxi cab services available in their areas. About a quarter of cities and counties have dial-a-ride services, and between a fourth and a fifth of cities and counties have employer-sponsored car or van pools. More than 90 percent of localities have special transportation services for elderly and disabled people as well.[75] The Minnesota legislature has appropriated funds to encourage the use of these kinds of paratransit services throughout the state.[76] Minnesota took this step at the urging of Minneapolis and St. Paul, whose officials had concluded that large-scale, heavy-duty public transportation systems made little sense given the Twin Cities' demographic patterns.

Cities are making headway in meeting the public transportation needs of their citizens, despite an absence of local leaders who are concerned with whole urban areas, competition among the various municipalities, and an inordinate suspicion of major cities felt by their surrounding suburbs. Despite these difficulties and obvious financial constrictions, an analysis of transportation policies in eight large cities concluded that there was reason to believe that local policymaking for urban transit was becoming increasingly democratic, systematic, and rational.[77]

The "Logics" of Transit Planning

More critical, perhaps, as impediments to cohesive public planning of urban transportation policy, are the relationships among the various "logics" of transportation politics in metropolitan areas. Despite the fact that urban transportation planning undoubtedly is the cities' single most powerful tool for attaining land-use goals, Frank Colcord has identified at least three conflicting logics of transportation policymaking that represent competing professional and political values: the logic of the technician, the logic of the planner, and the logic of the politician.[78]

The *technician's logic* continues to dominate the decision-making process in transportation at all levels of government, and it guides the thinking behind the present highway program. The technician assumes that his or her field, the highway, offers a "final solution" to a narrowly defined technical problem, that of transporting people and products from point A to point B with optimal efficiency. Unfortunately, the technician's logic fails to take into account such values as torn-up neighborhoods, razed homes, marred urban landscapes, displaced people, environmental degradation, and a politically alienated urban citizenry. These variables do not enter the calculations of an engineering mentality and are irrelevant to the logic of the technician.

The *planner's logic* is broader in scope, but, while the planner has the potential for considering the larger mission for the metropolitan community, this mission is nearly always unexpressed. This is not to imply that community goals larger than that of getting efficiently from one point to another are not present. In fact, it is the current preeminence of the technician's logic in transportation planning circles that has unwittingly encouraged the gradual emergence of the planner's logic as a means of achieving broader community objectives.

Finally, the *politician's logic* parallels the planner's logic of fostering the broader values of the community, but the politician also is susceptible to the short-range objectives of the technician. To the politician, temporarily relieving downtown traffic congestion by building a new freeway may be a most appealing alternative in the absence of expressed objections from various citizen groups or alternative policy choices offered by other planning groups. The logic of the politician, in brief, is supremely one of staying in power, and this is achieved by responding to the pressures of the moment as they relate to the politician's idea of building a "good record" over time.

These distinctive logics of transportation planning coexist in metropolises, and each has its uses. The planner must express the community's goals, present and future, and offer creative solutions. The politician must cooperate with and beneficially influence the planning process, provide leadership, and yield legitimacy. The technician must find efficient, novel, and effective means for implementing community goals as identified by the planner and the politician. According to Colcord, there may be a new trend in establishing a harmonious relationship among these traditionally discordant transportation logics in urban areas.

NOTES

[1]Don Allensworth, *Public Administration: The Execution of Public Policy* (Philadelphia: J. B. Lippincott, 1973), p. 32.
[2]National Research Council, *Towards an Understanding of Metropolitan America* (San Francisco: Canfield, 1974), p. 59.
[3]Allen D. Manvel, *Local Land and Building Regulations* (Washington D.C.: U.S. Government Printing Office, 1968), p. 31.
[4]Allensworth, *Public Administration,* p. 33.
[5]*Ibid,* p. 38.
[6]Scott Greer, *Urban Renewal in American Cities* (Indianapolis: Bobbs-Merrill, 1965), p. 76.
[7]Thomas Thorwood, "The Planning and Management Process in City Government," in *Municipal Year Book, 1973* (Washington, D.C.: International City Management Association, 1973), pp. 28-38.
[8]David B. Walker and Albert J. Richter, "Regionalism and the Counties," in *The County Year Book, 1975* (Washington, D.C.: National Association of Counties and International City Management Association, 1975), p. 15.
[9]Allensworth, *Public Administration,* p. 33.
[10]Mavis Mann Reeves and Paris N. Glendening, "Congressional Action Affecting Local Government," in *Municipal Year Book, 1976* (Washington, D.C.: International City Management Association, 1976), p. 55.
[11]Council of State Governments, *Land: State Alternatives for Planning and Management*

(Lexington, Ky.: Council of State Governments, 1975), p. 19. See also C. E. Little, *Shifting Ground: New Priorities for National Land Use Policy* (Washington, D.C.: U.S. Government Printing Office, 1976).

[12]Harold F. Wise and Bertram Wakeley, "The Practice of State Planning and Policy Development," *State Government,* 57, No. 3 (1984), p. 85.

[13]*Ibid.,* p. 88.

[14]*Ibid.,* p. 85.

[15]John F. Shirey, "National Actions Affecting Local Government: Cutbacks and Lowered Expectations," *Municipal Year Book, 1982* (Washington, D.C.: International City Management Association, 1982), p. 47.

[16]"Intergovernmental Focus," *Intergovernmental Perspective,* 8 (Summer, 1982), p. 5.

[17]Jane Roberts, Jerry Fensterman, and Donald Lief, "States, Localities Continue to Adopt Strategic Policies," *Intergovernmental Perspective,* 11 (Winter, 1985), p. 29.

[18]Samuel Kaplan, *The Dream Deferred* (New York: Seabury, 1976), p. 31.

[19]J. B. Lansing, R. W. Marans, and R. B. Zehner, *Planned Residential Environments* (Ann Arbor: University of Michigan, Institute for Social Research, 1970).

[20]J. Terry Edwards and Thomas D. Galloway, "Freedom and Equality: Dimensions of Political Ideology Among City Planners and City Managers," *Urban Affairs Quarterly* (December, 1981), p. 175.

[21]B. Douglas Harman, "City Planning Agencies: Organization, Staffing, and Functions," in *Municipal Year Book, 1972* (Washington, D.C.: International City Management Association, 1972), p. 63. Figures are for 1971.

[22]Francine Rabinowitz, *City Politics and Planning* (New York: Atherton, 1969).

[23]David C. Ranney, *Planning and Politics in the Metropolis* (Columbus, Ohio: Charles E. Merrill, 1969), pp. 147-150.

[24]See, for example, Paul Davidoff, "Advocacy and Pluralism in Planning," *Journal of the American Institute of Planners,* 31 (December, 1965), pp. 331-338.

[25]Herbert J. Gans, "The Need for Planners Trained in Policy Formulation," in Earnest Erder, ed., *Urban Planning in Transition* (New York: Grossman, 1970), pp. 239-245.

[26]Allensworth, *Public Administration,* p. 52.

[27]Edwards and Galloway, "Freedom and Equality," pp. 173–193.

[28]R. Robert Linowes and Don T. Allensworth, *The States and Land Use Control* (New York: Praeger, 1975), p. 46.

[29]Sarah McCally Morehouse, *State Politics, Parties and Policies* (New York: Holt, Rinehart and Winston, 1981), p. 425.

[30]The following discussion is drawn largely from Allensworth, *Public Administration,* pp. 46-47.

[31]Kaplan, *The Dream Deferred,* pp. 67-68.

[32]Alvin H. Mushkatel and Dennis R. Judd, "The States' Role in Land Use Policy," *Policy Studies Review* (November, 1981), p. 264.

[33]The arguments against zoning are drawn from Neal R. Peirce, "Municipal Zoning, Dinosaur of the 1970s," *The Arizona Republic* (June 3, 1977).

[34]Steve Carter, Lyle Sumek, and Murray Frost, "Local Environmental Management," in *Municipal Year Book, 1974* (Washington, D.C.: International City Management Association, 1974), p. 259.

[35]The following listing may not do justice to the myriad techniques of land-use planning, but it is indicative of some of the more important issues that have arisen over the use of these techniques and the motivations of policymakers and communities that underlie their use. Professional land-use planners classify land-use and growth management techniques into six functional categories (some examples of which are covered in the text's discussion): zoning and subdivision techniques, public improvement and land acquisition techniques, administrative procedures, numerical restraints or quota systems, environmental controls, and financial tax systems. See M. E. Gleeson et al., *Urban Growth Management Systems: An Evaluation of Policy-Related Research* (Chicago: American Society of Planning Officials, 1974); and D. R. Godschalk et al., *Constitutional Issues of Growth Management* (Washington, D.C.: Planners Press, 1979).

[36]Lisa Wogan, "Creative Zoning Balances Private and Public Land Use Needs," *Nation's Cities Weekly,* 3 (May 12, 1980), p. 2.

[37]Joana Battaglia, as quoted in William H. Whyte, "How to Make Mid-Town Livable," *New York* (March 9, 1981), p. 25.

[38]*Ibid.,* p. 26.

[39]The discussion of transferrable development rights is drawn from Gladwin Hill, "New Community Planning Tool Potential Boon," *The New York Times* (October 12, 1977).
[40]The following discussions of Ramapo and Petaluma are drawn from Kaplan, *The Dream Deferred,* pp. 77-79.
[41]Paul Davidoff and Mary E. Brooks, "Zoning Out the Poor," in Philip C. Dolce, ed., *Suburbia* (Garden City, N.Y.: Anchor, 1976), pp. 145-147.
[42]Richard P. Fishman, ed., *Housing for All Under Law: New Directions in Housing, Land Use, and Planning Law,* a report of the American Bar Association Advisory Commission on Housing and Urban Growth (Cambridge, Mass.: Ballinger, 1978).
[43]*Southern Burlington County NAACP et al.* v. *Township of Mount Laurel* (1975), as quoted in Davidoff and Brooks, "Zoning Out the Poor," p. 156.
[44]*Ibid.,* p. 161.
[45]*Southern Burlington County NAACP et al.* v. *Township of Mount Laurel* (1983), as quoted in "State Court Mandates Affirmative Zoning Plans," *Public Administration Times* (July 1, 1983), p. 1.
[46]Irene Smith, president of the State Conference of the New Jersey NAACP, as quoted in *ibid.*
[47]"Inclusionary Zoning Termed Inefficient," *Public Administration Times* (December 1, 1981), p. 11. Figures are for 1981.
[48]"States Prove More 'Enterprising' " *Business Week* (November 29, 1982); and Roberts, Fensterman, and Lief, "States, Localities Continue to Adopt Strategic Policies," p. 22. Figures are for 1985.
[49]Fred Bosselman and David Callies, *The Quiet Revolution in Land Use Control* (Washington, D.C.: Council on Environmental Quality, 1971).
[50]Alvin H. Mushkatel and Linda Mushkatel, "The Emergence of State Planning and Its Potential Impact on Urban Areas," *State and Local Government Review* (May 1, 1979), p. 56.
[51]U.S. Bureau of the Census, *Social Indicators III* (Washington, D.C.: U.S. Government Printing Office, 1980), Table 4/7, p. 192. Figures are for 1977.
[52]Drew Lewis, "Road Work Ahead—A Lot of It," *Washington Post* (November 28, 1982).
[53]*Ibid.*
[54]Douglas B. Feaver, "Cost of Roads, Rails, and Rivers Shifts to 'Users' Under Budget," *Washington Post* (March 9, 1982).
[55]Bruce B. McDowell, "Governmental Actors and Factors in Mass Transit," *Intergovernmental Perspective,* 10 (Summer, 1984), p. 9.
[56]National Transportation Policy Study Commission, *Compendium of Federal Transportation Policies and Programs* (Washington, D.C.: U.S. Government Printing Office, 1979), p. 35.
[57]Thomas F. Humphrey, "The States' Role in Policy Implementation: Transportation Policy," *Policy Studies Review* (November, 1981), p. 329.
[58]Yale Rabin, "Federal Urban Transporation Policy and the Highway Planning Process in Metropolitan Areas," *Annals of the American Society for Political and Social Science,* 451 (September, 1981), p. 21.
[59]Department of Housing and Urban Development, *The President's National Urban Policy Report* (Washington, D.C.: U.S. Government Printing Office, 1978), p. 110.
[60]"Transportation," *Book of the States, 1984-85* (Lexington, Ky.: Council of State Governments, 1984), p. 380; and McDowell, "Governmental Actors and Factors in Mass Transit," p. 9. Figures are for 1982.
[61]National Transportation Policy Study Commission, *National Transportation Policies Through the Year 2000: Final Report* (Washington, D.C.: U.S. Government Printing Office, 1979), p. 51. Figure is for 1979.
[62]"Transportation," *Book of the States, 1984-85,* p. 378. Local governments control 2.6 million miles of roads.
[63]Humphrey, "The State's Role in Policy Implementation: Transportation Policy," p. 332.
[64]James A. Dunn, Jr., *Miles to Go: European and American Transportation Policies* (Cambridge, Mass.: M.I.T. Press, 1981), p. 78.
[65]Humphrey, "The State's Role in Policy Implementation: Transportation Policy," pp. 332-333.
[66]McDowell, "Governmental Actors and Factors in Mass Transit," p. 9. Figures are for 1982.
[67]*Ibid.* In 1980, fares accounted for 41 percent of the operating budgets of public transit systems, local government subsidies contributed 27 percent, the federal government 17 percent, state governments 13 percent, and other sources 2 percent.

[68]Bureau of the Census, *Social Indicators III,* p. 158.
[69]*Ibid.*
[70]"Opinion Roundup," *Public Opinion* (June-July 1982), p. 29.
[71]McDowell, "Governmental Actors and Factors in Mass Transit," p. 8.
[72]Wilfred Owen, *Transportation for Cities* (Washington, D.C.: Brookings Institution, 1976), pp. 5-6, 10.
[73] Paula R. Valente, "An Assessment of Public Transportation: Current Issues and Future Trends," *Municipal Year Book, 1982* (Washington, D.C.: International City Management Association, 1982), p. 194.
[74]Thomas C. Burgess, "Creative Finance Next Station Stop for Mass Transit," *The Arizona Republic* (May 1, 1982).
[75]Valente, "An Assessment of Public Transportation," p. 194.
[76]Neal R. Peirce, "Transportation Planners Thinking Smaller," *The Arizona Republic* (June 17, 1977).
[77]Allen Lupo, Frank Colcord, and Edward P. Fowler, *Rites of Way: The Politics of Transportation in Boston and the U.S. City* (Boston: Little, Brown, 1971).
[78]Frank C. Colcord, "The Nation," in *ibid.*, pp. 204–237.

19

CORRUPTION AND THE COSA NOSTRA

Political corruption is a fact of public life in all industrial societies, but in America it has a culture uniquely its own. Some American political scientists, in fact, defend what they call "honest graft" on the basis that it "makes the system work." To a degree, this is true. The person who best explained what honest graft means was George Washington Plunkitt, the undisputed boss of New York's Tammany Hall in the late 1800s. "There's an honest graft, and I'm an example of how it works. I might sum up the whole thing by sayin': 'I seen my opportunities and I took 'em.' "[1]

Perhaps a more accurate description of Plunkitt's so-called honest graft would be individual graft. *Individual corruption* is conducted in the tradition of Plunkitt's seeing his opportunities and taking them. *Systemic corruption* is different—it is graft that "does not disappear when it becomes entrenched and accepted: rather, it assumes a different form, that of *systemic* as opposed to *individual* corruption."[2]

"HONEST GRAFT": AN AMERICAN TRADITION

Individual corruption, or honest graft, for better or worse, has always been a part of the American political panoply. As early as 1776, John Adams noted that a gunpowder supplier had been granted an "exorbitant" contract by the Continental Congress and would, "without any risk at all," make a "clear profit of 12,000 pounds, at least." The firm was the trading house of Willing, Morse, and Company, and both these gentlemen happened to be members of the Secret Committee of the Congress, which had devised the contract.[3]

Other examples are more up to date. In 1973, the late Otto Kerner, former governor of Illinois, author of the famous "Kerner Commission's" *Report on the Causes and Prevention of Violence,* and a federal judge, was sentenced to three years in a federal prison. He was found guilty of paying $50,000 for racetrack stock worth $300,000 as part of a deal to assure that certain racing groups would receive favorable race meeting dates during his tenure as governor. In 1977, Allen G. Hochberg, the former chair of the New York State Assembly's Ethics Committee, became the first sitting member of the Assembly in New York's history to be sent to prison because he was found guilty of attempting to bribe a potential opponent not to run against him.[4]

In 1981 a federal investigation that had been conducted during the previous three years found that "graft is routine and nearly ubiquitous in Oklahoma county government."[5] Investigators estimated that graft in nearly all of Oklahoma's 77 counties added as much as $10 million a year to the state's road maintenance costs alone. Prosecutors stated they had evidence against more than 250 people, and an assistant U.S. attorney stated that the corruption in Oklahoma's counties was "the largest investigation of public corruption in terms of sheer numbers in the nation's history."[6] According to one former county commissioner, the graft in Oklahoma's counties had been pervasive since statehood. "This thing's been happening since they made county commissioners. Sure I took kickbacks. I never asked the man for it; they always gave it to me."[7]

But the times are changing. Abusing the public trust is taken less lightly than it once may have been, and federal prosecutions of public corruption (data are not available for state and local prosecutions) have been steadily—in fact, dramatically—rising. As Table 19-1 shows, from 1970 through 1983, the number of public officials at all levels of government indicted for corruption by federal courts shot up by 17 times, and the number of convictions went up by 22 times! In 1983, there were almost 730 state and local public officials indicted, convicted, or awaiting trial for corrupt practices, more than 550 of whom were local officeholders. "Honest graft," then, may be waning as the American way of "making the system work"—if it ever was.

THE NEW BOYS IN TOWN

When organized crime enters the picture, the nature of political corruption changes, and this change is new because it undermines the political system *as* a system.

Organized crime is the most effective when it is the least noticeable. Indeed, to keep its relationship with government inconspicuous, organized crime has been known to pack up and move away from the cities that it controls to small towns, in order to avoid embarrassing the urban politicians it "owns." The most notorious such transfer was the move of Al "Scarface" Capone's organization from Chicago to Cicero, Illinois. Scarface immediately established his control in Cicero, as the following quotation from the Illinois Crime Survey of 1929 notes:

> On the Monday night preceding the election, gunmen invaded the office of the Democratic candidate for clerk, beat him, and shot up the place. Automobiles, filled with gunmen, paraded the streets, slugging and kidnapping the election workers. Polling places were raided by armed thugs, and ballots were taken at

Table 19-1 Federal Prosecutions of Public Corruption, Selected Years, 1970–1983

Prosecution Status	*1970*	*1975*	*1980*	*1983*
Total[1]				
Indicted	63	255	723	1,073
Convicted	44	179	551	972
Awaiting trial	—[2]	27	213	222
Federal officials				
Indicted	9	53	123	460
Convicted	9	43	131	424
Awaiting trial	—[2]	5	16	58
State officials				
Indicted	10	36	72	81
Convicted	7	18	51	65
Awaiting trial	—[2]	5	28	26
Local officials				
Indicted	26	139	247	270
Convicted	16	94	168	226
Awaiting trial	—[2]	15	82	61

[1] Includes individuals, not shown separately, who are neither public officials nor employees but who were involved with public officials or employees in violating the law.
[2] Represents zero.

Source: Bureau of the Census, *Statistical Abstract of the United States, 1981* (Washington, D.C.: U.S. Government Printing Office, 1981), p. 184, and *1985,* p. 175.

the point of a gun from the hands of voters waiting to drop them into the box. Voters and workers were kidnapped, brought to Chicago, and held prisoners until the polls closed.[8]

The Substance of the Syndicate

It is this kind of activity that makes political corruption in the twentieth century rather different from political corruption in John Adams's eighteenth century, or different even from the clubby corruption in Oklahoma's counties. The head of a major national firm that specializes in detecting white-collar crime has commented, "Never have kickbacks, bribes and conflicts of interest been such a dominating factor in U.S. society."[9]

Whether or not the assessment is accurate, kickbacks and other forms of payment have made organized crime a lucrative operation. By any standard, the economics of organized crime is impressive. Estimates in the 1980s usually credit organized crime with running a $150 billion annual business, with net profits at about $50 billion.[10]

Crime's volume of business makes it the second biggest industry in the United States; only the oil industry is larger. Figure 19-1 places the economic impact of organized crime in perspective. It is estimated that the average citizen pays a 2 percent tax on every dollar as a direct result of organized crime's cut and that criminal syndicates may add as much as 20 percent to the cost of running some American cities through their corruption of local governments.[11] It also has been estimated that between 15,000 and 50,000 business enterprises with investments totaling more than $20 billion are controlled directly or indirectly by

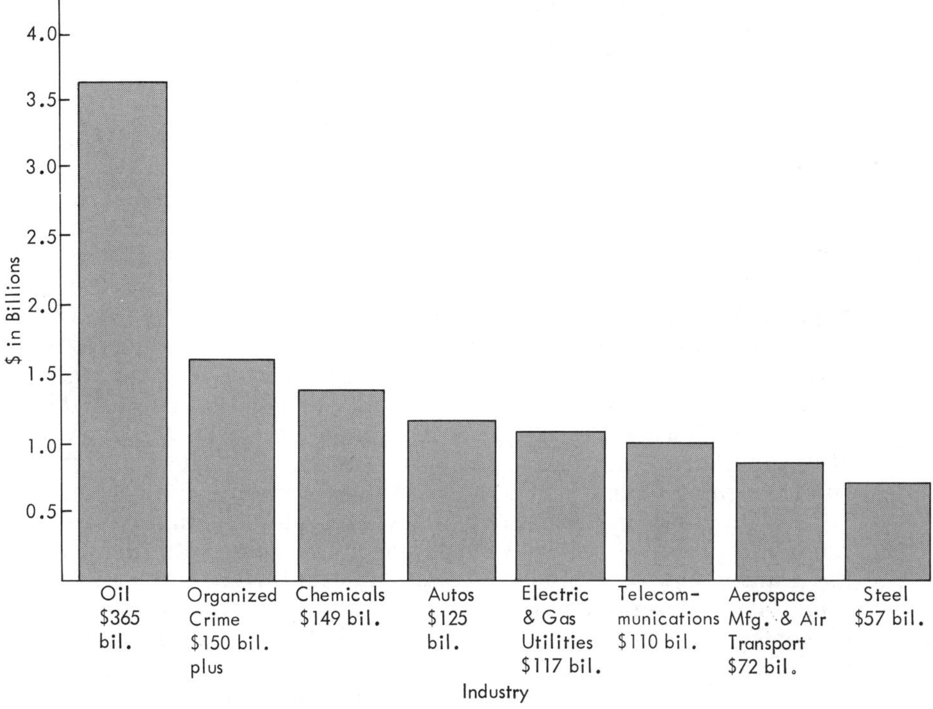

Figure 19-1. Revenues by U.S. industry, including Organized Crime, 1979. (*Source:* James Cook, "The Invisible Empire," *Forbes,* September 29, 1980, as derived from p. 61.)

criminals, and perhaps 10,000 of these businesses are owned outright by known members of the Mafia.[12] Much of the Mob's money comes from narcotics and gambling. Perhaps more than half is from narcotics alone and possibly a fifth from gambling.[13]

There can be no question that organized crime takes its toll far beyond the more than $150 billion that American citizens unknowingly shell out to it. It has been estimated, for instance, that as many as half of the street holdups in America are committed by drug addicts whose supplies are controlled by organized crime; the Federal Bureau of Investigation estimates that organized crime controls 85 percent of the heroin market in the United States.[14] And perhaps the most victimized of all by the Mob are the poor of the inner cities where drug usage is highest, loans most usurious, and prostitution cheapest.

The Glamor of the Godfather

While most people have some inkling that the Mafia hurts them economically, some believe that, as a political alternative to inept government, it does not sound so bad: justice is swift and sure, the organization guarantees that those who are loyal to it will not go wanting, and its "soldiers" are able to attain a sense of human dignity ("pursuit of happiness"?) within its ranks. The most lucid exposition of this view is contained in Mario Puzo's novel, *The Godfather.*

Facts belie this view. "Soldiers" often are sacrificed for the gain of the capo dons, and life in the Syndicate is more in the style depicted by the movie *Crazy Joey* than by Puzo. The Mafia does not offer an option to government. Instead, the Syndicate inevitably must try to destroy government. To quote the President's Commission on Law Enforcement and Administration of Justice, "The purpose of organized crime is not competition with visible, legal government but nullification of it."[15]

THE RISE OF LA COSA NOSTRA

Experts estimate that there are from 2,000 to 5,000 "made" (i.e., initiated) members (who, allegedly, must murder someone on the Mafia's orders to be initiated) and perhaps some 20,000 to 50,000 additional associates who comprise the Mafia; the usual estimate, however, is 2,000 "made" members.[16] Its alleged bank is the multibillion-dollar pension fund of the Teamsters Union, and as a consequence of its superlative organization and vast treasury, "the Mafia can rightly claim to be the reigning monarch of the American underworld."[17]

Organized crime has not always been with us.[18] In the early part of the century, a variety of relatively small-time gangs operated in the major cities of the country. One of the more successful ones was New York City's "Five Points Gang," headed by one Johnny Torrio. Among other luminaries who were members of Torrio's Five Points Gang was Charles "Lucky" Luciano and Al "Scarface" Capone.

The early years of the twentieth century were ones in which criminal gangs were dominated by local political machines. Often the machines hired thugs to get out the votes and occasionally to bring reluctant voters into line. This phase extended well into the 1920s, and there was never any question about who was in control: a local political machine gave the orders to the local gangs. On those rare occasions when the gangs did not follow orders, they could be relatively easily controlled by the local police, and usually were jailed or hounded out of town.

This relationship of small time local criminals working for relatively well-organized local politicians might have endured had not Prohibition been enacted in 1920. Prohibition forced change. It was becoming increasingly clear to all who were in the underworld that to supply the hundreds of thousands of speakeasies that had mushroomed across the country during the Prohibition years, the gangs would have to organize. "Organization" is the kinder term, however, since what happened far more frequently were outbursts of violence among the gangs. The year 1920 marked the beginning of the "beer wars" between various gangs in a number of cities over who would control the illegal liquor market.

The *Unione Siciliana* was a central organization during this period. The *Unione* listed on its membership rosters virtually all Sicilian immigrants in the country, and in 1928 Torrio took over the huge New York branch of the *Unione.* This event was a major step in establishing Torrio as a national criminal figure. In Chicago, Al Capone was at the same time waging his "war of the Sicilian succession" that revolved around who would control Chicago's *Unione Siciliana.* Although Capone won that war, it had been costly, and Capone was forced to establish an alliance with Detroit's mostly Irish Purple Gang, which also had New

York connections. These linkages marked the beginnings in the development of a national crime network.

In 1928, the first national meeting of the Mafia was held in Cleveland under Torrio's leadership, and in 1929, a second national meeting was held in Atlantic City. This latter meeting marked the tentative organization of a national crime syndicate, although the tensions that developed during the meeting eventually led to the "Castellamarri wars" of 1929 and 1931 between Joseph Masseria and Salvatore Maranzano in New York. Maranzano won, and became the first, and ultimately only, *capo di tutti capi,* or boss of all bosses. It was Maranzano who divided New York among the famous "five families" that still endure today and established the ground rules for a national crime network.

A "Mafia family" extends considerably beyond blood relatives. Figure 19-2 explains the organization of a large Mafia family, such as is found in New York City. As the chart shows, the authority of the "don" or head of the family is absolute. "Buffers" act as staff men, and their role is to transmit messages in a way that protects the top of the family hierarchy. The *consigliere* usually is an older member of the family and provides advice to the don. *Consigliere* are frequently the main corruptors of politicians.

As a result of Maranzano's victory in 1931, Lucky Luciano became the dominant underworld figure in Manhattan and quickly established an alliance with the German-American Dutch Schultz, who controlled the Bronx. In 1931 Luciano arranged the assassination of Maranzano and, together with Torrio in

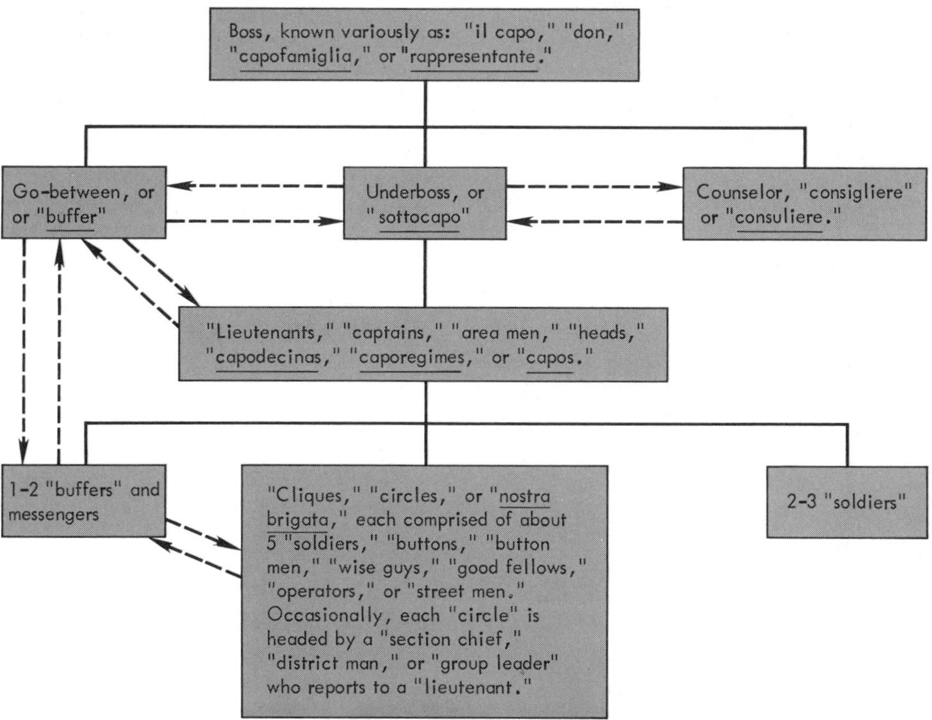

Figure 19-2. Organization of a large Cosa Nostra "family."

1934, called two crucial meetings of the new national crime commission that Maranzano had established. These meetings, which were held in New York and Kansas City, concluded with the formal division of the nation among 24 families. Figure 19-3 illustrates the basics of this national structure. It is not a particularly democratic organization in that the commission itself never has had more than a dozen members and, on occasion, membership has sunk as low as eight. The commission is controlled by the dominant Mafia families, and the five New York families listed in Table 19-2 always have seats on the commission; Chicago, Detroit, Buffalo, Philadelphia, and New Jersey are usually represented.[19]

In 1936 Dutch Schultz was murdered; Luciano was imprisoned; and Vito Genovese, who was Luciano's chief assistant, fled to Italy, and a new generation of dons emerged. During the 1940s, the Syndicate became involved in white-collar crime, Las Vegas was penetrated by a number of Mafiosi, and a Cuban connection was developed for purposes of narcotics transfers to the United States. The 1950s saw a series of wars between various families, particularly in New York City, and these episodes have continued without cessation. A recent example concerns the legalization of gambling in Atlantic City, New Jersey, which touched off a furious round of warfare between Philadelphia's Mafia family and New York City's Gambino family. Atlantic City had been in the territory of the Philadelphia family headed by Angelo Bruno, but with the introduction of casinos in 1977 to Atlantic City, the town became a considerably juicier plum than it had been earlier. As a result, in 1980 alone Bruno and five of his closest associates were assassinated by members of the Gambino family, possibly in cooperation with the Lucchese family as well. Thus, although there is a national commission, it does not control the 24 families comprising it to the degree that violence within the Mafia can be contained.[20]

Although its control is not absolute, the commission is charged with resolving disputes among families, approving the initiation of new Mafia members, recognizing new family bosses, and controlling relations with the Mafia still in Sicily, which is a separate enterprise.[21] The continued presence of New York's five families on the commission is significant, for it is believed that the Mafia families based in major cities other than New York follow orders given by the

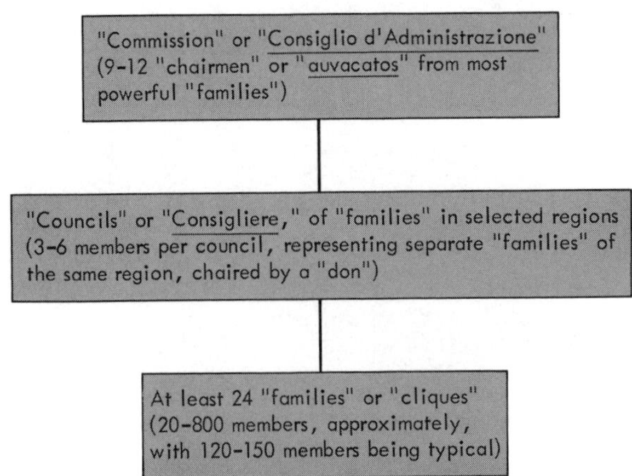

Figure 19-3
National organization of the Cosa Nostra.

Table 19-2 Major Mafia Families in the United States

City, State, or Region	*Reputed Boss (as of 1981)*	*Principal Enterprises*
New York City	"Five families" of New York: Bonano family (Boss: Philip Rastelli), Colombo family (Boss: Carmine Persco), Gambino family (Boss: Paul Castellano), Genovese family (Boss: Frank Tieri), Lucchese family (Boss: Anthony Corallo)	Loan sharking, narcotics, gambling, extortion, garbage and meat industries
New England	Raymond L. S. Patrarca (Providence) Underboss: Gennaro Angiulo (Boston)	Loan sharking, gambling
Philadelphia	Phillip Testa	Gambling, insurance frauds, arson, loan sharking
Cleveland	James Licavoli	Labor racketeering
Chicago	Joey Aiuppa	Gambling, loan sharking
Los Angeles	Dominic Brooklier	Garment industry, pornography
Las Vegas	"Open city,"[a] although the Chicago "Outfit" dominates Las Vegas	Gambling, prostitution
Arizona	"Open city,"[1] although the Chicago "Outfit" dominates Arizona	Land fraud, insurance fraud, bankruptcy fraud
Kansas City	Nick Civilla	Nevada-casino profit-skimming
New Orleans	Carlos Marcello	Political corruption, real estate
Florida	Santo Trafficante, Jr.	Gambling, hotel services

[a]An "open city" is one designated by the Mafia national commission (see Figure 19-3) as the preserve of no single family. Mafia families are free to enter such "markets" and plunder as they wish.
Source: Data from Aric Press, et al., "How the Mob Really Works," *Newsweek* (January 5, 1981), p. 38.

five families.[22] The five New York families alone are believed to have more than 850 "made" members and 2,000 associate members.[23]

THE MINOR MOBS

We should be aware that there are other criminal organizations besides the Mafia. The Federal Bureau of Investigation ranks motorcycle gangs as its second most important target after the Mafia among criminal organizations. Bikers now have a virtual monopoly on portions of the drug trade, as well as a number of other enterprises. The major motorcycle gangs are the Oakland-based Hell's Angels, with more than 5,000 members; the Outlaws, based in Chicago with slightly less than 5,000 members; the Bandidos out of Corpus Christi, Texas; and the Pagans, centered in Long Island City, New York.[24]

The Southeast is dominated in part by the "Dixie Mafia," which is a confederation of roughly 750 traveling criminals in 17 states who specialize in burglary, drugs, fencing, gambling, and white-collar crime. The "Dixie Mafia" emerged during the 1970s, and as many as a dozen gangs can be found operating in any one state at a given time. The "Dixie Mafia" is primarily white and is said to be responsible for as much as half of the crime in the region.[25]

In Florida, Cuban and Colombian organizations have begun to challenge the Mafia's Trafficante family's traditional control in that area. Like the

Mafia, both the Cuban and Colombian organizations are international and are particularly vicious in their methods of dealing with rivals.

In the Southwest, other ethnic-based organizations have made their presences felt, particularly in California. The two major organizations of Mexicans and Mexican-Americans are known as the Nuestra Familia (for "our family"), which is composed primarily of rural Chicanos from California's Central Valley, and the EME, which draws its members from the barrios of East Los Angeles, and was founded in the prisons of California. During the mid-1970s, both groups were at war with each other, and their battles left more than a hundred people dead in California alone.

California also is the center for an emerging "Israeli Mafia" that has virtually taken over the narcotics traffic in Los Angeles, but also specializes in terrorizing and extorting shop owners. The Israeli Mafia is comprised of ex-convicts and former Israeli army commandos who have since migrated to the United States.[26]

Chinese gangs are prevalent in California, particularly in San Francisco. Most of the Chinese groups are based on family ties and have formed organizations known as *tongs,* which employ Chinese youths as their enforcers. The major youth gangs in San Franciso are the Wah Ching Society, the Joy Boys, and the Golden Dragons. New York City also has its share of *tongs,* known as the Ghost Shadows, the White Eagles, and the Flying Dragons. Black organizations have been identified in both New York and Detroit, and in Harlem the narcotics trade appears to be controlled entirely by blacks.[27]

As the National Advisory Committee on Criminal Justice Standards and Goals concluded, "Organized crime is not synonymous with the Mafia or La Cosa Nostra. . . . Today, a variety of groups is engaged in organized criminal activity."[28]

NULLIFYING GOVERNMENT

The Mafia and other organized crime syndicates have as one of their priorities the elimination of government as a serious rival to their activities, and the Cosa Nostra's primary targets of corruption tend to be officials working at the state and local levels. One analyst has estimated that the Syndicate contributes approximately 15 percent of the cost of state and local political campaigns.[29] A survey conducted in Illinois found that three quarters of the respondents believe that criminals were corrupting or securing important favors from their politicians.[30]

The police are a frequent target of corruption efforts by the Syndicate, and the methods favored are inducing the police to agree to drop an investigation before the investigation should be dropped; not inspecting various locations where a violation could be occurring; reducing the seriousness of the charge against the offender; agreeing to alter testimony at a trial; influencing local governmental recommendations regarding the granting of licenses, such as liquor licenses; and altering departmental records of people who have been arrested.[31]

Through these and other methods, the Cosa Nostra has, on occasion, been able to take over whole police departments. In one investigation, one of the largest police forces in the nation found that police and other personnel in the department were accepting narcotics payments, passing on sensitive information to organized crime figures, dealing in drugs and illegal gambling, and fencing stolen property, among other activities.[32]

But it is in the courts where organized crime has been most successful in its corrupting influence, and the record of Mafiosi being dealt with leniently by judges is clear. Approximately 50 of the estimated 2,000 to 5,000 members of the Cosa Nostra are convicted and sent to prison in a typical year, and the average sentence ranges from three to four years.[33] At this rate of conviction, it would take nearly a century to jail the Mafia, a projection that assumes life sentences, not three- to four-year ones.

One reason why so few members of the Mafia are sent to prison appears to be a consistent pattern of preferential treatment by judges. One examination found that more than half of the organized crime figures convicted in federal courts were fined but received no prison sentences, and only a fifth received prison terms of two years or more.[34] Another federal study found that of those members of the Syndicate who were sent to prison, a majority were eligible for parole within eight months.[35] Yet another examination of federal sentencing found that of 247 Mafia cases heard by federal courts, four out of five sentences were six years shorter than the ten-year maximum sentences that could have been imposed and that parole practices seemed to be unusually lenient as well.[36]

Another investigation of more than a thousand criminal cases in New York that involved leading Mafiosi concluded that the rate of dismissals or acquittals for defendants who were connected with the Cosa Nostra was almost five times the rate of other defendants! For those defendants who were not connected with organized crime, local judges dismissed the indictments against them in fewer than 12 percent of the cases. But for those defendants who did have connections with the Mafia, more than 40 percent of all indictments brought against them were dismissed by local judges.[37]

Another study of New York's judicial practices found that of 536 organized crime figures who had been arrested for felonies in New York City during the previous decade, only 37 had actually been sent to prison. "The study showed conclusively that mobsters fare far better in the state courts than other criminals not affiliated with the Mafia."[38]

Still another examination of crime in New York, which centered on the city's illegal gambling operations that were run by the Mafia, found that

> seventy-one raids were conducted, resulting in a positive identification of 99 persons. These 99 individuals have totaled 356 arrests among them, because many of them have been arrested more than once. Of these arrests, 198 were dismissed, 63 were acquitted, 12 were found guilty and given suspended sentences, 77 were fined, and 5 served jail sentences. The average fine was $113 and the average jail sentence was 17 days. Although judicial corruption is evident, it is difficult to prove.[39]

In short, penetration by organized crime of the public safety and judicial systems may be more pervasive than local officials care to admit. To gain some flavor, however, of how the Mafia undermines a local political system, consider the following examples. The first is that of a state, and its inclusion is more for the sake of demonstrating how governmental structure can make criminal penetration easier or more difficult rather than as an example of a state government being controlled by Mafiosi (which, in this case, it is not). The second instance is of a city, and it is included precisely because it was a political system entirely under the thumb of organized crime. The final case considers the difficulties of reforming a polity that has been under the domination of systemic corruption, even after the rascals supposedly have been thrown out. The inevitable question is, Are some governments incapable of reform? Regrettably, the query can only be asked, not answered.

"The Outfit" in Arizona

Not enough is known about organized crime in Arizona to be able to compile a history of its evolution. It is clear, however, that the Syndicate exists in Arizona and that it has made inroads into the political hierarchy. The Mob's influence was exposed in 1976 when an investigative reporter on the state's major newspaper was killed by a bomb planted in his car, evidently because of his investigations of criminal activities in Arizona.

As a victim of Syndicate penetration, Arizona is not alone in the West. San Francisco, Los Angeles, and Las Vegas are all cities that have felt the impact of "the Outfit," as the Mafia family originating in Chicago is named; experts on crime agree that the Outfit is expanding its business into the West.[40] In Arizona, Chicago-based Syndicate figures have been joined by major dons from Detroit and New York, and some estimate that more than 200 major Mafiosi reside in the state.[41]

In Arizona, the Syndicate makes its greatest profits from land frauds and related swindles. A convicted federal prisoner claimed before the Arizona legislature that organized crime preferred Arizona for their land fraud operations because the state was well known throughout the nation in these circles for its corrupt public officials. He went on to say that he himself had bribed state, county, and federal employees within Arizona. The confidence game most favored by Arizona Mafiosi is to set up a phony land company that from the beginning is designed to go bankrupt within a few years. It is claimed that state officials are bribed to sign forms indicating that the state or locality intends to lay sewer lines, erect power lines, and so forth, thus fraudulently increasing the value of the land, the better to bilk investors.[42] The assistant attorney general for Arizona has noted that state officials permitted a "Mafia-connected" company to operate almost four years *after* learning that the firm was completely bankrupt, noting further that "incompetence and bribe-taking were common among public officials." He also observed that Arizona was a "haven for fraudulent insurance companies, making it one of the two 'easiest states' in which insurance companies could be formed."[43]

The Arizona House Task Force on Organized Crime concluded that defrauded land purchasers might have been better served if Arizona had never had a state real estate department, noting that "a Real Estate Department without the tools and resources to do a complete job ought not to be in business at all. At least the public would not be lulled into a false sense of security." By way of indication, the task force noted that fraudulent land promoters in the state had fleeced the public of at least half a *billion* dollars during the last ten years and that the state's real estate department, which was responsible for assuring honesty in property transactions, was grossly underequipped to deal with highly skilled land fraud swindles conducted by organized crime. In the 1970s, for example, the department had only three auditors and six investigators; they were responsible for handling more than 6,000 applications for real estate licenses every year, for monitoring the activities of more than 17,000 licensed salespersons plus an additional 6,000 licensed real estate brokers, and for following through on more than 2,000 complaints about land promoters, salespersons, subdivision frauds, and similar reports.[44]

In 1977, partly in response to a rising recognition that organized crime was a political force in the state, Arizona adopted a completely new and comprehensive criminal code. The new code was a product of a four-year review and represented the first revision of Arizona criminal law since 1910. As one legislator noted, "Arizona law is still in boots and spurs in many respects. We've looked at criminals involved in gambling and prostitution and said, 'Let's let them have their fun,' often failing to realize the money they are using came from violence."[45] So loose, in fact, were Arizona's statutes concerning white-collar and organized crime that crooked land companies had been allowed to operate in the state for generations simply because fraudulent land companies literally were not illegal until 1976. Under such circumstances, it is not difficult for land fraud swindles to flourish, and flourish in Arizona they did.

In enacting its new criminal code, Arizona fell short of passing the strongest possible antimob legislation. A few Arizona legislators, as well as the state attorney general, advocated passage of the Racketeering Influence and Corrupt Organizations Act, the model law adopted by Congress as part of the federal Organized Crime Control Act of 1970. The model legislation is controversial and can be a cause of injustice to innocent citizens. Arizona elected not to pass such legislation, which is perhaps unfortunate in light of the fact that in 1977 the U.S. Department of Justice officially warned the state of Arizona that the Chicago Outfit was setting up the city of Phoenix as another target city for the money-laundering racket and for establishing highly questionable corporations, notably in the areas of insurance and land speculation.

The new state code does make loan-sharking and usury illegal, which they were not prior to adoption of the Arizona revised criminal code, and crooked land companies also are illegal for the first time in Arizona. But, while Arizona's new criminal code is very tough on crime, it is rather weak on the organized part of crime. To quote one investigator, "The law that provides the tools to find Mr. Big, break his organization financially, repay his victims, and convince a jury that a syndicate does indeed exist—that law went down to defeat in Arizona."[46]

While the full extent of the Cosa Nostra's activities in Arizona is unknown, it is clear that the state's political structure is such that Arizona has become a prime target for penetration by organized crime and the corruption of local officials. Arizona became the forty-eighth state in 1912, at the height of the Populist movement, and its constitution reflected the views of a rural people who distrusted a strong executive. Thus, commissions and boards were created that were "responsible to the statute" rather than to the chief executive. Although the governor has the authority to appoint commissioners and boards (with legislative approval), he or she exercises no legal control over virtually any of them once the appointment is made. Whatever control the governor can maintain is done through the personal loyalty of the appointees and his or her own persuasive powers. Since 1912, Arizona's legislatures continued to create boards, commissions, and agencies, and a proliferation of commissions and boards resulted over the years. When the state was created, Arizona had only 31 government agencies. By 1971, the number of independent agencies reached a high of 176, which has since been decreased to fewer than 150. This decrease was due largely to a change in legislative philosophy. Working in concert with the governor, the legislature undertook to consolidate agencies of state government and to place the resultant "superagencies" under the control of the executive; 11 agencies since have been reorganized, consolidated, and placed under the direct control of the governor, including most of the major ones.[47] It was only in 1975, however, that the Arizona Real Estate Commission, which had been accused of gross corruption and bribe-taking by the assistant attorney general for Arizona in earlier years, was retitled the Arizona Real Estate Department and was placed under the control of the governor.

The point is that when an agency "reports to the statute," no one is in control. Thus, agency staff members, who often make the real policy (which then is "rubber stamped" by their board members), are extremely susceptible to pressures brought on by sophisticated and tough Mafiosi.

Of course, the opposite organizational structure of government can be corrupted, too. In a highly centralized government, in which all agency heads report to a chief executive, only the chief executive needs to be bribed or corrupted for criminal elements to gain a free hand. The most typical example of this occurrence is the average municipal police department, which usually is organized along hierarchical, military lines.

Normally, the more decentralized a government is, the more potentially susceptible it is to corruption—particularly if that government has been targeted by a highly centralized criminal organization. Certainly a paramount example of organized crime taking over a disorganized government may be found in Newark, New Jersey. During the period when the Syndicate first moved in (the 1920s), Newark had a commission form of government—possibly the most decentralized and ineffectual form of urban governance ever devised.

The Mafia as Government: The Nadir of Newark

Newark, with more than 380,000 people, of whom more than half are black and more than 7 percent are Latinos, is among New Jersey's largest municipalities and is conveniently close to New York City. During most of the prohibition era a no-holds-barred gangland war raged in New York City, and out of it emerged New York's first Godfather, Abner "Longie" Zwillman, who happened to be Jewish, not Italian, and who claimed Newark as his hometown. Soon Zwillman had set up a regular ferry schedule on the New Jersey coastline designed to supply New York with illegal liquor. It was by far the most extensive bootlegging operation on the East Coast, reaping an estimated $50 million between 1926 and 1931 and accounting for approximately 40 percent of the entire bootleg liquor supply being transported across the nation's borders. With this fortune, Zwillman established himself as the Democratic boss of Newark's third ward, using his bootlegged money to finance the gubernatorial campaigns of all candidates—on the understanding that he would be allowed to approve the winner's nominee for attorney general.

As Zwillman gained power in Newark's third ward, Ruggiero "Richie the Boot" Boiardo garnered control of the first ward. After considerable competition between the two dons, Zwillman and Boiardo supposedly had a reconciliation in 1930 and staged a two-day party to celebrate. Shortly after the close of the party, Boiardo was shot 16 times in true gangland style, but somehow survived;

evidently his life was saved when a bullet struck the Boot's $5,000 diamond belt buckle. After Boiardo recovered, he was sent to prison for two and a half years for carrying a gun when he was shot, but served only 20 months, 16 of which were in a minimum security facility. He returned to his first ward and negotiated a division of turf in Newark with Zwillman while the law stood quietly aside.

Longie Zwillman committed suicide in 1959 and was succeeded by Gerardo "Jerry" Catena, who controlled the entire Jersey wing of the Vito Genovese family, and Boiardo became a part of the Catena operation. The Mafia's grip on Newark, and particularly the grasp of Richie the Boot, tightened with time. The Boot eventually was succeeded by Anthony "Tony Boy" Boiardo, his son, who soon gained control of the city.

In 1962 Newark elected Hugh Addonizio, known to all as Hughie, who had served as a U.S. congressman from Newark for the past 14 years. Why did Hughie run for mayor? To quote Hughie, "There is no money in being a congressman but you can make a million bucks as mayor of Newark." Organized crime contributed heavily to Addonizio's campaign for mayor, with Tony Boy Boiardo himself setting a fine example by contributing $10,000. Addonizio, backed by Boiardo, soon started robbing the public till with such a vengeance that one Mafia chieftain complained, "The guy's [Addonizio] taking $400, $500 for little jobs!"[48]

Shortly after his election, Hughie quickly secured his position by appointing Dominic Spina, one of his campaign workers, as director of police, and Spina appointed Police Captain Rocco Ferrante to head the intelligence division of Newark's finest. It was the division's job to investigate gambling and vice in the city, and Ferrante also served as Addonizio's official personal bodyguard. Meanwhile, Ralph Villani, a former mayor of Newark who had been indicted for corruption but never convicted (mainly because the statute of limitations had run out), still served as an elected member of the city council, and in 1962 and 1966 Villani was elected by his fellow council members as president of the council.

While Addonizio and company were taking over the political structure of Newark, Tony Boy Boiardo founded the Valentine Electric Company, which, within ten years, became the largest electrical contractor in the region, receiving half the contracts awarded by the Newark Housing Authority and doing $5 million worth of business a year. Boiardo was the real boss of Newark.

The basic mechanism for stripping Newark was a model of managerial efficiency—unlike anything else in Newark—and was based on Boiardo's ability to shake down contractors doing business with the city, demanding 10 percent of their contracts. Phony bills written by a phony supply company (the address of which was actually a vacant lot) were sent to the contractors, who dutifully paid into a phony bank account; the money eventually was withdrawn and turned over to Boiardo, although sizable portions of this money went directly to the mayor and eight of the nine members of the Newark City Council. It was estimated that Boiardo, Addonizio, and their accomplices eventually bilked the city of more than $1.4 million in kickbacks alone, a sum that is by no means inclusive of all the money lost through their systematic corruption.

With Spina and Ferrante in charge of Newark's police, shakedowns by cops in the city's black slums became commonplace, and in 1967 one of the worst race riots in American urban history exploded in Newark, killing 23 people and resulting in property damage estimated at $10.4 million. New Jersey Governor

Richard J. Hughes quickly appointed a blue-ribbon commission to determine the cause behind Newark's violence of that year, and it found that the chief reason was "a pervasive feeling of corruption" throughout the city, continuing that "A former state official, a former city official and an incumbent city official all used the same phrase: 'There is a price on everything at city hall.'"[49]

A year after Newark's riots, the Nixon administration appointed a new U.S. attorney for New Jersey, Frederick Lacey, a distinguished lawyer who zeroed in on Newark's rampant corruption like a sharpshooter. Within a year, the mayor of Newark and a number of other city officials were indicted by a federal grand jury on charges of extortion and income tax evasion and, flouting precedent in such cases, actually were convicted—a rare, indeed almost unique, occurrence in New Jersey courtrooms when top Mafia dons and high political figures were involved. Addonizio was sentenced to ten years in jail, but Tony Boy Boiardo managed to avoid a trial until his death in 1978 on the basis that, because of a heart condition, his life would be in jeopardy as the result of the stress incurred by a courtroom proceeding.

Jersey City: The Legacy of Reform?

What happens after a town is cleaned up politically and a new, reform-oriented administration is swept into office? Obviously, it depends on the town, but consider the example of another New Jersey municipality, Jersey City, a metropolis that some analysts still consider to be the most corrupt town in America.[50] Jersey City was controlled for a number of years by the famous political boss Frank Hague, who ruled with an iron hand. So rapacious was Hague that he amassed a fortune of $8 million purely on the basis of his political position. So open in his avarice was Boss Hague that, when he died, an elderly woman attended his funeral holding a hand-lettered sign that stated, "God have mercy on his sinful greedy soul!" John B. Kinny, a lieutenant in the Hague organization, succeeded Hague as boss of the Jersey City machine, and his handpicked mayor, Thomas J. Whelan, soon was sent off to jail in 1972 for extorting millions in kickbacks from city contractors. Whelan was succeeded in a special election by a young public health physician, Paul T. Jordan, who was a vigorous reformist candidate. On winning the election, Jordan proclaimed, "We are free at last!" Jordan chose not to run for office in the next election, but picked a like-minded successor who lost by a landslide to a close associate of the imprisoned Mayor Whelan; soon the loan sharks and the gamblers were back in town.

Why did Jordan's reform candidate lose to a man of the classic machine mold? Reformer Jordan had abolished the kickback system on city contracts (which added anywhere from 8 to 15 percent on all items bought by the city); he had cleaned up the police department, created a Mayor's Action Bureau that acted on some 15,000 to 20,000 citizen complaints every year, and initiated a number of similar reforms. Yet, 51 percent of Jersey City residents, according to a poll conducted at the end of Jordan's term, stated they would leave Jersey City if they possibly could, and another poll taken at the same time found that only 5 percent of the people of Jersey City thought that the reformist Jordan had done a good job; 50 percent rated his performance as poor. According to one observer, the relatively unsophisticated, less educated, and elderly citizenry who populated Jersey City longed for the return of the "good ol' days," which they defined essentially as less crime. The sad fact of the matter is that this perception bore little relationship to reality, since Jersey City's crime rate (that is, street crime as opposed to political corruption) is actually lower than is that of other cities of comparable size. Moreover, Jordan himself appeared to project a somewhat aloof image and had lost the common touch, of which Boss Hague was a master. Thus, after six decades of openly corrupt politics, Jersey City granted itself a respite of five years, but it was soon back to its old ways. Apparently there is among some citizens a certain comfort to be derived from the corruption of others.

Graft and the Grassroots

Regardless of how the good citizens of Jersey City, and possibly other communities, behave, it is reasonably apparent that the average American is deeply concerned about political corruption and the role of organized crime. A poll by Louis Harris conducted in 200 communities found that state and local government leaders ranked far below garbage collectors in public esteem and that "corrupt politicians" and "lack of confidence in government" were issues second in importance only to that of inflation. Overall, public opinion polls indicate that roughly 70 percent of all Americans believe that there is dishonesty in their state and local governments.[51]

In a sophisticated analysis of an unidentified, midsized city that was in the pocket of organized crime, an in-depth survey was taken of a representative sample of the city's citizens concerning their "tolerance of corruption." It was found that the residents of the city had very little interest in local politics, were aware that their government was a poor one, and were extremely suspicious of local officials. It was also found that high social status, high level of education, youth, and a relatively long residence in the city correlated with a low tolerance of political corruption.[52] In sum, then, it appears that while corrupt politicians and high-level criminals in some cities may be working hand-in-glove, the public neither likes nor approves of it; they merely feel powerless to change it.

WHAT MUST BE DONE?

It is perhaps easy to become despondent after reading the sorry tale of political graft, the Cosa Nostra, corrupt politicians, and capo dons. Can those relationships be broken and, if so, how?[53]

Certainly the most obvious of policies that can be instituted to assure better government is the development of sound management. *Sound management* in this sense means:

1. Establishing centralized purchasing procedures.
2. Auditing to be conducted by truly independent auditors.
3. Enacting a single code concerning land-use development administered by a single agency and following prescribed rules of procedure.
4. Establishing tax assessment districts, each headed by a full-time and professionally qualified assessor.
5. The institutionalization of an absolutely open licensing and franchising procedure for such industries as cable television, liquor businesses, race tracks, and so forth.

Arbitrary governmental decision making also should be eliminated. Steps in this direction include qualifying bidders for construction jobs at the state level and improving the government's bidding system. They would require ending one-person rule in public purchasing policies, training public purchasing officials in the rudiments of construction management, and establishing state licensing agencies with the power to set criteria for issuing licenses.

Clear avenues of appeal should be established to permit private enterprises dealing with state and local governments to appeal decisions made at lower levels; such areas include appeals on contracts, zoning decisions, and building codes. State agencies should be created to advise businesspersons wishing to locate or expand in the state and to intercede in their behalf with government agencies when necessary.

Compromising relationships between public officials and private citizens should be prohibited. Each state should adopt a conflict-of-interest law and full-time boards to enforce such laws. Professionals such as those in medicine and law should also be prohibited from engaging in conflict-of-interest situations. Prohibitions should be set on campaign contributions, and bipartisan commissions should be created by the states to oversee elections and administer and enforce campaign and election legislation.

"Sunshine laws" and legislation that require the fullest possible public disclosures of personal finances by public officials, both elected and appointed, should be enacted; government agencies also should be required to publicize the names of all firms with which they do business. Complete financial disclosure should be mandated for all owners of real estate whenever the government is involved in the purchase or sale of their property. Political campaign funding should be fully reported, and "right-to-know" laws should be passed so that meetings of public agencies and legislative committees are virtually always open to the public.

Finally, citizens should adopt "the honesty ethic in public life," which encourages exemplary behavior by public officials and the enhancement of ethical standards among relevant professional societies. Significant in this effort is the attempt to judge whether or not police organizations are adequate to cope with political corruption.

WHAT IS BEING DONE?

Ethics Legislation in the States

While the list of the policies needed to help make public officials more resistant to graft is a good one, it obviously has not yet been fully adopted by America's state and local governments. Nevertheless, progress has been made, especially in the burgeoning enactment of conflict-of-interest legislation and financial disclosure laws. Still, the particulars of such policies frequently are controversial, and, with some 490,000 elected officials and 13 million state and local government employees, it is not surprising that it is often difficult for legislators to determine who should and who should not be covered by such laws. Forty-two states have major ethics legislation; of these, 37 apply the law to their own legislators. All 42 states apply conflict-of-interest and financial disclosure policies to major public executives, usually covering administrators who have judicial and regulatory duties, or who spend significant amounts of public money, or who form policy. Only 22 of the 42 states that have ethics legislation apply those laws to all or part of the judiciary and, in a few cases, to judicial employees. Nineteen states extend their ethics laws to officials of counties or municipalities, including, in some cases, members of school boards, special districts, and local commissions.[54]

Open meeting laws and related "sunshine" legislation also are increasingly popular in the states, and state governments in recent years have enacted more such reform measures than ever before. To quote the U.S. Advisory Commission on Intergovernmental Relations, recently enacted reform legislation has set up "a record unmatched since the turn-of-the-century Populist Era."[55] All 50 states have open meeting laws that apply to both state and local governments, and 33 of these passed such laws or strengthened them significantly in the 1970s. Seven states require advance public notice of meetings, and 34 states have enacted legislation that punishes officials who violate sunshine laws. Most states also require lobbyists to register, and 43 require lobbyists to report their expenses.

The City Manager: The Record of Reform

Similarly, important strides also have been made toward instituting sound management, particularly at the local level, with the growing adoption of the council-manager plan. Contrary to conventional wisdom, being an honest city manager is not easy. Merely because the manager cherishes political anonymity (at least in most cases), it does not follow that he or she is removed from the pressures of politics. Consider the experiences of LeRoy F. Harlow, a professional city manager with a wide background in urban administration. The following passage, written by a former member of his staff, indicates the reality of local political pressure:

> One week after I went to work as City Manager Harlow's principal assistant, a businessman telephoned to inform me that he was one of a group organizing to drive Harlow out of town. He suggested I quietly leave town before I was run out. As inducement, he said his group would secure for me a higher paying position in Minneapolis. This would reflect an advancement opportunity too good to ignore, and would look good on my record. A few weeks later, the police chief called me to his office to say he was securing legal counsel on how to separate me from my job. Both of these initial incidents were in response to major assignments given me by Harlow—to help establish a city merit system and centralized purchasing.[56]

While such "administrative" decisions as setting up a merit-based civil service and competitive bidding practices may not appear to be political at first glance, such professionalism can be intensely political. As the author of the preceding passage notes, city management "can be a rugged and vicious environment, not recommended for the faint-hearted."[57]

It is all the more surprising in light of these pressures that the city management profession has been able to resist political corruption as effectively as it has. As Paul N. Ylvisaker of Harvard University has noted,

> It is a remarkable profession, indeed, when you realize that for two generations, the pressures of America growing up and becoming too fat have not stalled you in your effort to perfect the [city managers'] code of ethics and to increase your

power to enforce it. The small number of city managers who have been a discredit to that code is one of the remarkable tributes still remaining on the American political landscape, and . . . that kind of integrity is now the quality that this country most needs.[58]

In short, though organized crime and corrupt politicians always will be with us, the 1970s witnessed a spate of "good government" reforms at the state and local levels. Sunshine laws, professional ethics codes, governmental reorganizations, watchdog boards, conflict-of-interest legislation, and financial disclosure policies all work toward the reduction of graft at the grassroots. Nevertheless (and trite as the cliché may be), it is the people who must ultimately be responsible for keeping government honest and efficient. While there are exceptions (such as when organized crime takes over an entire municipality by bribery or terrorism), it still is generally a fact that the people have the supreme power and may use it as they see fit.

There is no more fitting thought on which to close a book about democracy at the grassroots than that of the people's power.

NOTES

[1]William L. Riordan, *Plunkitt of Tammany Hall* (New York: E. P. Dutton, 1963), as reprinted in John A. Gardiner and David J. Olson, eds., *Theft of the City: Readings on Corruption in Urban America* (Bloomington: Indiana University Press, 1974), p. 7.
[2]Gerald E. Caiden and Naomi J. Caiden, "Administrative Corruption," *Public Administration Review,* 37 (May-June 1977), p. 306.
[3]Cited in George Amick, *The American Way of Graft* (Princeton, N.J.: Center for Analysis of Public Issues, 1976), p. 4.
[4]National Municipal League, "Legislative Ethics Chairman Convicted," *Public Officials and the Public Trust,* 5 (February 1977), pp. 5-6.
[5]"Oklahoma! Where the Graft Comes Sweepin' Down the Plain," *Time* (October 12, 1981), p. 31.
[6]William Price, as quoted in *ibid.*
[7]Cecil Parker, as quoted in *ibid.*
[8]Illinois Crime Survey, 1929, cited in Ralph Salerno and John S. Tompkins, *The Crime Confederation: Cosa Nostra and Allied Operations in Organized Crime* (Garden City, N.Y.: Doubleday, 1969), as reprinted in Gardner and Olson, *Theft of the City,* p. 150.
[9]*U.S. News & World Report* (October 29, 1973), as quoted in Amick, *The American Way of Graft,* p. 5.
[10]James Cook, "The Invisible Enterprise," *Forbes* (September 29, 1980), p. 60. The estimate is for 1980.
[11]Senator Denis DeConcini, as quoted in Albert J. Sitter, "Mob Crime Called Top U.S. Enemy," *The Arizona Republic* (November 9, 1979); and August Bequai, *Organized Crime: The Fifth Estate* (Lexington, Mass.: D. C. Heath, 1979), p. 153.
[12]Bequai, *Organized Crime,* p. 183; and Sitter, "Mob Crime," citing estimates by the U.S. Department of Justice.
[13]Cook, "The Invisible Enterprise," p. 60; Aric Press et al., "How the Mob Really Works," *Newsweek* (January 5, 1981), p. 40; and Michael Dorman, *Payoff: The Role of Organized Crime in American Politics* (New York: David McKay, 1972), p. 258.
[14]Leslie Maitland Werner, "U.S. Officials Cite Key Successes in War Against Organized Crime," *The New York Times* (November 7, 1983).
[15]President's Commission on Law Enforcement and Administration of Justice, *Task Force Report: Organized Crime* (Washington, D.C.: U.S. Government Printing Office, 1967), pp. 1-5, as reprinted in Gardiner and Olson, *Theft of the City,* p. 356.
[16]Sitter, "Mob Crime"; John Winters, "Bikers Ranked Number Two on FBI's Priority List," *The Arizona Republic* (November 19, 1982); and Werner, "U.S. Officials Cite Key Successes."
[17]Bequai, *Organized Crime,* p. 6.

[18]The source for the following history of the Cosa Nostra's evolution is *ibid,* pp. 31-39.
[19]Werner, "U.S. Officials Cite Key Successes"; and Stanley Penn, "Alleged Heads of Mafia Groups Charged by U.S.," *The Wall Street Journal* (February 27, 1985).
[20]United Press International, "Atlantic City Casinos Touched off a String of Murders in Philadelphia and New York," *The Arizona Republic* (December 21, 1980).
[21]Penn, "Alleged Heads of Mafia Groups."
[22]Werner, "U.S. Officials Cite Key Successes."
[23]Penn, "Alleged Heads of Mafia Groups."
[24]Winters, "Bikers Ranked Number Two on FBI's Priority List."
[25]Press et al., "How the Mob Really Works"; and Bequai, *Organized Crime,* pp. 22-26. Source for the "Dixie Mafia" is National Advisory Committee on Criminal Justice Standards and Goals, *Report to the Task Force on Organized Crime* (Washington, D.C.: U.S. Government Printing Office, 1976), pp. 11-13.
[26]Dennis A. Williams with Ron LaBracque, "And Now, the Israeli Mafia," *Newsweek* (January 5, 1981), p. 40.
[27]Bequai, *Organized Crime,* pp. 24, 26.
[28]National Advisory Committee on Criminal Justice Standards and Goals, *Organized Crime,* p. 8.
[29]Alexander Heard, *The Costs of Democracy* (Chapel Hill: University of North Carolina Press, 1960), pp. 154-168.
[30]ITT Research Institute, as cited in Chicago Crime Commission, *A Study of Organized Crime in Illinois* (Chicago: Illinois Law Enforcement Commission, 1971), p. 3.
[31]Herman Goldstein, *Police Corruption* (New York: Police Foundation, 1975), pp. 16-18.
[32]Bequai, *Organized Crime,* p. 160. The police department was unidentified.
[33]Robert Blakely, director of Notre Dame University's Institute of Organized Crime, as cited in Albert J. Sitter, "Mob in Five Cities Isn't Nearly as Crippled as U.S. Claims, Experts and Informers Say," *The Arizona Republic* (December 21, 1980).
[34]Sitter, "Mob Crime Called Top U.S. Enemy."
[35]General Accounting Office, as cited in Mary Thornton, "GAO Criticizes Strike Forces on Organized Crime," *Washington Post* (December 7, 1981).
[36]General Accounting Office study as cited in Jack Anderson and Joseph Spear, "Courts Handle Drug Kingpins Gently," *Washington Post* (May 2, 1985). The GAO examined the sentencing of 1,044 drug traffickers and Mafiosi in 37 federal district courts from 1962 to 1983.
[37]Bequai, *Organized Crime,* p. 164.
[38]Dorman, *Payoff,* p. 126.
[39]National Advisory Committee on Criminal Justice Standards and Goals, *Organized Crime,* p. 25.
[40]David Smothers, "Chicago Mafia Creating Empire in the West," United Press International (July 17, 1977), syndicated nationally.
[41]James Yuenger, "IRE: A Noble Experiment That Turned Out a Disaster," *Chicago Tribune* (April 20, 1977).
[42]Albert J. Sitter, "State's Infamy for Corruption Draws Fraud, Con-Man Claims," *The Arizona Republic* (November 10, 1977).
[43]Arizona Assistant Attorney General, quoted in Albert J. Sitter, "Expert on Crime Says Mob Directs Swindles at State," *The Arizona Republic* (November 20, 1977).
[44]Arizona House Task Force on Organized Crime, as quoted by Albert J. Sitter, "Land Agency Is a Liability, Panel Claims," *The Arizona Republic* (November 14, 1977).
[45]As quoted by Mark Adams, "Code Misses Mark in Effort to Control Mob," *The Arizona Republic* (December 12, 1977).
[46]*Ibid.*
[47]Nicholas Henry, "The Burgeoning Bureaucracy," *Of, By, and For the People,* research report prepared by the State Universities of Arizona, Nicholas Henry, editor and coordinator (Phoenix: Arizona Academy of Public Affairs, 1977), pp. 10-12.
[48]Quoted in Ron Porambo, *No Cause for Indictment: An Autopsy of Newark* (New York: Holt, Rinehart and Winston, 1971), as reprinted in Gardiner and Olson, *Theft of the City,* p. 87.
[49]As quoted in Fred J. Cook, "The People versus the Mob, or Who Rules New Jersey?" *The New York Times* (February 1, 1970), as reprinted in *ibid.,* p. 80.
[50]The discussion of Jersey City is drawn from Neal R. Peirce, "Saga of Reform Lost in Jersey City," *The Arizona Republic* (July 29, 1977).
[51]Louis Harris poll, as quoted in Amick, *The American Way of Graft,* pp. 9-10.

[52]John A. Gardiner, *The Politics of Corruption: Organized Crime in an American City* (New York: Russell Sage Foundation, 1970), as reprinted in Gardiner and Olson, *Theft of the City,* pp. 347-348, 393-394.
[53]The following discussion of recommendations on how to make governments more graft resistant is drawn from Amick, *The American Way of Graft,* pp. 160-230.
[54]Council of State Governments, *Ethics: State Conflict of Interest/Financial Disclosure Legislation, 1972-1975* (Lexington, Ky.: Council of State Governments, 1975), pp. 1-7.
[55]Advisory Commission on Intergovernmental Relations, *State Actions in 1976,* M-109 (Washington, D.C.: U.S. Government Printing Office, 1977), p. 61.
[56]Dwight Ink, "Foreword," in LeRoy F. Harlow, *Without Fear or Favor: Odyssey of a City Manager* (Provo, Utah: Brigham Young University Press, 1977), p. ix.
[57]*Ibid.*
[58]Paul N. Ylvisaker, "Keynote Address," 1973 Annual Conference of the International City Management Association, quoted in John M. Patriarche, "Ethical Questions Which Administrators Face," *Public Management,* 19 (June, 1975), p. 3.

GLOSSARY

Advocacy planning. A point of view espoused by members of the planning profession, which holds that professional planners should promote the interests of the poor and minority groups more consciously in their planning.

Affirmative action. A government policy encouraging the hiring of members of disadvantaged groups on the grounds that government positions should be open to as many people as possible.

Aid to Families with Dependent Children. A federal public assistance program designed to help poor people with children.

Annexation. The absorption of outlying areas by a jurisdiction, usually a municipality.

Appelate court. A court that reviews the decisions of lower courts.

Apportionment. Deciding on the basis of population how many representatives to a legislature that a district will be accorded.

At-large election. Elections in which candidates do not campaign in precincts or wards but, rather, are elected by the voters as a whole.

Bicameral legislature. A legislature with two separate houses.

Biennial session. The practice of convening a state legislature every two years.

Blanket primary. Primary elections in which voters may vote in both parties' primaries, regardless of their party registration.

Block grant. Money granted by one government to another that is tied to a general area of concern but that permits relatively greater latitude by the receiving government on how the funds may be used.

Board of Commissioners. The governing body for a county; usually the commissioners are elected at-large.

Board of Supervisors. The governing body of a county; usually the supervisors are elected from wards rather than at-large.

Bona fide occupational qualification. A qualification for a job that is really needed to do the job and is not present merely to disqualify certain classes of job applicants, such as women.

Bond. A certificate of indebtedness given by a borrower to a lender. A bond obliges the borrower to repay the debt with interest. The most common bonds are municipal bonds, which are issued by local governments to pay for needs that cannot be financed from tax and other revenues. See also *General obligation bond, Moral obligation bond,* and *Revenue bond.*

Bureaucracy. The executive side of government, characterized by specialization of functions, adherence to rules, and hierarchy of authority.

Categorical grant. Money granted by one government to another that is highly specific in its purpose. *Also called* project grant.

Caucus. A meeting of politicians usually held for purposes of nominating party candidates. See also *Legislative caucus.*

Central committee. The policymaking committee of a political party. *Also called* the Executive Committee.

Charter. The basic law of a local governmental body, such as a county or city; charters are granted by the states.

Chief administrative officer. The top appointed manager in either a city or county government. Unlike the city manager, the chief administrative officer reports directly to the mayor or the chief elected official of the county.

Chief state school officer. The principal state administrative official for elementary and secondary public schools; typical titles include commissioner of education, superintendent of schools, and superintendent of public instruction.

Circuit breaker. A device intended to render the property tax more equitable by reducing or eliminating the property tax when it exceeds a predetermined percentage of the personal income of the property owner.

City-county consolidation. The merger of a major urban area with its surrounding county for purposes of administrative and economic efficiency.

City manager. The chief administrative official of a city. The city manager is appointed by and reports directly to the city council.

Civil case. A court case of a noncriminal nature.

Civil service. The administrative service of the government exclusive of the armed forces.

Civilian review boards. Groups of private citizens who review accusations of misconduct by the police.

Class action suit. A legal action undertaken by one or more plaintiffs on behalf of themselves and all other persons having identical interest in the alleged wrong.

Closed primary. A primary election in which only members of a given political party may vote in that party's primary elections.

Collective bargaining. Joint decision making between representatives of employees and employers on such subjects as salaries, hours, and working conditions.

Commission plan. A weak executive form of local government in which city commissioners generally are elected at-large and each member of the city council is both a legislator and an administrator. In the counties, the commission plan is also known as the plural executive plan.

Community. The economic, social, and political interdependence among people who fall into broad social categories.

Community development. The effort by governments and private citizens to improve the physical environment, social aspects, and performance of municipal governmental institutions and to increase participation by local citizens in the policymaking process.

Comparable worth. A doctrine being developed by the courts that holds that public employees should be paid the same rate for performing tasks that involve roughly the same levels of importance, skills, knowledge, stress, and responsibilities, even though the tasks themselves may be quite different.

Comprehensive plan. A plan of development for a community that touches all facets of community development. Usually a comprehensive plan focuses on land-use issues.

Compulsory referendum. A statewide vote on an issue, usually on proposed constitutional amendments, that is required by the state's constitution.

Conference committee. A special joint committee of members from both legislative houses who are selected to iron out differences when a bill passes both houses, but in different forms.

Constituency. The citizens residing in an elected officeholder's district.

Constitution. A document establishing the mode in which a state is organized and the way in which power is distributed.

Constitutional commission. A variant of the constitutional convention in which the legislature generally appoints commissioners to study or prepare basic constitutional changes on an ongoing basis.

Constitutional convention. An assembly of representatives convened to draft or revise substantially a state's constitution.

Convention. A meeting of politicians and political party representatives generally held for purposes of nominating candidates. Conventions usually are more broadly representative than are caucuses.

Corruption. The buying and selling of political favors or improper behavior in political and governmental circles.

Cosa Nostra. A Sicilian term for "our thing." The Cosa Nostra refers to organized crime. Other terms for organized crime are the Mob, the Mafia, and the Syndicate.

Council-administrator government. A form of county government in which a county administrator is appointed by the county board of commissioners or supervisors and reports to the board; it is similar to the council-manager form of urban government.

Council-elected executive plan. A form of county government in which the executive branch is headed by a strong elected administrator who is comparable in power to a governor. An administrative officer reports directly to the county executive rather than to the county council.

Council-manager government. A form of urban government in which legislative and executive powers are separated as much as possible, with executive powers being vested in the city manager and legislative powers in the city council. In the counties, the council-manager form is known as the council-administrator form.

Councils of Governments. Voluntary associations of local governments that are designed to coordinate intergovernmental planning and policy.

County. The largest territorial division of local government within a state.

County manager. The chief administrative officer of the county. The county manager is appointed by and reports directly to the county board of supervisors. *Also called* the county administrator.

Court administrator. A relatively new official, now used in all the states, who manages state court systems.

Court order. A directive issued by a court that requires a person to do or abstain from doing a specified act.

"Creatures of the states." A phrase attributed to Judge John F. Dillon in 1868 and one that refers to the judicial interpretation that local units of governments have autonomy only as granted by their state governments.

Criminal justice. The system of police, courts, and prisons designed to control crime and provide justice to the citizenry.

Crosscutting requirements. A type of federal mandate that applies across a wide spectrum of federal grant programs for state and local governments; if a recipient violates a crosscutting requirement, Washington can withdraw its assistance programs in a large number of unrelated areas.

Crossover sanctions. A type of federal mandate in which Washington may reduce or withdraw federal assistance in one or more programs if its standards are not being satisfied in another program.

De facto. A condition that exists in fact if not in law, such as *de facto* racial segregation in northern school systems.

De jure. A condition that exists in law if not in fact.

Demography. The study of population shifts and characteristics.

"Dillon's rule." See *Creatures of the states.*

Direct federalism. The relationships between local governments and the national government that often involve the bypassing of state governments.

Direct initiative. A popular vote on issues placed on the ballot by a petition signed by a set percentage of voters; unlike an indirect initiative, a direct initiative does not involve the legislature.

Direct orders. A type of federal mandate in which Congress issues direct orders to states and localities as a condition of receiving federal aid.

Discrimination. The act of discriminating against a person on the basis of race, creed, or sex.

Double-filing. A mechanism that permits a candidate to seek the nomination for the same office in two or more parties during the same primary election.

Due process of law. The concept of limiting government by granting citizens protection against the arbitrary deprivation of life, liberty, or property.

Earmark. The practice of setting aside certain revenues for specific uses through legislation; for example, federal gasoline taxes are "earmarked" for the Federal Highway Trust Fund and are used to build more highways.

Electorate. The voters in a given political system.

Elitism. A point of view concerning political power that argues that power is concentrated in a ruling elite.

Enterprise zoning. Providing business firms with tax incentives to locate in economically depressed areas.

Exclusionary zoning. Zoning practices that are designed to restrict or discourage new housing for poor people and minorities.

Extradition. The return by one state to another of a person accused of committing a crime by the second state.

Federalism. The relations among governments, specifically, the series of legal, political, and administrative relationships established among units of government and that possess varying degrees of authority and jurisdictional autonomy.

Federal mandates. Conditions established by the federal government that must be met by state and local governments if they are to receive federal assistance. See also *Crosscutting requirements, Crossover sanctions, Direct orders,* and *Partial preemptions.*

Felony. A serious crime, in contrast to a misdemeanor.

Fiscal federalism. The financial relationships between American governments.

Fixed sentencing. A recent trend in many states that legally requires a judge to give a particular sentence to persons found guilty of particular crimes. Under fixed sentencing, the law gives judges little or no latitude in determining the nature of the guilty person's sentence.

Food stamp program. A federal public assistance program administered through the U.S. Department of Agriculture in conjunction with state and local welfare agencies designed to improve nutrition for the needy.

Formula funding. The method used by states to fund education on the basis of numbers of students enrolled.

Formula grant. Money granted by one government to another in which money is distributed among all eligible recipients on the basis of some prearranged method. An example is Supplemental Security Income assistance.

Functional plan. Specialized planning done by such agencies as urban and rural authorities, health departments, and the like.

"Gargantua." An argument advocating the centralization of government authority over large metropolitan areas.

General assistance programs. Welfare programs for those who do not qualify for categorical assistance programs and that usually refer to state-initiated welfare policies in contrast to nationally initiated welfare policies.

General obligation bond. Municipal bonds that are backed by the full faith and credit of the government that issues them; if necessary, the issuing jurisdiction can be legally required to raise taxes to repay the bonds' purchasers.

Gerrymandering. Division of a territory into election districts for the purpose of giving one political party an electoral majority in a large number of districts while concentrating the voting strength of the opposition in as few districts as possible.

Government. The continuous exercise of authority and the performance of functions for a political unit.

Government corporation. An independent, legislatively created monopoly empowered to build, maintain, and manage specified public services.

Governor. The chief political executive of a state.

Grand jury. A body of 12 to 23 members that hears evidence presented by the prosecuting attorney against people accused of a serious crime. The grand jury may indict the accused and send the accused to a formal trial if it believes the evidence justifies such a trial.

Grant-in-aid. Program under which the federal government awards funds to state and local governments. See also *Block grants, Categorical grants,* and *Formula grants.*

Gross national product (GNP). The total value of all goods and services in the nation produced in a single year.

Home rule. A high level of independence accorded by a state-issued charter to a local unit of government relative to the state government.

Impeachment. A formal accusation by the lower house of a legislature that brings a public official (such as a governor or judge) to trial in the upper house.

Implied powers. The authority of the federal government that is based on the inference of certain powers specifically delegated to the federal government in the Constitution. Through the doctrine of implied powers, the national government has broadened its authority relative to the states.

Incentive zoning. Providing developers with incentives (such as permission to build higher buildings) to build in pedestrian amenities in their urban construction projects.

Inclusionary zoning. Requiring housing developers to allocate a percentage of their developments to low-income families.

Income tax. A tax on personal income; favored by states and the national government.

Incorporation. The creation of a legal entity, such as a city, at the request of the area's inhabitants. Incorporated jurisdictions usually have a large measure of self-government.

Incumbent. An elected officeholder.

Indeterminate sentencing. The traditional method of sentencing persons convicted of crimes in which a parole board is granted authority to decrease a prisoner's term of sentence within broad parameters.

Indirect initiative. A procedure in which a successful initiative petition is sent to the legislature for action before being submitted to the voters; the legislature may preempt the voters by enacting the initiative into law.

Initiative petition. A document permitting a specified percentage of the voters to propose a constitutional amendment or similar basic change for purposes of putting it to a referendum vote. See also *Direct initiative* and *Indirect initiative.*

Interest group. A collection of people with a specified policy that they would like to see enacted.

Intergovernmental relations. See *Federalism.*

Intergovernmental service contract. An agreement by one jurisdiction with another to provide certain services to its residents.

Intergovernmental service transfer. The permanent transfer of a responsibility by one jurisdiction to another.

Interlocal agreements. Cooperative agreements entered into by local governments. See also *Intergovernmental service contract, Intergovernmental service transfer,* and *Joint service agreements.*

Interparty competition. The degree to which political parties are competitive in elections.

Interstate compacts. Agreements between states that require congressional approval.

Item veto. A form of veto power in which a chief executive officer may delete sections or items of a bill, usually an appropriations bill, while signing the remainder of the bill into law.

Joint service agreement. An agreement between two or more jurisdictions for the joint planning, financing, and delivering of certain services to the residents of all participating jurisdictions.

Judicial court. A form of special court used in some states to decide on the removal or retention of judges.

Judicial review. The power of the courts to declare laws and executive orders null and void because they are contrary to the constitution of the state or nation.

Judicial tenure commission. Organizations in the states that make recommendations on the removal or retention of lower court judges.

Lakewood Plan. An extensive network of contract service agreements between 32 municipalities in Los Angeles County.

Legislative council. A permanent professional staff that provides research on legislation on a continuing basis. Legislative councils are less *ad hoc* in nature than are legislative reference services.

Legislative reference service. A professional staff that provides research on upcoming legislation and often drafts bills for state legislatures.

Legislature. A body of peoples' representatives who make laws for a society. Legislatures normally refer to the lawmaking bodies of the states.

Legislative caucus. Legislators who belong to the same party and who confer on how to vote on upcoming bills. *Also known as* the party caucus.

Legitimacy. The degree to which the people trust their political institutions.

Lieutenant governor. A statewide elected official in 36 states whose chief function is to substitute for the governor in his or her absence; in 29 states, the lieutenant governor presides over the senate.

Lobby. See *Interest group.*

Long ballot. Elections in which the people vote for virtually every official, as opposed to minor officials being appointed by a few elected officials.

Machine politics. A tightly organized political entity that controls state or local elections and policymaking. The political "machine" is dominated by a political "boss" who may or may not hold political office.

Majority. More than half of the votes cast in any one election.

Mandates. See *Federal mandates.*

"Matthew effect." An electoral situation, usually associated with the single-member plurality vote system, in which the political party that accumulates the largest portion of a district's votes will garner even larger proportions of the district's legislative seats, while parties with relatively smaller percentages of the vote tend to acquire even less legislative seats.

Mayor-council government. A form of municipal government in which council members and the mayor are elected and manage the city directly.

Medicaid. A federal public assistance program designed to provide health care to the needy and that is financed jointly between federal and state governments.

Medicare. A federal social insurance program that provides comprehensive medical care for people over 65.

Meet-and-confer bargaining. Nonbinding negotiations conducted between public managers and unions of public employees that require only that management and labor meet and discuss differences with each other.

Merit system. A system of public personnel administration in which hiring, promotion, demotion, and firing of public employees is determined by their ability to complete a task efficiently and effectively.

Metropolitan district. A type of special district covering an entire metropolitan area.

Metropolitan Statistical Areas. Regions with at least one city of 50,000 people or more or an urbanized area of 50,000 people or more and a total MSA population of at least 100,000 (75,000 in New England). In 1983, the U.S. Office of Management and Budget dropped the use of Standard Metropolitan Statistical Areas and adopted in its place Metropolitan Statistical Areas.

Misdemeanor. A minor crime.

Missouri Plan. A method of selecting judges in which the governor appoints the more important judges and, after an interim in office, the judges are put up for popular election.

Mobility. Mobility can be both demographic and social. *Demographic mobility* refers to the movement of people across the country. *Social mobility* refers to people going up and down the economic ladder in society.

Modified one-party Democratic systems. States in which the Democratic Party has general predominance but can be effectively challenged on occasion.

Modified one-party Republican systems. States in which the Republican Party has predominance but may be effectively challenged on occasion.

Moral obligation bond. A type of municipal bond issued by public authorities but not protected by the full faith and credit of a government; the issuing jurisdiction has only a "moral obligation" to repay its creditors.

Multimember district. An electoral district from which several legislators are chosen on a proportional vote. *Also known as* an at-large district.

Multimember district system. An electoral formula in which the number of votes won by any particular political party is proportioned out according to that party in terms of seats in the legislature.

Multipurpose district. A special-function district that conducts more than one function of government.

Municipal bonds. See *Bond.*

Municipality. A city or town.

Mutual aid pact. A type of interlocal agreement that becomes operative only when some disturbance, such as a fire or riot, occurs.

Neighborhood associations. Local, neighborhood-based groupings of citizens dedicated to improving their neighborhoods and intensively lobbying city hall to do so.

Neighborhood corporations. Nonprofit organizations chartered by the state and managed for the public benefit in specified urban areas by that area's residents.

Nonpartisan election. An election in which the candidate's party is not listed on the ballot.

One-party Democratic systems. States whose politics are dominated by the Democratic Party.

Open primary. A primary election in which all voters may vote, regardless of party affiliation, in one party's primary.

Optional referendum. A "straw vote" in which legislatures may submit a proposal to the voters, but the outcome is not binding on the legislature.

Override. The ability of the legislature to enact legislation regardless of the veto by a governor or mayor. Usually an override requires at least two-thirds of the legislature.

Paratransit. Transportation services that stand midway between the private automobile and mass transit; examples include car pools, taxis, and jitnies.

Parole. The conditional release of a prisoner who has served part but not all of a prison sentence.

Partial preemptions. A type of federal mandate in which subnational governments are deprived in part of their traditional prerogatives because Washington sets standards for certain programs as a condition of receiving federal aid.

Party. A collection of people with an overarching political program.

Patronage. Awarding public office on the basis of political loyalty as opposed to professional merit.

Periodic registration. A system of registration in which voters must register periodically, such as every year.

Permanent registration. Registering as a voter on a permanent basis.

Planned unit development. A land-use planning technique used primarily in residential developments that establishes criteria and standards for an entire site.

Planning boards. Local agencies designed to devise a comprehensive community plan, make rezoning decisions, administer community subdivision regulations, and make policy in related areas. *Also called* planning commissions.

Plea bargaining. The negotiations that occur between the lawyer of a person accused of a crime and the public prosecutor. The objective on the part of the accused's lawyer is to reduce the charge, while the objective of the public prosecutor is to gain a conviction.

Plural executive plan. A form of county government in which members of the board of commissioners are usually elected at-large, and each commissioner functions as both a legislator and administrator. The plural executive plan is also known as the commission plan, especially when used by municipalities.

Pluralism. A point of view on political power that argues that power is dispersed among many competing groups and individuals.

Plurality. The most votes cast in a given election. A plurality can be less than half the votes cast but still be the most votes cast for any one candidate or issue.

Political Action Committee. The legally established fund-raising and fund-distributing arm of an interest group.

Political culture. The basic beliefs of a group of people regarding political activity, the role that citizens play in the political process, and the nature of that process.

Polity. The political system.

Poll tax. An obsolete and unconstitutional tax in which voters had to pay a tax in order to vote.

Popular referendum. An election in which voters may approve or disapprove legislation enacted by the legislature.

Postcard registration. Registering to vote by mail. The method is used by about one-third of the states.

"Poverty line." A measure devised in 1955 by the federal government as a definition of poverty. The official poverty line is a point slightly more than three times the average annual cost of what nutrition experts determine to be an adequate diet.

Precinct. Neighborhood political units that comprise, in their totality, a ward.

President *pro tempore*. The presiding officer of a state senate. State senates elect a president *pro tempore* when the state has no lieutenant governor or when the lieutenant governor is not charged with chairing senate sessions.

Pressure group. See *Interest group.*

Primary election. Nominating party candidates by means of direct popular election. See also *Blanket primary, Closed primary, Open primary,* and *Runoff primary.*

Privatization. The contracting out of public services by governments to private firms.

Probation. The suspension of a prison sentence by the court, but with conditions set for a period of time.

Progressive tax. Taxes are progressive when the ratio of tax to income rises as income rises.

Project grant. See *Categorical grant.*

Property tax. A tax levied on property owners and that is set according to the value of the property. Property may be real, such as land or buildings, or personal, such as cars, stocks, and bonds. See also *Circuit breaker.*

Proportional tax. Taxes are proportional when the ratio of taxes to income is the same for all classes of income.

Protective labor law. Legislation designed to protect classes of prospective employees, such as women and children, from exploitation in the workplace.

Public assistance. A federal benefit program funded out of general tax revenues. Public assistance includes Medicaid, Supplemental Security Income assistance, Aid to Families with Dependent Children, and food stamps.

Public authority. See *Government corporation.*

Public choice theory. A school of thought in political science and public administration that advocates an economic approach to policy issues.

Quorum. A particular proportion of the total membership of a legislature that must be present for any official action to be taken. Usually this proportion refers to at least a majority of the membership.

Quotas. As used in public personnel administration, quotas refer to the argument that the traditional entry and promotion qualifications of civil service should be reduced or waived until the number of women and minority group members working in government at all ranks at least equals their proportion in the population at large.

Ratification. Voter approval of action taken by state legislators or by members of a constitutional commission who have proposed amendments to the state constitution.

Reapportionment. See *Apportionment.*

Recall. A procedure than enables voters to remove an elected official from office prior to the next regularly scheduled election.

Recidivism. The number of persons who are sent back to prison for additional crimes that they perpetrated once they are out of prison.

Referendum. A vote by the citizens of a political system on a particular issue, such as Proposition 13 in California. See also *Compulsory referendum, Optional referendum,* and *Popular referendum.*

Regressive tax. Taxes are regressive when the ratio of tax to income falls as incomes rise.

Residence requirement. The stipulation that a potential voter must have resided in his or her community for a specified period of time before he or she is eligible to vote.

Revenue bond. A type of long-term municipal bond that repays its purchasers through fees collected from users of the service underwritten by the bond.

Revenue sharing. A policy initiated in 1972 by Congress that distributes federal funds to state and local governments on the basis of federal personal income tax funds provided by state and local jurisdictions.

Reverse discrimination. The act of discriminating against white males as the result of attempting to comply with affirmative action requirements.

Revision. Basic change in a state constitution.

Roles. In sociology the term "roles" refers to the behavior of individuals and groups in particular situations.

Row officers. Elected county officials who frequently have little policymaking authority.

Runoff primary. A second primary election held to choose a candidate when no candidate has received a majority of the primary votes.

Sales tax. A tax on goods, such as gasoline or liquor; favored by state governments.

School board. The policymaking body of local school districts in most states.

School district. The autonomous unit of local government that makes school policy in all the states except Hawaii.

Severence tax. A state tariff on natural resources, such as coal or oil, extracted in the state and exported to other states.

Shared tax. A tax that state and local governments divide between themselves.

Short ballot. Elections in which the people may vote only for a limited spectrum of candidates for highest-level offices.

Single-member district. An electoral district that sends one representative to a legislative body.

Single-member plurality vote system. An electoral formula under which each electoral district in the state may elect one representative to the legislature by plurality (in contrast to majority) vote.

Snowbelt. The states in the Midwest and Northeast. *Also known as* the Frostbelt or the Graybelt.

Social insurance. Benefits paid to individuals by the federal government, which are funded by compulsory payroll taxes. Social insurance usually is called "Social Security" and includes Old Age, Survivor's Disability, and Health Insurance (OASDHI), Medicare, unemployment benefits, and general health care.

Speaker of the House. The presiding official of the House of Representatives in the states.

Special authority. See *Government corporation.*

Special district. A government type with authority to perform a particular governmental function, such as fire protection or water supply.

Specialized local trial court. A court of relatively limited jurisdiction that deals primarily with minor cases.

Standard Metropolitan Statistical Areas. Urban areas of 50,000 people or more. This use is now obsolete. See *Metropolitan Statistical Areas.*

Stare decisis. Judicial precedent, or the reliance by the judiciary on past cases in making decisions.

State boards of education. The chief state policymaking body for elementary and secondary public schools in all states except Hawaii.

State departments of education. The chief state agencies responsible for educational planning and standard setting; increasingly, departments of education are displacing boards of education as the major state policymakers for elementary and secondary public schools.

Status categories. A Census Bureau term that bases certain social and economic measures on occupational type, level of education, and amount of income.

Suburbanization. The movement of people from the inner cities to the surrounding suburbs.

Suffrage. The right to vote.

Sunbelt. The states located in the Southeastern and Southwestern portions of the country.

Sunset laws. Legislation that requires a periodic legislative review of agencies for purposes of determining whether or not those agencies should be continued.

Sunshine laws. Legislation that requires the fullest possible public disclosure of personal finances by public officials, both elected and appointed.

Supplemental Security Income assistance. A federal public assistance program that, in 1974, combined Old Age Assistance, Aid to the Blind, and Aid to the Permanently and Totally Disabled and that displaced the states' role in these programs.

Supreme Court. The final court of appeals in the states. *Also called* Superior Court.

Tax. A charge levied by government for purposes of generating revenues. See also *Income tax, Poll tax, Progressive tax, Property tax, Proportional tax, Regressive tax, Sales tax, Severence tax, Shared tax,* and *Use tax.*

Town. A small municipal unit of local government.

Town meeting. The method of governance used by towns and townships. In an *open town meeting,* all the town's residents vote on issues; in a *representative town meeting,* a large number of elected representatives vote on issues.

Township. A small municipal unit of local government favored in the Northeast and North Central states.

Transferrable development rights. A variation on traditional zoning that separates the right to improve property from the right to own property. Under TDR, a community can directly give or withhold development rights from a private developer in order to restrict development in one area and to encourage development in another.

Trial court. A court that has general jurisdiction and the broadest authority in the state court systems.

Trial court of general jurisdiction. A court that deals with criminal felonies and civil cases.

Trial court of limited jurisdiction. See *Specialized local trial court.*

Two-party systems. States that are genuinely competitive between the Republicans and Democrats.

"Ultralocalism." A prevalent ideology that advocates a fragmenting of governmental authority.

Underclass. That portion of the population that seems to be permanently mired in poverty and that is characterized by family instability, poor job skills, poor social skills, and a dependency on public assistance.

Unicameral legislature. A legislature with only one house. Only Nebraska has a unicameral legislature.

"Urban hardship." A term developed by the Brookings Institution that compares inner cities with their outer suburbs and, from that comparison, derives a measure of how badly off or better off a city is relative to its surrounding area.

Urban Renewal. The attempts to improve the physical environment of cities through federal programs with local cooperation. In 1974, federal urban renewal was subsumed under the Housing and Community Development Block Grants Program.

Urbanization. The movement of people from the countryside to the cities.

Use tax. A tax on the use of particular amenities, such as a toll on highway use.

Veto. The ability of a chief executive to cancel legislation that has been passed by the legislature. See also *Item veto.*

Victimless crime. A violation in which it is difficult to prove there was ever a victim. An example would be public drunkenness.

Voting registration. Recording oneself as a voter in the community in which one resides. See also *Periodic registration, Permanent registration,* and *Postcard registration.*

Ward. The division of a city created for the purposes of electing members to the city council.

Welfare. See *Public assistance.*

"White flight." The phenomenon of white people leaving urban areas for the suburbs.

Women's liberation. The movement by women to have equal rights with men.

Zoning. A local land-use plan concerning how certain sections of the community may be used. See also *Enterprise zoning, Exclusionary zoning, Incentive zoning, Inclusionary zoning, Planned unit development,* and *Transferrable development rights.*

APPENDIX A

working at the grassroots

Now that you have read about governing at the grassroots, why not consider working there, too? Public administrators in state and local governments are in one of the world's most rewarding professions: the people's interests are served, the job security is high, the pay is good, and the field of public administration is fascinating.

JOBS! JOBS! JOBS!

Even better, there is a relatively high probability that you can get a good job in government. Employment in the public sector has been going up almost every year for the past three decades, and today there are some 16 million public employees, or about 1 for every 7 workers. Most are in local government (nearly 60 percent); state government accounts for about a quarter of public employment, and the federal government for a sixth. The fastest growth rates in public employment are among the state and local governments, and opportunities are quite good at these levels.

Professional Specializations: The Best Prospects

Dalton S. Lee and Cathy Osborn have explored which specialties in public administration are likely to offer the most opportunities for new public administrators. Lee and Osborn sent questionnaires to professors of public administration in those universities that are members of the National Association of Schools of Public Affairs and Administration (NASPAA), all state and territorial personnel departments, and a random sample of cities with more than 50,000 people. The most conclusive finding in the survey was that holding a Master of Public Administration (MPA) degree greatly enhances one's chances of being hired by a government. In addition, however, the study found differing opinions among respondents about the best career areas in public administration. These opinions are ranked as follows from most favorable career opportunities to least favorable:

Public Administration Educators	*State Personnel Specialists*[1]	*Local Government Administrators*
1. Budgeting	1. Policy analysis/program evaluation	1. Policy analysis/program evaluation
2. Finance	2. Program management	2. Planning
3. Policy analysis/program evaluation	3. Budgeting	3. Program management
4. Urban management	4. Finance	4. Urban management
5. Personnel administration	5. Planning	5. Budgeting
6. Program management	6. Personnel administration	6. Finance
7. Planning		7. Personnel administration

[1] Urban management was not ranked by these respondents.

Minorities and Women: Better Possibilities

More minorities and women are hired and earn more money in the public sector than in the private sector.

More than a fifth of all state and local employees (excluding educators) are members of minority groups (16 percent are black and 4 percent are Hispanic), and 41 percent are women. Nationally, blacks and Hispanics earn about 25 percent less than whites, and women earn a third less than men; but in state and local governments, these minorities earn 14 percent less than whites, and women earn 25 percent less than men. While these are not disparities easily swallowed, they nonetheless indicate greater equality of opportunity in the public sector than in the private one.

Moreover, state and local governments appear to have a better record of promoting minorities and women than does the federal government. Only 7 percent of the top federal executives are minorities, and only 4 percent are women. But 9 percent of top administrators and officials in state and local governments are minorities, and 23 percent are women! While the comparisons cannot be precise, it nonetheless appears that blacks, Hispanics, and women will find their best chances for rewarding careers in the grassroots governments.

MONEY! MONEY! MONEY!

Public sector pay rates have gone up from 4 to 9 percent every year since 1970, and, despite tax revolts in the states, pay rates for state and local employees have increased more rapidly than have pay rates for federal employees.

State Public Administration

There are nearly 2.2 million state employees, not counting an additional 1.7 million in education. The Council of State Governments reports that there are more than 120 categories of top state officials, ranging from directors of state lotteries to secretaries of education to directors of emergency management. Few data have been compiled about compensation rates for state public administrators. However, $70,000 to $80,000 seems to be the salary level for the top state administrative jobs in the more populous states, and in these states, salaries at all administrative ranks appear to be roughly comparable to federal pay rates. It is increasingly common to find top administrators in state government (particularly in higher education) to be paid more than the governor. One thing is clear: state administrators' salaries are rising rapidly, and the field of state public administration is more professional than ever—a trend that is certain to continue.

Local Public Administration

Local governments employ 4.2 million people, not counting an additional 5.1 million in education. Considerably more is known about administrative salaries at the local level than at the state level. In 1984, city managers earned an average salary of more than $42,000, and salaries were increasing by about 6 percent a year. However, in the largest cities, top urban administrators typically earn more than $100,000. West Coast governments pay their public administrators the most; Northeastern cities pay the least—often a third less than Western cities. Entry salaries are more difficult to assess, but some examples follow:

	APPROXIMATE AVERAGE SALARY, 1984	
POSITION	*NORTHWEST (Generally the lowest pay)*	*WEST (Generally the highest pay)*
Finance director of a small town (5,000 to 10,000 people)	$23,000	$30,000
Director of public works of a small town	26,000	30,000
Superintendent of streets of a small town	22,000	25,000
Planning director of a small town	18,000	30,000
Chief personnel officer of a small town	17,000	21,000
Superintendent of parks of a small town	17,000	22,000
Director of recreation of a small town	17,000	22,000
Director of data processing of a small town	15,000	26,000

Although the preceding examples are all department heads, it is not too unusual for college graduates, particularly those who have degrees in public administration, to enter local government as the department head in smaller jurisdictions. On occasion, a department head in the government of a small town may also be the entire department!

GETTING A JOB IN GOVERNMENT

When perusing the job announcements and want ads, it is important to know which jobs are appropriate for public administration students. Being new to the field, some students may not even be sure what job titles are related to public administration. For the most part, trainee and intern positions are for the less experienced and may not lead to permanent positions. A "I" after a title, such as Analyst I, usually indicates an entry-level position. An Analyst II or Analyst III would indicate that more extensive education or experience was required.

Summarize your abilities in a resumé format that presents your most important assets first. What things were you able to accomplish in your job and education? State your case in terms of projects that you have directed, designed, developed, implemented, researched, reported, managed, controlled, planned, organized, edited, or built. When stated in these terms, those new or returning to the job market are disadvantaged by using the traditional *chronological resumé.* They should use a *functional resumé* format that highlights their training, analytic skills, ability to get along with others, knowledge of organization dynamics, budgeting strategies, and management tools, for example. Both a sample functional resume and chronological resumé will be found on pages 543–545.

An excellent way to develop job contacts is to join the American Society for Public Administration, or ASPA. ASPA has local chapters in cities across the country comprised of public administrators from all levels of government. Typically, ASPA chapters sponsor monthly luncheons and regional conferences where new contacts are easily made. ASPA also publishes *Public Administration Times,* which announces job openings in government. To learn how to join, ask your course instructor, or write:

American Society for Public Administration
1120 G Street, N.W.
Washington, D.C. 20005

ASPA's telephone number is (202) 393-7878.

An internship, paid or voluntary, can be an important step toward gaining needed relevant work experience for students lacking public sector experience. Often, schools of public administration or departments of political science work with governmental agencies in developing local internship opportunities in personnel, budgeting, planning, policy analysis, and so forth. A satisfactory internship can provide strong recommendations and strengthen one's resumé.

CONCLUSION

If you are interested in becoming a public administrator, two recommendations are paramount. First, join the American Society for Public Administration. Not only does it provide unique networking opportunities, but it publishes a biweekly newsletter listing professional job openings around the country.

Second, consider entering an MPA degree program. Increasingly, these programs cater to the scheduling needs of students who already have jobs, and the MPA itself is regarded as an important qualification for entry and advancement in the public sector. To learn more about the Master of Public Administration degree, contact your local university or the National Association of Schools of Public Administration (NASPAA) and ask for its highly informative pamphlet, *MPA: The Master of Public Administration Degree,* which is available at no charge. NASPAA also publishes *In the Public Interest,* an informative newsletter on employment trends in the public service with a special emphasis on internships. A detailed *Directory* of more than 200 MPA programs is also available from NASPAA for $12.50. NASPAA's address is the same as ASPA's:

National Association of Schools of Public Affairs and Administration
1120 G Street, N.W.
Washington, D.C. 20005

NASPAA's telephone number is (202) 628-8965.

SOURCES

Book of the States, 1984-85 (Lexington, Ky.: Council of State Governments, 1984).

Bureau of the Census, *Statistical Abstract of the United States, 1985* (Washington, D.C.: U.S. Government Printing Office, 1984).

Dalton S. Lee and Cathy Osborn, "Employment Prospects in Public Administration," unpublished manuscript (Tempe: School of Public Affairs, Arizona State University, 1984).

Municipal Year Book, 1985 (Washington, D.C.: International City Management Association, 1985).

State Administrative Officials Classified by Function, 1985-86 (Lexington, Ky.: Council of State Governments, 1985).

SAMPLE FUNCTIONAL RESUMÉ

KENNETH L. MATTHEWS
1234 East University
Tempe, Arizona 85281
(602) 555-9876

URBAN PLANNING AND ADMINISTRATION

Responsible for initiating the Town of Snowflake's first general plan. Generated background information, organized all meetings, wrote news releases for local papers, created land-use maps, and developed fiscal impact statements.

Successful CDBG application for $110,000 (FY 84–85). Analyzed data processing needs and initiated purchases of computer system for Town. Skillfully performed a wide range of general administrative tasks.

POLICY ANALYSIS

Generated reports for the Office of Community Relations at ASU for submission to the state legislature on such topics as the need for a west side campus and the transportation crisis in Maricopa County.

Collected data and analyzed policy for the Town of Snowflake on water and sewer rate structures and employee pay scales. Also restructured all town policies and programs to meet federal antidiscrimination legislation.

RESEARCH METHODS

Strong academic background in research methods that included work in congressional voting behavior and immigration policy. Practical experience in conducting job attitude survey for the Town of Eager, community needs survey for the Town of Snowflake, and a multiplicity of analytic reports for the Office of Community Relations at ASU.

WORK EXPERIENCE

1983–85 Research Assistant, Office of Community Relations, Arizona State University
1984 Administrative Intern, Town of Snowflake

EDUCATION

1985 Master of Public Administration, ASU, 4.00 GPA
1983 Bachelor of Arts, Political Science, University of Washington, 3.67 GPA, cum laude, Phi Beta Kappa

SAMPLE CHRONOLOGICAL RESUMÉ

VIVIAN LOOK
5678 East University Drive
Tempe, Arizona 85281
(602) 000-0000 (work)
(602) 000-0000 (home)

OBJECTIVE

To work in an area of public administration related to legislation or public policy. The ideal position would allow me to utilize my skills in research analysis, interpersonal relations, and communication, both oral and written.

EDUCATION

School	*Dated Attended*	*Degree*	*Major Coursework*
Arizona State University Tempe, Arizona	1–83 to present	—	Public Administration
University of Michigan Ann Arbor, Michigan	9–79 to 8–80	MPH	Public Health
University of California	3–69 to 7–72	BS	Nutritional Science, Economics, Psychology

Other training: Food Services Division, Milwaukee Public Schools, Milwaukee, Wisconsin. 9-72 to 6-73. Administrative dietetic internship focusing on the management of school food service programs.

PROFESSIONAL WORK EXPERIENCE

Administrative Intern, Maricopa County Office of Management Analysis, Phoenix, Arizona. 1-84 to present.

Under the direction of the Deputy County Manager, assistant Management Analysts in conducting management audits of county departments and investigate efficiency and effectiveness of services provided. Assess present and future staffing requirements and make recommendations for improving the service delivery system. Perform other duties as assigned by the Deputy County Manager and Management Analysts. Other assignments have included assisting the Contracts Specialist in Materials Management in developing a master copier plan for use by the county in the next five years.

Research Assistant, Center for Public Affairs, Arizona State University, Tempe, Arizona. 8-83 to present.

Under the direction of ASU faculty member and Director of the Center for Urban Studies, assist in research, class preparation, and other duties as assigned. Work on research projects has included assisting in computer-based management and analysis of educational enrollment data for the Phoenix Town Hall, citizen surveys for the city of Glendale, and library research on public choice theory.

Project Nutrition Consultant, Bureau of Nutritional Service, Arizona Department of Health Services, Tempe, Arizona. 10-80 to 8-83.

Served as the primary contact person from the Bureau of Nutrition for county and tribal health departments, as assigned. In this capacity, monitored local agency programs for compliance to program and contract requirements, provided assistance in program management, and served as an advocate for local projects, participating in negotiations when appropriate. At the Bureau level, participated in planning, development, and review of policies and procedures and budget allocation process for state-subvened funds. As the lead consultant for the Bureau's Laboratory Quality Assurance Program from 1-83 to 8-83, researched alternative methods of carrying out the program and completed comparative cost studies. Developed and presented final recommendations for improving the program and reducing costs, which was ultimately adopted by the agency.

Nutritionist, Health Division, Lane County Department of Health and Social Services, Eugene, Oregon. 7-75 to 7-79.

Special Vocational Educational Teacher, Springfield School District No. 19, Springfield, Oregon. 9-74 to 6-75.

Trainer/Nutritionist, Community Nutrition Institute, Washington, D.C. 10-73 to 6-74.

RECENT PROFESSIONAL ACTIVITIES AND HONORS

1983 to present	Regents Graduate Academic Scholarship, Arizona State University, Tempe, Arizona
	Member, American Society for Public Administration, Arizona Chapter
1982–83	Co-editor, Legislative Newsletter, Arizona Dietitians for Legislative Action
1981–82	Community Nutrition Section Chairperson and Executive Board Member, Central Arizona District Dietetic Association
1979–80	U.S. Public Health Traineeship, University of Michigan, Ann Arbor, Michigan
1978–79	Member, Task Force on Dental Health, Nutrition, and Health Education, Western Oregon Health Systems Agency
	Member, Nutrition Task Force, Oregon Public Health Association

INDEX